"R.F.K. Must Die!"

By the same author
POPE, COUNCIL AND WORLD (1963)

"R.F.K. Must Die!"

A History of
the Robert Kennedy Assassination
and Its Aftermath
by
Robert Blair Kaiser

E. P. DUTTON & CO., INC., NEW YORK, 1970

First Edition

Copyright © 1970 by Robert Blair Kaiser
All rights reserved.
Printed in the U.S.A. by Vail-Ballou Press, Inc.

Published simultaneously in Canada by
Clarke, Irwin & Company Limited, Toronto and Vancouver

Library of Congress Catalog Card Number: 74–86074

SBN   0–525–19111–9

Sections of this book appeared first, in condensed form, in the
Ladies' Home Journal

Grateful appreciation is extended to
Harcourt, Brace & World, Inc., for permission to reproduce
the Location Chart portion of the Individual Record Blank, Revised,
used with the Rorschach Method of Personality Diagnosis.
Published by Harcourt, Brace & World, Inc., New York.
Copyright © 1960 by Harcourt, Brace & World, Inc.
Copyright 1942 by the Rorschach Institute, Inc.

For those who believe
that knowing is better
than not knowing

Acknowledgments

I would like to thank the following persons whose kind assistance and advice were indispensable to the writing of this book:

A. L. Wirin, Richard Buckley, Russell Parsons, Grant Cooper, Helen Smith, Emile Zola Berman, Michael McCowan, John Howard, David Fitts, Lynn Compton, Sidney Trapp, Janet Ward, Herbert V. Walker, Vesta Minnick, Alice Nishikawa, Harold Frediani, Charles Collins, Frank Patchett, Gordon McDevitt, Chic Guitierrez, Hank Hernandez, Michael Neilsen, Phil Sartuche, Bill Jordan, Roger LaJeunesse, Peter Pitchess, James Downey, William H. McCloud, William Conroy, Ralph Welch, Craig Carpenter, Gus Feederle, Rose Gallego, Val Clenard, David Smith, Bob Greene, Martin Kasindorf, Jordan Bonfante, Fernando Faura, Bob Mulholland, Jack Perkins, Jonn Christian, Abdeen Jabara, Issa Nahkleh, Bill Doerflinger, Peggy Brooks, Mary Solak, Henry Cuneo, Bernard L. Diamond, Seymour Pollack, Eric Marcus, O. Rod Richardson, Martin Schorr, Thomas Greening, John Frankenheimer, George Plimpton, Michael Creedman, Jules Witcover, Joanne Funger, Olive Hungate, Arthur Abelman, Charles Grobe, Saul Cohen, Paul Hilsdale, Max Becker and Rosanne Keefer.

I also wish to thank the Los Angeles *Times, Newsday,* NBC News, Radio Stations KMPC and KRKD, Dr. Bernard L. Diamond and *The Journal of Social Therapy* for permission to quote material which was theirs.

Acknowledgments

I would like to thank the following persons whose kind assistance and advice were invaluable in the writing of this book:

...

Contents

10   Contents

Preface

When yet another assassin's bullet took the life of yet another Kennedy, the whole world demanded to know who did it and why. They soon discovered who. It was a young Palestinian Arab refugee with a strange double name: Sirhan Sirhan. But the story of why he killed—which he propounded at the trial—didn't make any sense.

This is a book that tries to make sense of it. It is a book about the assassin and about those who probed him: police, prosecutors, defense attorneys, psychiatrists, psychologists, reporters.

I was one of those reporters. Out of curiosity, mainly, and out of a suspicion that the public would learn something less than the whole truth if it had to rely on either the assassin's unchallenged version or even the police estimate, I wangled my way inside the case.

Once I was inside, I was really in. I was able to talk to Sirhan's family and some of his friends, to sit in on the defense attorneys' conferences with Sirhan, to become a participant-observer in the attorneys' own private working sessions, confer closely with the psychologists and psychiatrists in the case. I had access to police and FBI files, and, most important of all, I was able to visit Sirhan in his cell two or three times a week until he left Los Angeles for San Quentin, condemned to die.

I doubt whether any reporter has ever gotten so deeply inside a major murder case.

Why was I given such entrée? I hesitate to say the answer was simply money. I did promise to provide funds for Sirhan's legal defense, and I probably would have gotten nowhere without such a promise—and delivery. Sirhan wanted a good private attorney and I made it possible for him to hire one. It wasn't that Attorney Grant Cooper demanded a big fee, or any fee at all. In fact, Cooper renounced any proceeds from my writings on the case in favor of the University of Southern California Law School. Still, he needed some resources: the district attorney's office spent $203,656 to prosecute Sirhan. Simple fairness would dictate that Sirhan's attorneys should have a fraction of that for their expenses (otherwise, the expression "fair trial" would have been a sham). And simple common sense told me that there was only one sure source for those expenses, the world press. The world wanted to know, the news media would pay. They did, in a modest way. By the end of the case, I was able to turn some $32,000, approximately half of what I had then received, over to Sirhan's attorneys.

But I provided more than money. I gave myself. The defense attorneys received most of the Los Angeles Police Department files and all of the FBI reports on the case through a legal "motion for discovery." But neither they nor their investigator had time to read and digest all this material. I did. They didn't have the time or the patience to draw out the assassin. I did. Soon, the attorneys began to need me, for, in my total curiosity, I soon knew more about the case than they did themselves. My reporter's dream was complete when Dr. Bernard L. Diamond, the chief psychiatrist for the defense, turned to me as the chief repository of knowledge about the case and began taking me into Sirhan's cell with him for his analysis of Sirhan under hypnosis.

I am not at all sure that every case would lend itself to such heightened personal involvement by a reporter who is trying to write about it. In this case, however, I got access to the assassin, without giving up the right to tell the story as I saw it.

"R.F.K. Must Die!"

One

On the Santa Monica Freeway, John Frankenheimer accelerated his Rolls-Royce Silver Cloud to sixty-five, glad now to have gotten Senator Robert Francis Kennedy out of the house and on his way to the Ambassador Hotel. Kennedy had been edgy that evening, unable to sit still during supper, preoccupied about the outcome of the California primary. No wonder, thought Frankenheimer, after the tumult of the most fevered campaign in the history of the Republic. For seventy-one days Frankenheimer, one of Hollywood's better movie directors, had followed Kennedy and shot thousands of feet of film for a new, ambitious documentary that could help beat Richard Nixon in the fall.

But Frankenheimer knew, when Kennedy had sagged the night before in San Diego, unable to finish his last speech, what a toll this kind of campaign had taken of the candidate. He and his wife had given Bob and Ethel their bedroom at Malibu and tried to provide them both with some respite from the crowds and the clamor that had brought Bob close to collapse.

But it was a mistake, Frankenheimer knew now, to have invited those people over for supper. Roman Polanski and his wife Sharon, Frank Wells and his wife, Luanne, Brian Morris and Anjanette Comer, Dick Sylbert and Sarah Hudson were show biz and wrong for Bob Kennedy on election night. Angry with himself for having so little foresight, Frankenheimer sped right by the Vermont off ramp and got tangled up in the Harbor Freeway interchange. He cursed angrily as he tried to get the Rolls headed back toward the Ambassador.

"Take it easy, John," said Bob Kennedy with a gentle touch. "Life is too short."

✻　✻　✻　✻　✻

Senator Kennedy frowned at the image on the Ambassador Hotel's seemingly unadjustable color TV and studied the tops of his shoes while Walter Cronkite patiently explained to the nation about the news delay in California. The old-fashioned ways of counting votes were good enough, apparently, in Mendocino and Modesto and Riverside and San Diego, and election officials all over the state had hustled their returns to the news services and the networks within an hour after the polls had closed.

The trouble lay in Los Angeles, the land of instant everything, where the powers that run the county had decided to let IBM do the counting job in a few milliseconds. To the delight of the children smoking grass on the Sunset Strip, the computers of Los Angeles, which controlled billion-mile space flights to the moon and to Mars, couldn't seem to scan a bunch of punch cards.

But Robert F. Kennedy was not amused. Forty-three percent of the vote was here. L.A. was the key to everything else: California's 174 delegates, the Democratic National Convention, maybe the Presidency of the United States. And now at ten o'clock on election night no one—not even the omniscient pol who was heading Kennedy's campaign in California—knew what the mostly unpredictable voters of the county had done that day.

The voter turnout was high in the black and brown communities, and that was good because those communities were largely Kennedy's. The Senator shook his head, chewed a little more vigorously on a stick of peppermint gum, moved away from the television set in the crowded sitting room of the Royal Suite with an abstracted look on his face, refused a Scotch and water, put his hands in his pants pockets and wandered into a bedroom area in the other half of the suite, also crowded, where David Brinkley, on another channel, was conveying his own unveiled disgust over the computer breakdown. Kennedy smiled, perhaps enjoying the revelation that someone else was as discomfited as he, plopped down on the floor with a sigh, hugged his knees and leaned back against the wall. He accepted a small cigar and a light from someone and turned to Dick Goodwin. Goodwin had served as a speech writer for Presidents Kennedy and Johnson and had now become a political strategist. He left the White House in 1967 to become a member of Robert Kennedy's shadow cabinet; then he joined Senator McCarthy when he began his campaign in New Hampshire. After Kennedy beat McCarthy in Indiana, Goodwin came back to the winner. Kennedy puffed lightly on the cigar. Goodwin started to speak. Some more people piled into the room. Kennedy smiled, got up again and motioned for Goodwin to follow into the privacy of the bathroom. In a few minutes he came out again, wandered around the suite and then, for no apparent reason, went out and stood in the corridor, leaned against the wall, folded his arms and looked down at the carpet. Two or three reporters, including Jack Smith of the Los Angeles *Times,* had been waiting in the hallway on the odd chance that Kennedy would appear. Now that he was there, they were momentarily too surprised to ask a question. Finally, someone asked him what he thought of the returns at this point in the evening.

"I can't talk about it now," said Kennedy. Smith observed that his voice was very low, almost inaudible, but tense and tremulous, as if charged with some vital current. "I'm not interested in figures."

One of the reporters started talking about the campaign that lay ahead and about "the politicians."

"I like politicians," Kennedy said quietly. "I like politics. It's an honorable adventure." Kennedy paused. "That was Lord Tweedsmuir." Kennedy paused again. "You don't remember Lord Tweedsmuir?" None of the reporters seemed to remember. Kennedy was pleased. He delivered a brief lecture on John Buchan, Lord Tweedsmuir, the Scottish author and statesman. "He wrote *The Thirty-Nine Steps,* you know, and several others. And then he was Governor General of Canada. He said, 'Politics is an honorable adventure.' " Kennedy savored the expression again, wanting to remember. Then he went back into the suite, went into the bedroom again and hunched on the edge of the bed, allowing himself to look small, vulnerable, edgy, tired. His son David, in a blue blazer and gray slacks and a striped necktie, walked up to him, bubbling because everybody said they were winners again, kissed him on the cheek and sat on the bed, close to his dad.

Only a week before, Kennedy had lost the primary election in Oregon, his first defeat after an unbroken series of wins for himself and his brother John, the former President of the United States. Kennedy preferred to win, played to win, or he didn't play. Most of his older advisers who didn't want him to challenge the leadership of Lyndon Johnson in 1968 had won their argument by insisting that this was a fight he couldn't win. Ultimately, he rejected this pragmatic political advice because it was a fight he and his wife Ethel finally decided he had to win. The Johnson Administration was overcommitted in Vietnam and undercommitted in urban America, and only new leadership could turn the country around. He forced the pace, plunged into one of the most tumultuous primary campaigns America has ever seen, became Bob Kennedy, the candidate-in-his-own-right (not Bobby Kennedy the little brother of John) and a surprising new symbol of hope and reconciliation in a time of division and dissolution. But here in California in the last of the 1968 primaries, Senator McCarthy, who had beaten him in Oregon, was leading in something called the "raw vote count."

Now the networks, impatient with minor officialdom in Los Angeles, decided to force their pace a little. CBS predicted a Kennedy victory by as much as sixteen percentage points. NBC held out, finally announced that a sampling of key election precincts, selected in advance to represent a cross section of the state, also indicated that Kennedy would win. The NBC sample was bad—it included no precincts from Los Angeles County—but the network took a chance. In the East, where it was already well past midnight, the audience was dwindling. Television producers urged Kennedy to claim his victory.

Kennedy stalled. What if the projections were wrong? Wasn't McCarthy ahead where it counted, in the raw vote? He took some time to talk to Goodwin again, to Pierre Salinger, his brother's former press secretary, to Jesse Unruh, leader of the California campaign, and Frank Mankiewicz, his own press secretary. He phoned Kenneth O'Donnell, a longtime Kennedy adviser, in Massachusetts. O'Donnell was flying from the East in the morning for a major strategy session because O'Donnell said he thought Kennedy could get the nomination. "I think I may," said Kennedy. If the predictions were correct in California, if Los Angeles County held up, then McCarthy would have to give a little and more than a little. Some of the McCarthy team, Goodwin said, were ready to defect to Kennedy. Some of them were coming to have breakfast with Kennedy in the morning. McCarthy would give, or McCarthy would not give. It didn't matter. The nomination would go to the man who could squeeze the delegates headed for the convention in Chicago, and the man who could do that best was Kennedy. Only he could call in some of the debts owing from his brother's administration.

And here on the fifth floor of the Ambassador Hotel in Los Angeles were many of those closest to both Kennedys: Bob's wife, Ethel; his sister Pat Lawford and his sister Jean, and Jean's husband, Steve Smith; Pierre Salinger, Fred Dutton, Richard Goodwin, Ted Sorensen, Larry O'Brien, who had all worked with John Kennedy. And some new faces too. There were the black faces of Roosevelt Grier, the gigantic tackle of the Los Angeles Rams football team; and Rafer Johnson, the decathlon champion of the 1964 Olympics from UCLA, who had quit a lucrative sportscasting job with NBC Television News to help Kennedy. There were the brown faces of Cesar Chavez, the unassuming organizer who had pulled together the grape pickers of California's central valleys and was here in Los Angeles, getting out the massive Mexican-American vote in East L.A., and his pretty lieutenant, Dolores Huerta, a mother of three and the farmworkers' chief labor negotiator. There were the alert faces of writers like Theodore White, Warren Rogers of *Look* magazine and Budd Schulberg, the novelist (who was giving most of his time these days to teaching blacks in the ghetto); the searching faces of *Life* photographer Bill Eppridge and *Look* photographer Stanley Tretick; the merry face of Richard Tuck, the political prankster, itching for another chance to needle Richard Nixon; the earnest face of Paul Schrade, a socially crusading leader in Walter Reuther's United Auto Workers; the patrician faces of George Plimpton and his bride, Freddy; and the strong face of John Glenn, America's first astronaut. On this night, June 4, 1968, all of the faces were happy faces. They were part of the team, almost as much a part of the family as young David, Michael, Courtney and Kerry Kennedy who were there with their springer spaniel, Freckles.

Downstairs in the Embassy Room, where Kennedy would speak when it was time to claim victory, the crowd had gone beyond capacity to an estimated 1,800 persons. Security officers and Los Angeles firemen were turning campaign workers away and sending them down one floor to the Ambassador Ballroom. Gabor Kadar, a Hungarian refugee with absolutely no credentials at all but more than enough enterprise, was turned away from the Embassy Room, went outside, made an unsuccessful try to go up the fire escape, finally found a clothes hamper on the west side of the building filled with soiled white cooks' uniforms. He took one of the uniforms out of the hamper, put it on over his suit, picked up two empty milk cans and carried them up a stairway to the kitchen. He dropped the cans in the kitchen and proceeded on to the Embassy Room from there, doffed his uniform in a corner, and squeezed up to the right side of the platform where Senator Kennedy was scheduled to appear.

Michael Wayne, a slight twenty-one-year-old with dark curly hair, a clerk at the Pickwick Book Store in Hollywood, had as much moxie as Kadar. He'd spent the earlier part of the evening picking up political mementos at the Rafferty headquarters on Wilshire and the McCarthy headquarters in Westwood, where he gathered such souvenirs as a hard-cover edition of Senator McCarthy's *Limits of Power*. He then hitchhiked to the Beverly Hilton Hotel and talked his way into a seventh-floor TV room where McCarthy was being interviewed by David Schoumacher of CBS.

McCarthy did not argue with the network predictions but tried to under-sell California's significance. "We made our real test in Oregon," said McCarthy. The idea was that any Democrat could pull the minority blocs. In November, he argued, he'd get those bloc votes and a lot of independents who wouldn't come near Robert Kennedy. The reasoning was strained but it was the best McCarthy could do. Robert Kennedy had the momentum now.

Michael Wayne got McCarthy's signature on the book, then followed McCarthy down to the Grand Ballroom of the Beverly Hilton where a rather subdued crowd waited to find out where they would go from here. "Go on and sing and have a pleasant time tonight," McCarthy told the crowd, "because we've just begun to fight." As he spoke, the running tabulation of vote totals still showed Senator McCarthy in front, 46 percent to Kennedy's 41. But his followers had seen the predictions on television. Some of them didn't feel like singing. Young Mike Wayne decided to hitchhike back down Wilshire to Senator Kennedy's party at the Ambassador where he knew there would be more action.

Now Kennedy was ready to move to live interviews with the TV networks. Though he was eager for the exposure on national television, he was equally anxious to avoid saying anything which would make his victory seem "ruthless." Kennedy was the epitome of grace, while both Sander Vanocur of NBC and Roger Mudd of CBS tried to draw him into spilling out his future battle plans to the world. Mudd came out with an expression he had obviously heard from Kennedy: "Are some of the delegates that are listed as leaning or even committed to the Vice-President, are they *squeezable?* Are they solid?"

"Roger!" said Kennedy, blinking hard. "Your language!"

Mudd laughed. "Well, that . . . you . . . isn't that the way you talk about it?"

Kennedy knew Mudd was aware that "squeezing" the Humphrey delegates was the only real job that lay ahead, and Mudd's choice of words was if anything too precise. "No, I don't go that far," laughed Kennedy. "I don't. I don't."

Mudd stammered. "Well, I . . ."

Before he could say too much, Kennedy gave him an out. "Probably somebody else does."

*   *   *   *   *

By now the Embassy Room five floors below was jammed with a singing, boisterous, laughing crowd. A security guard blocked the way of young Michael Wayne, but that didn't stop Wayne. He got into the press room through the kitchen, begged a rectangular blue and white badge that read "Kennedy Election Night Press" and a green badge reading "Kennedy for President—Press." He clipped the two badges together with his PT-109 tie clasp, a memento he had picked up two weeks earlier from Senator Kennedy himself at the Ambassador. Thus armed with "credentials," he drifted into the hotel lobby.

He grabbed two rolled Kennedy posters and several Rafferty buttons, then went up, unimpeded, to the Kennedy wing of the fifth floor, found the Presidential suite open, ordered a Scotch and water at the bar, begged another PT-109 tie clasp from a Kennedy worker.

In a small bedroom of the Royal Suite, Bob Kennedy was asking Budd Schulberg what he ought to say to the workers down below. Schulberg, who saw him then as something considerably less than arrogant, reminded him of the blacks and the chicanos who had helped him win in California. "Bob," he said, "you're the only white man in this country they trust." Kennedy smiled his small shy rabbity smile.

Ethel Kennedy opened the door. "Can't even get in my own bedroom," she cried in mock anger, really very pleased now that things were going well again.

The Senator went into the bathroom, this time with Sorensen, talked, fiddled nervously with the electric typewriter sitting next to the sink, came out into the sitting room, and lit a long cigar while he watched Frank McGee, who had taken over on NBC for the nettled Mr. Brinkley. The cigar hung from his hand, growing a fine ash, and then someone came up and gave him a ginger ale. He drank it down in one lusty gulp.

Frank Mankiewicz rushed in to say that it was time to move toward the Embassy Room. "Do we know enough about it yet?" asked Kennedy. He went back into the small bedroom to make one last check with Dutton— the points he ought to make, the names of the people he ought to thank.

Ethel Kennedy, three months' pregnant with her eleventh child, was lying down for a moment of rest. It would be her last calm moment for some time to come. "Ready?" said Bob.

"Ready!" said Ethel, rising brightly.

"Do you think we ought to take Freckles down? You know they say I win with an astronaut and a dog." It was a question that needed no answer. Things would be hectic enough downstairs without Freckles. They passed through the sitting room. Jack Smith of the Los Angeles *Times* saw Kennedy pass a long mirror, touch his necktie and make a final pass at his hair. "Then," said Smith, "he went down to pursue his honorable adventure."

In the corridor, Kennedy turned back to Budd Schulberg, watching him go down the hall. "Budd, stick around. We'll talk later." Schulberg nodded. Yes, later.

Jack Gallivan, one of Kennedy's advance men, had held an elevator for the Senator's party. They got in and then Kennedy asked if this would take them to the lobby. Someone said it would and Kennedy backed out. "I don't want to go through the lobby," he said. "I would rather go through the back way." He'd been mauled by large crowds for weeks. He didn't need another mauling before his talk. Uno Timanson, an Ambassador executive, led the party to a freight elevator. Kennedy and company piled into that. A contingent of writers and reporters got into another and Mike Wayne joined them. The two elevators reached the kitchen simultaneously, the groups combined and made their noisy way toward the Embassy Room. In the service pantry corridor, Wayne caught up to Kennedy, shoved a poster in his face and demanded an autograph. Kennedy stopped. The wave of people around Kennedy stopped. Kennedy signed the poster and moved on toward the Embassy Room.

Kennedy stopped a moment to talk to Bob Healy of the Boston *Globe* and Jules Witcover of the Newhouse newspaper chain, and invited them to The Factory, the currently fashionable discothèque in West Hollywood, for a victory party. Witcover remembered that Kennedy was as elated as he'd ever seen him in the entire campaign.

Steve Smith was talking to the crowd when Kennedy appeared, and the crowd roared its approval of the Senator and of Ethel, suntanned and pretty at his side in a white, sleeveless summer dress designed by Courrèges. Amid the tumult, someone told Kennedy that Cesar Chavez, the leader of the California grape strikers, would not be on the stage with him. Since Cesar's Lenten fast earlier in the spring, which had caused permanent damage to his spine, he tired easily and needed rest. Dolores Huerta, Cesar's organizing lieutenant, would take his place. Kennedy put an envelope in his pocket; on the back of it was Dolores' name, printed in haste, and her title, "Vice President, Farm Workers Union."

His talk was a disjointed mixture of the serious and the absurd. He wanted to acknowledge those who had helped in a special way. He wanted to entertain the crowd. And he wanted to throw in some sober words for folk watching from all over America. "I think," he said during one of those sober moments, "we can end the divisions within the United States, the violence."

Kennedy had a "high regard" for Don Drysdale, the Dodger pitcher who had just won a three-hit shutout an hour or so before, Drysdale's sixth in a row, to break a major-league record. He liked winners. He had thanks for Jesse Unruh "and all those associated with him" whose friendship and help and continuing perseverance helped him win. (For a time, it was not entirely clear that Unruh and his friends could do the job for Kennedy in California.) Kennedy thanked Congressman Tom Rees "who was an early supporter" and all those with him who worked so hard and "all of the students." Hundreds of them in the crowd cheered and wouldn't let him continue. He was grateful to his brother-in-law, Steve Smith, who was "ruthless but effective" and his sisters Jean and Pat and "all those other Kennedys." And to his old friend, Rafer Johnson, and to Rosey Grier, "who said he would take care of anybody who didn't vote for me."

Had he forgotten any of his friends? No. But how about his new enemy, Senator McCarthy? "Just a minute more of your time," said Kennedy. "Everybody must be dying from the heat." The crowd cried, "No! No!" Kennedy paused, then put in some good words for McCarthy. "The fact is," he said, "all of us are involved in this great effort . . . on behalf of mankind all over the globe . . . who still suffer from hunger." Kennedy had just won the California primary election, but his horizons were considerably wider just then. He was giving small expression to the ecumenicity that had been building inside him. Budd Schulberg had noticed it: to him, Kennedy was "a bridge between the best forces of the Establishment and the revolutionaries—the angry students and the angry blacks, the dispossessed."

While Kennedy went on, Fred Dutton turned to Uno Timanson and asked if the crowd of campaign workers waiting in the Ambassador Ballroom one floor below were watching all of this on television. Timanson said they were. Dutton indicated to him that there was no point in the Senator's going down there. "The Senator will go to the Colonial Room," said Dutton, "to have a session with the pencil press." Timanson left the stage to look at the Colonial Room and noted that there were no newsmen there, just a few teletype operators. He went back and told Dutton, "The press is here, in the Embassy Room." Dutton knew that. He had also visited the Colonial Room with his own aid, Thadis Heath. But some of the writers following Kennedy had been miffed because Kennedy seemed to give the TV reporters preferential treatment. Now was the time to even things up a bit—and if the Senator went to the Colonial Room, the writers would soon be there.

At the podium, Kennedy was almost finished. Time for a sally at Mayor Sam Yorty, a man for whom he'd had little affection since Yorty, a Democrat, had endorsed Richard Nixon instead of his brother in 1960. "Mayor Yorty has just sent me a message that we have been here too long already." Kennedy laughed and the crowd screamed approval. Kennedyites in Southern California disliked Yorty even more than Robert Kennedy did.

Kennedy concluded. They were his last public words. "We can work together [despite] the division, the violence, the disenchantment with our society, the division between black and white, between the poor and the more affluent, or between age groups or over the war in Vietnam. We are a great country, an unselfish country, a compassionate country. And I intend to make that my basis for running . . . So my thanks to all of you and now on to Chicago and let's win there." More screams and yells. Someone started to chant, "WE WANT BOBBY, WE WANT BOBBY." The crowd took it up, like a pro football crowd calling for a new quarterback.

There was a moment's hesitation on the stage. Someone wanted to lead Kennedy to his left through the Embassy Room past a gauntlet of pretty Kennedy girls costumed in red, white and blue. Indeed, his two bodyguards, Bill Barry and Rafer Johnson, were helping to clear the path. Edward Minasian, a maître d' dressed in a black tuxedo, started to lead Kennedy off to the right. But Karl Uecker, another maître d', had his way. He took Kennedy's right hand in his left, parted the gold curtain behind the rostrum and led Kennedy off the rear of the platform directly toward the service pantry.

Andrew West, a news reporter for radio station KRKD, a Mutual Network station, got to Kennedy for one question: "Senator, how are you going to counter Mr. Humphrey and his backgrounding you as far as delegate votes go?" It was clumsily put and ill timed, but perhaps West was only trying to see if Kennedy had a better word than "squeezable." Kennedy had no fancy coinage ready. He said simply: "It just goes back to the struggle for it."

By now, Timanson was in the lead, motioning frantically to Uecker who pulled Kennedy along. They turned to their right into a dim corridor, headed down a short incline and passed through the double doors of the service pantry, while Kennedy's entourage rushed along to catch up. "Slow down," cried Frank Burns, an attorney and close friend of Jesse Unruh. "Slow down. You're getting ahead of everyone."

Bill Barry, the ex-FBI man who had guarded Kennedy so closely through the hectic days of the campaign while Kennedy almost drowned himself in people, was lifting Ethel Kennedy down from the stage. "I'm all right," said Ethel. "Stay with the Senator." Barry turned and started for the pantry. He saw Frank Mankiewicz ahead of him and Jesse Unruh and Frank Burns and Pierre Salinger. They were also hurrying to catch up.

The one man who might have saved Kennedy's life, an armed security guard who was at the Senator's side when he reached the pantry, was hardly in condition to perform any heroics. Thane Eugene Cesar had worked a full day on his regular job as a maintenance plumber at Lockheed, on the 7:00 A.M. to 3:30 P.M. shift. He no sooner arrived home in Simi, some thirty-five miles from Lockheed, than his boss at the Ace Guard Service phoned and told him to show up at the Ambassador that evening. Cesar rushed into town—an hour and a half drive—only five minutes late. After six more hours of work, trying to "control drunks, break up fights and keep young children from sneaking into the Embassy Room," Cesar was assigned to escort Senator Kennedy through the crowd to the Colonial Room. He grabbed Kennedy's right arm and started pushing back the crowd in the pantry with his own right arm.

Senator Kennedy moved through the double door past Boris Yaro, a photographer for the Los Angeles *Times,* and Richard Drew, a reporter for the Pasadena *Independent Star-News.* Yaro had his camera up, trying to focus. Drew said, "Hey, Boris, you missed him." Yaro looked up and saw that Kennedy had rushed past. He started to follow, raised his camera again when Kennedy stopped to shake hands with some of the kitchen help, who were standing next to some stainless-steel warming tables. Taped on one wall was a large hand-lettered sign: THE ONCE AND FUTURE KING.

Lisa Lynn Urso, a dark-haired teen-ager who was a Kennedy volunteer in San Diego, had gone to the kitchen during the victory speech "to cool off." She was still in the pantry when Kennedy entered, and she turned as he came toward her.

Valerie Schulte, a student at the University of California at Santa Barbara, and a "Kennedy girl," hobbled in behind Kennedy (she was on crutches) and saw him stop in front of the kitchen boys.

"Senator Kennedy was smiling," said a bus boy, Juan Romero. "He held out his hand and I shook it." Kennedy moved on a step or two, turned to his left and shook hands with a waiter, Martin Patrusky, and then with a kitchen porter, Jesus Perez.

Out of the corner of her eye, Lisa Lynn Urso noticed that a slight young man in front of her, dressed in blue or beige, was reaching across his body with his right hand. Subconsciously, she thought "he was getting ready to shake hands with Kennedy." But when he continued the motion, she said to herself, "He's reaching for a gun." She saw him bring his arm back out in front of him and upward and he took a slight step forward.

Juan Romero noticed someone to his left, smiling and reaching a hand toward Kennedy. There was a gun in that hand and it was "approximately one yard from Senator Kennedy's head."

Lisa Lynn Urso saw no gun—just "flames coming from the tip of his hand."

Curiously enough, Freddy Plimpton saw no gun either. She'd been following her husband George through the pantry, and was still behind Kennedy when she saw him shaking hands with Jesus Perez. Then Kennedy gave a slight jump and his hands went up to the side of his face "as if to push something away." Freddy Plimpton's recall of the gunman is more vivid than that of any other eyewitness. "His eyes were narrow, the lines on his face were heavy and set and he was completely concentrated on what he was doing. I did not see a gun. I don't know why I didn't see a gun."

But Valerie Schulte saw it. "Kennedy turned back to shake hands and I was pushed sideways and forward. And then I saw this gun. It was a small gun. It looked like a cap gun."

Richard G. Lubic, swarthy president of a closed-circuit television company in Hollywood, stood at Kennedy's right, waiting for an acknowledgment. He heard a voice cry: "Kennedy, you son of a bitch," then heard two shots "which sounded like shots from a starter pistol at a track meet."

Cesar, the armed guard, also saw the gun. "I saw a hand sticking out of the crowd," says Cesar, "between two cameramen, and the hand was holding a gun." Cesar says he was blinded by the brilliant lights, moved toward the gun, then saw a red flash come from the muzzle. "I ducked," says Cesar, "because I was as close as Kennedy was. When I ducked, I threw myself off balance and fell back and when I hit . . . I fell against the iceboxes and the Senator fell down right in front of me."

Martin Patrusky, the waiter, recalled that, "The guy looked like he was smiling and he looked like he was going to shake hands with him, and he reached over like this, and then the firing just started, and the next thing I know . . . I seen Kennedy starting to go down on his knees."

Freddy Plimpton believed the first shot hit Senator Kennedy in the arm. No one can gainsay her, but most other witnesses reported that there were two shots in rapid succession, then a pause, then three more. "I was about three feet behind and to the right of him," said Boris Yaro, "and I was trying to find his head in my camera view finder when I heard what I thought were two explosions. My first thought was 'Some jerk has thrown some firecrackers in here.' "

Edward Minasian, who was on Kennedy's right and a little ahead of Karl Uecker, saw a flash and heard two shots. Then Uecker leaped on the man with the gun. "I immediately grabbed the man's gun hand," said Uecker, "and pushed him onto the steam table. During this time he continued to fire the gun."

"I pushed the two of them against the serving table," said Minasian. "The shots continued. No other people grabbed the suspect. I saw the fellow behind the Senator fall, then the Senator fell." The man behind Kennedy was Paul Schrade, who thought he had run into a bolt of lightning.

Uecker had his right arm around the assailant's neck and got his left hand on his right wrist after the second shot—or possibly the third. Uecker tried to push the gun away from Kennedy, with little success. Besides Schrade, four others were hit by the wild shots. Uecker tried to slam the gun hand against a nearby steam table and cried out, "Get his gun! Get his gun!" Then the shots stopped and he told Minasian, "Get the police; get the police." Minasian ran for a telephone.

Bill Barry was hurrying through the crowd to catch up and take his customary place immediately in front of Kennedy. He was perhaps six feet away when he heard a sound "like a firecracker." He charged through the remainder of the crowd, struck out with his fists, then got a headlock on the man being held by Uecker.

At the sound of the shots, Roosevelt Grier pushed Ethel Kennedy to the floor and covered her body with his, a huge human shield. Moments later, he was seen kneeling next to the steam table, his head in his hands, sobbing, "Oh, no! Oh, no!" Pete Hamill, a free-lance writer from New York who had been traveling with Kennedy, looked at his watch. It was 12:15 A.M., June 5, 1968.

In the dim light of the hallway, about three or four feet from the double doors leading to the pantry, Rafer Johnson heard a sound like "a bursting balloon." A second or two later, he heard another and started to move toward the pantry where he saw "smoke and pieces of paper in the air." He plowed through the crowd and entered the pantry just as Bill Barry hit the little man with the gun. He first saw Paul Schrade lying on his back with a bloody hole in his head, then Senator Kennedy almost flat but struggling to get up. Kennedy's right hand moved from his head in a slow arc to his side. Blood flowed from the right side of his head below the ear, his cheek and his chest were stained with it, and a pool of it, enough to fill a chalice, formed on the dirty concrete floor. Kennedy looked at Johnson, and they stared at each other for a moment.

Hugh J. McDonald, assistant press secretary to Kennedy, came to Kennedy's side, took off his own jacket and placed it next to Kennedy's head. Rafer Johnson moved toward the man with the gun who was struggling with Uecker and Barry.

Jim Wilson, a burly television cameraman, was on the floor, slapping it with his hand and screaming, "My God! My God! No! No!" His sound man, John William Lewis, a little blond fellow, was shouting in his ear, "You've got to shoot, Jimmy, you've got to shoot! You've got to shoot!"

Andy West, the radio reporter, had more aplomb. He burst into the room, took in the complete meaning of the scene before him, and flipped the switch on his portable tape recorder.

Senator Kennedy has been shot! Senator Kennedy has been shot; is that possible? Is that possible? Is it possible, ladies and gentlemen . . . it is possible, he has. Not only Senator Kennedy. Oh my God, Senator Kennedy has been shot and another man, a Kennedy campaign manager and possible shot in the head. I am right here.

By then, Frank J. Burns, Jr., and Warren Rogers had joined the macabre dance in the middle of the floor, spinning down the room to the last of three steam tables.

Gabor Kadar, the Hungarian refugee who had entered the area in disguise, vaulted onto the table and grabbed the hand of the man holding the gun. To dislodge the gun, he slammed the hand against the table several times, apparently without success.

Andy West's tape and the sound track of Jim Wilson's film (for Wilson had now gotten to his feet) recorded the cacophony of the moment. Screams, shouts of "Oh, my God!" and "Jesus Christ!" and more screams and "Somebody get a doctor!" In the middle of this chaos—by now, at least seventy * people had come into the room—there were two well-defined centers of activity: one around Kennedy and the other around the man with the gun.

From the floor, Thane Cesar watched others pile on the man with the gun. Then he rose, pulled his own gun and moved—too late—to the side of Kennedy, "to protect him from further attack."

Jack Gallivan and George Plimpton attached themselves to the twisting

* See Appendix A for the official Los Angeles Police Department list of the persons who were actually in the pantry when Kennedy was shot.

pile of men struggling for the gun. No one knew whether there were more bullets in it or not. "Take care of the Senator," said Gallivan to Barry. "I can handle him." Earl Williman, an electrician at Desilu Studios and an officer in his union, jumped up on the steam table and tried to stomp on the hand holding the gun. Suddenly, the gun was free, lying right on the table.

Barry called to Roosevelt Grier. "Take him, Rosey, take him!" As he spoke, he released his hold. The assailant seized the gun again and another struggle began.

Barry fought through the crowd that was now gathering around Kennedy. "Put that gun away," he said to Thane Cesar, the security guard. He put the coat lying next to Kennedy under his head.

Juan Romero, the little bus boy, had gone to Kennedy and cradled his head with his right hand. "Come on, Mr. Kennedy," he said. "You can make it." Kennedy's lips moved. Romero said he seemed to say, "Is everybody all right?" Someone next to Romero said, "Throw that gum away, Mr. Kennedy." Romero started to reach for a wad of chewing gum in Kennedy's mouth, but then he thought he'd better not. Kennedy's right eye was open and his left eyelid moved up and down. His right fist was raised as if he were clutching at something. Richard Aubry, a post-office clerk with a press badge on his chest, knelt down next to Kennedy and said a little prayer. A young man bent over Kennedy and repeated words the nuns had taught him in grammar school back in New Jersey: "Oh my God, I am heartily sorry for having offended you. . . ." It was an Act of Contrition, and the young man from New Jersey, Danny Curtin, dug into his pockets for his rosary, handed it to Romero and said, "Keep this, Mr. Kennedy." Romero wrapped the rosary around Kennedy's left thumb and folded his hand over it. Kennedy brought the rosary up to his chest.

Richard Tuck had pushed a path through the crowd for Ethel Kennedy. Before she got to her husband, she heard Ira Goldstein, who worked for something called Continental News, moaning, "What happened to Kennedy? What happened to that so-and-so?" Ethel stopped and scolded him. "How dare you talk about my husband that way!" Goldstein said she slapped his face.

"I am sorry, lady," Goldstein protested. "I got shot too."

Ethel softened. "Oh, I'm sorry, honey," she said, and knelt and kissed him on the cheek.

Finally, Ethel made it to Kennedy's side. She pushed Romero away and started talking to her husband in a low, soothing voice. His jaw worked. He was trying to speak.

Ethel left his side for a moment and, with more presence of mind than most of the screaming mob in that pantry, found a towel and filled it with ice from the ice machine that was such a dominant feature of the room, and came back with it just as Dr. Stanley Abo arrived. Abo, a radiologist from Midway Hospital in West Los Angeles, was the first doctor at the scene. He was literally pushed into the pantry, examined Schrade briefly, then turned to Kennedy. He pressed his ear to Kennedy's chest, found the breathing quite shallow. He found one wound, a small one just back of the right ear, hardly bleeding. He took Kennedy's pulse. It was slow, possibly because of something he termed "cranial pressure." Abo probed the wound with his finger to make it bleed and thereby relieve the pressure.

"Oh, Ethel, Ethel," Kennedy moaned. Ethel patted his hands. "It's okay," she said.

"Am I all right?" he asked.

"You're doing good," said Dr. Abo. "The ambulance is on its way."

"The ambulance is coming," said Ethel.

Kennedy took her right hand in his and brought it to the crucifix on his chest.

More and more people streamed into the room. The air became very heavy. Tuck took off his coat and started to fan the Senator.

"You'd better go see where the damn ambulance is," said Barry to Tuck. "Or how it can get in."

Across the room, Rafer Johnson lunged for the gun, grabbing it by the barrel with his left hand. Roosevelt Grier held the butt. Incredibly enough to Andy West, the assailant still had his finger in the trigger housing.

> Rafer Johnson has a hold of the man who apparently has fired the shot; he has fired the shot. He still has the gun. The gun is pointed at me at this moment. I hope they can get the gun out of his hand. Be very careful. Get the gun. Get the gun. Get the gun. Stay away from the gun.

[Someone in the background cries out, "Get his head."]

Joseph La Hive, president of the Van Nuys Democratic Club, followed right behind Grier and Johnson and he, too, grabbed at the gun. "Let me have the gun. Let go, Rosey. Let go, Rafer."

"Shut up!" cried Johnson. Then he shouted to Grier, "Let me have the gun."

La Hive let go of the barrel and chimed in. "Let Rafer have the gun."

Andy West cried out at La Hive:

> Get away from the barrel; get away from the barrel, man. Look out for the gun. Okay.

Johnson shouted at Grier again. "Rosey, give me the gun." Grier pulled and twisted—the little man's strength was fantastic—and finally got control of the gun. He gave it to Johnson.

West kept on recording.

All right, that's it, Rafer, get it, get the gun, Rafer. Okay, now hold on to the guy, hold on to him, hold on to him. Ladies and gentlemen, they have the gun away from the man; they got the gun.

Johnson looked at the gun in wonder and disbelief, small, snub-nosed, with a dull blue barrel. Then he put it in his left coat pocket. Uecker, Grier, Gallivan, Plimpton, Burns and Rogers continued to hold on. Burns dropped off.

West went on:

I can't see the man. I can't see who it is. Senator Kennedy right now is on the ground; he has been shot. This is a . . . this is . . . What is he?

The captive continued to struggle and others pounced in to strike. Kadar pummeled him in the chest and kicked him in the knee. Booker Griffin, an organizer from Watts and an aspiring politico, started chopping at his neck, and others seemed to be trying to twist his head off, as it hung over the edge of the metal table.

Wait a minute! [cried West] *Hold him! Hold him! We don't want another Oswald. Hold him, Rafer. We don't want another Oswald. Hold him, Rafer. Keep people away from him; keep people away from him.*

Jesse Unruh picked up on that and turned to the twisting tableau on the steam table. "We don't want another Dallas," he shouted, pulling away some of those who were still trying to strike the prisoner. "We don't want another Dallas." Unruh climbed up on the steam table and started an impromptu speech. "If the system works at all," he said, "we are going to try this one." The American people were cheated when Oswald didn't stand trial. Unruh, for one, was determined to see that this man did.

Several doctors reached Kennedy's side and called for air. Andy West tried to help.

All right, ladies and gentlemen, this is now . . . Make room, make room, make room, make room, make room. The Senator is on the ground; he is bleeding profusely, from apparently . . . clear back. Apparently the Senator has been shot . . . from the, in the frontal area, we can't see exactly where the, where the Senator has been shot, but, push back . . . come on . . . grab a hold of me, grab a hold of me and let's pull back, that's it . . . come on, get a hold of my arms and let's pull back, let's pull back.

Dr. Abo clamped the ice pack on the Senator's head. Dr. Ross Miller loosened the Senator's tie. Another unbuttoned his shirt. Someone took off his shoes. The doctors were told an ambulance was on the way. They decided that was all they could do for Kennedy at the moment. They looked at the others who were shot. At Paul Schrade, a man of forty-three, whose head rested on a white plastic campaign hat; at nineteen-year-old Ira Goldstein, hit in the left hip; at William Weisel, an American Broadcasting Company associate director, aged thirty, wounded in the abdomen; and at Mrs. Elizabeth Evans, forty-three, who had been touring the several election night headquarters with her husband and wound up with a slug in her forehead. Seventeen-year-old Irwin Stroll, hit in the knee, had already been carried off by his friends, put in a taxi and sent to the hospital.

Andy West was still talking into his recorder:

All right now, the Senator is now the . . . the ambulance has been called for and the . . . ambulance has . . . Bring the ambulance in this entrance. This is a terrible thing: it's reminiscent of the Valley the other day when the Senator was out there and somebody hit him in the head with a rock and people couldn't believe it at that time. But it is a fact. Keep room, Ethel Kennedy is standing by, she is calm, she is raising her hand high to motion people back, she's attempting to get calm. A woman with a tremendous amount of presence. It's impossible to believe. It's impossible to believe this. There is a certain amount of fanaticism here now, as this has occurred. They are trying to run everybody back. Clear the area, clear the area. Right at this moment . . . the Senator apparently, we can't see if he's still conscious or not. Can you see if he is conscious? He is half conscious.

Jesse Unruh tried to get some order in the room. He pulled one photographer off the steam table and pushed him into the corridor. He pushed out the merely curious and photographers and newsmen, including Andy West.

Is there some way to close these doors, Jess? [Someone's voice cried, "No."] *Is there any doors here?* ["No."] ["Out, out, out, get out."] *Out, out, through the exit, let's go. Out we go . . . Unbelievable situation.*

Inside the pantry, a woman yelled at Boris Yaro of the Los Angeles *Times,* "Don't take pictures."

"Lady, this is history," said Yaro. The woman started pulling on his right arm and so, says Yaro, "I shoved her into the wall and kept shooting —more."

Back on the steam table, Joseph La Hive tried to get the gunman's feet off the floor. He lifted one leg and gave it a savage twist. "Stop," the man said, "you're hurting my leg." At least he spoke English. His words triggered something in Johnson. He shouted in the man's ear, "Why did you do it?"

No answer.

Rafer Johnson moved around next to the man who was now pinned to the table by at least six others and looked into his eyes. To George Plimpton, who was holding onto the man's right arm, they were "enormously peaceful eyes." He couldn't remember the color of the man's shirt. "Being a writer, I'd think I would. And yet, God damn it, I can't tell you . . . I think his shirt was yellow brown, but if you told me it wasn't, I wouldn't be the slightest surprised. I could tell you all about his eyes. They were dark brown and enormously peaceful."

Johnson glared fiercely into those eyes and asked again: "Why did you do it?" Again no answer. Johnson clenched his fist and placed the back of it on the young man's forehead. "Why did you do it?" he growled.

Someone thought he heard the assassin say: "Let me explain. I can explain."

But someone else told him to shut up. And he did.

Grier, somewhat over his playing weight of 290 pounds, had pinned him down on the table. Even so, someone suggested tying the prisoner with a rope. Niwa Yoshio, a 22-year-old cook in the cold meat department who was holding on to the man's left arm, gave the arm to someone else while he dashed off for some rope. He didn't find any, returned, took the arm back and shouted to Henry Carillo, a room-service manager, "Get some rope." Carillo went to something called the head checker storage room, obtained a segment of rubber extension cord and returned with it.

"Don't tie him," said Grier. "The police will be here soon."

At approximately 12:15 A.M., Patrolmen Travis White and Arthur Placencia were cruising on Wilshire Boulevard when they heard a call for another car in the area, 2 A 51, to proceed to 3400 Wilshire where there was something called "ambulance shooting." That meant that someone was shot, an ambulance was already rolling and they should, too, as backup. White, the senior man, said, "That's the Ambassador! Let's go." He turned on his siren and red lights.

At the hotel, no one yet seemed to know what had happened, or where. Finally, some hotel employees took the two policemen to the kitchen area. Said one employee: "He's right here and they are killing him." Indeed, it looked and sounded like it. White and Placencia saw the struggle on the steam table. Rafer Johnson and Rosey Grier were still fighting off people "milling around the suspect and punching and kicking him." They heard cries of "Kill the bastard! Kill him!" The man they were looking for was spread-eagled on the table and Jesse Unruh had a knee in his back.

Other police arrived. Officer William Nunley pulled out his handcuffs, leaned over the table, snapped one cuff on the man's left wrist, but had trouble getting hold of the right. Unruh wouldn't let go. Neither would Grier.

"We are police officers," said White. "We are taking him in." He and Placencia rolled Grier off the man, and the man let out a great gasp of air.

"I charge you with the responsibility for the man," said Unruh. But he kept hanging on.

Finally, one of the policemen gave Unruh a violent push and started to move through the crowd. "All right," said Unruh, "you can take him, but I am coming too." Placencia and White moved off with the prisoner, and Unruh kept his hand on the back of the man's neck. "This one is going to face trial," shouted Unruh, a politician even in the middle of a murder scene. "Nothing is going to happen to him. He is going to pay. We aren't going to have another Dallas."

White led the way, almost running through the Colonial Room and into the carpeted lobby. Placencia was right behind him with the prisoner. They started down the twisting stairs to the ground floor.

"Slow down, slow down," cried Unruh. "This isn't a race." Placencia looked back and saw a horde of people behind him. He still didn't know why they were angry. "All I can think of," said Placencia, "is getting the suspect out of there. And here is Unruh—'Slow down, slow down, it's not a race.' And I just looked and I said, 'Come on, partner, let's go.' "

Just as the police led the suspect away, Kennedy's friend, Richard Tuck, arrived with the ambulance driver, Robert Hulsman, and a bulky attendant, Max Behrman. Both were dressed like police officers, with one difference, a shoulder patch that said "medical attendant." They wheeled their stretcher up to Kennedy. Hulsman took his feet, Behrman his head.

"Keep your hands off him. I'm Mrs. Kennedy," Behrman said Ethel Kennedy said.

"We are here from Central Receiving Hospital, Emergency Section. We are here to help you," said Behrman.

"I don't care who you are," said Mrs. Kennedy. Somebody else said to hurry and get the Senator on the stretcher. Behrman moved in roughly, put a blanket under and around Kennedy.

"No, please don't," said Robert Kennedy. "Don't lift me up."

Hulsman and Behrman each grabbed an end of the blanket and heaved it onto the stretcher. Barry told the attendants to go "Gently, please, gently." But they bumped and banged their way through the kitchen pantry to the elevator, where Rafer Johnson stood guard. Johnson allowed Mrs. Kennedy, Bill Barry, Fred Dutton, one of the chiefs of Kennedy's campaign, Blanche Whitaker, wife of Jim Whitaker, the mountain climber, Warren Rogers of *Look* and Dick Tuck to get into the elevator with the stretcher bearers. Pete Hamill looked at his watch. It was 12:32. Seventeen minutes getting Kennedy out. He looked at the pool of blood on the floor. Kennedy's blood. Could he survive that much loss?

At 3:31 A.M., Eastern Standard Time, President Lyndon B. Johnson was awakened in his White House bedroom by a phone call from Walt Whitman Rostow who told him Senator Kennedy had been shot in Los Angeles. The President turned on his TV console—three separate screens, one for each network—and put in a call to the Secret Service. He wanted the service to dispatch agents immediately to the side of all Presidential candidates and their families. No, he didn't have legal authority to do so. Yes, he was going to ask Congress to give it to him in the morning.

The dark young man named Michael Wayne ran out of the pantry into the lobby. "Get him," cried a voice, "he's getting away!" Several persons tackled Wayne on the rose-colored carpet. A security guard cuffed him and turned him over to the police, who led him off for questioning, through a crowd of people who assumed that Wayne was the gunman, or, possibly, an accomplice. As it turned out, Wayne was only running for a telephone. There was nothing sinister about that. A lot of people were running around in mindless frenzy. The Embassy Room was bedlam. Some persons tried to jam into the pantry. Others were frozen with shock and unbelief. Steve Smith, the Senator's brother-in-law, got on the public-address system and urged everyone to leave quietly. Women started crying hysterically.

Steve Arvin, a reporter for radio station KMPC, was at a bank of telephones at the west end of the Embassy Room, talking with Bruce Anson in KMPC's Hollywood studios when he got his first inkling of what had happened.

"Bruce?"

"Yeah?"

"Hang on." Arvin's voice turned giddy. "I think somebody's shot Kennedy. Hang on."

"Wait a minute," cried Anson.

"Hang on." Arvin left his wife, Anne, holding the phone, tried to find out what was happening and returned with what he could only call "an unconfirmed report" that Kennedy was shot. He didn't know where Kennedy was shot, or how serious it was, or who shot him. He wasn't even sure that it was Kennedy who was shot.

Finally, Anson was saved from utter despair by a report from one of the bank of police radios at KMPC's newsroom. "Steve, we just got a report from the police radio. It wasn't Kennedy. It was not Kennedy who was shot."

"Well," said Arvin hesitantly, "that's why I said this report was unconfirmed. But this gentleman from the media said he saw the Kennator. . . ."

Minutes later, Arvin phoned Anson again with a young man in tow who had been next to Kennedy in the pantry. The young man identified himself as Danny Curtin and Anson put him on the air. With great feeling, Curtin, who was twenty-one and a psychology major at Southwest College in Los Angeles, started to blurt out his story: how he had heard the shots from outside the pantry doors, burst in, saw Kennedy bleeding from the head, talked to him and gave him a rosary to hold. For some reason, Curtin felt that Rose Kennedy, the Senator's mother, would be listening. He wanted to reassure her. He, too, was a Catholic and he wanted Rose Kennedy to know that Bobby had a rosary in his hand. . . . It could have been a moving interview, certainly better than anything KMPC had at the moment.

But Anson cut him off in favor of a piece of teletype copy from the United Press. That was authoritative. The eyewitness was not. Anson announced with some relief that Kennedy was shot in the hip. He repeated the news. "The United Press International says Senator Kennedy was shot in the hip." Later, relying on another bulletin from the UPI, KMPC reported that one shot was fired at Kennedy and five shots pumped into his assailant, a man tentatively identified as "Jesse Grier."

At the hotel's automobile entrance, John Frankenheimer was waiting with his wife Evans in his Rolls-Royce Silver Cloud. "Get moving," shouted a policeman.

"We're waiting for Senator Kennedy," protested Frankenheimer, who had left the hotel immediately after Kennedy's speech and knew nothing of

the shooting. Again, the policeman told him to get moving, and Frankenheimer sensed something was wrong. He knew it for a fact when he saw
deputy sheriffs vaulting the west wall of the Ambassador property and
rushing toward the hotel. He turned on his radio and got the sickening
news.

Inside the hotel, knots of people wandered around aimlessly, some
cursing, some weeping, some arguing heatedly. Near a fountain in the middle of the lobby, a woman with a pair of rosary beads begged others to
pray with her and twenty of them knelt down. An apparent unbeliever
cursed and threw a chair into the fountain.

Andy West was signing off.

*At this moment we are stunned. We are shaking, as is everyone else in this
kitchen corridor at the Ambassador Hotel, in Los Angeles. They are blocking off the entrance now, supposedly to make room for the ambulance.
That's all we can report at this moment. I do not know if the Senator is dead
or if he is alive. We do not know the name of the other gentleman concerned. This is Andrew West, Mutual News, Los Angeles.*

In the elevator, Max Behrman bawled out instructions. "Please lower
your voice," Ethel Kennedy said. Behrman went right on shouting orders.
Blanche Whitaker was infuriated. She gave Behrman a light tap on the
mouth.

"Don't do that again, lady," he growled, "or somebody will get a
crushed head." The elevator reached the ground floor.

Behrman and Hulsman propelled the stretcher down a concrete ramp.
"Somebody grab that thing," cried Barry. Warren Rogers reached out and
slowed the stretcher down.

"For Christ's sake, let go!" shouted Behrman. Rogers held on.

"Only Mrs. Kennedy rides with him," snarled Behrman. Fred Dutton
shoved past him and joined Mrs. Kennedy inside. So did Blanche Whitaker. Behrman got in.

"But I belong in there too," said Barry.

Rogers grabbed him and they both got in the front seat next to the
driver, Hulsman. Ethel Kennedy signaled to Father James Mundell, a Mary-
knoll priest and close friend, to follow the ambulance.

Behrman picked up his call book and turned to Ethel Kennedy. "Just
for the records," he said, "I have to know what happened." Ethel said she

didn't care what he had to know. Behrman said she grabbed his call book and threw it out the rear of the ambulance.

In front of the Ambassador's canopied west door, police car 2 X 48 was ready to take the assassin away. A crowd of people there started screaming and surging forward. Patrolman Placencia pushed his suspect into the back seat, locked the door, went around to the other side and climbed into the back. White got in behind the wheel and Unruh jumped in beside him. ("We didn't ask him," said Placencia. "He just got in.") Others tried to crawl over Unruh to get to the prisoner. Unruh's friend Frank Burns pulled them away and shoved the door shut.

"Let's get out of here!" cried Unruh. And the police car pulled off.

White sped out the drive, across Wilshire onto Alexandria, right on Fifth Street, red lights flashing. Art Placencia thought his prisoner had a little smile on his face. He had seemed terribly frightened in the pantry area. Now, to Placencia, he looked "smirky."

Placencia turned on his flashlight and looked into the young man's pupils which were dilated and remained so despite the light in his eyes, an indication the gunman was either drunk or drugged.

Travis White noted what Placencia was doing and told Placencia (who had only been out of the police academy two short months), "You'd better give him his rights, partner."

Placencia took out his field notebook. On the inside cover was a standard formula which the Los Angeles police used to inform the suspect of his constitutional rights to remain silent, have counsel present, and be provided free counsel. After Placencia read the formula, he said, "Do you understand your rights?"

The suspect mumbled something. Placencia read the formula again. "Do you understand your rights?" he demanded.

"Yes," said the suspect.

"Do you wish to remain silent?"

"Yes."

Placencia addressed Unruh in the front seat. "By the way, who did he shoot?"

"Bob Kennedy," said Unruh.

The news jolted Placencia, but he tried not to show it. "By the way," he said, "who are you?"

"Jesse Unruh."

"Oh!"

Unruh turned around in his seat, and spoke to the man in handcuffs. "Why did you do it?"

"I did it for my country," Unruh said the suspect said.*

Unruh thought the young man looked like a Mexican. The Mexican-Americans, Unruh knew, were very high on Kennedy. Nine out of ten of them had voted for Kennedy that very day, and the ones who hadn't probably hadn't voted. "Why him? Why him?" demanded Unruh.

"It's too late. It's too late," said the prisoner, shaking his head. Unruh, too, shook his head. He couldn't figure it.

"He can't do himself any harm, can he?" asked Unruh when they arrived at the Rampart Street police station.

Sergeant Bill Jordan, the night watch commander, pointed out that the man was handcuffed. "And somebody will stay with him," he added. "You'd better believe that."

Grant Burr Cooper should have been asleep. He was "in trial" and when he was in trial, he stuck to a rigorous regime: home at 6 P.M., two or three drinks (Myers Rum and Tab) to relax, a quiet dinner with his wife Phyllis, and then to bed by 8 o'clock where he would use television as a soporific, to clear his mind of all the clutter of the day, the second-guesses and I-should-have-saids which, in his early days as an attorney, used to keep him tossing all night.

But Cooper wanted to see Kennedy claim the victory. He was not a rabid Kennedyite. He had voted for Eugene McCarthy and would end up dropping his ballot on November 4 for Hubert Humphrey. But this was a helluva election year, already full of stunning surprises, when the unexpected was likeliest to happen. Russell Baker, the political satirist of *The New York Times,* had written an entire book that spun out a fantasy ending up with LBJ, Nixon and Wallace deadlocked for the Presidency, and Robert Kennedy being voted into power by the U.S. Senate. Now it seemed Kennedy wasn't waiting for Baker's dream to come true. He had forced LBJ to abdicate and would take care of Nixon head on.

Kennedy was coming on strong, and Cooper now wanted to see what he would say. Cooper had to smile at Kennedy's exuberance, at Kennedy's happiness, at the happiness and exuberance of the Kennedy people.

Then Kennedy was suddenly off the tube. Cooper got up to go to the

* White and Placencia said they didn't hear the man say anything of the sort. Later, Unruh would say he wasn't sure where, when or if the man really did say, "I did it for my country."

bathroom, returned just in time to see there was trouble at the Ambassador. "Phyllis," he said. She had just dozed off. "Phyllis," he said. "Somebody's shot Kennedy." It was a scene being played in millions of homes across the nation. "Some son of a bitch," said Cooper, "has shot Kennedy."

Russell Parsons lay on his back in the dark, staring at the ceiling of his room at the Elks Club in Los Angeles, not far from the Ambassador Hotel. Why, he wondered, why all the sirens at this hour of the morning? To Parsons, sirens meant trouble and he sighed. All of his life he had stalked trouble. Through years as a prosecuting attorney in California and Utah, through years as a criminal attorney, he lived on the troubles of others. In his later years, he had undertaken to run several homes for the incompetent and the insane, mansions of misery.

Somehow the misery rubbed off on him. At seventy-six, toward the end of his life, at a time when he should have been retired and living a life of ease in his old home in the Hollywood Hills, he bunked alone in a dingy room at the Elks, while his second wife, Vicki, took her ease in Palm Springs.

Another siren in the night. That was the second one in a minute, coming down Sixth Street, right under his window. Here was a third. What was happening? He rolled over and tried to sleep.

John Howard was a big man with a sandy crew cut and a sunny, carefree disposition that belied his responsibilities as chief of the D.A.'s Special Investigations Division. He had prime administrative duties in an office of some two hundred lawyers and served as the D.A.'s chief attorney before the County Grand Jury.

Normally, on a Tuesday at midnight, he would have been at home, fast asleep. On this night, election night, he was with a friend, Lynne Frantz, who was losing a race for a Democratic nomination in the 17th Congressional District, the South Bay area of Los Angeles. If Frantz had been winning, Howard would have left the campaign headquarters at the Plush Horse Inn in Redondo Beach and gone home. But a friend who was losing needed consolation. Not that Frantz didn't have a lot of other friends. He did. And they, too, were there, heisting one last highball and talking, as losers will, about what they ought to do "next time."

All of a sudden, the babble of voices trailed off to nothing, and on the

television in the corner a reporter was trying to tell the world that somebody, possibly Senator Kennedy, was shot in the pantry of the Ambassador Hotel.

"God! Not again!" said Howard, hoping the report was wrong.

Howard was a Kennedy Democrat. He didn't even wait for confirmation, dashed instead to his car and sped up the almost deserted Harbor
Freeway to the D.A.'s headquarters downtown. By the time he got there,
the radio news told him Kennedy—and others—might have been critically
wounded. He called a platoon of other prosecutors down to headquarters
and headed for Central Receiving Hospital.

Robert Greene, a staff writer for Long Island's *Newsday,* was at home
in King's Park, Long Island, in bed. Most of his 287 pounds were asleep,
but part of his brain was awake. He had long been in the habit of keeping
the radio on all night, letting a little monitor inside him listen to the news
and, occasionally, jolt him awake when someone was saying something he
needed to know. Shortly after 3:00 A.M., in the middle of a desultory discussion on WNBC by "Long John Nebel," a bulletin on Kennedy came on
and Greene sat upright in bed, knowing something important was happening. His wife, Kathy, awoke at the same moment, listened and grabbed her
husband. "God, Bob, Kennedy's been shot," she cried.

Greene, who had been a friend of both John and Robert Kennedy,
hulked, Buddha-like, on the edge of the bed and lit up a Pall Mall, wondering what he should do. His editor at *Newsday* solved that problem for
him by phoning. "Get over to JFK," he directed, referring to New York's
international airport, "and get on American's Flight #9 for Los Angeles.
We'll have someone waiting there with your ticket and some money."

Officers White and Placencia deposited their prisoner in the "breatha-
lyzer room" (outfitted with special equipment used for testing suspected
drunks) at Rampart Street police station, then moved him immediately to
Interrogation Room B, a bare room with a metal table and a few metal
chairs and a microphone imbedded somewhere in the acoustical walls.
White searched him while Placencia and Unruh looked on. White found
four $100 bills, one $5 bill, four $1 bills in the left front pocket of a very
tight-fitting pair of light blue denims, $1.66 in change in the right pocket,
a comb, a car key, a David Lawrence column clipped from the May 26
edition of the Pasadena *Independent Star-News,* two unexpended .22-cali-

ber cartridges, one expended copper-jacketed slug, a songsheet handed out to Kennedy supporters at the Ambassador, and a five-inch-by-five-inch newspaper advertisement for a Robert Kennedy rally:

> You and your friends are cordially invited
> To come to see and hear
> **SENATOR ROBERT KENNEDY**
> On Sunday, June 2, 1968
> At 8:00 P.M.
> Cocoanut Grove
> Ambassador Hotel, Los Angeles
> Leon M. Cooper, Treasurer
> Jesse Unruh, Chairman

The Lawrence column was headed "Paradoxical Bob" and it began, "Presidential candidates are out to get the votes, and some of them do not realize their own inconsistencies. . . ." To Lawrence, Kennedy was inconsistent by opposing the war in Vietnam while he advocated help for Israel. White squinted at the prisoner. He certainly didn't look Vietnamese.

Sergeant John S. Locker entered the room, asked Jesse Unruh to step outside and assigned Sergeant E. H. Austin and Officer F. R. Willoughby of the Rampart Vice Division to guard the prisoner. Los Angeles Police Department brass started pouring into the Rampart station and Sergeant Bill Jordan took over. Jordan, like many older members of the Los Angeles Police Department, was an ex-Marine, but he hardly fit the stereotype of "Marine" or even "cop." His blond hair was long rather than crew cut. He was likelier to smile than frown, and his voice was low, not raucous. But now his face was grim. He told Willoughby and Austin to wait outside.

"This is weird," said George Plimpton to his bride. The two of them— six-foot, five-inch Plimpton and Freddy, barely five feet—were trying to lead huge Roosevelt Grier out of the pantry, through the Ambassador lobby and up to one of the Kennedy bedrooms on the fifth floor. Grier, the bodyguard. Robert Kennedy had just said moments before, "Rosey would take care of anybody who didn't vote for me." But Rosey was a hunk of blubber now, stumbling down the carpeted corridor, his body racked with sobs.

The Plimptons took the giant into Suite 135, a tiny, rococo bedroom with undersized furniture and a bed with a pink quilted coverlet on it which was barely broad enough to receive the bulk of Grier. It reminded Plimpton of nothing so much as a ballet dancer's dressing room. "It's

okay, Rosey," said Plimpton. "It's okay." Grier moaned. Plimpton looked
at his wife, shook his head slowly and motioned for her to follow him out
of the room.

In the ambulance, siren wailing, red lights flickering, Barry pleaded for
a smooth ride. Ethel Kennedy and Fred Dutton bent over Bob, and Ethel
made a motion with her hand, running it quickly up and down her throat.
It seemed to say, "He can't breathe." Dutton turned to Max Behrman, who
reached over and grabbed a clear plastic breathing mask.

"You keep your dirty filthy hands off my husband." Max Behrman insisted that that is what Ethel Kennedy told him when he lifted the Senator's
head. He said he ignored her. Roughly, according to Warren Rogers' account, Behrman stretched the elastic attached to the mask over Kennedy's
head, scraping across the bullet wound behind his ear. Ethel shivered with
horror, then, accepting Behrman for the moment, asked, "How do you know
the air is on?"

"You can hear it," said Behrman. Ethel nodded. And the tan-colored
ambulance, Unit G-18, sped on toward Central Receiving Hospital.
Behrman decided to try his luck again. "I want to know what happened,"
he said to Ethel Kennedy.

"I don't give a goddamn what you want to know," said Ethel.

Behrman shrugged. He said he picked up some gauze compresses and
applied them to the bloody side of Kennedy's head. He said Mrs. Kennedy
slapped him for this, on the right cheek. Then she called up to Bill Barry
in the front seat and asked him to throw Behrman out because "he's asking
too many questions."

Barry tried to crawl right over the seat, but Hulsman, the driver, pulled
him back without taking his eyes off the road. "Take it easy," he said.
"We're almost there."

At Central Receiving Hospital, a low rambling brick building at 1401
West 6th Street in Los Angeles, exactly eighteen blocks from the Ambassador Hotel, the patients who had been watching television started phoning
out to their families while calls from the Ambassador Hotel started pouring into the hospital switchboard. There Miss Norma Case handled the
calls as best she could and started using the hospital's public-address system (instead of the phones) for emergency messages. One of these went out
to Miss Bette A. Eby, Nursing Supervisor at Central Receiving. "Miss
Eby. Miss Eby." Miss Case's voice echoed all over the hospital. "Have a
room ready and be prepared to draw blood.

Nurse Eby selected Treatment Room 2, which was better equipped than any of the others, and closer to the ambulance ramp. She placed an intravenous standard in the room, cut some adhesive tape and attached it to the standard and readied some intravenous fluids on the back counter near the treatment table.

By now almost the entire staff had heard that Senator Kennedy had been shot and was headed toward Central Receiving. Dr. V. Faustin Bazilauskas, number one doctor on duty, waited at the ambulance entrance with some disbelief. Surely the report was false. There were a good many rumors floating around an emergency hospital. Then a taxi pulled up. A young man climbed out and limped over to him. It was Irwin Stroll.

"What are you here for?" said Dr. Bazilauskas.

"I got a bullet wound," said Stroll.

"Where was that?"

"At the Ambassador," said Stroll.

Dr. Bazilauskas sighed with relief. Then it wasn't Kennedy. It was just this young man and his wound was "insignificant." In the next instant, Central Receiving's ambulance Unit G-18 pulled out of the vehicle and wheeled it up to Dr. Bazilauskas, with Ethel Kennedy trailing closely. It was Senator Kennedy and he was unconscious.

Dr. Bazilauskas told a nurse to look after the boy and moved toward Kennedy. "Not here, doc," shouted Behrman, "in the treatment room where you belong." Bazilauskas hesitated in the glare of the neon lights, then plowed through the crowd with a nervous look over his shoulder. He had reason to be nervous. The crowd pushed around the stretcher and Behrman struggled through a tangle of television news crews. Finally Behrman got the stretcher into the hallway and Bill Barry was shouting, "Grab him! Get that man!" He was pointing to a photographer in shirt sleeves trying to focus his camera. It was John Malmin of the Los Angeles *Times*. Fred Dutton detached himself from Ethel's side, Dick Tuck joined him and they hit Malmin together. He went down and his Rolleiflex went flying.

Miss Eby and another nurse, Margaret Jane Lightsey, tried to pull the stretcher into the treatment room while the newsmen and camera crews hauled it back to get more pictures. Sergeant Gene Tinch of the L.A. Police finally broke up the tug-of-war and the hospital personnel got Kennedy into Treatment Room 2. Miss Eby and Mrs. Lightsey stood at the head of the treatment table while two other nurses, Miss Reba Nelson and Mrs. Alice Mejia, took their normal stations at the center of the table, opposite the stretcher, to receive the patient.

But Dr. Bazilauskas stepped between the stretcher and the treatment table, shouting, "Get him on the table! Get him on the table!" The stretcher was still being moved into position but Bazilauskas was impatient. He placed his hands under Kennedy's hips and started to lift. With this, the oxygen tank which was on the foot of the stretcher thundered to the floor. Miss Eby remonstrated with the doctor. "Let us do it properly," she cried. The ambulance attendants took matters into their own hands, seized the sheet Kennedy was lying on and flipped him on the treatment table. "Don't be so rough," cried Ethel Kennedy. "Don't be so rough."

The scream of the fighter jets at Hamilton Air Force Base made speech impossible. It was all right. None of the four men had anything to say, not Senator Edward M. Kennedy, nor his aide, Dave Burke, nor a cousin, Bob Fitzgerald, nor the editor of the Nashville *Tennessean,* John Seigenthaler.

They'd gotten the news at the Fairmont Hotel in San Francisco. Ted Kennedy had been slumped in a chair, watching television with Burke, exhausted after the clamor of a victory rally, but not too exhausted to catch the latest news from Los Angeles, where the vote was so slow. When the picture brightened before their eyes, they saw no happy victory party in Los Angeles but confusion and chaos and dire reports about a shooting at the Ambassador. Ted froze with the realization of what happened, then turned to Burke with a tremor in his voice.

"Dave," he said, "we'd better get down there."

And now an Air Force jet was ready. The four of them climbed grimly aboard and flashed south toward Los Angeles.

The prisoner was exasperatingly mum. Sergeant Jordan told him of his right to remain silent. The prisoner took the admonishment most literally: he would not tell Jordan his name.

Jordan turned to the items taken from the young man's pockets. "I want to count this in front of you so that you are satisfied that this is the right amount." Jordan fingered each of the items taken and named them. The interrogation rooms of the Los Angeles Police Department are all wired for sound; every word uttered goes on a tape recording "for the record." Jordan was getting the prisoner's property "on the record."

"Let's see, $100 bills. We have one, two, three, four $100 bills. . . ." Jordan made a second search of the prisoner who winced when Jordan grabbed his leg. "Sorry," said Jordan. "What happened?"

"I had—I had mentioned it to Officer 3949."

"Sorry, what was that?"

"I don't know his name, sir." Though the prisoner didn't know the names of the officers who had taken him in, he had noticed—and remembered—their badge numbers.

"You mentioned what?"

"My ankle and my knee—my knee."

Jordan realized what he was saying. "Okay," said Jordan, "I'm very sorry. I'll be as gentle as possible. If I get in an area that's uncomfortable, you tell me." The days of the so-called third degree, when policemen persuaded prisoners to talk by beating them with a piece of rubber hose, are long gone, and policemen in Los Angeles are somewhat aware that they are—thanks to a TV series called "Dragnet," written from official files of the Los Angeles Police Department—models of deportment for the entire nation. Jordan told the prisoner to sit down and brought Austin and Willoughby back into the room.

They came in and stared silently at the prisoner. He stared back at them.

Now, at the Ambassador Hotel, the crowd was not being asked to disperse. Instead, the police were trying to round up any and all witnesses to the shooting, get their names and addresses and take them to Rampart Street station for their statements.

Some of these potential witnesses were newsmen and they, too, along with dozens of other newsmen moved among the crowd, anxious to find out what others saw. Richard Aubry, a sometime newsman from the black ghetto, argued with Booker Griffin, a friend of his, who claimed he too was in the pantry during the shooting. "Did they get the other two guys?" asked Griffin, excitedly.

"Now, wait a minute here now, Booker," said Aubry, "who said anything about any other guys?"

A producer fed some of these witnesses to Sander Vanocur of NBC Television News who was standing in the lobby and trying to piece together what had happened inside. Often enough Vanocur, like the police, would run into a pseudowitness who made up in imagination what he had failed in actually seeing. And as if the situation weren't confusing enough, he had to contend with a young Kennedy worker named Sandy Serrano who said she'd seen a woman coming down the fire escape from the Embassy Room shouting, "We killed him, we killed him." Coconspirators? Oh, God!

Vanocur tried to get her story. "Miss Serrano . . . uh. Just take your time. I'll hold the mike in front of you. Tell me everything from the time you first saw the Senator come in the room, and what happened?"

SERRANO: Well, he, he—everybody was in the main room, you know, listening to him speak and it was too hot so I went outside and I was out on the terrace and I was out there for about five, ten minutes, you know. I started to get cold and then, you know, and everybody was cheering and everything, and then I was standing there just thinking, you know, thinking about how many people there were and how wonderful it was. Then this girl came running down the stairs in the back, came running down the stairs and said, "We've shot him, we've shot him." Who did you shoot? And she said, "We've shot Senator Kennedy." And aft.—she had —I can remember what she had on and everything, and after that a boy came down with her. He was about twenty-three years old and he was Mexican-American because I can remember that because I'm Mexican-American and I says, "What's happening?" and all of a sudden all these people start coming down that back end and I walked in and I was by the bar area and nobody seemed to know anything about it and I thought well, you know, maybe I misunderstood or something.

VANOCUR: Wait a minute. Did this young lady say "we"?

SERRANO: "We," she said.

VANOCUR: Meaning "We, the Mexican-Americans?"

SERRANO: No. She was not of Mexican-American descent. She was not. She was Caucasian. She had on a white dress with polka dots. She was light skinned, dark hair. She had black shoes on and she had a funny nose. It was, it was—I thought it was really funny. All my friends tell me I'm so observant.

VANOCUR: Did you work for Senator Kennedy?

SERRANO: I'm cochairman of Youth for Kennedy in the Pasadena-Altadena area. I worked very hard for him, and everybody in the Pasadena area worked very very hard for him. 1965 I met him, Washington, D.C., in an elevator. He stepped on my foot and I shoved him and it's an unforgettable experience."

Vanocur shook his head in some bewilderment. He wondered about Miss Serrano's story. She seemed a little hysterical. But she wasn't that hysterical and thousands of viewers all across the nation had a feeling that they had participated, by means of the magic of television, in the very beginnings of an investigation that would track down those who had conspired to kill Senator Robert Kennedy.

Kennedy's eyes were glazed and he didn't seem to be breathing at all. Ethel stood at his side. The doctor listened through a stethoscope for a heartbeat, then began slapping Kennedy's face. "Bob! Bob! Bob!" he shouted, slapping his face again and again. There was no response.

"His pupils are not dilated," said Miss Eby hopefully. The doctor began pushing with his palm on Kennedy's chest. Nurse Eby detected a slight ingurgling breath from Kennedy and turned to Mrs. Lightsey for some suction tubing. Miss Eby applied the tube to Kennedy's mouth, then turned and lifted the heart-lung machine from its table directly behind her. Dr. Bazilauskas and the other nurses on each side of the table lifted Kennedy's shoulders. Miss Eby slipped the heart-lung machine under Kennedy, handed Dr. Bazilauskas a hammer attachment for the chest, inserted an airway into the patient's mouth, placed the resuscitator mask over his mouth and immediately turned the dials to their proper adjustment. Mrs. Lightsey adjusted the hammer straps on the right, and another nurse, Mrs. Wilma McAllister, adjusted the straps on the left. Mrs. Kennedy shuddered each time her husband was moved.

When the heart-lung machine was in place and functioning, Miss Eby looked closely at Kennedy's right ear and observed clotting blood in and about the ear, powder burns outside of the ear, and behind the ear in the mastoid area she saw a wound with powder burns around it.

Dr. Albert C. Holt, a surgeon on duty at Central Receiving, entered the room and prepared to administer the intravenous fluids. Kennedy was still wearing his suit coat and shirt, both of them opened to his bare chest. Dr. Holt fingered Kennedy's dark blue coat sleeve. "Cut it off. Cut it off," snapped Ethel Kennedy. Dr. Bazilauskas called for scissors and cut Kennedy's left sleeve. Nurse Reba Nelson and Miss Lightsey removed Kennedy's pants and socks under the sheet. He was wearing no shoes and there were no personal items at all in his pants pockets. Miss Nelson also removed Kennedy's upper clothing with the help of Dr. Bazilauskas and Miss Eby. Ethel Kennedy told the nurses to throw the clothes away or destroy them, but Mrs. Mejia started wrapping them in paper according to usual hospital procedures. She didn't get very far. Mrs. Kennedy wheeled at the sound of rattling paper, and Mrs. Mejia took the clothes and the paper out of the room, finished her wrapping in the corridor, then brought the wrapped clothing—a dark blue suit, a pair of shorts, a shirt, belt, blue socks and a blue tie with silver stripes—back into the room. As Dr. Holt started to prepare the intravenous fluids, he suspected they would have to transfer Kennedy to Good Samaritan Hospital for surgery.

Dr. Holt tested Kennedy's reflexes. The Babinski reflex was good—toes curled normally in response to a touch on the soles of the feet. But taps on the knees resulted in hyperactive jerks, indicating some brain damage.

Miss Eby suggested an immediate transfer to Good Samaritan. Bazilauskas and Holt agreed, and told Mrs. Lightsey to warn Good Samaritan. Dr. Holt asked her to get Dr. Henry Cuneo on the telephone and, since a second bullet might have penetrated the chest, the thoracic surgeon at Good Samaritan, Dr. Bert Meyers, as well. Cuneo was one of the best brain surgeons in Los Angeles. Furthermore, both he and his associate, Dr. Nat Downs Reid, Holt knew, had had plenty of experience in dealing with gunshot wounds to the head, for both of them had served their internship and residency at the huge Los Angeles County General Hospital, where gunshot victims are a matter of course.

Miss Eby asked Ethel Kennedy if she wanted a priest. "Yes," said Ethel Kennedy. "There is one in the hall." Ethel Kennedy went out to the hallway to the double doors where she saw Father Mundell. Ethel asked the policeman on duty to let him in. The policeman looked at Father Mundell. He was dressed in a blue blazer and gray slacks. Maybe the policeman wasn't convinced that Father Mundell was really a priest. He wouldn't let him in.

"Look," said Ethel, "I'm . . . you know, Mrs. Kennedy."

"I," said the policeman, "am a policeman." Ethel blinked hard. She was unprepared at this moment for an officious cop and took characteristically direct action. She pushed the policeman aside. He wheeled and hit her in the chest with a forearm blow and that was the end for him. Several bystanders mobbed him, while a photographer took pictures. Bill Barry knocked the photographer down and out and ripped the film from his camera, and Ethel pulled Father Mundell into the hallway, and took him into Treatment Room 2. Father Mundell gave Kennedy Absolution, a short version in English of the traditional formula: "I absolve you from your sins . . ." and stayed at Ethel's side while she continued to observe the ministrations of the doctors.

Dr. Bazilauskas had ordered adrenalin for a heart needle, a long wicked-looking instrument, but when the nurse gave it to him, he took one look at Ethel Kennedy, listened again to the sound of Kennedy's heartbeat and then ordered the adrenalin to be given in the arm instead of directly in the heart. Nurse Nelson handled that operation. She looked at Kennedy's right shoulder. It was wounded, so she went around to his left shoulder and gave him the adrenalin there. In moments, Kennedy's heartbeat sounded better. Dr. Bazilauskas turned to Mrs. Kennedy, offered her the stethoscope so she could hear for herself. She listened and nodded with satisfaction.

At this point Dr. Holt was called to the telephone. It was Dr. Cuneo.

"Senator Kennedy has been shot in the head and the chest," said Dr. Holt.

"Oh, God, you don't mean it!" exclaimed Cuneo, who'd been awakened from his sleep.

"We'd like to take him to Good Samaritan," said Dr. Holt.

"I'll see you there," said Cuneo.

Outside Central Receiving, the crowd had swelled to more than 300. In the hallway, the photographer who had been knocked down staggered over to Richard Tuck and asked him his name.

"I'm Dick Tuck and I'd be glad to take the credit, but I didn't do it."

Pierre Salinger came running up. "How is he?" he said to Warren Rogers. Rogers couldn't reply. "Where is he hit?" demanded Salinger.

"In the head," said Rogers.

"Oh, no!" cried Salinger. He put his head on Rogers' shoulder for a moment, then walked away.

Other ambulances started pulling up with other victims.

Father Thomas Peacha, a young red-haired assistant pastor at St. Basil's Church on Wilshire Boulevard, was driving home from a sick call when he heard a radio bulletin that Senator Kennedy had been shot at the Ambassador. He drove directly to Central Receiving Hospital, gained surprisingly quick admittance to the Receiving Room and saw Kennedy lying flat on his back with a white sheet covering his body and an oxygen mask over his mouth. With a word to Ethel Kennedy, who sat calmly on a high stool, and a nod to Father Mundell, he anointed Kennedy's forehead with a bit of oil—a short form of the sacrament of Extreme Unction. The sacrament is a holdover from more primitive ages, a bit of concrete symbolism intended as a comfort to the sick and those close to the sick. Father Peacha felt that another word was needed: "Don't worry," he said to Ethel. "He'll be all right."

"Father," she said, very calmly, fearlessly, "say a prayer for him."

And the doctors had their own chrism: they applied polysporin ointment to both of the Senator's eyes and covered them with eye patches. In a coma, the eye may not react to bumps and jolts in ordinary ways. The ointment and the patches were protective precautions. Ethel Kennedy—uncomfortable with Behrman—exacted a promise from Dr. Holt that he would stay with the Senator all the way, something he intended doing in any event. They were ready to move, but the police informed them they had a security problem outside. The crowd had become a mob and who could predict what anyone's hysteria would prompt him to do? The police wanted Behrman and Hulsman to drive their ambulance to another entrance.

The crowd outside was chanting, "WE WANT BOBBY, WE WANT BOBBY." But no matter.

"No," said Dr. Holt. "We have no time for elaborate security measures. This is Senator Kennedy and he has a bullet wound in his head."

The police went out to see what they could do with the crowd, and Holt turned back to Senator Kennedy. A black man was there at his side with a stethoscope around his neck. "I'm Dr. Ross Miller," he explained. "I attended the Senator at the Ambassador." The doctors and nurses got the impression Dr. Miller wanted to take over. They tried to ignore him. He insisted on riding alongside the Senator to Good Samaritan, and there might have been a black-white confrontation then and there until the black doctor took himself out of contention by clumsily knocking the IV needle from Kennedy's left arm. Miss Eby, Bette-on-the-spot all the way, caught the tubing, clamped it off, threw away the contaminated needle and made a substitution in seconds. The doctors and nurses, who couldn't have turned Senator Kennedy over to Miller in any event, pushed past Miller, with the Senator on a stretcher, wound down the corridor and out through a police cordon to the waiting ambulance. Dr. Holt carried the IV bottles and, once in the ambulance, cradled Kennedy's head in his hands. Mrs. Kennedy sat next to him. Steve Smith and his wife Jean also squeezed in, and the rest of the Kennedy entourage followed in vehicles both private and public. Pierre Salinger and his wife Nicole rode to Good Samaritan on the back of a police motorcycle. It was 12:57 A.M. The ambulance pulled out with a police escort on the way. Police cars, their red lights flashing, had traffic stopped at every intersection. In three minutes —at exactly 1:00—they wheeled Senator Kennedy into the Hospital of the Good Samaritan where a spotlight shone steadily on a large white cross on the roof nine stories overhead.

Hans Korthoff, a desk clerk at the Ambassador, came forward to the police somewhat hesitantly with a sheet of legal-sized paper in his hand, folded in half and in half again. "I don't know if this is important," he said, "but some shabby-looking guy said he found this in the Embassy Room last night."

The policeman thought it was indeed important, for it looked like a map of the Embassy Room drawn in black crayon, with some suspicious notations in red ink on the top of the map: "Panic alarm not functioning." Behind the stage where Kennedy made his last speech: "Critical access." At the lower-left-hand corner of the map: "Kitchen." He turned it in to the detective division at Rampart Street station.

"I wonder," said Lieutenant Charles Hughes, "if this handwriting compares with that of our assassin—whoever he is. Or, if not, who drew it, and why?"

On the fifth floor, in the intensive care unit, two resident surgeons, Dr. Paul Ironside and Dr. Hubert Humble, started blood transfusions and a tracheostomy on Senator Kennedy. It would keep his airway clear of secretions and ensure a steady and adequate supply of oxygen to the brain.

The tracheostomy was highly successful, lowering Kennedy's blood pressure from 280 to a more normal 140.

At 1:10 A.M., Dr. Cuneo arrived outside the hospital. He was short and slight, and the police had a hard time believing he was Senator Kennedy's brain surgeon. "About six policemen were trying to get me in," recalled Cuneo, "and about fifteen were trying to keep me out." On the fifth floor, Dr. Holt gave him a report of what had been done, then Dr. Cuneo went in to examine the Senator.

There was an obvious gunshot wound in the right mastoid. A dark red splotch behind the ear, still running, indicated intracranial bleeding. From the ear itself oozed a bloody spinal fluid, indicating a basal fracture of the middle fossa of the skull. Two other bullet wounds in the right armpit seemed negligible, but the head wound was trouble.

Dr. Bert Meyers, the hospital's chief thoracic surgeon, joined the team working on the Senator. Dr. George Griffith, a cardiologist, taped electrodes from an electocardiograph to Kennedy's chest and extremities in order to monitor his heart. Dr. John Zaro, an internist, continued to monitor the blood supply. Dr. Robert Scanlan, chief of the hospital's radiology department, brought in a portable X-ray machine for X rays of the Senator's skull, spine and chest. While he took his pictures, Dr. Cuneo walked over to Ethel Kennedy, standing quietly some twenty feet away, and gave her a preliminary report.

"Extremely critical," said Cuneo. He told her of the "intracranial injury." But he said he was impressed with the Senator's improvement since the tracheostomy. "His blood pressure has gone down, his heart is beating strongly, his airway is free of obstructions and his color is good."

Now the news from *the* doctor who should know was too much. Ethel Kennedy almost collapsed, quickly recovered, then was urged to lie down. She was asked if she wanted a sedative. "No, thank you," she replied. "I want to be awake and alert."

Dr. Reid arrived—he'd been rushed there in a police car—and when he did, he and Dr. Cuneo went down to the department of radiology on the second floor with Dr. Scanlan to look at the Senator's X rays.

The X rays told Cuneo and Reid to forget the other bullet wounds. One bullet had passed completely through some soft tissue in the right armpit, the other had penetrated the armpit, then burrowed upward through fat and muscle, lodging just under the skin of the neck, two centimeters from the spine. But a third bullet inside the skull had shattered, and the doctors saw fragments scattered through the lower right side of the skull, some very deep. Dr. Cuneo believed that the bullet had also penetrated or torn the lateral sinus, a large blood vessel as big around as a man's little finger, and that fragments of the mastoid bone were also scattered into the brain.

There was only one thing to do: operate as soon as the Senator could take it, remove the blood clot which was surely forming inside the skull and remove as much of the bullet as they could find.

Cuneo and Reid went back upstairs, saw that Kennedy's heart and respiration were now stable, and all vital signs, including the blood chemistries, were good. The time was now. They talked to Ethel Kennedy again. "Now we know what we have to do," said Cuneo.

To all around him, Cuneo may have seemed like a man of steel. As a brain surgeon, he had to be. But he proceeded with an overwhelming sense of responsibility. "This man could have been our next President," said Cuneo. "He was the brother of John Kennedy. The father of ten children. And millions of people who loved him were looking over my shoulder."

"How long have you been in here?" said Officer Willoughby.

He got no reply. "Do you speak English?" asked Willoughby.

No reply. During the long silence that followed, Officers Willoughby and Austin had a chance to size up the guy who had tried to kill Kennedy. He was dark-skinned, had thick lips and wild dark hair and intense brown eyes. He had a bruise on his forehead and a cut near his left eye and his clothes were in disarray.

Jordan returned with a cup of hot chocolate for Willoughby and checked the prisoner's shoes, a pair of gray "Hush Puppies." Jordan took it easy on the prisoner's sore leg, inspected his right shoe, then his left, found nothing suspicious, then left the room again.

The prisoner complained about the handcuffs binding his arms behind him. "These are tight," he said.

"What happened to your leg?" asked Willoughby.

The prisoner didn't respond. He watched Willoughby sip his hot chocolate. "I'm thirsty," he said.

"Well," said Willoughby, waving his cup, "we're not going to give you any of this." The prisoner kicked the cup out of Willoughby's hand.

"That's enough, pal!" warned Austin.

"Yeah!" said Willoughby, practically strangling with rage.

"Yeah!" said Austin.

Both officers tried hard to suppress their anger. "Keep it cool," said Austin to Willoughby. Willoughby went out to get a rag to wipe the hot chocolate off the floor.

"You're not going to prove anything that way," said Austin. Austin had a hayseedy voice, reminiscent of Chill Wills.

The prisoner looked contrite, and said in the softest tones, "Later, please apologize for me to him."

"I will," said Austin.

Willoughby came in and tried to mop up the sticky drink. He had quite a blotch on his pants. "Did you get the worst?" asked Austin. Willoughby nodded. The three of them sat still. No one said a thing. The two officers looked at the prisoner, their veneer of kindness almost worn away.

"It's going to be a long night," said Austin.

"Yeah, you said it," said Willoughby. He searched himself for a cigarette.

"I've got some here," said Austin. He gave Willoughby a cigarette.

"May I smoke?" asked the prisoner.

The two officers merely glared at him. After a long pause, Austin spoke. "What color are his eyes?" He was making out a description for his report.

"Brown," said Willoughby.

"How much do you think he weighs?"

"Oh, 140. How much do you weigh? 140?"

He got no reply.

"How much do you weigh?" asked Austin. "Huh? 140? 150? 130? 120? 110? How tall are you? Makes no difference to me. I'm only a peon here."

"I like your humor, sir," said the prisoner with a smile.

The three of them sat there. And sat. "I hate to sit here and say nothing," said Austin. "Are you married?" No reply. "Do you have a family?" No reply. "We're all people, you know. You got a girl friend? Boy friend? Friends?" No reply. "Did the detective tell you that you have the right to remain silent? Did he?" No reply. "Did he tell you that? Do you understand that? Do you understand? Do you, or don't you? Shake your head no if not, or shake your head yes if you do." The prisoner merely stared at Austin, his face impassive. "The only things I'm asking you," explained Austin, "is things we're going to find out anyhow. You know that. . . . Do you speak English?"

No reply.

Willoughby sighed. "Silent Sam," he said.

"What happened to your leg?"

No reply.

"You won't even tell me that?"

"He's just trying to be sociable with you," explained Willoughby to the prisoner. "Can't you talk? Huh? We're going to be in here for a long time. You just as well be sociable. Hell, we're just trying to get along."

"We're not participants of voodoo," said Austin, "because we can't outstare each other."

Finally at 1:30 A.M., Bill Jordan came back in and broke up the staring match. First round to the prisoner. Now they would move him downtown.

Officers Willoughby and Jordan hustled their man down a rear stairway to the basement and out into the underground garage where Sergeant Frank Patchett was ready behind the wheel of an unmarked Ford with the motor running. Jordan pushed the prisoner, still handcuffed, into the back seat. Willoughby moved in next to him, and Jordan went around to the other side of the car and climbed in the back seat. Sergeant Adolph Melendres heaved his bulk into the front seat and slammed the door. "Let's go," said Jordan. Then he told the prisoner to get down on the floor.

Patchett looked behind him to see if a second escort vehicle was ready. The driver of that car, Sergeant Beryl Mick, blinked his lights and the two cars pulled out onto Benton Way, avoiding knots of curious and angry citizens front and back of Rampart and a handful of reporters who had guessed the assassin might be at Rampart Street. Jesse Unruh rode in the second car. He was the first of many public officials who would take a special interest in the case, and he was going to stick with it to see that nothing happened to the prisoner. In this instance, it was obvious that Unruh, shocked to the roots of his being by an assassination attempt before his very eyes, wasn't interested in "coddling" a criminal. Rather, he was eager to see that all the rules were followed so that the assassin's sentence in a court of law would stick. Violated rights could only lead to a higher court reversal sometime in the future. And Unruh didn't want that.

Quietly, the two cars headed downtown, preferring Beverly Boulevard, which was relatively empty at this hour, to the Hollywood Freeway, which would have gotten them downtown quicker. In four minutes, they arrived at Parker Center, a tower of aluminum and tinted glass that serves as the headquarters of the Los Angeles Police Department, and parked in the basement garage near a freight elevator. Police officers from the Metro Division were stationed there in anticipation; others were in the elevator, along the third-floor corridor and outside the doors of the Homicide Division. They were the elite of an elite police force, and they were here operating under a code designated "maximum security." Obviously the message had already moved through Parker Center, from top to bottom. "They lost their man in Dallas. We won't lose ours."

In the homicide squad room, they sat their man down and asked him his name. No reply. "Who are you?" demanded Sergeant Patchett. He got no answer. An officer came in to take a full set of fingerprints. "If you'd give us your name," said Patchett, changing his tone, "you'd save us an awful lot of work." He got no answer to that either. "What's the matter," said Patchett, shifting to a third gear. "Ashamed of what you've done tonight? "

"Hell, no!" said the prisoner, loud and clear.

Patchett shrugged, then went off to transmit the prints to the FBI lab in Washington, and the other officers took the prisoner to a smaller room, Room 319, which was bugged. He asked for a drink of water. But when Jordan returned with it, the prisoner wouldn't put his lips to it until Jordan tasted it.

Deputy District Attorney John Howard and his chief investigator, George Murphy, tried to get somewhere with the prisoner. They got about as far during this second interview as Sergeant Jordan did during the first. The prisoner understood his rights. He wouldn't tell them his name.

Howard said that when he felt like talking the prisoner could phone either himself or Murphy. "That's Murph." He pointed to Murphy, a huge Irishman with a florid complexion. "Now, I . . ."

"When will I have a chance to clean up?" asked the prisoner.

"Let me explain what will happen," said Howard. "They have to book you. That's legal procedure—fingerprints, pictures taken, everything like that. After that, I'm sure you will be able to clean up." Howard and Murphy were ready to go, but there were some security precautions that had to be taken. Anytime that the prisoner would be moved during the next twenty-four hours, the police department would take emergency precautions, freezing all movement within the entire realm of Parker Center. Sergeant Jordan went out to get the freeze put on.

While he was gone, the prisoner turned and inquired casually, "How long have you been with the D.A.'s office, Mr. Murphy?"

"Three years," said Murphy. "I retired from the police department and went over to the D.A.'s office three years ago."

"Do you remember Kirschke?" asked the prisoner.

"Very well," said Murphy. Jack Kirschke was an assistant district attorney who had been convicted of killing his wife and her lover.

The prisoner was curious about Kirschke. Murphy said it was a hard case to figure.

"Well," said Howard, "I knew Jack Kirschke. Did you read about it or . . ." Jordan returned. It was time to go. "We'll take it up again," said Howard. It was 2:20 A.M.

Premier Eisaku Sato had just finished delivering a speech in northern Japan when one of his aides whispered the news about Kennedy. A handful of reporters present recorded his reactions. Sato frowned, then he seemed to choke a little and muttered almost inaudibly: "What has happened to the U.S.?"

In the lobby of Tokyo's swank Hotel Okura, a crowd gathered around a teletype machine and followed the developments on Bob Kennedy, a man whom many had learned to admire when in 1964 he'd challenged a rabid anti-American student to a debate at Waseda University. Japanese television stations started to pick up a signal from the communications satellite Telstar and soon converted it on every television set in Japan into the swooping, shadow-filled film of the Ambassador pantry where Robert Kennedy lay prostrate on the blood-covered floor. The exposure was total.

Soon the Spanish state television replayed the same shocking footage to the Spaniards who were just beginning their working day. The Minister of Information, Manuel Fraga Iribarne, went on the state television to plug the need for "order and submission to law as the maximum political duty."

Flags all over the world were lowered to half-mast and prices dropped on all the stock exchanges in Europe.

From Harlem to Watts, the cry went out, "They got him." "They" were the perpetual enemies of the black man, and the one man who provided some hope was lying in a hospital in Los Angeles with a bullet in his brain.

Two

"We're all puppets."

They walked the prisoner from the Homicide Division down one flight of stairs directly to the felony booking section of the Central Jail on the second floor of Parker Center, and put him through the ordinary booking procedures. They took his thumbprint, had him strip down for a thorough "skin search." They told him to bend over and spread his buttocks. The prisoner objected very vigorously to this and they told him, "You'd be surprised at the way some things are smuggled into this jail." The prisoner bent over and smiled.

He was booked under Section 217 of the Penal Code, assault with intent to commit murder. But the custodial officer, Martin Dismukes, got no information out of the prisoner. "Okay," said Dismukes, "just sign 'John Doe' here on the booking slip." Dismukes noted that the prisoner was very composed and markedly at ease.

They took his picture, front and profile, and led him through a barred gate and into a kind of wire cage for another full set of fingerprints. The prisoner made no comment. He refused to fill out the handwriting exemplars or answer any questions at all. Officer Guadalupe De La Garza took him to a shower room and watched him take a very slow, very thorough shower. He dried himself just as slowly, put on some jail shorts and a pair of jail trousers. They were way too big. He didn't like that at all.

"May I call John Howard?" he asked. Officer Frank Foster gave him a dime and took him down the hall twenty feet to a pay telephone on the wall. Whoever answered the phone told him that Howard was still at Parker Center. "He's still at Parker Center," said the prisoner. Officer Kenneth Jones then called the Homicide Division and gave the message to Howard that the prisoner wanted to see him. Foster and Jones took him to a rather roomy isolation cell done in green-tinted tempered glass and put him in there along with Officer Foster. It was his job to stay in the cell with the prisoner until Howard was ready for him.

"It's a darn good-looking moustache you've got," said the prisoner.

"How's that?" said Foster.

"I like your moustache," said the prisoner.

At the Rampart Street station, detectives from the Homicide Division were trying to fit together their picture of what had happened at the Ambassador. At 2:35 A.M., Sergeant Jack E. Chiquet and Sergeant Edward Henderson were interviewing Sandra Serrano. She said that during Kennedy's speech she had been out on the fire escape outside the Embassy Room "because it was too hot inside" when three people came up the fire escape. One of them was a girl in a white dress with black polka dots, a Caucasian with dark brown hair, a girl about five feet, six inches. With her was a young man of about twenty-three, perhaps a Mexican-American, who had on a white shirt and a gold sweater. And another young man with "messed-up clothes and a lot of hair." Then, said Sandra Serrano, "the same girl, about two, two minutes later, three minutes later maybe, came running down the stairs. She practically stepped on me, and she said 'We've shot him. We've shot him.' Then I said, 'Who did you shoot?' and she said, 'We shot Senator Kennedy.' And I says, 'Oh, sure.' She came running down the stairs very fast. Then the boy in the gold sweater came running down after her, and I walked down the stairs. I went down to the first level where everybody was at."

Did she ever hear the sound of gunfire? "Well," she said, "I didn't know it was a gun. I thought it was the backfire of a car."

"What makes you think that these people were together?" asked Sergeant Chiquet.

"Because they went up together," said Miss Serrano.

"But you didn't hear any conversation?"

"No. No. No."

"But in your opinion, the three of them were together?"

"I'd say they were."

Chiquet looked at Henderson. "Do you have any questions?" He didn't. The girl's story seemed to hold together, it was 2:55 in the morning, and they had more witnesses outside that needed talking to. But there would be more interviews with Sandra Serrano. More than she ever dreamed.

*   *   *   *   *

At 2:55 A.M., Val Clenard reported the first official bad news to listeners of KMPC in Los Angeles, news that dashed the hopes of many who had prayed that a bullet wound in the head might not be as serious as they feared:

Frank Mankiewicz, the press secretary for Senator Robert Kennedy, just moments ago came out to a very crowded news conference in front of Good Samaritan Hospital and, amidst the shoving and pushing of the newsmen, he climbed on top a police car hood and told us that Senator Robert F. Kennedy is in very critical condition. The Senator was hit twice. A superficial wound—he didn't say where—but the critical wound—is in the mastoid area behind the ear. A bullet has lodged in Robert Kennedy's brain. A team of six neurosurgeons will attempt to remove that bullet from his brain within the next few minutes. This operation is expected to last almost an hour. They say that—or Frank Mankiewicz says—that Mrs. Kennedy is with her husband and watching very closely as we all are in this critical period of our lives. The breathing of the Senator is reported good. He is semiconscious at times, and right now he is just minutes away from undergoing brain surgery for the bullet that has been lodged within his brain. The doctors are quoted by Frank Mankiewicz as saying that he is in very—and I underline this word—very critical condition at this time.

Clenard's report echoed that of dozens of others on radio and TV. . . .

Abraham Lincoln Wirin, the chief counsel in Los Angeles for the American Civil Liberties Union, sat up watching TV. Wirin was a man who had spent a good deal of his life defending the poor and the downtrodden, and was an admirer, therefore, of Robert Kennedy, who'd been doing quite a bit of the same. He couldn't understand. The reports said Kennedy's assailant was a Mexican-American. The Mexican-Americans, Wirin knew, were all for Kennedy. What was happening? Why Kennedy?

At 3:15 A.M., Eason Monroe, president of the ACLU in Southern California, phoned and suggested the ACLU "do something to prevent another Dallas."

"What do you suggest?" asked Wirin.

"This fellow is at the L.A. Police Headquarters in Hollywood. Why don't you go over and see him?" Wirin said he would, hung up, thought it over and then phoned Monroe with some second thoughts.

"Eason?"

"Yes?"

"Al Wirin here."

"Yes."

"Eason, first, there's no reason to assume the man who shot Kennedy is at the Hollywood P.D. And second, nobody there would let me see him."

"Well, what do you think, Al?"

"I think I'll wire [Police] Chief Reddin and ask him to let me see him. I can put the pressure on by making the telegram public. And an identical wire to Mayor Yorty—'to prevent L.A. from becoming another Dallas.' "

Monroe agreed. But by the time Yorty and Reddin got Wirin's wires, the assassin himself had already asked for the ACLU.

"You've got your hands full, Henry," said Dr. Maxwell Andler. Dr. Cuneo admitted that, indeed, he did. "Is there anything I can do?" asked Andler.

Cuneo had known Andler for twenty-three years and he knew that he was good. Like himself and Dr. Reid, Andler had had extensive experience in World War II, treating gunshot wounds to the head. And all three of them had interned at County General Hospital in Los Angeles. "Stick around, Max," said Cuneo, thankful for another skilled brain surgeon at his side. Now he had Reid from the University of Southern California School of Medicine and Andler from the crosstown rival, the University of California at Los Angeles.

They started to move the Senator to the operating room on the ninth floor, but outside the double doors of the intensive care unit a mob of friends waited, 200 or 300 of them, blocking the only elevator to the ninth floor. "We can't go that way," said Cuneo. "They may be friends, but some of them may be coming apart. You don't know what one of them might do. . . ."

So the doctors, the nurses and the Senator made their collective way in stages. First, an elevator to the sixth floor, then a transfer to another elevator to the ninth-floor surgery. There, the doctors and nurses changed into surgical gowns, caps, masks and sterile paper shoes. At 3:00 A.M., they entered the operating room, got Kennedy into a position on his left side, shaved behind his right ear, stepped aside for a moment while a police photographer took a picture of the bullet wound before surgery (which would be used as evidence in court), then, with Dr. Earl C. Skinner, an anesthesiologist, standing by, commenced surgery at 3:10 A.M.

At 3:15 A.M., police officers took the prisoner to Interrogation Room No. 1, no more than fifteen steps from his isolation cell. John Howard and

Bill Jordan were there, and their superiors were watching from the darkened corridor on the other side of the one-way glass. "Hi!" said Howard.

"Hello," said the prisoner. Howard motioned for the prisoner to join them at the wooden table. He sat lightly in a wooden chair and complained to Howard about the clothes he'd been given. Sergeant Jordan admitted they weren't quite a perfect fit.

"Yeah, how about that?" said John Howard, laughingly, and fingered the waistband of his own trousers—size 42. "Do you want to trade?"

"I wish you could accommodate me more," said the prisoner seriously. He said he didn't look very presentable. Sergeant Melendres joined them. "There," said Melendres, "he looks better, all cleaned up nice." Melendres, Jordan and Howard all smiled sweetly. The prisoner had called them. Maybe this was the break. Maybe, maybe he'd decided to talk.

Yes, he did want to talk, but not about the assassination of Robert F. Kennedy. He wanted to talk about the Kirschke case. Kirschke's death penalty was later reduced to life in prison.

Said Howard, "Yeah, we were talking about Kirschke, weren't we? How come you followed that? I was interested to ask you."

"I was hoping you'd clue me in on it," said the prisoner. "You know, brief me on it, you might say." Howard scratched his head and looked at Jordan. Well, if the kid wants to talk about Kirschke, he thought, maybe I'd better talk with him about Kirschke. Maybe I'll loosen him up. "It was a tough lawsuit. You'd have to know Jack. He was a deputy. I worked with him. It's hard to . . ."

"No, I mean . . . I mean the substance of the case."

"The substance actually was whether or not he was the guy that . . . there is no question his wife and this friend of hers got shot. There's no question about that. The question was: who did it? The jury resolved that it was Jack Kirschke. It was a hard-fought case and went a long time."

"But how would the jury have reacted," asked the prisoner, "had Kirschke not been a . . ."

"A district attorney?" asked Howard. "It's hard to say. I think myself they probably would hold a district attorney to a higher standard than an ordinary citizen."

The prisoner had his own ideas. He thought of the district attorney as a villain who, by prosecuting others, was sowing the seeds of his own retribution. "The tables were turned, you might say." By now the prisoner was settling down to enjoy the situation as much as he could. It was 3:25 in the morning, he had shot Senator Robert Kennedy in the head just three hours before and he wanted to start a philosophical discussion—on crime and punishment. It was appropriate and inappropriate.

"Now," said the prisoner, "would you say that the death penalty is, in fact, just and should be issued?"

Howard said, "I didn't follow the case that much. I do not, I could not say that as a matter of, you know, I would, I have no reason to believe that it is not just, not fair. Now, that's a matter of semantics. Now, we're talking, you're asking me if it's fair and proper. The question is: did he kill two people? If he killed two people, then is it a proper sentence? Who knows?" It was a question which Howard himself would help this man's jury answer in eleven months.

"What's happening?" demanded Jordan. The show was going nowhere.

Howard, too, tried to get the conversation moving more productively. "It's hard to know other people. Do you know where we are now? I told you you've been booked."

"I don't know," said the prisoner.

"You are in custody," said Howard. "You've been booked. You understand what I've been . . ."

The prisoner broke in, "I have been before a magistrate. Have I, or have I not?"

"No, you've not," said Howard. "You'll be taken before a magistrate as soon as possible, probably will be tried."

"Are you going to take me up there?"

"I'll get you up there if worse comes to worse," said Howard.

"No, no, no, I mean . . ." The prisoner was worried about his pants. Jordan reassured him, "You'll be properly attired," he said.

It was past 3:30 in the morning and Howard hadn't come to the cell a second time to talk about the Jack Kirschke case. "Now, besides Kirschke," asked Howard, "now what, what else can we talk about?"

"Really, that's all I wanted," said the prisoner.

"Really?" asked Howard. "Did you read about it, or are you, you seem to know, did you know any of the parties in it?"

"No, I, I, I told you, sir. I think he, that I observed it from just seeing it."

"On television?" asked Jordan.

"Very fleetingly on television," said the prisoner.

"Uh-huh," said Howard. "Yeah, it had a lot of publicity. A hard lawsuit."

The prisoner turned to Sergeant Jordan. "You're a good man, Mr. Jordan."

"I don't know about that," said Jordan.

"How do you mean?" asked the prisoner.

"Well," stammered Jordan.

"If a person doesn't allow himself, sir, well, really."

"Well, okay, I think I am."

"Beautiful," said the prisoner. The prisoner turned to Howard, "How about you, Mister ———, you got any children, family, or what are you?"

"I've got children. How about you, huh?"

"Do you plan to train them in this business of prosecution?"

"No. They're girls."

"Oh, maybe they'd become good juries and judges, like Judge Cannon."

"Yes, they could."

"Do you think she will make it again?" asked the prisoner. Judge Noel Cannon, a petite and attractive blonde, had provoked the official disapproval of some three-fourths of L.A.'s fifty-two Municipal Court judges for appearing in a Los Angeles *Times* photo demonstrating the womanly art of self-defense. She held a Derringer revolver in one hand and wore a sensational dotted minidress. The judges censured her action as an attempt to gain "personal publicity" in her efforts for reelection. Howard said he thought she'd make it again.

"Why?" asked the prisoner.

"Because the last time I heard," said Howard, "she was ahead in the voting. I just heard it, some mention made of it."

"I like that lady," said the prisoner. "She is a little one, no? The little, little miniskirt-type of a girl?" The officers put their heads together over that one.

The prisoner turned again to Howard, "Your daughters going to Vassar?"

"Going where?" asked Howard.

"How old are they?"

"Pretty young."

"Oh, really?"

"Yeah."

"You must have married late."

"Yeah, they're . . ." Howard stopped. Who the hell was supposed to be asking the questions here? "How about you? You haven't told me yet, have you?"

"What?" The prisoner answered a question with a question.

"What, about what?"

"Your question."

"Your question. How about *your* kids?" demanded Howard.

"What about it?"

"I don't know."

"Hey," Officer Frank Foster called into the room. "What do you take in your coffee?"

"Black," said the prisoner.

"Just black coffee?" said Foster, "or would you like a little bit of sugar in it?"

"Well, if you've got any good cream, I would like a little bit of that, and little bit of sugar, please."

"We won't be bugging you much," said Howard. "I won't, anyway, because I'm going to sleep because I'm inherently lazy."

"Inherently?" asked the prisoner.

"Yeah," said Howard.

Both Jordan and Foster were out of the room. The prisoner noticed that. "Where are they?" he asked.

"I don't know. They went out, probably to get a cup of coffee, bring you one, I don't know. I'll remind me before I leave to tell them to get you some pants as soon as I can."

"No, no, some civil clothes, preferably my own, really. This is really, this is—" he pulled at his pants—"this is mendicant's, the pants."

"Mendicant's?"

"Surely."

"What is mendicant's?" asked Howard. "You mean priest's?"

"Mendicant."

"I don't know the word," said Howard.

"Well, really? Gee, Mr. Howard, don't tell me that."

"How do you spell it?" asked Howard.

"I don't really know. You know, I've heard it, picked it up here and there." The prisoner laughed.

"Well, what are you laughing about?" asked Howard. "What are you thinking?"

"Your predicament. You're fencing."

"Not that."

"Why not?" asked the prisoner.

"Huh? Why would I pick that? You have me wrong." Sergeant Jordan came in with the coffee. "Now, you want me to take a swallow?" asked Jordan.

"Sure," said the prisoner lightly.

Jordan took a sip of the prisoner's coffee. "It's all right," said Jordan. In effect, Jordan was a court taster. If he didn't keel over and die from it, neither would the prisoner.

"Another one." The prisoner was asking Jordan to try another sip.

"All right, fine. I hope you like sugar. Like I said, if anything happens, we go together now."

"Right, right—all the way, huh?"

Deputy District Attorney John Howard made to leave. He gave the prisoner his telephone number again, and told him that if he called after hours, he would be able to reach someone else because, "I mean, you know, as I told you, I'm that lazy so I don't want to come down here."

"Inherently," said the prisoner, rubbing it in. "Inherently."

Howard went out of the room. "What are you thinking, Sarge?" asked the prisoner.

Said Jordan, "I'm the low man on the totem pole. Do you follow me?"

"You are the best man," said the prisoner.

"Well, that's . . . thank you . . . that's . . ."

"I mean that, sir, with all my sincerity."

"As long as you're with this department," said Jordan, "you will be treated properly. That's a . . . I promise you."

"I will hold you to that."

Sergeant Melendres broke in. Now he was going to make a stab. "Young man?"

"Yes, sir."

"Let's be friendly and manly here for a second, will you?"

"Yes, sir."

"We have a job to do," said Melendres.

"Yes, sir."

"I'm Sergeant Melendres and this is Sergeant Jordan, and you have been talking to Mr. Howard. Now, do you want to talk to us about the incident at the Ambassador, or don't you? Were you at the Ambassador tonight?"

The prisoner reminded them that he didn't want to waive his constitutional rights to remain silent. Howard who was listening outside came back in to assure him that, indeed, he did have those rights and that if he wanted to give them up, that was his choice, his choice alone, and no one else in the world could make it for him. "We would like to talk to you tonight," said Howard. "We'd like to bring a stenographer in here, take down your statement—"

"Uh-huh," said the prisoner.

"—as to what occurred within the last four hours before you came here. That's what we'd like to do. You have no obligation to make that statement."

The prisoner didn't want to play this game anymore. "Hell, I'm no movie star that wants all that much—"

"Fine. That's up to you."

"Jee-sus Christ!" said the prisoner.

In Rome, Pope Paul VI told the vast audience of pilgrims who fill St. Peter's Basilica every Wednesday at midday that he was praying for Senator Robert Kennedy—"for the life and health of this young man who was offering himself to the public service in his country." Hundreds of Americans in the crowd gasped in astonishment. What had happened to Robert Kennedy? In a moment the news flashed through St. Peter's, one pilgrim who knew about the shooting uttering a name that was universally understood to the man or woman next to him who didn't know about the shooting: "Robert Kennedy." And then the inevitable gesture, understandable in any language: a forefinger to the temple, and a wagging thumb. Robert Kennedy shot. The Pope waited some moments, then added in English: "We deplore this new manifestation of violence and terror."

The surgeons cut the overlying skin and muscle behind the Senator's ear and laid it back. They bored through the skull with an air drill and an air saw. They removed a segment of bone. Then, while Reid helped control bleeding, Cuneo probed the wound. He shook his head grimly. If the bullet had hit one centimeter or more nearer the midline of the skull, the Senator might have been in fairly good condition. The thickness of the occipital bone, uncommonly thick in Kennedy's case, might have deflected the little bullet. But the mastoid, which looks much like a honeycomb, was easily penetrated. When it was hit, it shattered, sending bone fragments into the brain, bone fragments which were sharp and dirty, medically speaking, and they had to be removed.

Cuneo first removed the blood clot, irrigated out bits of destroyed brain tissue, then went to work on the fragments of bone and bullet.

"What time is it?" asked the prisoner.

"It's twenty minutes to four."

"I'm allowed seventy-two hours before I'm brought before a magistrate, no?" The prisoner had obviously done some homework before he shot Kennedy. But he hadn't done it very well.

Jordan corrected him. "Maximum is forty-eight."

"Forty-eight. Well . . ." The prisoner paused. He could have been making a mental calculation. "You have that many hours, minus—before I'm brought before a magistrate."

"Right. That's correct," said Melendres.

"I'll talk to the guy out there," Howard added, "and see if they've got any smaller pants, okay?"

The prisoner thanked Howard politely.

In an adjacent room, Evelle Younger, the district attorney of Los Angeles, his chief deputy, Lynn D. (Buck) Compton and George Murphy, John Howard's chief investigator, sat and watched the entire scene. "You know," said Murphy, "the kid seems to like Jordan."

By 6:30 A.M. (3:30 Los Angeles time), Rose Kennedy was up and about in Hyannis Port, getting ready for seven o'clock Mass. Then she turned on the TV to see how Bobby had fared in the California primary. Earlier, Ted Kennedy had phoned Cape Cod with the news that Bob was shot and told Ann Gargan, his cousin, who had attended Joseph Kennedy since his stroke, not to awaken his mother but to wait until she arose. But the matriarch of the Kennedy clan, who had given so much of herself and of her family to the public, who had lost two children in plane crashes and another to an assassin's bullet, learned about yet another assassination attempt, as much of the nation did that morning, over television.

Quietly, she finished dressing for Mass, put on a shawl and sunglasses and headed for the front pew of St. Francis Xavier Church in Hyannis Port with a family friend, Attorney John Driscoll of Boston, just as President Lyndon Johnson was issuing a statement from the White House:

> There are no words equal to the horror of this tragedy. Our thoughts and our prayers are with Senator Kennedy, his family and the other victims. All America prays for his recovery. We also pray that divisiveness and violence be driven from the hearts of men everywhere.

The Mass of the day was one in honor of St. Boniface, an English Benedictine monk of the eighth century who took the faith to Hesse, Saxony and Thuringia and earned the title Apostle of Germany. The Lesson and the Gospel for the Mass of St. Boniface had been read to many congregations for a good many centuries, but those scriptural passages may have never meant more to anyone than they meant to Rose Kennedy who heard the celebrant read them in English:

> Now let us praise famous men, and our fathers in their generations. In them the Lord has wrought great glory and shown his majesty from the beginning.

There were the men who exercised authority in their dominions and were re-nowned for their achievement. Then there were those who were gifted with wisdom and expressed themselves in prophecies; those who led the people by their prudent counsels and instructed them with words of wisdom; those who composed melodies with their skill and wrote songs in poetry; those who were rich in virtues, endowed with strength and living in peace in their homes. All these were the glory of their generations and the praise of their times. The children whom they begot have left behind a name that their praises might be prolonged. . . .

At the same moment, a continent away, in the board room of Good Sa-maritan Hospital, Ethel Kennedy and Jean Kennedy Smith and Patricia Kennedy Lawford knelt for a private Mass said especially for them by Monsignor Joseph Truxaw, pastor of the nearby Immaculate Conception Church. It, too, was the Mass of St. Boniface, but the Lesson sailed over their heads, for Monsignor Truxaw, a pastor of the old school, mumbled the entire Mass in Latin. Perhaps Ethel and Jean and Pat recognized the more familiar Latin words of the Gospel, the beatitudes of Jesus as re-counted by St. Matthew:

Blessed are those who are persecuted in the cause of right, for theirs is the kingdom of heaven. Blessed are you when people abuse you and persecute you and speak all kinds of calumny against you on my account. Rejoice and be glad, for your reward will be great in heaven.

Officer Frank Foster stayed with the prisoner in the isolation cell. His first duty: to see that the prisoner did nothing to harm himself. His second: to get him to talk. If there were some coconspirators, better to find out sooner than later. Was there a girl with this guy when he poured the shots into Kennedy? Foster tried to establish some rapport. And somehow—it is not clear now who brought the subject up—the conversation got around to "The Boston Strangler," a sexual psychopath, who in 1962–63 murdered thirteen women. "Surprisingly enough," said Foster, "The Strangler didn't go for notably attractive girls. One was twenty-two. One was twenty-three. And all the others were sixty-five, sixty-eight, sixty-three, fifty-five—pretty old, you know."

"Gee, man," said the prisoner, "that's something. I wonder often what would provoke or cause such a man to do that."

"Well," said Foster, "no doubt that the man's, you know, demented sex-ually. The way they feel now possibly is that it's a younger person and that he has a psychological factor that he should kill his mother."

"Oh," said the prisoner.

"Because he apparently had a bad childhood. This is the way the psychologists have been setting up the pattern."

"But, correct me if I'm mistaken," said the prisoner, "is it when—is this the—the man is self-admitting. He admits that he's, wasn't trying, but they won't believe him? Is this related to it?" The prisoner's question was a contorted one. But he had obviously read enough about The Boston Strangler to know that whatever he'd done he'd done in some kind of dissociated state. He "wasn't trying." What meaning did this story have to the prisoner? How was it related to his own state of mind when he shot Kennedy? Foster didn't pursue that line. The two lapsed into silence.

Finally the prisoner asked Foster, "Any children?"

"I have two," said Foster, "a little girl and a little boy." He told the prisoner about his children. The two of them discussed the miracle of birth and growth, and the high cost of birth in this day and age. The prisoner indicated he was opposed to socialized medicine or the kind of care one gets in a Kaiser Hospital—"just like in a gas station."

"You—you don't usually sit with the prisoners?" asked the prisoner.

"No, no, ah. It's just this particular case. They wanted me to sit in here."

"I enjoy your company."

"We don't normally—we don't normally sit with everyone that comes in because we wouldn't have enough policemen."

"I know it. I'd hate to pay for them, man, you know, as a taxpayer."

"Yeah, now, well, you can understand why they, on this particular case, where they are more concerned than—"

"Really, man?"

Outside the hospital the crowd of newsmen and the curious grew and grew. They had seen the familiar figures of the Kennedy entourage come and go, their faces lit by flickering red flares and the eerie white lights of the television trucks now parked in a street covered with telephone cables. John Glenn, the astronaut, Andy Williams, the singer, Dick Goodwin, Jesse Unruh, Dick Tuck, Rafer Johnson. A police car, its siren screaming, brought Senator Edward Kennedy, who had swooped down at Central Receiving Hospital in an Air Force helicopter.

After Rafer Johnson had satisfied himself that there was nothing more that he could do for the Kennedys, he had a policeman drive him to Rampart detectives where he personally turned over the assassin's weapon. It

was an 8-shot, Iver-Johnson .22-caliber revolver with eight empty cartridges inside.

Henry Carreon, a handsome student at East Los Angeles Junior College, sat transfixed in front of his television set, waiting for further news
about the shooting. Maybe the young man who shot Kennedy was the
strange little guy he and David Montellano had seen practicing the day before at the San Gabriel Valley Gun Club in Fish Canyon. The news broadcasts said the man who shot Kennedy was short and dark and thin, and so
was this guy at the range. "I wonder," he said, "if the police have the gun.
If they do, and it is an 8-shot Iver-Johnson .22, I am going to call them."
    Finally, Carreon got the word on TV: the gun was an 8-shot Iver-John-
son .22. He phoned his friend, David Montellano. "David," he said, "remember that guy we talked to on the range? The little dark guy? I think he
is the guy who shot Kennedy." Montellano remembered. Carreon called
the police, told them his story, and said if they wanted him, he would be at
Montellano's house.
    The police did want him. Sergeant Louis R. Estrella of the LAPD
Homicide Division, arrived at 4:00 A.M. and got from Carreon and Montellano a full account of their day at the gun range. The fellow they remembered on the range didn't seem to know very much about guns, didn't
even know, for example, whether his .22 was a "single action" or a "double action" revolver. He was also hesitant in some of his replies to their
questions, and sometimes, when he did respond, he talked so fast they
could hardly understand him. He was shooting very, very fast, rapid fire,
which was against the range rules, and he was shooting Mini-Mags. Montellano recalled asking the young man about that. He said they cost twenty-five cents more a box, but they were "hollow points." "They spread a
lot more on impact," he explained to Montellano.
    Then Estrella showed each of them a spread of photos, all of them pic-
tures of dark, slim young men. Each fingered the same one, and that, Es-
trella knew, was the young man now being held for shooting Kennedy.

In London, Prince Stanislaus Radziwill got the news by telephone and
immediately put in a call to his sister-in-law Jacqueline Kennedy in New
York.
    "How is Bobby?" demanded Stash.
    "You heard he won in California," replied Jacqueline sleepily.

"Yes, but how is he?" asked the prince.

"I just told you. He won in California," insisted Mrs. Kennedy.

Radziwill realized that he was the first bearer of the bad news about Bobby to the widow of John. It was difficult for him but he forged ahead, told her quickly what he knew and that he would catch the next plane to join her in New York.

George Murphy said they ought to make one more try. "Let Jordan talk to the kid," he said. Jordan said he'd see what he could do. They had Officer Foster bring the prisoner back to Interrogation Room No. 1. Murphy and Jordan joined him there shortly. Jordan had another cup of coffee for him and went through the tasting ritual again. The prisoner told him to take some more—much as if he wanted to share his coffee with Jordan. Jordan declined and the prisoner insisted. "Really, I couldn't finish the other one. I . . ."

Jordan said he had his own coffee. They all had coffee. Murphy drank a toast. "Here's how. This will keep us awake anyway, huh?" He looked at his watch. It was 4:02 A.M.

Jordan paused for a moment, wondering where to start. "You obviously had some knowledge of the Kirschke case." Back to crime and punishment.

The prisoner said he had no special knowledge. It was just that he felt Kirschke had prosecuted innocent people and that reminded him of a book (or a movie, he wasn't sure), *To Kill a Mockingbird*. But neither Jordan nor Murphy had read the book. Then for some reason the prisoner suddenly realized that the conversation in his cell was not a private one. "Is this being bugged in? Are you bugging me?"

Maybe the honest approach was the way to go. "Yeah," admitted Murphy.

"Sure. You know that," said Jordan. "We wouldn't lie to you."

"Sure," said Murphy. "You know that."

But Murphy's admission didn't make things any smoother. "No, I mean, hell," said the prisoner, "if you want to tape me, bring the fuckin' microphone in. Don't, don't play this bullshit with me."

"No, we're not playing bullshit with you," said Jordan. "That's just routine. I mean, everything in the whole building . . ."

Jordan explained that all of the cells were bugged.

"It's coming from behind," the prisoner announced, somewhat gleeful that he'd figured that out all by himself, delighted that he'd caught the cops acting like crooks. He shouted to one wall where he thought a microphone might be imbedded, "Hello there!"

The three of them talked again about the Kirschke case. "Sometimes it's part of your job," said Murphy, "to prove a man innocent."

"That's right," said Jordan, "and we try to do our job the best we can. And let me ask you this: Would you purposely try to hang some guy on a case if you thought he was innocent?"

Philosophically speaking, the prisoner was a modern. "Well, really, I, I'm such a—how should I say?—indifferent. I mean, it depends. It's an indifferent attitude toward this business because really the falsehood and truth, sir, really, they're relative. Really, you, there's no factual, there's no facts directly to say this is false, or this is wrong, or this is right, you know. Everything is what you think it is, in fact, no? "

"Would you work hard to convict a person that you really, sincerely believed was innocent?" asked Jordan.

"I don't really know," said the prisoner. "You're asking me this question as if you're putting me, you're giving me the responsibility, me the responsibility of something so fantastic that it's beyond my mental and physical ability to, to cope with, really."

"I don't really think it's beyond your mental ability," said Jordan quietly. "I think you've got a lot of mental ability. I think you've been putting us on a little bit here."

The prisoner turned to Murphy, "What's he talking about?"

"See," said Jordan, "right now, right now, you're doing it. You're, you're very sharp. You're very sharp."

It was 4:25 A.M. and Sergeants Patchett and Melendres had a very interesting visitor closeted in Room 318 of Parker Center's Homicide Division. He was Thomas Vincent DiPierro, tall, dark, lean, nervous and, up to this point, the most intriguing eyewitness of all the persons who said they had been in the Ambassador pantry shortly after midnight.

Young DiPierro, son of one of the maître d's at the Ambassador, said he'd seen the assassin moments before the shooting and he was with a girl —a girl in a polka-dot dress. Sandra Serrano had seen a girl in a polka-dot dress fleeing the scene. The detectives took DiPierro downtown, where the men who were talking to the assassin could cross-examine him. If there was a conspiracy in the wind, the LAPD had better get its weather vanes adjusted before too much time elapsed.

DiPierro repeated his story for Patchett and Melendres. He had walked into the pantry right behind Senator Kennedy. He saw the assassin move toward Kennedy "with a stupid smile on his face" as if to shake his hand, and then there were two or three shots and DiPierro's spectacles were spattered with blood, and Paul Schrade fell back into his arms.

Moments before the shooting, DiPierro said, he had noticed the gunman hanging onto a tray stand (a tall wheeled cart used for stacking waiters' trays) some four inches off the floor. He was looking around, and a girl was with him. Patchett wanted to know why he thought the girl was "with him."

John Howard entered Room 318. He was getting nowhere with the assassin. From what police detectives had told him, DiPierro had an angle he couldn't ignore. Howard stood there and listened carefully to the young man's story.

"Well," said DiPierro, "she was following him . . . She was holding on to the other end of the tray table and she—like—it looked like as if she was almost holding him."

"Did you see him get off the tray stand?"

"Yes, I did."

"And then he walked toward the Senator?"

"Yes."

"This girl—"

"She stayed there."

"At the tray stand?"

"Right. I glanced over once in a while. She was good-looking so I looked at her."

"What is it in your mind that makes you think they were together, the fact that they were standing together?"

"No, no, he turned when he was on the tray stand once, and he had the same stupid smile on, you know, and then he kind of turned and said something. I don't know what he said."

Howard broke in: "Did you see him speak to her?"

"He turned as though he did say something. . . ."

"Did she move her mouth like she was speaking to him?"

"No, she just smiled."

"And would it seem to you that she smiled at something that had been said?"

"Yeah. . . ."

DiPierro described the girl. Between twenty-one and twenty-four. Brunette. Very shapely. And she wore a white dress with either black or dark violet polka dots on it.

"Okay," said Patchett. "Just to sum this up, what's the thing that sticks out in your mind?"

DiPierro paused a moment. His most vivid memory was not of the girl, but the assassin. "The stupid smile he had on his face."

"Smile on his face?"

"It was kind of like an envious smile, like, ah, you know, villainous. I don't know how to describe it."

With perhaps the same kind of smile on his face, the prisoner indicated he'd like to talk about the stock market.

He got a short lecture on it from Jordan and Murphy. "I never had any money to fool around with the stock market," said Murphy. "Policemen don't make that much money."

"I wish I had. I wish I had some," said the prisoner. "Really, that would be a good adventure to, to experiment with."

"Oh, it's a lot of fun, I guess. I don't feel . . ."

"Well, if you got a few dollars to throw away . . ."

"If you've got it," said Jordan, "that's the clue." They all laughed about that. "Right there, if you've got a few dollars."

Jordan had to leave the cell. The prisoner told Murphy he looked like Dean Rusk. Murphy said he didn't know about that. "Now, the one interesting thing is to find out exactly who John Doe is. That's what we're interested in."

"Really, you know, that's beautiful, beautiful. Maybe we should keep it interesting."

"We have to, I guess," said Murphy, "because you're the doctor there. But, it's going to be interesting to see who John Doe really is, and we . . ."

"Speak up, man." The prisoner was getting bolder.

Murphy looked at the prisoner searchingly. "You're just sort of matching wits with us."

"You know, there's a horse named that," said the prisoner.

"What?"

"Matching Wits."

"Is there?" asked Murphy.

"Or something to that effect."

"Anyway, that's sort of what we're doing, aren't we?" asked Murphy.

"Well, I, I think it's like I said, you know. I'm always open for any kind of an intellectual, educational—anything that would, you know, benefit my mind. Really, what can, what more can you ask for?"

"Well, of course," said Murphy, "you can have a nice conversation and everything."

"It's up to you guys."

"But you could also make our job a lot easier."

"Again, you might lose the interest in the mystery."

"Oh, we're not going to lose interest." The two of them laughed over that.

At 4:45 A.M., the doctors took some hope: Senator Kennedy had started to breathe completely on his own. All the bleeding was stopped and most of the metallic fragments were removed. Drs. Cuneo, Reid and Andler stayed with it, to finish removal of the bone fragments that had been driven into the brain.

Frank Mankiewicz walked out to the street, puffing hard on a cigarette, approached the crowd of newsmen, waited a few moments while the newsmen who had been waiting in a hospital auditorium across the street were alerted, took a final puff and threw the cigarette away. He climbed on top of a police car and told the reporters the surgery would take "another hour and perhaps two." Jules Witcover, the news correspondent with the Newhouse chain who had been traveling with Kennedy, stood there in the first gray dawn and frowned. To him, no news was bad news.

Jordan returned to Interrogation Room No. 1 a little more chipper than he was when he left a few minutes before. He thought he might have the first break in the case. "Hi! Miss me?"

"How about some more coffee?" asked the prisoner.

"Do you want some more coffee?" asked Jordan.

"Make it a little warmer," said the prisoner. "It's a little cold. Please, if it's no inconvenience at all."

It was Jordan's moment for irony. "Now, what could be inconvenient," he said, "at four-thirty in the morning?"

"Is it four-thirty or five?" asked the prisoner. "A quarter to five."

Murphy noted that it was exactly a quarter to five. "You mean you can tell what time it is?" he asked incredulously. There was no clock in the room and the prisoner had no watch.

To Jordan, that was interesting, but irrelevant. He now thought he knew who the prisoner was.

Officers had taken the prisoner's car key back to the Ambassador and tried it on every car nearby. Finally, success. It fit a 1958 Chrysler registered to Robert Eugene Gendroz, a waiter at the Ambassador. "Okay. Let me have you try this on for size. What about Robert Eugene Gendroz?"

"Hell," said the prisoner, airily, "that's a good name—Gendroz."

"I think," said Jordan, "I think we're in pay dirt now." There was a note of triumph in his voice, at last. "Roberto, or Bob?" asked Jordan.

"That's a nice name."

"It's a nice name. And your car?" asked Jordan.

"Cadillac?" asked the prisoner.

"No," said Jordan.

"Rolls-Royce?" asked the prisoner.

"How about a Chrysler?" asked Jordan.

"Beautiful," said the prisoner.

"Beautiful. Nothing wrong with a Chrysler, is there? A 1958 Chrysler?" asked Jordan. Jordan thought he had the prisoner pinned down, but he was mistaken. The prisoner continued with the put-on.

"Wonderful," said the prisoner. "The mystery is beginning to unfold now, huh?"

"Now, listen," said Jordan.

"Pieces are all starting to fit together," said Murphy.

"Right," said the prisoner. But it was wrong. "How did you know I had a '58 Chrysler?" asked the prisoner. "The key? Beautiful." He smiled. His own car was a '56 De Soto. If the key fit the Chrysler, it was a simple coincidence.

"Well, listen," said Jordan, "now, you're a taxpayer. Now, wouldn't you be disappointed if we, if we didn't come up a little bit for you?"

"You're God damn right," said the prisoner. "Slowly, but surely, you're driving there."

"But we get there," said Jordan.

"You get there," said the prisoner, smiling again because the police were getting exactly nowhere.

By 6:00 A.M. Murphy and Jordan were exhausted and they hadn't learned much, only that their prisoner was very tough and very clever.

He was clever enough to ask about the one-way mirror and the tape recording he'd guessed they were making. Jordan admitted that persons outside could look in. "But nobody is trying to trick you."

"Do you ever do any censoring on the tape?" asked the prisoner.

"Censoring?" asked Jordan.

"Yeah."

"Well . . ."

"Anything or something, you know, modify it?"

"If you edit at all it loses whatever limited value it would have." And having such a tape, Jordan might have added, was a protection for both the police and the defendant. Incredibly, the Dallas police have no record of their sessions with Lee Harvey Oswald and critics have been asking ever since: what did they have to hide?

"Is any of what I am saying, sir, would be used against me in court?" Jordan said it could be.

"You really send them to the slaughter, no?"

Jordan protested. "No, no, I don't feel that way. Do you—do you think I send people to the slaughter? I mean . . ."

The prisoner admitted he was speaking about "a stereotype."

Murphy, who had ducked out momentarily, ducked back in again. "We're going to arraign you in a little while. You're going to court."

"Please make sure about my attire," said the prisoner. He wanted to wear his own clothes. "Why not? I don't see why."

Jordan said, "You look very presentable compared to when I first saw you. You are clean. You are neat. Your eyes are clear. . . ."

Though only a few hours had elapsed since the shooting, big bundles of evening newspapers were thumping down on city sidewalks in Europe, and the people who didn't know what to think pressed their coins into news vendors' palms to see if the journalists had a clue. The London *Daily Mirror* filled its front page with a huge picture of Senator Kennedy with open but sightless eyes and a black headline reading, "GOD! NOT AGAIN!" The *Mirror*'s editorialist could express only revulsion: "What is this dreadful sickness that lurks beneath the surface of the richest country on earth? Again and again, it sickens us all." On the Continent, where plots, poisonings and coups are the most memorable part of everyone's history books, whispers of a political conspiracy became an assumed fact. *Le Soir* of Brussels judged that "a sinister and systematic conspiracy against the most eminent American liberal leaders has been organized by a kind of Mafia composed not only of killers but supported by influential and powerful circles." Most commentators in Paris took up the conspiracy theme, but *Combat,* a Paris daily, theorized about a worldwide sickness. "America does not have exclusive rights to violence: she is merely the magnifying mirror of all the phenomenons of dispute which are taking over the Western capitalist democracies. America is mad with France's own madness, sick with our sickness. She is not the nightmare of our dreams. She is the focal point of this fever which is mounting slowly in our veins." Others reexamined the rhetoric of violence. The *Neue Zürcher Zeitung* said: "Even before the shots were fired on Bobby Kennedy the international political life of our days was befogged by myths carrying too much violence. Since President Kennedy's murder, the New Left has been working with pseudophilosophical legends of obscure powers which kill the bright figures of the assumed guarantors of a better future."

These editorialists were only guessing; none of them knew then how right they were or how much impact the rhetoric of violence (and violence itself) had had on the assassin.

But now the prisoner, sitting in the isolation cell of the L.A. City Jail, didn't seem to be violent at all. His voice was very very soft.

"Your leg hurt you?" asked Officer Frank Foster.

"Kind of," said the prisoner softly.

"How did you hurt it?"

"I don't know."

"Did you fall down, or something?"

"No."

"When did it happen?"

"I don't remember."

"You don't remember?" Strange. Either the prisoner was very very cagey or he had a very convenient loss of memory.

Foster told the prisoner he wasn't being recorded—a lie—and they started in on small talk: Foster's dog, his motorcycle.

"What made you become an officer?" asked the prisoner.

"Oh, I don't know. I've always been kind of interested in law enforcement. I had a real good friend back home that was a state trooper, highway patrolman, and he kind of got me interested into it. And I just felt that that was my way or my little bit of helping society a little bit."

The prisoner said he was impressed with Foster's mind and wondered about other policemen. Were they like Foster?

"Oh, a lot of them feel very similar ideas, I'm sure. It's like any profession, there are cases where there's injustice, and everything else connected with all professions."

"I agree," said the prisoner emphatically, as if he had had some encounter with injustice in high places.

"I don't care if it's the person that—maybe he's just a common laborer, maybe he does—maybe he washes out toilet bowls, I don't know, or the highest person that can gain a position in the world; there's still injustice and maybe misuse of his powers even though it's his powers."

That pleased the prisoner. "Let me shake your hand," he said. "You're the first man—please, please, you're the first man that ever said that and expressed it, you know, in the same way as I feel it."

They traded some compliments. Then Foster said, most broad-mindedly, "Well, maybe—maybe you're just the victim of circumstances."

"Beautiful," said the prisoner. "Overintentional"—meaning perhaps that Foster was closer to the truth than he knew.

"Well, you know, you can never tell. I mean if—I know maybe if circumstances were different it would be vice versa, I'd be on the bench and you'd be over here, you know, you never know."

Said the prisoner, "We're all puppets."

Three

"Tell my mother to clean up my room. It's a mess."

Frank Mankiewicz and Steve Smith were waiting in the hallway when the doctors emerged from surgery at 6:20 A.M., blinking their way back to the real world after the intense, time-stop concentration of the operating room.

"The next twenty-four to thirty-six hours should tell," said Dr. Cuneo.

"Should tell what?" asked Mankiewicz.

"Whether he'll live or not," said Cuneo simply.

"And if he lives?"

Cuneo put it to them directly. "There is some evidence of damage to the midbrain." If a bullet or a bone fragment had hit the midbrain, the body's most important neural pathway, they wouldn't, of course, have been standing there talking, for Kennedy would have been dead. But the concussive shock of the bullet and the indriven fragments of bullet and bone resulted in tiny hemorrhages to the midbrain. Just how bad they were only time would tell. The blood clot, now removed, and the swelling of the brain had cut off a certain amount of oxygen; that might or might not have caused permanent damage.

Even if Kennedy survived, he would not be the same Bob Kennedy. He would be totally deaf in one ear and the right side of his face would be paralyzed. His left field of vision would be impaired, and he would have a degree of spasticity in his arms and legs. "But," Dr. Cuneo added, "the higher centers seem to be unaffected. He would still be able to think and reason."

Senator Kennedy was wheeled down to the elevator, taken back to the intensive care unit of the fifth floor, placed on an ice mattress to lower his temperature and decrease the metabolic rate. This reduced the strain on his heart and protected the brain, which needs less oxygen at lower temperatures. The doctors continued to monitor the cardioscope and kept a critical record of all the other vital functions. Ethel Kennedy was given a cot at her husband's side. Sometimes she sat, sometimes she lay down. Almost always she held his hand.

Mankiewicz told Dr. Cuneo that the press would appreciate his telling them what happened. "You tell them," said Cuneo, who was just then beginning to come back to reality. "While the patient was draped and under the sheet," said Cuneo later, "I forgot he was Bob Kennedy. Afterward, the import began to hit me again."

Mankiewicz directed Cuneo to Senator Edward Kennedy, who was with Ethel now on the fifth floor. But even, perhaps especially with Ted Kennedy, Cuneo was at a loss for words. Cuneo thought to himself: What do you tell a man who has lost one brother, a President of the United States, to an assassin's bullet, and has another brother, a U.S. Senator, in critical condition as the result of yet another assassin's bullet?

But it was Ted Kennedy who did the talking. He told Dr. Cuneo that he had asked Dr. James Poppen of Boston's Lahey Clinic to come out to Los Angeles—in fact, an Air Force jet scheduled to fly to Anchorage, Alaska, had scrapped its flight plan, under orders from Vice-President Humphrey, and was ready to leave Boston at any moment with Poppen aboard. Cuneo knew Dr. Poppen from various professional meetings around the country. He had looked after John F. Kennedy's back, after Ted Kennedy's multiple injuries when he suffered a plane crash in 1964, and attended Joseph M. Kennedy, still lingering from his stroke of 1961. "I don't know anybody else I would have been any happier with," said Cuneo. He turned to Ethel Kennedy, assured her that her husband was "better than he was when he had arrived" and breathing now on his own. He told her there would be some impairment in any event, but they'd know more in twenty-four hours.

Cuneo and his colleagues went down to breakfast in the hospital cafeteria, and Mankiewicz tried to figure out what he ought to tell the press. While he did so, reporters waited and tried to pick up some clues about the Senator's condition from the army of nurses, doctors, police, Secret Service men and friends of the Kennedys who came and went. According to one early rumor there was no brain damage and some preferred to report that, with hope. Others were completely noncommittal but their tones were gloomy.

At 7:20 Frank Mankiewicz was outside the hospital again, telling the newsmen all he dared. He did not tell them about the shattered facial nerves, the hemorrhage into the right temporal lobe, the certain deafness of the right ear. Why talk about certain horrors when the doctors weren't even sure that he would live? He told them simply, "There may have been an impairment of the blood supply to the midbrain."

Downtown, another army of reporters waited outside Parker Center for further news about the mysterious gunman who wouldn't give his name. No one except members of the Los Angeles Police Department were allowed in the building, which was so absolutely unprecedented that local newsmen could only conclude that the assassin was there in Parker Center. Finally, credentialed newsmen were searched, then allowed into the auditorium on the first floor for a 7 A.M. news conference to be given by Chief Tom Reddin.

Reddin had little news. The suspect was still unidentified. He declined to give his name. The police had sent his fingerprints to the Washington headquarters of the FBI. Reddin did not say that the State of California's Criminal Investigation and Identification Division was trying to trace the gun which Rafer Johnson had finally wrested from the gunman's grip. Nor that Judge Joan Dempsey Klein was heading downtown to her courtroom on the seventh floor of the county's Hall of Justice for the arraignment of the prisoner. Nor that Officer Donald Day was backing his own camper truck up to the elevator exit in the police garage so that the police could transfer the prisoner three short blocks to the Hall of Justice as unobtrusively as possible. But then, that was the point of this news conference. It was more of a diversionary action than an attempt to communicate information, for the police wanted to avoid news media coverage of the prisoner's transfer to the Hall of Justice. It was during a much more public transfer, attended by a tangle of newsmen, that Jack Ruby shot the assassin of President Kennedy. And so Reddin stalled for time and tried to talk about the assassin. "I spoke with him for about fifteen minutes," lied Reddin, "and he sounds well educated. Speaks good English and is a good conversationalist. We talked about many things. He was very relaxed and wanted to talk about just about everything except the events last night. If I were to judge him strictly on the basis of our conversation and that were the only basis, I would say he was a gentleman." Reddin went even further, attempting to show the newsmen where the gunman's bullet struck Senator Kennedy. A UPI photograph of that conference shows Reddin standing in front of a forest of microphones and poking a pencil into his upper jaw.

"Can we have an interview with the suspect?" asked one newsman.

Said Reddin, "After Dallas, nobody is going to get within a thousand feet of him."

Nobody did, except for half a hundred sheriff's deputies who stood guard in Department 40 of the Hall of Justice, while the chief public defender, Richard Buckley, a lean, nervous man with a tanned bald head, huddled in the jury box with the man to be arraigned. Buckley looked up and asked the deputies within earshot to give him some privacy. They moved some fifteen feet away, and Buckley resumed his conversation. The prisoner said he wanted to talk to someone from the American Civil Liberties Union. Buckley said he would pass the word along. "In the meantime," he advised, "you don't have to tell them anything if you don't want to. Not even your name." This prisoner nodded soberly. "You don't even have to tell me." The prisoner nodded again, uncertain whether this was friend or foe, then tentatively deciding he was friend when Buckley told him: "And don't sign anything. Don't even sign a booking slip."

Buckley's advice was entirely proper under the circumstances, and something the prisoner had half figured out for himself somewhat earlier that morning. He had signed the booking slip "John Doe."

At 7:40 A.M. the prisoner was moved into a chair in front of the bench and surrounded by deputies, then advised of the charges against him. "Do you have a name?" asked Judge Klein. She was rather attractive but judicially severe.

"Mr. Buckley is my attorney," said the prisoner unresponsively.

"Do you have a name?" repeated the judge.

"John Doe," said the prisoner. In white hospital pants, a blue denim shirt, and black slippers, he certainly looked like a John Doe.

"Do you have an attorney?"

The prisoner said he didn't. Not yet.

Judge Klein officially appointed the public defender.

The judge said he was charged with violating Section 217 C of the Penal Code, assault with a deadly weapon with intent to commit murder. He was informed of his rights to a speedy and public trial by jury or judge, his right either to testify or refuse to testify. "Do you have any questions?"

"Not at this time," he answered. He seemed quite composed.

Chief Deputy District Attorney Lynn Compton suggested the defendant be held without bail. He outlined his reasons:

(1) There was a strong possibility that one of the victims (Compton was

thinking of Kennedy) would die, and those charged with murder don't get out on bail.

(2) The defendant refused to identify himself, which made it impossible to conduct any investigation of his background to determine how high his bail should be.

(3) There might be others involved in the shooting who could conceivably want to kill this man.

Compton pointed out, "This man *did* attempt to assassinate a United States Senator."

Buckley disagreed. He said the court had to fix bail and in a reasonable amount.

"What do you consider a reasonable amount?" asked Judge Klein. She said she had difficulty even considering the question of bail at this point. "I even heard some news reports that many persons had expressed the thought that the defendant should be killed, hung or strung up."

Buckley knew his law. There was no murder—yet—and some kind of bail should be set.

The judge complied. "All right," she said. "I'll set bail at $250,000 at this time." She also set a time for preliminary hearing—8:00 A.M. Monday. But even then, Deputy District Attorney John Howard was making arrangements for the Grand Jury to meet on Friday, hear evidence in the case and return an indictment.

A dozen sheriff's deputies surrounded the defendant, handcuffed him and led him through a back hallway to the jail elevators, sped him down to the basement and into a waiting station wagon. They pushed him down on the floorboards and sped through a tunnel, up on to Spring Street and north toward the jail that would be the defendant's home for the next thirty days.

The New County Jail was a squat, gray, concrete structure, unadorned except for a few shrubs well away from the building. The deputies entered from the rear, through a gate controlled electronically from a tinted glass tower directly overhead, and into a large asphalted yard, past several black and white prisoners' buses, and screeched to a halt outside the north entrance to the jail. The jail was on something called "extreme alert." All prisoners and all trustees were in their cells, the booking area was deserted except for two veteran officers, who put the prisoner quickly through the formalities. He gave no answers at all but they measured him and weighed him—he was five feet, three inches and 120 pounds—moved him through two blue-green electronically-controlled steel gates, gave him an exchange of clothing, blue denim trousers (that fit) and a blue chambray shirt, took his picture and his fingerprints (again), then marched him through a long, echoing first-floor corridor, now completely deserted, 150 feet west to the jail hospital. The prisoner limped into the clinic, looked around curiously and sat down. A medical technician swabbed his left arm with a piece of cotton and picked up a needle and syringe. The prisoner recoiled. He didn't want a needle in the arm. "It's just a blood sample," said the deputy.

The prisoner shuddered and stuck out his arm. "How much you taking?"

"Ten cc's." The prisoner nodded. They took him into a room next door dominated by a huge green X-ray machine, and X-rayed his left knee and ankle and his left hand.

His radiologist was Dr. Henry Williams, a graduate of Howard University and the City College of New York Medical School and a member of the faculty of three medical schools in Southern California. From the bit of small talk that went back and forth between them (for there was a certain rapport between the black doctor and the prisoner), Dr. Williams concluded the prisoner was "self-satisfied, smug and unremorseful." "It seemed," Williams said, "that he anticipated all this—like he wasn't surprised he was here, and was ready to accept the penalty."

The X rays of the leg showed no fractures, but the prisoner's complaints convinced the sheriff that he'd be better off in a wheelchair. One was brought in and he was wheeled off to a large blue and stainless-steel elevator, up to the southwest wing of the second floor infirmary, vacated that morning for the prisoner's exclusive incarceration. They put him in a bleak little concrete cell, #7057, furnished in jailhouse modern—a bed of iron pipe and a mattress, a sink, and a seatless toilet. They clanked a steel door on him, and left a two-man guard watching him through an ample window.

At 9:32 A.M., Dr. Philip Attalla, a staff doctor at the New County Jail, came up to the prisoner's cell to put a splint on his left index finger. Attalla was an emigrant from Egypt and he looked searchingly at the prisoner. Was he an Arab? He spoke a few words in Arabic to the prisoner, but got absolutely no reaction.

Across town, one half block south of Wilshire, on New Hampshire Street, three blocks from the Ambassador Hotel, an officer assigned to the Los Angeles Police Department's traffic division found a pink and white 1956 De Soto Fireflite, license number JWS-093, parked in a red zone. He wrote out a citation, #39-43559 M, and put a yellow copy under the windshield wiper. The officer couldn't have searched the car without a warrant, but if he had, he would have found nothing more incriminating inside than two spent .22 cartridges on the front seat and a book in the back entitled *Healing: The Divine Art.*

By now, the police learned that the assassin's Iver-Johnson pistol had been purchased at the Pasadena Gun Shop by Albert L. Hertz of Alhambra for his daughter's "protection" during the Watts riots of 1965. He told officers his daughter, Mrs. Dana Westlake, had moved to Marin County, north of San Francisco, and sheriff's deputies there telephoned Mrs. Westlake to find out what she'd done with the gun. "I gave it to a neighbor in Pasadena named George Erhard," she said. "He was a collector and I didn't want the darn thing around. I have two small children." In Pasadena, police found Erhard working at Nash's Department Store. "Sure, I had the gun," he said. "I sold it to a guy named Joe. He works in the store here."

As a matter of fact, "Joe," who preferred to be called by his real name, Munir (pronounced Moo-NEAR) Sirhan, had reported early for work that morning, heard about the shooting of Robert Kennedy and recognized the picture of his unknown assailant, being flashed intermittently now on television, as his brother, Sirhan Sirhan. He dashed out of the store, hopped in his boss's car and sped home. Home was a modest frame cottage at 696 E. Howard with a large, blooming magnolia tree in the front yard. His mother, he noted with relief, was already at work and he awakened his older brother, Adel.

"Sirhan didn't come home last night, did he?"

"I don't know. Did he?" Adel was a professional player of the oud, the large gourd-shaped guitar of the Middle East. He worked nights and slept mornings and for him 9:00 A.M. was the middle of the night.

He snapped to quickly enough, however, when Munir told him that the police were holding Sirhan for the shooting of Senator Robert Kennedy.

Within fifteen minutes, the two brothers, Adel, twenty-nine, and Munir, twenty-one, were presenting themselves at the Pasadena Police Department. "Have you got a morning paper?" Adel asked the desk sergeant timidly. "No," he barked and turned away. The two went outside. Adel spied a newsstand up the street. "I'll go get a paper," he said (for he wanted to show the police his brother's picture on the front page, rather than tell them).

"I'll go take my boss's car back," said Munir.

Adel returned to the station alone with a copy of the Pasadena *Independent*. "I think this is my brother," he said, tapping the picture of Sirhan on the front page. The police took him upstairs for questioning. An FBI man soon joined them.

Back at Nash's Department Store, Munir parked the car, went up to his boss's office and met some gentlemen from the FBI who said he'd better come with them. "What for?" he demanded.

"You bought a gun from George Erhard?" As an alien and a convicted felon on probation, Munir had no right to have a gun.

"No," said Munir. "My brother did."

The agents brought George Erhard into the office. "Is this the fellow who bought the gun?" said one of them to Erhard. Erhard said it was, but Munir insisted he was mistaken. It was his brother, Sirhan.

Munir insisted on taking them to see Adel. He and Adel had already gone to the Pasadena Police Department on their own volition. They had nothing to hide.

By the time they got to the police station, Adel had already departed, with a contingent of police and Federal agents, to 696 E. Howard. They did not place Adel under arrest but were careful to read him his rights: "You have a right to remain silent—anything you say can and will be used against you in a court of law—you have a right to an attorney. If you cannot afford an attorney, the state will provide you with one gratis." To Adel, already overwhelmed with the enormity of what his brother had done, or what the police had said he had done, those words made him shake, for he knew they meant that *he* was in trouble.

"You have nothing to hide here, do you?" asked Los Angeles police sergeant William Brandt, who had been dispatched to see if he could find any evidence of a conspiracy.

"No," said Adel.

"Then you don't mind if we come in and take a look?"

Adel looked around him. A crowd of several hundred persons had formed in front of the house, dispatched there, in effect, by Mayor Yorty himself, who had just called a news conference to announce that the assailant was an Arab immigrant named Sirhan Sirhan who lived at 696 E. Howard in Pasadena. "No," said Adel. "You can come in."

The Los Angeles police officers soon found more than they'd hoped for in the bedroom of their suspect. On the floor next to his bed lay a large spiral notebook. On his small table, which served as a desk, was another spiral notebook. Some other odds and ends included a handbill summoning voters to a Senator McCarthy rally in Pasadena; the May 23 issue of the *Christian Science Monitor,* Western edition; a small spiral notebook with annotations on only two pages; a good deal of Rosicrucian literature; other readings in the occult; an honorable discharge from the California Cadet Corps (ROTC) by reason of graduation from high school the thirteenth day of June, 1963; a brochure advertising a book on mental projection by Anthony Norvell; and a large brown envelope from the U.S. Treasury Department Internal Revenue Service on which someone had written, *"RFK must be disposed of like his brother was,"* while at the bottom of the envelope another scrawl read "Reactionary." Sergeant Brandt thought this was hardly evidence of a conspiracy. But it was pretty damn good evidence of "willful and deliberate premeditation." So, in fact, were the two notebooks.

In his cell at the New County Jail the prisoner whistled. Then he smiled. Then he made a face and hunched his shoulders a bit. Dr. Marcus Crahan, the medical director of the jail, wondered what was the matter. "It's chilly."

"Are you cold?" asked Crahan.

"Not cold."

"What do you mean?"

"No comment."

"You mean you're having a chill?"

"I have a very mild one." It was an interesting admission, one that would later arouse the curiosity of a psychiatrist interested in what really happened on the night of June 4.

Dr. Poppen arrived at Good Samaritan at 10:15 A.M. Dr. Cuneo gave him a complete rundown and took him to the Senator. With Ethel Kennedy looking on, Dr. Poppen made his own examination, timed the beeps on the cardioscope, checked the blood pressure and the intravenous records and the X rays, then turned to Ted Kennedy, Smith and Mankiewicz and told them the team in Los Angeles had done it all. There was nothing left to do but wait.

"I'm Peter Pitchess. I'm the sheriff of Los Angeles County and I'm here to tell you why I'm here."

"Yes, I know," said the prisoner, "I recognized you."

Pitchess was elected in 1958 and reelected in 1962 and 1966 and he will probably continue to be reelected for as long as he wishes because (1) he is a good administrator of the largest sheriff's office in the United States, and (2) he is the kind of sheriff who maintains a very high visibility in that county. The prisoner had seen him many times, as much of the nation has, leading the Rose Bowl Parade every New Year's Day in Pasadena, astride his palomino, One in a Million, Jr.

"Let me explain our interest here," said Pitchess. "You're committed to our custody and our care. We have a responsibility to see that you're protected—from yourself and from the outside. There have already been threats against your life. We'll do everything possible to see you provided with the full protection of law and of our facilities. I want a clear understanding from you that you will do everything possible to help us do that."

The prisoner blinked and said quietly, "Do you really care about my safety?"

Pitchess said sternly, "I asked you a question. I want an answer."

The prisoner smiled, "Yes. I'll do whatever I can to help." Then he asked Pitchess about his rights.

"You have a right to counsel, either of your own choosing or appointed by the court."

"I mean," said the prisoner, "what are my rights in jail? What privileges do I have?"

"You have the same rights any other prisoner has."

"Do I get to read the newspapers?"

"Yes, it's our custom to provide the L.A. *Times* and the *Examiner*. They're circulated every day. If you want 'em, you can buy 'em. You have money. You can also buy magazines."

"How about books?"

"There's a circulating library. Or you can make specific requests through the county library."

The prisoner nodded. He said he'd make a request for some books later and asked Pitchess for a morning paper.

Pitchess left, aware that A. L. Wirin of the ACLU was scheduled to arrive at any moment. In the corridor, he relayed his impression to Undersheriff William McCloud. "A very unusual prisoner," said Pitchess, "a young man of apparently complete self-possession, totally unemotional. He wants to see what the papers have to say about him."

*   *   *   *   *

Aside from the columns and columns of news and sidebars about the shooting itself, the newspapers reflected a national anguish that yet another Kennedy was struck down in his prime and a sharp division of opinion on where to place the blame.

Liberals implied that somehow American society itself provided the climate in which an assassin could flourish, while conservatives maintained there was nothing wrong with society, only a few individuals within it. Mayor Jerome P. Cavanaugh of Detroit said the shooting "reveals just how deeply sick America is." Mayor Carl B. Stokes of Cleveland, a black man who knew—personally—many, many other men whom society had made sick, prayed that the nation could "free itself of hate and violence." Mayor Richard J. Daley of Chicago thought of a first step which his liberal advisers hoped wouldn't be an only step: Congress should pass a Federal gun law "because there are too many people with guns that should not have them." Some in Congress did call for stiff gun-control measures, which had been favored by Kennedy, while some Republicans in the House said they preferred immediate approval of anticrime legislation carrying relatively mild gun controls. Senator Mike Mansfield, the Senate Democratic leader, proposed creation of a special committee "to find ways and means to cope with violence on the American political scene."

Dr. David Abrahamsen, a governor of the Lemberg Center for the Study of Violence at Brandeis University, had as much insight as any psychologist who was quoted on this day. Lemberg said America's stress on materialism bred violence. "We're not a melting pot," he said. "We're a damn pressure cooker. Our society is not built on the restraints of family or class, it's built on success. If you don't have it, you're frustrated." Lemberg called this frustration "the wet nurse of violence."

Arthur Schlesinger, Jr., a close personal friend of both John and Robert Kennedy, spoke on this day at commencement exercises for forty-eight postdoctoral graduates at the City University of New York. He said that Americans are the most frightening people on this planet "because the atrocities we commit trouble so little our official self-righteousness, our invincible conviction of our moral infallibility."

Almost on cue, two California politicians stood up to exemplify Schlesinger's point. Governor Ronald Reagan went on national television to tell the country it should feel no collective guilt. "Two hundred million Americans did not do this. One young man did it, and for not even an American reason." And Mayor Sam Yorty said, "This could have happened anywhere." But it didn't happen anywhere. It happened in Los Angeles,

California, U.S.A., and a pervading sense of gloom settled down over the nation. A television station in New York started out the day by canceling its show of children's cartoons and projecting a single word, without sound, for two and a half hours: SHAME. And in Los Angeles, one of the country's best sportswriters, Jim Murray, turned away from Drysdale and the Dodgers, sat down to his typewriter and asked savagely: "What have the Kennedys ever done to deserve ambuscades every five years at the hands of people they ask only to serve? What apology can we offer to a noble family except to resolve to stop being ruled by our refuse, our human refuse, that is? How many good men have to die before we wrest weapons from the terrible hands of our barbarians, demand respect for our institutions, stop glorifying hate?"

And Yevgeny Yevtushenko, the Russian poet, who had had a three-hour conversation with Senator Kennedy on a visit in 1966, wrote a poem of eighteen irregular stanzas called "The Freedom to Kill." It began:

> The color of the Statue of Liberty
> Grows ever more deathly pale
> As, loving freedom with bullets,
> You shoot at yourself, America.

A small man with bright, probing eyes and a magnificent gray beard appeared in the prisoner's cell. "I," he said simply, "am from the ACLU. I'm Al Wirin."

The prisoner nodded vigorously and motioned for Wirin to sit down on the bed. "You know I did it," he whispered. "I shot him." He pulled an imaginary trigger on an imaginary gun. "I shot him." Wirin nodded. Something about Wirin's reticence warned the prisoner. "Are they bugging this cell?" he asked.

"The sheriff assures me they are not."

The prisoner pointed at one of two electric sockets in the east wall. "What about those?" he asked.

"The sheriff assures me they are not bugging this cell. However, it would be safer to assume they are."

"Well, I'd like the sheriff himself to tell me they are not bugging me." He knocked on the door and asked the deputy if the sheriff was still in the area.

He was. "Can I help you?" asked Pitchess.

Wirin told him that the prisoner was concerned about the possibility that his cell might be bugged. "He wants your word that it isn't."

"Absolutely," said the sheriff. "This cell is not bugged."

"Will you put this in writing?" asked the prisoner.

"Hell, no," said the sheriff. "My word is my bond."

The prisoner shrugged and smiled. After the sheriff left, the prisoner switched his pillow to the west end of his bed and pulled Wirin very close. "I haven't told them my name," he said, "but I'll tell you." He whispered in Wirin's ear: "Sirhan Sirhan." Wirin had him repeat it. Phonetically, it came out *sur-han sur-han,* each syllable about equally accented, and the second one rhymed with man. He told Wirin about his family in Pasadena. He wanted Wirin to go out and see if they were all right, and to tell them that he was all right. He was also concerned about his car. "I parked it near Kuchel headquarters," he said, "on a side street not far off Wilshire. There are some bullets in the car."

Wirin asked him if he could tell the police about the car. Sirhan paused. Wirin said the police now knew who he was. He'd just heard the mayor announce it on the radio. Sirhan said he could tell the police. They'd find it sooner or later anyway. Wirin asked him why he'd called for the ACLU.

"It represents the minorities. . . ."

"Yes," admitted Wirin, "it does."

"You'll represent me?"

"No," said Wirin.

"Why not?"

"Well in the first place," said Wirin, "I'm Jewish."

"Ohhh," groaned Sirhan. "I'm dead already."

"I'll try to be honest and fair," said Wirin. "I'll help you find an attorney. The ACLU is interested in due process of law and constitutional rights. But there's no constitutional right to . . ." Wirin spread his hands, unable to say "assassinate."

The prisoner nodded. That was fair enough. He decided a disclaimer was necessary. "Now I'm not against Jews," he said. "I'm against Israeli imperialism." He asked Wirin to see if he could get him a morning paper. Wirin went to the door and rapped.

"Can we get this man a morning paper?" asked Wirin.

Pitchess himself walked in with a copy of the Los Angeles *Times.* "This is on the house," he said.

"Oh, no!" protested Sirhan. "I want to pay my way."

"Forget it," said Pitchess. "It's nothing."

Indeed it was, as far as Sirhan was concerned, for as soon as Pitchess had left, he noted that it was a copy of the *Times*'s Preview Edition, which had hit the streets at five the night before and so contained no news at all about the assassination. To himself, Sirhan said in disgust, "It's the same damn paper I got from Mistri last night."

Wirin said he'd see about an attorney for Sirhan.

"I want a good one. I want the best." Wirin nodded, wondering whom he could get to take on what would surely be an unpopular case. Sirhan had one more request. "Tell my mother," he said, "to clean up my room. It's a mess."

Sirhan may have been fastidious or may have been hoping his mother would discover (and destroy) the notebooks which he'd left lying in his room. But it was too late for that. At the moment Sirhan was telling Wirin to tell his mother to "clean up the mess" in his room, the LAPD was scanning the notebooks with more than a little satisfaction. One page was a detective's dream:

> May 18 9:45 AM—68
> My determination to eliminate R.F.K. is becoming
> more the more of an unshakable obsession . . .
> R.F.K. must die—R.F.K. must be killed Robert
> F. Kennedy must be assassinated R.F.K. must
> be assassinated R.F.K. must be assassinated . . .
> Robert F. Kennedy must be assassinated before
> 5 June 68 Robert F. Kennedy must be assassinated
> I have never heard please pay to the order of of of
> of of of of of of of of this or that please pay to
> the order of

If that didn't prove premeditation nothing did. In the detective division of Rampart Street station, police grilled Adel Sirhan and Munir Sirhan in separate rooms. Both disclaimed any knowledge of the notebooks. Both disclaimed any knowledge of their brother's intentions. Both disclaimed any knowledge of their brother's actions. And both were obviously scared to death.

Munir Sirhan had a record, but he was obviously nothing more than a restless kid. He'd run away from home at fifteen; he'd been picked up for vagrancy in Flagstaff, Arizona; he'd been convicted of illegal possession of marijuana in Los Angeles County in 1966 and served nine months in jail. And, it seemed, he had bought a gun from George Erhard in February, 1968.

Adel Sirhan didn't even have a record. He was soft spoken, polite, a gentleman. He played the oud at The Fez. He made picture frames. He was good to his mother. Did he know anything about a girl? No. Did his brother have a girl friend? No. A brunette? No.

Nevertheless, at 12:30 P.M., the police put out a teletype bulletin to every law-enforcement agency in the land:

I RAM 6–5–68   APB E M E R G E N C Y
ASSAULT WITH INTENT TO COMMIT MURDER. IN CUSTODY SUSPECT SIRHAN BIS-
HARA SIRHAN AKA SIRHAN SHARIF BISHARA . . . PRIOR TO SHOOTING, SUSPECT
OBSERVED WITH A FEMALE CAUC. 23–27, 5–6, WEARING A WHITE VOILE DRESS,
¾ INCH SLEEVES, WITH SMALL BLACK POLKA DOTS, DARK SHOES, BOUFFANT
TYPE HAIR. THIS FEMALE NOT IDENTIFIED OR IN CUSTODY. . . .
ANY INFORMATION ON SUSPECT AND DESCRIBED FEMALE CAUC. RUSH RAMPART
DETS.
ATTN. . . . ALL HOMICIDE DETAILS
          LAPD CENTRAL HOMICIDE
          FBI LOS ANGELES
          CII SACRAMENTO
          PASADENA PD
          REFER DETS. LT. HUGHES / MELENDRES
          GL / MAC 1230 PDT LOS CJT

A police car led the way with its siren screaming and Senator Eugene McCarthy, looking grayer than ever, pulled up to Good Samaritan Hospital in a four-car caravan. Now, as McCarthy climbed out of the big black car that had brought him, the scream of the siren trailed off into a mournful wail. McCarthy had prepared a statement an hour and a half before to decry the lone lunatic theory. To McCarthy, the question was why? He talked about the "neglect which has allowed the disposition of violence to grow here in our own land," and said that violence at home was a "reflection of the violence which we have visited upon the rest of the world."

McCarthy went into the hospital, found that Ted Kennedy and Ethel were "resting" and paid his respects to them through Richard Goodwin and Pierre Salinger. Guarded by the Secret Service, he left the hospital without making a further statement, flew directly to Washington and suspended his campaign for the Presidency.

In New York, a Secret Service detail set a guard on the Fifth Avenue apartment of Richard Nixon, who canceled his appointments for the week and remained in seclusion. Governor Nelson Rockefeller and Vice-President Hubert Humphrey also called a moratorium on the campaign.

Goodwin and Salinger went up to the fifth floor and noted at noon that the doctors started monitoring Kennedy's brain waves. The first electroencephalogram at 12:05 P.M. showed a rate of ten to thirteen cycles per second—which was a little fast—and a moderately high-voltage disorganization. Dr. Cuneo ordered tracings to be taken intermittently every ten to thirty minutes.

In the corridor of Rampart station, no less than 25 newsmen interviewed one another while they awaited more official word about Sirhan. "You can bet that anything important will come from the mayor himself," said Martin Kasindorf of *Newsweek*.

Kasindorf was a prophet. The tip-off came shortly thereafter when a police sergeant emerged from an inner office and said he'd gotten a request from the mayor's office. "How many of the press are here? Whom do they represent?" The newsmen called out their affiliations. AP. UPI. Reuters. L.A. *Times*. *Life*. *Newsweek*. KHJ. Channel 2. Channel 4. Channel 5. Channel 7. Channel 9. The San Francisco *Chronicle*. *The New York Times*. Clearly, the media were here. A newsman wondered if the mayor would come rushing out. "He will," said Kasindorf, "if it will get him on the tube."

The mayor did come, but not before the police laid a smoke screen for the Sirhan brothers. They called a news conference at 12:30 and then, while everyone—including Paul Udell of Channel 2, who had been crying, "We want a shot of the brothers. Where are the brothers?"—poured into a basement conference room, the police slipped the brothers out a back door.

In the basement, a brightly lit room with all the blandishments of a mausoleum, Inspector K. J. McCauley gave the press some of the particulars he had on Munir and Adel Sirhan. "Munir Sirhan said his brother Sirhan Sirhan had bought the gun from someone named George Erhard some five or six months ago for $25. Yes, it was an Iver-Johnson .22-caliber revolver. It seems that Sirhan was an exercise boy at Hollywood Park. Munir showed up at the Pasadena Police Department early this morning. Far as we know none of the family are citizens. He has a mother. Sirhan went to Pasadena City College. He is well spoken. Speaks other languages. Russian."

Did Sirhan have political reasons for shooting Senator Kennedy?

"We asked Munir about that," said Inspector McCauley, "but I don't want to go into that now."

And that was the end of the conference. But not quite. As the newsmen trooped out, Mayor Yorty just happened to saunter down the stairs.

"What can you tell us about Sirhan Sirhan?" asked a newsman stringing for *Life*.

"Well," said the mayor, "he was a member of numerous Communist organizations, including the Rosicrucians."

"The Rosicrucians aren't a Communist organization."

"Well . . ." puffed Yorty. The television newsmen turned on their lights and started shooting, and the reporters rushed their mikes up to the mayor. He stopped and looked around. The party was hardly complete. Maybe, he suggested, we'd better go inside where we can be more comfortable.

Back in the basement conference room—it was now 1:15 P.M. and Yorty was into his second news conference of the day—the mayor spilled as much prejudicial information as any public official would. "It appears," he said, "that Sirhan Sirhan was a sort of loner who harbored Communist inclinations, favored Communists of all types. He said the U.S. must fall. Indicated that RFK must be assassinated before June 5, 1968. It was a May 18 notation in a ringed notebook. When he was arrested, he had a column by David Lawrence about Robert Kennedy wanting the United States to supply arms to Israel." The men from the wire services galloped for the exit and dashed to the telephones and Kasindorf muttered to himself, "Yorty's done it again."

By 2:15 P.M., a couple of hundred curious citizens stood in front of the Sirhan home at 696 E. Howard in Pasadena. Many of them paid an enterprising young man with a Polaroid camera one dollar to take their pictures in front of the house of the assassin. The police had cordoned off the street to vehicular traffic, and a team of police stood guard around the house. Inside, FBI agents were questioning Saidallah Sirhan, yet another older brother of Sirhan Sirhan, and reporters found a friend of Adel Sirhan sitting gloomily on the bumper of his tan Volkswagen. She was an attractive girl of Arab descent who couldn't understand what had happened. "Sure," she said, "we were shocked when America started helping the Israelis and we demonstrated against the Zionists with a parade on Hollywood Boulevard and another one outside the Hollywood Bowl. But there was never any talk among us about killing Kennedy." As a matter of fact, neither she nor her friends had ever identified Robert Kennedy as an enemy of the Arab cause.

The backyard of the home was unweeded and overgrown. A rusty lawn mower sat next to the garage, alongside a pile of empty Pepsi-Cola bottles.

But a bougainvillea bloomed in the backyard, and the white blossoms of a magnolia tree prettied up the front. Tacked up over the front door was a small horseshoe. Good luck.

Neighbors viewed the passing parade, and some of them volunteered their view of Sirhan Sirhan. One said he was "very religious." Another said he "hated people with money." Another said he was "just a normal kid. He took cars and bikes apart and put them back together again." They talked of a sister, Aida, now deceased, who had lived in Palm Springs. They talked about Sirhan's brothers—Adel and Munir, who lived at home, and Sharif and Saidallah, who lived apart. One neighbor reported that Sirhan had run away from home several years ago (she was wrong: it was Munir who had run away) and said that "Sirhan had things he couldn't get clear with himself." His mother worked in a nursery school, over at the Presbyterian church. The kids in the neighborhood, a mixture of blacks and whites, said Sirhan was "nice." Was he an angry fellow? "He didn't show it," said one black girl, "he didn't show it." But a conspiracy buff, an intelligent young man in his early twenties named Arthur Bean, swore that "someone talked that kid into gunning down Kennedy." A postal clerk who knew Saidallah stood in the shadow of an orange tree across the street and said there was nothing suspicious about Sirhan's carrying $100 bills on his person. "That's the way these Sirhans keep their money. In $100 bills. Loose."

A. L. Wirin made an appearance, talked to the police, discovered that the mother, Mary Sirhan, was staying with friends, got her address and went back to his car, which he'd parked at the corner.

And then Saidallah burst out of the house in slacks and a white starched shirt, no tie. The crowd shrank back from him and he stumbled up the street, in tears.

Oliver Brindley Owen, also known as "Jerry" and "Curly," eased up to the LAPD's University substation in his Chevy pickup truck. He was there to tell the police he had some information on Sirhan. Owen was a roly-poly, raffish preacher who hawked the old-time religion, along with free pony rides for children, at supermarket parking lots in L.A.'s Bible Belt —Bell, Southgate, Downey, Lakewood and points southeast. He billed himself as the "Shepherd of the Hills," and he knew 31,816 Bible verses by heart, but he had a few extracurricular interests which were, for a preacher, somewhat peculiar. He owned a piece of a professional boxer named Rip O'Riley, and a string of horses, and he hung around with a slightly shady crowd of gamblers and ex-pugs. He also had a police record.

He said he'd run into Sirhan and another "Mexican-looking kid" thumbing a ride in downtown L.A. on Monday, June 3, and taken them up Wilshire Boulevard to Vermont, where both of them had jumped out, talked to a tall, dark fellow and a girl of about nineteen or twenty with dirty blonde hair. Then, he said, Sirhan jumped back in the cab, asked Owen if he could ride on with him toward Hollywood. Sirhan, possibly noting the horse ornament on the hood of Owen's pickup, told Owen that he was an exercise boy at the racetrack and was looking to buy a horse. Owen said he had a horse for sale and told him he could have it for $300. Sirhan said he was interested, then asked Owen if he'd mind stopping for a minute so Sirhan could see a friend who worked in a kitchen nearby. Owen pulled off Wilshire, parked not far from 7th and Catalina, waited ten minutes, decided he'd waited long enough and started to turn his truck around and leave. At that moment, Sirhan dashed back. Owen noted he'd come from "a tall building with many rooms." He later identified it as the Ambassador Hotel.

Owen took the young man to the Hollywood Ranch Market parking lot on Vine Street. During that phase of the ride, Owen's hitchhiking friend said he was a Jordanian, that he had come to the United States when he was thirteen, that his name was Joe. He gave a surname that sounded like "Zaharias." Owen completed an errand or two—he was getting some boxing gear ready for his fighter, O'Riley—and then, as he drove his thumber back down Sunset Boulevard, he made a deal to sell him the horse for $300. He let him off on Sunset near a bowling alley and a topless bar, and agreed to meet him there at eleven o'clock that evening when they would make final arrangements about the horse.

When Owen returned shortly before eleven, he saw Sirhan climb out of a 1958 or '59 white Chevy. In the car were two other men and a girl, possibly the same girl he had seen on the corner of Wilshire and Vermont earlier in the day. Sirhan showed him a $100 bill and said he would have the rest of the money early in the morning.

At seven or eight the next morning, in the parking lot of his hotel, Owen found a tall, well-dressed man waiting at his truck. It was the man he'd seen with the girl at the corner of Wilshire and Vermont. "He was a sharp fellow," said Owen, "a seasoned guy like a Vegas, a gambler, he's playin' the track or somethin', and he wore a cat's-eye ring and alligator shoes." The man said, "Joe can't make it." But he offered Owen a down payment on the horse, and asked him to deliver it that night near Wilshire and Catalina, when he would have the rest of the money. Owen said he had business in Oxnard, left the man his card and told him to have Joe get in touch later if he was still interested in the horse. Owen noticed the same girl in the same Chevy sitting nearby, and Sirhan's companion of the day before was with her.

Then Owen was off for Oxnard where, he said, he preached at the Calvary Baptist Church, spent the night and returned to Los Angeles on June 5 with his horses.

About midday, Owen stopped at the Coliseum Bar and Grill near the Los Angeles Memorial Coliseum, heard the news about the Kennedy shooting, saw Sirhan's picture on the TV and heard a newscaster describe him as an exercise boy. Owen took a closer look, bought a copy of the Hollywood *Citizen-News,* studied Sirhan's picture, concluded he was the kid who wanted to buy the horse and drove over to the police with his story.

To the officers, Owen was an obvious gasbag. He talked nonstop, from a little after 3:00 P.M. until seven in the evening. But if what he said was true, others might have been involved with Sirhan. Maybe Sirhan had planned to escape from the Ambassador and make his getaway in Owen's horse trailer. Or maybe Sirhan's companions were setting up a pseudo-escape for a gunman who really didn't have a prayer of getting out of the Ambassador.

Irwin Garfinkel, one of the crack deputies in the public defender's office, paid a call on Sirhan. Sirhan didn't think he could trust Garfinkel, who, after all, got his pay from the same people who paid the district attorney. "I don't remember much about the shooting, sir," said Sirhan. "Did I do it? Well, yes I am told I did it. I remember being at the Ambassador. I was drinking Tom Collinses. I got dizzy. I went back to my car so I could go home. But I was too drunk to drive. I thought I'd better find some coffee. The next thing I remember I was being choked and a guy was twisting my knee."

In effect, Sirhan was saying that he didn't remember anything from the time he went back to his car until moments after the shooting.

At 5:30 P.M., Dr. Cuneo looked at the electroencephalograph tracing and noted with alarm that the hills and valleys of the tracing were beginning to level off: the higher centers of the brain were no longer getting any blood. By 6:30, the tracing had leveled off to a straight line: no cortical activity at all, which meant that the brain itself was dead. But the cardioscope indicated the heart was still pumping: *Beep . . . beep . . . beep . . . beep . . . beep.* How long would it continue?

That evening, President Lyndon Johnson appeared on the nation's television screens for a special message. He said he would charge a special Presidential commission to seek the causes for violence of the sort that struck down Robert Kennedy. Johnson said, "It would be wrong—it would be self-deceptive—to ignore the connection between lawlessness, hatred and this act of violence." On the other hand (it was Johnson the politician speaking), "It would be just as wrong, just as self-deceptive to conclude from this act that our country is sick, that it has lost its sense of balance, its sense of direction and common decency. Two hundred million Americans did not strike Robert Kennedy last night no more than they struck John F. Kennedy in 1963 or Martin Luther King in April of this year. But those awful events give us ample warning that in a climate of extremism, of disrespect for law, of contempt for the rights of others, violence may bring down the very best among us. A nation that tolerates violence in any form cannot expect to be able to confine it to just minor outbursts."

Johnson said the commission would look into the causes and the control of physical violence across the nation—"from assassination that is motivated by prejudice and by ideology, and by politics and by insanity, to violence in our cities' streets and even in our homes."

On the fifth floor of the Good Samaritan Hospital in Los Angeles, members of the Kennedy entourage who were keeping their vigil were drawn irresistibly to the outside world as reflected on television, saw the President's craggy face and heard the President's strident voice, and laughed scornfully when he announced that Senator Roman Hruska of Nebraska, a champion of the nation's gun lobby, would sit on his commission to investigate the violence.

The other eight represented a cross section of what is sometimes known as the Establishment:

- Dr. Milton S. Eisenhower, president emeritus of Johns Hopkins University in Baltimore and brother of former President Eisenhower.
- Archbishop Terence Cooke of New York.
- Albert E. Jenner, Jr., a Chicago lawyer who was on the staff of the Warren Commission.
- Patricia Harris, a law professor at Howard University.

- Eric Hoffer, a San Francisco longshoreman and self-made philosopher.
- Senator Philip Hart of Michigan, a leading civil-rights advocate and an opponent of gun controls.
- Representative Hale Boggs of Louisiana, the House majority whip and a member of the Warren Commission.
- Representative William M. McCulloch, of Ohio, a member of the House Judiciary Committee.
- A. Leon Higgenbotham, Jr., a U.S. district judge for Eastern Pennsylvania.

Harris and Higgenbotham were both Negroes.

By 7:00 P.M., the doctors noted that the Senator's brain tracing continued as before: no activity. A stethoscope was too insensitive to record the blood pressure. But Kennedy's heart continued to beat and his breathing, aided by a positive pressure machine, was good.

Then Jacqueline Kennedy arrived with the husband of her sister, Lee, Stash Radziwill. Only God knows what feelings were in her heart as she saw Bob Kennedy lying there high on the ice mattress, stuck with the tubes and wires that monitored his ebbing life-forces. It was like Dallas and it was different. Strange, idiotic, unexplainable, yes, but not chaotic, not chaotic at all, because the police and the doctors were beginning to learn how to handle Kennedy assassinations. But the pain could not be any less.

In June of 1968, I was a free-lance writer working on a novel and some magazine assignments when I got the news from Sander Vanocur on the "Today Show" that someone had shot Bob Kennedy in the pantry of the Ambassador Hotel. I choked, cried, cursed and, instead of sitting there weeping in front of the TV, tried to do something. Doing something meant using my journalistic excuses to be curious. I phoned *Life* magazine in Los Angeles, found that the bureau needed my help and tried to get on the track of the man who shot Kennedy.

With *Life* photographer Howard Bingham I found Saidallah Sirhan in his one-room apartment with bath at 1659 North Lake Street, a couple of blocks from the Sirhan home on E. Howard. The apartment sat over a garage at the back of the lot. Saidallah demanded that Bingham and I sign in with our names and addresses. He wanted to see some identification too.

While Bingham signed, I looked around. It was a messy bachelor apartment, with two large rugs on the floor. One was green with white flowers on it. That lay over a multicolored striped rug, just a bit bigger than the flowered one on top. Sixteen-ounce Budweiser empties lay about the room, and Saidallah guzzled on a Bud while he talked with me.

I asked him about his family. Mother, father, Adel, Sirhan, Munir and Aida arrived in the United States on January 12, 1957. Three years later, the two eldest brothers, Sharif and Saidallah, arrived. "Is your father now deceased?" I asked.

Saidallah looked at me piercingly. "What?"

"Is he dead?"

"I do not know."

"What?"

"I do not know."

"Where is he?"

"I do not know."

"When did you last hear from him?"

"Two months ago. Two months ago, he was in Israel, Jerusalem."

"In Israel, huh?"

"No, not in Israel," he shouted. "Israel doesn't exist. In Palestine. I am a Palestinian Arab. Do not forget that."

"Did Sirhan have Communist sympathies?"

"This is a fake," shouted Saidallah, enormously agitated. "This Yorty statement is a fake! That kid never did, he had no intention, he had no idea about firing a gun. This kid never did appear to me that he is of such character. Did he have even a police record?" Saidallah took a long quaff of beer. He emptied the can, went to the refrigerator and popped the top on another Budweiser. "Look," he said, "there are a lot of actors in this town. There are actors who could have shot Kennedy. But my brother! Shit, no! According to my life experience, man, Sirhan Sirhan, he has nothing to do with such movements."

"Did Sirhan ever say he wanted to see Kennedy out of the way?"

"No."

"Did he discuss the Arab-Israeli War?"

"Not to my knowledge." I looked around the room more carefully. I saw an oud hanging on a wall over the foot of his narrow bed. A cheap print of Jesus before Pontius Pilate dominated another wall. A twenty-five pound dictionary sat on a stand. An Admiral radio rested on a shelf over the bed, and next to the bed was a portable television and a record player. A pile of long-play albums sat on the floor. Middle Eastern music. Ravi Shankar.

Saidallah came back into the room, zipping up his tight black pants, and got another beer out of the refrigerator. Bingham asked him what the stringed instrument was. Saidallah then played a very coy game, finally took down the oud, explained what it was and let himself be persuaded to play it. The music was sad and became even more plaintive when he stopped playing with his finger and used an eagle feather instead.

I looked over at a copy of the Pasadena *Independent* on Saidallah's pillow and saw the headline in red letters: KENNEDY SHOT—LAST RITES GIVEN. Saidallah stopped playing. "What are you doing?" he shouted. I shrugged. "Go ahead! Look!" Saidallah cried.

I kept my eyes fixed on Saidallah. "I understand Sirhan was an exercise boy at a racetrack?"

"After he fell from a horse," said Saidallah, "my mother says Sirhan has been in a nervous condition."

"Did you say nervous?"

"No!" shouted Saidallah. "I said Sirhan seemed to be in a mental condition."

"As a result of the fall?"

"I do not know 'result.' It was after the fall."

One of the neighbors had told me Sirhan had gone back to Jerusalem a couple of years ago. I asked Saidallah about this.

His answer came very slowly, very evenly, murderously, with flashing eyes: "He . . . was . . . raised . . . under . . . U.S. . . . . culture . . . P! C! C!" PCC was Pasadena City College.

Bingham tried to get Saidallah to agree to a picture. No. For a half hour, Bingham sported around with Saidallah. He went to his wallet, finally, and pulled out a smaller-than-passport-size photo of himself, moustachioed, rather than clean shaven, as now. "Take a picture of this," he said. Bingham tried, in vain, to take a picture of the picture. Finally, Bingham and I, both of us discouraged and depressed by all this, said good-bye. "Beg me again," said Saidallah.

Outside the Good Samaritan Hospital, it seemed that all the lonely people in town had come to join the vigil for Bob Kennedy. Shatto Street, in front of the hospital, was nothing more than a footpath now for policemen and firemen and newsmen traveling back and forth on official business. Across the street, the mobile television units hummed and their lights shone down on the scene, making the darkness into day, while the television cameramen focused their long lenses on the hospital's entrance. It was here that Jackie Kennedy had tried to come in and was turned away to another entrance because the police feared for her safety in this crowd.

But it was not a violent crowd, nor a noisy crowd, nor even a mobile crowd. Most of them were young people, many of them dressed in a style that would have to be called "Sunset Psychedelic," and they sat silently on the hill north of the hospital, looked, listened . . . and prayed. Many of the boys and girls had pasted across their chests orange and black bumper stickers hurriedly printed by an unknown believer in the hours since the shooting: PRAY FOR BOBBY.

Hundreds of cars paraded back and forth on Wilshire, their radios on, their occupants listening for the latest word from inside the hospital. Some stopped and picked up a bumper sticker from a man standing on the corner, passing them out free.

Over in the Good Samaritan auditorium, which now served as a makeshift press room, newsmen sprawled on the floor, keeping their red-eyed vigil. Many of them had not slept for forty-eight hours. Many would have given a year of sleep if they thought it might help Robert Kennedy.

1:33 A.M., Thursday, June 6. The longest day was almost over. Senator Kennedy's heart, a strong heart that kept pumping far longer than doctors ever thought it could, started slowing down. The interval between the beeps on the cardioscope was growing longer, the little white dot on the viewer growing more sluggish. *Beep* . . . . *beep* . . . . *beep* . . . . *beep* . . . .

beep. There was a flurry of activity. Those closest to Bob Kennedy who had kept their vigil at the hospital were called in to pay their last respects to the live, barely live, Bobby. George Plimpton's heart almost broke when he entered to see Ethel Kennedy holding tightly to her husband's hand and all the other Kennedys seemingly busy, checking this tube or that machine or the reading on this or that chart. Finally, only family was left, only family and the doctors who were still standing by. *Beep* . . . . *beep* . . . . *beep* . . . . *beep*.

Finally at 1:44 A.M. the beeps stopped, the pattern on the cardioscope leveled off completely and Drs. Cuneo and Poppen put their heads together and nodded. Senator Robert F. Kennedy was gone. Senator Edward Kennedy moved over to Ethel's side, put both his arms around her and held her tightly.

At 2:00 A.M., Frank Mankiewicz entered the press room across the street for the last time. He faltered once or twice as he spoke, but finally he said what he had to say: "I have a short announcement to read which I will read at this time. Senator Robert Francis Kennedy died at 1:44 A.M. today, June 6, 1968. With Senator Kennedy at the time of his death were his wife, Ethel; his sisters, Mrs. Stephen Smith and Patricia Lawford; brother-in-law, Stephen Smith; and Mrs. John F. Kennedy. He was forty-two years old." Mankiewicz later added the name of Senator Edward Moore Kennedy, whom he had simply forgotten.

Some fool asked what the specific cause of death was, and Mankiewicz, instead of ignoring that stupidity or raging at the man, replied quietly, numbly, "The gunfire attack . . . the bullet . . . that went into the head . . . near the right ear."

That first night in jail Sirhan couldn't sleep. His energy seemed completely gone, but he couldn't sleep. Maybe it was because his bowels were locked and his knee ached and his finger throbbed and his throat kept going dry. He dozed fitfully through the earliest morning hours. At 6:00 A.M. he was awake, staring at the door of his cell, wondering what this day would bring.

A. L. Wirin would return. Wirin had promised him that. Yes, Wirin would return to talk to him. But what if his goddamn cell was bugged? He rose quietly, checked to see if the deputy outside his door was watching, then went over to the east wall of his cell and started pulling at the metal wall plate covering an electric socket. Maybe the bug was there.

The deputy who turned to observe him assumed that Sirhan did not have eavesdropping in mind but electrocution. Maybe he was trying to kill himself. Within minutes the sockets were covered by solid metal plates and a deputy was posted to sit in Sirhan's cell itself. Sirhan lay back on his iron bed watching the deputy through half-closed lids and cursed silently to himself.

Across the hall, workmen were fitting steel armor plate on the windows of three rooms that faced onto a potential sniper's nest, a railroad trestle off the Southern Pacific mainline, called Signal Bridge #1. Anyone up on that bridge could have a command view of the corridor (which the prisoner would be using, from time to time, to get to a shower room, to take some daily exercise). Sheriff Pitchess was aware that someone, some nut maybe, might take the law into his own hands and try to execute Sirhan Sirhan in jail. Stories were being told around Los Angeles of the mindless violence at the Ambassador Hotel when it became clear that it was Kennedy who was shot: about the man who methodically smashed three trays of highball glasses, throwing them down at his feet, one by one, about the women who dashed headlong into the hedges east of the hotel, scratching and bruising themselves in their grief, about the security guards who milled about aimlessly and finally said the hell with it and sat in the lobby listening to their walkie-talkies, while senseless fights broke out all about them.

After breakfast Dr. Crahan popped in for one minute, then returned at 10:25 with his stenographer John Plake. Crahan said he'd been reading about Sirhan in the newspaper. "I understand you were aspiring to be a jockey?" Sirhan said he'd been instructed by his lawyer to remain silent. "To remain silent entirely with no response to any questioning?"

"Depends," said Sirhan, "on what you question . . . anything pertaining to the case."

They talked about Sirhan's finger. The swelling had gone down. His ankle and knee. Not much different. Crahan observed that Sirhan's fingernails were badly bitten.

Sirhan flared and his words didn't seem very well connected. "That's a presumption there, only. Now, sir, are you trying to judge me here? How shall I put it? Psychically, with psychiatry in mind? Or medicine in mind, internally?"

"Both," Crahan admitted, then tried to regain control again. He was asking the questions, wasn't he? He asked a few and got nowhere. Finally Crahan lapsed into silence and smiled apropos of nothing.

Sirhan said, "I like your smile, Dr. Crahan. It seems very sincere."

"I try to be," said Crahan. Sirhan lay back in his bed hardly looking at Crahan, wiggling his toes, puffing on a cigarette, smiling as inanely as Crahan. He pointed at the stenographer who was busily noting Sirhan's actions. "Does he practice spiritualism, sir?"

"I sometimes think he does," said Crahan, not quite understanding Sirhan's meaning.

Sirhan explained: Plake was writing even during the silences. Why? Crahan shrugged, thinking to himself that here was an unusual prisoner indeed, alert, wary and composed, his attitude even "light and happy."

Then A. L. Wirin appeared for his second visit, carrying a number of newspapers under his arm, and Crahan and Plake left the cell. "I don't want to read 'em," said Sirhan.

Wirin sat down on the edge of the bed with the papers on his lap. "Kennedy's dead," he said.

Suddenly Sirhan's manner changed. He dropped his head, then looked up at Wirin with moist eyes. "Mr. Wirin," he said, "I'm a failure. I believe in love and instead of showing love . . ." He didn't finish his sentence. Wirin recalls that Sirhan added something else—about a betrayal of his own primary beliefs. Then almost immediately Sirhan closed off the tear ducts and noted as if in extenuation: "Kennedy was a millionaire. I was poor." That led to another thought: the $400 he'd had with him when he was arrested. He wanted Wirin to get it and give him $25 for incidental expenses in jail, then turn the rest over to his mother.

"Oh, yes," he added, "please send $10 to the Rosicrucians in San Jose." To the Rosicrucians? Did Sirhan owe some debt to the Rosicrucians? Wirin said he would send the money. (They sent it back.) Then Sirhan asked him if he could get him some books. What books? *The Secret Doctrine,* he said, by Madame Blavatsky, and *Talks at the Feet of the Master* by C. W. Leadbeater.

Sirhan's request was something Wirin felt he could report to the newsmen who clambered all over him when he left the jail. Soon, the whole world knew of Sirhan's predilection for the occult, and amateur criminologists pondered the significance of it all.

Madame Helena Blavatsky, who was born in Russia, and traveled all over the world, came to New York City in 1875 and founded the Theosophical Society. She wrote a book on the occult, *Isis Unveiled,* then transferred the headquarters of her movement to Madras, India, presumably to be in closer touch with Tibetan mystics, and later produced her 1,300-page masterwork, *The Secret Doctrine,* in six volumes. After she moved to England, she continued to write and lead an inner circle of theosophists—whom she called Illuminati—until her death in 1891.

The Secret Doctrine is a very, very dull book, but it created, according to an advertising blurb of the Theosophical Society in America now headquartered in Wheaton, Illinois, "a storm of controversy." Madame Blavatsky's followers, who include a popularizer named C. W. Leadbeater, claimed that her ideas were somewhat ahead of their time. Indeed she aimed to form a brotherhood of adepts, without distinctions of race, creed, sex, cast or color, to encourage the study of comparative religion, philosophy and science and investigate unexplained laws of nature and the powers latent in man.

The latent powers. These are what intrigued Sirhan the assassin, because in some way he'd used his own latent powers to kill Robert Kennedy. But how? It scared him to think about it and yet . . . he was fascinated.

In Dallas, President Kennedy's aides literally stole their boss's body from the bureaucrats at Parkland Memorial Hospital who insisted on going by the book. In Los Angeles, again, things would be different. On his own initiative, Dr. Thomas Noguchi, the county's coroner and chief medical examiner, had hurried into Good Samaritan's basement autopsy room at 3:00 A.M. ready to go to work; the Kennedy party would leave for New York with the Senator's remains as soon as possible.

Autopsy rooms are generally chill, hollow places where the echoes of the examining pathologist's voice are heard only by a tape recorder. This room, partly because of the second guesses and unexplainable gaps that occurred in the matter of President Kennedy's autopsy, was hardly empty. For more than six hours, from 3:00 A.M. to 9:15, Noguchi and two assistants, Dr. John E. Holloway and Dr. Abraham T. Lu, labored under the gaze of a dozen pairs of eyes, including those of Dr. Cuneo, who had worked so nobly to save Kennedy; three of the U.S. Government's top pathologists from the Armed Forces Institute of Pathology in Washington, who had jetted to Los Angeles for precisely this purpose: Colonel Pierre Finck, chief of Military Environmental Pathology and chief of the Ballistic Wound Branch of the institute; Commander Charles Stahl, U.S. Navy, chief of the Forensic Branch of the institute; Dr. Kenneth Earle, chief of the Neuropathology Branch; and representatives from the LAPD, the sheriff's office, the FBI and the Secret Service.

Noguchi had a twofold task: to make an exact determination of what, precisely, killed Robert Kennedy and to recover any relevant "evidence." Noguchi and his aides discovered three separate bullet wounds:

Bullet number one penetrated the right mastoid, shattered and lodged in the right hemisphere of the cerebellum.

Bullet number two entered the back of the right armpit, penetrated some subcutaneous tissue and muscle structure in a right to left direction and upward, and exited in the front of the right shoulder without striking any bony structure or leaving any lead fragments in its track.

Bullet number three entered the right armpit one-half inch away from wound number two, burrowed through the muscle structure of the back and lodged in the lower portion of the back of the neck, just short of the sixth cervical vertebra.

At 8:45 A.M., Noguchi retrieved this bullet by making a small incision in the back of the neck and pulling it out with a gentle right index finger. This could be key evidence, for bullet number one was shattered and bullet number two was lost. Noguchi scratched his initials on the base of the bullet and the last two digits of this case's serial number: #68-5731: TN 31. He handed it to Sergeant Bill Jordan at 8:49. Jordan nodded grimly, took it and warmed it in his hand.

It was the doctors' judgment then and there that neither wounds two or three could have been fatal. Bullets two and three both took the same course, but ended up in different places, they reasoned, because Kennedy's body rotated clockwise as the assassin fired from his slightly crouched position. Bullet number one did the job, and this shot left a powder tattoo one inch long on Kennedy's right ear. From that clue, Noguchi guessed that the gunman had gotten very, very close. (His guess was later upheld when police experts performed extensive powder pattern tests with an Iver-Johnson .22. Their judgment: the muzzle of the gun that killed Kennedy flamed from an inch away.)

Four

**"The question of a conspiracy has come up.
The public, the Congress and
the President of the United States want to know.
They have a right to know."**

The Los Angeles police had been somewhat more than busy. Eyewitnesses Sandra Serrano and Thomas Vincent DiPierro had given them sufficient reason to suspect that there were others involved. Was there a conspiracy? If so, who were the coconspirators? The police (and the FBI) fanned out to Pasadena, Hollywood Park Race Track, the town of Corona, where Sirhan had once worked for several months, and the barns at Santa Anita Race Track. Purpose: to talk to everyone who had ever known Sirhan Sirhan.

Although the police had difficulty finding anyone who admitted to more than a nodding acquaintance with Sirhan (thus giving a false impression that Sirhan was "a loner"), they did ferret out a short, pudgy fellow named Walter Crowe. He admitted that he and Sirhan had been pals from the sixth grade through two years at Pasadena City College. Afterward they drifted apart. Crowe transferred to UCLA, where he got his degree in history, and Sirhan went to work with the horses. "Back in March," said Crowe, "I saw Sirhan for the first time in two years. His mother asked my mother why I never saw Sirhan anymore, and so I phoned him up one night and we met at Bob's Big Boy near Pasadena City College. We went to two topless bars together and drank beer and ended the evening eating tacos at Ernie's on Colorado near Fair Oaks."

FBI Agents Robert H. Morneau, Jr., and Irvin B. Wells asked Crowe what they talked about. "About my schooling at UCLA," said Crowe. "About the Mideast. About politics." What about the Mideast? Crowe said that while at one time Sirhan had had high hopes in Abdel Nasser, he now felt that the Arabs could never regain the territory lost in the Six-Day

War. They talked about the Arab commando organization, Al Fatah. As far as Crowe could tell, Sirhan had had no contact with the organization. Crowe said he believed that Al Fatah had helped raise the morale of the Arabs, but he personally believed that the real solution in the Mideast would come when the Arab half of the population in Israel organized, took seats in the Knesset (parliament) and helped change Israel's theocracy into a secular state. Crowe said that Sirhan seemed to be less interested in politics, was skeptical, in fact, about any ideological thrust. What Sirhan wanted to do now was make money. Lots of it. Crowe felt that some sort of barrier had arisen between them—possibly because he had gone to UCLA and Sirhan's education had been cut short. "Sirhan was a moody fellow," he told the agents. "Up one day, down the next. Kind of withdrawn."

Crowe did not tell the FBI all this in that first meeting. "They asked me stupid questions, like, 'Did Sirhan masturbate?' 'Did he pull his hair?' 'Engage in self-destructive activity?' I told them he was never violent, but I later corrected that."

Crowe had a chance to correct it the very next day. The same FBI agents pulled up to his family home in Pasadena, took Crowe out to their car and put him in the back seat. "We know all about you now," said one of the agents. "You're a Communist."

Crowe was frightened as the car pulled away, but the agents only drove him a few blocks, parked near a neighboring golf course and questioned him there. "The question of a conspiracy has come up," said one of them, "possibly a conspiracy which might involve the Communist Party. The public, the Congress and the President of the United States want to know. They have a right to know." Crowe nodded. "You may have to testify in court or before Congress itself about this. You understand this?" Crowe said he understood and proceeded to tell all. In 1965, Crowe said he had helped start an ad hoc committee to agitate for rights of black men. In fact, he was the principal organizer. He also tried to start a chapter of the Students for a Democratic Society at PCC, but found the students— including Sirhan Sirhan—too apathetic to get it off the ground.

At UCLA, Crowe had joined the W. E. B. Du Bois Club, and in 1966 he attended the Du Bois National Convention in Chicago. In late 1966 or early 1967, the club at UCLA folded. Crowe and seven others formed a Student Club of the Communist Party, U.S.A. Purpose? Political discussion.

What about Sirhan? Crowe said Sirhan was never a member of his Du Bois or Communist clubs. He leaned left politically, but he was erratic.

And that last meeting with Sirhan? Crowe's memory was better this time. The meeting was on the night of May 2, the day after Crowe began a job with the County Department of Welfare. "I told Sirhan about my ties with the Communist Party," said Crowe nervously. "I told him the party in Russia and the party in the United States functioned differently, and that the party in Russia was supporting the Arabs with arms against Israel."

Did Crowe think this news might have influenced Sirhan? "How can I know what influenced Sirhan?" asked Crowe, his voice quavering. "Sirhan never told me this was significant information, he showed no surprise when I told him, he gave no indication of startled enlightenment, he just seemed to take it all in."

How about the other seven members of Crowe's club? "I never told Sirhan who they were. I don't walk the streets recruiting Communist Party members. Sirhan wasn't interested in the SDS. Why would I recruit him for the CP?" Crowe paused. The two agents, both sitting in the front seat but turned halfway around in their seats, regarded him coolly.

"Look," said Crowe. "I'm aware of the awful implications here. I heard Mayor Yorty say that Sirhan believes in the objectives of the Communist Party. I just hope to God that the dates on these notes the mayor is referring to are prior to my meeting with Sirhan on May 2. This is on my conscience. I hope to God I did not influence Sirhan to kill Senator Kennedy. I cannot believe that anything I said to him could have provided him with a motive. But I do not know of anyone else who could have influenced him. All I know is that I was with him and a few weeks later he killed Kennedy. I have an ache in the pit of my stomach. I have a dreadful fear that I might have been responsible—for one of the crimes of the century."

It was quite a speech. If anything, however, Crowe's anguished admission that he might have been responsible for one of the crimes of the century gave the agents some suspicions that this bespectacled idealist was no conspirator. Agents Morneau and Wells drove him back home.

Other investigators tried to check on other leads. Some of these leads were false, generated by the perverse (though nonmalicious) desires of some to be directly involved in a matter of such moment to the Republic, and some may have been entirely legitimate. All of them caused the police a great deal of work and almost all of them led them exactly nowhere.

W. J. Wood, a geologist who used to work in the Middle East, told police that he was doing some volunteer work at the Kennedy campaign headquarters at 5615 Wilshire Boulevard on Sunday night when he over-heard a conversation in Arabic. "There were three men," said Wood, "and they began speaking a distinct Jordanese dialect. One of them said, 'He won't be in the hotel tomorrow night, but we can get him the next night.' "

An attractive blonde who will be known here as Cynthia Kean had a story which was not inconsistent with Wood's. Sometime between 3:00 and 4:00 P.M. on Monday afternoon, June 3, she told police she was parked facing west on Melrose Boulevard near St. Andrews Place when a shiny blue 1959 Ford pulled up to the curb in front of her. A young man matching Sirhan's description jumped out of the car and started arguing heatedly with two other men in the front seat. His jacket flew open and Cynthia noted with alarm that he had a gun stuck in the waistband of his pants. She heard someone say "Kennedy" and "get in the car, we have to get him tonight" and "don't want to" and "afraid." Then, she said, the man with the gun suddenly noticed that she was watching him. With a frightened look on his face, he jumped back in the car. By now, Cynthia had put her car in gear and was moving slowly around the blue Ford. She looked into the Ford, noted a white fur rug above the back seat and on the seat, two rifles.

Juan Romero, the little busboy who had held Kennedy's head in his hands on the pantry floor, had already told the police about two strangers of uncertain description who had come to the Ambassador kitchen on Sun-day, June 2, looking for some white coats similar to those worn by the waiters. A waitress in Alhambra, a town not far from Pasadena, told the police that on the morning of June 4 at about ten o'clock, she noticed someone who looked like Sirhan with another man. The two of them, she said, were drawing some kind of map together. It looked like a floor plan. Could this have been the same floor plan drawn in red ink and black crayon that was found and turned in to the front desk of the Ambassador Hotel at 1:30 A.M. on the morning of June 5? George Green, a cochairman of a black organization called "New Images," told the police that approxi-mately a half hour before Kennedy was shot, he saw Sirhan Sirhan in the Ambassador kitchen on the edge of a crowd of newsmen interviewing Frank Mankiewicz or Pierre Salinger. With him, he said, were a tall, thin man with dark hair and a girl in her early twenties. The girl had a good figure and wore a polka-dot dress. Green said that he was coming into the kitchen just as Kennedy was shot and that he saw the same tall, thin fellow and the girl in the polka-dot dress running out of the kitchen. "They seemed to be the only ones who were trying to get out of the kitchen," said

Green. "Everyone else was trying to get in." Albert Ellis, a roommate of the Ambassador Hotel's convention manager, John Shamel, told the FBI that, during the chaos that followed the shooting in the pantry, he heard a female voice cry, "We shot him!" He did not see who said this nor could he characterize the voice in any special way.

Finally, late in the afternoon of June 6, a woman who identified herself as Edith Goldstein, called the police and told them she'd just discovered in an alley near her home in West Los Angeles a brown paper shopping bag containing a perfectly good lady's outfit: black shoes, size 9-B; a black purse containing assorted cosmetics and a nine-ounce can of Lanolin Plus hairspray; a Lovable bra, size 34-B; a Lovable panty girdle; one pair of pink panties, size 7; a black slip, size 34; a pair of nylons; and—a gray dress with white polka dots.

Since Dallas, nothing that happened in the aftermath of a Kennedy assassination was too bizarre to be dismissed out of hand. Thus, when a chemical salesman who shall be known here as Robert Duane presented himself to the FBI with a story indicating that he had spent Tuesday, June 4, with a girl who might have been the one in the polka-dot dress, he got a serious hearing. He told Special Agents Lloyd D. Johnson and Eugene B. McCarthy that he had gone to the Ambassador about 9:00 A.M. Tuesday to meet a fellow salesman, failed to find him and met a shapely blonde girl in the arcade near the coffee shop on the ground floor. Robert bought her breakfast. He told her his first name. She told him hers: Virginia.

During breakfast, she also told him her name was Alice and Betty and said more than once that she wondered if she could trust him. She finally told him her name was Gilderdine Oppenheimer. Duane said something to her in German. She said she did not understand German, but spoke some Arabic. She said she was from Virginia. Duane said his mother was from Virginia. "Well, I'm not really from Virginia," she said, "I'm from New York." But she had been traveling extensively and had just come from Eilat, Beirut and Cairo. Gildy asked Duane if he had connections in Australia. She wanted to go there. Alone. Duane asked her if she was in any trouble. "Never mind," she said. "I don't want to get you involved." She asked him his preference in the Presidential primary. He told her he was for McCarthy. She said, "Kennedy's no good." And she added: "They're going to get him."

At this point, Gildy told Duane she was being watched. Duane looked up toward the entrance to the coffee shop and noticed a man watching intently. The man continued to stare at them while they finished breakfast. Duane told the girl that he had to make a business call in Oxnard, some fifty miles up the coast. She said she wanted to go with him, and Duane said that would be all right with him.

"Are you going to the victory reception here tonight?" asked Gildy. Duane said he didn't intend to. "If you come, you will be really surprised. They are going to take care of Kennedy."

"How do you know?" asked Duane.

"Forget it," she said. "I don't want to get you involved."

On the trip to Oxnard, up the Pacific Coast Highway through Malibu, Duane noticed that the girl kept looking behind the car with some trepidation, and he saw that her hands were wet. "What's the matter?" he asked.

"There's someone following us," she said.

Duane looked into his rearview mirror, saw a dark blue Volkswagen behind him. He slowed down. The VW slowed down. He accelerated. So did the VW. He pulled off the highway onto a sight-seeing promontory dominated by two large boulders. The VW pulled in and parked about fifty feet away. Duane saw that there was only one person in the car, a stocky man with dark gray hair, who stared at him, then backed the VW around behind one of the boulders. Duane pulled out and sped north toward Oxnard. The VW did not follow.

"They use radios to communicate with one another," said Gildy.

"Do you belong to some kind of group?" asked Duane.

"Once you get involved," said Gildy, "you belong. Or they take care of you."

"Where do you live?" asked Duane.

"I live near the Ambassador. On Kenmore. But I've only lived there a few days." Duane and Gildy went on to Oxnard and Ventura, and returned back down the coast. About 5:15 P.M. they stopped at the Trancas Restaurant for an early supper (or a late lunch). Gildy said she had a long night ahead of her and wanted a drink. Duane said he didn't want to drink with her. He took her back to the Wilshire District of Los Angeles, and asked her address on Kenmore. She told him first to drop her at Olympic and Kenmore, then decided he should let her off near the Ambassador. She asked him again if he were going to attend the "victory reception." He said he wouldn't, and at approximately 7:30 P.M. he saw her, for the last time, walking up the canopied sidewalk leading from Wilshire Boulevard to the Ambassador Hotel.

Duane gave the FBI descriptions of the girl. Her hair was dirty blonde, puffed up on top, long enough to be drawn to one side and clipped near her left shoulder. She wore a tan A-line dress and tan shoes and carried a tan purse. Her hose seemed to be of a different texture than the current fashion in Los Angeles and her shoes were fastened with a narrow strap that struck Duane as faintly foreign. She did not smoke and her body gave off a somewhat musky odor.

One of the agents looked at him searchingly. "I didn't screw her," said Duane. "I didn't. But I'd appreciate it if you keep my identity a secret."

"We have to tell the Los Angeles police. They have jurisdiction here."

"I realize that," said Duane. "But I wouldn't want my wife to know about this. If you phone, please don't identify yourselves as FBI."

"How about the man who stared at you in the Ambassador coffee shop?"

Duane gave a description that could have applied to any of the Sirhan brothers. The agents showed him all the Sirhan brothers. Duane said the man looked most like Munir, but it wasn't Munir, he said, it wasn't any of the Sirhans.

On the next day, Duane paid the FBI another call. He had something to add. Another car might have been following him and the girl who called herself Gilderdine Oppenheimer. Maybe a dark blue 1966 Ford. Anything else? Well, yes, Duane said. He didn't call on his two accounts in Oxnard at all. He reminded the FBI not to say anything to his wife.

One team of officers visited every person who had signed in at the San Gabriel Valley Gun Club on June 4. Henry Carreon's story had checked out: it was Sirhan Sirhan who had been firing there on Tuesday, for the roster showed, among the names and addresses, the apparent signature of Sirhan Sirhan, 696 E. Howard, which was strange, because the rangemaster hardly cared whether anyone signed in or not. Neither Henry Carreon's name nor that of his buddy, David Montellano, was on the list. Nor was Michael Soccoman's. Soccoman, a college student from nearby Monrovia, presented himself to Los Angeles police officers because he had handled Sirhan's gun at the range and he was afraid the police might find his fingerprints there and charge him as an accomplice. Detective T. L. Brown showed Soccoman a picture of Sirhan. "Yes," said Soccoman, "that's definitely the same person I met at the range. I fired his gun and he fired mine. He said he'd purchased the revolver for $40 and had been practicing with it for four months up north. He was a good shot. He came over and said, 'That is a pretty nice gun you have there. Sort of heavy. Can I see it?' I asked him if he wanted to try it and he shot it a couple of times. His were the two best shots in my target. Then I went over to his position and I fired his gun a couple times. I put it down because I didn't want it to blow up in my hand. He was firing hollowpoints and the gun looked like a piece of junk. I asked him why he was shooting hollowpoints on a range, and he said they were all he had. But I saw he had several boxes of cheaper ammo. He said he was going to do some hunting. I told him he would have a pretty hard time hunting with a .22 pistol. He said, 'Well, it could kill a dog.' "

Was Sirhan alone at the range? Soccoman, Montellano and Carreon said that he was. But the rangemaster, Everett C. Buckner, had a different recollection. Buckner told LAPD Detectives Dave Warren and Robert Singhause that a young and rather attractive blonde who wore a light dress had come to the range office with another man shortly after Sirhan arrived. "This is the first gun I've ever owned," she said, showing Buckner a pistol. Her companion, who had a rifle, left her and went to the south end of the range, which was set aside for rifles, and she went to a position near Sirhan. Then Sirhan came over and said, "Let me show you how to shoot." Then, Buckner told the police, she said, "Get away from me, God damn it, someone will recognize us."

Sirhan's car turned up some evidence and some leads. Pursuant to Search Warrant #1793, issued on the afternoon of June 5, Lieutenant Albin S. Hegge impounded the car and catalogued its contents. He found two bullet slugs on the front seat and an unfired .22-caliber bullet. In the glove compartment, he found a black leather wallet containing Sirhan's driver's license and other identification cards, and a Canadian dollar; a key ring with six keys on it and a tag with the De Soto's license number, JWS 093, printed on it; an empty box, labeled Mini-Mag .22 long rifle, H.P., 150 Blue Chip stamps, a variety of cashier's receipts; a raffle ticket from St. Elizabeth's Western Fiesta May 20 and 21 (Grand Prize, 1967 Pontiac Firebird); two photos of a man on horseback and one of several sheep; some matchbooks from Shakey's Pizza Parlor on Foothill Boulevard in Pasadena. In the back seat lay a book, *The Divine Art of Healing,* by Manley Palmer Hall, a paper bag labeled "Jack in the Box," and four newspapers: the Los Angeles *Times* for June 4 and 5, 1968, and the *Christian Science Monitor,* June 2 and 4. But the most interesting items were a business card reading: "Lock, Stock 'n' Barrel. Fine guns. 8972 East Huntington Drive, San Gabriel," and a sales receipt for $3.99 from the same gun shop dated June 1, 1968.

Was Sirhan alone when he bought the .22's on June 1? Larry Arnot, a former Pasadena fireman retired on disability, who clerked at the Lock, Stock 'n' Barrel on that day, said that Sirhan had come in about 3:00 P.M. with two other men. They were very serious, hardly talkative and left

quickly after Sirhan had bought two boxes of .22-caliber Mini-Mag ammunition, hollowpoint, with a muzzle velocity approximately 25 percent
stronger than that of the average .22 bullet, and one of the others had
bought two boxes of Super-X Westerns. Arnot put the four boxes on one
sales slip, #2372. Who were the other two men? Arnot was shown pictures
of the Sirhan brothers. He identified Sirhan Sirhan as the young man who
had bought the Mini-Mags and Munir Sirhan as one of his companions.
He couldn't say who the man was who bought the Super-X Westerns.

Now that Kennedy was dead, Sirhan had to be charged with murder.
At 4:25 on Friday, June 7, he was given a perfunctory arraignment in the
infirmary chapel. It was the first proceeding in the action to be known as
People vs. *Sirhan,* Case No. A-233-421. One hundred sixteen members of
the press were duly searched and watched during the entire proceeding by
five sergeants and thirty-nine deputies as the Grand Jury murder indictment was read. Judge Arthur Alarcon issued an order that, in essence, for-
bade any public official from giving information on the case to anyone.

In trials which trigger a good deal of public interest—and this one
would, in terms of media coverage, be the biggest in U.S. history—there is
an understandable desire on the part of popularly elected officials to give
the public information, even when some of that information may prove to
interfere with the proper administration of justice. In the United States, a
defendant is considered innocent until proven guilty in a court of law—
and not in the court of public opinion. A jury trial is a very formal kind
of battle waged by lawyers for the defense and lawyers for the prosecution,
refereed according to stringent legal rules by a judge whose very profession stands for scrupulous fairness. Trial by a newspaper is hardly hedged
by the same safeguards. It is often one-sided, incomplete and biased in
favor of the most sensational revelations (which are often irrelevant, and
therefore inadmissible in a court of law). Worst of all, trial by newspaper
usually precedes a jury trial. That means that a court can be hard-pressed
to find twelve ordinary citizens who have not already decided, in their
heart of hearts, that the defendant is as guilty as the newspapers said he
was.

Mayor Yorty could protest later that he made his revelations about Sirhan's notebooks because "the people had a right to know," but Judge
Alarcon's order was designed to stop any public official who might be
tempted to serve the public in such a manner. After all, the notebooks
were seized without a warrant, and the defense would surely challenge

their admissibility. Alarcon's order regarding publicity prohibited counsel, witnesses and public officials from revealing to the public (among other things) any statements, documents, exhibits or other evidence whose admissibility might have to be determined by the court. On Monday, June 10, Sheriff's Inspector Bill Conroy served the order on Mayor Yorty in person.

After that, most of those embraced by Judge Alarcon's order complied scrupulously. News sources like Mayor Yorty, for instance, who had access to the files of the police on "his payroll" were not anxious to risk a contempt of court citation by testing Judge Alarcon's ruling, thus effectively cutting off all authoritative news on the Sirhan trial during the pretrial stage. The police kept mum, the sheriffs and the FBI revealed nothing. Evelle Younger, a district attorney who was more than a little politically ambitious, would obey the order—until the last possible instant, on the eve of the trial.

On June 7, FBI Special Agent Richard Burris took Sandy Serrano back to the Ambassador Hotel and asked her to reenact her midnight adventures with the girl in the polka-dot dress on the night of June 4. After taking some time to reorient herself, she took Burris to a pair of double fire doors leading out of the Ambassador Ballroom to a fire escape and repeated her story.

The story seemed to accord fairly well with the one she had told and retold to L.A. detectives on the morning of June 5. But what happened to the girl in the polka-dot dress? And to her friend in the gold sweater? Thomas Vincent DiPierro had seen a girl in a polka-dot dress before the shooting, a fact that FBI Agents William A. Bailey and Robert Pickard were confirming at that very moment from DiPierro himself. Well, maybe Miss Serrano wasn't as hysterical as Sander Vanocur believed. Maybe she could pick the girl out of the crowd that was filmed by the TV cameras earlier in the evening.

Movie time in Burbank. Burris took Miss Serrano out to the NBC Studios for a screening of all the film and tape the network had retained from the night of the fourth. They were joined by five other investigators: LAPD Detectives Charles Hughes, Charles Calvert, Lyle Sandlin and Thomas Strong, and U.S. Secret Service Agent Anthony Sherman, Jr. But Miss Serrano failed to find the girl in the polka-dot dress.

Finally, FBI Agent Burris took Miss Serrano to Parker Center for a covert observation of a pretty young dancer named Cathy Fulmer, who had phoned the sheriff's office a few hours earlier with the suggestion that maybe she was the girl in the polka-dot dress. She said she had been in the pantry and she was wearing a white dress with a polka-dot scarf. "I was scared," she said. "The guy next to me got shot. I was running, and on the way out somebody yelled, 'What happened?' I yelled, 'Kennedy was shot.'"

"Is that the girl?" asked Burris.

"No," said Miss Serrano. "Definitely not the girl I saw on the stairs." But no one asked DiPierro to take a look at Miss Fulmer.

Reporters had some difficulty finding out much about Sirhan's life. Almost every medium, however, had the essential details.

Sirhan Sirhan had grown up as a Christian Arab in the Old City of Jerusalem, apparently the most polite, diligent and attentive of five sons born to Mary and Bishara Sirhan. Bishara beat the children, and neighbors said he once held a hot iron to Sirhan's heel. In 1948, Sirhan was subject to the horrors of war in Jerusalem itself. He came to the United States with his mother and father, two of his brothers and a sister in January, 1957. Six months later, his father abandoned them all and went back to Palestine. Sirhan was a shy student at John Muir High School in Pasadena, graduated and attended Pasadena City College for two years, then tried to become a jockey.

Sirhan exercised mounts at Granja Vista Del Rio Horse Ranch in Corona, California, then his ambitions were shattered early one morning in September, 1966, when he was badly thrown from a galloping horse and taken to the hospital with cuts and bruises. He quit racing and applied for damages under California's workmen's compensation law.

While he fought for those, he found employment as a stock boy and driver for a health food store in Pasadena, then quit when he won a $2,000 settlement for his injuries, from which he received $1,705 after medical and legal fees. He was said to have writhed inwardly over Robert Kennedy's support of Israel in its fight against the Arabs. In the editorial judgment of *Life* magazine, Sirhan "seemed formed in the classic mold of political assassin—small, proud, polite, repressed and aboil with a secret, almost religious sense of cause: Arab nationalism."

Experts in medical journalism offered some speculations about "the psycho-biology of violence," suggesting that men become assassins for reasons that are at once psychiatric and biological.

But much of this was only guesswork. Why did Sirhan kill Kennedy?

Had he suffered brain damage when he fell from the horse? Was he a schizophrenic? Would there be a trial? Judging from the history of American assassins, there was only a fifty-fifty chance that Sirhan would ever see a jury. Neither John Wilkes Booth nor Lee Harvey Oswald lived very long after they were captured. Leon Czolgosz, the assassin of President William McKinley, was put on trial four days after McKinley's funeral in Canton, Ohio, and defended by two attorneys who accepted their appointments with obvious reluctance two days before the trial, presented no witnesses and failed to persuade Czolgosz to take the stand. The trial ended in eight hours and twenty-six minutes, including the time it took to impanel the jury, which brought in a guilty verdict in thirty-four minutes and condemned him to death. Of all the assassins, only Charles Guiteau and his hardworking attorneys presented a complete profile in court. But even then, almost everyone in the country, except the jury who condemned him, wrote him off as a simple madman, for Guiteau claimed he killed President James Garfield to give a religious tract he had written the public attention it needed. During the trial, moreover, he called on President Chester Arthur and everybody else whose political career had been advanced by the assassination to show their gratitude by contributing money for his defense.

By Friday, June 7, the third day after the shooting, when the Grand Jury returned an indictment for murder, I felt that the story of this assassination lay locked in the mind of Sirhan Sirhan. I phoned A. L. Wirin, the civil liberties lawyer whom Sirhan had asked to help him find an attorney. "Is there any chance of getting in to talk to Sirhan?" I asked.

"No," said Wirin, "I'm afraid not."

I said I was surprised Wirin was so quick to say no. "I just talked to Grant Cooper about the legal ramifications, and he said a request like this isn't absolutely out of the question." There was a thoughtful pause at the other end of the line. I knew that Wirin was one of the leading constitutional lawyers in the land and that there might be a constitutional issue here: a man doesn't lose the protections of the Bill of Rights as soon as he is accused, and among those protections is the right of free speech. If Sirhan wanted to talk to me . . .

"Do you know Grant Cooper?" asked Wirin.

Almost every reporter in town knew Grant Cooper because, aside from the fact that Cooper had tried some of the most highly publicized cases in recent California history, including the two trials that had ended with hung juries * for Dr. Bernard Finch and his loving nurse, Carole Tregoff, who

* They were convicted, in a third trial, without Cooper.

were charged with murdering Mrs. Finch, he had also served on a number
of Bar Association committees and a special state commission studying the
relationship between law and psychiatry.

"Do you think," said Wirin, "that Grant Cooper would take this case?"

I said Cooper couldn't. On the following Monday, in fact, the Federal
Government would begin its case against six gambling gentlemen who
were accused of an interstate conspiracy to cheat some of Hollywood's
notables out of many thousands of dollars at gin rummy. One of the
men—who was accused of hiring a mechanic to fix a peephole in the
ceiling at the Friars' Club in Beverly Hills and relay signals to him with
an electronic device—had retained Cooper.

"Well, " said Wirin, "if Mr. Cooper would like to take this case, we can
get a postponement. Would you talk to him again? I'd like him to seriously
consider taking this case." Cooper was an obvious choice. Aside from his
skills as a criminal attorney, he was a fine spokesman for the legal profession. Moreover, after the Friars' Club case, for which Cooper's client was
paying a handsome fee, Cooper could afford to take on something in the
public interest.

I wondered why Wirin didn't ask Cooper himself. Wirin said reporters
were following him everywhere. He'd rather not be seen talking to Cooper.
And naturally he didn't want me to report any of this at that time. Later,
maybe. . . . When I hung up, I began to guess at Wirin's rationale in using
an unofficial go-between to approach Cooper. If Cooper said no, Wirin
would not be compelled to tell another that he was a second choice. And
he had requested the Los Angeles County Bar Association to appoint an
attorney, a matter still under the consideration of the board. As far as I
was concerned, this service might lead to the interview I wanted.

On Sunday, June 9, I found Grant Cooper surrounded by stacks of financial records half a yard high—his evidence in the Friars' affair—in an
office area overlooking the swimming pool at his home.

"I think Al Wirin is going to have trouble getting an attorney to take
this case," I said. "No one wants to defend the accused assassin of Robert
Kennedy."

"I know," said Cooper. "One of my wife's friends said to her yesterday,
'Surely, Grant's not going to defend Sirhan?' and yet, dammit, he has a
right to a fair trial. Everybody does in this country, and I've been preaching that for years." He paused, looked at the material surrounding him and
sighed. He was tanned now from a recent fishing trip to Baja California,
but by the end of the Friars' case he would be pale. "What's wrong with
the Public Defender's Office?" The Los Angeles County Public Defender's

Office is the oldest in the land. It has authorization for 250 attorneys and a large, efficient staff of investigators.

"It's good," I said. "You know that and I know it and Wirin knows it. But in some states, and in most of the world, a public defender means pauper justice. How would this look to the rest of the world?" I didn't know it at the time, but Sirhan had already expressed himself trenchantly on his chances with the public defender at his side: "Yes, the district attorney sits at one table, and the public defender sits at the other, but they both get paid at the same window."

Cooper was an Establishment attorney. He had far more work than he needed to make an interesting and profitable career, and therefore no real reason to take on a thankless case—as this one would surely be. Except that he liked challenges. In June, 1967, Cooper had gone to Da Nang in Vietnam to win acquittal for a Marine corporal charged before an eight-man military court of "unpremeditated murder." The corporal had military counsel. Why did Cooper go to Da Nang, in the middle of a war zone? "I'd never been asked to defend a man before a military court before," he said.

"All right," said Cooper. "I'll take it." I had accomplished my mission, so I could hardly ask why Cooper said yes. I guessed it might be because Cooper had never been asked to defend an accused assassin before. Cooper said he had two conditions. First, he had to get an okay from his client in the Friars' affair; and second, the Sirhan case would have to be postponed until the Friars' case was over. "That may not happen," said Cooper, "until sometime in September." Cooper paused and looked out to the blue water of his swimming pool. "What I'd really like to do then is go fishing. But I'll take the case."

The police and the FBI, still in pursuit of "the girl in the polka-dot dress," brought Thomas Vincent DiPierro and Sandra Serrano back to the Ambassador Hotel for replays of their encounters with her. They soon learned that Miss Serrano and DiPierro had compared notes before they ever talked to the police and had decided on their own that they had each seen the same girl.

Now the police pinned each of them down separately, and asked them to compare a dozen dresses brought in for the occasion—collars, sleeve length, waistline, frills, flares, number and size of polka dots. DiPierro and Miss Serrano each gave widely varying descriptions.

Because their recollections differed, the police were ready, perhaps too ready, to conclude that both DiPierro and Miss Serrano must be lying.

FBI Agent Richard Burris took Miss Serrano to the Embassy Room, showed her the stage where Kennedy had spoken and the route he had taken to the pantry. He then walked Miss Serrano from the spot where Kennedy was shot, back through the Embassy Room (which, he noted, had been jammed at the time with 1,100 people, 50 percent over capacity), through the fire exit doors and onto the outside fire escape stairs where Miss Serrano said she was sitting when she saw the people coming down and shouting. "This is a distance of some 170 feet," said Burris, "and yet some thirty seconds after, you heard what you thought to be six backfires. Now, after seeing where Senator Kennedy was shot, do you still feel you heard the gunshots?"

"I never heard a gunshot in my life," said Miss Serrano. "I never said I heard gunshots. I said I heard five or six backfires." She was right. But that didn't stop Burris. He wanted to challenge her about some other discrepancies. Why, when she phoned her mother in Ohio shortly after the shooting, didn't she mention that she had seen someone she felt was connected with the crime? "I've always had difficulty communicating with my mother," she wailed. "I wanted to talk to my father."

Burris wouldn't let go. "On television, with Sander Vanocur, you didn't say anything about seeing a girl and two men going *up* the fire stairs. You only said you saw a girl and a man coming *down*. And later you told the police you saw two men and a girl going up together *and one of them was Sirhan Sirhan*. That was the most significant thing you had to tell the police and yet you didn't say anything about this in your first interview, your interview on television."

Miss Serrano was close to tears. "I can't explain why," she cried. "You're trying to trick me. You're lying to me and you're trying to trick me."

"Now, where have we lied to you, Miss Serrano?" asked Burris.

"Well," she sniffed, "once you said it was a black polka-dot dress, rather than a white dress with black polka dots."

The investigators were breaking Miss Serrano into little pieces. Their intuitions may have been correct. Maybe Miss Serrano had seen nothing significant. But they were using force, not logic, to prove that. Later, in the same way, they would break down DiPierro, too.

On Monday, June 10, Sirhan received a letter from John Lawrence of New York City, the director of an organization called F.A.I.R.— Federated Americans against Israeli Racism—telling him that although he

was an S.O.B., F.A.I.R. would stand by him. He enclosed three issues of a
periodical called *Insight,* the official organ of F.A.I.R., and $5, which was
held by the sheriff's office. Lawrence told him he was a soldier in the
cause of justice for the Arab people, and that all men ought to forgive his
mistake, for he had made it in pursuit of justice.

To establish his credentials with Sirhan, he presented an item about
himself in *The New York Times,* reporting that Lawrence had "declared
that 'There are no tears in us for Robert Kennedy' whom he called 'the advocate of sending American jet bombers to Israel so Jews may kill more
Arabs.' " It is possible that this was the first news Sirhan had that Kennedy
was such an advocate. Kennedy did say the United States should send fifty
jets to Israel. But he didn't say so until May 26—more than a week after
Sirhan wrote in his notebook that Kennedy must die. Even then, the news
was not widely reported: the newspapers in Portland, Oregon (where Kennedy made the statement) didn't carry it; neither did the Los Angeles papers or even *The New York Times,* until a reporter there, checking the
Arab angle after the assassination, discovered what Kennedy said in Portland on May 26, and pointed it out in a piece on June 7. The Associated
Press, however, did report Kennedy's words in a late night wire. It is possible that some radio stations picked up the quote.

Lawrence got no response from Sirhan. He then made a series of abu-
sive phone calls to Sheriff Pitchess and sent Sirhan wires on June 10, June
11 and June 13, offering encouragement and advice. Sirhan wired Lawrence on the thirteenth:

> RESPECTED SIRS: GRATEFUL FOR MONEY ENJOYED
> "INSIGHT" PLEASE SEND MORE ISSUES ANXIOUS
> ABOUT MIDEAST REACTION. Sirhan. 718-486.

But that didn't satisfy Lawrence. On June 14, he wrote Sirhan a long letter
informing him that he was being deprived of his right to send and receive
mail and select the attorney of his choice. He also enclosed a copy of a letter he was sending to Abdul Hamid Sharaf, the Jordanian Ambassador to
the United States, asking for an investigation into the entire matter.

The sheriff decided on an investigation of his own—of Lawrence
himself—and found that he was born John Lawrence Pawluk on December 4, 1921, in Fort Worth, Texas, and, judging from police blotters in
Los Angeles, Denver and New York, was the kind of man who went looking for trouble, often going out of his way to help the weak and the downtrodden.

Once, in 1966, he pleaded with a judge to be put *in* Nassau County, New York, jail so he could advise prisoners of their legal rights.

He was a fighter, no doubt about that, but Sirhan wondered whether Lawrence's assistance was really what he needed. Though Lawrence admitted he wasn't a lawyer, he had done "legal research" and concluded that Sirhan didn't have a chance of acquittal. He therefore advised that Sirhan plead mitigation upon the extenuating circumstances. Lawrence suggested putting American society, government and the victim, Mr. Kennedy, on trial for their sociopathic conduct.

In the meantime, he urged Sirhan to model himself upon the example of John Brown, who had fought in a just cause—to free the slaves of the South—and was nevertheless captured, tried and hanged.

> John Brown's body lies a mouldering in the grave
> [quoth Lawrence in his certified letter to Sirhan, No. 298290]
> John Brown's body lies a mouldering in the grave
> John Brown's body lies a mouldering in the grave
> But his truth goes marching on.
> Glory, glory hallelujah
> Glory, glory hallelujah
> Glory, glory hallelujah
> His truth goes marching on.

It is not recorded in the sheriff's log that Sirhan ever sang this song audibly to himself—or to anyone else—during his sojourn in jail.

I left a message at Wirin's office on Spring Street, telling him Cooper would take the case. Then, on Tuesday, I ran into Wirin in the hallway outside his office. Wirin looked pleased. The Bar Association had decided to stay out of the case completely, so if Wirin was going to succeed in getting counsel for Sirhan, he needed Cooper now more than ever. "I'm going up to see Sirhan right now," said Wirin. "I have already discussed a whole list of our top lawyers with him. He recognized Cooper's name right away. He'd like to have Cooper. I'm going up to tell him now, and have him sign a retainer." I went to the Federal Court to catch Cooper at the noon recess.

Channel 2's Paul Udell, one of the brightest TV reporters in town, was waiting for Cooper. I wondered if there had been a leak. No. "I'm here," explained Udell, "to see if I can get Cooper to comment on the difficulty of finding a lawyer for Sirhan."

At the recess Cooper said he'd be glad to comment on that, say, at eight o'clock in the morning. As soon as Udell left, I moved Cooper away from the crowd in the corridor and told him Sirhan was signing a retainer at that very moment asking that Cooper represent him.

Cooper looked down the corridor at Udell who was on his way out. "That changes things a bit, doesn't it? I'd better not have that interview." He started to go for Udell. I suggested he wait until later to cancel that appointment, not anxious that Udell suspect I was the bearer of some news hot enough to get Cooper to change his mind.

Cooper nodded and drew me along with him for a two-block walk to the Redwood Room, a popular noon-hour restaurant next door to the Los Angeles *Times*. "My client says it's all right with him if I take the Sirhan case," reported Cooper, "but his wife doesn't like the idea. It might prejudice the jury." Cooper stopped on the sidewalk, raised his eyebrows and looked over the top of his horn-rimmed spectacles. "And she's right," he said, poking his forefinger at me for emphasis. Cooper's speech was a succession of emphatic explosions. "She's right. It might." And so Cooper had another condition. He said he would take the case if Wirin could find another attorney who would be willing to direct the defense until Cooper was able to come in. We also talked about my potential interview with Sirhan. At that time, all I had in mind was a single magazine piece.

I met Wirin early the next morning at his home in the hilly section near Griffith Park called Los Feliz. He was still in his robe and slippers, somewhat indisposed with a cold. "Sirhan wants to tell you his story," he said immediately. "If you've got any money for him, he'll turn it over to help young Arab refugees." Getting in? That was a problem. "The man hasn't lost his basic rights guaranteed him under the Constitution. One of these is the right of free speech. But he's under tight security. Nobody gets in to see him. A public defender has been appointed and I'm not sure that I'll be allowed more visits myself. You'll have to work this out with Cooper and the sheriff." Wirin dug into the pocket of his robe, found three sheets of paper that had been torn out of a small spiral notebook. They were tentative retainers for Cooper and the two other lawyers whom Cooper wanted to work with him in the case: Joseph Ball, a most prominent Southern California attorney who had served on the Warren Commission, and Herman Selvin, one of the best appeals attorneys in the state.

Wirin was sure that the court would grant a postponement until the end of the summer. That would not be extraordinary. But who would be the attorney of record until then? Wirin had several options he thought Cooper should think about. Cooper could get one of his potential associates to handle the preliminary motions, or ask the public defender's office to do so, or utilize one of the other attorneys on Wirin's list, or get some other attorney of his own choosing. I gave Cooper this message outside the Federal Building at noon. Cooper said Selvin and Ball had already turned him down. "Who are the other men on Wirin's list?"

"Russell Parsons and Luke McKissack."

"Let's have Parsons take over," said Cooper. "I don't know McKissack and I've worked with Russ before."

What to do about the girl in the polka-dot dress? Chief of Detectives Robert Houghton had to make a decision. Despite the discrepancies in Sandra Serrano's story, there were still some other witnesses whose stories indicated there was a mystery girl. For one thing, there was Robert Duane's musky pickup who was so nervous because somebody was going to "get Kennedy." There were the clothes found by Edith Goldstein that hadn't yet been analyzed or traced to any owner. There was the black man, George Green, who told the FBI that he had seen a woman in a polka-dot dress running out of the kitchen after the shots. And now, two more witnesses had come forward. Susan Locke, a pretty "Kennedy girl" who was at the Ambassador on June 5, told the FBI she had noticed a girl in a white shift with blue polka dots standing expressionless in the Embassy Room just before Senator Kennedy was ready to speak. She was in her early twenties, well proportioned, with long brown hair pulled back and tied behind her head, hair that appeared to be dried out, like that of a girl who "does a lot of swimming," and she looked so out of place there at the time that Miss Locke pointed her out to Carol Breshears, who was in charge of the Kennedy girls, and Mrs. Breshears told a guard to watch the girl. And there was Evan Phillip Freed, a student at Cal State, Los Angeles, and a free-lance photographer for the Culver City *Evening Star-News,* who said that immediately after the shooting he had seen a man and a woman running out of the pantry. The man was tall, thin, had a dark complexion. The girl? Freed had no description of the girl. He thought she might have been wearing a polka-dot dress.

And what had DiPierro seen in the pantry? Was there a girl with the assassin or not?

Hawk-nosed Robert Houghton, a veteran of some twenty-six years as a Los Angeles detective, a man who could have been Chet Gould's prototype for Dick Tracy, decided to forge ahead. He had a team of thirty men and he could have more if he needed them. Houghton was aware that books and magazine articles were still being written to discredit the Dallas police for their shoddy handling of the John Kennedy investigation. If Houghton had anything to say about it, no one would be able to criticize the LAPD for not trying.

Investigators still roamed the city, looking for the girl in the polka-dot dress, and for the dark young men who had been seen with Sirhan. Sergeant Gordon McDevitt cruised Cynthia Kean's neighborhood for days, looking for the shiny blue Ford with the white fur in the back seat, and he spent hours checking the department's Vehicle Information Index, an elaborate file identifying autos previously stopped by the police according to noted oddities: bent license plate, missing front fender, red racing stripe, . . . He found no card on a Ford with a white fur in the back seat.

The court-appointed psychiatrist, Dr. Eric Marcus, paid his first visit to Sirhan on June 15 and soon learned that his job for the defense would not be easy.

Sirhan didn't even rise. From a prone position, he greeted Marcus with: "So you're the doc who's supposed to see whether or not I'm crazy." It was a statement and not a question, and, before Marcus could fashion a diplomatic reply, Sirhan challenged him. "Are you Jewish?" he demanded. Marcus shrugged and simply didn't answer. "Where do you stand politically?" Again Marcus demurred. "Are you a Zionist?"

Marcus said he wasn't. "What I am," he explained, "is a doctor and I'm here to draw you out so I can be of some assistance to you and your attorney, Wilbur Littlefield." (Public Defender Richard Buckley had assigned the case to Littlefield, one of his top assistants.)

Sirhan sneered. "Littlefield is from the public defender's office. He's only the attorney on [sic] record." Sirhan was obviously not counting on Littlefield for anything and he had a similar contempt for Marcus. They were both being paid by the county, and he didn't see how the same public crying for his blood could also pay for his defense counsel or his defense psychiatrist, or how they, in turn, could give him a fair defense.

Marcus shrugged. "Suppose you give me an account of the events on June 6."

Sirhan laughed. "I was in jail on June 6."

Marcus spluttered. "Well, let's see, when was it? The night of the shooting? Tuesday, June . . ."

"I don't remember," snapped Sirhan. He turned away from Marcus and stared at the wall.

Marcus waited. He'd had no experience with assassins before, but during his eight years of practice as a psychiatrist, the last three as a member of the Superior Court panel, he'd encountered more than thirty murderers. If they didn't want to talk on a first interview, there would be other chances. Besides, Marcus had recently adopted the methods of Gestalt therapy—a relatively new school of thought within psychiatry, which can find a patient's actions as significant as his words, his silences as meaningful as his verbal meanderings.

Sirhan broke the silence. "I'm just not going to discuss the case with you. You're not open with me. I will not be open with you."

Marcus told him that his own openness was hardly relevant. "You have to be open with me so I can help you. It's that simple." Sirhan thought that over and finally shrugged, which Marcus took to be a kind of acquiescence. He asked Sirhan what he'd been doing in the past year.

"Worked three or four months. Had difficulty finding employment." Marcus had already made a tentative conclusion that Sirhan was rather shallow and hardly sophisticated enough to come up with any deep responses even if there were a rapport here, which there wasn't. But he took a long chance and asked Sirhan about his dreams.

"I dream," said Sirhan, "of fixing my car and being useful."

He asked Sirhan what he meant by "useful."

"Employed. I wanted a good job."

That wasn't the kind of dream Marcus was asking about. "Belong to any political organizations?"

"No." Marcus asked him about his future. "I don't want to think about it," said Sirhan.

"Were you ever married?"

"No."

Marcus asked him how he did in school. Sirhan said he achieved little. "But I did accumulate forty units of junior college credit."

"What are you proud of?"

"I'm proud," said Sirhan, "of being an Arab." He added quickly: "And I'm ashamed of being an Arab—a second-class citizen—in Western society." He told Marcus of his interest in political science and of his fervent political debates in school.

"How about your brothers?"

"Two of them live at home," said Sirhan. "My youngest brother, Munir, got in trouble with the police. He was railroaded into jail." There was a bitterness in Sirhan's tone and Marcus tried to get Sirhan to amplify, but Sirhan decided he'd said enough already.

It was a disappointing interview, a charade in which Sirhan had cast himself as a recalcitrant delinquent and Marcus as the boys' vice principal. But it was not completely useless. At least Marcus could report that Sirhan was competent to stand trial. He left some screening tests behind—some personality inventories—for Sirhan to complete at his leisure.

Sergeants Lyle Sandlin and Thomas Strong were trying to get the Sirhan family history from Sharif Sirhan, the second eldest of the Sirhan brothers. This was the courteous and polite Sharif Sirhan. At other times in the past —and at other times to come—his controls would break down and the seething volcano inside him would explode into behavior which some might call antisocial. Once, thwarted in love, he was caught tampering with the brakes of his ex-girl friend's car and arrested for attempted murder. But here in Room 317 of Parker Center, he was courteous and polite, and he did not even get angry when the officers failed to understand his slightly accented English.

"You learned English in the old country?" asked Sergeant Sandlin. "What school did you attend there?"

"St. George's." It sounded like "Suds-es."

Sharif told the officer he and his older brother Saidallah had come to the United States in 1960 (three years after Sirhan and the rest), joined their mother in Pasadena and got jobs as machinists. Sharif said he lived at home, but he also had a room in a small hotel close to his job. "From '64 to '68, I have three or four accidents, and my mother always say to be careful while driving, so when I have this job, there's a place where some- times I stay there when I work overtime. My mother says it's better not to drive the car to Pasadena since I—she didn't want any more accidents. I almost got killed."

They talked about places where Sirhan had worked, and his fall from the horse. Sharif was very vague about places and dates. But he was very clear about the change in Sirhan after the fall from the horse.

"After he fell, we noticed that something went wrong with him because he started to change gradually. Now, we noticed the change not all at one time. It just became gradually, gradually, gradually, little by little, little by little. The last two or three months we couldn't even talk to him or say— he was always, you know, avoiding us, and we tried to avoid him just so that we would pretend, if he wants to do something wrong instead of not to do it, because if we keep after him, he might get worse and worse and worse. So we thought it better just to leave him the way he is. Not to bother him, and get out of his way."

"You say he started to get worse," said Strong. "What do you mean? In what way?"

"Before—before he fell, when you talk to him he listens to you and he —I mean he was considerate. He was that way. Whatever you give him a job, he give it to you the way you wanted it—sincere and honest and wanting to do whatever you want him to do. He used to listen. But after that, he just started not to listen to anybody. He used to take care of his room, keep it clean, take care of his bed. My mother says, 'Go clean the lawn outside,' he used to do it. After that, he just didn't care for anything, not for his room, not even for himself, or nothing at all."

Sharif said that neither he nor his brother Saidallah had spoken much with Sirhan since his fall. They found that speaking to Sirhan only led to fights, and so they just decided to ignore him. And that seemed just fine with Sirhan.

Sandlin asked him about Sirhan's friends. "Did he have a close friend? Who is his closest friend?"

"Recently?" asked Strong. "Within the last year?"

"The closest friend," said Sharif, "was his bedroom and his books."

"Who was his best girl friend?" asked Sandlin.

"This—once again—I have been asked this question many times. This is really strange. This is the only brother that I never saw with a—with a girl. This is the only brother."

"Did he ever talk about girls?"

"He may have talked about them, he may have talked to them on the phone concerning school, but never with a date. I don't know if he ever went to date a girl, outside of—not to my knowledge. I don't know." Outside of whom? Sharif did not want to say. "Not to my knowledge" meant "yes, but I don't want to say."

The officers asked Sharif about Sirhan's interest in guns, organizations, politics. Sharif didn't know. "He never indicated which side he was on politically, or what he felt, huh?"

"No. Not to my knowledge."

They asked him about Sirhan's car. Sharif said that he never touched Sirhan's car and Sirhan never touched his. "In other words," said Sandlin, "you lost this brotherly feeling with each other, didn't you?"

"No, no," protested Sharif. "Not me."

"Well, you wouldn't speak to each other."

"Always," said Sharif, his voice softening, "our hearts were with him, because we knew that something was wrong—"

"Oh, I see—"

"With him. So we just—Mama discussed this with me and Adel several times, several times, several times. And all the time when we come—it is our idea there must be something wrong with him."

"Did you ever suggest to your mother that he should go to a doctor?"

"Sure."

"What did your mother say?"

"She said that he was seeing a doctor." But the doctor Sirhan was seeing heard nothing of Sirhan's withdrawal from the family, only his complaints about a pain in his eye. "He ended up with no people. No friends." In lieu of friends, said Sharif, Sirhan took up with the garbage man.

"The garbage man?" asked Sandlin.

"Yes, the minute he sees the man, he goes running out there and says, 'How's the weather out here? Don't go.' And he goes back and makes coffee and cake and cookies and he gives them to him."

"To the garbage man?"

"Yes. He stays there and he drinks coffee with them."

Sandlin and Strong puzzled over that. "Tell us, in your own words now, just what you think about your brother."

"I should think that you wanted to ask," said Sharif. "I'm ready to answer. To me, I think it's just unbelievable. I can't believe it. There must be something wrong with him, otherwise—just a—I—I can't believe it. I can't believe it." They asked Sharif if Sirhan used to display fits of violence, or get into fights at school with boys.

"No fights," said Sharif. "He has no police record, no citations."

"Did he used to get mad and cuss a lot, a lot of profanity?"

"Nothing in our business, because at that time, even to disobey my mother, or anything like that, I used to slap him."

"You used to chastise him?"

"I used to hit him sometimes if he does something wrong. So that's why I tried to avoid him in those last two years, because he's man enough, and I would just keep, you know, hitting on him."

At 5:00 A.M. on June 18, the girl who told the police she had seen Sirhan with some coconspirators, Cynthia Kean, phoned Sergeant Gordon McDevitt at home. "Sergeant McDevitt," she cried, "you've got to come quick!"

"Where?" asked McDevitt, sensing the urgency in her voice.

"My house."

"You all right? Your mother there?"

"Yes," she said, "but hurry."

McDevitt drove directly from his home in Torrance to the home of Cynthia Kean's mother in Hollywood. She had told him of strange events in the past few days. A girl had been to her home twice at odd hours, pretending to be looking for someone else, and a man in an expensive car followed her home one night. McDevitt had to identify himself through the keyhole.

"My God, thank heavens you're here," said Cynthia. "Look what I found under the front door this morning!" She handed McDevitt a crude assembly. It was Boris Yaro's picture of Robert Kennedy lying on the pantry floor, his head cradled in the hands of Juan Romero. A single word from the L.A. *Times*'s headline, TRIUMPH, gave the picture an ironic tag, and pasted in the lower left-hand corner of the whole were some printed words cut from a magazine: DON'T TALK OR I DO ANYTHING TO PREVENT IT.

Actually, McDevitt learned, it was Cynthia's mother who found the threatening note under the front door. He couldn't tell who was more upset, Cynthia or her mother. But some sixth sense told McDevitt there was something strange about this girl. It was obvious to him that Cynthia had a strong love for Robert Kennedy. Maybe her anguish over the assassination had taken an imaginative outlet. He took Cynthia and her mother downtown to Parker Center, deposited the mother in a waiting room, and asked Cynthia if she'd mind undergoing a polygraph examination. Not at all. McDevitt introduced her to Sergeant Hank Hernandez, a handsome, confident officer with a great deal of experience in lie detection.

Hernandez had a soothing manner, and he slowly drew the entire story from his subject, a recap, really, of what she had told McDevitt. Then he was ready to ask Cynthia some key questions, while the polygraph monitored her autonomic reactions. He explained how the polygraph worked, attached a cardio band on her left arm and pumped it tight. That would record the reaction of her heartbeat. He attached electrodes to the first and third fingers of her right hand. That would record something called a "galvanic response." And he fastened a band—a pneumonograph—around her chest. She giggled nervously. "I'm not going to hurt you," said Hernandez.

But in a very few minutes, Hernandez had her in tears. She failed each key question miserably. It was clear to Hernandez she'd made up her entire story, and he told her so. As she wept quietly, Hernandez handed her Kleenex and talked to her, as he said, "like a big brother."

"You're not the first person," he said, "who has made up a story. But let me tell you something. You are the first person who has come up here, of all the people who have come up with stories, you are the first person who, I think, really loved Senator Kennedy. All the others were here for personal publicity. But you did this because you loved Kennedy. But how old are you? Twenty? You've got a long life ahead of you. Maybe you can help us now by telling me why you made this up."

With this, Cynthia's tears turned to sobs. "I can't tell you," she cried.

"If I can just get some insight into why you did this," pleaded Hernandez. "You don't have to be ashamed."

"Oh, but I am," she cried. "I'm ashamed of myself. I'm so ashamed of myself!"

"Well, what first decided you to make up this story?" asked Hernandez, handing her another Kleenex. Cynthia spent some time blowing her nose. "You do want to help us, don't you?"

"Oh, yes, I do," she moaned.

"Well, when did you first get the idea?" asked Hernandez. "When you were watching TV, or where?"

The girl paused, sniffled for several more minutes, then plunged into an explanation, rambling and filled with irrelevancies, which amounted to this: she was a firm believer in various theories of a conspiracy in Dallas, and she wanted to make sure that the Los Angeles police investigated every possible angle in this Kennedy killing. "I didn't want to let it happen again," she said. "But I don't know how I could have carried it so far."

Hernandez told her he'd have to make out a report, to clear up the record. No, on second thought, he'd go out and get Sergeant McDevitt, and he could make a report. Moments later, Hernandez and McDevitt were back. Hernandez assured her the police would do their job and investigate every possible angle; in fact, he would demonstrate that right now by tying up all the loose ends in her own story. "When did you make up that note, Cynthia? Yesterday?"

"Last night," she sobbed, "after my mother went to bed."

"Your mother was in bed when you put it under the door?"

"Yes. Oh, I'm really ashamed." Cynthia looked at McDevitt and started crying more loudly now. "Oh, it would have been so simple to say I just made it all up. It's just wrong. I'm really ashamed. The whole thing. A big, fantastic fantasy. Of course, they're going to find out," said Cynthia, possibly referring to her friends, or to her husband, who was away in the service. "What will they think? Oh, God," she sighed. "I can say I'm sorry. But that really doesn't mean anything right now." Hernandez gave her some more Kleenex. "Oh, this is so damn bad. So damn bad. So damn rotten."

"Well," said McDevitt, "you know, the only one you really caused any trouble was me. You got me out of bed at five o'clock this morning, but apart from that—"

"I don't know how you can be so nice." She looked at McDevitt gratefully. McDevitt smiled a fatherly smile. But he wished people like Cynthia Kean wouldn't try so hard to "help."

On June 18 I phoned A. L. Wirin to see if he had made any moves toward Russell Parsons. He hadn't. I asked Wirin if he'd seen a story in the L.A. *Times* which reported that four Arab attorneys from Amman, Jordan—Fouad Attallah, Ahmad El Khalil, Mohammed Baradeh and Hassan Hawwa—were planning to come to Los Angeles for the legal defense of Sirhan Sirhan.

"Yes," said Wirin, "I saw that and your point is well taken." I had made no specific point, but my message calling attention to the wise men from the East had its import on Wirin, a lawyer who was extremely anxious to see the Sirhan trial prove to the world that even an assassin could get justice in America. And it was obvious that Cooper and Parsons would fare better in Los Angeles County Superior Court than a quartet of Arab lawyers who would have to work with California attorneys in any event. Wirin said he would move right away, phoned the sheriff's office for an appointment with Sirhan and was refused on the grounds that Sirhan was now being represented by the public defender. Well, no matter. Sirhan had already signed a retainer for Parsons, and Parsons was the man he would have. Sirhan had asked Wirin if one of his attorneys couldn't be a Jew. Neither Cooper nor Parsons fit that requirement. But, then, Sirhan couldn't have everything.

Sheriff Pitchess was having his own problems. The Jordanian consul in Los Angeles, a liquor store owner named George Zraikat, had been demanding to see Sirhan. A visit to Sirhan from anyone, in a city where the police, the FBI and the Secret Service were still investigating the possibility of a conspiracy to commit political assassination, was the last thing Peter Pitchess had bargained for. But Zraikat had gotten to the public defender's office, which had assured him that he had every right to see Sirhan —if Sirhan wanted to see him. Littlefield told Sirhan of the consul's interest, Sirhan addressed a telegram to Zraikat (REQUEST TO SEE YOU EARLIEST CON-

VENIENCE [OFFICIAL HOURS]), and now Zraikat was here at the New County Jail to see Sirhan.

He spent only seven minutes with Sirhan, more than a little intimidated by all the precautions the sheriff's office had taken. He was first served with a copy of Judge Alarcon's order forbidding him to discuss the case with anyone, then he was put through a triple search of his person, ushered with Wilbur Littlefield through a maze of barred steel doors, and sat in front of a special visiting screen with two sheriff's officers hovering over him, insisting politely but firmly that he could not speak to Sirhan in Arabic.

While Sirhan was then ordered down from the second floor, Zraikat expostulated about these arrangements to no avail. After a few words with Sirhan, the consul left hurriedly, went home and phoned Washington. The next morning, Robert Newman, an officer on the Jordanian desk of the U.S. State Department, was phoning long distance for Sheriff Pitchess. Newman pointed out to Pitchess that a U.S. citizen jailed in Jordan had the right to speak English with the American consul in Amman. Diplomatic protocol demanded that a Jordanian citizen jailed in Los Angeles should have reciprocal rights. It was a point well taken, but Pitchess was unimpressed. "Listen, sonny," he said firmly, "the consul accepted our conditions before he came here. Furthermore, this kid grew up in Pasadena. He speaks good English and so does the consul. That's good enough for me. I take no chances with this prisoner. He's *my* responsibility."

Newman asked Pitchess what he suggested he should do about American citizens in Jordan. "That's *your* responsibility," said Pitchess.

On June 19, A. L. Wirin and Russell Parsons met for breakfast at Manning's Cafeteria on sleazy old 3rd Street in downtown Los Angeles. Wirin told Parsons that Cooper wanted him to handle everything until the Friars' case was finished. "So, until then," said Wirin, "you're it." The two of them agreed that they each ought to compose separate telegrams to Sirhan Sirhan, and that Parsons ought to see Sirhan immediately.

Wirin scrawled his message first in a little notebook:

> THE LAWYER OF YOUR FIRST CHOICE HAS AGREED TO
> REPRESENT YOU. SO HAS RUSSELL PARSONS TO WHOM
> I HAVE DELIVERED YOUR WRITTEN RETAINER. HE WILL
> WIRE YOU AND SEE YOU IMMEDIATELY. A. L. WIRIN.

Parsons composed his wire:

MR. A. L. WIRIN HAS HANDED ME A RETAINER AGREEMENT
SIGNED BY YOU REQUESTING THAT I REPRESENT YOU. I
AM ACCEPTING THIS RETAINER AND WILL REPRESENT YOU
WITHOUT FEE AS A PUBLIC SERVICE. I INTEND TO SEE
YOU IMMEDIATELY. RUSSELL E. PARSONS.

He sent it to the Western Union office in his building at 2nd and Broadway and phoned the public defender to give him the news.

At noon, Parsons and Richard Buckley, chief public defender, appeared at the sheriff's office in the graystone Hall of Justice, discovered that neither Wirin's nor Parsons' telegrams had yet been delivered by Western Union. "It's all right, gentlemen," said Undersheriff William McCloud. "You can certainly go up to see Sirhan." McCloud knew that an attorney of Parsons' standing wouldn't be presenting himself fraudulently and the note in his hand certainly looked as if it was signed by Sirhan.

Buckley and Parsons were driven to the New County Jail, given a triple search and taken to the second floor infirmary, southwest wing. Buckley introduced Parsons to Sirhan, stayed seven minutes and departed. Parsons found Sirhan immensely pleased that at last he had his own attorney, remained for a simple twenty-minute, get-acquainted chat and left to talk to the newsmen, who had gotten few words indeed from Wilbur Littlefield as long as he was the attorney of record.

Parsons would change all that.

News crews from seven local television stations and two networks swarmed into Parsons' office, along with a chorus of radio reporters and newspapermen. At home in Westlake Village, on the western edge of the county, I watched Parsons' performance, wondering what it would be like to work with him. On the tube, he came across as a fighter. Someone asked him about his health. "That's a prying, personal question," said Parsons. "I come from a family of champions. I walk two miles every night. I take exercises every morning." Someone else asked him his age. "In the late sixties," lied Parsons. "That's good enough. What the hell does it matter? Who're you going to tell? Some girl?" When a reporter asked him why he was taking the case, Parsons put the burden of proof back on the reporter. "Don't you think this man ought to get a fair trial?" he demanded.

"What are you going to plead?" asked another.

"We have to study that, young man. We have to study that. I remember when I was a prosecutor in Beaver County, Utah, I had a fellow once who wanted to plead guilty and the other fellow . . ."

"Will Sirhan take the stand in his own defense?"

"We have to study that too. That's something you never know until the eleventh hour. I had a client once who didn't want to take the stand. I never did get paid for that case, but if you look in the records you would see . . ."

I smiled to myself and thought of Casey Stengel, probably the canniest manager in the history of baseball, who talked a lot and said nothing, and won the American League pennant ten times. But as far as John Lawrence, the Arab sympathizer in New York, was concerned, Parsons said too much, for Parsons had also talked about the possibilities of deportation to Jordan and of an insanity defense. In two consecutive news releases from the Organizing Committee for Clemency for Sirhan, Lawrence denounced Parsons for "floating trial balloons of 'possible' defense theories" and inciting zenophobic statements from hatemongering elements in the U.S.," and charged that neither Sirhan nor his family had any say in choosing Russell Parsons.

On that day, however, Parsons took Adel Sirhan, the family's most responsible member, up to see Sirhan. Adel, who had been talking to Lawrence via long distance, challenged Sirhan. "Is this the man you want?" he said to Sirhan.

"Yes, it is," said Sirhan calmly, and he told Adel that Grant Cooper was also coming into the case soon. In the meantime, Parsons would handle things. Sirhan liked Parsons.

And so, by the way, did a good many individuals on the outside who saw him as some latter day St. Jude, a new patron of lost causes. The persecuted and the paranoid who walk the streets of Los Angeles started walking right into Parsons' office as into a shrine, hoping he would undertake their case. One woman wanted Parsons to stop her fellow workers from giving her the evil eye. One day another woman left a brown paper bag for Parsons. Inside was a canister of instant tea and perhaps a half a pound of hamburger. Inside the bag was a note: "This tea made me sick. When I stopped using it, I got okay. The round hamburger doesn't look right to me." The woman signed her name and that was all.

Another woman, hardly psychotic, but burdened with sufficient excuses for a dozen breakdowns, walked slowly down the cool, refrigerated corridors of Parker Center. She was Mary Sirhan, the mother of the assassin. Fifty-five, she could have passed for seventy, but she carried herself bravely, chin up, under control. She had had police interviews, FBI interviews, Secret Service interviews, and she would have many more, for she, a law-abiding woman, wanted to cooperate with the law. But it was not easy, not at all. She told herself that her son Sirhan couldn't have killed Kennedy. But the police, they kept implying that he did. And that destroyed the fiction she attempted to maintain.

Sergeant Hank Hernandez thanked her for coming down. He didn't tell her, but they were sitting in the very same room where Sirhan was first interrogated on the morning of June 5. He told her he and his partner at this moment, Sergeant Tom Strong, were responsible for the background investigation on Sirhan. "We want to find out why this happened. We know what happened, and we're trying to find out if we can from talking to the family whatever they can tell us about the surrounding circumstances."

She told them very little, nothing which would help them in their investigation. Sirhan hadn't worked for a long time, was rendered immobile because his car had broken down and he couldn't afford to get it fixed, read a lot, went to bed early and rose early and spent a good deal of time at the public library. He had few friends.

"When was the last time he had a friend over to the house?" Hernandez asked.

"He had an elderly man from the Bible study. A real elderly man around seventy, and they used to sit in the dining room and study the Bible." She didn't know the man's name. He was from a church that used the slogan, "Your Bible talks to you."

Hernandez asked her about Sirhan's girl friends.

Mary Sirhan said she had a few pictures of Sirhan in school and there were some girls in the pictures. But he had no girl friends. "You know," she said, "we're different. I said. I should say I—it's something. If we don't want to marry a girl, we won't walk with a girl. It's against our— we're different. And my sons, you can see them all unmarried because it's a different way."

Hernandez tried to help Mrs. Sirhan recall what her son's actions were on the five days preceding the shooting. As far as she could recall, he was home most of the time. On Monday? Oh, yes, he was home on Monday. Then he asked her about the gun. "Did you know that he had a gun?"

"No."

"Did you ever ask Adel since this happened how he got the gun?"

"No."

"Why?"

"Because I don't know. I haven't seen a gun. I have never heard. Is there—was there—a gun?"

"Oh, yes," said Hernandez, "he had a gun.

Mary Sirhan was obviously unable to say anything negative about her son. Hernandez asked if he was a normal boy like any boy or did he have a temper. "Never, never temper, no."

Sirhan never fought with his brothers? Mary admitted that he had had his differences with his two older brothers, Saidallah, who drank a little bit, and Sharif. Both of them wanted to impose the rules on the household and that led to arguments. Finally, she asked the two older boys to find somewhere else to live.

Hernandez reminded her of a fight Sirhan had had with Munir over some hot water on the stove. Mary explained that away. It was nothing. Nothing at all. "The last time you saw your boy, did you know if there was anything—on Tuesday, when he left, did you think there was anything wrong with him yourself?"

"No," said Mary. "He just got up and washed his face. I know he washed and just go and get the paper. He didn't say anything, nothing."

"He didn't say that he felt bad or that he—to you he didn't look any different than he did the rest of his life that you have seen him?"

"No," said Mary Sirhan. The poor woman didn't know what to conceal and what to come out with.

The interview ended on a sad note. The officers asked about her daughter, Aida, and Mary talked about her last painful days when she lay dying of leukemia. "I think that's all," said Strong. "We don't want to burden you anymore, but I think we pretty well covered—"

"I'm so sorry for what happened," said Mary Sirhan.

"We believe that you are," said Sergeant Hernandez.

"I'm really hurt and that's not the way that I wish to end. I was hoping that my son would be a great something that—good, not to be a killer." She sobbed. "Oh, I just can't take it."

"We realize this," said Strong, with sympathy. "We understand this."

"Why do you think he did what he did?" asked Hernandez.

"I'm asking why," said Mary Sirhan. "I just don't know. Please, if you know it, just let me know."

Hernandez sighed and looked at Strong. "Yes, ma'am. That's what we're trying to find out."

By June 20—more than two weeks after the assassination of Robert Kennedy, the FBI had finally found Sirhan's seemingly closest friend. He was Ivan Valladares Garcia, a native (and still a citizen) of Guatemala. He was tall, well spoken, serious and extremely agitated about this interview on the campus of Pasadena City College.

"No," he told Special Agent Lloyd D. Johnson, "I will not give you my home address. You can reach me at work. My mother is nervous and I do not want her disturbed." Garcia told Johnson that he had met Sirhan at PCC, that they had never discussed politics, that Sirhan had never discussed Senator Kennedy or the Arab-Israeli conflict, except to note that his success as a jockey might be thwarted by the rich Jews who owned most of the racehorses in California. Sirhan did not have a strong interest in girls, did not have an interest in guns. Garcia volunteered the opinion that Sirhan was not part of any conspiracy. Why not? "Because," said Garcia, "the whole thing was so poorly planned." Any conspirators would have chosen a gun of larger caliber, would have found a better place to kill Kennedy, would have planned a better escape route. "Frankly," said Garcia, "I'm puzzled by all this. I never knew Sirhan to violate any laws of any kind."

All in all, Garcia had reported a lot of the things that Sirhan didn't do. But nothing of what he did do.

Sergeant DeWayne Wolfer, a criminalist for the LAPD, approached the Ambassador pantry with a sound level monitor in one hand, a .22-caliber Iver-Johnson Cadet Model revolver in the other (identical to the weapon wrested from Sirhan's grasp on the night of June 4) and a box of Mini-Mag ammunition in his pocket. He made some test firings and discovered that the shots could not be heard on the south fire escape where Sandra Serrano was sitting when Kennedy was shot.

To the police, this proved Sandra Serrano was lying. She had never told anyone she had heard shots. That notion came from the police. Now, however faulty their logic, they would move in on Miss Serrano.

Sergeants Hank Hernandez and Tom Strong welcomed Sandra Serrano to the warmth and comfort of their lie detector room on the fourth floor of Parker Center, and Hernandez tightened the cardio band around her left arm. It was 10:15 P.M. "Now, Sandra," Hernandez plunged right in, "I'm going to ask you some questions just so we can get the true facts on the previous statements that you made before. You know that you shouldn't be afraid, and I hope you're not. The whole thing that we are trying to resolve here is what actually happened at the Ambassador Hotel, and I well understand, as you have explained to me, that this thing was magnified out of proportion with people that you said messed you around up there. So if you will tell me the truth about what happened, and I could ask you questions—"

"Uh-huh," said Miss Serrano, not wildly enthusiastic about all this.

Hernandez tried to clarify her story for her. She had had one drink, a screwdriver, in the Embassy Room. She went out to the fire escape about 11:30 P.M. and sat down. Sometime later, she saw a girl in a white dress —not polka-dot—and a few other persons come down the fire escape. The girl said "something about shooting Kennedy." Later, Miss Serrano talked to Thomas Vincent DiPierro who said he had seen the gunman with a girl wearing a polka-dot dress.

"So that's where that thing about the polka-dot dress, that's where it started?" asked Hernandez.

"I guess," said Miss Serrano.

Hernandez asked her when she first realized her story was getting out of hand. It was, she said, when she went to the Rampart Street police station. Hernandez wondered why she hadn't corrected the story then. She said she had told the police what she thought they wanted to hear. "I was sitting there hearing descriptions and descriptions of these people, of these people, of these people. Oh, God, no, maybe that's what I'm supposed to have seen. It messed me up, that's all; and I figured, well, they must know what they're doing."

"Well, at least you're being a decent, honest woman right now, aren't you, you know?"

"Yes, yes, yes." Then Sandra changed her mind. "I don't think I'm very decent."

"Well, you are being decent. You're telling the truth now."

"Yeah, in a way. But you know what I think? Some changes should be made. You know, when somebody sees something," stammered Miss Serrano, "keep them away from other people who have seen it. Because you don't know—you don't know what happens." That thought trailed away into a bit of incoherence. Then Sandra thought she might blame the press a little, too. "Well, you see another thing, too, you know, that is that, that other newspapers came out with that somebody else had seen it, and then I—I kept thinking to myself, maybe—you know, gee—"

"Regardless of what they saw, you know we just want to get the facts, and the facts that you saw were partly, apparently, were misquoted, or misprinted, or mistelevised to the actual true facts?" Hernandez was too understanding.

"Well, they can't have been mistelevised because I said that. I actually said that. None of them—I don't know. Somewhere I heard it. I don't know why I said it, but it just fitted. Then it happened that it all fitted in, and I couldn't understand it, you know. Then, yeah, I really thought there was something behind it. I was scared. I tell you I've been scared all this time."

"Okay, well, don't be scared anymore, okay?"

Sandra Serrano smiled ruefully. "Okay. But don't tell my aunt, okay?"

"Well, I'm not going to tell anyone here," said Hernandez. "Of course, we're going to have to cancel all these reports, you know that."

"I know that."

But Hernandez went too far. All he had proved was that Sandra Serrano was confused. He never got her to deny she'd seen a girl running down the fire escape shouting, "We shot him!" Only that her description of the girl's dress was adjusted to agree with Thomas Vincent DiPierro's polka-dot girl.

Not content with talking to the FBI, Robert Duane, after reading a story in the *Valley Times* about the mysterious girl in the polka-dot dress, phoned the reporter whose by-line ran over the story.

"Fernando Faura?"

"Yes."

"You the guy who wrote the story about the girl in the polka-dot dress?"

"Yes."

"I'm interested in knowing what you know. I think I spent the day with her on June 4."

"Don't hang up," said Faura. "I want to talk to *you.*"

The police had their red herrings. Now the press, represented by Fernando Faura and *Life* magazine, would go sniffing off on an unproductive lead as well.

On June 21, Mary Sirhan, accompanied by Adel, went to see Sirhan for the first time. A jail matron searched her thoroughly and escorted her, along with Adel and Russell Parsons, into a glassed-in room on the first floor of the New County Jail. She had instructions to speak only English. Sirhan limped in and sat across from her on the other side of a glass screen. Her eyes filled with tears for a moment and her voice broke. But soon her tones became accusatory and she poured forth instructions for Sirhan. "You never were a Communist," she said. "The newspapers can make you a Communist. But you're not a Communist. And you never received any money."

The visit was a brief one, for all traffic on the floor was stopped as long as Mary Sirhan was with her son. Parsons led her away, and neither she nor Adel could speak in either English or Arabic.

That night, Sirhan told the guards he wasn't well. He was dizzy and he had a stomach ache. A male nurse gave him two aspirins and a half ounce of rhubarb and soda. And for several weeks more, Sirhan got a half grain of phenobarbital each night to help him sleep.

Deputy Chief Robert Houghton had figured out the scope of the investigative task that lay ahead for the LAPD. He assembled the best detectives he could spring loose from other assignments—the team that started with thirty men grew eventually to a squad of forty-seven—into a "Special Unit" working under the code name "Senator." Eventually the team called itself the "Special Unit, Senator," and finally, S.U.S. for short.

Houghton set himself a pretty task: to investigate every shred of evidence relating to the assassination. That meant that the police had to search out every possible witness to the shooting, and anyone else at the Ambassador on the night of June 4 who had seen any suspicious moves on the part of the assassin, or had seen him with any other persons, in polka-dot dresses or otherwise.

That meant the detectives had to interview all the hotel employees and attempt to track down some 5,000 persons who were at the hotel that night. They had to make the standard ballistics test on Sirhan's gun, check the weapon for the fingerprints of others who might have touched the gun, and account for each of the bullets fired in the pantry. (See Appendix B.)

One group developed a file on Sirhan's medical history, another group was set to examine files from other agencies and pursue any leads they might offer and an office team set up shop in a large sound stage on the eighth floor of Parker Center to prepare and maintain a case history, including some large charts to plot a critical path through all this maze. Their target date was August 27, for the district attorney's office expected to go to trial in September.

The most intriguing line, of course, was the possible conspiracy. If Houghton's men uncovered one, they would be heroes. If they didn't, at least they would preserve the professional reputation of the LAPD and forestall years and years of subsequent criticism from the conspiracy buffs whose theories on the plot to kill President John F. Kennedy had provided the publishing industry with a rich new lode, and given the nation a new parlor game to boot. "Which do you prefer? The grassy knoll theory? The railroad bridge theory? The eight-bullet theory? The theory of the other Oswald?"

And now Truman Capote, a friend of Jacqueline Kennedy and of her sister, Lee Radziwill, had a theory on the Robert Kennedy assassination. Capote, who was considered something of an expert on murder after *In Cold Blood,* went on the NBC "Tonight" show and speculated that Sirhan and his accomplices might have been intensively trained, brainwashed trigger men of a type envisaged by novelist Richard Condon in *The Manchurian Candidate.* Their purpose, Capote claimed, could be to drive the United States to its knees by assassinating all its leaders. A goal, he said, that was once expounded by Madame Helena Blavatsky, whom everyone now knew Sirhan was reading in the county jail.

Houghton appointed Sergeant Phil Sartuche to mine that vein, and Sartuche, with no real background for such a task, plunged into the morass of mysticism and the occult.

Others stayed with the girl in the polka-dot dress. And other teams looked into the possibility that Sirhan might have been in touch with others who could have wanted Kennedy killed: the Mafia, the right-wing extremists, left-wing extremists, the Al Fatah.

With a little more diligence than they exercised and a great deal more intelligence than they had, the police might have established links between Sirhan and the underworld, between Sirhan and the right wing, between Sirhan and the left wing, between Sirhan and the Al Fatah. Sirhan had Arab friends, for example, who had left the United States and returned to the Middle East for no apparent reason, but neither the police nor the FBI had enough interest in them to interview them there. There was one young man who showed up in some still photographs of Robert Kennedy's last talk on the Embassy Room stage. He was standing on Jesse Unruh's left in one picture that was printed in the June 14 issue of *Time,* and he had a camera around his neck. A Kennedy worker named Teddy Marie Nafius said this same young man had visited Kennedy headquarters in mid-May, identified himself as Ali Ahmand and said he was employed at Microdot in Pasadena. By the time detectives got around to Microdot in August, however, fellow workers said the man had quit Microdot and gone back to his homeland of Pakistan. And his name wasn't Ahmand at all, but Iqbal. Judging from police reports and FBI records of the investigation on file in the L.A. district attorney's office, neither the police nor the FBI bothered to check on Iqbal in Pakistan, ask him why he'd given a false name to the Kennedy worker in mid-May, or what he was doing on the Embassy Room stage. There would be other investigative avenues opened but never traveled. Perhaps they were discouraged too often by boys who cried "Wolf!"

Major Jose Duarte, an anti-Castro Cuban with American ties in Miami and Los Angeles, was one of these. He opened up a whole new line of inquiry for the police when he claimed that Sirhan was a militant member of the Students for a Democratic Society. On May 21, in Los Angeles, Duarte had attended a meeting of the Peace and Freedom Party—which nominated the black militant Eldridge Cleaver for President of the United States—and got into a heated argument there, he said, with Sirhan. Yes, he was damn sure it was Sirhan and his description certainly matched Sirhan's. The police interviewed seventeen people who were at the meeting. Fourteen of them remembered the altercation involving Duarte. He had asked for permission to speak during a slide show on the Bay of Pigs invasion. Duarte said he had participated in the invasion. A dark young man with an accent called him a mercenary. Duarte and the dark young man had a shouting match. But the young man wasn't Sirhan. He was Reza Jalalipour, an Iranian student, who was a little bigger than Sirhan, but certainly a look-alike. "No," insisted the fighting major, "it was Sirhan I had the argument with. I know it." Later, at Parker Center, Sergeant Michael McGann and Officer Jerry Mount confronted the feisty little freedom fighter with Reza Jalalipour in the flesh. "Is this the man?" asked McGann. "Yes," admitted Duarte. "It looks like him."

But how about the girl in the polka-dot dress? The LAPD still couldn't be sure. Special Unit, Senator visited television news agencies and newsreel cameramen to inspect every foot of film they'd shot on the night of June 4. Maybe Sirhan was with the girl. A UCLA student named Alvin Tokunow, who was shooting some documentary footage at the Ambassador, started scanning his film, much like the photographer hero in the movie Blow-Up, David Hemmings, who found a murderer with a gun lurking in the shadows of some innocent stills he had taken in a London park. Object: to find Sirhan Sirhan in the crowd around Kennedy. He failed to find him in one reel taken on the night of June 4. But he had another reel, shot at the Kennedy rally on Sunday night, June 2. And there he saw Sirhan—or somebody who looked just like him—right next to a pretty girl in the middle of the crowd in the Cocoanut Grove. He went to the police with it, and a colleague named Teddy Charach went to *Life* magazine. Charach thought he had struck oil. It was another Zapruder film, at least, and he suggested *Life* might want to pay him $40,000 for it. A team for the S.U.S. got sore eyeballs looking at the incredibly bad rushes. Aside from the fact that they couldn't find Sirhan in any of the takes, much of the film was out of focus and jerky. Was this some new kind of experimental cinema? Had the camera been held by some go-go dancer? The hell with it.

Their main job was to be sure to convict the man they had in custody, Sirhan Sirhan, and to do that well they had to gather all the real eyewitnesses they could find. Sifting out the pseudo eyewitnesses was a long, painstaking task. They had a few photos of the pantry in the first chaotic moments after the shooting, a good enough check but not entirely sufficient. The police and the district attorney's office trooped more than 100 persons into the Ambassador pantry and had them re-create what they saw in front of a television camera, and they preserved the interviews on video tape. "Thank God for the early inaccurate accounts of the scene on the radio," said Sergeant Charles Collins sometime later. Collins, who, with Sergeant Frank Patchett, handled the trial preparation, blessed the Almighty because early radio and newspaper accounts had the assassin seized by Roosevelt Grier and Rafer Johnson. An "eyewitness" who came in and told police that version was automatically suspect, for it was not Grier and Johnson who first seized Sirhan, but Karl Uecker, a maître d' at the Ambassador Hotel. Said another investigator: "Put everybody together who *says* they were in the pantry and you could fill the Coliseum."

Five

**"Monsters. Wickedness.
Too many entanglements. Blood."**

On June 25, the Los Angeles County Board of Supervisors authorized spending $25,000 to remodel the Deputies' Ward Room on the thirteenth floor of the Hall of Justice where, the sheriff's office decided, they could provide Sirhan with maximum security close to the courtroom where he would be tried. Hearings in the chapel of the New County Jail provided the jailers with too many headaches. For an upcoming hearing on June 28, for example, one memo on the security arrangements ran to thirty-eight pages of precautions. Included in the supervisors' authorization were plans to build a bulletproof shield of glass around the defendant so that during the trial no vigilante could slip in and personally avenge the Robert Kennedy assassination. Already workmen were remodeling an adjacent section of the thirteenth floor to accommodate Sirhan for the remainder of his stay in the sheriff's custody. That meant that Sirhan's jailers would soon have to transfer Sirhan. In anticipation, Inspector Ralph Welch started timing various routes from the New County Jail to the Hall of Justice. He wanted the fastest route he could get and one that would avoid major traffic arteries and potential bottlenecks. Welch soon found this way and drove it over and over at various times of the day and night so that he would be ready whenever the sheriff gave the word.

For his first scheduled hearing on June 28, Sirhan Sirhan was pushed the considerable distance from his cell to the infirmary chapel in a wheelchair. A huge crowd of newsmen gathered, including David Smith of the Los Angeles *Times,* Gladwin Hill of *The New York Times,* Martin Kasindorf of *Newsweek* and an old-timer named Walter Winchell.

Forty-three deputies stood by to search them all, then accompany them to the chapel. The search took almost an hour. The proceeding before Judge Richard Schauer took seven minutes.

Parsons simply asked for additional time to prepare his plea because one of the court-appointed defense psychiatrists, Dr. Edward Stainbrook, had declined the appointment and Parsons had no report yet from Dr. Marcus. Judge Schauer then appointed Dr. George Y. Abe to replace Stainbrook. Schauer was in no hurry; courts often postpone trials to let community prejudice die down so that the scales of justice are not weighted too heavily against the accused. The only thing that remained was to secure Sirhan's waiver of his legal right to be tried within sixty days. He waived, and that was that. By now, after sifting the evidence they had, Prosecutors Compton, Howard and Fitts decided there were only two possible defenses open to Parsons: insanity or diminished capacity. Both of them were psychiatric defenses calling for expertise they didn't possess. So they had hired a psychiatrist of their own, Dr. Seymour Pollack, a distinguished forensic psychiatrist from the University of South California, who there headed a special Institute on Psychiatry and the Law. As an agent of the district attorney's office, Pollack could not talk to the defendant, but he could observe him in court. During this seven-minute session he sat to Sirhan's right with a direct view of him across the counsel table and took notes on his behavior. Once he noticed that Sirhan had held Parsons' hand like a little boy with his father.

The proceeding was a dull letdown for the members of the press. But Sirhan was upset. He went back to his cell, complaining of a stomach ache and was again dosed by a jail nurse with a solution of rhubarb and soda. The next morning Sirhan purchased a copy of the Los Angeles *Times* to read about himself, not anxious to read anything hateful, but fascinated with the publicity nonetheless.

Others, too, may have been fascinated in other ways. That day, a middle-aged black woman was arrested in the jail lobby with a loaded Colt .45 automatic in her purse. She was the second armed black woman seized and arrested in the jail that week.

After the court appearance, Parsons answered a reporter who asked him if he would plead insanity for Sirhan. "That's not for me to say," said Parsons. "That's for the psychiatrists and the jury."

John Lawrence heard Parsons' words on network television and fumed. In a final note to Sirhan he pointed out (correctly) that Parsons was playing with the truth, for it is not the psychiatrists or the jury who decide on a plea, but the defense attorney. Lawrence made one last attack on the way Sirhan's defense seemed to be going, charging that Drs. Eric Marcus and

George Y. Abe were both on the state's payroll and working under the police state. But then, Lawrence tipped his hand and bespoke his real fears, which were not for Sirhan but for Lawrence himself. If Sirhan took the psycho route in his defense, he warned, he would be compromising all the Arab sympathizers in America, for they, like Sirhan, would be called crazy every time they cried out against injustice to the Palestinian Arabs.

It was the first time such an argument was used with Sirhan but it would not be the last, for political considerations (which Sirhan succumbed to) were destined to blunt the effectiveness of the only defense he really had.

When the Kleig lights around Defense Attorney Russell Parsons had finally dimmed, he began to realize that his problems were almost identical to those of the Los Angeles Police Department. For he, too, had to find out why Sirhan had killed Kennedy. On the face of it, such a task seemed easy enough. After all, he had something the police didn't have: access to the assassin. But Parsons got amazingly little from the assassin himself, partly because it was his practice never to ask one of his criminal clients a direct question about the crime. The clues to Sirhan's behavior had to come from others. There the authorities had an advantage over Parsons, for they had detectives everywhere and all he had was one lonely investigator, Michael A. McCowan, an ex-Marine and an ex-cop who had worked for the LAPD ten years before he finished law school. When Parsons asked him to work on the Sirhan case—without fee—he hesitated hardly a second, plunged into the case and became Parsons' good right hand.

There was something phony about Munir Sirhan's account of how his brother bought the Iver-Johnson .22. But the police polygrapher, Sergeant Hank Hernandez, was so heavy-handed and inept, he never came close to finding out what it was.

Hernandez gave what was becoming a canned spiel. "Now, Munir, I can certainly appreciate the fact that Sirhan is your brother and I can certainly appreciate the fact that you're, the way you are feeling right now about this as a brother, but I want you to be aware that this investigation— twenty years from now people are going to be reading about it. A hundred years from now they're going to be reading about this. When you went to school, you read about Abraham Lincoln and I'm certain that a hundred and two hundred years from now, if there is still this world in existence,

that somebody is going to be reading about Senator Kennedy. So please—
I'll ask you again. Don't become involved in this thing by telling something that you know is not the truth because from one step people will
figure another step and another step. Now, is there anything about your
statement concerning that gun that you—"

"Well," said Munir, "what is it that you want to know?"

"Okay. Did you buy the gun from this fellow George?"

"No."

"That's what I want to know."

"No, I didn't."

"Did you buy the gun?"

"No."

Hernandez wasn't satisfied with that because George Erhard had told
him that he sold the gun to Munir, not Sirhan. For almost two hours they
went round and round and nothing was resolved.

Finally, Hernandez intimated that Munir had known all along that his
brother wanted to kill Kennedy.

"Are you insinuating," asked Munir, "that I knew he was—"

"I'm not insinuating anything. I'm just talking to you about this thing."

"I didn't know that he was going to use it for shooting Kennedy, sir,"
Munir said evenly.

"What did you think he was going to use it for?"

"As I said, he said he was going to use it to go to the rifle range. He
used to belong to the ROTC. It's been a long time since he's had a gun in
his hand. He liked it, so he could just go out there and shoot."

Finally Hernandez thought he had the story straight and he concluded,
"You helped him get the gun, Munir. And you feel guilty about this, don't
you?"

"Yes, sir, I do."

"Because you got the gun for him."

"Right. Without me he wouldn't have been able to get a gun."

"That's right, right. That's the whole thing there. You put it right there
in a nutshell, and I think you do feel guilty about it."

"Yes, sir, very."

And that was as far as Hernandez could proceed. Both he and his subject were far too exhausted at that point to go through with a valid polygraph examination. On the next day, however, Hernandez submitted sixty-three questions to Munir about the gun. The polygraph made it clear
that Munir himself was the one who purchased the gun.

*   *   *   *   *

In his cell, Sirhan puzzled over the screening test Dr. Marcus had left for him. Parsons had urged him to cooperate "because these doctors could really help us," but Sirhan went only halfway. He put aside a test instructing him to draw certain figures—of a man, of a woman, and one of himself as seen by himself. And he shrugged off a sentence completion test as silly. And then, perhaps because it required less effort, he completed the true-false answers to more than 500 statements on something called the Minnesota Multiphasic Personality Inventory (MMPI).

Expert psychologists would later interpret Sirhan's answers according to a set of statistical norms arrived at over the years by testing thousands of patients in and out of mental institutions. Some of Sirhan's nonresponses (which are usually considered more important than the yes or no responses) were significant:

291. At one or more times in my life, I felt that someone was making me do things by hypnotizing me.
293. Someone has been trying to influence my mind.

On July 1 at 12:52 P.M., in Room 402 of Parker Center, Thomas Vincent DiPierro reneged on his story about the girl in the polka-dot dress. Sergeant Hank Hernandez was aware that neither the S.U.S. nor the FBI could find the girl in the polka-dot dress, and the LAPD at least was beginning to look silly. For days, hundreds of citizens tried to help the police by reporting girls seen around town wearing polka-dot dresses, and one of the clerks in the S.U.S. chamber itself irritated her frustrated colleagues by wearing polka-dot dresses to work every day. Hernandez had to break down young DiPierro. He did. Then he called in a stenographer to take down a kind of summary interview.

"As a matter of fact," said Hernandez, "you have told me now that there was no lady that you saw standing next to Sirhan."

"That's correct," said DiPierro.

"Okay. Now, I can appreciate what you would have or could have been going through on that evening."

"Yes."

"But I think what you have told me is that you probably got this idea about a girl in a black and white polka-dot dress after you talked to Miss Sandra Serrano."

"Yes, sir, I did." This reply should have given Hernandez some pause, for on June 20 Sandra Serrano had told Hernandez that she had gotten the polka-dot part of her story from DiPierro. Now, under prodding from Hernandez, DiPierro was saying just the opposite.

"You did not see a girl in a polka-dot dress. You did not see a girl in a black and white polka-dot dress standing behind Sirhan on that evening?"

"No," said DiPierro. DiPierro had been persuaded that there was no polka-dot dress. Now he was saying there was no girl either.

"Is there anything else that you have told me previously or that you have told Sergeant Patchett or anyone else that . . . is not the truth?"

"No. Nothing," he said. "Only about the girl."

To Hernandez, that was a relief. DiPierro was a very good eyewitness. He was right behind Kennedy, he got blood spattered in his face and his descriptions of all else were sharp, accurate and confirmed by others.

"Only about the girl?" repeated Hernandez.

"Yes, sir. That good enough?" DiPierro was making the admission to please Hernandez.

Hernandez got up and left the room for a few moments, then returned, at ease. "Okay, Vincent, I think that we are pretty well cleared up as far as the girl with the black polka-dot dress. The time is now 1:00 P.M. and this interview is now concluded."

Hernandez was too eager. Granted that the police had destroyed Sandra Serrano's absolute credibility. What negated DiPierro's account? Nothing except the insistence of Hernandez. DiPierro's description of Sirhan—and the girl—in the pantry was vivid. He had said he saw Sirhan in a crouch with the gun—which is the way Sirhan practiced at the range. Moments before that, he had reported, he saw Sirhan standing on a tray rack, holding on with one hand, and with him a girl. DiPierro didn't get these details from Sandra Serrano. Whether the girl DiPierro saw was wearing a polka-dot dress or whether she was the same girl Miss Serrano saw was beside the point. What of the girl DiPierro saw? The one who "was standing up next to him on—behind, and she was holding on to the other end of the tray table and she—like—it looked like as if she was almost holding him"? The girl Sirhan turned to once "as though he did say something"? The girl who "smiled back at him"?

It was poor police work simply to wish her away, but that is exactly what the LAPD was doing. As Sergeant Hernandez told several witnesses in his canned spiel, the LAPD was trying to prove there was no conspiracy. For a time, Hernandez, for one, was trying to prove there was, but Deputy Chief Houghton told him to forget it, and Hernandez was nothing if not obedient.

Others in the department got the message: cool the conspiracy. Life was already complicated unnecessarily by the overactive imaginations of Sandra Serrano and Cynthia Kean and Everett Buckner. Buckner was the rangemaster at Fish Canyon who said he had seen Sirhan with a blonde on June 4. But investigators found Buckner's story full of discrepancies. The girl herself came forward and identified herself as Claudia Williams, a barmaid in the San Gabriel Valley with a husband and two children. She said a young man she had never seen before had responded to her request for help, showed her how to shoot her new gun, let her shoot his and then left. It was Sirhan. Did she tell Sirhan as Buckner had reported: "Get away from me, goddammit. Someone will recognize us!"? No, she certainly didn't.

Police did a little more checking on Buckner, discovered he was anxious to tell anyone who would buy him a drink all about the plot he had seen abuilding right in front of his eyes at Fish Canyon.

Finally, the police confronted Buckner with Claudia Williams. He was 98 percent sure she was the woman he'd seen with Sirhan. Was he sure what she'd said to Sirhan? No. "Since reconsidering," he told Sergeant Hank Hernandez, "I do not know what she said to him. But she said something."

"Uh-huh," said Hernandez.

Sergeant Hernandez didn't much like the Reverend Oliver Owen. He'd found Owen in San Francisco, given him a lengthy interrogation on the polygraph and found his answers far from satisfactory. But, instead of trying to figure out why Owen told the story he did, Hernandez moralized with him. "You're a preacher, a man of God, supposedly. What does the Bible say about lying?"

Owen responded automatically with a verse: "Psalms, 120 and 2. 'Deliver my soul from deceitful lips and a lying tongue.' " Hernandez got a little rough with Owen for quoting the Bible on the one hand and lying to the police on the other. Owen maintained he wasn't lying.

"You failed to identify Sirhan in ten photos," said Hernandez calmly. He pushed a picture toward Owen "That's not Sirhan."

Owen allowed as to how he could have been mistaken. "I said that has to be him because he looked it. It could be an incidence." (He meant coincidence.) "I—listen, I might be wrong. It might not be the guy. Maybe I picked up someone else. I don't know. I don't know. . . . If I saw him face-to-face, or heard his voice or something, then I would—I'd come out and make a definite statement. I don't know. It looks like him to me."

That didn't satisfy Hernandez. He told Owen he was lying when he said he had no record of arrests. Owen exploded. He rose to his feet and advanced on Hernandez, then raised his arms to the sky and cried, "Get me out of here, please God! God, please! Please, God, listen! Please God!"

"Try to calm yourself," said Hernandez, not moving a muscle.

"Oh, God help me!" shouted Owen. "God, help me. I'm not goin' to do it. I'm goin' to have a nervous breakdown, pret near."

"Just try to calm yourself."

"No! You're not going to talk to me like that."

Hernandez looked at him innocently. "How am I talking to you?"

"The way you are."

Hernandez paused. "There's no fool like an old fool," he said.

That roused Owen again. "Are you calling me a fool?" he demanded.

"No," said Hernandez.

"You know what the Bible says, 'If you call a man fool . . .' " Owen switched in midquote. "Do you want me to tell you who the biggest fool in the world is? Psalms 53 and 1, 'The fool hath said in his heart there is no God.' That's·the biggest fool in the world."

Hernandez was finished with Owen. He didn't think that Owen had ever seen or talked with Sirhan. Hernandez had ignored or dismissed as insignificant an incautious admission to the police on July 2 by Adel Sirhan that his brother Sirhan "wanted $300 to buy a horse with." His judgment was that Owen was simply "a blowhard." He asked Owen if he wanted to tell his attorney, George T. Davis, that he was lying, or did he want Hernandez to phone Davis right now? Owen sputtered.

"Just wait here," said Hernandez. He left the room, and while he was out, Owen delivered what he thought was a soliloquy, apparently to his attorney, George T. Davis:

"No! I'll tell you, George, what you ought to do. You're not going to get away with anything like this, George. Come on, George! No! No! I won't, George! They're doing everything to break me. No!"

Then, all of a sudden, Owen stopped speaking out, and trailed off in a mumble. When Hernandez returned, Owen asked him if the room was bugged. Hernandez evaded his question and wondered what it was that George T. Davis was trying "to get away with."

4:30 A.M., July 3. Saidallah Sirhan is driving north on the Pasadena Freeway. He has been in Los Angeles' Chinatown to see a reporter for the Los Angeles Free Press. Couldn't find her. Two cars follow him for about six miles. One is a Volkswagen bus with four men in it. The other is a green

1969 Chevrolet, with three men inside. Near the end of the freeway, in Pasadena, the two cars pull alongside, the VW on the right, the Chevrolet on the left. Then someone in the VW, possibly the driver, points a gun at Saidallah, and fires. The first shot strikes Saidallah's coat in the back seat. He ducks. The second zips over his head and buries itself in the door beside him. He pulls off the freeway, the two cars pull away from him, and he proceeds directly to the Pasadena police. That is Saidallah's story.

The police did not believe Saidallah. Knowing that Saidallah had already given them one false report—about a *Life* reporter and photographer who sent two toughs to beat him up in his apartment on Lake Street—they guessed this might well be another, calculated to draw further attention to a man who, amid all the notoriety attached to his family, was being sorely neglected. Saidallah believed he could sell "his story" for big money, but the *Free Press,* a cheap underground paper with the budget of a lemonade stand, seemed to be the best Saidallah could do.

The police examined Saidallah's car. Two neat bullet holes, side by side, in the wind wing. If Saidallah were going to pump two slugs into his own car, that was the cheapest place to do so. And that was pretty neat shooting at fifty miles per hour or more from a moving vehicle. One bullet in the wind wing, okay. But two? Not so likely. Furthermore, the bullet which landed in the door would have had to pass through Saidallah's body first if he had been sitting in the driver's seat.

The police gave him a lie detector test. Some of his answers—to key questions—were unsatisfactory. Still, Saidallah's charges were news and the implication—that someone was trying to do him violence—helped justify the twenty-four-hour police guard that had been established at the Sirhan residence. The Pasadena police informed the press about the shoot-out on the freeway and advised Saidallah to move in with the family.

In Rome, Bishara Sirhan, en route from Jerusalem to the United States to see his son, read the newspaper accounts of desperadoes shooting at his son Saidallah on the Pasadena Freeway and made a snap decision: it might be safer for him to return to Jerusalem and take his chances with the rapacious Zionists than subject himself to the cowboys of Pasadena. He caught the next plane back to Tel Aviv, and wrote Sirhan a letter postmarked Taybe:

> I am very angry with you for the deed you have committed and I don't encourage you or any other persons to kill another. Son, you forget all the bad

acts committed against the Arab people. Learn to forgive and forget what happened in the Palestine wars . . . Pray God and Jesus Christ.

Bishara made no mention of Sirhan's crime in any very direct manner. The closest he came was to write: "I am deep in sorrow from the incident that took place concerning you and Mr. Kennedy." He ended his letter with a combination of concern and anger:

> Are they torturing you, are they hitting you, are they belittling you or are they treating you well? Also, please tell me why did you appear on television strapped to a chair?

Sirhan had never appeared on television strapped to a chair, but those writing letters to Sirhan were not in notable contact with reality.

On the same day, Independence Day, July 4, someone from Daytona Beach, Florida, who signed himself "Wise American" wrote one of many fan letters to Sirhan:

> Sirhan Bishara Sirhan,
>
> You did a great service to the American Public in eliminating that sly-looking shanty Irishman in a fashion adopted by De Valera and his intolerant South of Ireland Roman Catholics who, when they disliked anyone, adopted the method you did to get rid of them. You also prevented that ugly intolerant wife of RFK from gracing the rooms of the White House; in her hot heated rage she bashed one of the persons wounded. A bitch totally unfit for our great White House. The bastards have been having kids almost every year of their marriage to satisfy the anti-Christ, the Pope of Rome, and the rotten Roman Catholic Church.
>
> No Roman Catholics for President of these U.S.

Dr. Eric Marcus paid a second call on Sirhan Sirhan, still incarcerated in the southwest wing of the New County Jail east of the railroad tracks. He found that Sirhan had not completed the screening tests he had left behind. Marcus shrugged. It made no difference, for he had already decided to employ a clinical psychologist to give Sirhan a complete battery of diagnostic tests.

He asked Sirhan about his notebooks. Marcus had been allowed to pore over them, and to him some of the pages seemed strikingly similar to certain mad writings he'd seen emanating from the state hospital for the insane at Atascadero. Marcus had done some reading on assassination in various medical journals—notably "Presidential Assassination Syndrome," by Dr. David A. Rothstein in the *Archives of General Psychiatry*. Rothstein had examined the records of nine inmates at the U.S. Medical Center for Federal Prisoners at Springfield, Missouri, who were serving terms for threatening the life of the President of the United States. And parts of Sirhan's notebook resembled the writings of these persons—all of them classified as schizophrenics. One of the Springfield prisoners (a man born in Italy) wrote: "I wish to advise that if the President of the United States resists my commands, I will bash his brains in alive. . . ." An earlier letter of his, sent to Russia and returned because it had an insufficient address, contained the comment that ". . . the capitalists are the Big Fish in the sea who eat up the people." And he also stated that he would like to give the President a different brain so he could understand how it felt when people did not have enough money to clothe and feed themselves properly.

Sirhan wrote, on page 123 of one of his notebooks:

> I advocate the overthrow of the current President of the fucken United States of America. I have no absolute plans yet, but soon will compose some. I am poor—this country's propaganda says that she is the best country in the world—I have not experienced this yet—the U.S.—says that life in Russia is bad . . . I believe that the U.S. is ready to start declining, not that it hasn't—it began in November 23, '63, but it should decline at a faster rate so that the real Utopia will not be too far from being realized during the early 70's in this country.

"What about these notebooks of yours?" asked Marcus. Sirhan said he had no recollection whatever of writing anything in the notebooks.

On numerous pages, Sirhan had written "Peggy Osterkamp" over and over again. Once, he had written, "I love you, Peggy," and in another place he had written "Peggy Osterkamp Peggy Osterkamp Peggy Osterkamp Peggy Sirhan." "Who," asked Marcus, "is Peggy Osterkamp?"

"Just a girl I met a few times at the ranch in Corona."

"That's all?"

"That's all."

"You ever date her?" Sirhan shook his head. Marcus turned to the night of the shooting and asked Sirhan about that. This time, Sirhan was more cooperative. He told Marcus the complete story he had told the public defender and Russell Parsons. When the range closed at 5:00 P.M. on June 4, Sirhan had not expended all his ammunition. He went to Bob's Big Boy and had a hamburger with a friend, a foreign student whose name (he told Marcus) he couldn't recall. They talked about horses and Sirhan showed him some bullets he had in his pocket. He read a notice in the paper about a Zionist rally on Wilshire Boulevard. He became very angry over this and decided to go to the parade. However, he could not find the parade and wandered instead into the campaign headquarters of Senator Kuchel. There, his mood improved, and he heard that there would be a good deal of excitement at the Ambassador Hotel nearby. When he got there, he was fascinated by the television lights. He went to a bar, but was refused a drink because he had no identification with him to certify that he was over twenty-one. He entered another bar and ordered two Tom Collinses at once. He gulped the first one down and sipped the other. He may have had another drink or two. He got dizzy and said to himself that he'd better go home. He was reluctant to drive, however, in the condition he was in and then, the next thing he remembered, he was being choked in the Ambassador pantry.

Marcus was unimpressed by the amnesia. He'd encountered too many accused murderers who claimed liquor-induced amnesia, only to discover later that other witnesses had found the men lucid before, during and after their crimes. Amnesia, Marcus knew, was a convenient and unsophisticated cover-up for something the defendant didn't want to remember.

Still, Marcus wanted to pursue the claimed drunkenness. He would suggest that Parsons obtain information about any blood alcohol tests which might have been taken after Sirhan's arrest. And he would request clearance with the authorities to give Sirhan an electroencephalogram under the influence of three Tom Collinses and allow him to interview Sirhan immediately afterward.

Something about this interview angered Sirhan. After Marcus left at 11:15 A.M., the sheriff's deputy on duty noted in the log that at 1:11 P.M. Sirhan started pounding on the wall of his cell.

Sunday, July 7. D day. Inspector Ralph Welch was given the word by Sheriff Pitchess to move Sirhan. He was ready. At 3:00 P.M., Welch put a heavy-duty station wagon through a rugged test in the parking lot of the New County Jail, trying all the gears, jamming the brakes on and off, turning the electrical system on and off, double-checking the gas and water and oil. At 3:30, three other sheriff's cars pulled into the parking lot. Undersheriff Bill McCloud and Inspector Welch—the only ones beside the sheriff who knew this was the time and the hour—moved nonchalantly up to the southwest wing of the infirmary and told Sirhan he was about to be moved. "Just listen to us very carefully," said Welch, "and do what we tell you and everything will be okay." He handcuffed Sirhan, took him down a never-used stairway on the south side of the infirmary into an alcove full of garden tools, surrounded by a high concrete wall. They passed through a crosshatched metal gate and into a courtyard, across a strip of lawn and over to the station wagon and three escort cars. Somehow, the prisoners on the third floor of the southeast wing of the jail knew that Sirhan was being moved. As Sirhan was helped into the back seat of the station wagon and told to lie down at the feet of three deputies, the prisoners started crying out through their bars: "KILL THE SON OF A BITCH! KILL THE SON OF A BITCH!"

McCloud hopped onto the front seat, and Welch got behind the wheel, started the car and backed up. He put the car in "drive" and stepped on the gas. The car continued to go backward. He couldn't get the damn thing out of reverse. With cries from the southeast wing of the jail still filling the heavens, Welch's surreptitious journey was already aborted and now he couldn't get the car in drive. He tried shifting two more times with no luck, then decided to waste no more time. He climbed out of the station wagon and commandeered one of the escort vehicles, transferred everyone into that car, a black and white sedan, and left the station wagon sitting there. He pulled out onto Bouchet Street, turned north on Vignes, went under the railroad overpass to Main and turned north. That took the caravan away from the Hall of Justice and McCloud looked nervously at Welch.

"It's okay," said Welch. He cut through a small, deserted section of the downtown industrial district toward Broadway with both escort cars following close behind. The route purposefully avoided the Sunday jam around Olvera Street. Broadway should have been clear. But suddenly, Welch found himself in the middle of some sort of Chinese parade, halted in the intersection of Sunset and Broadway by an auto accident in its path. Welch slowed almost to a stop, let one of the escort cars lead the way through a small opening in the traffic jam, stared straight ahead and squeezed through, afraid even to look at the standers-by.

Across Sunset, they were almost home. Up the hill to Temple, and around the Hall of Justice to the east side, through the gate and into a large dark tunnel, lighted with four small tungsten bulbs. It was the delivery entrance for the county morgue. Welch didn't stop at the morgue, but pulled the car up to a small elevator and slammed on the brakes. A team of deputies was waiting at the elevator, and the man who would be Sirhan's chief jailer for the next ten months, Lieutenant Craig Carpenter, took over.

By the time the FBI interviewed Jerry Owen in San Francisco on July 8, he had acquired two bodyguards—Ben Hardister, a private detective, and Wesley Gardner, a former deputy sheriff in Napa County. The body-guards were presumably with him because of some threats he said he'd received back home in Santa Ana, near Los Angeles ("Keep your mother fuckin' mouth shut about the horse deal," an unidentified caller had warned him on the phone.) But why were they with him here? Had he been threatened in the Bay Area? He didn't say.

"Go easy on him," Gardner told Special Agents Robert B. Herrington and H. Ernest Woodby. "He's been under sedation and he's kind of tired."

The agents told Gardner and Hardister to wait, then took Owen to an interrogation room to tell them about his activities on June 3, 4 and 5 in Los Angeles. Owen told the agents the same story he had told the LAPD, except for a few minor changes, and/or embellishments.

Though Owen avoided the press (a fact that tended to negate the LAPD theory that Owen was "a publicity seeker"), he consented to tell his story to a senior editor of *Ramparts* magazine, a former agent for the FBI named Bill Turner. And what did his story add up to? Despite the harassment he had received from Sergeant Hernandez, of the LAPD, Owen clung to the story that he was being set up as the unwitting driver of Sirhan's getaway vehicle, a plan he claimed he had foiled by failing to appear on election night at the Ambassador.

Turner and a colleague named Jonn Christian, a bright, bearded fellow with a conspiratorial view of history, followed up on Owen's story. Christian found a friend of Owen named Jonathan Perkins, an elderly preacher who lived in the Embassy Hotel in Los Angeles. "Yes," Perkins told Christian, "I remember those days quite well. Curly said he went to that spot and the kid never showed up."

"What spot?" asked Christian.

"On Catalina Street, near the Ambassador."

"When?"

"On the night Kennedy was killed. About 11:00 P.M."

Later, when Christian was told that Owen had flunked his lie detector test by the LAPD, Christian replied that he had known Owen was lying all along. This only proved his suspicions that there was more of a tie between Owen and Sirhan than the police believed.

Walter Crowe sat down with Sergeant Hank Hernandez at Parker Center full of apprehension about this meeting. He didn't want to be there. What good would it do him? And yet, he didn't want to refuse compliance either. That would only give the police some reason to think he was part of a Communist conspiracy to kill Robert Kennedy.

Hernandez explained he was giving Crowe a polygraph test to clear up the record. He said that the LAPD was anxious to tie up every loose end so that, if someone wanted to write a book in twenty years about the Sirhan conspiracy, he couldn't say the police had ignored Walter Crowe. Then he asked Crowe twelve key questions and found "deceptive physiological responses" to three of them:

"If I ask you questions about Sirhan, will you tell me the truth?"

"Yes, sir," said Crowe. The needle jumped.

"When you talked with Sirhan [on the night of May 2], did he tell you he was planning to shoot Senator Kennedy?"

"No." Again the needle jumped.

"Did Sirhan ever tell you he was planning to shoot Kennedy?"

"No." The needle jumped a third time.

Hernandez looked searchingly at Crowe. "Is there some other question that you are afraid I will ask you during this test?"

"Yes," stammered Crowe. On that reply, he was telling the truth.

Hernandez shut off the polygraph. Crowe noticed that Hernandez was excited, on edge with expectation. Crowe, too, was nervous and he fumbled for a cigarette. Hernandez jumped to light it for him. "I would say that I have to share the guilt," said Crowe.

Hernandez wondered why Crowe felt so guilty. "Is there anything that you discussed, discussed with Sirhan that could have been something that induced him or helped him to do the deed that he did do?"

"I'm—I'm sure there must have been," stammered Crowe. "That's very important, isn't it? Right. You know, revolutionary—you know, plain revolutionary influence. I was right there. I'm—you know, I was—you know, you know—an influence on his life."

Hernandez wondered if Crowe could recall more of that conversation on the night of May 2.

That was difficult for Crowe because he didn't like the implications of what Sirhan had said. "Now—I mean, he said that, geez, you know, I mean, he said that to be a revolutionary, you know, it requires a total commitment."

"What did this mean to you, Walter?"

"It was bullshit."

"No, but when he said this, you have to have total commitment, what did this mean to you?"

" 'I am more of a revolutionary than you are.' You know. That's what it meant to me. But it was, you know, it wasn't for real. He wasn't living that way. He wasn't doing those things in his daily life and so it was just—it was talk, you know."

But then again, maybe it wasn't just talk. With prodding from Hernandez, Crowe admitted: "I told him that the Arab-Israeli struggle was akin to a national liberation struggle."

"And how do you think this had an effect on him deciding to shoot Kennedy?"

"Well, I don't know if that—you know, I don't know if that did or not. Actually, I don't know that any of it did. I just don't know. But speculating on telling him that Al Fatah had given new respect to Arab people and morale—we could expect, you know, long internal struggle in Israel. That it would be like a liberation struggle. I mean, that—that could have put some ideas in his head. Terrorism."

"So he says, 'Well, then it's up to me.' He probably could have very easily said, 'Well, it's up to me to—' "

"Right."

" '—do it here.' "

"Right. Right. Exactly. That's it. You know that he could have seen himself," said Crowe, "as a fighter."

"Well, Walter, it's late. I appreciate the fact that you—you have indicated to me you want to go home. No report will be made, I'll tell you this. However, I do have to continue talking to you and I can tell you this on my own right now. In all honesty to you, no report will be made."

Crowe's lip curled. "You guys say one thing and you do another." He leaned back and reflected to himself about the twists and turns this interview had taken. He was very unhappy. He decided that Hernandez was a God damn son of a bitch, and told him so.

Hernandez stood. "Now, Walter, you've told me you're nonviolent. You've told me you're a gentleman. Now, look at yourself, Walter." Hernandez walked out of the room. Crowe sat there, shaking, sweating a little bit, staring at the wall.

Dr. George Y. Abe, a psychiatrist and the director of the Metropolitan State Hospital at Norwalk, California, came to see Sirhan on July 12 and 13. He was the second of the psychiatrists appointed by the court under Sections 730 and 952 of the Evidence Code of the State of California as an adviser to the lawyers for the defense, and a stolid professional of Japanese-American background who, like Dr. Marcus, served on the Superior Court panel of psychiatrists.

He found Sirhan affable enough and so cooperative that he believed the prisoner was enjoying the attention, apparently fascinated with the idea of another psychiatric examination. "Seems like a game," he told Dr. Abe. "Like a scientific experiment."

Through the first long interview, Sirhan told Abe about the night of the assassination, and he told Dr. Abe about his political philosophy, which, to Abe, was rigidly anti-Zionist. "The Zionists in this country," Sirhan said, "have money and power and any political candidate who wants to win has to listen to them." Kennedy listened to them, Sirhan maintained. Nevertheless, he would have voted for Kennedy, "because Kennedy was for the underdog." Abe was puzzled by that, and noted as he left the jail that Sirhan had "paranoid-inclined ideations, particularly in the political sphere, but there is no evidence of outright delusions or hallucinations."

On the following day, Abe asked Sirhan to tell him about his early life, and helped him remember key details with a standard set of questions. Abe turned up a chain of childhood neuroses: Sirhan wet the bed, he had bitten his nails all his life, had repetitive nightmares of walking into a great darkness, and feared walking into a dark room, was squeamish about killing bugs, was overly fussy about his food, and didn't care to swim because he felt shy and sensitive about exposing himself. His parents were both "disciplined" and his father was very strict and unreasonable at times. When his father left the family in 1957, Sirhan maintained he did not feel any sense of loss because he was "too preoccupied with getting along in America."

Though Sirhan seemed breezy enough during the interviews, they obviously upset him. He sat up most of the night in an anteroom to his cell, staring at the wall and wondering whether Dr. Abe would think he was crazy. The deputy on duty noted that Sirhan was talking to the wall and slamming it with his elbow. Did Dr. Abe think he was crazy?

Sergeants L. L. Sandlin and Thomas Strong, Special Unit, Senator, Los Angeles Police Department, paid their umpteenth visit to the Sirhan family in Pasadena. They were still trying to clear up the Jerry Owen file, and had asked Adel Sirhan to talk to his brother about the preacher who said he was with Sirhan on June 3.

"I asked Sirhan these questions," said Adel. "Sirhan didn't recall anything there. Sirhan never hitchhiked. He was never in, down in that area—"

"On Monday, June the 3rd?"

"Monday he was here all day long. All day and all night long. He was here Sunday also. That's what he told me."

Sirhan was lying. Later, he told his attorneys about some of his movements on June 2 and 3. But the police were anxious to close the Owen file and they would later use Sirhan's denial to help them do just that.

Sergeant Sandlin was glad Adel "cleared this up." Then he asked Adel if Sirhan attended a Kennedy rally in Pomona on May 25.

Adel said quickly, too quickly, "Nah."

"I just wondered if he might have mentioned it," said Sergeant Sandlin.

"We have a possible witness," said Sergeant Strong.

"I doubt that very much. The 25th?"

"—of May," said Sergeant Strong. "I think that was on a Tuesday." Strong and Sandlin had their dates wrong. Kennedy was in Pomona on May 20, not May 25.

"He very seldom went anyplace," said Adel. "Hardly, you know."

"Why should we bother ourselves?" said Mrs. Sirhan. "These things nobody knows but Sirhan himself and there will be time, so you can ask him when the time comes. I feel like I should not say one word. I'm sorry."

"I'm sorry you feel that way," said Sandlin, "because actually if you'll think back over our past conversations, I don't think that we've asked you anything that has—would be detrimental to him at all."

"Don't you go and give your report to the district attorney?" asked Mrs. Sirhan.

"No, ma'am," lied Sergeant Sandlin. "This is police department business. I give them nothing."

Mrs. Sirhan eyed Sandlin skeptically. "How can I—but how can I believe you?"

"Well," said Adel, "that's your business if you don't believe him."

"I'll tell you one thing now, Mrs. Sirhan," said Sergeant Sandlin. "I won't lie to you. The district attorney has his own staff of investigators, you see. I don't have to give them any. They've got their own sources."

"That's good," said Mrs. Sirhan. The officers and the Sirhans spent some time congratulating one another on their mutual honesty.

"We all know this," said Sergeant Sandlin, "that the truth, the truth has never hurt anyone about anything."

"And there's nothing but the truth," said Sharif Sirhan.

"And let's be honest with each other. Now, a lie will go around the world six times while the truth is getting its pants on."

"Right," said Sharif.

"I wonder," said Mrs. Sirhan, "if sometimes the truth will be exactly the truth. Now, it is not because Sirhan is my son. If you go to him since he was a little baby, there is not—I don't remember—or he gave me a problem or make me—not one trouble."

"He has no record," said Adel.

"He's never been in trouble," said Mrs. Sirhan.

"I don't think he was ever even engaged in a fight," said Adel.

"He never, never," said Mrs. Sirhan.

"He went to work," said Adel. "He was a model all over the place."

"All over," said Mrs. Sirhan. "Wherever he goes. And you—I think you found that out already. The manager of the school, he says he's a genius. Every year he goes up, up, up, up and he goes—when he was only eleven years old he was through with all these elementary and beginning to the secondary."

The officers knew Sirhan was only average in school, but they went along with the game. Sergeant Strong told the Sirhans he prayed for them every night, and Sergeant Sandlin reminded them that they had become very good friends.

Russell Parsons' investigator, Michael McCowan, pored over a pile of books given him by Adel Sirhan—Sirhan Sirhan's own collection, some of them obviously stolen from the Muir High School library or the Pasadena Public Library. McCowan's initial reaction to Sirhan's books was unsympathetic. "This guy," said McCowan, "is a fuckin' Communist."

For this judgment, there was pretty slim evidence. Sirhan had a book called *History Will Absolve Me* by Fidel Castro, which—judging from a stamp on the inside front cover—had come from something called the "Fair Play for Cuba Committee," a onetime affiliation of Lee Harvey Oswald. Another book called *New University Thought,* an anthology, had one chapter in it full of underlined and framed passages concerned with U.S. policy toward Cuba. The rest of the books were hardly Communistic. One of them was a book on Gandhi by Louis Fischer.*

Most of them dealt with the science of the mind, mysticism and the occult. *The Power of Positive Thinking,* by Norman Vincent Peale. *The Faith of Great Scientists,* an anthology. *The Edinburgh Lectures on Men-*

---

* Sirhan had written "profound" next to a passage that read: "The British were masters in somebody else's home. Their very presence was a humiliation. . . . Even if the British had converted India into a land flowing with milk and honey, they would have been disliked. Imperialism, like dictatorship, fears the soul, degrades the spirit and makes individuals small, the better to rule them. Fear and cowardice are its allies. Imperialism is government of other people, by other people, and for other people. . . . Subjection stimulated a desire for liberation . . . history has known no good colonizers. Every empire digs its own grave. Imperialism is a perpetual insult, for it assumes that the outsider has the right to rule the insiders who cannot rule themselves; . . ."

tal Science, by Thomas Troward. *Meditations on the Occult Life,* by G. Hodson. *The Astral Plane,* by C. W. Leadbetter. *Cyclomancy: The Secret of Psychic Power Control,* by Frank Rudolph Young.

In these books there were no indications what passages Sirhan had favored. But *Isis Unveiled* by Madame Helena Blavatsky was, according to McCowan's report, heavily underlined for the first 477 pages. Some 225 pages that remained were unmarked.

McCowan noted that *The Integrity of Personality,* by Anthony Storr, had "Sirhan" scrawled on the inside front cover, in Sirhan's hand. Evidently, he had challenged several significant passages in Storr's book. On page 25:

> The pursuit of the millennium, as Professor Cohen has recently demonstrated, is not only a mythical but also a destructive question to which men become ready to sacrifice not only their lives but those of others to an illusion and to annihilate their fellows in the name of brotherly love.

Sirhan had placed a question mark in the margin next to that and three question marks beside a sentence on page 34:

> The more isolated a man is, the less he is an independent personality.

And on page 43, Sirhan wrote "profound" beside a sentence that read:

> To identify with another person is to lose one's self, to submerge one's own identity in that of another, to be overwhelmed, and hence to treat one's self ultimately as less than a whole person.

And then there was *The Law of Mentalism,* by A. Victor Segno. Underlined on page 16:

> What is a fact to one is an unreality to another. . . .

and on page 71:

> Many a genius is ruined by his first success.

In a book called *Readings for College Writers,* purchased in the Pasadena City College bookstore on January 30, 1964, Sirhan gave some indication that he might have been thinking dark thoughts even then, four and a half years before he killed Senator Kennedy. Sirhan marked a passage that read: "The enemy is not necessarily a bad man. Indeed, he may be a man of high character and considerable good will." And on page 331, he dared a bold answer to a rhetorical question. "There is therefore no escape from the choice that lies before us. Shall we renounce war or shall we bring our species to an end?" Sirhan replied: "The latter." It was a sentiment that paralleled a thought on page 21 of Sirhan's own notebook, probably written on June 2, 1967, for that was the date at the top of the page:

> A Declaration of War Against American Humanity
> when in the course of human events it has become
> necessary for me to equalize and seek revenge for
> all the inhuman treatment committed against me by
> the American people. the manifestation of this
> Declaration will be executed by its supporter (s)
> as soon as he is able to command a sum of money
> ($2,000) and to acquire some firearms—the
> specification of which have not been established yet.

> The victims of the party in favor of this declaration
> will be or are *now*—the President, vice, etc.—
> down the ladder.

> The time will be chosen by the author at the
> convenience of the accused.

> the method of assault is immaterial—however the
> type of weapon used should influence it somehow.

> the author believes that many in fact multitudes
> of people are in harmony with his thoughts and feelings

> the conflict and violence in the world subsequent to
> the enforcement of this decree, shall not be
> considered likely by the author of this memoranda,
> rather he hopes that they be the initiatory military
> steps to WW III—the author expresses his wishes
> very bluntly that he wants to be recorded by history
> as the *man* who triggered off the last war—

There was other evidence in Sirhan's books that he had been thinking about violence applied to the political order when he was still in high school. In *A History of the American People,* by David Saville Muzzey, Sirhan had underlined a paragraph on the assassination of President McKinley:

> It was his last public utterance. The next day, as he was holding a reception in the Temple of Music, he was shot by a young Polish anarchist named Czolgosz, whose brain had been inflamed by reading the tirades of the yellow press against "Czar McKinley." After a week of patient suffering the President died,—the third victim of an assassin's bullet since the Civil War.

Below that, Sirhan wrote: "and many more will come." Another book, the *Transformation of Modern Europe,* from the John Muir High School Library, by Louis Gottschalk and Donald Lash, summed up the assassination of the Archduke Ferdinand, and someone, presumably Sirhan, underlined most of the paragraph:

> It is conceivable that if the chauffeur of the Archduke's car, having taken the wrong road on the way back from the official reception at the town hall, had not backed up to correct his error, the assassin would not have been successful. On the other hand, another assassin might have been, because the plot to kill the Archduke had been carefully laid under the direction of the colonel in charge of the intelligence division of the Serbian general staff, and more than one assassin was lying in wait that day.

These passages clearly prove that Sirhan had had assassination on the brain from the time he did the underscoring and wrote the notations. The only question was: did Sirhan really do the underscoring and if so, when? Russell Parsons did not care to know. He ordered McCowan to make no mention of these in his report and hid the books on a lower shelf in his office. To Parsons, these passages only proved one thing: premeditation. This was evidence best left unrevealed.

On July 19, James Earl Ray, the assassin of Martin Luther King, a man whose name would be linked in the press with Sirhan's for the duration of the case, was flown from London in an Air Force jet to Memphis, Tennessee, met by a caravan of police vehicles and taken downtown to the Criminal Courts Building. It was shortly after 4:00 A.M. when Ray arrived in a parking area thick with uniformed police and plainclothesmen carrying shotguns, machine guns and carbines. Ray's hands were manacled in front of him to a special belt, and he wore a bulletproof vest that looked like a chasuble. A picture wired around the world by The Associated Press showed a gloomy-looking Ray with his head sunk far down on his breast.

A picture of Sirhan Sirhan, taken later that same day on the thirteenth floor of Los Angeles County's Hall of Justice and given the same worldwide wirephoto treatment, showed Sirhan with his head high, smiling brightly. Parsons had told him in his cell to cooperate with the news photographers and TV cameramen shooting for the news pool. Sirhan's first reaction to this request was slightly negative ("Fuck 'em," he said to Parsons), but he obviously had changed his mind.

Exactly 100 members of the press, including an array of artists sketching the principals for the evening's television news, filled the new 46′ × 50′ courtroom after the usual shakedown. A frieze of uniformed deputies stood around the perimeter of the room, the windows of which were shielded from the outside by one-quarter-inch armored plate. Extra deputies were posted at every entrance and exit to the building, and a helicopter carrying armed deputies fluttered protectively over the Hall of Justice. Today was the day when Sirhan would enter his plea.

Judge Schauer asked Parsons what his plea would be. Parsons told the judge he still hadn't received the psychiatrists' reports and asked the court's permission for Dr. Marcus to get some help in the persons of Dr. O. Roderick Richardson, a clinical psychologist, and Dr. Edward Davis, a neurologist, who would submit Sirhan to some tests in his cell. Schauer gave the permission and set August 2 as a firm date for the plea and the setting of a trial date. Though the postponements were not at all unusual in the criminal court, the public, which usually ignored such matters, would begin to pressure the County Board of Supervisors with querulous comment on the delays. Cooper, of course, was still tied up with the Friars' Club affair in Federal Court.

On August 2, Parsons appeared with Sirhan in the makeshift courtroom on the thirteenth floor to enter a plea of not guilty—no surprise to the district attorney's office, which knew that the plea could always be changed. "Not guilty" was the best kind of temporizing plea until Cooper came into the case. In the meantime Evelle Younger, the district attorney himself, was in court that day to argue against the order forbidding his office (among others) to talk to the press about the Sirhan case.

Younger claimed that he wanted the freedom to tell the public there was no conspiracy to kill Senator Kennedy. "If irresponsible sources suggest through the news media the existence of a national or international conspiracy," Younger stated, "responsible law-enforcement authorities ought to be allowed to discredit the purported claim." But of course no one had made any serious claims about a conspiracy. What Younger wanted (it was an open secret around the courthouse) was free rein to comment on the Sirhan case before trial and thereby gain the kind of national publicity that would further his own political ambitions. At one time, he had his aim set on being Governor of California. Now, with Ronald Reagan firmly seated in Sacramento, and Lieutenant Governor Robert Finch next in line, and a new-breed Republican like Houston Flournoy waiting in the state comptroller's office, Younger set his sights elsewhere. During the Presidential campaign, he'd presided over a special citizens' commission for candidate Richard Nixon on law and order. Some of Younger's friends said Younger had high hopes of becoming the Attorney General of the United States.

Parsons and A. L. Wirin, who appeared as a "friend of the court," opposed Younger's motion with a simple citation of the Supreme Court's decision on the Sam Sheppard case, and Judge Richard Schauer hardly gave the matter a second thought before he agreed with Parsons and Wirin and denied Younger.

Schauer had a simple operating principle and clear directives from the highest court in the land: the principle that a defendant—even an accused assassin—is innocent until proved guilty in a court of law, and not in the court of public opinion. The precedent was *Sheppard* vs. *Maxwell* (384 US 333). In 1954, Dr. Sheppard was convicted of second-degree murder for the killing of his wife and sentenced to life imprisonment in the Ohio State Penitentiary. In 1966, the U.S. Supreme Court reversed that conviction and ordered Sheppard released from custody on the grounds that he was denied due process—that is, convicted by a jury beleaguered by outside influences. The U.S. Supreme Court agreed with the Ohio Supreme Court that:

> Murder and mystery, society, sex and suspense were combined in this case in such a manner as to intrigue and captivate the public fancy to a degree per- haps unparalleled in recent annals. Throughout the pre-indictment investiga- tion, the subsequent legal skirmishes and the nine-week trial, circulation-con- scious editors catered to the insatiable interest of the American public in the bizarre. . . . In this atmosphere of a "Roman holiday" for the news media, Sam Sheppard stood trial for his life.

The U.S. Supreme Court didn't censure the press. It did blame the trial judge for allowing such a situation to develop. The judge could have lim- ited the number of reporters at the trial, insulated the witnesses to prevent their testimony from being revealed in the press before the trial and, above all, prohibited the release of information by police officers, witnesses and lawyers on both sides.

To let District Attorney Eville Younger speak out, then, in a case of this magnitude, where his every word would be reported verbatim, would amount to trial by mass media, make it impossible to find an unprejudiced jury and surely lead to reversal in the higher courts and a new trial for Sir- han.

But Younger persisted. Through the summer and fall, he appealed Schauer's decision to the Second Appellate District Court of Appeals and to both the California and the U.S. Supreme Courts. All the courts turned him down, for none of his arguments could counter those of Joseph A. Ball, one of California's most respected attorneys and a member of the Warren Commission, whom the Superior Court chose to prepare its brief against Younger's appeals. Said Ball: "At the time of trial the District At-

torney will have full opportunity in his opening statement and in presenting his evidence to inform the jury and the public. . . . If the District Attorney has information which he feels is nonprejudicial and needs to be
disseminated to the press at this time, he can apply to the court for permission to do so. . . . The only feasible procedure is to limit disclosure
until such time as the information is disclosed to the court and the defendant has had an opportunity to object to its dissemination to the press."

While the authorities maintained their silence about the case, enterprising reporters like Fernando Faura tried to develop their own leads. Faura
was convinced that Robert Duane had really run into a coconspirator in the
assassination of Robert Kennedy, and that Duane could lead him to the
mystery girl in the polka-dot dress. He took Duane's description of the girl
to an artist in Long Beach who made a tentative sketch, then took the artist to see Duane. He offered a few suggestions, the artist made the corrections and Faura had the sketch photographed in color.

The *Life* bureau in Los Angeles thought Faura's theories worth a test,
and set out with Faura to find the girl. Maybe she was still in the area of
the Ambassador Hotel. *Life* reporters, with copies of the Duane-Faura
sketch, roamed the area. Finally, success. Fernando Faura found the girl at
the Sheraton West near the Ambassador and called for Bureau Chief Jordan Bonfante and a free-lance photographer, Julian Wasser.

Bonfante and Wasser stalked the girl in her hotel lobby, and Wasser
moved in bravely, snapping away with his Leica. The girl, who was supposed to be hiding from the police, reacted unpredictably. She called the
police.

"Girl in the polka-dot dress, huh?" fumed Wasser to Bonfante as they
awaited questioning in the detective bureau at Rampart.

"She *looked* like the girl in the picture," said Bonfante. At first Bonfante was abashed and angry, but then, as the humor of the situation
struck him, he roared with delight.

"She *looked* like the girl in the picture," he later told Fernando Faura.

"Well," shrugged Faura, "she was just a look-alike, that's all." Faura
decided, however, to double-check his sketch with Thomas Vincent Di-
Pierro.

"That's her," said DiPierro. "She's the girl in the polka-dot dress. The
girl's face is a little fuller than this sketch has it, but this is the girl."

That was all Faura needed. He persuaded Duane they were onto something that would make them both heroes, and took him to Chris Gugas,

one of L.A.'s best polygraph examiners. Gugas had insisted on a thorough briefing before the test, and when Faura arrived with Duane, Gugas let Faura pace the floor outside his inner sanctum while Gugas put Duane through the test in private.

"How'd he do?" asked Faura anxiously after the test.

Gugas played it like a medical technician. "Patience, patience. I'll let you know tomorrow."

The results, apparently, were good, for Faura phoned Duane the next night and told him: "You passed, Bob. You passed the test. You passed it like a champion." With that, Duane became more confident in what he had seen and heard. So did Faura and so did Bonfante. What more did Duane recall? Well, not much more, not much at all. So Faura took Duane to a doctor who specialized in hypnosis. Maybe Duane could be induced to remember more.

Duane approached this test with reluctance and some skepticism. He really didn't believe the doctor could do anything for his memory and he was afraid of possible side effects. As it turned out, the side effects were good: the ache in Duane's jaw from recent oral surgery stopped. And Duane's memory was given a boost, for, under Faura's questioning, he suddenly remembered that the girl told him she was leaving Los Angeles for San Jose where, she said, she would visit the headquarters of some organization called the Rosalyns, or something like that.

"San Jose?" cried Faura. "The Rosicrucians?"

"Yeah," said Duane. "That's it. The Rosicrucians."

In the first week of August, Parsons summoned another enterprising reporter—me—downtown to discuss the case. I found Parsons less formidable in person than he'd appeared on TV. He had a gray face and a back beginning to hump with age and a gray suit he might have purchased at a thrift shop on Broadway. "This," said Parsons, in a resonant, almost hammy voice, "is the greatest story in the world." He was referring, I gathered, to the Sirhan story. It might be, I thought, but it wasn't anything until someone sat down to write it.

"I'd like to write it," I said.

"You and two hundred other guys," said Parsons.

I reminded Parsons—somewhat cruelly—that he wasn't running the case, Cooper was.

"You're still in the picture," said Parsons, unable to withstand an attack like that. "What do you want to do?"

I told him what I wanted—a wide-ranging interview in which Sirhan would talk about himself, his family, growing up in America, the state of the world, his hopes, his fears, in short, whatever he felt strongly about—and how I hoped to do it, and how such an interview might help pay for the expenses of the case.

Parsons nodded. "Nobody's taking up a collection to help this boy. That's a cinch." But he had a problem. The protection of his client came first. Since he'd taken the case, he'd permitted no one, not the police nor the district attorney nor the FBI to talk to his client. How could he trust me? How could he trust me not to leap in print with damaging material before the trial? Or, if he could trust me to mark time, how could he prevent the district attorney from issuing me a subpoena and making me testify? His solution to the second difficulty was ingenious, but relatively simple: he would make me an investigator, a secretary and clerk for the defense, which would bind me into the confidential lawyer-client relationship, something Cooper had had in mind all along. Despite this move, Parsons never gave any indication that he completely trusted me. But he was stuck with me.

Parsons took me out for coffee. Two little black boys appeared to be joyriding on the automatic elevators. Instead of being annoyed, as I was, Parsons dug into his pocket and gave each of them a quarter.

"What do you want out of all this?" I asked Parsons over coffee. "Fame or—?"

"Money, dammit," said Parsons. "Money. I said I would take this case without fee, but we've got expenses. I'd like to bring a psychiatrist here from Chicago and we need some other expert witnesses, and . . ."

Parsons, it turned out, talked about money much of the time—probably because he had a guilty conscience for handling it so badly. Mike McCowan joined the kaffeeklatsch. He was a natty Irishman with clear blue eyes and a roguish smile.

"You know that man who was in to see you a half hour ago?" asked McCowan.

"Yes?" said Parsons.

"You forgot to ask him for a retainer."

"Yes, I guess I did."

"I asked him for it," said McCowan offhandedly and handed Parsons a check, then burst into laughter at the look on Parsons' face. Though Parsons dreamed of money, he was surprised whenever any came his way and he would get very little here. What Parsons would really acquire for himself in the Sirhan case was the kind of recognition he'd always needed and never attained. A good trial lawyer is, of necessity, a good actor and he has the normal actor's sensitivity to public attention. Now, though Parsons had given fifty years of his life to criminal law, few singled him out for special praise—possibly because few are inclined to laud those working for the burglars, bookmakers, madames, murderers and extortionists whose activities draw the unusually zealous interests of the police.

In theory, most citizens who watch Perry Mason on television agree with the idea that everyone in America has a right to "equal protection under the law" and "due process." In practice, policemen haven't worried too much about those abstractions. They play cops and robbers and they play to win, because in real life the objects of their pursuit are not the kind of invariably innocent clients Perry Mason seems to draw. "Evidence?" asked Parsons. "The judge never asked the police how they got it. The only question he asked was, 'Did you have it?' That was the only question."

Parsons helped change that with an appeal brief to the California Supreme Court on behalf of a bookmaker named Charley Cahan whose business—conducted from his plush Hollywood apartment—could hardly stand the intrusion of a dozen police microphones beaming Charley's most private conversations to their tape recorders in the next apartment. Parsons argued that this violated the fourth amendment to the U.S. Constitution—that a man's home is his castle and no one could cross his threshold without his permission. The California Supreme Court agreed and reversed Cahan's conviction. On August 5, 1961, the U.S. Supreme Court upheld the reversal and set forth a ruling that evidence obtained illegally, even by the police, could not be used in local or Federal trials in the United States. "Cahan was later convicted for second-degree robbery," reported Parsons, with a glint in his eye. "But the cops got him legally that time."

"The law is designed for the protection of every poor bastard in the country," said Parsons. "If it can't protect a Cahan, it might not protect you." Parsons recalled the case of Edward John Caruso, a large (six feet, one inch, 238 pounds) mechanic who was tried in 1965 for a $3,500 holdup in North Hollywood, even though three reliable witnesses had testified that he was talking with them at the time of the robbery in a restaurant forty miles away. The trouble was that on the morning after the robbery the two victims fingered Caruso in a police lineup. Result: a conviction for Caruso. When Parsons took the man's appeal, he looked into the question of that lineup and discovered that the four other men in the lineup were a head shorter and a hundred pounds lighter than Caruso, and two of them were blond, to boot, while Caruso had jet-black hair. "Didn't that make it hard for the witnesses to finger anybody *but* Caruso?" asked Parsons, in effect, in his appeal brief. "Yes," answered the California Supreme Court in a 1968 decision. Since that ruling, when police hold a lineup for identification purposes, they must assemble a group of men who bear some rough ethnic and physical resemblance to one another.

"Yes," admitted Parsons, in falsely sepulchral tones, "I am one of the guys who put handcuffs on the police." But McCowan, who had been a Los Angeles policeman for ten years, pointed out that Parsons had no grudge against the cops. He had helped clear nineteen of twenty policemen charged with various malfeasance, and the twentieth was then on appeal before the U.S. Supreme Court.

Russell Parsons told Sheriff Peter Pitchess he was employing a new investigator to help him with the Sirhan case. Who? Robert Kaiser. The sheriff deferred approval. He wanted to run a check on Kaiser. Without too much difficulty, the sheriff's investigators found ample information right in their own files, for I had had sheriff's press credentials when I was a correspondent in Los Angeles for *Time*. And, interestingly, my name was in the Sirhan investigation file. A report by the Pasadena Police Department indicated that one of Sirhan's older brothers, Saidallah, had told officers that I had interviewed him on the evening of June 5 shortly before two strange men had entered his apartment, threatened him with violence if he didn't cooperate with *Life* magazine and beat him up a little to show him what they had in store. If Kaiser had had anything to do with that violence, reasoned the sheriff's office, he shouldn't be allowed near the high-security chambers of Sirhan Sirhan. Parsons was asked to bring me in for a personal interview.

"Mr. Kaiser is one of my investigators," Parsons told Assistant Sheriff Jim Downey. Downey smiled at the transparency of Parsons' ruse. I told Downey what had happened with Saidallah on the evening of June 5. "We'll check it out," said Downey. "We'll check it out."

Dr. O. Roderick Richardson entered Sirhan's cell with some trepidation. Dr. Marcus had told him that Sirhan was apt to be sullen and uncommunicative—which he was with Marcus. Marcus was Jewish, of course, and that was undoubtedly off-putting to Sirhan. In addition, he was a small fellow with dainty, almost girlish manners. Richardson was a tall burly WASP with a handsome smile, and he moved into the cell like the athlete he was, for he had won all-county honors playing high-school football in San Jose. Maybe it was the contrast with Marcus that did it. At any rate, Sirhan ushered Richardson in as if he were Nasser himself, apologized for his inability to provide more comfort and seemed eager to cooperate with the test. He sat on the edge of his narrow bed and gave Richardson a heavy wooden chair.

Richardson was momentarily taken aback, and, while he was gathering his aplomb, he decided to administer the Rorschach inkblot test before Sirhan tired of the battery he was about to receive, for the Rorschach was the most valuable of them all. A good Rorschach test can give a psychologist perhaps a deeper insight into the patient than any of the series of perhaps thirty to forty tests currently at his disposal. In a Rorschach, the subject is merely supposed to say what he "sees" in the ink blots. The blots are, of course, only blots. But that is why the test is considered so valuable, for the cooperative patient is forced to verbalize not what he sees outside himself, but rather something of that mass of impressions, thoughts, judgments, fears and hopes that lie inside himself, sometimes so deeply inside and so guarded that they "come out" only in this indirect and necessarily unreflective way.

Sirhan didn't disappoint the doctor. "I was afraid I'd get into the most important case in my life and find my patient telling me they just looked like a lot of ink blots to him. Instead, he came through with a torrent of response."

In Ink Blot No. 1 (see Appendix E for reproductions of the ten standard Rorschach inkblots), Sirhan saw nine different items, and Richardson let him go. A chicken. A butterfly in flight. A frog. Two doves. A coastline. Mountains. Clouds. Cliffs. A bowl. Later, Richardson would ask him where he had seen all these things, but the only accepted method calls for the patient to go through all of the cards first.

On Card 2, Sirhan saw a crown, a diamond, a space satellite, a blood smear on a microscope thing, a cross, blood, a face of a person, an elephant or a bear. On Card 3, dancers, lungs, cauliflower, sternum, rooster. On Card 4, underwater plantations—plant life—kelp, a medieval castle —abandoned, an X ray of the chest, abdominal muscles, very dark— serpents, an animal on hind legs, the hoof of an animal. On Card 5, a big eagle, a chicken leg—fried chicken, horns—like the ears of a kangaroo, a ballet dancer, a seal. On Card 6, a cat, another chicken, a lamp, a rocket, an owl, high altitude, the bust of a female, the claws of an eagle or predatory bird, walking in a very dense forest, a lot of foliage, vertebrae. On

Card 7, a monkey with tail, stuffed bears, a jigsaw puzzle, a dam, a canal, a map of Egypt, a river delta, towers. On Card 8, the California bear, flags, the spine, a desert plant, guns—mortars, boats. By now, Sirhan was becoming somewhat upset, and he put his head in his hands while he talked about the last two cards. On Card 9, plant life under a microscope, apples, fire. "It's weird," he said, shaking his head. "Whew! It has depth. It's too deep. Whew!" Cards 8, 9 and 10 were in color and it was the color that upset Sirhan. On Card 10, he said, "This whole color! It throws me off! Monsters!" He paused a full sixty seconds. "It's really about all on this one?" Sirhan asked, as if to be let off then and there.

"You seem upset," said Richardson.

"It's frightening. It frightens me. They all seem the same. Wickedness! Too many entaglements! Blood!" Sirhan grimaced and put the card away quickly.

On a second go-round, Richardson asked for clarifications. On Card 1, he asked where Sirhan had seen the chicken. "It's the whole thing," Sirhan replied, and pointed to the middle of it, "this being the center. I've eaten some chicken," he announced almost proudly as if it were some bit of unusual news. "I never used to like that part, if I could avoid it. It's very bony." The rest of his explanations on Card 1 were normal enough, but on Card 2, Sirhan stopped describing what he saw in the blots and started describing the configurations of the white spaces: crown, diamond, space satellite. Then he went back to the blots again. Richardson asked him about the elephant or bear. He pointed to it and said it was the "GOP elephant."

Richardson asked him about the dancers he saw in Card 3. At first, they were "a jovial bunch of Negro drum players. Watusi." Then he saw something sinister in them. They looked "like foxes, more animal than human . . . like a werewolf."

"What sex?" asked Richardson.

"Oh," said Sirhan easily, "men."

Among themselves, psychologists call Card 4 "the father card." Sirhan saw no father images at all. Where others often see a penis, he saw an X ray of the chest, and grimaced as he reported it. Where others often see other phallic symbols, he saw serpents ready to strike.

Card 6, too, commonly elicits sexual responses. Sirhan found none. Finally, at the end of the inquiry, Richardson asked him, "Can you find anything of a sexual nature in this particular blot?"

"Yeah," Sirhan answered quickly. "You mean this being the vagina?"

Richardson didn't pursue that, and asked him whether he saw something which many others see: "What about an animal skin or a hide that's often seen on this card?"

"Oh, yeah, the whole thing. That's beautiful. Looks like the fur side."

Card 7 was unexceptional. On Card 8, Sirhan became excited once more at the colors. "The colors shock me," he said. "No. I don't know. I feel very jittery. I can't hold still. It stirs me. I read this magazine article on the twentieth anniversary of the State of Israel. It was in color. That color. I hate the Jews. There was jubilation. I felt that they were saying in the article, 'We beat the Arabs.' It burns the shit out of me. There was happiness and jubilation."

His agitation carried through on Card 9. "The smear of a botanical slide," he said, indicating the whole blot. "The color clashes. I am not used to it. Too many of them at the same time. It confuses me. It just increases in degrees!"

And on Card 10: "It's a cacophony of colors, a hodgepodge. All those legs!" He pointed to a brown area, avoiding the red. "This here looks like some kind of rat. No, not a rat, it flies. A bat. The whole thing looks like monstrosities. It's more vulgar. I'd avoid it." Sirhan paused, breathing hard. "Everybody wants to catch on to you, with all those legs! The minute you're within reach, you're in their clutches."

Richardson asked him about the blood. "I seem," said Sirhan, "to associate the whole thing negatively with blood."

"What about the red area?"

"It looks like liver to me, some kind of meat." He grimaced. "I'd rather not even discuss it. I'd rather not even discuss it. All those legs."

Richardson would find Sirhan's color shock very significant indeed, and so would a whole team of psychologists, save one, who came just short of calling Richardson a liar on the witness stand for telling the court that Sirhan said, "The colors shock me."

Richardson told Sirhan he did very well on the Rorschach and he brightened at the praise. Then Richardson dug into his kit and pulled out a stack of heavy cardboard cards imprinted with drawings. "You're supposed to tell me a story about each picture," he said. "And give each one a title." This was something called a "Thematic Apperception Test" (TAT).

The first card presented a boy with a violin. Sirhan dubbed it, "A Master in the Making," then thought of a better title: "A Master Musician."

The second card presented a pastoral scene, a man plowing, a woman heavy with child, a young girl with books in her arms. "Well, I don't like it," said Sirhan, reflecting a certain antifeminism. "It's the girl that has the books and not the man. Although I can understand the man has to do the harder farm work—there is more sadness, the girl is not indigenous to this atmosphere. Actually the books don't blend in with that condition of the mother—and the plowman." The farm looks fairly rich to most respondents, but Sirhan sees it as a scene of "desperate impoverishment. They are trying the best they can but they still can't make it." He titled it: "The Rich and the Poor."

Sirhan saw something of suicide in Card 3, a very vague picture of someone sitting on the floor, shoulders slouched, head turned away. He wants to "come back to this one" but goes ahead anyway. "She must have killed herself," he says. "Or she's doped up. Or cowardly. She can't face it."

"It's a girl?" asks Richardson.

"Yeah, maybe her boy friend ran out on her. She's depressive, melancholic, thinking, 'Should I or shouldn't I?' She's thinking, the hell with it. She's tired, you know."

The fourth card (designated 12-M in the standardized TAT literature) depicted a man lying on a bed with another hovering over him, a hand outstretched. "This is really odd," said Sirhan. "It's the story of Edgar Cayce. Psychical readings, a man who controlled his subconscious. . . . I don't know if it's a good or bad man here. Maybe a priest saying a prayer. He looks Oriental, though. I wonder if he's kneeling. If he's kneeling then he's trying to heal the sick. I wish he were praying for me. I wish that patient good luck. But there's a little mysticism in here. It's dark. The man with his hand out, to put him into a trance . . ." He recalled the biography he had read about Cayce. *"There Is A River.* I think the man's name is Sugrue."

The fourth card, designated 13-MF in Richardson's kit, depicted a girl only half covered with a sheet, lying in bed, and a man, who was clothed, standing with his back to her. Sirhan first wondered whether the man had strangled her or raped her—a violent interpretation indeed. "Nevertheless," said Sirhan, "he doesn't seem to be satisfied. He's hiding his face. I don't know why." Then Sirhan laughed. "I saw a movie," he said, "where a detective tried to catch a guy with this woman. When he was leaving her bed, they snapped a picture of him."

In the fifth card, 6-BM, an older woman has her back turned to a young man. Sirhan smiled. "Maybe he is asking her for money. She has refused. Or he's going to get married and she doesn't respect his wife. The mother seems negative toward his request. He wants what she wants, but doesn't want to hurt her feelings. That's about all. She is maybe the grandmother. Looks a lot older. He's making a request of some sort."

The sixth card, 8-BM, was disturbing to Sirhan, as well it might have been. In the foreground, a boy with rifle, in the background, a man lying down with a doctor hovering over him. "Boy," breathed Sirhan. He paused a good long time, indicating he couldn't (or didn't want to) verbalize about what he saw in the picture. Finally, he had a way of explaining away what was at first so obvious. "Oh, I see. The background is just a fantasy of this boy's—I don't like it." Richardson noted that Sirhan "looked rueful." "Maybe dreaming of shooting this guy or somebody else. And they are operating. He [pointing to the boy in the foreground] is now, whereas this [pointing to the background] is past. Just maybe imagining more than . . ." Sirhan trailed off and then lapsed into silence.

Using the standard Wechsler Adult Intelligence Scale, Richardson found Sirhan ranged from bright normal to superior in intelligence. In a test on similarities, he said a dog and a lion were both "carnivorous," an egg and a seed "both fructify." These are pretty big words, used properly. With a fly and a tree, Sirhan had no problem. Both have life. But with air and water, he struck out. "I'm not a scientist," he said by way of explanation. He knew what has life, but he didn't recognize what gives or sustains life.

On the vocabulary test, he came to the word "matchless." "One and one only," he said, sitting up suddenly very straight on his cot, "one of a kind." But he missed four of the last six words, the most difficult on this test.

Finally, Richardson administered a Bender Gestalt, in which Sirhan was asked to look at a series of designs one by one and reproduce them, one by one, on a blank piece of paper. Richardson had forgotten to bring in some paper, so, rather than destroy the rhythm of a session that had gone so well, he simply presented Sirhan with the back of TAT Card 2. There, Sirhan did a fairly normal job. And that was that.

Six

**"I didn't know he had that many children.
I didn't know he had so many children."**

The sheriff's office had checked on my story, and apparently cleared me. Now Parsons and I were back at the sheriff's office for a final clearance. Assistant Sheriff Jim Downey phoned and asked Lieutenant Craig Carpenter, Sirhan's chief jailer, to come to his office. Downey was an amiable Irishman with the kind of friendly face anyone likes to see behind a bar (and doesn't mind seeing behind a badge either). "Okay," he said. "Everything's set. And by the way," he added, "the sheriff would like a copy of your book." I laughed: "What book?" Downey laughed.

Then Carpenter arrived. His manner was crisp—a contrast to the heartiness of the assistant sheriff—and entirely befitting the most important jailer in the world. Carpenter had a special team of thirty deputies, ten of them at a time around the clock with one important duty: to watch Sirhan.

Lieutenant Carpenter led Parsons and me back down the marble corridor on the east side of the Hall of Justice, down eleven steps to the main lobby and over to an elevator which services the jails on the eleventh, twelfth and thirteenth floors. The elevator car was a big one and its insides had been battered by twenty-seven years of violent bookings, scarred by the traffic of murderers, extortionists and thieves, permeated with the effluvium of society's losers. The black deputy handling the controls raised an eyebrow. Carpenter told him I was "okay," and smiled a tight, nervous smile, hoping that I was, indeed, "okay."

So far, the persons who had turned up in or near the jail with concealed weapons only served to put Carpenter more on guard. And threatening letters for Sirhan continued to come to the attention of the sheriff and of Russell Parsons.

"I am going to Vietnam to get killed for my country," one man wrote Parsons on a postcard, "but before I go, I have a bullet for you and another for Sirhan."

There were other hateful letters, too, but their hate was directed to Sirhan's victim. One man wired a telegram of congratulations: "GOOD SHOT." Another said he did a great service to the American public by eliminating "Ruthless Robert."

But a major part of the mail that was piling up in Parsons' already-cluttered office at 205 South Broadway consisted of hate-the-sin, love-the-sinner letters. Some of the letter writers saw only the humanity of the accused and offered their prayers and their efforts to understand. Parsons eliminated the crank letters and passed the rest on to Sirhan.

On the thirteenth floor, Carpenter led the way out of the elevator and tapped three times on a heavy steel door. A brown-uniformed deputy looked through a viewing window, saw Carpenter, opened the door (which turned out to be two doors) and let Parsons and me come in. We followed Carpenter through the icy, air-conditioned room (where some preliminary motions in the Sirhan case had already been disposed of), and then into Carpenter's office. There we removed our jackets, belts, watches, and everything from our pockets. Our pens? Our notebooks? We would have to leave them in Carpenter's office. "We'll supply the pen and paper inside," said Carpenter, as he, too, stripped himself of all extraneous objects. He led us back through the hearing room and over to a low gate. Another deputy pushed a button. That triggered a latch and the gate opened. Inside the gate in a narrow corridor, another deputy invited us to face the wall and lean against it with our hands outstretched. The deputy went over every inch of our bodies with his hands and covered Carpenter in the same way. "Okay," he said finally.

We moved on to another door where a deputy was peering out through a small, wired-glass square. Carpenter nodded. The deputy opened the door and checked our identification cards—Parsons' card, with his fingerprints and a picture, and mine with blanks yet to be filled in, lay on a small counter. The deputy checked the cards, had me sign mine and nodded, then had us each climb three steps to a platform and stretch our arms like gliding birds. He then picked up a battery-operated electronic paddle, called a "Transfrisker." On the metal of his badge, the Transfrisker clicked. He passed the paddle over arms and trunks and legs and shoes. Nothing clicked, which proved that we were not carrying even the tiniest bit of metal, and, presumably, no weapons or saws. Then we were ready for the final door. Behind it was Sirhan.

It seemed as though Sirhan's steel and concrete apartment was filled with uniformed deputies. Actually, there were only three men inside. But the entire area—a converted day room for deputies—was rather small though it did include a small kitchen outside the cell where a deputy prepared Sirhan's meals. A deputy started pulling back some heavy sailcloth drapes around Sirhan's double cell, and opened a barred cell door leading to Sirhan. While he did so, Parsons and I signed in on a mimeographed form. The deputy took that in to Sirhan for his signature. It was the sheriff's official proof that Sirhan wanted to see us. Sirhan signed it on his bunk and then emerged into a kind of barred antichamber to receive his guests.

Sirhan was smaller, much smaller than I had imagined. And very thin. He was wearing a pair of forty-nine-cent Japanese thongs made of a sponge plastic and some faded-blue bell-bottomed prison jeans. No shirt at all. Hairy chest. Sirhan was puffing on a cigar, and in between puffs he was smiling—apparently amused by all this—and his white teeth shone in contrast to his heavy two-day stubble of a beard. One of the deputies slid two heavy wooden chairs into his cell. It was four feet wide and eight feet long, with a seatless toilet and a sink at the far end under a shelf that held a pair of slippers, a shirt and some toilet articles.

Sirhan shook hands with me—a strong, confident handshake that said, "I trust you. I want you to trust me." And then he crinkled his eyes, friendly-like, and patted me conspiratorially on the knee and winked. Parsons told Sirhan to put aside his smelly cigar and tell me his story. Sirhan apologized about the cigar, stubbed it out in a heavy paper cup and in a semiwhisper plunged right in and started pumping out his recollections about the fatal night of June 4, 1968.

A deputy sat in a heavy wooden chair about fifteen feet away, watching every movement inside the cell. He was hardly able to hear the conversation because Carpenter had ordered a large, old-fashioned, table-model radio outside the cell turned on loud to a middle-brow music station. It was one of the little ways the sheriff could give Sirhan and his attorneys some privacy, but the popular music became a bizarre counterpoint to conversation in a cell. Sirhan went through his actions on the night he killed Kennedy. His recitation sounded rehearsed, or at least oft told (which it was), for it was the same basic story he had told to (1) Garfinkel, (2) Littlefield, (3) Marcus, (4) Parsons, and (5) McCowan. And as he finished, Nancy Sinatra was singing stormily about some boots she had which were made for walking but would, someday, walk all over her two-timing lover. "I felt a choking" *boots* "in my throat," *boots* "and people were holding me," *boots* "and beating me, and twisting my left knee, and pounding my head on the table." *are gonna walk all over you* "They hurt my left eye. It still hurts."

I noticed a bony protrusion around Sirhan's left eye. I reached over to touch his temple and heard the deputy stir noisily in his chair, ready to move quickly, no doubt, if I made one more extraordinary motion. I pulled my hand back at the same moment I realized that Sirhan had a bony protrusion around the right eye as well. The bone protrusions were natural to Sirhan. He simply had a very angular face dominated by large limpid dark eyes that fled from any direct confrontation.

I asked him about his recollections of the wild scene in the kitchen after the shooting. He frowned. "I don't remember the kitchen," he said. "I was looking for coffee. I had the feeling it would sober me up." His voice trailed off. Sirhan looked as if he were trying to think of more, and I waited. "Two policemen dragged me right out," he said. "They told me later,"—Sirhan laughed here with some satisfaction, and it was at this point that I noted a crazy incongruence between what Sirhan was saying and the feeling behind it—"I was on television!"

Parsons asked Sirhan if he had seen any friends at the Ambassador. He hadn't. Parsons asked Sirhan if he'd talked to anyone at all. It turned out that he'd talked to several persons. A Danish electrician. A few waiters. A couple of Mexican-looking fellows. "In the garden," he said, "I met two Mexican boys, dressed as I was. We talked about Robert Kennedy. They were afraid to go inside. I said they shouldn't be afraid. 'If he doesn't like the way we're dressed, the hell with him.' The younger fellow convinced the older one about this. I agreed with the younger fellow."

Where had he seen these fellows? Sirhan tried to explain and I gave him the yellow legal pad I was using. Sirhan drew a crude map of the Ambassador's second floor and placed the Danish electrician and the waiters and the two Mexican-looking fellows, and the bars where he had ordered Tom Collinses. How many drinks did he have? He didn't remember. Where was the Embassy Room on this map? He didn't know. He didn't remember the Embassy Room? No. He didn't know where the Kennedy party was? No. I paused, letting him stir uneasily with his evasion, giving him a chance to say that yes, he knew where the Embassy Room was, it was right here, or come up with a reason why he didn't know—which might have been far more significant.

But Parsons took him off the hook, and started pursuing another line of questions, calculated to stir up Sirhan's latent anti-Semitism. "Oh, yes," said Sirhan, as if Parsons' prodding reminded him of "a line" that he would have to develop for the trial, "once I even denounced my brother for going to work for a Jewish man."

Surely, I thought, Parsons wasn't going to try the case by appealing to the hidden anti-Semitism of the jury? Maybe he was. He nodded with obvious satisfaction when Sirhan said, "Anytime there's anything Jewish, I walk away from it." Through the rest of this conversation, and in subsequent conversations, at odd times and in odd contexts, Sirhan's anti-Semitism would come to the fore. He could not, in fact, speak for very long about anything without dragging "the goddamn Jews" or "the fuckin' Zionists" into the act in one way or another. The other night, he said, the cell radio blared forth with the musical theme from *Exodus,* the Preminger movie about the founding of modern Israel. "I saw that movie, Mr. Parsons," said Sirhan. "Every time I hear that song, I shut it off. It bugs me. The memories. Those Jews"—he snapped the back of his right hand against the palm of his left—" 'The fuckin' Arabs' is what they're trying to say every time they play that song."

And so, I was inclined to believe Sirhan when he said, "Anytime there's anything Jewish, I walk away from it." So why did he go out of his way looking for a "Jew parade" on Wilshire Boulevard on the night of June 4? That didn't make sense.

Parsons asked Sirhan about his growing up in Jerusalem. Sirhan said he was with his mother once as a child when a bomb dropped nearby. It might have been a traumatic experience, but Sirhan's quick dispassionate account of it seemed to indicate that the bombings didn't have much meaning for Sirhan. But that was only a surface impression. There were layers of feeling deeper within him of which he was unaware and which would only be tapped later by a skilled psychoanalyst.

"Did you have any malice toward Robert Kennedy?" asked Parsons.

"Well," said Sirhan, with some hesitation, "I didn't like Kennedy. The same way I don't like Humphrey. I heard that Kennedy was giving arms to Israel." He explained that that was why he was carrying the David Lawrence clipping in his pocket. He was upset because Kennedy was advocating arms for Israel. But again, as he spoke of his upset, he didn't *sound* upset. His dislike of Kennedy—you could hardly call it so much as anger —seemed remote and detached. It was only later that I concluded that this arms-to-Israel story was a fabrication.

Parsons asked him about the details of his arrest and incarceration. He told the story, with few digressions, and recalled that once, in the New County Jail, Dr. Crahan asked him if he were a homosexual. That angered Sirhan and the recollection in his cell angered him again. "I could have belted him!" he said through clenched teeth.

On the floor under his iron bed, there was a dictionary and a Bible, a copy of the Los Angeles *Times,* the August *Reader's Digest* and a library book. I wondered what he was reading. *"A New Basic History of the United States,* by Charles A. Beard," he said, reading from the title page. "There's this part called the North and South at war." He flipped to a paragraph he had underlined in pencil. It was a summation of the state of the nation under President Andrew Johnson. He read it aloud, thoughtfully, then turned to me. "The same kind of animosity and unrest exists now, under another President Johnson, as it did then, during the presidency of Andrew Johnson." I wondered why that was significant to Sirhan, but Parsons stood and said it was time to be going.

Sirhan seemed reluctant to let us go, urged us to come back soon and then stood there grinning as Carpenter, who had been standing by, reached for a Polaroid camera so he could take my picture. A deputy pulled the heavy sailcloth curtain back across the bars.

"Well," said Russell Parsons out on the sunny sidewalk of Broadway, "that interview should be worth a hundred thousand dollars." I shook my head. It wasn't an interview. Parsons had asked 95 percent of the questions and Sirhan, well, I thought Sirhan had given me a canned spiel about the assassination itself. I wouldn't ask any editor to buy that, and, furthermore, now that I was officially an investigator for the defense, I was automatically preempted by the court order from writing about anything before trial which bore directly on the crime.

"I'll need a lot more from Sirhan before I can go back to New York." Parsons shook his head. He didn't understand. "What I need," I said, "are some more interviews with Sirhan. I need to know his whole life history. And I need a contract with Sirhan which will give me the exclusivity the magazines will demand."

"I see," said Parsons dubiously. His doubt was cleared up the next morning when he read on page 1 of the Los Angeles *Times* that James Earl Ray had agreed to tell his exclusive story to a writer named William Bradford Huie.

Mid-August. The FBI had sent Sirhan's notebooks (see Appendix C) back to its crime lab in Washington, D.C. There, the pages were subjected to a complicated photo and chemical analysis, to see when each of them was written, or, at least, in what order the pages were written. There, the experts decided that Sirhan had penned the items somewhat haphazardly, skipping around in the notebook, writing at random. It seemed that two significant pages, dated June 2, 1967, and May 18, 1968, were actually written on those dates.

As for the content, one of the notebooks in particular seemed to be filled with entries reflecting a preoccupation with (1) money, (2) the girl named Peggy Osterkamp and (3) a new Mustang. "Please pay to the order of" appeared 14 times throughout the notebook, often in connection with the name of Robert Kennedy. Peggy's name appeared 58 times, over and over again. Peggy Osterkamp. Peggy Osterkamp. Peggy Osterkamp. Peggy Sirhan. And over and over again the word Mustang, almost like an incantation: "Today I must resolve to come home in a new Mustang. Today I must resolve to come home in a new Mustang. Mustang. Mustang."

Just what Sirhan had intended by the phrase "please pay to the order of" was locked in the mind of Sirhan. There were no clues in the notebook. Sometimes the phrase was followed by some numbers, which Sirhan would repeat, not on a line, but in a kind of diamond pattern. "Please pay to the order of" is, of course, the language one finds on a check, but whose check was Sirhan talking about?

Detectives for both the FBI and the S.U.S. interviewed Peggy Osterkamp, which was hardly unpleasant, for Miss Osterkamp was a tall, willowy blonde, and highly attractive. She was the daughter of an affluent dairyman in Corona, and a horse lover who had once worked on the Altfillisch ranch, Granja Vista del Rio, where Sirhan had also worked. Did she know Sirhan? Slightly. She had been introduced to him at the Pomona Fair in 1966 and seen him around the ranch in Corona. Once, while she was having a Coke in a small luncheonette in Newport Beach with two of her girl friends, Sirhan had sped by her table, picked up the check that was lying there without a word or a nod, paid it himself and left the shop. Did she ever date Sirhan? It seemed unlikely to the detectives. Peggy was a couple of inches taller than Sirhan, in her boots almost a half a foot taller, and the kind of girl who would be rated and dated by someone more in the mold of a Barry Goldwater, Jr., not a Sirhan Sirhan. No, she said, soberly, wonderingly, she had never dated Sirhan.

And the Mustang? Sirhan, it seemed, had never come close to getting a Mustang either. After he cashed his check for $1,705 from the Argonaut Insurance Company, he had enough for a down payment on a Mustang. But strangely, he made do with his old De Soto.

Maybe the Arabic passages would give the officers some clues. They had them translated. Nothing. Some Arab song, a snatch of Arab poetry, some verbs, conjugated. Sirhan's own name in Arabic, over and over again.

There was a jotting on a page the FBI designated as Q1-23. "Tom, my warmest salutations. I do not know what has prompted you to write to

me." On Q1-37: "Hello Tom   perhaps you could use the enclosed $ Sol
perhaps you could use the enclosed $" On Q1-39: "11 o'clock Sirhan 11
o'clock Sirhan Sirhan Sirhan 11 o'clock Sirhan Livermore Sirhan Sirhan Pleasanton . . . Hello Tom racetrack perhaps you could use the enclosed $"

Who was Tom? Tom in Pleasanton? They soon guessed it was Walter
Thomas Rathke, for Rathke, according to Sirhan's first employer at the
track, Trainer Gordon Bowsher, was a friend of Sirhan. The FBI found
Rathke working as a groom at that time up north at the Pleasanton Race
Stables. Pleasanton was a small town east of Oakland, near Walnut Creek,
a bedroom community for people working in the largely war-related indus-
tries of the East Bay and a short distance from the Lawrence Radiation
Lab at Livermore. Rathke was forty-one, bearded, thoughtful and apparently lacking in any interests whatsoever except the occult. He had gone to
college, had married and had worked for the telephone company. But now,
he was satisfied with just getting along, lived alone in the stables and
worked as a simple groom.

Yes, he told Sergeant Phil Sartuche of S.U.S., he had known Sirhan. They
had "compared notes on the occult." He had written to Sirhan twice and
had asked him if he needed any money. I later discovered that Rathke had
far more influence on Sirhan than he cared to admit. But Sartuche saw
nothing sinister about Rathke and the LAPD dropped him.

By now, both the LAPD and the FBI were inclined to believe that none
of Sirhan's associations had had anything to do with his plans to kill Kennedy.

On August 16, Parsons phoned me, elated with the arrival that day of
his first complete psychological report—from Dr. O. Roderick Richardson. He read excerpts from the report: "schizophrenic paranoid," "possibility of brain damage factor," "strong depressive elements," "suicide
potential." Parsons was practically cackling: "And get this, this is what
the doctor says about paranoid schizophrenia: 'paranoid schizophrenia
disturbs and impairs moral-ethical functions.' In other words, Sirhan's
crazy as a bedbug. How the L.A. *Times* would like to hear me say that!
'Crazy as a bedbug!' " The *Times*'s Dave Smith, he knew, was preparing a
long profile of Sirhan, and editor Bill Thomas was hoping that Parsons
would make Smith privy to just such reports as this.

Richardson's report was impressive. He did not rule out the possibility
of brain damage, but found ample evidence of "a paranoid schizophrenic
process."

"His personality makeup," wrote Richardson, "includes particularly strong needs to demonstrate that he himself is shaping and controlling events in all respects rather than that events or other figures control him. This feature of his personality may generate daringly individualistic behavioral expressions which represent acts defending and preserving his sensitive sense of personal integrity and autonomy."

Richardson said this was an orientation which could, under conditions of maximum emotional stimulation, reach psychotic proportions, i.e., be manifested in "gross paranoid misinterpretation of social reality, intense, uncontrollable fear and anger, and marked disturbances of impulse control."

Richardson cited Sirhan's remarkable responses to Cards 8, 9 and 10 of the Rorschach Test, "as intense as if he were actually witnessing a jubilant Israeli celebration . . . resulting in a sudden paranoid, psychotic behavioral response.

"Under conditions of minimal stress," Richardson said, "Sirhan is capable of presenting himself in a logical, plausible fashion: however, his personality structure or organization is highly fragile, so that his best and most adequate level of functioning is not stable or reliable, but subject to episodes of acute and rapid deterioration. At such times, his behavior and thinking become psychotic and are characterized by paranoid, projective distortion of the characteristics and motives of others, loss of judgment, loss of discrimination, loss of control over impulses, particularly hostile, aggressive impulses. Under these conditions, there is marked inability to judge or interpret his interpersonal environment in socially consensual terms, i.e., he loses his ability to respond conventionally, realistically and adequately in a moral-ethical sense.

"In this psychotic ego state," wrote Richardson, "he could not 'know' the difference between right and wrong, as non-disturbed individuals in our culture would judge this difference. . . ."

Richardson's conclusion, of course, suggested the possibility of a simple insanity defense, but Parsons had never had much luck getting a jury to accept a plea of insanity. "There is one trouble with an insanity defense," said Parsons. "It becomes a battle between doctors. One doctor says the defendant doesn't know right from wrong. The other side says he does. This only confuses a jury."

If a jury is confused by insanity pleas, no wonder. The legal norms for insanity—couched under something called the M'Naughton Rule—have nothing to do with reality as modern psychology knows it. The

M'Naughton Rule (the "knowledge of right and wrong" test) was formulated in 1844, and even then it was moldy with age.

In 1949, however, California began to formulate something better: the California Supreme Court, the most "advanced" high court in the country, took up the case of Wesley Robert Wells, a life prisoner at San Quentin, who had put a guard on the critical list by slamming him in the head with a brass cuspidor. The guard recovered from his injuries, but Wells was tried and condemned to death under a rigid statute making the death penalty mandatory for any life prisoner who commits assault with malice aforethought. Although, on appeal, the Supreme Court did not overrule the sentence, it held that the trial judge erred in not allowing Wells to present medical testimony that his mental condition prevented him from forming a specific criminal intent.

At the time, few lawyers and no psychiatrists recognized the far-reaching implications of this decision. Very slowly, in a few trials from 1953 onward, psychiatric testimony was used to disprove premeditation, malice and criminal intent. That testimony didn't keep nutty killers out of prison, but it kept them out of the gas chamber. Then in the 1960's came a string of cases in rapid succession, and a new kind of criminal defense in California, now usually called diminished capacity, was evolved.*

It was good law—for society had always recognized gradations in criminal responsibility, and the law had been making an effort since the nineteenth century to apply updated psychiatric concepts to help solve the problem. The trouble was that the M'Naughton Rule forced the doctors who testified to assume an expert's stance in areas where they were incompetent. A psychiatrist does not deal in the stark contrasts of "right and wrong," after all, which are ethical and legal concepts, but rather in sickness and health along an infinite gradation. Bringing psychiatrists into court to argue about meaningless legal categories turned into an exercise that frustrated the lawyers on both sides and demeaned the doctors. How much better simply to let the doctors come into court and speak as doctors! Because of the progressive Wells-Gorshen-Wolff-Conley decisions, wrote Dr. Bernard L. Diamond in the *Stanford Law Review,* the court was, in effect, telling the expert medical witnesses:

> Forget about the legal definitions and the technicalities; forget about sanity and insanity; premeditation, malice and *mens rea*—that is our concern. Tell us everything that you, as a medical expert, know about this defendant. What kind of a person is he? What is wrong with him emotionally and mentally? How did he get to be the way he is now? What made him do what he is ac-

* See pages 409–415 for an account of that evolution.

cused of? What hidden mechanisms in his mind caused him to behave in the way he did? What kind of treatment does he need to insure his rehabilitation? Is he likely to respond to treatment? What kind of protection does Society require to prevent something like this happening again? Tell us all that you know about this defendant, and we will give full consideration to what you have said; we will put it together with all the evidence from other sources: then we will decide what is best for society to do with this defendant.

Diminished capacity was the best and the only bridge between psychiatry and the law. It did not mean total exculpation, for those convicted of second-degree murder or manslaughter under this rubric would still bear partial responsibility and go to prison like any other felon. But they wouldn't be executed and that, in a state split too badly to give its legislators a clear mandate to abolish the death penalty, was no small victory for those who consider capital punishment for the mentally ill offender a latter-day barbarity. If Sirhan's defense counsel could only show the jury that Sirhan was suffering from diminished capacity, they might be able to save him, not from prison, but, at least, from death by gas at San Quentin.

August 20. Parsons and I had another visit with Sirhan. Again the ritual of search. Hot outside. Hot in Sirhan's cell too. Again, he wore no shirt and again he had a growth of beard, and was puffing on a cigar—a Muriel Perfecto. Sirhan was smoking ten of them a day.

Parsons led off by reading Sirhan some of the milder parts of the Richardson report. Sirhan seemed to be listening intently, blinking. "How will this influence the court and jury?" he asked.

"It will help your case with both," said Parsons.

Sirhan asked about the encephalogram. Parsons said he was making arrangements to have it done soon. Soon, for Parsons, would mean two months.

During all this I looked around the cell, noticed a paper cup full of quarters—his newspaper money—on the shelf across from Sirhan's bed and a Bible open on the floor to the twelfth and thirteenth chapters of Proverbs. Then Sirhan turned to me and I took the opportunity to explain my intentions: to find out who Sirhan was, and what he was, and why he was, to open up areas of discussion about his background, his family, his early years, his acculturation in America, his friends, his foes. "You are a human being," I said, "and I want to see you as a person and not a symbol or an abstraction. It is too easy to hate an abstraction and the world has too much hate in it already."

Sirhan listened to this spiel halfheartedly. He still had some unfinished business with Parsons. He dug out some notes he had written to himself in pencil, which he had hidden under his thin, sheetless mattress. He looked at his notes and turned to Parsons. "What about Unruh?" he asked. He was referring to the Speaker of the Assembly, the most powerful Democrat in California, and the man who helped save his life in the pantry. "He ought to help us," said Sirhan. "He's got a son who's in trouble." Another unrealistic idea, but Parsons humored Sirhan.

"Yes, he ought to help us."

Sirhan consulted his notepad again. He turned to Parsons and expressed his dismay about "all the evidence the district attorney has against me." Sirhan said it looked to him (he had been getting the L.A. *Times* every morning) that Evelle Younger wanted to use the case "to advance his own political aims."

"We'll object to that," said Parsons. "We'll object."

Sirhan had clipped something from the paper which vindicated his feeling of persecution. It was a book review in the Calendar section of the L.A. Sunday *Times. The Crime War: The Manufactured Crusade,* by Robert M. Cipes. The book pointed out American society's obsession with security and told of the ways politically ambitious prosecutors furthered their careers by exacerbating something they called "the crime war." Sirhan read aloud and with relish a quote from Cipes:

> The jury is an electorate before whom the prosecutor exercises his skill in manipulation, perfecting the style which will carry him to a higher office. Every summation to a jury closely resembles a campaign speech in an appeal to emotion and prejudice . . . The war against organized crime is a convenient vehicle for one seeking public acclaim. It is in the courtroom where he gets the headline that promotes his political career.

Sirhan looked at Parsons for a confirmation of his own triumphant feeling. He saw himself as the victim of a manufactured crusade, to be used by those who were thirsting for his blood. Parsons nodded and agreed with Sirhan. "That's right," he said, "that's right." That reminded him of a story . . .

Impatient with the interruption, Sirhan sat there nodding and fiddling with the notepaper on his knee and finally, when Parsons was through, Sirhan observed that in this case, "We probably need a very sophisticated jury and probably a politically oriented one."

This suggestion, too, was unrealistic. The trial would go on according to the normal protocol of the Superior Court of Los Angeles County. The law, like the church, has a way of moving ponderously toward reform. Instead Parsons suggested that, if Sirhan couldn't have a blue-ribbon jury, maybe he'd be pleased to know he would have blue ribbon lawyers, and told him that Grant Cooper had secured an initial agreement from Edward Bennett Williams to help on the case.

As a young man who, it was becoming clearer, nourished himself on the mass media, Sirhan knew about Williams. He was one of the best criminal lawyers in America and the best that money could buy. He was Jimmy Hoffa's lawyer. "Beautiful," said Sirhan, smiling his crinkly-eyed, almost-winning smile. Then he asked about the psychologist from San Diego whom Parsons had been telling him about.

"He's a wonderful man," said Parsons. He told Sirhan how much money the psychologist—Dr. Martin M. Schorr—made per day in a San Diego hospital and in his private practice. "But," said Parsons with feeling, "that man is willing to come up and help us with our case!" Sirhan was supposed to look grateful, nodded in mock appreciation to Parsons and smirked in my direction.

Then, for the next two hours, with a minimum of interruptions from Parsons, Sirhan talked about his origins in Jerusalem and growing up in America. It was an exhausting session, for the details had to be dragged out of Sirhan, and it was depressing as well, for Sirhan had an overwhelming negativism about practically everything.

"Tell me about some of the happy moments you spent with your father," I asked.

Sirhan thought long and hard, squinting, trying to remember. "I was on a bike," he said, "with Adel. And I had my arms out like a bird and my father was laughing. Oh, he was laughing. Oh, he got a kick out of it."

I waited. Silence. "Some more?"

Sirhan could not think of any other happy moments.

Out of the lengthy conversation, however, I was able to draw some significant self vignettes out of a young man who felt very sorry for himself.

It is the eve of the family's departure from Jerusalem, December, 1957. Bishara Sirhan has secured the sponsorship of an American citizen and passage from the U.S. Government. "This," says Adel, "is the best thing that ever happened to us." But Sirhan doesn't seem to think so. He has run away from home to Ramallah, a suburb of Jerusalem. He stays there all day in the park. He buys sandwiches and soda pop and finally, when his coins run out, he appears back at the family apartment dirty and disheveled. Bishara raises a heavy hand to teach Sirhan another lesson. But Adel shields him. "Father," he says, "let's leave here in peace." The family composes its differences at a dinner of tabooleh, *a cold mixture of cucumbers and tomatoes, mixed with grain. But the city is not at peace. That night they hear shooting in the distance.*

Sirhan's first look at U.S. shores on January 12, 1957 is nothing special. "I'd seen a lot of ports by then," he says. "They all look the same." He does not remember seeing the Statue of Liberty. But America does represent for him at a subconscious level, at least, an escape from his hated condition as a Palestinian Arab, a member of a mini-minority. "When we become citizens, Mama," he asks his mother, "will we get blond hair and blue eyes?"

In July, 1957, Bishara and Adel are doing some work in the backyard and Sirhan, feeling coltish, tracks mud on some newly washed concrete. "Don't do that!" shouts Bishara testily. But twelve-year-old Sirhan soon forgets and makes muddy tracks once more. Bishara is ready to maul him and Sirhan escapes into the house to his mother's protection. Bishara rages, but Mary will not let him discipline the child.
"All right," he says darkly, "it's either him or me."
"You are my husband," says Mary, with the children cowering behind her, "and these are my children." But that isn't good enough for her husband, who by now has learned to resent the independent American ways that even his own wife is now adopting. He cannot hold a job, but he scoops up some $500 which Adel and Aida and Mary have earned and buys a plane ticket to Jerusalem. A taxi picks him up at the home in Pasadena and takes him off to meet the airport limousine. The family never sees him again, but they trump up an official story: Bishara had to go home to care for his mother who is ill.

In junior high school in Pasadena, Sirhan tries to become Americanized. He has his own bicycle and a paper route and the common slang that passes for language in the Pasadena of the late fifties. Nobody can bullshit him or hand him any jazz. But when graduation time rolls around, he shows the others something about himself which is special: in their yearbooks, he signs his name in Arabic.

At John Muir High School, his eyes are opened to the differences between the haves and the have-nots. The school is typical of the huge American high school, its student body of 3,000 a cross section of the general population of Pasadena, now more mixed than most of the many "cit-

ies" that make up Los Angeles. At Muir, some teen-agers drive to school
in their own Jaguars. Others walk—on shoes with holes in the soles.
"That's when I became aware of the differences between me and them,"
says Sirhan. "That's when I knew I was different. They were among the
elite with their blond hair and blue eyes, and their different clothes every
day and their cars, their very own cars, and their cliques."

A dance at Muir. Sirhan's first. He is scared and he bolsters his courage
by getting a boy friend to come along and he fortifies himself with "a little
bit to drink." He watches from the sidelines. Everyone but him seems to
be out of their minds with joy as they squirm and twist to some loud,
frightening music. What are they doing? The twist? "Goddamn!" Sirhan
says to no one in particular. "I don't want any part of it."

Byroneseque intellectuals. This is more Sirhan's speed. Walter Crowe.
Tom Good. Brilliant. Against anything the majority was for. "I'd spend
my last drop of blood to defend my country," says one kid with a crew
cut in history class.

"That sure isn't going to help you very much," quips Walter Crowe.

The class roars and Sirhan is glad Crowe is his friend. Clever. After
class, Sirhan gives Crowe a book he'd borrowed. C. Wright Mills's The
Power Elite. "Terrific," says Sirhan. "It opens your mind. What a contrast to the bourgeois stuff around here." Crowe has some more for Sirhan. Paul Goodman. Albert Camus. The Stranger. The Plague. "Bitchin'."

August, 1963. Sirhan sits on a kitchen chair tilted back against the refrigerator. His brother Saidallah knocks the chair down and Sirhan with it.
"What the hell's the matter?" shouts Sirhan. "Haven't you got a tongue?"

Saidallah stabs at Sirhan with a can opener he has in his hands. The two
of them scuffle. Mary breaks up the fight.

"What's the matter? cries Sirhan. "This drunken brother of mine!
That's what's the matter. Either him or me. I'm tired of this." Saidallah
had disgraced himself in the family with his drinking. He drank up most of
Aida's gallon of Oso Negro which she had bought in Tijuana. He had almost destroyed a '53 Nash and now he was jabbing at Sirhan with a can
opener. Sirhan calls the police.

"Is there any place you can go to live for a while?" asks the Pasadena
patrolman with a sigh. Sirhan says there is. He goes to live with William
Beveridge, a gardener who has found Sirhan a willing assistant. Beveridge
has a camper in back of his house. Sirhan can stay there.

696 E. Howard. Sirhan lies on the floor on a flowered carpet. His eyes half closed, dreamy. An L.P. record jacket in his hand. "A Memorial Album. Highlights of speeches made by our beloved President, J.F.K."

John Muir High School. Foreign Relations Club. Sirhan is invited to talk about the Middle East. He wears a clean white shirt and his best tight pants and his shoes are shined so he can see his face in them. "Goddamn!" he says to himself when he arrives. "They are all Jews!"

He gives his talk. Is amazed that everyone sits and listens civilly. When he is finished, one very pretty girl who is also very fashionably dressed rises brightly and wonders why the Arabs can't accept the status quo instead of making more war and talk of war. "Can't you accept the peace?" she asks seriously.

"We're hospitable," says Sirhan sardonically, "but give up our own houses? You want us just to give up our own houses?" Sirhan is gentle with her, for she is very pretty and very fashionably dressed. He is, you might say, attracted to her. But God damn it, he tells himself, she is still a Jew!

Pasadena City College. Huge. An education factory. Impersonal. Long lines of kids. Class begins. Kids still chatting, but the lecturer goes right ahead, simply not caring if anyone is listening or not. Sirhan's head jerks from side to side and up to the teacher. He can't believe it. This is higher education?

"The way they did things at PCC," said Sirhan, "helped detach me from society, or at least campus society. But for me, that *was* society. I majored in political science, foreign languages. Diplomacy was my main interest. But soon I gave up on the idea of being a diplomat. When I figured the score, I saw that the odds were stacked against me. You gotta be rich to be a diplomat. You have to give big parties. You could blow your entire year's salary in three months. Ralph Bunche? Yeah, he made it in diplomacy, but he has a manufactured eminence. He spoke at PCC once. After that, I realized that being an Arab is worse than being a Negro. Oh, I worked hard, but . . . I hate that interjection: 'but.' I worked, but . . . I stood out in one class—anthropology. Just my name gave me away. I stood out for that teacher as an example to prove the points he wanted to make to the class about 'acculturation.' Once, during a discussion of adaptation, the problem, the issue of Palestine came up. This was my chance to speak. I really wanted to clobber this fellow, this blond son of a bitch, and I did. I put him where he really belonged. I talked for one solid hour. There were two or three colored people in the class. They had to applaud: I was on their side when they got up to tell about their grievances. My argument? Well, I said that if the U.S. was really as benevolent as it claimed to be, why did it send Hitler's Jews to Palestine? Why not to the Mojave Desert? Then see how much milk and honey they could produce!"

The class, said Sirhan, was so violently in favor of his talk that the wall maps shook with their applause. But that was the exception. In general, the Jews on the faculty, numerous enough, were against him. "The Jews are behind the scenes wherever you go. You tell them your name and they freeze. 'SUR-HAN?' "

I saw that Parsons was getting restless, but I was unwilling to leave Sirhan on that depressing note and asked him what he was reading.

Sirhan leaned over and fingered a new book with a bright blue dust jacket, *The Decadence of Judaism in Our Time* by Moshe Menuhin, but he made no comment on that. Then he picked up a worn library book, *Les Miserables* by Victor Hugo. He said he felt an affinity for Jean Valjean, the persecuted hero, and, while Parsons started shifting his weight and clearing his throat and saying, "We'd better be going," Sirhan read aloud a passage he'd underlined:

> ". . . 'Teach the ignorant as much as you can; society is culpable in not providing instruction for all, and it must answer for the night which it produces. If the soul is left in darkness, sins will be committed. The guilty one is not he who commits the sin, but he who causes the darkness.' "

"Sorry we had to stay so long," I said insincerely after we left the cell.

"I don't really like to come here," said Parsons. "I don't like jails. It's really not very nice up there. When I took the mother up there, she looked around and said, 'Death is better than this.' "

But there were already some indications that Sirhan was happier and more at peace with himself in the rigid life of the jail where he enjoyed high status after all as the star prisoner, than he was when he floated free in the chaotic unstructured life he had led outside in that large and lonely mass called "L.A." In L.A., he had had no connection with power, beauty, love, wit, courage, loyalty or fame, or the pride he might have taken in these. In L.A., he had little sense of "self" in any total way. What little satisfaction he enjoyed, I later discovered, seemed to come from a disembodied spirit world, the world of the mind. In jail, reading about himself now in the daily newspapers and magazines and beginning to see himself as an Arab patriot, he had attained a new form of security. What threatened that security more than anything, it seemed, was the fear of being found out. He was afraid that I would, in effect, take away his precarious new identity. In this interview, Sirhan had refused to discuss his notebooks or his experiences with the occult. Later he would make far more forceful objections to inquiries about the Rosicrucians, and it was only when, at another time, I suggested that Sirhan was a lonely, disembodied nothing who had never even touched a woman that he plunged into a history of his sex life. This was important for Sirhan's new existence. What he feared most was being understood. Understanding was a kind of fire that threatened to consume him. Indeed, at the very end of my first interview, Sirhan complained that he was "drying up in here." And after this second interview, the deputy who watched outside the cell noted in his report under the rubric "unusual behavior" that Sirhan had a session of "talking out loud to himself." Finally, Sirhan called the deputy over and told him he wanted a book called *Psychology You Can Use*. He didn't want to give himself away. Perhaps he needed further guidance on how to cover up.

My first meeting with Mary and Adel Sirhan was arranged outside the Hall of Justice. Their clothing said they were happy (Mary Sirhan wore a bright green knit dress and Adel a green checked sports jacket), but their postures bespoke a visible burden: their shoulders sagged, their eyes drooped, their jaws were clenched. Mary Sirhan was eager to exonerate her son and blurted almost immediately: "Sirhan never received any money. He never was a Communist. Sirhan was a good boy. Everybody says he was a good boy. So, is he not a good boy anymore?" I nodded sympathetically. Mary Sirhan wore her graying brown hair pulled back in a bun at the nape of her neck. Her left eye was afflicted with a cataract condition and her thick lower lip protruded abnormally. She had suffered. "Sometimes," I said, "even the best of us do bad things."

Mary sighed and offered a platitude of her own. "The cloud overhead," she pointed upward, "either falls or it moves on. Sometimes it is better if it falls. Something new will grow."

"Sometimes," said Adel, taking me aside and speaking in a lingo which was surprisingly idiomatic, "I think she is gonna flip." Adel was thicker than Sirhan, had a handsome smile and, it turned out, a love for things more substantial than mysticism or the occult: good music, good food, beautiful women. He knew his brother didn't have much of a chance—

which made him more realistic than his mother, clinging to a naïve faith that in some miraculous way her son would be acquitted. It was her only out. She couldn't take much pleasure in a sympathetic telegram, for instance, from the mother of Lee Harvey Oswald, although letters from solid Christians were a help to her present peace of mind. She was no longer on the mailing list of her Arabic Orthodox church and that hurt. So did the stares of her neighbors. One day when she was shopping at a nearby supermarket, one woman got a side view of her, wheeled her cart down another aisle and right up in front of her.

"Yes, I am the one," said Mary Sirhan. "I am Mary Sirhan. You want something? You want to ask me some questions?" The curious woman flushed, mumbled and walked away.

In McCowan's air-conditioned Cadillac, Adel talked about the brilliance of his brother Sirhan. "He always went to the heart of everything. If he got interested in something, he read everything he could get his hands on." When he went to work with the horses, he tried to learn everything he could. Once, he saved a horse's life because he noticed some symptoms that even his trainer had missed. When he went to work at the health food store, he learned about vitamins and organic foods from the ground up. He bought books about health food.

At 696 E. Howard in Pasadena, a policeman stood on duty in the driveway and two other officers slouched in a patrol car with the doors open, and the police radio was humming and crackling its lo-fi symphony of static. He asked me for my credentials. I gave them and McCowan said, "He's working with me." The home was nicely furnished with big overstuffed chairs and a color television. A large tape recorder sat in one corner and, on a mantelpiece over the fireplace, fourteen carved wooden camels marched westward. I told Mary and Adel that I wanted to help people understand the complexities of a young man who was, after all, like them in many ways. "I want to tell them about a human being. It is reality versus an abstraction. A real human being. An abstraction is easy to hate. And there is already too much hate in the world."

Mary liked that and said that maybe my inquiry could be a kind of "gift to the world." She had resumed her old job, mornings, at the Westminster Presbyterian Church's nursery school, several blocks away. Munir had his old job back at Nash's Department Store. Adel had prospects of another engagement in Reno, for $350 a week. Mary was reading everything she could get concerning Sirhan's defense, which at that stage was mostly idle speculation. She kept the assassination issues of *Time* and *Newsweek* on a buffet table in the dining room, and the special Kennedy Issues of *Life* and *Look* on the coffee table in the living room. Now and then, she picked up *Time* and talked to the face of Robert Kennedy as drawn by Artist Louis Glanzman, telling him how sorry she was. Kennedy, moreover, talked to her. "It's okay, Mary," she says he says. "I forgive you. It's okay."

"I should have hated to look at his picture," said Mary Sirhan, "but I have to look at it. The look on his face—I keep going back to it." At this point, she started to weep. "I prayed that he wouldn't die, that he would be all right. And, when I finally heard that he was dead, I started to cry. I couldn't help it."

Mary Sirhan and Adel recalled some vivid scenes from the troubled days in Jerusalem:

Sirhan is four. St. Paul's Street in New Jerusalem, where the Sirhan family lives in a four-room home, complete with a garden shaded by eucalyptus trees, is itself a dividing line between the Palestinian Arabs and the Jews. A driverless truck full of dynamite just happens to roll down a grade toward the house of the British High Commissioner for Palestine not far away from the Sirhans. The explosions rock the entire neighborhood, and young Sirhan clutches his private parts and shudders uncontrollably for hours.

In the spring of 1948, St. Paul's Street is a mass of barbed wire. In the darkness of night, Zionist commandoes move in boldly on a British radio station above the Sirhans' home. They dynamite the upper story and make the Sirhan bathroom into a machine-gun nest commanding the street, while the family cowers in the basement. "It's all right," soothes Mary Sirhan. "The fighting will stop in a day or two."

There is still shooting in the streets. The Sirhan family prepares to leave with scores of other Palestinian Arabs in the neighborhood to the safety of an Orthodox convent perhaps a mile away. "We will return soon," says Mary Sirhan. Sirhan Bishara Sirhan, age four, turns and takes a last look at his stuffed tiger, almost life-size, which sits on wheels and can be ridden like a hobbyhorse.

Bishara Sirhan returns to the convent, pokes his head through the hanging blankets that separate his family from the other refugees. There is a look of defeat on his face. "I have signed up with the United Nations Re-

lief and Welfare Association. We are refugees," he says. "That's official now."

In an old temple in a former Jewish sector of Old Jerusalem, the Sirhan family has a single fifteen-foot by thirty-foot room with a domed ceiling and a grilled window overlooking the street. Mary Sirhan is trying to make dinner on a Swedish-made camping stove, which is six inches high and six inches in diameter with a tiny reservoir at the bottom for the kerosene that fuels it. "I don't like this. I don't like this," whimpers Sirhan. "Why don't they stop fighting so we can go home? I want to go home and play with my tiger."

"You have to be a man now," says Mary Sirhan sternly.

Games.
Sirhan is a prisoner. The prison is imaginary. But Sirhan sits there glumly nevertheless. He is not very good at aseer. Any number can play aseer, evenly divided into two teams. The boys fight over a heavy medicine ball stuffed with rags and use it to assault the opponent's goal. If the goalie drops the ball, he becomes aseer, a prisoner. If he catches it, the thrower becomes captive. Sirhan doesn't throw it very hard. He doesn't catch it very well.

Sirhan's eyes widen and his pupils catch the reflection of the dirty little flame before him. He and his friends giggle maniacally as the kerosene-soaked rag consumes itself. Then they soak another rag and this time it is Sirhan's turn to strike the match there in the shadows of the fetid toilet.

In the street the boys shout and kick away a stuffed soccer ball. The ball squirts away from the pack. They chase it and leave Sirhan standing in a kind of trance. Later they return and Sirhan is still standing and staring. They take him home where he remains for several days.

Sirhan runs screaming to the family apartment with a water bucket half full of water. Members of the other families in the crowded compound pour out of their rooms to see what Sirhan is crying about. They find him in the hallway, staring down at a human hand floating on top of the water. Sirhan is quivering with fright.

Mary Sirhan hauls herself up the narrow stairway. She has had a hard day washing clothes at a local laundry. She finds Bishara beating Sirhan. "What are you doing?" she cries.

"Making a real man out of him," shouts Bishara.

She makes him stop immediately, eyes blazing. "Not anymore," she says. "Sirhan is not like the others. Look at him, how pale and weak!"

Sirhan kisses her hand. "Give me your blessing, Mama," he says. Bishara smolders for a moment, then he leaves the room and does not return until it is very late.

When Parsons and I came to see Sirhan on August 21, Sirhan was reading a current issue of *Esquire*. "They've got an article here on Edward Kennedy," said Sirhan with a satisfied smile.

"Yeah!" I said. "What did you think of it?"

Sirhan tapped the magazine with the back of his hand, and laughed. "Teddy never worked a day in his life!" Sirhan said this triumphantly, much as if he'd always *known* this, but was glad now to see it in print. In the *Esquire* piece, a heckler at a factory gate where Kennedy was making a pitch to represent Massachusetts in the U.S. Senate asked if Ted had ever worked with his hands. He admitted he hadn't. Sirhan missed the punch line of the story, which came from a worker who clapped Kennedy on the back moments later and said, "You wanta know something? You ain't missed a thing!" To Sirhan, the salient morsel was that Ted Kennedy had never worked with his hands. But if Sirhan had had his way, neither would he. He played nothing but long shots at the racetrack and his dreams of success counted heavily on magic to make them come true.

"Say, kid, you've got a way with horses."

"Really?" Sirhan is flattered. He'd been trying his damndest to do good as a stable boy for Gordon Bowsher, a trainer at Santa Anita. In his heart he knew he was chicken. But he tried not to let anyone see that. Now, here is the groom Tom Rathke, telling him he had a way.

Rathke says he'd noticed that Sirhan had an almost mystical power, as if he almost communicated things to the most ornery horses with thought waves.

"Really?" says Sirhan. "Thought waves?" He is interested and he asks Rathke to tell him more.

Sirhan ponders over the advertisement in the magazine, and wonders about the significance of the triangle and the rose, and the all-seeing eye. Something called the Ancient Mystical Order of the Rosae Crucis, based in San Jose, California, offers him a chance to develop his inner powers.

He takes out his notebook and practices several versions of a letter begging admittance into their fraternity. He encloses $20.

"Frank," says Sirhan, "can you give me a job?"

Frank Donnarauma shrugs. "I don't know. What's the matter with the one you've got?"

"The one I had you mean. I quit. Bowsher wasn't moving me along fast enough. I want to be an exercise boy and he's got me cast as a hot walker."

Donnarauma says he doesn't have anything for Sirhan. And he doesn't know of anything either. Soon the meet at Hollywood Park will be over. He just doesn't know.

Next night, however, at 10:00 P.M. Donnarauma phones Sirhan at home. Maybe there's a job for him out at the Altfillisch ranch near Corona. "Where?"

"Corona," says Donnarauma. "It's in Riverside County. You just come out the San Bernardino Freeway . . . can you be there at 7:00 A.M.?"

Could he? Of course. He hangs up and calls to Adel. There is excitement in his voice. "Adel! Adel! Can I borrow $25?"

Sirhan has a job on a real ranch! Granja Vista del Rio at Norco, a big green ranch with a big white fence around it and a huge crew working the barns. "You'll do everything," says the owner of the ranch, Bert C. Altfillisch, a small, grizzled man with a face that could have been battered in the ring.

"Exercise boy?"

"Yeah, you'll get a chance at that too." Norco is too far from Pasadena for a commute, so Sirhan has to find a place to live. But on $200 a month to start, he ought to be able to find something in Norco, a little town that sleeves the arm of California State Highway 71. Where can he stay? Sirhan drives along slowly in his '56 De Soto. Ahh. The Highlander Motel. He stops in a cloud of dust. It doesn't look too swift; maybe just right for him. He knocks on the door that says "Manager." No answer. Disappointed, he shuffles back toward his car.

"Looking for a place?" says a boozy-looking fellow who is leaning against a door of one of the units. Sirhan nods glumly. "You can sleep here on my couch tonight if you want."

"Really?" says Sirhan. He can hardly believe it. "I can stay with you tonight? Gee, my name's Sol. What's yours?"

"Van Antwerp."

The Huddle, a poolroom in Corona. Terry Welch has cleared all the stripes off the table. He chalks his cue with vigor, takes aim and laughs, "Eight ball down here in the corner." Sock, thump . . . plunk. "Hey," shouts Terry to the waitress, "more beers here."

Losers buy the beers. But when the girl brings them, Sirhan, who can't even get in the game, insists on paying for them. He pays. He takes a measured sip of his 7-Up.

Terry Welch, on a Detroit, Michigan, television station, after the assassination: "Sirhan wanted to know about everything. He read everything. He could talk about everything like an expert: art, music, electronics, law, the manufacturing of glass, paper, metal. You name it, he knew about it. He was like a geisha girl."

Noontime. Granja Vista del Rio. The exercise boys all stand behind Sirhan as he faces off with Bert Altfillisch. The boys are ready to go on strike. Exercising the colts in the morning is okay, but that's it. No grooming in the afternoon. No stable work. No nothing in the afternoon. Sirhan is their spokesman. And he has a speech full of words that impress Sirhan and all of his hearers, even if no one, including Sirhan, quite knows what those words mean.

Altfillisch stands there with a peeved expression on his craggy face, his thumbs stuck in the front of his Levi's. Finally, when Sirhan is finished, Altfillisch says, "I don't quite know what you just said, but the hours remain the same. If you don't like it, you're through. All of you."

The boys grumble a bit as they walk off for lunch, but they aren't angry at little Sol. "You done good," says Terry Welch, slapping Sirhan on the back.

September 25, 1966. A foggy morning at the ranch, foggier still on the exercise track set down on the Santa Ana River bottom. Several owners aren't happy. They have driven all the way from Los Angeles to see their quarter horses run, and now the trainers do not want to run. Trainer Lynn Wheeler says he doesn't care how far they've come. It is just too foggy. The owners wait around, kicking at the gravel, grumbling about the fog.

"Well," says Trainer Larry Heinemann finally, "I guess the fog has lifted enough." He gives the word to the boys: "Sol," says Heinemann, "you take Hy-Vera."

Lynn Wheeler shakes his head. "On a foggy morning like this," he says, "you've got to have better boys."

Owner Millard Sheets agrees. He withdraws his colt. "It'll have to be a three-horse race," he says.

Up the track in the saddling area, the horses, too, are snorting. By the time they break out of their canter into a full run, the fog is starting to bond again, then closes in completely as the horses thunder by the owners and the trainers. Sirhan is up on Hy-Vera, a chestnut mare, and he seems to have a half-length lead on the other two, and they are going awfully fast. "Oh, God!" says Millard Sheets. His fears are justified. In moments, a crash. Horses squeal. A young man screams.

Sheets and Heinemann vault the fence, run down the track and see one boy wandering around in a daze and another one—Sirhan—crumpled up against a metal post on the outer rail. "I found him," says Sheets, "and I thought he was dead. He didn't—he didn't move and I—as I got real close to him, I didn't see him until I got about ten feet from him, it was so foggy, and I saw him lying there crumpled up like a little hurt bird, and I got down and he began to moan, and as he turned his head over I could see this blood in his ear and I thought, Oh, my God, he's hemorrhaging from inside, and then, only a matter of a few seconds later, I realized that it was from outside cuts running into his ear. He had the damndest bunch of mud and blood all over his face and he thought he had gone blind. He was scared pissless. He was just screaming." Sheets starts to feel Sirhan's legs.

"My face!" yells Sirhan. "My eyes! I'm blind." Sheets takes hold of Sirhan's hands, puts his head in his lap and holds him for fifteen minutes before Sirhan, who is in a semicoma and uttering piteous little cries which Sheets takes to be prayers, stops fighting him. Finally, the ambulance comes and takes him to Corona Community Hospital.

Dr. Richard A. Nelson, being interviewed by Special FBI Agent Sanford L. Blanton: "Sirhan questioned all of the medical applications and all medicines administered to him and appeared unduly frightened of the various treatments. He was one of the most reluctant patients I ever had."

"It's too bad," says Bert Altfillisch, when Sirhan leaves his office with his last check on December 6, 1966. "The kid had a lot of ambition, but he never coulda become a jockey. He sort of lost his nerve."

January, 1967. The Fez, a dimly lighted supper club on North Vermont in Los Angeles. A darkly handsome young man named Adel Sirhan finishes a number on the oud, takes the applause with a warm smile, hops

*down off the stage and hurries over to the bar. He expects to see his
brother Sirhan, who has borrowed his Volkswagen for the day, but he is
surprised to see him drinking. "How did it go?" he asks Sirhan.*

*"Jet Spec came in second." It was a creditable showing for the colt's
first out, but Sirhan's voice was glum. He wanted to see Jet Spec win because the owners, the Prestwoods, were good people. They liked him and
they were going to make sure he got a chance as a jockey, their jockey,
someday. But that was not to be. Sirhan was finished as a jockey and this
outing to Caliente today with the Prestwoods only served to remind him of
his failure. "Give me another one of those," says Sirhan, lifting his glass.
"What do you call 'em? Tom Collinses?"*

*By the time Adel is finished for the evening, his brother is helplessly
drunk. Adel slings him over his shoulder and carries him out to the car.*

*Winter and spring, 1967. Sirhan's life is a montage of magic: mysticism
and the track. He spends a good deal of time at Broughton's Used Book
Store near Colorado on Lake Street, browsing through the $20 volumes of
Madame Helena Blavatsky. He spends a good deal of time at Santa Anita,
either with his friend Tom Rathke or alone near the pari-mutuels, trying
to make a living by betting long shots.*

*At home in his room before a little mirror on his desk, he practices
white magic, turning candle flames red or green or blue, staring intensely
at them by the hour.*

*Later in the spring at Hollywood Park, during the parade before the last
race, he tries his magic on a horse. A horse named Press Agent, owned
not so incidentally by Bert Altfillisch. He concentrates intensely on the
starting gate. At the bell, Press Agent breaks smartly and—runs right into the rail. Sirhan lingers at the rail, staring intently across the infield,
wondering about the powers he has been building up within himself. He
is still staring when all the fans have poured out of the park, a lone figure
on the rail, standing in a many-colored carpet of discarded mutuel tickets.
Later, he will write in his notebook: "I believe that I can effect the death
of Bert C. Altfillisch."*

*As Sirhan watches television in May, he thrills a little at the sight of
half a dozen Black Panthers armed with rifles and marching through the
capitol in Sacramento. Like him, they are underdogs and, at last, they are
doing something about it. In June he sees television coverage for five
nights running of night fires in Cincinnati sparked by the arrival of H. Rap
Brown, who comes to say that "SNCC has declared war." In July the war*

breaks out in Newark: fires, looting, bombings—and guns. In Cambridge, Maryland, Rap Brown exhorts his black militants to tear down the white man. "Don't love him to death," he says. "Shoot him to death." In Washington, D.C., he tells them, "There should be more shooting than looting, so if you loot, loot a gun store."

Of course, says Brown at the time, this is nothing new. "Violence is as American as cherry pie." Just so. That is clear to Sirhan when he sees the currently popular blockbuster, Bonnie and Clyde. Clyde Barrow in real life was a seedy crud. But Warren Beatty as Clyde Barrow, seen through the eyes of Arthur Penn, is a romantic figure, romanticized even in an orgasm of death. On TV, killings and rumors of killings become common. In Vietnam the body count goes up and up. In Newark, in Plainfield, Fresno, Des Moines, Erie, Cairo, Minneapolis, Durham, Englewood, East Harlem, Detroit. And Sirhan writes in his notebook:

> *I advocate the overthrow of the current president of the fucken United States of America, I have no absolute plans yet—but soon will compose some I am poor. . . .*

Parsons interrupted the autobiographical flow with a bit of news about the Russian invasion of Czechoslovakia. Sirhan immediately related this to the Russian invasion of Hungary in 1956. That reminded Sirhan that the United States supported Hungary [after a fashion] and, speaking of U.S. support, he said, "I can't see why the U.S. would want to support Hungary and yet not support Arab refugees in the Middle East." Neither Parsons nor I asked him to elaborate on this, but he did. "The Arabs have been in exile for twenty years on world charity, living on four cents a day. And they were used by the USSR in debate after the Six-Day War. That's very unfair. I don't like it."

That put Sirhan back in the middle of his autobiography. The Six-Day War was, he said, his "denouement." He meant it was the beginning of the end, his final psychological defeat.

Trouble in the Middle East. Another war in the works? There are troop movements in the Sinai Peninsula. Troop movements by both sides, Israelis and Arabs. And stepped-up reportage in the press. In Pasadena, Sirhan is powerless. All he can do is read the barrage of Israeli propaganda reported in Time *and* Newsweek, *which he reads avidly in the Pasadena Public Library along with the* B'nai B'rith Messenger, *and compounds every evening by tuning in the local six o'clock news shows and Huntley-Brinkley at seven o'clock and George Putnam at ten o'clock. "That goddamn Putnam," Sirhan tells Adel and Munir, who is now home after a nine-month stay in the county jail on a marijuana conviction. "Putnam has to plug the Jews in every newscast. If I had only been a newscaster!"*

Sirhan is building up to a crescendo of hatred and he is impotent to do anything about it. Well, he can, at least, spill off something with his ballpoint pen. On the night of June 2, after one of Putnam's "plugs for the Jews," Sirhan goes to one of his spiral notebooks from school and writes a unique manifesto.

> *2 June 67 12:30 p.m.*
> *A Declaration of war against American Humanity*
> *when in the course of human events it has become*
> *necessary for me to equalize and seek revenge for*
> *all the inhuman treatments committed against me*
> *by the American people. . . .*

On June 5, Israeli jets attack the Egyptian Air Force, catch every one of its planes resting on their air strips and blast them before they can get off the ground. The Israeli Army marches into the Gaza Strip and the Sinai Peninsula and to the shores of Lake Galilee, ignoring the pleas for ceasefire from the United Nations General Assembly. In six short days, the Arabs have lost yet another war and, more important, lost complete control of all the land that was once Palestine.

Sirhan feels that the Jews are "rubbing it in." How does he know? The media tell him so. The television news shows use garish maps of the Middle East before and after the "war" to display the extent of the Israeli take-over. Channel 9 digs out old movies about the Israeli struggle for freedom: Hill 24, Where Are You? *with Kirk Douglas. One of the networks replays the stirring Paul Newman movie* Exodus *about Zionist terrorism in Palestine. The local radio stations interview half a hundred celebrities from Hollywood's movie colony and relay their appeals for funds to help the Israelis' fight for freedom.*

Time *magazine features the eye-patched Moshe Dayan on its cover and replays the best of Yiddish humor on the war. At one point in the campaign, an Arab division spots a lone Israeli sniper on a sand dune. The commander dispatches three men to get him. When they do not return, he sends a dozen men. None of them comes back. He sends an entire company. Two hours later, a blood-spattered Egyptian soldier crawls back. "It was an ambush," he explains. "There were two of them." "It was our finest hour," boasts an Israeli spokesman. "Or did it take longer than that?" Darryl Zanuck announces plans for a zillion-dollar war movie enti-tled* The Shortest Day. *Cassius Clay doesn't like "Muhammed Ali" any-more, changes his name to Morris Steinberg.*

In July, Sirhan seethes over the July 14 cover story in Time *on King Hussein, a contemptuous piece called "The Least Unreasonable Arab." "Instead of trying to salvage what they can," says the story's lead, "the Arabs are busy blaming just about everybody but themselves for the fact that great gobs of territory lie in Israeli hands."*

Along with the story is a Time *essay, "Araba Decepta: A People Self Deluded," which angers Sirhan even more. "Desperately in need of sur-vival training for the 20th century . . . a case of arrested development . . . emotional and political instability . . . suffering from one of history's worst inferiority complexes." The phrases make Sirhan's eyes water.* Time *calls pan-Arabism "a Mittyesque dream" and calls for "one courageous Arab leader to call reality by its name" and lead his people to "find sources of pride and confirmation of manhood in causes other than holy war."*

Sirhan chokes and slaps the magazine down on the library table. He doesn't even bother to put it back on the shelf. He'll show them! Mitty-esque dream!

To the Strathmans, Patricia and John, who rather like Sirhan because he is thoughtful and sensitive, none of Sirhan's seething is apparent, for he does not let his friends know when he feels sad. He has not told the Strath-mans that he was asked to leave college. He has not told them that he couldn't make it with horses. All the Strathmans see is this mild, good-in-tentioned but ineffectual young man. One night in August he takes them out to dinner to a modest but "great" Armenian restaurant in Pasadena where he orders only tea for himself and insists on ordering them the spe-cialty of the house. "I'm not hungry," he says, "but I'll have some dessert with you."

He spies a Middle Eastern pastry on the menu and orders it because he knows they will "flip over it." But when the waitress brings it, Sirhan stares in disbelief. It is round and crumbly, about as big as a saucer. Sir-han grabs a table knife and cuts it in half, gives half to the Strathmans' three-year-old daughter, then cuts the other half in thirds and doles out the sections with solemnity to John and to Patricia.

Patricia sees through Sirhan's carefully disguised depression and offers the only cure she knows: an invitation to come home with them and chat over coffee. Sirhan soon fills her sympathetic ear with tales of his magic. He has acquired the ability, he says, "to see mystical bodies" out of the corner of his eye and to conjure up his guardian angel. In fact, he made him appear momentarily for the Strathmans. Did they see? No? Well, he only appeared for a fraction of a second because Sirhan's powers are not yet fully developed.

John sputters and finds something to read, but Patricia does not scoff and Sirhan tells her more: one night as he is lying in bed, he says, he performs an experiment on his mother, who is sleeping in the next room. He concentrates on her intensely and tells her—in pure thought, not words— that she must get up and go to the bathroom. For some minutes he sends his thought waves and then he hears her stir, get up and turn on the light in the bathroom. The flushing toilet is music to his ears, and he stares at the ceiling, unable to sleep with excitement over his new magical powers.

But Sirhan's magic cannot produce the money he needs to wage his own war on America. To get that he decides to file an insurance claim with the Industrial Accident Commission. His claim is thwarted for a couple of weeks, for the lawyer he retains whose name is Hansen turns out to be a Jew who has changed his name from Blumberg, and Hansen fails to file his papers because, of course, Sirhan is an Arab.

He gets another lawyer, a woman, whom he knows is not a Jew because, after all, she helps him get his claim going. In the meantime he starts looking for a job. He checks the job listings at the Pasadena City College Placement Bureau, sees one for retail stock clerk, $135 a week. Not bad. Qualifications: Union membership, forty-five completed units at PCC. Okay. He has the units and he can join the union. He walks home, almost three miles, to shave, shower and shine up.

He makes application for the job, but the woman in the placement bureau knows automatically that Sirhan is a foreigner. She makes him wait fifteen minutes and then she asks him for his green card from the U.S. Department of Immigration. He blows up. "Goddamn it, lady, give me that application back! I want to withdraw!" The woman calls her superior. He tells her not to give the application back, but to throw it in the wastebasket. Sirhan goes around the counter and tears it up into finer bits, furious at the treatment he has received, furious that the woman would think he is a foreigner.

Through Friday, Saturday, Sunday, Sirhan cannot get the incident out of his mind. On Monday, he goes back to Pasadena City College and demands to see the president of the college. His secretary tells Sirhan the president is in an important budget meeting. "Lady, I don't give a shit!" says Sirhan. She invites him to see the college's vice-president.

"What's the trouble?" asks the vice-president.

Sirhan tells him the story, the vice-president takes him back to the placement bureau and the woman in charge seems "more pliable." But Sirhan can feel her resentment.

She shrugs. "We all have to live," she says.

"You're goddamn right!" says Sirhan, emboldened now and wanting to "look like a winner." He fills out another application. The woman gives him the name and address of the prospective employer. It is a job as a stock clerk at the Safeway Market—where Sirhan had seen a card in the store window, soliciting applicants for the identical job. "Hell," says Sirhan, "I had to go through all this to learn something I already knew?"

Though the Black Panthers thrill Sirhan, the Black Muslims intrigue him even more, for they are, after all, closer to him culturally, aren't they? Aren't they even speaking Arabic? Sirhan gets Munir to go down and pay a visit with him to the Black Muslim temple in Central Los Angeles. Disappointment. He and Munir get no farther than the vestibule. The brothers at the temple let him sign their register. They let him buy a book about Elijah Muhammed for $3. Sirhan is an Arab? Well, now, how do you pronounce this here word right here? And this one? And this one? Sirhan catechizes them on the words and feels that perhaps they may relent and let him into their meeting. But no. They cannot. He may be an Arab, but he is not black. And as it says on the sign outside, this temple is for Black Muslims.

Mary Sirhan is worried about her son Sirhan. He spends too much time in his room alone. It is nice that he also spends some time playing Chinese checkers with the two old ladies down the block, but this is not normal. Nor is it exactly normal to serve cookies and lemonade to the man who comes every week to pick up the garbage. What Sirhan needs is a job. She gets him one with John Weidner, owner of the health food store down on Lake Street, who is a Seventh-Day Adventist, always eager to help a backslider like Mary Sirhan and help her into the fold again.

Munir is frightened by the look in the eye of his brother Sirhan. Sirhan seems to fondle that box with the gun in it a little too lovingly. "You're not going to—you know?"

"No," says Sirhan.

"You swear?"

"I swear."

"On sis?" His dead sister, Aida.

"On sis," says Sirhan.

On Thursday, March 7, 1968, Senator Robert F. Kennedy breaks more than a year's careful evasions on the war in Vietnam by appearing on the floor of the Senate and asking whether the United States has the authority to kill tens and tens of thousands of people "because we say we have a commitment to the South Vietnamese people?"

"Are we like the God of the Old Testament," he asks, "that we can decide in Washington, D.C., what cities, what towns, what hamlets in Vietnam are going to be destroyed?"

A careful Kennedy watcher hears the radio report of Kennedy's Senate speech as he is driving along the San Bernardino Freeway in John Weidner's delivery wagon. To Sirhan Sirhan, the speech is a tip-off. Kennedy has already decided to run for President. Sirhan returns to the store. Weidner chides him for almost nothing. He was supposed to make a delivery first in Monterey Park and then in Downey. Sirhan reversed the order.

"No," says Sirhan. "You said first Downey, then Monterey Park."

"No," says Weidner. "Monterey Park, then Downey."

"You're calling me a liar? I quit." Weidner blinks. That is not a reason to quit his job.

But it is not, of course, the real reason.

Sirhan's suspicions about Kennedy's candidacy are upheld on Saturday when Kennedy denounces the pro-Johnson forces in New Hampshire who have said that a significant vote in that state's Tuesday primary for Senator Eugene McCarthy would be "greeted with cheers in Hanoi." Kennedy is edging into the campaign.

On Sunday, all the L.A. television news shows carry extensive footage on Kennedy's sudden appearance in Delano, California, to participate in a Mass of Thanksgiving with Cesar Chavez, the leader of the farmworkers' more-than-a-union, who has been fasting as a witness for nonviolence for forty days. The huelgistas *mob Kennedy. He is not a candidate? Sirhan smiles. He looks like a candidate.*

At the end of the week, in the Caucus Room of the Old Senate Office Building in Washington, D.C., and in millions of homes in America via live television coverage, Senator Robert Kennedy is officially a candidate for the Presidency of the United States.

In the presence of his wife, Ethel, and nine of their ten children, Kennedy says in his reedy Bostonese that he runs to seek new policies— "policies to end the bloodshed in Vietnam and in our cities, policies to close the gap that now exists between black and white, between rich and poor, between young and old in this country and around the rest of the world."

Sirhan sneers. But then, so do Lyndon B. Johnson and Eugene McCarthy. Johnson tells a group of businessmen in Washington that "these are days when we have to take chances. Some speculate in gold—a primary metal—and others just speculate in primaries." In Green Bay, Wisconsin, McCarthy says, "An Irishman who announces the day before St. Patrick's Day that he's going to run against another Irishman shouldn't say it's going to be a peaceful relationship."

On April 5, a large, brown envelope comes to 696 E. Howard for Sirhan. It is from the Argonaut Insurance Company. It is his $2,000, the $2,000 he has been dreaming about. He opens it hurriedly with his finger, finds a check inside for $1,705. Shit. Two hundred ninety-five dollars deducted for medical and legal fees . . . Still, $1,705. With $200 already saved that made it some $1,900. Enough for a Mustang? Not quite. Sirhan will "invest" a few hundred at the track. He ought to be able to build a few hundred up to a few thousand and pay cash for the Mustang. No time payments for him.

But Hollywood Park is not lucky for Sirhan. In a week he has lost a few hundred. Now he is further away from a Mustang, not closer.

In April, Sirhan is fascinated by the television coverage of the King assassination. Amazed that the assassin could kill and get away while he killed.

Sirhan has pissed away much of his insurance money, most of it at the races. He tells himself he has never had so much fun. Sometimes just for the hell of it, he picks out a total stranger standing near him at the rail, *asks him what horse he likes and buys the stranger a $2 win ticket. At other times, he buys admission to the Turf Club and books his bets at the $50 window. That is fun! Or is it? What does he gain by it? Does anybody ever buy him a ticket? Or does he win enough for a new Mustang?*

No. No Mustang for him. So here he is, fixing up his old De Soto all by himself. He has the De Soto jacked up on the driveway of his home, hammering the hell out of a bent axle, listening to the Kentucky Derby. If he were at Churchill Downs, he'd bet Don B., 35 to 1. All of a sudden the jack slips. The car lurches and Sirhan is pinned painfully under the axle. "Goddamn!" cries Sirhan. "Even my own car turns on me." Contorting himself with great effort, he slips out. Is he hurt? No. Just a greasy bruise on his left shoulder. He still has a good right arm to hammer the hell out of that axle and file away the camshaft for hours.

In three days he is finished. The axle seems to turn properly. The left-rear-wheel bearings seem to turn smoothly enough. He takes the car for a test drive on the San Bernardino Freeway. Will the left side hold up? It does. He gets over into the fast lane, and is spinning along when the right bearings start to lock. With luck he edges back to the right just in time to catch the next off ramp, the back wheels scraping and rasping like a son of a bitch. His De Soto wheezes to a stop. Sirhan hops out and looks at the smoking right rear. "Fuck it," he says. "Fuck everything. It isn't worth it."

Somehow, the conversation came back to the current political situation in the United States. The Democratic Party would be in convention in Chicago the following week, and it looked as if Hubert Humphrey would get the nomination. "Hubert Humphrey!" cried Sirhan. "That chicken-faced son of a bitch?" Why was Sirhan upset with Humphrey? "Because," said Sirhan, "even after the assassination [of Robert Kennedy], Humphrey said he would send bombers to Israel—just to spite me! He said that just to spite me!" Then he added his own warning for Humphrey: "Humphrey, you better have a million guards around you, because you're gonna get it, you goddamn bastard!" He didn't say how Humphrey would get it. Or who would give it to him.

I said there was some talk of Edward Kennedy's getting the nomination in Chicago. "Ted Kennedy?" Sirhan laughed scoffingly. "That would be like putting the exercise boy on Damascus. The horse is gonna run away with him." Parsons agreed with Sirhan. Encouraged by that, Sirhan added: "Ted doesn't know the other side. He's starting from the top." Then he stopped and mused: "But if he should become President, maybe he would pardon me. . . ." He shook his head. No. It was more likely to Sirhan then and there that Lyndon Johnson might yet take the nomination. "You can't discount Johnson yet." Then Sirhan spun out another of his dreams. Maybe he could blackmail President Johnson right now. How? "Either he gets me out of this" —Sirhan waved at the cell walls— "or I tell the world he paid me to kill President Kennedy."

"President Kennedy? "

"I mean Senator Kennedy."

"Well," I said slowly, "could you prove that?"

"I wouldn't have to," snapped Sirhan. "Just saying it would be sufficient. I couldn't prove it but I'd die with the story. . . ."

Did he see himself as another Oswald? Or . . .

"You think you'll get the death penalty?"

Sirhan shrugged. "A death penalty would only be vengeance. What would it gain?" He paused, then added reflectively, "I know I've killed a man. At least, I'm told of it. I have nothing in my conscience about it, but . . . I'm told I killed a man, so I deserve some punishment, but maybe I could serve humanity by working ten years in a hospital, to pay my debt, you might say." I wondered whether Ethel Kennedy or Bob Kennedy's ten (soon eleven) children would consider that any kind of a bargain. Ten of Sirhan's valuable years for Bob Kennedy's life. . . . "I don't regard myself as a criminal," said Sirhan flatly.

As what then?

Sirhan talked about Gandhi, and the black revolution. He identified with both. "The Negroes," he said, "can see everything, but they can't eat it. Their only solution is to dig in and eat it." Immediately, Sirhan added: "I wanted a new car. I always wanted a Mustang. I said, 'All I need is money and how am I gonna get it?' They're not giving Mustangs away." In this context, Sirhan was implying that he might have killed Kennedy for money. That would explain a lot of the writings in his dream book. *Please pay to the order of Sirhan . . .*

At this point, infuriatingly, Parsons reentered the conversation. "In other words, you don't believe in coercion for selfish reasons but to correct an injustice?" That was somewhat less than a perfect paraphrase of what Sirhan was saying, but it served to take Sirhan off the hook before I could reel him in.

"Yes," said Sirhan.

I gave Parsons an ungrateful look. Sirhan said, "Martin Luther King came too early in history. He tried to oversell his cause." I didn't even care to pursue the thought. Sirhan went back to the notion of Edward Kennedy's giving him a pardon. "In that way," said Sirhan, "America could correct its conscience. Make me an example of a person who could rise again and pay for his mistakes to society." His face brightened. "That would be beautiful. Yes. I think I could do it."

Parsons asked Sirhan about the Kennedy dynasty. Parsons, it was becoming more apparent, didn't like the Kennedys. Sirhan's answer was not right to the point, unless the Kennedys were, for him, the concrete symbol of haves who exploited the have-nots: "We claim to live in a democracy," said Sirhan. "Poor, rich, black, white, all equal before the law, whose votes and opinions count. *I* never experienced this. Rather the contrary. I experienced the injustice that these people have committed against me."

"But why Kennedy? Why kill Kennedy?" I demanded.

"It was a warning to the U.S.," said Sirhan. His voice became a bit sepulchral. "You'd better listen. Be more cautious. Be more fair. Remember Kennedy. Remember Kennedy."

I asked Sirhan why he bought the gun. His answer was almost totally unbelievable. "Because," he said, "I was living in a mixed neighborhood."

And what about the notebook? "Well, that's another story," said Sirhan. "That had nothing to do with the killing of Kennedy."

"On one of the pages, you wrote that RFK must die, must be assassinated before 5 June 68."

"June 5 stood out for me, sir, more than my own birth date. I felt Robert Kennedy was coinciding his own appeal for votes with the anniversary of the Six-Day War."

Kennedy, of course, hadn't set the date for the California primary election, but somehow, in the twists and turns of Sirhan's mind, Kennedy was powerful enough to do anything, and somehow, because he was big, Sirhan was justified in killing him. Remorse? Apparently, there was none. Sirhan came close to it once when he recalled a television documentary about Kennedy which he had seen on May 20. It was "The Story of Robert Kennedy" and it got its Southern California premiere on Channel 2, CBS, in Los Angeles. Midway through the half hour, Sirhan sat up very straight. The announcer was telling him Kennedy was in Palestine in 1948 *with the Jews.*

"In 1948," said the announcer's voice, "he went to Israel as a war correspondent. He began to find some answers." War scenes flashed on the screen, and then shots of refugees fleeing the battle zone. "Living with Israeli troops," continued the voice over, "seeing war and death at close hand for the first time . . . seeing the River Jordan red with blood of Jews and Arabs . . ." On the screen the refugees dissolved into Arab-Israeli war headlines and the logo of the Boston *Post* with a by-line by Robert F. Kennedy: "He wrote his dispatches and came to a decision." A decision? What was his decision? On the screen in color the Israeli flag waved in the breeze: "Bob Kennedy decided his future lay in the affairs of men and nations."

The documentary did not say in so many words that Robert Kennedy had cast his lot with the Jews. In fact, the words of the announcer said Kennedy decided on nothing more specific than "a future in the affairs of men and nations." This was the way a propaganda film suggested more than it said: The Israeli flag waving in the breeze carried its own message to thousands of Jewish viewers. But it said something to the lone Palestinian as well, and the lone Palestinian consulted his local paper again to note: This was Kennedy's own documentary presented by the Kennedy for President Committee, Jesse M. Unruh, Chairman.

Sirhan remembered little more about the documentary. Oh, he did recall that in one scene, Kennedy was playing with a lot of children. "I didn't know who they were," said Sirhan. Then he paused, leaned over and confided in a low, somber tone, "By the way," he said, "I want to get one thing straight. I didn't know he had that many children. I didn't know he had so many children."

Seven

"With that power, I could have been a millionaire."

I had told A. L. Wirin that Sirhan could expect something close to $10,-000 from a U.S. magazine like *Look* or *Life* for a satisfactory interview. But Parsons and McCowan had a bigger bonanza in mind. "Ten thousand dollars is peanuts." said McCowan to Parsons.

Parsons challenged me. "Ten thousand dollars is peanuts," he said. "I've been approached by a writer who wants to do a book on my life."

I pointed out that one magazine interview was only the beginning. The proceeds from a U.S. magazine piece could be matched by sales to European magazines. Eventually, there was a book to be done on the Sirhan case.

"Yes," said Parsons, "and there's my book, too. *Parsons for the Defense.* I figure if Louis Nizer can do it, so can Parsons. Whoever heard of Louis Nizer before? Now 'Parsons' is a household word in Tasmania."

"And television rghts, too," said McCowan. "Don't forget about that."

"How much money do you think you can put together?" asked Parsons. "We need money. I don't have to tell you we need money. Those dirty bastards at the D.A.'s office aren't going to help us."

"They're telling witnesses not to talk to me," complained McCowan.

I said I ought to be able to get publishing commitments by the end of September, if Parsons would draw up an exclusive agreement. "You do it," said Parsons.

I did it and showed a draft to Parsons and Cooper.

Cooper said he didn't want any money. I insisted he take a share. Cooper said he'd take his expenses and turn the rest over to the University of Southern California Law School. I did another version, Cooper made a few more emendations and Parsons found the whole thing acceptable. But the Sirhan family had other ideas, for McCowan had already promised them $100,000 "off the top" of a deal he had tried to promote on his own.

I wondered why the Sirhans were ever led to expect anything at all. It is not uncommon for a family to go into debt to secure a good lawyer for a loved one accused of murder. Who tries to make money on misfortune? But no matter. The Sirhans had great expectations. And now there was trouble. They wanted a bigger share.

In a showdown conference at Parsons' office, Adel Sirhan said, "Look, you can write other books. Parsons and Cooper can handle other cases. But this is our only chance."

I shouted: "You want to set yourself up for life on one deal?"

"Can you guarantee my brother's safety?"

"After killing Robert Kennedy?"

Adel shrugged and said that if no one could ensure Sirhan's "safety," the family ought to make the best of it.

"Is there any reason," I asked, "why the Sirhan family should make a pile just because Sirhan Sirhan killed Senator Robert F. Kennedy?"

Adel spread his hands. "Look, as long as there is money to be made . . ."

I was appalled at the thought that anyone could dream of making money on the death of Senator Kennedy, then realized that I myself intended just that. "Look," I said, resolving that dilemma quickly in my own mind, "I'm going to do a lot of work for this. Mr. Parsons is going to do a lot of work. Mike McCowan is going to do a lot of work. What are you going to do?"

Parsons became the conciliator. He pointed out to Adel that Kaiser was a pro who knew what he was doing. Adel conceded that.

"Maybe you ought to get another boy," I said wearily.

"Maybe we should," said Adel.

Parsons didn't want that. "We're losing time here," he said. "We've got to get going on this investigation. We need money."

Adel was silent. I finally told him to "shit or get off the pot."

Parsons blanched, and said apologetically to Adel, "Mr. Kaiser is a lot like me; he says what's on his mind."

Adel looked up at me with sad, glistening brown eyes. It was apparent this wasn't easy for him either. "I don't see," he said softly, "why you can't take one-third and let us split fifty-fifty with the attorneys."

Silence. Everyone waited for me. I looked down in my lap at the contract. What I really wanted was to get the story and be able to write it the way I saw it without interference from anyone. "Okay," I said, "I'll take one-third."

Adel said to Parsons, "Fifty-fifty?"

Parsons was weak. He turned to McCowan. "What do you think?"

McCowan was weak. "I don't know," he said.

"All right," said Parsons. "I'll go for fifty-fifty." Later, Cooper would go along with that, too, but he demanded and got the Sirhans' agreement to split the trial expenses fifty-fifty, as well.

Parsons and McCowan took the contract to show Sirhan. Through lunch, Parsons read it to him, clause by clause, and then Sirhan signed it without hesitation. "Any percentage is okay with me," said Sirhan. "I just want the attorneys to have enough."

As they made ready to leave, Sirhan remarked over the friendliness of the deputies. "Those guys have only one aim," warned McCowan. "To put you in the gas chamber."

Sirhan got a wild look in his eye and a silly vision of great power. "If I go to the gas chamber," he growled, "I'll tell you this: I'll take the whole fuckin' world with me."

After Labor Day, the LAPD had its investigation pretty well wrapped up. The trails leading to potential coconspirators ended up in box canyons of frustration with no way out, no resolution, except mere surmise and a heavy leaning on probabilities.

They never found the Arabs whom W. J. Wood, a volunteer worker, overheard at Kennedy headquarters, the ones who said they could "get" Kennedy Tuesday night at the Ambassador. They assumed that Wood had only picked up a snatch of innocent conversation between some Kennedy supporters, friends of Kyber Khan, an Iranian playboy who had spent a lot of his time in May at Kennedy headquarters, offering his services and those of his many Arab friends to the Kennedy people.

Larry Arnot, the clerk at the Lock, Stock 'n' Barrel in Pasadena who had seen Sirhan on June 1 accompanied by two other men, turned out to have a fertile imagination. Under a polygraph examination, he admitted to Sergeant Hernandez he did not remember seeing anyone with Sirhan on that day. In fact, he did not even remember Sirhan. He had a sales receipt all right, but he could not remember the sale. Two other men? He guessed he was thinking of another dark-skinned trio who came into the store that day.

The mystery map found at the Ambassador turned out to be the product of an enthusiastic Kennedy supporter named William Crosson who had wanted to help with security on the Kennedy campaign.

Sergeant Hernandez tried to dismiss Robert Duane as well. Wired to the polygraph, Duane clung to the story that a young woman he knew as Gilderdine Oppenheimer had told him of a plan to assassinate Senator Kennedy on June 4, and that he had not lied to any police officer. But Hernandez told him his answers were "indicative of deception" and "untruthful."

Hernandez said Duane's answers would have to be changed. "Either you change them, or I change them," said Hernandez. Duane wondered if he could return later to make his own corrections. Of course he could.

At 7:30 P.M. on September 9, Duane appeared at Parker Center for a chat with Hernandez and Sergeant Phil Alexander, while a stenographer stood by to take down the conversation verbatim.

Hernandez drew some concessions from Duane. The man following him and the girl on their way to Oxnard might have been a jealous boy friend or a husband. And nothing that happened to him on June 4 had "even the slightest connection with the assassination of Senator Kennedy."

Alexander suggested that it was the reporter, Fernando Faura, who had helped him make the connection between that girl and the Kennedy assassination. Alexander seemed to want to ignore the fact that Duane had himself made the connection when he first talked to the FBI.

"Right," said Duane. "He romanced me."

"That wasn't your idea?" said Alexander.

"No, sir. It was his idea."

"Right."

"Naturally, I fell into it, and I went along with it because, well, like he said, possibly she could be the girl or she is the girl and toward the end he kept saying, well, she's the girl. I went along with it. And when he would tell me that another witness has identified my picture, the girl that was with me, that gives you a little strength, and you begin to wonder and you become feared—"

Hernandez suggested that Duane had concocted this story to cover up his illicit interlude with the girl called Gildy. "No, no," said Duane. "I didn't state all this to cover up anything." But he did ask the police not to bother his wife about this. Hernandez said there would be no reason for the police to do that. "I appreciate that," said Duane. "Believe me. Because I love my wife and, gentlemen, I want to keep her."

Duane wondered whether the police could help him get rid of Faura.

"Sure," said Hernandez. "This is your inherent right. Nobody can go around bothering you, Bob."

Hernandez and Alexander breathed a sigh of relief. Maybe that would be the end of Fernando Faura. But how about *Life* magazine? Alexander said he'd talk to *Life*. He did. He paid a call on Jordan Bonfante, *Life* bureau chief, in an effort to talk him out of doing a story on the girl in the polka-dot dress in general, and on Robert Duane's story in particular. Bonfante pointed out that Duane's story seemed to check out with one polygraph examiner. "I don't think you've really proved that Duane was mistaken," said Bonfante. He was right. It was practically impossible to do so. But if the police didn't do so, the implications were that there was a girl who knew something about the Kennedy assassination and that the police couldn't find her. That was a black eye for the department.

To Bonfante, this sounded too much like *Catch 22* to be true. He decided to discover how important this was to the LAPD and let Alexander talk. Six hours later, Alexander was still talking, and had not yet managed to persuade Bonfante there was no "girl in the polka-dot dress."

Walking down Spring Street with Russell Parsons is strolling with a star. Every other senior citizen nods at him or points. He is fast becoming a pop hero in the Serutan set, living proof that a man can find fame at seventy-six. Lawyers and judges stop to chat and ask Parsons whether he will accept the judge who has drawn the Big Assignment. Herbert V. Walker will preside over the Sirhan trial. The Los Angeles *Times* carries Walker's picture on its second front page in the middle of a story that calls him the "dean of the county's criminal court bench." The *Times* notes that he is the judge who sentenced Caryl Chessman to death and says he is "firm but fair."

Parsons turns the question back on the lawyers. "What do you think?" Parsons responds. "What's your opinion?" According to the rules, Parsons can ask for another judge and he is wondering if he should. On the way to lunch, he picks up eight votes for Walker and two against. Parsons knows there are judges who would give the defense a better break. But he has no way of telling whether he would get one of them or someone far worse than Walker. "What does your friend think?" Parsons asks me.

"Cooper?"

"Yes."

"They're chummy, they serve on a bar committee together. Cooper knows Walker and Walker respects Cooper." Parsons nods.

At Mannings' Cafeteria, Parsons plops down in a well-worn and oft-painted booth, picks at a pineapple and cottage cheese salad. A younger lawyer happens by. "Sit down, sit down," says Parsons. "You've had cases with Walker. What do you think?"

The lawyer tells an interminable story, utterly lacking in suspense. By his singular account, Walker is an opinionated old bastard who made up his mind too fast and browbeat a hapless young deputy D.A. into doing something he really shouldn't have done. "Well," says Parsons after he leaves, "that makes it eight to three."

Late that week, Judge Walker would ask Parsons if he would ask the court for another judge. "Hell, no," said Parsons. "If we wanted you out, we wouldn't go about it that way. We'd ask you to step aside on your own. But we're not going to."

Walker seemed relieved. This would be a big case. His biggest by far. He asked Parsons if he liked the idea of a glass cage in the courtroom around Sirhan. Parsons said he was intending to discuss that with Walker. "It wouldn't help us a bit to make the courtroom into some kind of penitentiary. Let's downplay the security aspect. Could have a bad effect on the jury."

Back in his office, he pushes aside a pile of papers on the edge of his desk and sits a spell, then turns to his favorite subject: "Where," he says, "is the money?"

My trip to New York had been somewhat less than successful. *Look* bought an exclusive story on James Earl Ray from William Bradford Huie and didn't want to feature two assassins back to back, although the editors might have considered doing so if there was a conspiracy to kill Bob Kennedy (as they *knew* there was to kill Martin Luther King). "*Look* is buying conspiracies this year," said one of the editors. "It's too bad you don't like conspiracies." *Life*'s editors had considered buying world rights to the Sirhan story for $200,000, but they were vetoed by higher authority on the grounds that it would be bad for their "public relations." Only *The Saturday Evening Post,* in a losing battle to stay alive, could commit for American magazine rights. There were editors at big New York book publishing houses who liked the idea of getting the assassin on record. But the men holding the purse strings, the presidents and the board chairmen, didn't "feel right" about helping the Arab.

I reminded Parsons my agent was making deals at the Frankfurt Book Fair. I said I hoped I could get Parsons the money he needed from Europe.

"You're setting me up for a letdown, aren't you?" asked Parsons. "You're not going to have the money by the thirtieth, are you?"

"Commitments, yes. Cash, no. If you want me to withdraw then, I will."

Parsons squinted and waggled his bony finger. "You've said that two or three times now. Is that your intention? You going to pull out now? You could make a lot of money on this now. Maybe you already have. Maybe you've sold your services to somebody else."

I shrugged and admitted the thought had crossed my mind. Parsons was frightened; he didn't want to lose control before the trial, so he cajoled and wheedled. "Well, you know I have faith in you," he said. "I'm counting on you to produce. You're my banker." But, until his banker produced a big check from Europe, he wasn't going to let me anywhere near Sirhan.

Okay. I would work with McCowan for the time being on the investigation. To find out what the prosecutor knew about Sirhan, there were discovery motions to be made, should have been made long before. They wouldn't be filed until McCowan and I prepared them. And there were some key witnesses to be seen.

Walter Crowe was a key. McCowan and I visited him on his coffee break at the antiseptic cafeteria of the Los Angeles County Public Welfare Building on 2707 South Grand. Crowe ordered tea. He was short and pudgy, wore a slightly soiled pinstripe, button-down shirt with a dark knitted tie under an unbuttoned collar, and a tweed jacket which was much too heavy for a day when the weather man had forecast ninety-two degrees. Crowe was nervous and became edgier when questions interrupted his thought flow and destroyed his own careful continuity. He recalled his first encounter with Sirhan. They might have been sixth graders at the time and had adjoining paper routes. Sirhan had offered to fight him. Crowe (who wore thick spectacles then, as now) made some alternative proposals to a fist fight. Sirhan laughed and said, "When the U.S. and Russia fight, they do not use peashooters!"

Crowe admitted he was with Sirhan on May 2, 1968. Crowe recalled that Sirhan had lost some of his old idealism, that he had seemed set on a particular course now. "What I really wanta do," said Sirhan to Crowe, "is make a lot of money. A lot of money." Then Sirhan phoned his friend Ivan Garcia and asked Garcia to meet him at Bob's Big Boy Restaurant. He was buying the beers.

Ivan arrives with Joseph Marcovecchio, a friend from Colombia, and the foursome heads for the Hi-Life at 1958 E. Colorado. The Hi-Life is a dark tunnel of a place with two pool tables under a spotlight at one end near the door and a tiny spotlighted stage at the other. "SURPRISE NIGHT WEDNESDAY" reads a poster on the left wall. And another: "AMATEUR

CONTEST UPCOMING." *A hundred young men or so drink mostly in silence and wait morosely for the next act. Sirhan, Walter, Ivan and Joe find a table about halfway down, sit, order a pitcher of beer and wait. Sirhan pays. Then a young lady with a figure which is not unlovely, skips out on the stage wearing little but a smile. The jukebox on her left belches forth with rock music and she dances, not so violently as she might if she wore a bra, but enough to make her boobs jiggle and bob. It is apparently bad form for anyone to look as though they are enjoying this display, but few take their eyes off the girl while they sip their drinks. Four pitchers of beer and three dancers later, Sirhan is unhappy. He cannot understand a lovely girl like this demeaning herself in front of all these men. If he were in her shoes, he would be ashamed of himself.*

The four of them shuffle out. Where to? "Let's try the Cat Patch," says Ivan. The Cat Patch on 2211 East Foothill features not one, but two or three topless girls at once, and they do not dance up on a stage, but rather on a runway right in the middle of the bar. The choicest seats border the runway, giving the luckiest lookers an unobstructed view of the breasts bobbing above them in tune with the jukey rock. "A pitcher," says Sirhan to a petite waitress who seems absolutely suffocating in a bikini.

Four pitchers later, neither the beer nor the bosoms seem to cheer Sirhan. When he speaks he expresses his contempt for the entire proceeding. Neither Crowe nor the other two pay him much attention.

"Relax, Sirhan," says Ivan Garcia.

Sirhan settles back. Jiggle, jiggle. Bump, bump, bump.

Crowe said he was now one frightened little social worker. He'd stopped going to his Communist meetings and was seriously considering becoming an undercover agent for the FBI. Why? Because he was "filled with shame and guilt that I may have had some influence on Sirhan." How? "We are all, all of us, the sum total of all the influences on our lives. I was one of those influences." He paused and wiped his glasses. "What could I have done," he said, hoping he might get the investigators' answer to a question that had been keeping him awake at night, "that caused Sirhan to kill Kennedy?"

"What I hear you saying is that Kennedy's death filled you with anguish."

"Yes," said Crowe.

"You're blaming yourself for the assassination?"

"I guess I shouldn't," Crowe said ruefully. But it was clear that he did

—though not in any of the senses that the police were trying to uncover. Before he took his last sip of tea and hurried back to his office, Crowe asked about Sirhan. "Do you think he has a chance?"

"We definitely do," said McCowan, who would remain unrealistically confident to the very end.

Crowe weighed that, nodding quietly and thinking very hard. Then he shook his head in disbelief. "Will you see Sirhan?" he asked. "Well, tell him, tell Sirhan that killing Kennedy had no political justification whatsoever." Crowe was close to tears. Then he spun around and headed through the hallway alone.

Cooper was a man of one book. As long as he was in court with the Friars' Club case, he didn't want to think about Sirhan. Parsons had to. The case was set for trial November 1 and he had to come up with some kind of defense.

Could he claim that Sirhan had suffered brain damage when he fell from the horse at Corona in September, 1966? Probably not. Though the State of California had paid Sirhan $1,705 as a result of his claim, the medical records showed that Sirhan's injuries were not serious. But Parsons had to be sure. He ordered an electroencephalogram for Sirhan, and on Saturday morning, October 12, Dr. Edward H. Davis, a brain specialist from Beverly Hills, appeared in Sirhan's cell with his technician, Helga Kaye.

Sirhan hoped the electroencephalogram would show some abnormal brain waves. In fact, he had asked McCowan if he should prepare for this test by banging his head against the wall of his cell. "You don't have to do that," said McCowan. "Bumping your head against the wall isn't going to cause brain damage. If you've got any, the machine will show it."

No such luck. Sirhan's tracings, taken over an hour's period, were normal. Then Dr. Davis prepared the equivalent of four Tom Collinses— according to a recipe he had himself obtained from the Ambassador Hotel. Main ingredient: six ounces of Gordon's gin. Davis returned to Sirhan with the container and a paper cup, and Sirhan downed the mixture in eight minutes. It wasn't the most enjoyable way of getting high and hardly the way he had drunk the Tom Collinses on the night of the assassination. Dr. Davis wasn't sure whether the method mattered. What he wanted was to see whether Sirhan's EEG was changed under the influence of Gordon's best. Again, over a period of seventy-eight minutes, the EEG showed nothing significant.

But Sirhan did get interestingly drunk, and that gave him leave to put on a not entirely convincing show. For at least ten minutes he shivered violently. He was irrational, agitated and restless. At various times he cursed, and once he cried. Dr. Eric Marcus was observing all this from the sidelines. "Dr. Marcus is here," someone said.

"Get that bastard out of here!" cried Sirhan. Marcus had the deputies take Sirhan back to his inner cell. Sirhan seemed confused. "What the hell is going on here?" he asked. He grabbed his throat and appeared to be choking. He looked at Marcus again inquisitively.

"This is Dr. Marcus," said one of the deputies.

"I hate his guts," said Sirhan. "I'll get even with those Jews, goddamn it." Sirhan asked the pretty young technician to get him a drink. She shook her head and smiled. He asked her again and she declined. "You're a hell of a waitress!" said Sirhan. Marcus noted that Sirhan was in a sort of delirium. His notes had Sirhan saying, "Twenty years is long enough for those Jews!" "Got to have justice." "Didn't have to help them by sending planes." "That bastard just can't, he can't help those bastards!" "One year and those goddamn Jews are still left!" Marcus tried to talk to Sirhan, but Sirhan called Marcus "Adel" and asked him to take him home. "Speak Arabic," he cried.

"I'm not Adel. I'm Dr. Marcus."

"Get out of here," said Sirhan. "You're one of them."

"And who are they?" Marcus pointed to the deputies outside the cell.

"They're Jews," said Sirhan.

"Do you wish to kill Kennedy?" asked Marcus.

"The bastard isn't worth the bullets," said Sirhan. Marcus (who would fail in a later visit to loosen Sirhan's tongue with forty milligrams of a drug called Ritalin) attempted to provoke Sirhan by making derogatory comments about his Arab identity and the power of the Jews. "They'll have to drink every drop of my blood," responded Sirhan. Sirhan was still quite drunk when Marcus left and, Marcus believed, totally irrational.

On my next visit to the cell with Parsons, Sirhan asked about the outcome of the EEG. "I'm studying these reports," said Parsons. Dr. Davis' report ran less than two typewritten pages and needed no "study." I blurted what I knew.

"No abnormality?" said Sirhan. He was disappointed. "Not even with the liquor?" Sirhan could have accepted a report saying he had brain damage. He didn't like the idea of "mental illness," but brain damage was okay. Now, with no brain damage, he feared he'd be held fully responsible. He sat up straighter on the edge of his bed. "Well," he said, "if it's going to cost me my life, I want to help the Arabs."

That pleased Parsons, for he himself had resolved on a defense that would appeal to a moneyed consortium of Arab-Americans who wanted to air their grievances against the Israelis in the Sirhan trial. Parsons had started to spout their line: "Sirhan was an Arab patriot. He had every reason for hating Kennedy." And he and McCowan had flown to Chicago to reach an understanding with Abdeen Jabara, a young moustachioed attorney from Detroit who spoke for the Arab group on how to substantiate this approach.

The meeting was highly secret, which was supposedly why it was held in Chicago, but it is better than even odds that the police and the FBI knew all about it. Los Angeles police tailed Parsons to the departure gate at American Airlines, Los Angeles International Airport, and there was something about the man who followed them when they arrived in Chicago that spelled C-O-P to McCowan. No matter. Jabara said his group was anxious to have "the story of Palestine and the Palestinian Arabs" told at the trial, and they could get money to bring two experts in Middle East history to Los Angeles to tell that story. "Good," said Parsons, "that's what we need."

On Monday, October 14, it was the same scene at the Hall of Justice: the same elaborate security, the same thorough search of everyone, including Russell Parsons, the same deputies on guard in the tiny makeshift courtroom, the same armed helicopter overhead, the same warnings from Captain Fields: "Everyone remain seated. If anyone stands, he will be removed immediately." But a different judge, Judge Herbert V. Walker. Walker rumbled in exactly five minutes late. He was more than serious and his huge gray eyebrows stood out like a pair of horns. He took immediate charge, making clear to Parsons that he would certainly order the district attorney to let the defense attorneys examine the numerous witness statements and reports gathered by the police in the Sirhan investigation. The case law on "discovery" was clear. To give a man a fair trial, the state must make available any competent and relevant evidence that would tend to "turn light on" his defense.

Deputy District Attorney David Fitts was soon on his feet with a formidable pile of reports—the statements of some sixty-seven persons who had seen Sirhan at the Ambassador Hotel on the night of June 4. He plopped them down in front of Parsons. "Do you want to count them?" he asked.

"Not now," said Parsons, slightly surprised to see such a stack of paper. Fitts took ten minutes to read the names of each of the witnesses. He added fifteen more who had seen Sirhan at the San Gabriel Valley Gun Club on June 4. The judge and the attorneys plowed through some thirty-seven categories that Parsons had asked to be apprised of.

Sirhan spent most of the proceedings sizing up the caliber of the opposition: David Fitts, the meticulous one, looked most formidable; Chief Deputy District Attorney Lynn Compton, a onetime right guard at UCLA, looked like a crew-cut Lee J. Cobb; and John Howard like a friendly teddy bear. At only one point did Sirhan seem disturbed, when Fitts read the names of four young men who were with Sirhan early on the night of June 4: Maroof Bedran, Abdo Malki, Gaymoard Mistri and Amwar Sayegh. Were these four possibly coconspirators? The prosecution didn't think so. In fact, all the information turned over to the defense concerning "other suspects," said Deputy District Attorney Buck Compton, was negative. Later, at a press conference, Parsons supported Compton: "We have seen no evidence," he said, "of a conspiracy." That got top line next morning in the L.A. *Times:* "BOTH SIDES AGREE SIRHAN WAS ALONE." Deep in this story was more detail—some of the material Evelle Younger was fighting to release to the press, which was an obvious leak to the L.A. *Times*'s man in the courthouse, Ron Einstoss. Jonn Christian, the *Ramparts* writer who liked the conspiracy theory, refused to believe. "They're bureaucrats," he said. "They got the gun. That's enough." Christian was hardly a fan of the Dallas police, and he feared a cover-up by the LAPD. "The police," he said, "would probably like to bury the conspiracy and let it lie."

As a matter of fact, some investigators in the LAPD and the FBI had grown skeptical and more than a little weary running down leads that were either false or inconclusive.

The FBI learned that some Americans on a tour in the Middle East heard rumors in mid-May that Robert Kennedy had been shot. But how did the FBI assess the significance of a report like that? Did the Al Fatah order the killing of Kennedy and was the order ground out of the rumor mill as a *fait accompli?* Who could say? *

---

* The Los Angeles police finally assumed that this rumor was started by a Reuters dispatch from London that Senator Kennedy had been struck by a stone hurled at him as he was leaving San Fernando Valley College in Los Angeles in an open car. The report gained something in translation by Israeli radio. According to *Kol Yisrael,* the missile knocked Kennedy out of the car, the police could not control the crowd, and additional details were not yet available.

The bag of clothing (including a polka-dot dress) that was found and turned over to the police was a good symbol of the plight of the LAPD. Sergeant Chic Guitierrez inspected the garments in the property room of S.U.S. They were mostly new. The underthings had been worn only once or twice and never laundered. All the clothing was mass produced. There might have been a million Lovable bras sold in 1968. Who bought this one? And where? How did it all add up? In private, Guitierrez would say with philosophic despair, "Somebody just wanted to make me work." But the police couldn't make public admissions like that, which would only draw criticism on the department itself—and on the mayor, too, in an election year. Like most things in this life, nothing would be resolved in a nice neat package, much less tied with blue ribbon.

Still, the police and the FBI hardly did all they could. They used faulty logic and browbeat witnesses to eliminate "the girl in the polka-dot dress." They failed to find some old friends of Sirhan who were not beyond suspicion. They failed to exercise enough zeal in questioning other friends of Sirhan who obviously knew more than they admitted.

There was, for example, the man named Edward Van Antwerp, with whom Sirhan had lived for five months at Norco. Van Antwerp had disappeared without a word to anyone at 9:00 A.M. on June 4. When the FBI found him in Eureka, California, on June 16, he said he had never known Sirhan, much less lived with him. His wife said he knew Sirhan? She probably said that, he said, to get the FBI's help in locating him, for he had run away.

Special FBI Agent Richard G. Miller reinterviewed Van Antwerp the next day and took a picture of Sirhan along with him. After a good deal of conversation with Agent Miller and a good deal of squinting at the picture, Van Antwerp came to the sudden realization that Sirhan was the man he had lived with for five months. His face, reported Miller, showed "total amazement."

Apparently, however, Van Antwerp's initial denial and too-obvious surprise added up to nothing. Apparently, the bureau was content with Agent Miller's sum-up: "Van Antwerp has no knowledge of Sirhan's associates, social organization affiliations, political beliefs, ethnic background, family, or anything else of a personal nature."

Parsons stood in front of Judge Walker and asked for another postponement until the first of the year. Reason: his cocounsel was still busy on another case, and the holidays were coming up. Parsons didn't say his cocounsel was Grant Cooper, but the deputy D.A.'s and the judge knew Cooper was coming in and bringing another lawyer in with him from the East—not Edward Bennett Williams as first rumored, for Williams had other commitments, but Emile Zola Berman of New York City.

Walker said he'd give—but not that much. "There's no question," he said, "that the defendant has a right to counsel of his own choosing." If his counsel is not ready, the court would just have to wait. But not until after the holidays. Walker set a date of December 9 and indicated that the attorneys might be able to select a jury before Christmas adjournment.

It seemed silly to pick a jury and then adjourn for Christmas vacation, but Judge Walker had his reasons: (1) A new presiding judge would be selected after Christmas and if the trial had not yet begun, the case might be reassigned to another judge. Walker wanted to try this one—badly. (2) A politically ambitious television commentator named Baxter Ward (among others) was starting to criticize the County Board of Supervisors for letting the case drag on while the taxpayers were paying handsomely for Sirhan's supersecurity. By the end of September, the county's auditor-controller reported that extraordinary costs for the Sirhan case had run to $145,636. The supervisors, in turn, were putting pressure on Judge Walker, and Walker was anxious to calm them down because he had another idea that would end up costing the county $23,367 in hotel bills. He intended to keep the jurors at the Biltmore Hotel to protect them throughout the course of the trial—not so much from their friends and relatives who might force their own prejudices upon them, but from the press. "I know," said Walker, "there is a responsible and an irresponsible press. But I can't control either one of them."

It was not that Judge Walker was hostile to the press. In fact, when more than 150 requests came in from newsmen all over the world for some fifty available press seats in Walker's little courtroom, he conceived the idea of transmitting the proceedings to an auxiliary courtroom by means of a concealed television camera. "In effect," he said, "this is one way of expanding the courtroom."

But Walker balked at a suggestion from Los Angeles County Supervisor Kenneth Hahn that the same video feed be transmitted to the nation on network television. The U.S. Supreme Court had already reversed one major conviction (of Billy Sol Estes for swindling the Federal Government of millions) because some of the Estes trial was carried on live TV. But the Supreme Court's reasoning in the Estes case was not absolutely compelling. If Sirhan didn't object, why should the courts? Were not the courts, in fact, discriminating against the rather complete coverage of television in favor of the necessarily incomplete coverage of the newspapers? Sirhan could have asked that question and thereby forced a judicial review. But he didn't, and Walker resisted pressure from the politicians, even ruling that no video recording could be made of the trial, not for later broadcast, not even for posterity. In this decision and in many more to come, Judge Walker avoided whatever was daring and different, on the stated premise that the defendant could always appeal to a higher court.

Thus, on October 22, when Russell Parsons tried to get a ruling that Sirhan's notebooks were seized by the police illegally—that is, without a search warrant—Walker relied on long-standing precedents and ignored some newer decisions he might have applied.

Parsons argued that the officers had no evidence of a conspiracy, yet there they were rummaging around in Sirhan's room to see what they could find. Later in the day, the officers got a search warrant to look in his car, but they didn't get one to look in his room. Why not? "They may have suspected they couldn't get a search warrant," thundered Parsons. "Maybe that's why they didn't ask for one!"

But Walker turned aside his argument, ruling the evidence was not illegally seized. Later, if Parsons wanted, he could argue its admissibility in court. Under the circumstances, said Walker, the officers had reason to believe Adel Sirhan had the authority to let them take a look.

"We're going to get two Arab experts to testify," Parsons told Sirhan. But Sirhan was more interested in whether any decision had been made about him.

"Will *I* testify?" he asked.

"We'll see," said Parsons. "Maybe your mother—"

Sirhan objected. "My mother! Oh, no! She's too emotional. Her language is bad . . ."

"Well," said Parsons, who was learning that legal cunning pleased Sirhan more than almost anything, "there will probably be mothers on the jury."

"Ah," said Sirhan, kenning quickly, "yeah!" He smiled. Lowering his voice several notches, he asked Parsons about the Washington deal. He was referring to pleas he had made way back on September 24 that Parsons negotiate with the U.S. State Department for extradition to Jordan in return for his "not blowing the top off this thing." Sirhan never explained how he thought he would blow the top off anything, but he hinted that when he did, it would damage U.S.-Arab relations.

Parsons, who hadn't made any such move, misunderstood the reference to Washington and told Sirhan that he'd lined up a psychiatrist from Washington who had worked with the Secret Service on an analytical study of those who had made threats against the life of the President. The doctor was Edwin A. Weinstein of the Washington School of Psychiatry and the Division of Neuropsychiatry at the Walter Reed Army Institute of Research, and he had delivered his conclusions at the annual meeting of the American Psychiatric Association in 1965. But for Sirhan's benefit, Parsons gave Dr. Weinstein a figurative cloak and dagger. "This Washington doctor has access to Secret Service information," said Parsons in a conspiratorial tone, "and we can get it from him. Otherwise," Parsons whispered, "we couldn't get it, not even if President Johnson himself told 'em to give it to us."

Distracted then from his question about the State Department, Sirhan discussed his meeting with Dr. Marcus. He was wary of Marcus, whom he suspected of "trying to warm me up." "I don't know how to react to that," he said.

Sirhan had just read an article presenting Romain Gary's theory of the assassination in *West,* the Los Angeles *Times*'s Sunday magazine. There, Gary had said that Senator Kennedy's "talent, looks and power acted as bait" for a paranoid personality. "By choosing such a great victim, the assassin hoped to rise to a similarly high level, if only for a moment." Gary said Sirhan "could not resist competing with the work of Lee Harvey Oswald, trying to rise to a similar level of tragedy."

But Sirhan didn't buy that judgment from Gary, the famed French writer and then adviser in America to General Charles de Gaulle. He didn't want to be portrayed as anything less than a perfect human specimen. "I wasn't envious of the Kennedys," he protested. "It was just a political motive on my part." He said he didn't want any psychiatric defense to "sugarcoat" him. All he wanted was the truth. His truth.

Parsons went right along with that. "This," he said, meaning Sirhan's Arab nationalism, "is your principal defense. They're not going to like it." He didn't say who "they" were. "But we'll take it all the way to the Supreme Court."

"Oh, boy!" said Sirhan, squirming gleefully as if he'd just been handed a bag of *im la bas.** He patted Parsons on the knee.

---

* Sugar-covered almonds.

Encouraged, Parsons continued in the same vein. "They'll try to rebut, but I'll—"

"Well, I'm not psychotic," said Sirhan. "That article they wrote about me in *West* says I was psychotic, that I envied the Kennedys. I'm not psychotic!" He shook his head with vehemence.

"You may not be psychotic," I said, "but you've got to cooperate with your doctors." I drew a box on the bottom of my yellow legal pad and scored it with horizontal lines. "You see," I said, "this is the whole Sirhan, all these layers. You may only be conscious of this top layer. But if you open up with the psychiatrists and psychologists, they may be able to discover things you don't even know about yourself." I had a psychologist friend named Tom Greening who had outlined eleven factors in the making of an assassin, including the man's set of values, his intellectual assessment of reality, the cultural climate he lived in and his underlying psychodynamic motivation. Obviously, if this exhaustive study of Sirhan was going to get anywhere and if the study would reveal anything of value to the world at large, Sirhan's cooperation—even if unwitting—was absolutely necessary.

Sirhan nodded dubiously. Parsons seconded my suggestion. The conversation wandered a bit, then I asked Sirhan about his notebook.

"Let me explain about that," said Sirhan, in an unusual fit of candor. "It all has to do with psychic phenomena, the occult. I got a lot of my ideas from *The Edinburgh Lectures on Mental Science,* by Thomas Troward. In that book, Troward talks about the philosophy of mind, the objective mind in relation to the universal mind. If you give your subjective mind an intense command by your objective mind, your subjective mind will gather the information to carry out the commands of the objective mind. When I listened to RFK—I was sitting there watching his television documentary and drinking tea—I said, 'you S.O.B. If I had a million dollars, I'd put you in the White House!' I was with him. I really wanted him. But at the end when the bit about Israel came on, I had a fit. Then, when I heard he was at a Jewish social club in Beverly Hills, I had a double fit. That's when I determined to stop RFK." It was a long speech for Sirhan and on a subject he had avoided up to then and would often avoid in the future. "I sat in front of a mirror in my room." This was, apparently, soon after he'd seen the offending image of Robert Kennedy reporting in 1948 on the Arab-Israeli war in Palestine. "I concentrated on RFK in the mirror: I had to stop him. Finally, his face was in that mirror instead of my own. Then I went to my notebook and started writing. It was part of the auto suggestion necessary to get my subjective mind to get my objective mind moving. I read in the Rosicrucian magazine how if you wanted to do any-thing, you should write it down. It automatically works toward the realiza-tion of what you want. With that power," said Sirhan, with great intensity, "I could have been a millionaire! A millionaire! Ohh, shit!"

In quick succession, he rolled questions before his visitors: "Why did I not go to the races that day? Why did I not like the horses? Why did I go to that range? Why did I save those Mini-Mags? Why did I not expend those bullets? Why did I go to Bob's? Why did Mistri give me that news-paper? Why did I drink that night?" As Sirhan rattled this litany of deeds, he clenched his fists and planted his feet solidly on the floor as if protest-ing and resisting—what? "It was," he said, "like some inner force."

"But you wrote in your notebook 'R.F.K. must die'—"

"After the bit with the mirror," said Sirhan, "I forgot it all. The idea of killing Kennedy never entered my mind, sir. I just wanted, sir, to stop him from sending planes to Israel."

At the very end of the interview, I asked Sirhan if he was at the Am-bassador Hotel on Sunday, June 2. "I was home," he said quickly. "I stayed home, sir, that day." I said that some movies taken at the Kennedy rally at the Ambassador Hotel might show that he was present there. Sir-han frowned. "I don't think I was at the Ambassador that day."

"You 'don't think' you were there?"

"Well," he said, "everything about those days were so hazy." Then, a light. All of a sudden, he remembered something. "I drove to Corona," he said.

"To see whom?"

He hesitated. "To see the countryside. I like the scenery out there," he added weakly, and I started making some noises which indicated I didn't believe.

Parsons came to the rescue. "It *is* nice out there," he said to me. "Beau-tiful scenery out that way." Sirhan turned to Parsons and smiled gratefully, and Parsons went on to relate some stories about his own experiences in that part of Riverside County.

I produced a picture of Crispin Curiel Gonzalez from a newspaper clip-ping, telling of his arrest in Juarez, Mexico. "Ever see this kid before?" I asked.

"No," said Sirhan. "Who is he?" I told him he was a young man who had been picked up in Mexico with some puzzling notes on his person that indicated he'd known Sirhan and known Sirhan planned to kill Kennedy. "Where is he now?" asked Sirhan.

I said he was dead. "He was found hanging from his cell bars one morning." A brief look of dismay passed across Sirhan's face. Why? *

As Parsons and I moved to depart, I said, "We've got to talk more about your Corona period." Sirhan greeted this suggestion with no enthusiasm at all. "I mean, it *was* a significantly successful part of your life." Still no reaction. "You got five raises in five months?" No reaction. "Didn't you?"

"Yes."

"Well, that's a side of you I haven't seen." Sirhan nodded. I shifted gears. "Have you read *Witness* yet?" I had recommended it to Sirhan some weeks before.

Now Sirhan showed some life. "Yes!" he cried. "Three times!"

"Three times?"

"Yes, it's great! Is he still writing for *Time?*" I told him Whittaker Chambers was dead. "Oh," said Sirhan.

All in all, it was a valuable session, one in which Sirhan revealed something that could help his defense, though this was so minimally apparent to Sirhan that he called for Parsons and McCowan the next day to tell them to suppress the story about seeing Kennedy's face in the mirror and the writing in the notebook. "I don't want that to come out anywhere," he said. "Ever. And tell Kaiser he can't write about that."

He'd been thinking about something else: his activities on June 2. He confessed to Parsons and McCowan, "I really was at the Ambassador on Sunday. But I didn't want to tell Kaiser." Why not? "Well, because Kaiser's only interested in writing a book. I'm worried about the trial." Neither Parsons nor McCowan reminded him that I, too, was an investigator specifically charged with developing "all the background material he could obtain for the purpose of establishing Sirhan's mental state at the time of the shooting for the benefit of the psychologists and psychiatrists working on the case." McCowan had something else in mind: he was thinking about writing his own book.

On November 9, Federal authorities in Brooklyn, New York, picked up two men for plotting to assassinate President-Elect Nixon. Both of the men were Arabs. The men were subsequently tried and acquitted.

* I learned why a week later when Sirhan implied he knew Gonzalez.
"That kid didn't have to die," said Sirhan. *"He* didn't do anything."
"Who would have wanted to get him out of the way?" I asked.
Sirhan paused reflectively for a moment, then smiled. Then he changed the subject.

"What the hell's this about the conspiracy in New York?" demanded Sirhan in his cell on Monday, November 11. He was angry because some other goddamn Arabs were crabbing his act.

"Well," said Parsons, "it's not good for us. It's not good. I'm sorry. I have to comment on it for the press."

Sirhan nodded soberly and avoided looking at me. He had already told me too much; he had already made that clear to Parsons, and so Parsons seized control of this interview. I sensed Sirhan's hostility and let Parsons go, hoping he would ask Sirhan about the Corona period of his life—from June, 1966, to mid-December. Instead, he asked Sirhan to tell the story of his fall from the horse, a story he and other eyewitnesses had already told.

I fumed quietly while Sirhan and Parsons rambled on together. Finally, when Parsons ran out of questions, I asked Sirhan what he thought of the election's outcome.

"Nixon!" he said. "He's worse than Kennedy. To get the Jewish vote, he said he'd help the Israelis. But what good did it do him? Hell, he only got 4 percent of the Jewish vote. Humphrey got most of it, the son of a bitch. Nixon! Hell, I gave him the election." He glared at me. "Hell, I gave it to him!"

In his next interview with Parsons and McCowan, Sirhan repeated his election analysis. He'd given Nixon the Presidency. Therefore, Nixon ought to arrange his freedom, a passport to Jordan and a million dollars. Sirhan had his demand all printed out carefully on a long sheet of paper. He didn't want to go to trial. "We are desperate!!!" he wrote, underlining the phrase three times for emphasis.

Judge Walker was counting on Cooper's coming into the case by mid-November so he could get the Sirhan trial started, at least, on December 9, as he had planned. But no. Now, it seemed, the Friars' case would stretch on until the first week in December, which would give Cooper no time at all to prepare.

Judge Walker was sitting in his chambers across the street in the Hall of Justice when Parsons gave him this news. He cursed angrily, then settled down a bit. The pressures from the public hadn't lessened, and Walker was taking much of the brunt. "But let's face it," said Parsons later on the corner of Temple and Spring, "there really isn't a goddamn thing he can do. The case law is clear."

"Yeah," said McCowan smartly, recalling the best of the cases holding that a defendant is entitled to the attorney of his choice, *"Powell* vs. *Alabama."*

"Okay," I said, "then let's worry about something else. Let's worry about getting Dr. Schorr up here." Dr. Martin M. Schorr was the psychologist from San Diego whom Parsons had been playing with for months. Parsons had gotten letters from two San Diego judges recommending Schorr as a good man in the courtroom, with a gift for making complicated psychological matters clear to an ordinary jury. Why hadn't he followed up with Schorr?

Parsons flared. "I'm not too sure I want Schorr in this case," he said. "He's too goddamn eager." But then, a minute later, Parsons announced that he would phone Schorr that evening and bring him to Los Angeles. Then he took McCowan and me out for coffee, and treated us to a series of fond reminiscences.

A session with Parsons was a dizzying experience; his mind was a centrifuge, and anyone trying to follow his thoughts was led into a space voyage without direction. McCowan reminded Parsons he was overdrawn at the bank. Bank? Oh, yes, that led to another story: Bob Kennedy, it seemed, had paid a call, as an investigator for the Senate Rackets Committee, on Parsons' banker in L.A. "Kennedy wanted to know if Parsons was holding any funds for Murray Chotiner." Parsons sang the name of Chotiner in a basso profundo, for Chotiner, who once shared an office with Parsons, was an associate of Richard M. Nixon. "The Senate Rackets Committee checking on me with my banker!" exclaimed Parsons. "That hurt me. I had an application in for a loan, and I didn't get it. I didn't get it. Kennedy hurt me with my banker. He was a dirty son of a bitch and I never forgave him for that. I saw Kennedy at a McClellan hearing later and I told him that anytime he wanted to know how much I had in the bank to come and ask me." Now that Parsons was wound up, it was hard for him to wind down. He said he was glad Nixon had won. "This country needs a change," said Parsons. "I mean, could you or I start a riot and get away with it?"

Eight

**"Lawyers are not magicians.
We should enter a plea of guilty."**

Dr. Martin M. Schorr might have been nervous under the best conditions. He suffered from (among other things) acrophobia and ill-fitting contact lenses that caused him to tilt his head back in an eyeball-to-eyeball confrontation and crane this way and that like some barnyard fowl on the lookout for stray bits of grain. And here he was, in Sirhan's cell, intimidated not only by the elaborate security arrangements and a team of deputies looking on, but also by the presence of Russell Parsons and Mike McCowan.

Parsons had kept Schorr wondering for months whether he'd get into the case and now that he was "in," Schorr wasn't inclined to object to the conditions imposed on him. He had become interested lately in murder, handled a good many murders for the district attorney in San Diego County, and was convinced that men killed their wives, mistresses, friends, enemies, business partners and Vietcong villagers to get even with their overcontrolling mothers—or possibly their fathers—for past wrongs—or possibly only imagined wrongs. He wanted to write a book about this psychodynamic pattern called *Murder Is a Family Affair*.

So Schorr proceeded to administer the Rorschach Inkblot Test, the Bender-Gestalt, the TAT and the MMPI while Parsons and McCowan tried to stand by and keep their mouths shut, sometimes with little success. McCowan could hardly conceal his dislike for Schorr, and, at one point, Parsons even cackled at one of Schorr's questions to Sirhan. "I don't know who's crazier," he said in jest, pointing at Schorr, "you or Sirhan."

Despite these intrusions and the breakdown of his tape recorder, Schorr made the best of a bad situation. And, like Richardson, he was pleased that Sirhan had been able to respond so well to the Rorschach. The tests showed some immediately obvious signs of severe emotional disturbance. But some responses also made startling good sense. At the end of the interview Schorr asked Sirhan, "If you had three wishes, what would they be?"

Said Sirhan, "One, a pardon from President Nixon. Two, two million dollars. Three, the freedom to spend it."

As they left the jail, Parsons told Schorr how lucky he was to be in the case. "You couldn't buy publicity like you're gonna get for $100,000."

"You may be right," said Schorr. "I'll bill you for my expenses, but I'll put the fee on the cuff."

"Shit," said Parsons. "We could get 50,000 psychologists for free. In fact, they'd pay us!"

"Well," said Schorr, "when I get up on the stand, I like to say I'm getting paid. It looks more professional."

"Oh, fuck!" said McCowan.

McCowan and Parsons were disturbed by Schorr. So, too, was Sirhan. The next day he asked his jailer to send Parsons right up to see him.

"I want to plead guilty," Sirhan said. "I don't want a trial. I don't want the doctors proving I'm insane." Parsons and McCowan tried to soothe him, but he wouldn't be soothed. He pulled a sheet of paper out from under his mattress. It was a note for Judge Walker, berating him for turning down Parsons' motion to suppress the notebooks. "You're a bloodthirsty bastard," it read, "so take a good deep drink of my blood because justice will not be served." He said he knew he wouldn't get a fair trial because of "the Kennedys' power and the judge's bias." Said Sirhan: "I want to plead *nolo contendere.*"

"That's funny," said McCowan, who was learning how to coddle Sirhan, "you must be psychic. We've been thinking about pleading guilty for two months now and we didn't know how you'd react. The only thing is, we feel there's material we couldn't put in if we pleaded guilty."

"What material?" asked Sirhan.

"About the Arab-Israeli war," said Parsons. "The atrocities of the Jews."

"Oh," said Sirhan. "Oh, yeah."

"The problem is," said Parsons, "to admit you shot Kennedy without losing our defense."

Sirhan nodded, convinced as Parsons was that the Arab-Israeli conflict could be replayed in the Los Angeles County Hall of Justice.

Cooper came into the case on December 2. That day the Federal jury finally reached a verdict in the Friars' affair (of guilty for all the defendants) and Cooper was free at last to acknowledge what had been an open secret around town: that he was indeed going to defend Sirhan. Reporters surrounded him outside the Federal Courthouse on Temple and Spring, got his confirmation and wondered why he was taking the case. "Lawyers have a duty to take on unpopular causes," said Cooper. "Otherwise, some of the accused wouldn't enjoy due process. I've been preaching this for years and now it's time for me to practice what I preach."

Why had he denied a wire-service story that he would defend Sirhan? Cooper explained his dilemma. If he was forced to admit he was Sirhan's attorney, his obligation to his client in Federal court would force him to withdraw as Sirhan's attorney. Acknowledgment then was tantamount to withdrawal. So the only course was a diplomatic lie. Cooper didn't use the term but that's what it was, a diplomatic lie, a dutiful response that would harm no one. Cooper had had a similar conflict situation in Federal court only a few weeks earlier. One of his cocounsel had obtained a volume of the Federal Grand Jury transcript and given it to Cooper. When the judge asked him where it had come from, he said he didn't know. Saying he did know, or even declining to answer on the grounds that an answer would violate the attorney-client privilege, would have incriminated his client, and he had a duty not to do that. From the other side of the table, however, the U.S. attorney had a different view, and his investigation of the matter would cause Cooper a good bit of trouble he didn't need at a time when he was entering the most important case of his distinguished career under pressure of the greatest public scrutiny.

An immediate example of Cooper's high visibility came in the next morning's Los Angeles *Times,* which had not one story about Cooper, but three: a lead story on the Sirhan case, a sidebar on Cooper, and another (which had been sitting in cold storage) on his difficulties over the Federal Grand Jury transcript.

Parsons and McCowan met in Cooper's office to decide on their direction. Parsons felt the Federal Government could be "very vindictive" with Cooper. Cooper said he wasn't going to worry about it. He'd done his duty to his client, which is a lawyer's first duty, and that was that. It wouldn't be the first time he was in trouble. In the Finch case, he'd protested so bitterly when the judge had tried to tell the deadlocked jury which witnesses were "more believable," that he was cited—twice—for contempt of court. He appealed to the California Supreme Court on that, and won, on the grounds that he was merely doing what a good lawyer should do for his client.

Now, Cooper wanted to get on with the Sirhan case, for he hardly expected Judge Walker to postpone it much longer. Cooper's crisp manner was in real contrast to Parsons' woolly ways. His first consideration, he said, was to save Sirhan's life. He'd read a brilliant summary of the state's evidence prepared by McCowan. To Cooper, it was a clear case of first-degree murder.

"Not necessarily," said McCowan.

"He was lying in wait, wasn't he?" asked Cooper. "Didn't some witnesses see him waiting around for Kennedy in the kitchen?"

"They might have seen someone else who looked like Sirhan," said McCowan. "A kid named Michael Wayne."

"Well, would we be derelict in our duty," asked Cooper, "if we pleaded guilty in return for a sentence of life, rather than death in the gas chamber?"

Parsons pointed out that there was a good chance for second degree, based on the California law of diminished capacity. "Yes," said Cooper, "the psychologists' testimony could reduce what looks like first degree to second degree. And there's the matter of the alcohol. We've got to see the results of that blood test."

McCowan suggested a chromosome test be given to Sirhan, for there was some indication that chromosomic abnormality caused impulsive violence in some. In Sirhan, it could be further extenuating evidence. Parsons had asked for time to think about it. Cooper agreed on the spot. "It won't hurt," he said.

Parsons told Cooper about Sirhan's desire to make a deal with the U.S. State Department. Cooper shifted his weight impatiently when Parsons began to ramble off on several tangents. Finally, Cooper shook his head. "Not at this stage," he said. "After the trial maybe." Cooper went on with instructions to McCowan. He wanted him to check thoroughly on the movements of Michael Wayne. Parsons tried to interrupt four times. "Wait," said Cooper, "let me go on here." McCowan's eyes glistened with admiration. He was getting more decisive action in one morning from Cooper than he had gotten from Parsons in a month.

Cooper and Parsons were indeed men of differing styles. In the forties, while Russell Parsons was defending some well-known members of what is sometimes called The Mob, an assistant district attorney named Grant Cooper had tried to run them out of town.

Parsons' creative arguments before the California Supreme Court had established new law in the state (and the nation), but he never seemed to charge enough or collect the fees that should by now have given him the normal affluence of any average attorney. The best Cooper could get for his most publicized clients were stalemates, but he collected handsome fees.

Parsons was a lonely man who slept in a dingy residence hotel. Cooper, surrounded by a wife, five children and ten grandchildren, lived in the solid, modest opulence of Hancock Park.

Parsons' cramped downtown office was a ruin, his desk a bramblebush of correspondence and briefs and opened lawbooks, his walls devoid of any personal mementos, his floor crowded with briefcases and half-forgotten files. Cooper's office, off the Hollywood freeway, was spacious and oak-paneled, decorated with teakwood furniture, fishing trophies, pictures on the walls of Cooper and some prize marlin taken off Baja California.

Plaques behind Cooper's desk indicated he was president of the Los Angeles Bar Association and a member of the Board of Governors of the State Bar. Parsons served on no legal committees, Cooper on many, including the American Bar Association Committee on Free Press and Fair Trial.

Parsons lunched at Mannings' cafeteria, Cooper at the Brown Derby. Cooper drove a Thunderbird, Parsons a Cheverolet. And, while Parsons bored reporters with stories that never seemed to come to the point, Cooper knew what the newsmen needed and delivered it with heart and wit.

But both were good legal technicians, both of them loved the law and both of them were as determined as Wirin to prove to the world that even an accused assassin could get a fair trial, even and especially in Los Angeles County.

"Have you thought of a change of venue, Mr. Cooper?" asked a reporter when Cooper appeared at the Hall of Justice to see Sirhan the first time.

Cooper smiled weakly: "Where would we go?" Parsons wryly suggested Caribou, Maine. The point was clear. Who in the United States had failed to hear about the death of Senator Kennedy? Who wasn't already convinced that Sirhan, the assassin, should get the ultimate penalty? What major American assassin's life had yet been spared?

Even Cooper's friends, who were frank in their admiration for his taking the case, wished him bad luck. A lawyer from San Francisco wrote:

Dear Grant,

A lady who is near, dear and precious to me and has been for over 52 years asked the following question: "Is it ethical and proper for a lawyer to defend a man like the one who killed Robert Kennedy?" I answered, "It is not only ethical and proper, it is practically compulsory. Also, in this particular case, it evidences the pinnacle of legal ethics; the lawyer who takes such a case is a defender of the Constitution. I know the lawyer you mean. He is Grant Cooper. I think that he has done a great favor to the Bar and great credit to himself. Don't you ever think anything else."

As you may guess I was talking to a female. She said, "He couldn't be my lawyer." So I said that he could be mine.

All of the foregoing nonsense is to congratulate you on defending an accused criminal who is now the best-hated man in America.

I hope that you lose your case.

On Tuesday, December 3, Cooper went up with Parsons to see Sirhan. "All I want to do today," said Cooper, "is get acquainted with you and see whether you want me to represent you, along with Russ."

"You bet!" said Sirhan with enthusiasm.

Cooper wanted to make sure of that. He told Sirhan about his troubles in Federal court. Sirhan had read about them in the morning paper. "There may be some unfavorable publicity because of this," said Cooper. "I don't want to hurt your case."

"How much could they hurt my case?" said Sirhan.

"Well, if the jury thought your lawyer was no good . . ." Sirhan said he wasn't worried about that. He'd read about Cooper during the Finch-Tregoff case and he knew he was good. "Okay," said Cooper. "As long as you know."

Parsons said, "We're just trying to be frank with you, you know."

Cooper told Sirhan he had secured an agreement from Emile Zola Berman to come into the case. Cooper said Berman was Jewish, "but he's a helluva able lawyer." Cooper said there was a lot of responsibility here, and three lawyers could share the work load and the decisions. "We're not going to make any decisions until we have all the facts," said Cooper, "but Russ tells me you might want to plead guilty."

"I can plead *nolo contendere,*" whispered Sirhan. He didn't understand the exact legal meaning of the phrase or the implications of such a plea, but it rolled nicely off his tongue.

"Well, I guess we could," said Cooper, "but we're looking into the possibility of pleading guilty and arguing to the penalty. The main thing we're trying to do is save your life."

Cooper suggested he might even ask the jury to spare Sirhan's life so he could be traded in the future for some important U.S. prisoner, as the Russian spy Abel was traded to the Russians for U-2 pilot Gary Powers. "The situation over in the Near East is very hot now," said Cooper, "and it could develop into a red hot war where—"

"That's what I mean," said Sirhan earnestly. He lowered his voice even more. "Hell, I could, I could trigger it just like that."

Cooper cut him off. "Well, these are some of the factors we're thinking about."

"My life is in your hands," said Sirhan. But he wanted his attorneys to open up the diplomatic channels immediately. Cooper told Sirhan that was premature. Sirhan started to object, and Parsons stepped in with a long rambling story about a visiting newsman from Beirut that had no relation at all to Sirhan's request, and ended with a promise from the Beirut newspaperman that the Arabs would indeed raise some money for Sirhan's defense. Bags of money, it seemed, always bobbed at the end of Parsons' streams of consciousness.

But Cooper interjected here. "I want to make one thing clear. You're going to get a defense whether we get any money or not."

Next day in the makeshift courtroom on the thirteenth floor, Sirhan spoke out loud and clear when Judge Walker asked him if he wanted Grant Cooper as his attorney: "Very much so, Your Honor!"

Cooper told the judge he needed more time to prepare his case and asked for a postponement to January 7. He promised that the association of a third attorney, Emile Zola Berman, of New York, would not mean another continuance. Walker thought the postponement was reasonable and granted the motion over the *pro forma* objections of the prosecution. One month was really not enough time to prepare properly, but Walker had already indicated he would give no more. For the duration of the case, Cooper would have to improvise.

Deputies did not search Cooper on his second visit to Sirhan's cell. It was a point of personal protocol Parsons had waived, but Cooper insisted on the right of an attorney to see his client without going through a search that had a certain symbolism that was offensive to him as an officer of the court. It was Cooper's first full interview with Sirhan and he asked him all the hard, obvious questions.

"One of the most important things in the world for a lawyer," said Cooper, "and more important for you, is that I get the complete truth. A lawyer's just got to have the truth—and that means the whole complete truth—because I can't operate any other way. I know how to soft-pedal it if we have to soft-pedal it, but I don't care what you have told anybody in the past, you see? Whatever you give me as the truth, I am going to operate on. Now, let me tell you, if you give me something that's not the truth—"

"That hurts," said Sirhan.

"It's going to hurt you," said Cooper, "because I am going to rely on what you tell me and I am going to predicate our defense on what you tell me. If you give me a wrong steer, it's going to be your fault and not mine. It's not going to be Russ's—I don't care what you have told Russ in the past, I don't care what you have told any of the psychiatrists in the past, I want, for your sake, not for mine, for your sake—and I don't care how bad it is—I just want the complete unvarnished truth. Now, I suppose the thing for me to do now is to shut up and let you tell your story. I don't mean going back from your boyhood—I am not interested in that at the moment—I am interested in now when you first determined you were going to kill Kennedy, because it's written down in books and everything, and they have it, so you tell me—forget what you said to them—"

"Well—"

"You level with me."

"I will level with you," said Sirhan. "Really, I can't deviate much from what I have told Mr. Parsons." He told Cooper the same story he'd been telling everyone else. Sirhan admitted he'd vowed in his notebook to kill Kennedy. "But honestly, sir, I had no intention of carrying it forward."

"But, nevertheless, you still wrote it down."

"I still wrote it down," said Sirhan.

"Well, is there something in your Rosicrucian teaching that says to you, 'If I am going to do something, I will put it down and then I will do it'?"

"Well, it's auto suggestion, you might say."

"Now, where was it, though, that you very definitely decided to do it?"

"I honestly did not decide to do it, sir—very definitely. Objectively, I had no awareness of what I was doing that night. I will swear to anything on that point. How I really got to go to that area—that Ambassador area, on Wilshire Boulevard—was that evening when I saw an advertisement in the newspaper, June 4, about the Israeli—a parade to celebrate the victory of last year's war."

"But you had the gun with you?"

"I had the gun with me, yes."

"Why were you target practicing?"

"I was tired. I was at the races. I was losing all the time, and that day I did not like those horse entries. Why—I still don't know why the hell I didn't go—I wish I did. I decided to go target shooting instead of going to the races, I think, and that's how I went—"

"Well, you must have gone out there with a purpose—in other words, to me, your lawyer—"

"I understand that—"

"I am on your side—but as I view it—in other words, you heard Kennedy make a statement, in substance, that he wanted to send these airplanes to Israel [Cooper was accepting Sirhan's post-factum rationalization here]—this burned you up, and then you write down in the book 'Kennedy must go,' 'Kennedy must go'—or words to that effect—something to that effect, several times—and you had a gun—and you were angry, and I can understand that you decided on the one hand that you would do it, but you didn't actually believe that you would do it?"

"No—I never believed that I would do it."

Sirhan said he'd gone to the Ambassador to see Kennedy on Sunday June 2.

"Did you have your gun with you?"

"No, sir, I didn't. I just went there as a guest. Like the advertisement invited."

"Did you see him?"

"Yes, I did."

"And what did you do? How long did you stay there?"

"I stayed there to hear him talk, you know—10:30, or whatever it is there."

"Did you hear him talk?"

"Yes, yes, sir, I did."

"What did he say? Did he say anything about the Israelis that night?"

"No, he didn't. He just encouraged people to get out and work and campaign for him."

Cooper asked Sirhan to tell him what he had done all day Tuesday, June 4. Sirhan told him about practicing on the range, going to Bob's for a hamburger, looking for the Jewish parade and ending up at the Ambassador. Sirhan said he didn't know until later that Kennedy was even there. But then he thought he'd start drinking. "Everybody was—it was like a party— Hell, what do people go to parties for? Fun—you know—celebration. So I started drinking."

"When you left your car," asked Cooper, "what did you do with your gun?"

"I left it in the car."

"You did?"

"Yes, sir."

"All right. You didn't take the gun with you?"

"No, no—the gun was already gone. It was past. I had forgotten all about it when this Jewish thing got into me. The parade."

"All right." Cooper said "all right" but his tone was skeptical.

"When I started going down to the parade that gun was completely out of my mind, sir."

"All right, go ahead."

"I am not pulling your leg, or anything. That's the gospel truth. You will never believe it, but I'll keep on—"

"All right," said Cooper impatiently. "All right—go ahead."

Sirhan told about his drinking, meeting a few people who were standing around, talking, deciding he was drunk, going back to his car. "I got into the car, but, hell, I couldn't drive. I was too drunk. The idea of driving in the condition that I was in doesn't appeal to me. Then I said, 'Sober up, try to run around the block if you can, get coffee,' and that's what hit me —go and get some coffee at the Ambassador. And I went down again. I don't remember taking the gun with me."

"Obviously you did."

"I did. Obviously I did. But I have no recollection of taking it with me."

"You really don't?"

"I honestly don't. Really, that's all that happened."

"Well, what was the next thing you remember?"

"Then this choking business—"

"You don't remember anything else?"

"I don't remember what happened after that."

"Well," said Cooper, "who do you think killed him?"

"Obviously I must have—but I have no exact—no objective of what I was doing."

Cooper shook his head at Sirhan's syntax and had Sirhan go over several areas again. He wanted to get straight Sirhan's story about watching the Kennedy film. "Now, let me see if I can get this. You were so mad that you almost immediately went and wrote this down in the book?"

"Well—"

"Within a short time."

"Sometime that evening."

"Now, why did you write that down in your book?"

"Because—I couldn't believe it. He was—that was the last straw"

"Let me ask you this. You felt that he should be dead?"

"I didn't like him at all. So whatever in hell happened to him, I didn't give a damn."

"Well, obviously you felt that you were the one to stop him."

"Yes, I did."

"Obviously."

"It's obvious."

"Now, then, it's obvious that at least that subconscious idea went through."

"It did."

"In other words, you felt on the one hand that I have got to do it—'I have got to do it'—at the same time you told yourself it was stupid."

"It was. It was. It is stupid. Very. It was."

"Is that the way you felt?"

"That's the way I felt and that's the way I feel now, but more so, now that it is—"

Cooper said that surely Sirhan was angry with Kennedy when he went to see him at the Ambassador on June 2.

"No, I wasn't," said Sirhan.

Sirhan's story didn't make sense. "Why not?" asked Cooper.

"This is—well, you have to hit me at the time. At the time I heard these things I was mad, but again, sir, the madness, this feeling, this emotion or whatever, had subsided. This is where I came in—I had to do it, but I didn't, but I couldn't or shouldn't—this double feeling here, and that's why, I thought I decided to like him again when I went down there to see him."

"Well, did you see him on Sunday."

"I did see him on Sunday."

"Now, tell me this. Where did you spend all day Sunday?"

"I was home Sunday."

"Didn't you go to some Corona—or something—"

Sirhan said, "I could have driven there. I have driven there almost every day since I fixed my car."

"Don't you have a friend in Corona?" asked Cooper.

"I had some friends there, yes, but I wasn't—" Cooper asked about Peggy Osterkamp. "No, I didn't see her at all, sir."

"You are sure, now?"

"No, I am sure I did not see her."

"Now, let me ask you this—did anybody suggest that you do this?"

"No, sir, nobody."

"Did anybody talk to you in a way that agreed with your point of view about him? In other words, that he was a no-good so-and-so?"

"No. No, this is all mine, sir. This Israeli business—it really bugged me. I couldn't believe it. I would rather have died, sir, rather than live with it. I have a—the shock of it, the humility—the humility, and all this talk about the Jews being victorious—"

Cooper asked Sirhan about his earliest recollections, his life in Palestine and some of the bombings and the violence of the war. "All right," said Cooper, "now, here's what I understand. You had this inborn hatred, which I can understand, and then Kennedy made this switch—Bobby Kennedy, I am talking about—and then you decided to kill him. Obviously you did, because you wrote it down in the book. There's no question about that. Why did you cool off, through? I don't understand why you cooled off, if you had this inborn hatred and he was the personification of those —of one who was going to give aid to the enemy?"

"He could have just said that story for the votes, and then maybe he could have decided not to send those arms after he—after, you know, those Jews voted for him. But I have this feeling, sir. It was instantaneous at that minute, and it was good for while it lasted, you might say." Sirhan smiled, and it still didn't make sense to Cooper.

"Well, let's analyze it. It's obvious to me that you finally found out somehow that he was going to come through the kitchen area, or you thought he was going to come through the kitchen area, and he did come through the kitchen area, and you did pull the gun and you did keep pulling it until you—until you—"

"I don't know," said Sirhan.

Cooper allowed that Sirhan's lack of memory might be legitimate, but he wasn't comfortable with it. "All right," he said with a sigh. "Now, let me tell you this. Since that's the situation, I am going to prepare, based on what you have told me."

"It is the truth."

"All right now. If this doesn't work, don't blame me."

"No," said Sirhan.

"See? I mean I am relying on what you tell me."

"This is the truth—as far as I can objectively be, sir. That's the truth."

If that was the story, then Cooper could see only one way to go. "Lawyers are not magicians," he said. "My own feeling is that we should enter a plea of guilty. I haven't made up my mind yet—don't misunderstand me —because I want to talk again with Zuke Berman—I call him Zuke—he will be out next week. My tentative feeling is that it would be wiser to enter a plea of guilty to the offense of murder, and I think from what you have told me—in other words, murder is an unlawful killing of a human being with malice aforethought. Now, obviously, the malice was there—I mean, from what you have told me—and certainly you thought about it ahead of time. I mean, you wrote it down in the book. And my best judgment is—probably, probably they will find you guilty of first degree. The real issue, of course, is going to be life or death. But that's the real issue, you see? Whether you are going to die in the gas chamber or whether you are going to—" Cooper didn't finish. He said the final decision would have to be Sirhan's.

Cooper told Sirhan he wasn't insane enough not to know "the difference between right and wrong." But maybe it would pay to let the prosecution psychiatrist see Sirhan. "One of the psychologists," he said, "has indicated that, in his opinion, you are psychotic."

"Yeah, that—"

"But I mean—in talking to you, you seem as normal as apple pie." For that reason, Cooper didn't see how a jury could give Sirhan anything less than death. He had nothing to lose, then, by letting the prosecution psychiatrist, Dr. Seymour Pollack, see Sirhan. If Pollack found Sirhan mentally ill, Pollack's opinion might help him strike a bargain with the district attorney.

"Strategically," said Cooper after he returned to his office, "this is the wisest thing to do. There's no question about the facts: he killed Kennedy, and he planned it in advance." Furthermore, Cooper said, he wasn't at all happy with Sirhan's story, particularly his altogether too-convenient loss of memory. He wasn't sure he believed it. He didn't see how a jury could either. "It would be better for Sirhan if he could remember, if he could say, 'Yes, I got mad at Kennedy and set out to kill him and I did!' "

"But he doesn't remember," said McCowan.

"Yes, I know," said Cooper bleakly. "What the hell you gonna do? You got to go with what you've got. That's why I lean to a plea."

"He's amenable to a plea," said Parsons.

"Yes," said McCowan with a smile, "but his reason for pleading guilty is that he doesn't think he can get a fair trial from Walker."

Cooper peered at McCowan over his horn-rimmed glasses and unloaded his pipe. "We want to make sure Sirhan doesn't say *that* when he pleads guilty!"

I listened to a tape recording of Cooper's long interview with Sirhan and wrote Cooper a memo about it. I wasn't convinced that Sirhan was telling the whole truth. I wondered who had taught Sirhan this "autosuggestion" he had talked about. I thought his story about going to the Wilshire

District on the night of June 4 shot with contradictions. "My whole mission to Wilshire," he had said, "was a failure." But when Cooper asked him if he had intended to shoot up the "Jewish parade," he replied, "I don't know." It didn't sound as though he had had such high (but dashed) hopes for that evening. On Sunday, June 2, Sirhan said he went to the Ambassador loving Kennedy. "My madness had subsided. I started to like him again." But then, what retriggered him? I had always suspected that Corona (where Sirhan worked as an exercise boy) might be a place where some undue influence was exerted upon Sirhan. And in this interview, he told Cooper something that was news to me: "I drove to Corona practically every day after I fixed my car." But he wouldn't say why he'd gone there so frequently, or whom he'd seen there. And it really wasn't too much help for Parsons to explain away Corona by saying there was "beautiful scenery" in Corona.

"Before we do too much more research on the death penalty," I wrote Cooper, "or call in too many more experts, *we* ought to do a little suggesting of our own—that maybe Sirhan has been programmed to do something he *now* considers 'stupid'—possibly without his complete awareness that he was being so used."

"Do you mind if I show your memo to Sirhan?" asked Cooper over lunch at the Brown Derby.

"I've got enough problems getting him to open up with me," I said. "I'd rather you wouldn't."

Cooper nodded and put the memo in his breast pocket.

Sirhan's oldest brother Sharif was a problem. He had threatened Parsons on the telephone and told McCowan he'd get him too. Late one night in November, McCowan saw someone tampering with his car in the parking lot of his Burbank apartment. He sped downstairs, tiptoed up behind the man and slammed his head into the side of the car, toppling him over, unconscious. McCowan peered at him. It was Sharif. McCowan climbed back to his apartment and looked out of his window for a time while Sharif lay there unconscious. Then McCowan got sleepy and went to bed. When he awoke, Sharif had left, presumably wondering what had happened to him.

Sharif's stated problem was that he felt left out of the family's affairs. Now, with Cooper in the case, Sharif decided to make another appeal for inclusion and came to Cooper's office. Cooper welcomed him warmly— with McCowan at his side, sat him down and wondered what he could do. Sharif had some questions: about a possible change of venue, about Judge

Walker, and about the court order regarding publicity. He complained that Parsons had ignored him. Cooper gave Sharif some forthright answers that seemed to satisfy.

"I'd give my eyes to save Sirhan's life," said Sharif. "But *he* wasn't thinking about his family when he did this. I can't get a job now. I won't be able to get a job for the rest of my life." Cooper nodded sympathetically. "I'm mad at my brother Adel too," said Sharif.

"Why's that?" asked Cooper.

"Because a few days before the fifth of June, Sirhan told Adel, 'Soon I'll be famous and you'll be famous too.' I'm angry with Adel. He should have stopped him."

"Well," said Adel later in exasperation when he was challenged about this, "if I had suspected anything like this, I *would* have stopped him!" What about Sharif's story? "He's lying," said Adel.

The truth, the truth, nothing but the truth. It was hard to come by in this case in any kind of complete form. How could Cooper learn the truth?

Judge Walker would later refuse to authorize lie detectors or truth serums for Sirhan, but Cooper's next move would bring him closer to the truth. Cooper phoned Dr. Bernard L. Diamond at the University of California at Berkeley and asked him if he'd consider coming into the Sirhan case.

"Who wouldn't?" said Diamond frankly. As associate dean of the University of California's School of Criminology and a full professor in both the School of Law and the Department of Psychiatry, Diamond welcomed the chance to work with someone who brought to focus all three of his disciplines.

Cooper was elated. He explained that he and Diamond had worked together on a commission appointed by Governor Pat Brown to make legislative recommendations on insanity and the criminal offender, that no one knew more about the subject than Diamond, that he was, moreover, the state's leading expert on the defense of diminished capacity. Things were going well. If the D.A. wouldn't accept the plea, Cooper would still be able to present a good defense with the help of Diamond and of Emile Berman. Berman was a lawyer who knew how to put a doctor on the stand, and law schools across the nation sought him out to teach their students how to do just that. In Cooper's mind, Berman and Dr. Diamond were an unbeatable combination, and if they were both Jews, all the better, for if Cooper could get Jews in court to help the young Arab, he would diffuse some of the public hostility he felt himself for daring to undertake the case at all.

On December 17, Berman jetted out to Los Angeles from a snowstorm in New York to reconnoiter. He arrived at Cooper's office in a heavy top-coat and a felt hat, which looked odd in informal Los Angeles. Cooper, Parsons and McCowan briefed him on the entire case, held meetings for him with the Los Angeles Police Department and the district attorney's office, took him to the Ambassador Hotel pantry and got his help on some legal decisions.

The meetings began and ended with a subtle battle between Parsons and Berman over the questions of replaying the Arab-Israeli war in the courtroom. Parsons had had more sessions with Abdeen Jabara, the Arab-American attorney from Detroit. He didn't say it out loud but Jabara had some money for Parsons if he could only get a couple of experts in court to tell about the Zionist take-over in Palestine. "To put on Arabs as a counteroffensive in court," said Berman quietly, "would be a very serious step."

"In a defense of diminished responsibility," said Parsons, in his courtroom voice, "damn near anything that influences a man is admissible."

Cooper came between the two. "I won't exploit the Arab-Israeli problem unless and to the extent it helps Sirhan," he said, which satisfied Berman. "However, I am thinking about having an Arab observer here at the trial," which pleased Parsons. On a defense team that was growing by the day, Cooper played the role of peacemaker.

The three attorneys considered the pros and cons of a guilty plea. Berman paced the floor in Cooper's office. He was afraid that a plea might destroy Sirhan's right to a fair trial. "I shudder to think of that," he said.

Already somewhat swayed by Berman's hesitation, Cooper explained the law on his second alternative—the California law on diminished capacity—to Berman. It was a law so new in California that many criminal attorneys ignored it. What it was, said Cooper, was a psychiatric defense that was unencumbered by the impossible terms of the M'Naughton Rule, one that would allow psychiatrists to speak their own language in court and not a legal lingo they didn't understand. Berman nodded. He liked that, and asked for the case law on diminished capacity. He got an armload of it, including Dr. Diamond's article on the subject in the *Stanford Law Review*. "It we're speaking about a psychiatric defense," said Berman, "that means going back to the time he was four years old."

"Right," said Cooper.

McCowan interrupted them with a thought of his own. "I got a feeling in the back of my mind that somebody put him up to this." He explained his funny feeling stemmed from Sirhan's reluctance to talk about the influence on his life of the occult, and his insistence that McCowan and Kaiser stay away from the Rosicrucians.

"Okay," said Berman. "But how does that help our situation?"

"I just give out the facts," said McCowan defensively. "What you do with them is up to you."

"I don't think we're under an obligation to tell the police to investigate the Rosicrucians," said Berman, "unless you can come up with something solid." He reflected a moment and came as close as he ever did to laughter. "But, by God, that *would* shake up this town, wouldn't it?" Berman asked about Sirhan's present state of mind.

Parsons had been with Sirhan earlier in the day, escorting a lab technician who had come to take a blood sample for Sirhan's chromosome test. "He seemed very concerned about the trial," reported Parsons. "He stopped reading the newspapers, he wondered whether I'd gotten in touch with Nixon yet. I held his knee. He looked up at me like a little boy. He's subject to sudden changes, though. He can get violent. He's insane. And very dangerous. He might even kill us if he had the opportunity." Parsons paused a moment, enjoying the attention at last, then added: "But I think he likes us."

"He'd better!" laughed Cooper.

The press, at least, liked them. When Cooper introduced Berman at a news conference as "Zuke," a newsman asked him how he got the name. Emile Zola was a name he bore proudly, he said (for his mother's wandering escape from Russia as a young girl and her asylum in Paris were engineered by the famous French author), but "on the sidewalks of New York, you can't survive with a name like Emile Zola."

On those first days, Berman took nothing for granted. He asked the right questions about the peculiarities of California law, about Sirhan's background, his mental condition and his activities on the night of June 4. He walked through the Ambassador service pantry fourteen times. "You mean he was standing here?" cried Berman. "You mean he got in here?" he demanded. "I don't believe it. How do you know? Oh, you don't know which way he came in? You do? Oh. Well, how the hell did he know Kennedy was coming this way? Cameramen? Standing here waiting, too? Oh."

He talked little and said practically nothing during the first full-scale confrontation between the attorneys on both sides. The meeting was held in a large office in the district attorney's Special Investigations Division, a room dominated by a large oak table and a mass of file cabinets, with strange beige draperies on all four walls. Why the hangings? "For security," said Howard tersely, as he lit a big cigar, for large charts on the Sirhan case were concealed behind the draperies.

David Fitts reported he'd discovered that jail medics had, indeed, taken a blood sample from Sirhan about eight hours after he was arrested. "I went over to the jail myself," said Fitts. "They took it, all right."

"I knew it!" said McCowan. "Sirhan remembered. A black man took ten cc.'s from his right arm."

"Well, I don't know if it was a black man or not," said Fitts. "A fellow named Max Schotts was the chief lab technician at the jail and Max Schotts doesn't sound like a black man to me." Then Fitts reported the results of the test. There was no analysis to see if Sirhan was under the influence of drugs or liquor. It was a test for syphilis and a corpuscle count. That's all.

Cooper tried floating a couple of trial balloons. He said he'd be glad to cut down the time of trial by admitting certain facts about the shooting and going on from there. Fitts said that his boss might not want to stipulate as much as the defense would like. "I was afraid of that," said Cooper. He knew that the prosecution would want to etch the details of the mad pantry scene on the minds of the jury as vividly as it could. He wondered, however, about the prosecution's witness list (which ran to eighty-seven names). "What's Larry Sloan doing here?"

"He'll testify that the handwriting in the notebooks is really Sirhan's."

"We'd be glad to stipulate to that," said Cooper.

Howard was embarrassed. "Yeah," he said with a grin, "we'd like to see that, too. But we've got a problem. People *want* to testify in this trial. It's a kind of a showcase. Sloan has spent his life becoming a handwriting expert and this is his big chance. We told Paul Schrade he probably wouldn't have to testify. He said, 'What do you mean, not testify? I'm one of the guys who got shot standing next to Kennedy, and I can't testify?' This is his niche in history, you see? We can't tell him he doesn't count."

Cooper had a list of some more names that had popped up in the investigation. He wanted to know if Fitts and Howard would agree to make the police and FBI reports available.

Fitts said they certainly would. "You've got a right to 'em. When I told the police we were going to give 'em to you, some jaws dropped and some teeth clicked. But I told 'em I didn't want to have you come back later and say there was stuff I didn't give you." This was a nice spiel, but, in fact, the D.A.'s office did quite a little holding back. Berman, sensed something phony and challenged Fitts.

"Well," Berman said in his deliberate twang, "would you like to let us look through it all?"

"I'd like to," said Fitts. He didn't finish his sentence. But Howard gave Cooper a copy of Sirhan's notebooks.

The police, it turned out, were resisting such complete disclosure. Cooper, Berman, McCowan and I paid a visit on Deputy Chief Robert Houghton and found him closemouthed and defensive. "We have work to do here," he said. "We can't give you anything without a court order."

Cooper pointed out that he had a court order. Houghton phoned Howard in the D.A.'s office, ostensibly to confirm what he already knew, found him away from his desk, drummed his fingers and filled in the time waiting for a call-back by demonstrating that he'd done some checking on Berman. "You're a negligence lawyer, aren't you?"

"I like to say I'm in trial work," said Berman. "That covers both criminal and civil." Indeed, Berman's biggest national case was the defense of Sergeant Matthew McKeon, a Marine drill instructor at Parris Island, North Carolina, boot camp. McKeon had led his platoon into a coastal flat called the Ribbon Creek Estuary. In a fast-rising tide, one recruit who couldn't swim panicked. Soon the whole platoon was floundering hysterically. Six of them drowned and McKeon was charged before a military court with murder and dereliction of duty. Under Berman's defense, McKeon was given a mere six months in the Navy brig, but Berman got even that verdict reversed by the Secretary of the Navy.

Finally, after Houghton had established his authority, he let Cooper and Company into the high-security chamber of the Special Unit, Senator on the eighth floor of Parker Center to see some exhibits. It was a huge soundproofed room full of desks, and the walls seemed to be covered with something that looked like chicken wire. In one corner of the room were intricate scale models of the lobby floor of the Ambassador Hotel and the serving pantry where Kennedy was shot. "This ice machine," quipped one of the officers standing by, "makes real ice cubes." That was just a joke. But the film the police had produced wasn't. For some reason never made clear, the LAPD had spent some several thousand dollars on a twenty-minute color documentary on the assassination, which proved nothing, since none of the news film they could assemble showed the shooting itself. Cooper and Company watched it. The kids shouting in the Embassy Room over the sounds of a musical combo. Ethel Kennedy, who was radiant, and Robert Kennedy in good-humored, low-keyed triumph, then mass confusion, hysteria, wild shouts, a stretcher moving out of the hotel, a prisoner being hustled down the stairs by police into a squad car, and then suddenly a stretcher on a ramp where voices were crying, "Hold it," and a cut to the rosy glow of the ambulance's red lights. The film ended with shots of young people carrying signs that read, "PRAY FOR BOBBY," backed by the mournful cry of a dying siren. It was moving. No doubt about that. "But the jury will never see it," said Cooper.

After the visit with the district attorney, Cooper and Berman returned to Cooper's office with a copy of Sirhan's notebooks. They pored over the books, heads together, and Cooper read some excerpts aloud. "Get this," said Cooper, " 'Kennedy must fall Kennedy must fall please pay to the order of Sirhan Sirhan the amount of Sirhan Sirhan and do not forget to become any more of a he Senator R Kennedy second group of American sailors must be disposed of we believe that Robert F Kennedy must be sacrificed for the cause of the poor exploited people . . .' Here," said Cooper, " 'the so-called President of the United States of America must be advised of their punishments for their treasonable crimes against the state moreover we believe that the glorious United States of America will eventually be felled by a blow of an assassin's bullet b bullets bullets by an assassin's bullet today I must plan to come home in a new car today I must plan to drive home in a new car new new new Mustang in in a new Mustang in a . . .' Look at this," said Cooper. " 'I advocate the overthrow of the current President of the fucken United States of America, I have no absolute plans yet but soon will compose some . . .' 'I believe that the US is ready to start declining not that it hasn't it began in November 23, 63 —.' " Said Cooper, "What happened on November 23, 1963?"

"That was the day Kennedy, no Lee Harvey Oswald was killed on November 23, 1963. And this, 'How will I contact you after I arrive at the airport I am coming up sometime Tuesday afternoon Sirhan Sirhan Sirhan of afternoon did you really please pay to the order of Sirhan afternoon afternoon afternoon the amount of fifteen thousand dollars sometime in the afternoon Miss Miss Peggy Osterkamp Osterkamp did you really seven fifty seven fifty seven fifty seven fifty let us do it let us do it let us do it do it it it it Sirhan Sirhan let us do it.' "

Said Berman, "Hell, there was somebody else in this with him."

Sirhan saw Dr. Diamond for the first time on December 23, when Cooper brought him up to the cell, introduced him and left him there to speak for himself. Diamond did little talking but he seemed so relaxed and his speech was so liberally salted with colloquialisms (learned from his six teen-aged children and updated by his students at Berkeley) that Sirhan was encouraged to go ahead and tell him in a long monologue all he could remember about the night of the assassination.

When Sirhan got to the point where his memory went hazy, Diamond urged him to try to recall any details he could, even though they might seem disconnected to him now. Sirhan said it was like a dream. Even so, said Diamond, you can sometimes recall details from a dream. Sirhan remembered seeing someone in the kitchen wearing a uniform, a policeman, perhaps, or a fireman. He was leaning on a table, and then he was being choked.

After he was taken to the police station? Sirhan said he didn't remember much of that either. "Did you remember kicking a cup of hot chocolate out of an officer's hand?" Sirhan did. He was thirsty and asked for a drink and they wouldn't give him one. So, he told Diamond, "I said, 'You goddamn bastard.' I kicked it out of his hand. I remember that. When I'm mad, sir, I don't give a damn what happens." Sirhan's courage had grown considerably since that night. He did kick the cup, but he apologized meekly after he did it. And he didn't indulge in any name-calling.

Diamond asked him why he didn't talk about the killing with the police. Sirhan stammered badly, finally said, "They kept telling me about my constitutional rights."

"You wouldn't even give them your name?"

Sirhan had no answer. He stuttered. "Wuh, wuh why should I?"

"Uh-hummmm," said Diamond. He would have to come back to that.

Sirhan talked about the lack of any Arab voice in America. "Have you ever heard the Arab side of the story?" asked Sirhan. Diamond said he had. He had a lot of Arab students. That didn't count. "I mean on the TV, the radio, in the mass media?" said Sirhan. "That's what bugs me! There's no Arab voice in America, and goddamn it, I'm gonna show 'em in that courtroom. I'm gonna really give 'em hell about it."

"You think you can get your point across?"

"I think I can."

"You're willing to take the stand?"

"Yes."

"You know, if you take the stand, you have to tell everything. You can talk about the Arab-Israeli situation, but you have to answer questions about the shooting, too."

"Well, they have me there."

"Sometimes," said Diamond, "the truth is the best defense."

"It is, but that's it, sir."

"You don't think you'd be afraid?"

"I don't think I would be, sir. I have nothing to hide."

"What do you think the truth about the shooting is?"

"I don't really know, sir."

"You sure of that? How do you know this wasn't a put-up job?"

"I don't know." Sirhan sighed.

"How do you know it wasn't some kind of fix?" asked Diamond.

"Well," said Sirhan, "it could have been. I don't know."

Diamond waited. When Sirhan said nothing more, he asked, "Do you believe deep down inside that you shot him?"

Sirhan paused. "I hated him, sir. I loved him before. He would finish what President Kennedy started. President Kennedy tried to help the Arab refugees. But then, when I watched him on the television how he was trying to get all that Jewish vote behind him and how he was always for the persecuted people—meaning the Jews, sir!—my whole . . . feelings toward him—suddenly—changed, and sharply. I hated his guts, sir."

"Did the thought you wanted to kill him occur to you then?"

Sirhan said intensely, too intensely, "Never. Never. Never."

"Well, how about when you wrote it down in the notebook?"

"Ah, I, the, the thing that really bugged me was those jet bombers that he wanted to send to Israel." Diamond reminded him what he'd written in the notebook. "Did I write that?" Sirhan said he couldn't recall how or when he'd written that. "But every time that I heard about him, sir, I'd just . . ." Sirhan paused. "I can't describe it."

"Try to describe it," said Diamond kindly. "Try to put it in words."

"I wanted to grab him, sir, and just . . . what the hell. Just because those Arabs are helpless, it doesn't mean that you can—" Sirhan's hands moved upward in a choking motion and he made an ugly farting sound with his lips—"fuck the hell out of 'em just because they can't vote for you in the election."

Diamond asked him about his gun. Sirhan said he just bought it for target practice. Diamond, himself a gun lover, pointed out that a short-barreled gun is not a good target gun. "Well, hell," said Sirhan, "I only paid $25 for it." He said he'd priced other guns at stores, but they were much more expensive.

"Do you think what you did sort of helped things?" asked Diamond.

"I'm not proud of what I did."

"What do you mean, you're not proud of it? You believe in your cause, don't you?"

"I have no exact knowledge, sir, that this happened yet. I'm all, it's all in my mind, but goddamn it, when my body played with it, I couldn't understand it. I still don't believe it. My body outsmarted my brain, I guess."

"What did your body do?"

"Pulled that trigger."

"Does your body remember it, even if your mind doesn't?"

"I don't give a damn, sir, in a way. Now, I don't even care."

Diamond pointed out that Sirhan had to care. Otherwise the sacrifice of Kennedy's life, and maybe his own, would mean nothing. "What would the Arab people get out of this if you don't remember? You see, your body *is* you, Sirhan. And there is no difference between you and your mind. It isn't two people, and if this sacrifice isn't going to be in vain, people have to know the truth. No one is going to believe you about the Arabs if you're not going to tell them the truth about everything. To convince people, you have to tell the truth about everything."

Sirhan didn't know how to respond to that, except with another oration against the Jews. "Did you feel Robert Kennedy had betrayed you?" asked Diamond.

"Yes."

"What sticks in your mind about him?"

"His solid promise. Saying he would give fifty jet bombers to Israel."

"When did you decide to do something?"

"I don't think I ever decided. I'm mad, and it's good as long as it lasted, for the duration of the aggravation."

"So you don't think you carefully planned this, then?"

"Oh, hell, I never planned it. Sir, I wake up every morning and I say, 'Oh, hell, what's this all about?' My dreams are more pleasant than this, than this predicament."

"You dream now? What do you dream about, Sirhan?"

"I dream about being out of this place. I'm more free in my movement in my dreams."

"What does your mother think of all this? Did you hurt her?"

Sirhan paused. "I think I hurt her. Oh, a helluva lot. You see, it's against my grain to have done this. 'Thou shalt not kill.' And here, pow! I blast the S.O., the son of a bitch. It doesn't figure. I had three or four Bibles in my room. I don't understand it."

"And yet, it was you who did it. It was something inside of you. It was you who pulled that trigger." Sirhan couldn't explain.

Diamond asked him what he dreamed last night. He couldn't remember. He'd anticipated Diamond's coming and possibly asking him about his dreams, but he couldn't remember. Diamond asked him what the Arabs thought of him now. Sirhan said that Parsons had tried to persuade him that he'd be a hero if he went back to Jerusalem, but he didn't feel like a hero.

"What do you think is just, Sirhan? What do you want the jury to say?"

"Sir, for this, let me tell you: For the loss of a human life, I think I should be dead. Unquestionably. But for stopping Robert Kennedy, a fuckin' politician, who would have been a killer if he had been elected, he would have sent those fuckin' jets, I don't think I should be convicted at all."

"What would happen if you spent the rest of your life in prison?"

"I couldn't take it," said Sirhan. "I'd lose my mind."

"Do you want to live?" asked Diamond. "Have you lived your life? Have you thought of suicide, hanging yourself?"

"Oh, hell, no. I couldn't do that."

"Why didn't you turn the gas on yourself, ah, why didn't you turn the gun on yourself after you killed Kennedy?"

Sirhan waved his hand in front of his face. "It was all mixed up. Like a dream."

Diamond asked him about his experiments in the occult. Sirhan told him about some weird happenings with thought transference. He showed Diamond a book he had in his cell on yoga philosophy by Yogi Ramachuraka concerning the adept. Diamond read aloud:

It must not be imagined that this budding consciousness springs full blown into a man's mind at once. It has done so in some cases, it is true. But in the majority of instances, it is a matter of slow growth. But the man is never just the same after the growth commences.

"Is this what happened to you, Sirhan? Did it come slowly, or did it come all of a sudden?"

"It comes in spurts," said Sirhan.

Diamond continued to read: " 'He apparently may lose his full consciousness of the truth.' Have you ever lost it?"

Sirhan said he didn't know. Diamond read more:

But it will come back to him again and again, and all the time it is working gradually to make over that man's nature, and his changed mental attitude manifests itself in his actions.

"What about your change? Did it help you, Sirhan?"

"If I had any change, sir, I—I—I fucked it up, you might say on June 5."

"On June 5 by the killing?" asked Diamond. Sirhan nodded. Diamond continued to read the underlined passage:

He becomes more cheerful and happy. Things that worry his neighbors seem to have little effect on him. He finds it hard to manifest a respectable amount of regret and grief over things that bear heavily upon those around him.

"Except now, the Jews."

"The Jews, uh-humm. Do you have any regret for killing Kennedy?"

"A human life, sir? Very much so."

"Um-humm. You didn't want to hurt any life?"

"Hell, no! My mother, sir, used to beg me to kill the cockroaches in the kitchen. That was none of my business. I didn't want to do anything like that."

"But what about what you've done for the Arab people? What about the effect on the United States? You know this had something to do with the election of the President. You know that, don't you? What effect do you think it had, offhand?"

"I think it gave Nixon the Presidency."

"Uh-humm. Your single act? Otherwise Kennedy would have been President?"

"At one time, sir, I wished he were, but not after he came out with this Israeli thing."

"Not after he betrayed the Arab people?"

Sirhan paused, then told Diamond he wasn't sure Diamond got the point of the passages he had underlined in the book the doctor still had in his hand. Diamond read some more:

He is apt to be regarded as unfeeling and heartless notwithstanding his heart may be full of love and kindness. His mental attitude is changed. His viewpoint is shifted. He finds himself ceasing to fear. And those around him are apt to consider him reckless or thoughtless.

"Is this true about you?"

"Could be, yes."

Time [read Daimond] has less meaning to him, for the idea of eternity has come to him. Distance ceases to appall him for is not all space his?

Such a one had better keep quiet or he will be sure to be considered a queer fish and people may tap their foreheads significantly when speaking of him behind his back.

"When did you underline this, Sirhan? Since you've been here, or was this before? Is this an old book of yours or—"

"No, sir. This is—they brought it in."

"Did you underline this?" Sirhan nodded. "Do you think you're crazy, Sirhan? Do you think you are a queer fish?"

"I think I am just as normal as anybody else. Although I am a fanatic about the Arab-Israeli."

"Is that all you're fanatical about?"

"I don't know."

"Do you think you're fanatical about the occult?"

"No, sir."

Diamond asked Sirhan what he thought about the psychologists' reports. Sirhan said he had to laugh. He said he'd gotten off the track momentarily maybe, but that wouldn't make him mentally ill. Diamond wondered how badly Sirhan wanted to remember what had happened when he went "off the track." Would he be willing to take truth serum or a lie detector test? He would. "All right," said Diamond. "I'm coming back after Christmas. I'm going to try to help you remember."

Nine

"This is political. This is a politically motivated—this is,
heh heh, political, heh heh, politically motivated."

Both sides took their last little vacation during Christmas week before a
trial which no one thought would be brief. I took the opportunity to get
my first taped interviews with Sirhan, my first sessions alone with the assassin.

"Mr. Cooper told me that you'd come," said Sirhan. "But he didn't say
you were coming alone. I didn't expect you to come." It was 5:30 on a
Friday evening, and, even with a court order from Judge Walker, it had
taken me all day to get the official okay from the sheriff. No one wanted
to okay anything without checking it with Sheriff Pitchess, and he was
busy. The astronauts, Frank Borman, James A. Lovell, Jr., and William
A. Anders, were having an easier time getting to the far side of the moon.

The weather had changed since my last visit, and a chill penetrated even
to Sirhan's cell. He wore a T-shirt and a blue denim shirt over that. And
slippers instead of the Japanese thongs. He was chain-smoking cigarettes
now and seemed much more on edge. "Yes," he admitted, "I feel pretty
much the way I felt before June 5. I was near my breaking point then. I'm
unsteady. I'm very unsteady now."

"Do you dream?"

Sirhan flared at this direct probe. "You're not the psychologist now!
. . . It's not a dream. It's a physical feeling." He paused and thought for a
moment, as if he was trying to think of a way of describing the feeling,
then decided to go back to his dreams. "I dream, too. I dreamt that Parsons was in Washington, somehow." He was putting little hope in his trial.
He didn't want a trial. He didn't want to beg for his life. He wanted to
make a deal with the State Department.

"You wouldn't rather have the gas chamber than a period of time in the
penitentiary?" He said he'd rather die. I pointed out that there was a possibility of parole: "Better than nothing."

"The best years of my life are between twenty-five and forty."

"I understand. But I'd rather have half a loaf than no loaf."

"That's not me."

"No?"

"No. I go all the way or nothing. That's always been my habit. When I work, you know, at home, I could leave everything for weeks, and the yard, the house, everything. I could loaf, read, watch television, whatever. But when I'd start to work, goddamn it, better get out of the way because I plan to work, and I want no interruptions from my work. And that's the way it's always been."

Sirhan was curious about the progress of "his investigation." He wanted to know about the outcome of the chromosome test. The results weren't in yet. He wanted to know what it all meant. I told him what the theory was. —that only three out of a thousand people have an abnormal XYY chromosome, but in a prison population, the ratio goes up as high as twenty-five out of a thousand.

Sirhan caught the implication immediately. "Maybe that would lessen the penalty."

I pointed out that chromosome research was still in a primitive stage. But I told Sirhan about my understanding of the law in California: "In this state, you almost have to be a perfect specimen to get first-degree murder."

Sirhan said he'd get first degree. "With all those notebooks of mine?" I admitted that the D.A. could prove premeditation by citing the notebooks. "Well," said Sirhan, "that's all they need."

I said the law demanded more than that: the premeditation had to be the product of a healthy mind, not a sick compulsion. "The fact is, if you had written it once, that would have shown premeditation. But you wrote it—I saw it the other day for the first time—"

"See those dates? I don't remember all that."

"Not only did you write it on different days, but on one day when you wrote it, on May 18, you wrote it over and over and over again."

Sirhan seemed genuinely amazed. "I don't remember that, by God. Somebody's gotta bring me that notebook so I can look at it."

"It's a very interesting document. It could just as well save your life as it could convict you—just the fact that you would write it over and over and over again like that. I am not a psychiatrist. To me, you're as normal—"

"I am. I am. But when it comes to the Israelis, when it comes to anything about the Jews, shit, I, I go to pieces."

"I've seen that. Sure. I know that."

"Where have you seen that?" asked Sirhan.

"Right in here. We start talking about the Russian invasion of Czechoslovakia and in about thirty-five seconds, you're talking about the Arab-Jew situation."

Sirhan laughed. "Well, the more I am exposed to the Jewish people, the more this momentum just takes hold of me and, you know, by June 5, I couldn't control it anymore."

I told him that I was still trying to find the TV documentary that helped Sirhan identify Kennedy with the Jews. Sirhan thought it might have appeared on May 18, when he wrote in the notebook that Kennedy must die.

Sirhan found it extremely important here to tell how the narrator's voice on that documentary affected him emotionally. "It was designed to do whatever it was supposed to do."

"Stir your emotions?" I asked.

"That's right. And goddamn it, it did."

"Well, that seems to be the connection between your feelings about the Jews and Kennedy. It's hard to fit. You know, there are a lot of people that favor the Jews, but, you know, nobody shot them."

"No, but I was thwarted," said Sirhan intensely. "That's what bugged me. I was thwarted."

"Almost like a rejected lover. Like a girl friend?"

"Yeah," said Sirhan with feeling. "Well, with Kennedy, I loved him. I loved him from a different view. I associated him with the President. And to me, President Kennedy was infallible. He was a man, you know, I loved him! And I thought Kennedy, Bob, would do the same, you know, do the same. But, hell, he fucked up. That's all he did." His passion flattened here and his tone became matter-of-fact. "He asked for it. He should have been smarter than that. You know, the Arabs had emotions. He knew how they felt about it. But, hell, he didn't have to come out right at the fuckin' time when the Arab-Israeli War erupted. Oh, I couldn't take it! I couldn't take it!" He paused, to listen to the echoes of what he had just said. It seemed as though he was practicing this story for presentation later on.

I asked him how he felt when John Kennedy was assassinated. Sirhan said, "It hurt me, but it didn't grab me as much." It seemed that he wanted to get off this subject, and so I deliberately lingered there. I was in Europe in 1963, but during a visit to the United States at year's end, I was overcome by a television replay of the JFK assassination. I said: "They crammed everything into a half hour or so. The assassination, the killing of Oswald, the Kennedy funeral, the clopping of the horses' hoofs on the

avenue, the riderless horse with the boots backward in the stirrups . . ."
Through this recitation, Sirhan kept trying to interrupt. He didn't want to
hear about it. I went on. "And when they played the trumpets, when that
sound—that's when really—"

Sirhan finally stopped me. "I don't think I had any tears," he said. "But
I think I felt very sorry. There was no reason for it. Oswald fucked up, I
think. There was no reason. I saw no motivation, no legitimate reason for
that."

"Do you think he acted alone?"

"I don't know. I'm in no position to judge that. There's a lot of questions about that." Sirhan changed the subject again. He thought JFK's death
was "more tragic than Robert's. I regret it more than Robert's."

"Well, both of them had a huge effect on history."

"I don't know about that."

"You don't think that Robert would have been President today?"

"I think he would have been. He could have been. I don't know. Hell,
he got money. That's all it takes. Hell, Kennedy had a billion dollars. Hell,
he could rule the world with that."

"Well, the President of the United States does rule the world in many,
many ways."

"It depends."

"Doesn't he?"

"It depends. Does he rule the world?" Sirhan paused reflectively. "One
little punk—" he tapped his chest with his thumb, then aimed his forefinger at my forehead and made a popping sound in his mouth. "That's all
that rules the world. Lee Oswald ruled the world for that moment that
trigger was pulled."

I was astonished, not so much by the logic of what Sirhan had said, or
by his insight into the frailty of power, but rather because he, RFK's assassin, had verbalized so neatly the rationale of magnicide. But Sirhan was
quick to deny the implication: "But I'm not putting myself in that attitude
here. I told that to Dr. Diamond. I'm not proud of what I did. I'm not.
Every time they try to take a picture of me, I don't want it. I shy away.
I'm not proud about it. I don't know what they have about me—the press.
I haven't read the papers for the last three months."

"Was there anything particular in the papers that started you to turn
off?"

"That's it. Everything you read. This guy murdered this guy. This guy
shot this guy. You know, this is what I thought set me up for the whole

business. Fuck it," said Sirhan. "What the hell is it? It's all violence, chaos, unrest. Whatever happened to the old days, you know, peace and quiet?"

Then both of us laughed and agreed that the history of the world has never been marked by too much peace and quiet. "What have you been reading lately?" I asked. "You were reading a lot there earlier in the summer, weren't you?"

"I was."

"You know, I wanted to talk to you about *Witness.*"

"I loved that book. I loved it."

"Did you? It's very well written."

"Well, hell, the chief editor of *Time.* He can pretty well manipulate—"

"Put words together."

"That's the way I want you to write my book."

"That's the kind of a book I want to write. Remember the scene in the preface in the form of a letter to his children?"

"Yeah, I read that."

"And he talks about when he went out to the barn to commit suicide?"

"Yeah, I read that," said Sirhan nervously.

"And the little boy sensed it and came out into the dark."

"Yeah, yeah." Sirhan put up his hands, warding off my words as if they were darts.

"And started calling, 'Daddy, Daddy,' and then he finally found him and he put the gun away and the kid grabbed him and said, 'Daddy, don't ever go away like that again.' God, I just . . . I just had chills."

"Isn't it funny though," said Sirhan, getting away from the discussion of that father-son relationship, "when I started reading it, I had the same fucking book he had, was referring to, *Les Misérables.* He had a whole chapter on that. That book must be the New World Bible, you might say."

"Had you read *Les Misérables* before?"

"I read it before, but in the condensed form."

"What made you ask for it here?"

"I don't know. I . . . I belong to those people. I don't know. It seems to give me some—what? Solace? I felt that way. It was quite . . . encouraging. The words don't come too well. . . ."

"They're coming pretty well now," I said. "This is the kind of session that the real YOU comes out," I added. "We're getting somewhere now. I'm so delighted now that the obstacles are clear." I moved into another area of inquiry. Sirhan's propensity to pick up the tab, wherever, whenever he could.

"Yeah, why not? I enjoy it. I enjoy getting it."

"And then another time, when that girl was running for campus queen—"

"Don't talk about that, please," said Sirhan.

"Huh?"

"Don't talk about women to me." I was taken aback at the strength of Sirhan's objection to an apparently innocuous question. "Don't talk about women to me." It seemed significant enough to warrant a further probe, and I asked why. "This is political," said Sirhan. "This is a politically motivated—" He started to giggle nervously. "This is, heh heh, political, heh heh, politically motivated."

I hadn't implied that Sirhan's relations with girls had had anything to do with the crime, but in Sirhan's mind there was a connection he felt compelled to deny. I dropped the discussion for the time and then Sirhan was reminded of the Rosicrucians. Did I find anything in the police reports about the Rosicrucians?

"A little." The reports indicated Sirhan had been seen by a dozen or more persons at a Rosicrucian meeting in Pasadena a week before the assassination. He was alone, hardly spoke to anyone and left early. Nothing sinister seemed to occur there.

"I don't want that to come up at all," said Sirhan.

"Oh, yeah, Parsons gave me that little message of yours."

"Nothing. Nothing. If anything comes up at the trial—"

"Well, we'll see about that. Diamond and Cooper still haven't made up their minds. They still don't know what makes you tick. They're going to have to draw you out more about those notebooks. None of it may be relevant and all of it may be relevant."

May 28. 2030 East Villa Street, Pasadena. Headquarters of the weekly Tuesday meeting of the Akhraton Chapter of the Ancient Mystical Order of Rosae Crucis. 7:45 P.M. Some two dozen members are filing in, most of them dumpy, defeated-looking people in their forties. There is one guest this evening. He wanders in, shows his current membership card to the chapter secretary, signs the guest book Sirhan Sirhan, 696 E. Howard and adds absentmindedly the date the last guest signed in above him: "April 16."

A member, Willamay Harrison, introduces herself to the young man. He says his name is Joe, and he isn't familiar with the procedure here. She gives him an apron which he puts on over his tight-fitting jeans. Another

*member, Mrs. Verna C. Miller, gives him a name tag and on it he writes
Sirhan. Then Mrs. Harrison introduces Sirhan to her granddaughter Luana
Acob, who is fourteen. She is called a "colombe," literally a "dove," a
title given to young virgin members of the lodge who participate in the
lodge rituals. She would guide Sirhan through the evening.*

*Luana leads Sirhan up to the front of the lodge room shortly before the
ritual team enters in their purple robes. Sirhan is curious. He wants to
know who the officers are and what they do, and who the colombe is who
is standing next to the Shekinah on the stage.*

*Ted Stevens, the lodge master, asks for a volunteer. Sirhan says to
Luana, "Why not you?"*

*She says, "Why not you?" Indeed, why not? Sirhan rises, starts to cross
in front of the Shekinah. Stevens tells him that isn't proper. Sirhan, embarrassed, goes around the other way. On stage, Stevens gives Sirhan a chair
and a blindfold. Another volunteer? A woman comes forward, Mrs. Sally
Hardman, and she, too, takes a seat and a blindfold. Then Stevens performs an absurd experiment proving absolutely nothing, which few except
Sirhan take seriously. Stevens touches Sirhan's hand with a pin. "How
many pins do you feel?"*

"One."

"Now, how many?"

"Two."

*"Right." But as Stevens moves farther up the arm, Sirhan is less and
less able to tell how many pins he feels, one or two. Amazing. Willamay
Harrison falls asleep.*

*"Will you stay for coffee?" asks Luana Acob. Sirhan says he will. She
goes off to the rest room. When she returns to Sirhan, he is terribly en-
grossed in a display of books on the occult.*

"Uh, sorry," he says, "I have to go." He hurries off into the night.

*"Say," says Sherman Livingstone, an official of the Rosicrucians, who
has only chatted momentarily before the meeting, "where's that new young
man? I want to talk to him."*

"He's gone," says Luana.

I was back the next morning, talking to Sirhan about his reading. He
read *Time* every week at the Pasadena Public Library's branch on Catalina Street. And *Newsweek* and, he said, even *U.S. News and World Report.* And the *London Illustrated News* and *The Economist* and *The New*

Republic. "The New Republic, I love. That's my favorite." He liked Andrew David Kopkind—particularly.

I had by now realized that I got more out of Sirhan if I didn't ask direct questions. Sirhan was suspicious by nature, and direct questions only made him more suspicious. So we moved from magazines to the cinema. Sirhan saw a lot of movies. He couldn't think of too many movie stars he liked. But he hated Paul Newman, who led the Jews in *Exodus.* "I didn't want to see some goddamn Jew fuck off on the screen," he said. How about *Lawrence of Arabia?* Sirhan refused to go, even when some friends bought him a ticket. "The movie was anti-Arab, and the producer of the movie was a Jew." Sirhan paused here to make a face. "Sam Spiegel." Sirhan was developing an actor's sense of timing.

As he talked, Sirhan left his breakfast—some nicely fried eggs, a piece of coffee cake and some fruit—untouched, while he smoked an entire pack of cigarettes. "How many packs a day?" I asked.

"Six," said Sirhan. "Three different brands."

Like the cigarette smoke itself, Sirhan's face had started to turn gray. "Do you really think you ought to do that?" I asked.

He laughed grimly. "Nothing else to do."

What he did do was read. And now, instead of the romantic *Les Misérables* or the passionate *Witness,* he had a college text on logic and a dry book on Indian philosophy.

I tried to draw Sirhan out a bit on his family. Sirhan, it turned out, could not bring himself to make a single negative comment about his life with father, and forced himself to deny what he knew were facts. He couldn't recall the fact that his father had trouble holding a job during his six months in the United States. He never felt that his mother had a certain contempt for his father. I reminded him that after about six months in America, Bishara Sirhan scooped up money earned by his mother and his brothers and took off for Jerusalem alone.

"His mother was ill," said Sirhan.

I pointed out that his father, at the present time, was hardly acting like a devoted son to his sick mother. "He hardly ever sees his mother now. She's living in relatively straitened circumstances and he's living in a very, very nice house."

"I've never seen the house," said Sirhan. In a kind of detached, flat tone of voice, Sirhan explained away his father. "What you're saying might be completely true, but yet I was raised here. My whole mind is engulfed in the American way of life, American line of thinking, my mind operated

American. Now, my father . . . all this stuff is pretty well ingrained in him. And he's all Arab. One hundred percent Arab. Today, he would be a complete stranger to me. His line of thought, his background and heritage are not mine. I don't think I could reconcile myself with him, you know, on a cultural basis."

I tried to see what Sirhan really felt about his father. He felt nothing, he claimed. He and his father were just on two different roads. "I don't identify with the Arabs politically or any other way except for the fact that their blood flows in my veins. Their food I don't go for. Their clothing I don't dig. Their robes and all that bullshit. Their politics I can't understand and I don't want to understand. Their religion? I'm a Christian. Their language I don't speak very well. Hell, I'm an American. That's the way I look at myself."

That self-portrait didn't sound much like an Arab patriot. So why did Sirhan keep reiterating, as he had done to Diamond, that he killed Kennedy "to stop him from sending bombers to Israel"? I wanted to get back into that area Sirhan had been avoiding, his feelings about his father.

His father, he said, didn't "bother" him very much. Then, he protested about this line of inquiry. "They're all trying to dig into my family background. That had no effect on my actions. Nothing. Hell, I was an adult. I knew my own life. I knew my destiny. I was responsible for my own self. My background had nothing to do with it. Had I killed my wife, had I killed my brother, had I killed a neighbor, had I killed a bank attendant in a robbery, I can understand their trying to delve into my background. But, you see, this was political. It involved more people than just Sirhan."

"What do you mean by that?"

Sirhan paused, obviously searching within himself what to say. "There were too many Arab refugees . . . that helped me move against Kennedy."

I said I believed that Sirhan's Arab patriotism was working "on an overt and conscious level"—although I had serious private doubts about that—but I wondered what was going on at a subconscious level.

What it was, Sirhan said, was his experimentation in the occult. "That stuff really worked on me. It worked, I'm convinced of it. This whole incident." He told about his introduction to the occult, his membership in the Rosicrucians, his visit to their Pasadena headquarters, his attempts at autosuggestion, which he learned from a friend named Tom and from a book called *Cyclomancy*. And it was that that gave Sirhan his power. "But I'm not psychotic," he added immediately. "I don't feel psychotic."

"I don't think you are. Dr. Diamond doesn't think so."

"When did he tell you that? I want to know."

I explained what I thought I understood about psychosis. "A true psychotic would not have the ability, the strength, the power, the cunning to be able to do the necessary things to pull off something like that. A psychotic gets sidetracked. He gets confused. He is just not in touch with reality."

"I'm not psychotic," said Sirhan again. "I don't think I am. Except when it comes to the Jews."

"I'll tell you something," I said. "Sometimes when we are talking about this, it comes up naturally, and I feel as if it really is part of you. And other times, I feel as if you are putting me on. As if you are overplaying that."

"I could be sometimes," admitted Sirhan easily. "But it's in me."

"At times I think you are overdoing it."

"I could be. I could be. But I have to prove my point. That is my main weakness."

"You can't overplay it," I said. "You can't come across as one big mad-on against the Jews. That's unbelievable."

Sirhan nodded, but he wasn't convinced. His hatred seemed to him the only acceptable defense he had.

But that was not much of a defense. And so, I tried to get Sirhan talking more about himself. Maybe I would find some clues to Sirhan's real motivation. Neither his father nor his mother, he recalled, had expressed their affection for him with hugs and kisses. I asked him how he felt about his own body. "How did you feel," I asked, "when you were growing up? For example, were you smaller than the rest of the kids?"

"As a matter of fact," said Sirhan, "I was pretty well satisfied with my body. I could outdo, outmaneuver the big fellows. Hell, I could compete just as well as any big guys."

"And when you came to this country?"

"I could have been a little bit too small," he admitted. "But I, but I didn't let it bother me. That's the way I am. I could say, 'Fuck it,' you know. That was my attitude."

"Did you do anything to build up your body?"

"I did some exercise, but it didn't bother me too much. But, hell, that's the way I am. Why do anything to make it bigger when you obviously cannot increase the size of your bones?"

"But some guys lift weights."

"I don't go for that," said Sirhan.

Sirhan had been closemouthed with everyone about sex. The psychologists saw certain signs within him of a possibly repressed homosexuality. He had given no indication to any of them that he had had any normal heterosexual relationships. I was determined to challenge Sirhan on this. "How do you feel about screwing?" I asked.

"I think it's very terrific."

"Whether you're married or not?"

"There again I have to draw the line. If the girl's clean, I wouldn't want to touch her. But if she's promiscuous, as long as I keep my own health in shape, as long as I don't have to expose myself to any disease."

"Have you ever slept with a whore?"

"Not too much a whore as a promiscuous girl."

"Not a pro then."

"Not a pro."

"Not for money?"

"No."

"So you have had it?"

"I've had it. Twenty-four years old. What the hell you talking about? Did I ever tell you how I got my first piece?"

"No. Tell me."

"This girl used to come into that gas station where I was working. That garage, you know? She came in maybe three or four times before I really got . . . But she'd come in late at night when there was no business and I thought I'd stall her as much as I can. But one time she pulled into another station and some friends of hers had written under the hood. When I opened the hood, I saw written out, 'I trade ass for gas.' I was checking the oil. She didn't know the other guy had put it up there and she was embarrassed. And that sort of broke the ice between me and her. This time we felt each other and the next time she came in, we got a little warmer and I took her up on it. It happened. I took her back and had her in the back part of the station. But she was a beautiful girl."

"And she didn't pay for her gas that night?"

"She had her credit card."

"She used her credit card?"

"Yes."

"Then it wasn't really a trade?"

"Then I took her out to breakfast in the morning 'cause I worked till four o'clock in the morning."

"You did it in the garage? Standing up?"

"I think I had her against some tires. I think I was in a hurry."

"That's not a very good surrounding for the first time."

"Well, hell, it seemed she wanted it more than I did."

"Sounds like it was pretty quick though."

"Oh, hell, yes, it was. Just like that." Sirhan snapped his fingers. "But there was nobody else to take care of the station. Hell, it was late at night. What if some policeman came around? 'Hell, what's going on here?' She was a hell of a beautiful doll, though. She was training to become an airline stewardess."

"Did you ever lay her again?"

"In a more comfortable area, yes, in the back seat of my car at a drive-in movie, in my '49 Cad. A Burt Lancaster movie."

"What happened to the '49 Cadillac?"

"When I got the De Soto, I sold the Cad."

"I feel as if I'm prying and I guess I shouldn't. But I'm gonna forge ahead. Tell me more about your sex history."

"Really, I'd rather not."

"I feel embarrassed to even ask," I said.

"Well, I've had it. I know what it's all about. I've had my share."

"I'm surprised. I would have guessed that you probably didn't."

"Why?"

"I don't know." I paused, wondering how to put it. "I'll be very frank with you. I would think if you had a good sex life, you wouldn't be so upset by other things. You wouldn't have let the Arab-Israeli situation bother you that much if you'd had a wife and a good sex life or a girl-friend and a good sex life. You wouldn't have let this upset you as much as it did."

"Maybe that could be. But sex for sex's sake, I've had it. But sex with love, I don't think I had too much of that."

"So my feeling is kind of correct then?"

"Well, I guess."

"You made a nice distinction between sex and sex with love."

"But, hell, when I'd go down to Sunset Boulevard, shit, you don't need any introductions. You buy 'em a pop or a Coca-Cola or something and you got it made."

"Have you, in fact, done that?"

"Oh, hell, yes. In fact, the night before my sister died. It was my nine-teenth birthday. I was down on the Sunset Strip having a big time. I had had enough of all that trouble."

"You wanted a release?"

"Change."

"Change of scenery, bright lights "

"A release."

"Yesterday," I said, "when I mentioned this girl—"

"I still don't wanta talk about her."

"Yeah, you didn't want to talk about her and your next phrase was, 'The motivation was political.' Now, I hadn't implied that your relations with any girl had anything to do with the assassination. But you made the connection. Now, I'm wondering if you were so vehement in denying it there wasn't a connection? You follow me?"

"I follow you."

"In other words, maybe there was also a rejection from a significant female and that, added to every other goddamn thing in life—"

"I just don't want to talk about it."

"Well, I am not going to use any of your girl friends' names."

"You know," said Sirhan, "women, money and horses were my thing. But I still maintain this thing had a political motivation. There was no other . . . involving factor. And I will keep it political."

"Uh-huh."

"I don't want to get any women or any girls in trouble. I'll take the rap for everything. I don't want to involve them or ruin their life."

"All right. I understand. Because that's the way I'd feel. There was no implication you were rejected?"

"No."

"No rejection of you by a significant female that you loved?"

"No. Not exactly. That first girl I had at the gas station . . . she was great. Anything she had on her mind, she'd say it."

"Real direct, huh?"

"Informal. Very friendly, you know? She'd say things like, 'Why didn't you get a shave today?' Things like that. 'Take all that bullshit off your face.' That girl was very informal. I didn't worship her. I don't believe in worship. But I could charm her so I could get whatever I wanted out of her."

"Once you told Parsons and Parsons told me, you said you believed in 'fucking 'em and forgetting 'em.' That didn't ring true to me. I didn't think, and I still don't think, that you're that crass."

"I think I would be. You know, when you're on Sunset Boulevard. You don't know the girl. You pick her up. You take her in the car . . ."

"All right. I didn't know you did that. I didn't know that was your scene. I didn't know . . ."

"That's a part of my scene."

"All right," I said. But it wasn't all right. Now I wasn't quite sure how accurate my reconstruction would be of Sirhan's life with the ladies. Police reports had given me one picture of Sirhan—so shy he would drive around a girl's home for days at a time without even stopping to say hello—and Sirhan was trying his best, now, to tell me that he was quite a stud. Except on one notable occasion:

A warm, spring night at Pasadena City College. Night-school recess. Sirhan is sipping coffee in the cafeteria with several girls. One of them in particular, a little brunette, has attracted him for some time. Can he drive her home tonight? They get into his old Cadillac. He drives east on Colorado Boulevard. "You don't mind if I make one stop along the way, do you?" She doesn't mind. They chat and she stiffens as he pulls into a large, walled estate in San Marino. "It's all right," he says, "I work here. I take care of the lawns here." He parks behind some trees and a high hedge, goes out and turns off the sprinklers, returns and begins to explore the girl's body in the dark while the two of them talk about school. It is a beautiful night for lovemaking, and soon the girl has her dress all unbuttoned and her bra and panties off and is lying on the back seat.

"Goddamn!" says Sirhan fervently as he starts to mount her. "I wish I owned this estate instead of this goddamn Jew!"

"Ohhhh, Sirhan," she sighs, her arms outstretched. "I'm a Jew."

"Oof," says Sirhan, as if he'd just been kicked in the groin. Suddenly detumescent, he rises, removes his rubber and drives the girl back to PCC. "I'm sorry," he says, like a real gentleman. "I'm sorry."

"All right," I said. "To get back to that first question I was posing. You said sex you had, but a good love relationship was something else again. Did you ever come close?"

"I did. Yes, I did. But economically, I didn't have anything. For love, you need security, a home. Love? I could feel it. I could want it. But I can't afford it. How can you have security without money? How can you have real love without money? Ninety percent of the breakup in marriages are due to money problems. And, hell, why get married and love a woman and be unable to provide for her? Hell, I wouldn't want my children to be deprived or whatever. It all depends on economic security and I didn't have it. So without that, I didn't—whatever love relationship I had would be very much meaningless, very short."

"Was the last love relationship you had, was the breakoff mutual or—?"

"I think it was . . . I don't know. She was better off than I was. I think it was my part. I didn't want any part of it. I couldn't afford it. That's what ruined it."

"You got so far and then you said, 'If I keep going this way, then I've gotta get married, and I can't get married.' "

"I couldn't back up myself, you see? Sure, I could support this," said Sirhan, grabbing his genitals. "But I couldn't support the mouth."

"Uh-huh."

"You get me $100,000, I could be pretty well set up. With that security, I could work, I could go to school . . . but the way it is now, what do I have? Besides, what girl would marry me now?"

"So you sort of withdrew?"

"Well, no." Sirhan explained that he and his friend just started to drift apart. "I kept going to these races. Maybe I would bet it big someday."

"Now, just off the record, was Peggy Osterkamp this girl?"

"No."

"Okay. Because in your notebook, you wrote, 'Peggy Osterkamp' many times."

"You know why?" said Sirhan softly. "Because she looked beautiful on a horse, and I loved horses. That name, the first time I heard it, I loved it. The name 'Peggy.' *P* is the tight; the *g* is loose. Pe-gee. I don't know how to express it."

"Well, it's obvious there were fantasies."

"But she was beautiful on a horse."

"Well, it's obvious from the notebook there were fantasies in your mind about her. You wrote Peggy Osterkamp, Peggy Osterkamp, Peggy Oster-kamp. . . ."

"No. You know why? Maybe it was Peggy L—a racehorse. And then Peggy Osterkamp got on my mind."

"Well, I wondered whether there was a love relationship there or you wished there could be one."

"I never wished."

"Then why," I asked, "did you write 'Peggy Sirhan'?"

Sirhan sagged. "I don't remember that."

"You wrote 'Peggy Osterkamp, Peggy Osterkamp, Peggy Osterkamp, Peggy Sirhan.' "

"Really, I can't account for that."

"Judging from the description I've seen of her, she was pretty beauti-ful."

"She was. How'd you know that?"

"The FBI report ended up saying she was very attractive. Around school now, Walter Crowe told me you used to spend your lunch hours sitting alone in the midst of a bunch of girls. And you had a great time. You were really giving them a great line and you were enjoying yourself."

"Why not?"

"Yeah. If you can do it, that's great."

"Really, I have no complexes about that."

"All right. Now, for the first time, I've been able to sit down with you and throw out some ideas and have you say, 'No, that isn't so,' and have you able to talk about what is so."

"I'm glad you said that."

"I don't want to write a book about you and imply that you were an asexual being, that you never had it and had never been laid, or anything like that. I've heard people—who don't know a damn thing about Sirhan —they're psychologist types and they're Freudians, and they feel that a guy who'd been getting it wouldn't have done this. They've got it all worked out in their minds, but they don't know. And that's why I want to talk about it. You know, the truth has a power all its own. That's why I want—I'm glad I brought it up." I put my notepad down and leaned back in my chair.

"They don't realize that I'm not a psychotic," volunteered Sirhan. "I will be appreciated not now, but the next time the world goes to war, the next conflict comes up. That's when they're gonna think of Sirhan. Appreciate my own political views."

Later, Sirhan would clarify this: he was in the vanguard of "The Third World."

On New Year's Eve, I was again alone with Sirhan. My antismoking commercial had had some effect. Sirhan wasn't smoking at all. He was chewing gum. And he came as close as he ever would, with me, to absolute candor. Instead of playing the role of Arab patriot, which would later harden under the urging of the Arabs who could reach him during the trial, Sirhan was simply puzzled. He didn't know why he killed Kennedy and he couldn't account for his *modus operandi*.

"I don't understand," said Sirhan. "That's what I don't understand. Why did I leave that notebook behind?"

I nodded vigorously and added, "Also, why did you shoot him in a crowded room?"

"Oh, shit, yeah! I don't understand it."

I said earnestly, "Let me propose something. It may be a wild idea. You know, there may be a possibility that you were programmed to do this."

"Ohhh," said Sirhan, shaking his head. "I don't know." He put his head down between his knees. This suggestion was truly depressing.

I had been puzzling over some of the material in the notebook that suggested Sirhan was trying to drum some orders into his own head, orders that could have been given to him under hypnosis in the form of a post-hypnotic suggestion. Sirhan had written over and over again, "I have never heard Please pay to the order of . . ." "The fact is," I said, "you did have some contact with some people who did fool around with this mentalism." He had told me once that he had visited Manley Palmer Hall's Philosophical Research Society off Los Feliz Boulevard in Los Angeles.

"Oh, yeah," said Sirhan, "but they wouldn't do anything like this, Bob."

I paused, wondering how direct I could be at this point. "Well, what do you know about 'em?"

Such a thought was unthinkable to Sirhan. His friends who were interested in the occult had no political involvements.

I said they ought to be "checked out." Not by the FBI, perhaps, but maybe by some undercover agents for the defense. I presented a hypothesis to Sirhan. Maybe some people who wanted to get rid of Kennedy met Sirhan by accident and found him to be a tool they could manipulate. A bitter, disappointed—and highly suggestible—young man.

"Oh, no," said Sirhan. "Oh, no."

I reminded Sirhan again of his notebook. "You told me once you had written in your notebook, in fact, on the page where you wrote 'Robert F. Kennedy must be assassinated, assassinated, assassinated,' that you wrote it immediately after you had spent some time staring at yourself intensely in a mirror."

Sirhan said that he was merely following instructions from a book that he had had at the time.

"Who gave you the book?" I asked.

"I bought it," said Sirhan, "at Broughton's Book Store in Pasadena." I learned later that he bought it at the suggestion of a friend he wouldn't name. Here, Sirhan was worried. The whole scene in front of the mirror and the writing in the notebook "might imply that I was crazy."

"No," I said. "It would imply that you were a tool to be used by others. Why did you write it all down and leave it behind?"

Sirhan shook his head. "How could I be so stupid!"

I pointed out that some of the notebook writing seemed to have been written in a trance. "You wrote certain things over and over and over again," I said. "And when you wrote about killing Kennedy, you join to it the unexplainable phrase 'I have never heard Please pay to the order of of of of.' "

Sirhan said he didn't know about that. He couldn't remember writing that.

"We'll bring it up here," I said, "and show it to you. From my reading of the notebook, it seems there was some money passed and you were told to forget it."

"No, no," said Sirhan.

"Or," I said, "you were promised some money or shown a check."

"Oh," said Sirhan, shaking his head furiously, "I don't know. I don't know."

"I admit it's pretty farfetched," I said, "but on one page you wrote 'Please pay to the order of,' and then there were some amounts written down. '750, 750, 750, 750.' But they weren't all written in a straight line. Each of the numbers was placed on the four points of a diamond. And then there were some meandering writings about meeting somebody at the airport." My statement was more of a question, and I waited for Sirhan's response to that.

Sirhan didn't know.

"All right," I said. "Let's just admit this might be a possibility. How would you backtrack and find out when this all started? Maybe there was someone someplace whom you might have met who would have wanted Kennedy dead?" I tried to prime the pump a bit, bringing up various of Sirhan's friends to get his reaction to them. Negative. Negative. Negative. I asked Sirhan about the preacher Jerry Owen. Sirhan didn't say he didn't know Owen. He said that he was home Monday, that he raked up the leaves, that he slept quite a bit, that he read the papers, that he went to Corona later in the evening.

"Anyway," said Sirhan, "he proved out false, didn't he?" Sirhan was referring to the police lie detector test which Owen had failed.

"Yeah," I said, "but the interesting thing is he knew more about you in that first interview on June 5 with the police than he should have."

"Bob," said Sirhan, "I know a person doesn't have to meet you to know all about you."

"But he had more details than he should have."

"Well, I was home Monday," said Sirhan.

"But later you went to Corona?"

"Yeah," said Sirhan, "I drove out there." But he was evasive about why he had driven out there, whom he had seen or what he had done. "Why," asked Sirhan, "why would Owen go to the police? Maybe," Sirhan suggested, "maybe he was just seeking some personal publicity."

"Well," I said, "maybe that's all. Maybe that's all it was."

But then Sirhan volunteered a suggestion of his own. "Maybe," said Sirhan, "he could lead to someone who was playing with my mind." Sirhan talked about the dangers of putting one's mind under the control of others whom he did not know. "I always try to guard against that," said Sirhan. But now he had his doubts. He asked me to look into it, to look into every possibility, that maybe he *had* put his mind under the control of another.

"All right," I said. "But now if we're going to go into this, we ought to know more about the people that were in the same mind science thing with you."

"The only one," said Sirhan, "is Tom. I told you about him. But I don't want to involve him. He's much too good a man for this to fuck up with my mind." This was Walter Thomas Rathke, the groom who had introduced Sirhan to the occult.

"Yeah," I said.

"Much too good," said Sirhan. "He offered me a little protection at one time, but that doesn't involve this case. He's too good a man for this, Bob."

"What kind of protection did he offer you?" I asked.

Sirhan paused for some moments. "Mental protection," said Sirhan.

"Mental protection?" I waited for an explanation.

Sirhan evaded the question. He said something almost meaningless about Tom's protecting him from pernicious influence of other minds, something innocuous, as if Tom were warning him away from certain dangerous books. But that wasn't mental protection in any sense of the word, and I said so. "What did you mean, mental protection?" Sirhan declined to go into it any further. "Tell me more about Tom," I asked.

"No," said Sirhan. "I don't think he would . . ."

"Well, let's say there was somebody, somebody who could have influenced you. Wouldn't it likely be—"

"You know," said Sirhan, "isn't that funny? Goddamn it. You're not the only person who thought about that!" He said that one of the deputy sheriffs in jail, whom he had gotten friendly with, had talked about the possibility. Then the deputy was transferred to another post.

"Well," I said, "it's a possibility. We live in an age when these techniques have been developed."

Sirhan put his head down between his knees, shook it. "But why the hell me?" He looked up at me.

I told Sirhan about the case of Stig Wennerstrom, a disgruntled officer who had been picked out of the Swedish Air Force by some astute Soviet agents, and then led subtly step by step through a series of escalated acts of espionage, convinced by his "handler" to believe that he was acting in the interests of all humanity when he turned over NATO secrets to the Soviet Union.

"Well," said Sirhan, "I know this. I have this propensity. There are many things about me which cannot be explained by laboratory science. But I don't want anybody to call me crazy, if I tell about it."

I told him that being able to talk about it would demonstrate a higher degree of health than if he insisted on holding it all in.

"There's so much chaos in my mind," said Sirhan.

I wondered whether Sirhan wanted me to forget the whole line of inquiry.

"No," said Sirhan, "I don't want to mark it off."

"Do you want me to talk to Tom?"

"No," said Sirhan. "He was my friend. He was my friend."

"Would a guy who wanted to use you," I asked, "be a friend? Or an enemy?" I was thinking of Stig Wennerstrom's handler. Wennerstrom sometimes greeted his handler with an emotion so intense that it could only be compared to young love. When Wennerstrom was unable to meet his case officer at frequent intervals, he was in the position of an addict in need of a fix.

"He's not that kind of a man," said Sirhan.

"But he was in a position," I said.

"He could have been. He could have been. But I wouldn't want to influence *myself* to do such a thing."

I wondered whether there might not be other persons as close to him as Tom.

"There wouldn't have to be," said Sirhan. "Someone could have influenced my mind directly."

I hesitated. This was too much. "You mean by somebody you didn't even know, somebody you'd never seen? Just direct thought waves?"

"Yes," said Sirhan.

"That's harder for me to take," I said.

"I'm not trying to bullshit you guys," said Sirhan. "This is the real *me* now, no cover at all. This is beautiful stuff," he said, referring to his mind science experiments. "The relaxation of the mind!" He explained that he had read many many more books on mind science than he had had at home. He browsed a lot at Broughton's Book Store in $20 and $30 books. And with the knowledge he had gained in these readings, he was able, he said, to control himself. "I had the willpower," said Sirhan, "to control myself sexually and use that sexual potency in other creative ways."

I asked Sirhan to explain further. He tried, but then broke down. He couldn't describe it. "Did you live your whole life this way?" I asked.

"I tried a little bit of it," said Sirhan. "For four or five months. But I couldn't hold it any longer." And then, without any suggestion from me that the killing of Robert Kennedy was some sort of a sexual explosion, Sirhan volunteered, "But if I had need of some sexual outlets, I'd go out and get a girl. I wouldn't go out and shoot that bastard!"

"What you're saying is," I said, "you weren't all tied up?"

"I *was* all tied up," said Sirhan. "The Arab-Israeli—"

"Well," I said, "you had a real burning gripe."

"This is what puzzles me," said Sirhan. "I have had hatred, but not that much. Hatred was very foreign to me. That bothers me. I can't understand it."

According to a widely accepted cliché, propagated in the main by stage hypnotists and others who have a commercial interest in hypnosis, no one can be induced through hypnosis to do anything against his own moral code. The history of hypnosis, however, and the annals of crime itself are proof enough that skilled operators can lead certain highly suggestible subjects to do "bad" things by corrupting their sense of reality and appealing to some "higher morality."

On July 17, 1954, Bjorn Schouw Nielsen was convicted in Copenhagen Central Criminal Court and sentenced to life imprisonment for "having planned and instigated by influence of various kinds, including suggestions of a hypnotic nature," the commission of two robberies and two murders by another man. This man, Palle Hardrup, is free today because Dr. Paul Reiter, chief of the psychiatric department of the Copenhagen Municipal Hospital, spent nineteen months on an exhaustive study of the weird— possibly homosexual—relationship between the two men, which began in prison years before.

According to Dr. Reiter, Nielsen created a blindly obedient instrument in Hardrup, who would go into a trance at the sound (or the sight) of a simple signal—the letter X—and do whatever Nielsen suggested. Nielsen convinced Hardrup, in hypnosis, that he was a chosen instrument for the unification of all Scandinavia. Hardrup would form a new political party, would work under the direction of a guardian spirit—X—(who would communicate to him through Nielsen). Once this attitude was instilled, Nielsen induced Hardrup to raise money for the new party by robbing banks (and turning the money over to Nielsen). Hardrup robbed one bank successfully, and then, in the course of another, he killed a teller and a director of the bank and was arrested soon afterward by Copenhagen police.

It was Reiter's conclusion that Nielsen had created in Hardrup a split personality, a paranoid schizophrenic, who was never aware, until Reiter's work with him, that he had been programmed for crime, and programmed to forget that he had been programmed. Reiter's complete account * is a chilling tale of mysticism and murder—and of some very persistent detective work by Reiter perhaps unparalleled in the history of psychiatry and crime.

So it was not impossible. Sirhan could have been programmed and programmed to forget.

* Paul J. Reiter, *Antisocial or Criminal Acts and Hypnosis, a Case Study* (Springfield, Ill.: Charles C Thomas, 1958).

Ten

"Sirhan, did anybody pay you to shoot Kennedy?"

On January 2, Dr. Eric Marcus, the court-appointed psychiatrist for the defense, paid a call on Grant Cooper. To Marcus, Sirhan was extraordinarily like others whom the U.S. Government had locked up in institutions for the mentally ill because they had threatened various political figures with assassination. And now Marcus had a psychiatrist in tow who had made a study of these individuals. He was Dr. Edwin A. Weinstein, recently of Walter Reed Hospital's Division of Neuropsychiatry.

"The people making these threats," said Dr. Weinstein, a scholarly-looking man of very serious mien, "are invariably disturbed. Seventy percent of them have been in a hospital for some neuropsychiatric reason. Most of them are suicidal. Most of them are loners with a profound sense of anomie—of not knowing who they really are. And most of them have had unrealistic expectations and a long life of disappointment."

Sirhan, it seemed to Dr. Marcus, would have been institutionalized long ago if he'd ever been tested—if, for example, he'd been drafted into the military service where recruits acting "strangely" are often given a battery of psychological tests. (Sirhan should have registered for the draft, but he never got around to it.)

Dr. Weinstein reported that most of those he had studied put their own personal problems into a political idiom. Mrs. Oswald herself, he said, was a good example of that. In her testimony before the Warren Commission, she blamed everything on some institution or other, nothing on herself, or on her son Lee Harvey Oswald. And many of them reinforced their thinking by including themselves in certain organizations. They were "Communists" or "Nazis" or even members of clubs that didn't exist, like the "Down with America Association." As such, said Weinstein, they were members of "pseudo-communities." They never actually attended meetings or showed any other signs of membership, merely used these groups "as highly stereotyped condensed metaphors." For example, said Weinstein, John Wilkes Booth never joined the Confederate Army. Nor, said Marcus, did Sirhan ever join a young Communist cell or make any effort to communicate with Al Fatah.

Often, said Weinstein, the language of a man's threat was related to his own particular ailment. Thus, one man who was obsessively concerned with masturbation warned the President, "I will kill you with my bare hand." Another young man of eighteen planned to kill President Johnson by standing on a roof with *a good view* of the street, that he would not *be seen,* but make sure he himself could *see* the road, he would find the President's fat face in his *telescopic sight* and aim right between the President's *eyes.* He would then drop the rifle but turn for *one last look* of the President crumpling and catching his *face.* The young man was a small fellow who wore thick spectacles.

And Sirhan's language? One thing was clear: there was a strong sexual component in Sirhan's hatreds, for he leaned very hard on one particular implied metaphor. He wrote in his notebook about the "fucken U.S.A." He talked about Kennedy, the "fucken politician" who "fucked up" by advocating that the United States send those "fucken jet bombers" to Israel so the "fucken Jews" could "fuck the Arabs." What did it all mean? No one asked Marcus at the moment, and he was hardly ready to say, for he tended to shy away from all psychodynamic explanations that were frequently farfetched and often depended on mere theories whose general validity was yet unproved. Marcus was ready to go to court however and tell the jury that Sirhan was so mentally ill that he suffered from diminished capacity under the California law.

Cooper nodded. That would help. He needed something. He had just received the negative EEG report from Parsons indicating no evidence of brain damage in Sirhan, and Sirhan's chromosome test revealed that he had forty-six XY chromosomes, which was normal. Marcus was glad to hear that. In the Jack Ruby trial, he said, Attorney Melvin Belli had already demonstrated the iffy character of a defense based on funny-looking EEG's, and Marcus wasn't anxious to get in the middle of a trial like Ruby's with experts battling it out for both sides. A neurological defense could be justified, Marcus believed, only if Sirhan had had a previous history of psychomotor seizures, amnesia, sleepwalking or hallucinations, and Sirhan, as far as anyone then knew, had had no such history.

Later, however, I discovered that Sirhan had had at least one interesting hallucination.

A sunny Saturday at Santa Anita. Sirhan and Adel are each poring over their copies of the Daily Racing Form, *sitting on a bench in the infield. For twenty minutes, Sirhan concentrates intensely, finally decides he will bet on the 9 horse, puts down his paper and lo and behold there is Tom Rathke about fifty yards away from him, standing all alone and smiling at Sirhan.*

Sirhan folds up his form and walks over to Rathke. Suddenly, Rathke is no more. He has vanished.

At the stables on Monday, Sirhan sees Rathke at work. "Were you in the infield at Santa Anita Saturday?" demands Sirhan.

"No," says Rathke.

"Well, goddamn," says Sirhan, "I saw you there!"

"I know," says Rathke solemnly. "I know."

John Strathman talking about Sirhan and Rathke: "Tom Rathke?" says Strathman. "He was the groom, wasn't he? No. I didn't know him. Sirhan used to talk about him a lot, though. I think he was the guy who introduced Sirhan to the occult. He seemed to have Sirhan sort of transfixed. From what Sirhan told me, I got a sinister picture—of Sirhan and Rathke riding around in this old car. Rathke is driving and talking and Sirhan is listening and filling his head with all this junk on the occult."

"He was very intelligent," said Munir. "He could have been a general in the Arab army."

Munir had come to the jail with a suit of new clothes for Sirhan to wear to the trial. He sat down with Dr. Diamond in the Sheriff's Information Bureau. Dr. Diamond uncoiled the mike on his Sony Cassette Recorder. "Why not a leader here in America?" he asked. Munir didn't have an answer for that. "Did he ever talk about joining the guerrillas?" No. How then did Munir account for his brother's strange seizure of responsibility?

"When I got out of jail," said Munir, "let's see, it was in August, 1966, no, 1967, yeah, 1967, I had been in jail for nine months; I sensed that something was wrong with Sirhan. He'd say hello, but he didn't seem to mean it. He seemed *hurt,* but he concealed it, or tried to, anyway. And, once, he punched me right in the face and broke my glasses. Over practically nothing. A cup of tea. That wasn't like him."

"Any craziness in your family?" asked Diamond. Munir shrugged.

Diamond spent the lunch hour alone with Sirhan in his cell. Sirhan said he was "starting to tense up." Why? Sirhan groaned and groped for words.

Andy Williams was singing on the jail radio: "Call Me Irresponsible."
"I'm a criminal. I'm a murderer. I don't want to face it. I don't think I can
take the pressure, tension, you know, the seriousness of it all."

"What do you think's going to happen to you?" asked Diamond.

"I don't *know*." Sirhan's voice quavered.

"Worried to death, huh?"

"Huh?"

"You worried?"

"I don't know," said Sirhan. "Maybe after the trial starts, when I have
to get in there and fight for the Arabs . . ."

"What about fighting for yourself?"

"I don't know, sir."

Diamond asked Sirhan if he had had any more thoughts about what happened. "Bob Kaiser tells me your thoughts are getting a little bit clearer."

Sirhan said he and I had been talking about all his studies in the occult
and looking into the possibility of "somebody trying to influence my mind.
But I really don't know about that." Diamond skipped over the occult for
the moment and directed Sirhan's attention to the time of Sirhan's arrest.
He was still puzzled about Sirhan's reluctance to give his name. "Why not
keep my mouth shut," said Sirhan, "until I could see what the hell's going
on? Even when the public defender got to me later in the morning, I was
still dazed. Even when Wirin came later. I was still—dazed."

"You joked."

"I didn't give a shit."

"You think you were out of contact with reality?"

"I think I was high, sir."

"You were very talkative," offered Diamond. "You were willing to talk
about anything except yourself."

"Hell," said Sirhan, "that's what I don't understand!"

Diamond asked him about his going to see Kennedy on June 2. Sirhan
said he had seen an advertisement inviting people to come and meet Senator Kennedy at the Cocoanut Grove. To a humble little fellow like Sirhan,
that was overpowering. "A guy like me!" he exclaimed. "A nobody getting
a personal invitation to go down to the Ambassador! Too much out of my
class!" If he took the clipping with him, he explained, "they couldn't
throw me out of the place. That was my reason for taking that advertisement with me."

"How close to Kennedy were you?"

"Oh, shit, I was very far. I was in the crowd watching. Kennedy told the
people to get started on the last drive."

"Did he talk about the Jews, Israel?"

"No, he was very quiet *that day*."

"Was that the first time you actually ever saw Kennedy?"

"It was, sir—in reality." He added: "I'd seen him on TV." Then he vol-unteered quickly: "It was a thrill to see him." There was a note of fond recollection in his voice, like that of a four-year-old boy after his first visit to Santa Claus.

"It was a thrill to see him?" Diamond's eyebrows went up.

"Shit, yes, really. Hell, you know, a Presidential candidate, my first time." Now, Sirhan's tone became flatter. "And especially the advertise-ment, the public is invited. Really," he said, in a tone that sounded as if he were trying to convince both Diamond and himself, "I enjoyed it."

"You had no idea," said Diamond, "that three days later you were going to kill him?"

"Goddamn it, no, hell, no, I didn't. I don't know what the hell made me, sir. I seemed to have went in such a straight line." Sirhan put on imag-inary blinkers, bringing his two hands up to his temples. It seemed to him that he had "just been railroaded into this thing. But, hell, would I have left so much evidence behind me? I'm not that stupid!"

Sometimes, Diamond pointed out, people who don't care about being caught don't bother to cover up things.

"No, sir," said Sirhan. "I care what happens to me."

"You care."

"You're goddamn right, I care, sir! That bastard is not worth my life, sir. He isn't worth a minute of all the agony I've had up here."

"And yet," said Diamond, "the Arab cause is worth all this, isn't it?"

Sirhan paused. The notion of himself as an Arab hero hadn't yet taken hold. "I think it's worth—not my life. I—I think it's worth being told to the American people."

"Um-hmmm. And this is one way of telling it to them?" Shoot Kennedy so you can get a forum for your views?

"I don't know, sir. I never thought of it this way. Shit, no."

Diamond asked Sirhan about his notebooks. He didn't remember what he wrote in the notebooks, or when. The writing on May 18? "Very vaguely, sir." How did he feel? "Tensed up. Muscles tight. Blood going."

"And you were in that kind of mood in May?"

"I must have been. The thing that bugged me was the way—I never thought he would come out for Israel."

"Did you think he was going to be elected President?"

"I don't know. I don't know."

Diamond nodded. He seemed to have a good preliminary rapport with Sirhan and decided that now he would begin to see if Sirhan would take to hypnosis. "Sirhan, you know what hypnosis is?"

"Isn't it domination of the weaker will by the stronger?"

"No," said Diamond, "it isn't that at all. It's simply a way of demonstrating one's own ability to concentrate, and the hypnotist is not dominating over the will of the other. No one can be hypnotized against his own will, and the hypnotist really just gives suggestions and encouragement to a person so that he can use his own willpower to strengthen his own abilities. There's a lot of phony baloney about hypnosis."

Sirhan said he'd never really studied much about it. The Rosicrucians talked about a fellow named Mesmer.

"Would you have any objection to trying hypnosis here with me?" asked Diamond. Sirhan quickly agreed. "It might help you remember," said Diamond. Once, Diamond had worked with an Air Force captain who was willing to plead guilty to a charge of sending a bomb in the mails from Saigon to the United States. Under hypnosis he remembered facts that clearly proved he was innocent. Who knew what lay beneath the surface of this assassin? Diamond picked a quarter off the shelf behind his head and had Sirhan lie down and concentrate on the coin. "Relax. Take it slow. Don't be afraid." Diamond's voice was smooth and soothing. "Breathe slow and deep."

Sirhan said something by way of objection.

"This is just a practice session," said Diamond. "Nothing much is going to happen today."

"No. No," said Sirhan.

"You're afraid of something," said Diamond. "You're nervous." What was it? Some profound fear? No. It was the way Diamond held the quarter. George Washington's picture was askew and that offended Sirhan's sense of order. He reached up and straightened the coin and soon, surprisingly soon, as far as Diamond was concerned, he was under. "Are you aware you're all relaxed?" asked Diamond. "Except for a few muscles in your throat, you're all relaxed? I think you've always underestimated yourself, Sirhan." Diamond suggested that as a child Sirhan might have daydreamed, might have dreamed of leading his people. "Did you ever hope you could do that?" asked Diamond. "Are you aware that you could have helped your people?"

Sirhan started to sob. Diamond was unaware of what had triggered this display, but it could be a real key to the mystery of why Sirhan killed

Kennedy, and he urged Sirhan to let his feelings come out. "Don't be afraid to cry. Because these are your true feelings. Don't be afraid, Sirhan. Don't be afraid to let your feelings come out, Sirhan. Let your feelings come out, Sirhan. Don't be afraid." Now, Sirhan was sobbing strongly. "Let your feelings—"

"I don't know any people," cried Sirhan suddenly and loudly. They were his first words under hypnosis and they were perhaps more significant than any he would ever say again, because they were said in contradiction, really, of what Diamond was suggesting. Sirhan spoke them in a high-pitched, piteous tone, and the plaintiveness of his words was strangely accentuated by the voices of a church choir now emanating from the jail radio.

Diamond may have failed to hear what Sirhan said. Sirhan had said he knew no people. Diamond said: "Go on, tell me about it, Sirhan. What about your people?" Sirhan sobbed violently. "Say what you feel, Sirhan. Sirhan, say what you feel."

Sirhan's face was now contorted with grief and rage. His eyes were tightly closed, tears ran into his ears, he twisted his head in agony and sobs came from deep within him. Then he took two great sobbing breaths and said: "What the hell did they do?"

Then the moment passed. Sirhan tapered off, failed to respond to Diamond's pleas to tell him what he was feeling, or volunteer an explanation of who "they" were. "Sirhan, what happened to you just now? What did you feel deep down inside you?" No response. He was in too deep a trance. Diamond tried to rouse him. "Wake up, Sirhan. Wake up." He slapped his face lightly. "Wake up. Open your eyes. Open your eyes. Open your eyes, Sirhan. Sirhan! Open your eyes."

And then as Diamond pulled him to a sitting position, Sirhan sang two musical notes of self-affirmation: "Surrr-haaannn."

"Do you know what happened to you, Sirhan?" asked Diamond.

"I don't know." He shook his head and made wheezing sounds. "Whew! Whew!"

"Do you know what happened, Sirhan?"

"I don't know what the hell you're doing, doc."

"Sirhan, look at me." Triumphantly, Diamond said, "You see, I did hypnotize you! Do you remember what happened?"

"Where's that coin?" asked Sirhan. It was his last recollection.

"Were you surprised that it worked?"

"I don't know."

"Are you afraid?"

"I don't have any fear," he asserted.

"Oh, yes, you do. You are full of fear back there."

"It's cold, doc." He started to shiver, hugging and caressing his own upper arms. "Cold." Strange: Dr. Crahan had noted that Sirhan was shivering when he saw him on the morning of the assassination.

"Just calm down," said Diamond. "It'll be all right. In just a moment. Things came up like a torrent and overwhelmed you. A torrent of rage and fear." Diamond put Sirhan right back under hypnosis and asked him almost immediately why he pulled the trigger.

Sirhan snored. Again, he was under too deeply.

Diamond tried to wake him up again. Then he gave Sirhan instructions that would hold for the rest of their sessions in hypnosis. At a count of 1-2-3-4-5, Sirhan would go to sleep. At a count of 1-2-3, he would wake up. "All right, now, Sirhan, one, two, three, wake up. You're awake now."

Sirhan came out of it, but again he couldn't believe he was under. "Is this a game, doc?" Diamond assured him it was not, and, hearing Cooper's voice now outside the cell, he put Sirhan under again. One-two-three-four-five, a gentle touch from Diamond, and Sirhan was snoring.

Diamond went out. "There's something here I want you to see, Grant," said Diamond, leading Cooper back to Sirhan's inner sanctum. He sat on the edge of Sirhan's bed and counted to three. "Wake up, Sirhan. Wake up. Sit up, Sirhan. Look who's here."

Sirhan stirred, opened his eyes slowly and saw Cooper standing over him.

"Hi!" Cooper laughed from deep in his chest. "Glad to see ya!" He laughed again. "Been asleep?" Sirhan shook his head dazedly. "Quite a guy, isn't he?" said Cooper, nodding at Diamond.

"Hell of a guy! Hell of a guy!" admitted Sirhan.

Diamond put Sirhan under again, but Sirhan went into such a deep sleep that he could not answer Diamond's questions. "Did you kill Kennedy?" No response. "Did you kill the Senator?" No response. "Who shot him, Sirhan?" No response. "Were you there at the time?" No response. "Were you there in the kitchen?" No response. Cooper was impressed with the authenticity of the trance. But he was impatient with the results. What good was it? What good was it if Sirhan couldn't recall anything while he was under? Or remember anything when he came out?

Diamond knew that he still had a good deal of work ahead of him, pulling data from Sirhan and, equally important, convincing his attorney that it was information he could use.

*   *   *   *   *

On the eve of the trial, Emile Zola Berman arrived at Los Angeles International Airport on American Airlines Flight No. 11 with a copy of *The New York Times* under his arm. In a page-1 story, reporter Douglas Kneeland, in Los Angeles to cover the trial for *The Times,* wrote about the significance of the case: Sirhan would be the first assassin of the sixties to be tried in a court of law. Maybe. Kneeland suggested that the trial would surely be delayed if Cooper's troubles in Federal Court forced him to withdraw from the Sirhan case. Neither Parsons nor Berman, he implied (correctly), were ready to go ahead without Cooper.

Alex Sullivan of KNXT, CBS Radio, interviewed Berman in front of the shining stainless-steel baggage carousel (where Berman claimed a set of golf clubs he would never get a chance to use on this trip) and pursued him out into the parking lot. "My only desire," said Berman, concluding hurriedly as a chill fog started to blow in from the Pacific, "is to save this man's life. I'm not defending his crime, only his rights."

Berman and I met Cooper, Parsons and McCowan for supper at the Ambassador Hotel coffee shop, and the team adjourned afterward to Berman's cottage for a conference that lasted until 11:00 P.M. In Room 102-G, a large suite with a bilious green paint job starting to peel off the walls, Cooper told Berman he was staying in the case. He'd like to have more time to prepare his legal motions, but the judge was determined that the trial would begin right away. Cooper wondered whether he'd be forced to make another motion for continuance on the grounds that the press was linking the Federal matter too closely to the Sirhan case. In a classic example of oversimplified reporting, radio stations had been presenting one-line news broadcasts all weekend: "Grant Cooper, Sirhan Sirhan's attorney, says he lied in Federal Court. The striking teachers at San Francisco State College defy Chancellor Robert Dumke. Eleven killed in a Pennsylvania plane crash . . ." Cooper asked McCowan to subpoena the radio stations for copies of their news releases.

When Cooper picked up the Los Angeles *Times* off his porch at 6:00 A.M. next morning, he had all the proof he needed to argue that the press was making it exceedingly difficult for the court to pick an unbiased jury. Dave Smith's story on page 3, "Sirhan Trial Due to Start Today, but Defense May Request Delay" was flanked by Gene Blake's and Howard Hertel's: "COOPER ORDERED TO COURT TODAY OVER FRIARS' TRANSCRIPT."

It was somewhat unrealistic for Cooper to expect that the press would not trumpet his every move. Doug Kneeland suggested in *The New York Times* that Kennedy's absence from the political scene "contributed to the nomination of Richard Nixon, the divisive party bitterness and bloody street scenes of the Democratic Convention in Chicago, and to the acknowledged public apathy toward much of the subsequent campaign between Mr. Nixon and Mr. Humphrey." And Bob Greene wrote in *Newsday* that the trial of Kennedy's accused assassin promised to become "one of the most celebrated in American judicial history."

Indeed, the Hall of Justice was aswarm with no less than fourteen camera crews and several dozen radio newsmen toting their tape recorders when Cooper and Berman arrived shortly after 9:00 A.M. Up on the thirteenth floor, a UPI photographer and a single camera crew, shooting for all the television stations in the world, recorded Sirhan's historic emergence from his cell area. The two courtrooms were jammed with representatives of all the world's great news-gathering agencies. Those important enough to rate with Court Administrator Harold Frediani got seats in Judge Walker's tiny bulletproofed courtroom itself: Harry Rosenthal of The Associated Press, Jack Fox of the United Press International, Dave Smith of the Los Angeles *Times,* John Douglas of the Los Angeles *Herald-Examiner,* Sy Korman of the Chicago *Tribune,* John Hemphill of the Nashville *Tennessean,* George Lardner, Jr. of the Washington *Post,* Kneeland of *The New York Times,* Greene of *Newsday,* Ron DePaolo of *Life* magazine, James Brodhead of *Time,* Martin Kasindorf of *Newsweek,* Bruce Russell of Reuters, Val Clenard of KMPC, Bill Brown of KHJ, Jon Goodman of KNX, Bill Stout of the CBS network, Jack Perkins of NBC, Al Wiman of ABC, Dick Shoemaker of Channel 4, Paul Udell of Channel 2. On the fourth floor, another hundred newsmen or so watched the proceedings on two identical television sets affixed to the wall of the auxiliary courtroom.

Sirhan himself, in handcuffs, was escorted by two deputies to an elevator, taken down a back corridor on the ninth floor, the windows of which were covered with bulletproof quarter-inch steel shields, past a line of deputies and down a private stairway to a windowless holding room directly behind the judge's bench. There, the deputies took off his cuffs, and the three of them waited for the trial to begin.

"Everyone rise," intoned Willard Polhemus, "standing facing our flag, recognizing the principles for which it stands, Department 107 of the Superior Court is now in session, the Honorable Herbert V. Walker, Judge presiding." Walker settled down in his chair, surveyed the entire scene: the defendant, who looked entirely presentable in a neat gray suit and a light blue tie; the attorneys for both sides; two court reporters in place below his bench, hands poised over their stenotype machines; a sound technician below and to his right fiddling with the dials controlling the four court microphones; Inspectors Bill Conroy and Ralph Welch standing on the alert on the east wall, along with Lieutenant Craig Carpenter, whose eyes were fixed firmly on Sirhan; Sirhan's two guards directly between Sirhan and the rail; two uniformed bailiffs at the desk inside the rail; detectives from the Los Angeles Police Department strung along the inside of the rail to the west wall; a whole row of artists employed by local TV stations and the networks; and way in the back of the room, little Mary Sirhan and a son in dark glasses. All of them, even the law-enforcement officers intermingled among the crowd, Walker knew, had been scrutinized as they passed through two heavy locked doors, searched by a team of deputies in the hallway, scanned by the electronic "Transfrisker," ushered through a third locked door past a bank of press telephones and thence to the double doors of the courtroom itself. Everyone wore color-coded plastic badges, and everyone seemed to be holding his breath. *"People* versus *Sirhan,"* mumbled Walker, ". . . note that defendant and counsel are present, no one in the jury box. . . ."

At this suspenseful moment, Cooper asked the court to adjourn to chambers. Everyone exhaled. Some newsmen moaned. Others started to leave the court for the phones. Walker warned them they were not free to leave like that en masse, then called for adjournment.

For almost an hour, the attorneys argued in chambers. Cooper asked for thirty days' "continuance"—postponement—because of the "prejudicial" news reports before trial. He quoted from the "ABA's Reardon Report," a compendium of recommendations designed to conciliate the conflicting constitutional claims of the press and the courts.

Berman argued on behalf of Cooper. "Nobody in the role of principal counsel can persuade a jury about anything when his sincerity has been destroyed." Speaking of the potential jurors, Berman pointed out that they were "not eclectic people" and would necessarily look askance at Cooper.

Judge Walker was somewhat at a loss. Cooper had brought the matter up with Sirhan the day before in Walker's presence and Sirhan—with the advice of A. L. Wirin—had insisted Cooper stay in the case despite the possible prejudice. Yet now, Cooper was using the press stories to ask for a delay. And why? Was Cooper really tainted? "I gave a great deal of credit to you," said Walker, "because you came out and said you lied instead of trying to cover up, and I know that other people feel the same way." Walker said he'd think it over. In the meantime, he asked if Cooper would go back in open court and make his other motions. He did. Walker denied his unprecedented requests for two separate juries (one on guilt-or-innocence, the other on penalty) and gave Cooper the rest of the day ostensibly to marshal arguments on his other motions. Actually, the delay gave Cooper the time he needed to appear again in Federal Court where he was ordered to answer forty-five questions pertaining to the Friars' transcripts. From there, he went to the secret session of the Grand Jury and declined again to answer because he could not violate the confidential relationship between attorney and client.

To the readers of *Newsday* and the fourteen other U.S. newspapers that subscribe to the *Newsday*'s service, Bob Greene tried to explain the legal import of all these motions:

> The fact that the defense will lose most of those motions now is not a matter of prime concern to Sirhan's attorneys, because, if Sirhan is convicted of first-degree murder, the case will be appealed all the way up to the U.S. Supreme Court and, over the past 14 years, the Supreme Court has shown an increasing disposition to re-examine the trial process and to sharply define the rights of defendants in criminal cases. A few of many such decisions have been the prohibition on the admission of illegally-obtained evidence and the ruling that a defendant must be fully informed of his rights before he is questioned by police about any crime he is suspected of having committed.
>
> "No one can predict where or how the Supreme Court will move next," Emile Zola Berman, another of the defense attorneys, said. "In making these motions, we are citing every step of the trial process that we feel to be inequitable. If there is a conviction and the case goes up on appeal, we hope that the higher courts will agree with one or more of these arguments. If this happens, we have new law. And we also have a reversal of the conviction."

Dave Smith's story in the Los Angeles *Times* was more impatient, less reflective. "LEGAL MOVES STALL TRIAL OF SIRHAN," said the L.A. *Times* in a three-inch banner on page 1 on January 8.

Inside the *Times,* on page 22, was a report from Taiybe, Israel, indicating that Sirhan's father saw only one reason for a trial at all: to establish the fact that Palestinian Arabs had a legitimate cause: "A nation of our own, not Israeli, not Jordanian, but Palestinian."

Bishara Sirhan had now changed his tone. He said he didn't blame Sirhan for what he did. "He was a very good boy, a very studious boy. If he did this—and the facts seem to say that he may have done so—it was because he was doing something for his country. We know he is a hero." As much of a hero, he implied, as the Palestinian commandos who, on that very day, blew up the Damiya bridge, one of two essential links across the Jordan River in Jerusalem.

*   *   *   *   *

For Dr. Diamond, the legal delays were helpful, for he had only begun to scratch the surface with Sirhan. On Saturday, January 11, he visited the cell for the third time and put Sirhan into a trance almost immediately. Then, in order to check the authenticity of the hypnotic state, he pulled a safety pin from his jacket, sterilized it with an alcohol-soaked pad he had brought along for the purpose and stuck the pin through the skin on top of Sirhan's left hand. He told Sirhan he would feel no pain. Apparently, he did not. The guard outside the cell called Lieutenant Carpenter over to look. Carpenter said it was okay. Diamond had already checked it out with him.

"Did that hurt, Sirhan?" asked Diamond. Sirhan only mumbled. "Are you comfortable, Sirhan?" Another mumble. Then Diamond went directly to a series of questions suggested by Cooper. "Now, listen to me, Sirhan. Nod your head if you can hear my voice. That's it. Are you comfortable, Sirhan?"

"Yes." His voice was very low, almost inaudible.

"Sirhan, did anybody pay you to shoot Kennedy? Did anybody pay you to shoot Kennedy, Sirhan? Yes or no."

Sirhan sighed.

"I can't hear you."

"No."

"No? No one paid you to shoot Kennedy. Did anybody know ahead of time that you were going to do it, Sirhan?"

"No."

"No. Did anybody from the Arabs tell you to shoot Kennedy? Any of your Arab friends?"

"No."

"Did the Arab government have anything to do with it, Sirhan?"

"No."

"Did you think this up all by yourself?"

Sirhan paused five seconds. "Yes," he said.

"Yes. You thought this up all by yourself. Did you consult with anybody else, Sirhan?"

"No."

"Are you the only person involved in Kennedy's shooting?"

Sirhan blocked again with a three-second pause. "Yes."

"Yes. Nobody involved at all. Why did you shoot Kennedy?"

Sirhan had no answer.

"Why did you shoot him, Sirhan?"

"The bombers," mumbled Sirhan.

"What? The bombers? You mean the bombers to Israel?"

"Yes."

"When did you decide to shoot Kennedy?"

"I don't know."

"You don't know. Umm-hmmm. Are you sure nobody else was in on this, Sirhan? Tell me the truth."

"No."

"Nobody else besides you. Are you sure? Are you absolutely positive?"

"Yes."

"Was there any conspiracy at all, Sirhan?"

"No."

"No? No member of your family helped you?"

"No."

"Did you consult with anybody, did you ask anybody whether you should kill Kennedy?"

"No."

"No? Are you telling me the truth, Sirhan?" *

"Yes."

At the time, Diamond saw no significance in Sirhan's blocking on two key questions and took his answers as essentially true ones to questions the defense had not up to that moment really resolved. Diamond hardly succeeded, however, in getting Sirhan to reveal the events at the Ambassador on the night of June 4. Finally, Sirhan remembered a moment when Kennedy came into the pantry. What else? Nothing. Through the better part of an hour, Diamond tried and got little more than mumbles from Sirhan, who was going into a deeper and deeper trance. It was important that Sirhan remember what he was led to recall while in the trance, and Diamond gave him a posthypnotic suggestion that he remember more. Diamond brought him out, finally, and when Sirhan woke up, he was astounded to see the safety pin stuck in his hand. "Jesus Christ!" he cried. "What's that?" Sirhan was upset by the trickle of blood that flowed when he jiggled the pin, and he ran excitedly over to the bars to show the guard what Dia-

---

* Under hypnosis, a man can (and usually does) tell the same lies and make the same evasions he does when he is awake. And so, the reader should take care not to conclude that Sirhan, in hypnosis, always told "the truth." Thus, when Sirhan replies that yes (five–second pause), he did think up the assassination all by himself, the reader has to take that answer with a grain of salt. There were, however, some facts and feelings which Sirhan had suppressed in ways that were entirely unconscious— his anguish over the horrors of war, for example and when he came forth with these under hypnosis and at no other time, they had the definite ring of truth.

mond had done to him. He returned to Diamond. "You've got a lot of guts, doc."

"No," said Diamond. "You're the one who's got the guts. You do. You're the one who controlled the pain."

"You put that son-of-a-bitchen pin right in there."

Diamond admitted he had and then tried to see if his posthypnotic suggestion that Sirhan remember more would have any effect. It did.

What did Sirhan remember about that night at the Ambassador? He recalled seeing a man in a uniform. Sitting down. Sirhan was leaning on a table. What kind of table? Sirhan paused and tried to think. On the jailhouse radio, someone was singing "Friendly Persuasion."

"Not sure, but I recollect giving a girl a cup of coffee. I served myself. I didn't remember paying for it. . . ." He couldn't remember where he had the gun. For the first time, he remembered mirrors. They bugged him. Too much light. Then he started for the coffee. And then? He didn't know. He found a girl. He said to her, "Here's coffee." He remembered meeting a girl. Remembered giving her coffee. She looked Armenian. Or Spanish. She said she was tired and sleepy. "I might have tried to hang around with her," said Sirhan. "She could have been a fast one."

"Did you laugh with her, joke with her?"

"Don't remember."

"Did you talk about Kennedy with her?"

"Kennedy was out of my mind then."

Diamond sagged, now somewhat tired. Someone on the jailhouse radio sang, "Do you know the way to San Jose?" San Jose was simple. Did anyone know the way to Sirhan? Now Diamond wanted a cup of coffee. The guard brought in two cups, one for Diamond and one for Sirhan. Diamond leaned back. "How did you get the coffee?" referring now back to the Ambassador.

"I don't remember."

Diamond told Sirhan what he'd remembered in hypnosis, that he was in the pantry and Kennedy came in. Sirhan couldn't remember. Diamond told him he had to. "The jury will be very suspicious. They'll think you're covering up something." Diamond drew a rough floor plan of the hotel's lobby level. He suggested Sirhan might have gotten to the kitchen through a certain set of swinging doors, not through the Embassy Room, which was crowded.

"Wait a minute," said Sirhan. "Wait a minute. This is the press room? There was a lady there. A teletype machine. Western Union. I was there."

But he couldn't recognize where he'd gone after that. He wished he could go down to the Ambassador to refresh his memory. Diamond said he doubted Cooper could swing that.

"Hell," said Sirhan. "This girl kept talking about coffee. She wanted cream. Spanish, Mexican, dark-skinned. When people talked about the girl in the polka-dot dress," he figured, "maybe they were thinking of the girl I was having coffee with."

Diamond asked Sirhan if he always bit his nails. If he had wet the bed. Yes to both questions. He wet the bed to age twelve. Did he have any fits or spells? Sirhan thought he did, but couldn't describe them.

Diamond put him to sleep again. This time, he promised, he wouldn't stick any pins in him. He kept Sirhan sitting up, so he wouldn't go in so deeply. On a hunch, Diamond told Sirhan to think about the bombers flying over Israel, dropping bombs on Jerusalem.

Sirhan started weeping. Within a minute, he burst out into loud sobs. "He can't. He can't," cried Sirhan.

"What's happening to you, Sirhan? Don't run away from your feelings, Sirhan. Think of the bombers, Sirhan. Did Kennedy send the bombers?"

Sirhan stopped sobbing. "He was going to."

"Were you going to stop him?"

"I don't know." It seemed that any talk about the bombers triggered this spell in Sirhan, but the mention of Kennedy didn't have the same effect. The bombs and the bombers were genuinely traumatic, but Kennedy wasn't. What then was the connection? No one would ever be able to say with certainty. But this session was valuable enough to Diamond, for he found in Sirhan a remarkable reservoir of feeling and learned how to tap it. Here, in the bombs of Jerusalem, it seemed, were the seeds of disturbance. Maybe Diamond's scheduled meeting that afternoon with Mary Sirhan would tell him more.

Diamond came right to the point with Mary Sirhan. "Can you tell me about the bombings," he asked.

"Yes," said Mary Sirhan simply and clearly. "That's why we came to this country." When the sounds of violence would ring out in the streets —explosions from mortar shells or dynamite, rifle shots, screams from the victims—the children would "cry and scream and shake all over."

"Would Sirhan shake all over like that?"

"Very much."

"More than the other children?"

She looked over at Munir who was sitting there listening and nodded. "Yes."

"Could you describe what he would look like?"

Mary described the aftereffects of one bombing near their home: a soldier was blasted to bits and Sirhan saw his foot hanging from a church steeple.

"How did this affect Sirhan?"

"He was pale for some time. Wouldn't move for some time. Couldn't move. Fainted." Mary added, "After a truck full of dynamite exploded near our home, Sirhan wouldn't go out of the house for days."

"Did he have nightmares?"

"Sometimes he'd talk in his sleep."

"Do you remember if he ever woke up screaming with fear?"

"One night, living in Old Jerusalem, I felt him and he was cold like stick. More than any of his brothers, he had less blood and more fear."

Diamond described Sirhan's fit in his cell. "Did you ever see Sirhan like this?"

"Yes," said Mary Sirhan. "That's what I'm describing now." She didn't quite understand and told of Sirhan's spell—"from the freezing."

"Any other spells?" asked Diamond.

Mary told of a bomb—a mortar shell perhaps—that had blasted a storekeeper across the street from their home in Old Jerusalem. Sirhan saw this, she said, and some bystanders thought he, too, was hit. She ran out to get him and bring him in the house. "When we got in, he was just—gone —blacked out."

"Was he stiff or limp?"

"He was—just blacked out and after that—"

"What did he look like to you?"

"Pale, very pale."

"Were his hands clenched, or was he relaxed?"

"Clenched."

"Was he in a kind of trance?"

Mary couldn't say. But what she described may have indicated as much: he didn't know where he was or who was trying to help him. There were other times when Sirhan fainted on the street. A man phoned the bakery across from the Sirhans' home and told them that their boy had blacked out. Why did he black out? Mary didn't know. But they had to carry him home. Another time Mary Sirhan recalled how when Sirhan was seven, he had seen a nine-year-old girl who had gotten hit with a piece of shrapnel in the knee and blood ran from her leg as from a faucet. "What did she do? What did she do?" cried Sirhan, and he fainted.

What else? Nothing. Mrs. Sirhan was obviously not trying to tell Diamond what he wanted to hear or even embroider events that aroused Diamond's interest. But finally, almost as an afterthought, Mary Sirhan added that some days in Jerusalem Sirhan would faint twice in the same day. What would trigger that? "From fear. A bombing. Or when the bomb stops, people would go around to see what happens. If Sirhan would see blood on the ground, he used to faint." When he fainted, would his eyes be open or closed?

"Well," said Mary, "sometimes open."

"Open? Like in a trance?" asked Diamond.

"Yeah," said Mary Sirhan.

Diamond asked about Sirhan's experiments with the occult. Mary knew nothing about them. But Munir did. He took Diamond back to his room— formerly Sirhan's room—and showed him how Sirhan would stare into a mirror on his desk and look into candle flames and make them jiggle. There was a lead fishing weight still hanging on a string from the ceiling. "Sirhan said he could make this move back and forth just by concentrating on it real hard. I'd come in the room and he'd be staring at it real hard and it would be swinging back and forth."

From the Sirhan home, Diamond and I went directly to Cooper's office, where Cooper and Berman were waiting. "Sirhan is sick," said Diamond, "and this is a sick murder. I feel that Sirhan killed Kennedy while he was in a dissociated state. I really don't think he knew what he was doing." Diamond reported his own quick reconstruction: Sirhan consumed three or four Tom Collinses at the Ambassador, went back to his car to go home, discovered he was too drunk to drive, picked up his gun off the back seat of his car because he thought someone might steal it and returned to the Ambassador to get some coffee. Then, at some point, surrounded by mirrors and a great many lights, he became confused, possibly went into a dissociated state, perhaps a kind of a trance, then—after the shooting— suddenly found himself being choked and beaten by an indefinite number of men in the pantry. Diamond told the lawyers about his visit that day with Sirhan and the paroxysms that burst forth from the seething volcano inside Sirhan. He told them about his house call on the Sirhans and Mary's confirmation (though she hardly knew its significance) of the fact that Sirhan had suffered the same kind of "spells" when he lived through the shocks of the war in Jerusalem.

"They weren't epileptic fits, were they?" asked Berman.

"No," said Diamond, "not that. He had a sardonic grimace on his face, his face was flushed, he had tears in his eyes, he was full of moans and groans, a most profound culmination of fear and rage. Something very different from the cool Sirhan we know. There's no doubt about the authenticity of his dissociated state. And I have no doubt that we could even show it to the jury."

"You mean," said Cooper, "that you could even demonstrate that in court?"

"I could hypnotize Sirhan in court," said Diamond, "and he would manifest the same reactions. But I don't know whether the judge would allow it."

"I don't know why not!" said Cooper emphatically. "I don't know why not!"

Diamond's scholarly mind didn't lean to courtroom histrionics. He said that if the lawyers got the testimony of the psychiatrists and psychologists out in open court, they'd have "no problem getting a verdict of first-degree murder with life, even with the toughest jury." With the evidence that they had at this point, he felt that the lawyers had a "most legitimate negation of premeditation *and* malice."

Berman had a problem with that. No premeditation? "What about this?" he said, pushing a Xerox copy of Sirhan's notebook along the desk toward Diamond. Diamond looked at it for some minutes in silence. Berman shifted his angular frame and flipped to the page where Sirhan had written that Kennedy must be assassinated before 5 June 68. Cooper kept quiet, too, for he was intensely interested in Diamond's reaction. "How," demanded Berman, "how do you explain this?" He tapped the page with a bony finger. "How do you square this with his killing Kennedy in a dissociated state?"

"With this notebook," said Cooper, "the prosecution has as good evidence as anybody ever had of premeditation."

I suggested that Sirhan might have been under a quasi-hypnotic state when he wrote in the notebook. Cooper, forgetting that Sirhan had once told me he wrote that he would kill Kennedy after a staring session in front of his mirror, pooh-poohed that speculation.

Diamond said, "Well, could be, but you're fishing . . ."

Berman said, "You wouldn't expect to get legitimate writing under hypnosis anyway, would you?"

Diamond said it was entirely possible that you could. He paused for a moment, trying to collect his thoughts. He was patient enough to wait and see how the notebooks fit into the entire picture, but Cooper and Berman were not. He said that he thought the notebook writings were the day-dreams and the fantasies not of a cool, cold-blooded killer, but rather those of "a little chicken shit" who didn't think he'd ever kill Kennedy.

"Yes," said Cooper, "but he did kill Kennedy!"

"When he did," said Diamond, "it was under a very special combination of circumstances. He fulfilled his fantasy in a dissociated state."

I asked how Diamond could prove that Sirhan was in a dissociated state when he killed Kennedy. Diamond said there was really no way of "prov-ing" that. All he could prove was that Sirhan was capable of going into a dissociated state and talk to the jury about probabilities.

Cooper shook his head. "It seems like too damn big a gamble." He as-sured Diamond that even if there was a plea, "the D.A.'s office would still put on their whole case and we'd have to demonstrate the psychiatric evi-dence."

I said it would be extremely bad public relations for the D.A. to accept a plea and deprive the public of a real trial.

"I'd let them stage anything they want," said Cooper.

"When would you make the plea?" asked Diamond.

"When the evidence was in," said Cooper, "we'd have a conference with the judge. But it would all be worked out ahead of time."

"You wouldn't need a jury then?" I said.

"What?" said Cooper.

"You wouldn't need a jury then."

"Well, I wouldn't say that!" He talked about putting on the complete case before a jury. "The verdict—of first-degree murder with life imprisonment—would just be predetermined, that's all."

I said I couldn't see a mock trial. And if Sirhan got a death sentence despite the psychiatric evidence, I'd put my money on the Supreme Court.

"Dammit," said Cooper, "you can't tell me! With all the heat the courts have been taking, don't you think that the Supreme Court doesn't have its ears attuned to the public?"

"They've reduced every case like this so far," said Diamond.

"*Where* there was unanimity on the part of the doctors," said Cooper.

"No," said Diamond, "in *Bassett,* the Supreme Court rejected the psy-chiatrists' conclusions. One doctor didn't even examine Bassett. One doc-tor only spent twenty minutes with him. And one doctor said he was in-

sane under M'Naughton but had the capacity to premeditate. The court
said he didn't understand the law and reduced it to second degree."

Cooper laughed at that. "Not even the lawyer understood the law in that
one!"

On January 13, the court bailiffs marched exactly twenty-four
veniremen—potential jurors—into Judge Walker's courtroom. They put
some of them into the jury box and others in the first two rows of seats.
But they searched no one. It was not that they were unlike all the others,
including the deputy sheriffs themselves, who were searched when they entered the area. In fact, the sheriff's men were afraid that all their super security in the past six months would go for naught if just one kooky venireman took it upon himself personally to avenge the death of Senator
Kennedy by executing Sirhan right there in front of the hidden TV camera
in the dummy air conditioner. It was a real risk. And more than two
dozen extra plainclothesmen from the sheriff's office stood around the potential jurors and sat among them and followed their every movement with
extreme interest. "We wouldn't have had to do this," said one sheriff's officer, "if the defense attorneys had let us search them."

"We are trying hard," Parsons explained to the press, "not to emphasize
to the jurors that this is any kind of an unusual case."

So here were the potential jurors. Lean, lame, sleek, humble, casual, excited. A mixed lot, and no surprise. For they were selected by reason of
their position on the voting rolls: every fifth name in every sixth precinct,
minus a few doctors, lawyers, teachers and others commonly exempted
from jury duty. Now, it was the job of the judge and the attorneys on both
sides to see how competent they were to serve. They did this by asking the
jurors to give them honest answers to questions about themselves and their
beliefs, a process of inquiry known as *voir dire,* an expression from the
Old French meaning to say the truth. Out of the *voir dire* would come,
eventually, the twelve jurors and six alternates who would listen to the evidence and decide whether Sirhan was guilty, what crime he was guilty of
and what his penalty would be.

Obviously, anyone who would prejudge these matters was ruled out,
"for cause." Mrs. Jeanette Hendler, a pale, birdlike blonde, said she could
not serve on the jury because she was against capital punishment.
"Couldn't you just decide on the defendant's guilt or innocence?" asked
Cooper.

"I could not find him innocent," she said firmly.

"Well," persisted Cooper, "couldn't you find him guilty of a lesser crime?"

Mrs. Hendler stared across the counsel table to the slim figure at the far end, and the fluorescent lights glittered on her horn-rimmed spectacles. She said carefully: "He performed an execution." Cooper put his head down and agreed with John Howard that Mrs. Hendler could be dismissed for cause.

Attorneys for both sides tried to discover if the potential jurors had any prejudices. Cooper tried to discover any associations the veniremen might have with law-enforcement agencies that could prejudice them against the defendant. David Fitts wondered whether any had ever crusaded against capital punishment.

Some of the panel never even got that far in the examination: they had to admit frankly that serving on the jury would be a hardship. The judge was going to keep the jurors sequestered from the outside world in a hotel for two or three months? They couldn't do that. Mac Jensen had a mother at home with cataracts who needed his assistance. Mrs. Nadine Echols had three young children who demanded her attention. Robert R. Becold, a bachelor and a traveling salesman, who lived in hotels four days a week, said, "After a week or two, I'd be climbing the walls." They, and literally dozens like them, were excused.

Eventually, however, some tentative jurors were seated. And while they sat listening to the examination of other potentials, the attorneys on both sides took the opportunity to lay the foundation for certain arguments they intended to pursue later. Grant Cooper announced immediately that the defense would not deny that Sirhan killed Kennedy. His mental state was the only issue. An honesty point for Cooper. Fitts couldn't let him get away with it. "All right," Fitts asked Mrs. Rosa Molina, "counsel has suggested to you that insofar as the strategy of the defense is concerned, he will not urge that the defendant is entirely free from responsibility for the death of Senator Robert F. Kennedy."

Cooper was on his feet. "Pardon me, your Honor, please."

"I am about to amend—"

"I would strike the 'strategy' from the question," said Cooper. "It isn't a question of strategy."

"Well, let us not be so naïve—" said Fitts.

"Well, one minute," interjected Walker. "Don't get into a discussion. The word 'strategy' will be stricken and the jurors should disregard it as though they never heard it."

Fitts conceded. "But surely there is some plan and Mr. Cooper knows what he is doing. May I use the word 'plan'?"

"Your Honor, please, it is just the fact," said Cooper.

"All right, then," said Fitts, "the fact in this case . . ." He asked Mrs. Molina if Cooper's excessively honest concession would make her disposed to believe that whatever defense was offered would be automatically worthy of credence.

"What?" asked Mrs. Molina. "Worthy of what?"

Fitts fingered his wilting collar. It was hot in the courtroom and crowded and the fans seemed to contribute nothing but noise. "Credence," said Fitts. "Belief."

Judge Walker admonished Fitts to eliminate such words as "credence."

Fitts balked. "Well, if the court please, one of the things I like to find out is whether a juror understands the word 'credence.' "

Mrs. Molina's answer was no, Cooper's excessive honesty wouldn't sway her one way or another.

Cooper wanted to find out if the potential jurors had any preconceived ideas or notions or bias against psychologists? Any prejudice against psychiatrists? "You don't think," he asked, "that they are headshrinkers, as some people jokingly refer to them? Do you have objections to the use of hypnosis as a scientific tool? Or inkblots?"

David Fitts wanted to make sure that the jurors wouldn't be intimidated by the psychiatric experts the defense was sure to produce. "There are a lot of words that end in 'iatry' and 'ology': palmistry, astrology, phrenology. You don't have the sort of blind belief I have heard some people entertain that any word that ends in 'iatry' or 'ology' is necessarily something like Holy Gospel and must be accepted blindly? You don't feel that way?"

Most of the potential jurors gave attorneys for both sides the answers they seemed to want to hear. In this important trial, it wasn't as hard to get jurors as the lawyers originally feared. By their own testimony, it was a group surprisingly free of any preconceived notions on anything. Though polls in California indicated roughly half the population was against capital punishment, only two veniremen said they were. They reacted to questions about the Arab-Israeli conflict, wrote *Newsday*'s Bob Greene, "as though they had been asked about the possibility of life on Mars." They had no opinion on the Arab-Israeli question.

And so, while Cooper and Fitts took the major responsibility of picking the jury, both of them took the opportunity to make what amounted to preliminary arguments. "You may be listening to the testimony of witnesses for the prosecution for a whole month," said Cooper to a young, honey blonde named Carolyn Freeman. "And because we must sit silent during that period of time, you are only going to hear one side of it. Do you feel that you can heed the court's admonition and do your dead-level best and say to yourself from time to time, 'Now, I mustn't make up my mind about this until I have heard both sides'? Now, that's not easy. Do you feel you will do your dead-level best to do that?"

"Yes," said Miss Freeman.

But Fitts made it clear where he thought Miss Freeman would find herself at the end of the trial. "Do you believe that some months hence," he asked, "when this defendant is not as unfamiliar to you as he must at this time be, that having arrived—using the law and the evidence—at a decision that this is a proper case for the imposition of capital punishment, would you have the courage to walk down from the jury room, look at this defendant and say in essence by your verdict: 'Sirhan, for the murder of Robert F. Kennedy, you must die in the gas chamber'?" It was the first public announcement that the district attorney's office would seek the death penalty. And Sirhan put his elbows on his knees and looked as if he was going to become ill.

"Yes, I would," said Miss Freeman firmly. Emile Zola Berman shook his head. In his mind, Miss Freeman was a hanging juror. The defense would have to get rid of her later with a peremptory challenge.*

But Berman, Cooper and Parsons really wanted the next panelist to stick. She was Mrs. Alvina Alvidrez, a middle-aged woman who had worked for Kennedy in the California primary, but who did not believe in the death penalty. "Are you telling me," said Judge Walker, "that it would be impossible for you to think of any set of facts that would in accordance with your conscience enable you to vote for a guilty verdict wherein you knew there was a possibility that a death penalty might follow?"

"A guilty verdict, yes. A penalty, no," said Mrs. Alvidrez firmly.

"Now, are you telling me you could vote on the question of guilt or innocence?"

"Yes." She could in conscience in the trial's first phase.

"But you could not vote for a death penalty in the penalty phase of the trial?"

"Yes."

John Howard challenged her for cause.

Cooper resisted the challenge. Not only would it be a good idea to have

---

* A peremptory challenge allows each side to excuse a juror for no stated cause at all. Both defense and prosecution were allocated twenty such challenges.

Mrs. Alvidrez on the jury, but if she were eliminated, despite the protest, there might be grounds later for appeal.

Without further argument, Judge Walker allowed the challenge.

"What?" said Cooper, somewhat surprised.

"I said I am going to allow the challenge."

"Well, your Honor, please, I will resist it and I feel the juror, she indicated . . . she would follow the law and all the law as your Honor gave it."

Walker said he would allow Mrs. Alvidrez to remain on the jury on that score. He would take her off because she couldn't in conscience levy the penalty of death.

"Your Honor, please," said Cooper, "we resist that challenge on the ground that we have a right to this juror on the issue of guilt or innocence."

Judge Walker reversed himself and agreed with Cooper.

This gave everyone pause. John Howard suggested that the judge and the lawyers take five minutes to discuss the import of all this—outside the hearing of the jury. The judge called a recess.

While the lawyers discussed the matter in chambers, the newsmen poured out of the courtroom for the telephones, and others who weren't on their deadlines bubbled with excitement over the problems created by Mrs. Alvidrez. Eliminating a juror such as she had been standard operating procedure in the courts, but the judge would take a chance if he did so here, for the appellate courts seemed to be saying that juries so chosen in the past were "death-oriented." Were the newsmen gleeful merely because at last they had something to write about? Or, were they beginning, perversely, to root for the underdog? Adel and Munir Sirhan, who joined in the general glee in the hallway, preferred to believe that the defense was gaining some sympathy with the press.

That, of course, is what Cooper was trying for. He treated everyone—judge, jury, opposing attorneys and newsmen—with excessive candor, courtly manners and warmth.

You can't help liking Grant Cooper [wrote Francis Meredith in *Los Angeles* magazine]. He has a firm handshake and he looks you in the eye and he really remembers your name without consulting the yellow legal pad before him. In the corridor outside Dept. 107, where he and his defense cohorts Russell Parsons and Emile Zola "Zook" Berman repair during morning and afternoon recesses, the press glom around him, virtually ignoring his colleagues and probe insatiably for tidbits that have been overlooked in the dialogues inside. Almost all call him "Grant" and soon he has even on-duty and supposedly stern sheriff's deputies grinning a bit from under their crewcuts. "God, in a trial like this, the last thing you want is a conservative Republican on the jury," he says, and notepads flip over. He has a hearty, booming laugh that creases his face and warms the listener.

On the morning of January 16, Judge Walker gave his opinion on the Alvidrez matter: she could stay on the jury through the guilt-or-innocent phase. If she were then challenged by the prosecution, he could substitute one of the alternate jurors.

John Howard argued that the California Supreme Court had taken a position in several cases—he cited Beivelman and Nicolaus—that exclusion of a juror like Mrs. Alvidrez did not deprive a defendant of a fair or impartial trial.

Cooper and Berman pointed out that the Anderson and Satterfield case before the California Supreme Court would entitle the defendant to have Mrs. Alvidrez on his jury. Berman said California's bifurcated trial represented a real solution for the court.

Fitts objected. It would mean, he said, that the whole trial would have to be replayed for the new juror. "A juror who had not participated in the deliberations in any way, who had been sequestered from the other jurors, would suddenly enter the box, having had no responsibility for thrashing out the factual background of the case, and who has suddenly been thrown into the hopper with twelve people who had managed to work it out, and the deliberations would necessarily start over, your Honor, on the question of guilt or innocence."

"That happens," observed Walker, "in many cases where you take out a juror and put an alternate in. It's been going on for years."

"That's the best we can do under the circumstances," said Fitts.

"That may be the best we can do under these circumstances," said Walker. But then, after sleeping on the matter, Walker decided that Mrs. Alvidrez must go, after all. He cited Beivelman as his authority. Cooper took exception to the ruling: in the Beivelman case, none of the jurors was asked whether he could serve, at least, on the guilt-or-innocence phase. To exclude a juror like Mrs. Alvidrez, who said she could, made it likely that Sirhan would get "a hanging jury."

Six jurors were tentatively seated by the time Benjamin Glick appeared in the box. Glick, the owner of a small retail clothing business in West Los Angeles, was a Jew. Would the fact that Sirhan was an Arab make it difficult for Glick to sit in judgment? No. Did he believe he could give Sirhan a fair and impartial trial, no matter what his background? I do believe I can, said Glick.

This was a question that had occurred to Mary Sirhan, as well, except that it wasn't Glick, the potential juror, she was worried about, but one of the defense attorneys, Emile Zola Berman. Abdeen Jabara, the Arab-American attorney who had come now from Detroit for the trial, had told her that Berman was a Zionist, and she fluttered back and forth between McCowan and me, wondering if that report were true. Berman's Jewishness, she was told, seemed to be the least important thing in his life and a Zionist he was not. But Jabara was not convinced. Berman *was* a Jew, and maybe that was enough to hurt the cause that claimed his exceptional devotion.

To Cooper at the time, this was a peripheral issue. What he wanted at the moment was to get the best possible jury he could. With Glick, he attempted to explain the defense of diminished capacity. He said that full criminal responsibility could only be borne by someone whose mental condition was "absolutely normal."

Fitts objected. "I think that somehow the law doesn't say that. It's misleading." It was not misleading at all, but Judge Walker told Cooper he was getting "a little broad."

During the *voir dire,* Cooper would get no closer to explaining the law of diminished capacity. Neither would Fitts. Fitts told Glick that the state had to prove a certain "joint operation of act and intent" to convict of first-degree murder. In proving second-degree murder, however, there was "a lesser burden."

"Pardon me, your Honor please," interrupted Cooper. "I don't understand. The burden upon the prosecution is always the same, beyond a reasonable doubt, and I don't know that there is any lesser burden in second degree or manslaughter or any one of them. They must be established beyond a reasonable doubt and I don't think counsel's statement, as I understand it, is a correct statement of the law."

"I agree with you," said Fitts quickly. "You see how difficult it is to talk about these things?"

Cooper may have agreed with Fitts that the law was "difficult," for he settled finally on the most general of qualifying questions that demanded no revelation from Glick about his real feelings concerning the law of diminished capacity.

I did a brief story on Sirhan in *Life* magazine. The story, checked and rechecked by Sirhan's attorneys, said nothing about the case itself and gave only the briefest insight into the fact that Sirhan was, after all, a human being. Still, for the Sirhan family itself, the story said too much, for there, in black and white, Sirhan was exclaiming in some awe, "And Cooper's defending a punk like me!"

Adel Sirhan objected to the word "punk" and demanded Russell Parsons take him up to the jail to see his brother. There, he told Sirhan that he ought to demand a right to censor my articles. Furthermore, Adel relayed to Sirhan the worse fears of Abdeen Jabara—that the defense wasn't going to introduce "the Arab-Israeli situation as evidence in the case."

"I checked with the sheriff," said Adel to his brother, "and he told me that you had a right to telegram me at any time and that you could stand right up in court and tell the judge if you aren't satisfied with your lawyers. You can dismiss your lawyers," said Adel, "and defend yourself!"

Parsons offered then and there to withdraw from the case.

"You don't have to do that," said Adel.

McCowan suggested that maybe Sirhan better have a chat with Cooper and me. Sirhan said he'd like that.

On the afternoon of January 15, I went up to see Sirhan alone. He wanted the right to censor my stuff. I told him I wasn't his press agent, but an independent writer and contemporary historian. Sirhan scoffed at that pompous self-description, but I said I didn't care what words Sirhan wanted to use, I wasn't going to let Sirhan tell me what I could or could not write. "My main purpose is to tell the truth," I said.

"And to make money," added Sirhan. "I understand you want to make money and that's okay. But I don't want to be exploited."

I didn't think I was "exploiting" Sirhan, but whatever my intentions, my actions spoke for themselves. To keep his story about James Earl Ray "exclusive," William Bradford Huie had suggested to Attorney Percy Foreman that Ray not even take the stand in his forthcoming trial. Unlike Huie, I hardly dared interfere with the legal machinery merely to enhance a literary property. I wanted Sirhan to go to trial, and, now that Cooper had made up his mind to let the prosecution's psychiatrist, Dr. Seymour Pollack, see Sirhan, I thought Cooper's chances of saving Sirhan's life better than ever.

And so, at 9:00 A.M. on Friday, January 17, as Cooper was buckling his seat belt and I was wheeling my Cougar out into the stream of traffic on the Hollywood Freeway, I handed Cooper a rigorous memo that summed up my feelings about all this:

1. If Dr. Pollack agrees with Dr. Diamond about Sirhan's diminished capacity to form criminal intent, Sirhan is entitled under the laws of the State

of California (I speak in an absolute sense) to a judgement of second-degree murder (or possibly manslaughter). The proper plea in this case, then, would be second-degree murder (though the proper sentence might be the same as the one you are proposing, life imprisonment).

2. Wouldn't it then be a disservice to your client to plead him guilty to first-degree murder? You don't appeal after a plea, do you? No. But another attorney might be retained later by the family to challenge the entire proceeding, and then everyone would surely look bad. American law is here on trial as much as Sirhan is.

3. You have answered: "Pleading first degree, life, in this way will surely keep Sirhan out of the gas chamber." But what is the real chance of that? Diamond maintains that it is unlikely Sirhan would ever go to the gas chamber, since some 85 men are waiting for the death penalty now at San Quentin. As that number grows, Diamond says, it becomes less and less likely that any of those men will die at the hands of the state, more and more likely that the people here will abolish the death penalty, or at least object to the mass murder which would ensue if the Reagans have their way for a time (and then, in reaction, abolish it).

4. Isn't it more likely, as Dr. Diamond said last week, that if you got all the facts in the record which prove that Sirhan is, in fact, a paranoid schizophrenic subject to fits of dissociative reaction, the California Supreme Court would reverse a jury verdict of first-degree murder? Types like Sirhan, says Diamond, are unable to form the requisite intent for first-degree murder, possibly even unable to harbor real malice.

5. What's more, you may even be able to prove this now and convince the jury of the real facts. Maybe you are too modest about your own abilities. Or maybe you don't yet see how the facts of the case seem to be weighing in favor of a verdict of second-degree murder by reason of diminished responsibility.

6. On our drive to the airport last Saturday night, Dr. Diamond seemed a little shaken that you would consider a plea of first-degree murder when the facts of Sirhan's mental incapacity seem to be so clear (to him, though not *yet* so clear to you). Diamond, of course, sees this case as an opportunity for him (and Pollack) to trailblaze some new frontiers in forensic psychiatry. The trail has already been blazed, but few realize that it has been. *This* case, by reason of unprecedented public interest, is the one which would make the trail into a superhighway. Okay, maybe there are those in our society who do not want to build a superhighway as an escape route for idiotic felons. But isn't it about time for what Dr. Menninger calls the crime of punishment to give way to something more worthy of our relatively enlightened age? Or is that notion still too advanced for 1969?

7. Diamond said he had profound reservations about some kind of prearrangement between you and the D.A. whereby you would agree in advance

to the penalty and then *stage* some kind of trial. I don't know enough about the ways of the law here, but as a layman I see Diamond's point: either you have your client plead guilty, or you engage in a genuine, if friendly, adversary proceeding, where supposed truth is given a good test according to the rules of evidence as evolved through centuries of good Anglo-Saxon jurisprudence. I don't see how you can combine the two.

8. If you go ahead and plead guilty, the American public might feel cheated. They felt cheated when Lee Harvey Oswald didn't stand trial. They would feel doubly cheated if Sirhan Sirhan doesn't make it either. There are plenty of paranoid types in this country (and abroad) who would smile knowingly and claim that this is a big cover-up, that there's more here than meets the eye, that this case is too hot to handle, that there's a vast conspiracy, and that you, Grant Cooper, have been co-opted into it by the Establishment. Whatever that is.

9. But no cover-up is necessary. The facts are clear, and, if Drs. Pollack and Diamond can cooperate in a joint search for the truth, they are demonstrable as well. Dramatically so.

In the parking lot west of the Hall of Justice, Cooper folded the memo and put it in his pocket. "You've summed it all perfectly," he said. "Perfectly." But he wanted to think it all over some more. It all sounded good on paper, but he was worried about the practicalities and the irrationalities of the average jury.

So that Sirhan could never say that Parsons had denied him the opportunity to get independent advice, Parsons took Abdeen Jabara up to see Sirhan. Jabara was grateful to Parsons and told Sirhan immediately that only Parsons was doing a job for him (which was a lie, for Jabara had told Parsons' law partner, Eddie Gritz, only hours before that Parsons wasn't doing a good job). Then Jabara delivered his message: Cooper, he said, was only giving the case partial attention because of his problems in Federal Court. And as for Berman, well, he wouldn't let the Arab-Israeli situation "come out."

Sirhan sized up Jabara and a glint came into his eye. "Okay," he said, "if the Arabs are so anxious to help me, where's the money?"

Jabara shrugged. "It's coming!" he exclaimed. "It's coming." He didn't say so then and there, but he was holding some $16,000 until he could be assured that Cooper and Berman didn't intend, consciously or unconsciously, to overlook the Palestinian conflict and its long-term effect on Sirhan. They had a world forum here for a replay of the great powers' injustice to the Palestinian Arabs and they wanted to make the most of it.

Very earnestly, Jabara asked Berman to have a private lunch with him. Berman replied gravely that he would be most pleased. I sensed that Jabara intended to make the encounter into some kind of showdown and asked if I might join the party. "I'd like you to come," said Jabara, "I'd like you to come."

We walked to the best Chinese restaurant in town, Yee Mee Loo in Old Chinatown, and ordered a fine won ton soup and some deep fried shrimp. "This is a serious matter," said Jabara immediately, his voice cracking with the strain of the situation. Then, without touching his food, he launched into a brilliant lecture on the history of the Arab-Israeli conflict.

It all seemed to begin, said Jabara, in 1897 when Theodor Herzl founded the Zionist movement at Basel, Switzerland. Herzl believed that Jews could be saved only if they had a country of their own, preferably in Palestine. Herzl found a great deal of initial resistance to this idea among many European and American Jews. How could they build a Jewish state in Palestine? In two ways, said Herzl: through the purchase of land and political pressures. In 1902, Herzl's World Zionist Organization set up the Jewish National Fund to purchase land in Palestine, which was then predominantly an Arab land. Jews owned 2 percent of the real estate and comprised less than 8 percent of the population. After World War I, Britain assumed military control of Palestine in order, among other things, to fulfill its commitment to the Balfour Declaration byullowing unlimited Jewish immigration into Palestine and suppressing any rebellion by the indigenous Palestinian Arab population. In May of 1948, the Zionists, with the political and financial support of the United States, proclaimed the creation of a Jewish state in Palestine. Since that time, that state had continued to receive U.S. support, including arms. By 1968, incredibly to the Arabs, after decades of indignities and a final defeat in the Six-Day War of 1967, the Jews had assumed complete control of the territory formerly known as Palestine. What had started out as "a new national home in Palestine" ended up with the dispossession of some two million Palestinian Arabs from the new State of Israel.

Jabara had a point, to be sure. The Palestinian Arabs had certainly suffered outrageous fortunes. Berman, the Jew, didn't even bother to offer an amendment to Jabara's recital or present an extenuating circumstance or two. Berman, the lawyer, asked Jabara how it all added up. "The only question is, how do we bring it home to Sirhan? The judge isn't going to let us present a history lesson in court, is he?"

"The conflict," said Jabara, "has to come into the trial."

"Of course it does," said Berman, wondering to himself just how the judge could be persuaded to let that happen.

"And I've got some books," said Jabara fiercely, "that ought to go in evidence."

"I'd like to have them right away," said Berman. "And anything else you've got on the subject."

Jabara smiled and relaxed enough to enjoy the greatest fried shrimp in town. "Okay," he said. "Okay."

"Here," I said, pushing a plate at Jabara, "have a fortune cookie and see what the fates have in store."

Jabara took a sip of tea, opened his cookie carefully and burst into a roar of laughter. He handed over a tiny scrap of paper imprinted with the message: "DON'T LET YOUR ENTHUSIASM OVERRIDE THE REALITY AROUND YOU." Jabara laughed again.

While the lawyers settled down to the weary task of picking twelve jurors and six alternates, I continued to read the Federal Bureau of Investigation's Office File 56-156, Bureau File No. 62-587. It was impressively heavy, comprising at least 4,000 pages of reports from special agents all over the United States who looked into the case of Sirhan Bishara Sirhan "upon request of the Attorney General of the United States under the Civil Rights Act of 1968 and the Voting Rights Act of 1965."

And it was well written. The report of the assassination itself by Amadee O. Richards, Jr., of the Los Angeles office was a model of telegraphic clarity.

At approximately 12:15 A.M., 6/5/68, Senator ROBERT F. KENNEDY proclaimed victory in California primary election in crowded Embassy Room, Ambassador Hotel, 3400 Wilshire Boulevard, Los Angeles. As SENATOR KENNEDY and party were leaving Embassy Room through kitchen exit, a series of shots were fired by an unknown individual, subsequently identified as SIRHAN BISHARA SIRHAN. SENATOR KENNEDY fell backward onto floor, critically wounded with bullet in brain. SIRHAN wrestled to floor, disarmed and turned over to Los Angeles, California, police department (LAPD).

The reports gave me a chance to verify many of the associations Sirhan had already told me about. Here were summaries of FBI interviews with persons who had known Sirhan in school and with some of those who had known him at the ranch in Norco-Corona. Strangely, the FBI couldn't seem to find Frank Donnarauma, the man who had hired Sirhan at Corona, who also had an alias, Henry Donald Ramistella. (The FBI didn't find him until April 6, 1969.) But all these persons seemed to have been processed in an automatic way with no real guiding intelligence behind the perfunctory series of questions they were asked.

The reports then, added up to very little, except where they disclosed the identity of certain persons associated with Sirhan whom he had concealed from McCowan and me. But there was no indication in the reports that any of these persons had less than the greatest love for Robert Kennedy.

What the robots seemed to do best was compile all the numbers that various bureaucrats had conferred upon Sirhan in his short and mostly anonymous life. His passport number: 142 026. His visa number: 1669, issued under Public Law 203–4 (A)1(14). His alien registration number: A 10 711 881. His unit number in the California Cadet Corps: 138 Battalion, B Company. His Social Security number: 569–30–3104. His number at the State Racing Board: 1–031944. His California driver's license: M–238867. His booking number at the Los Angeles Police Department: 495 139. His booking number at the Los Angeles County Jail: 718 486. And, of course, the serial number of his Iver-Johnson revolver: 53725.

Eleven

"We're doctors, Sirhan, and we want to help you.
We're Jews, Sirhan, but we want to help you."

During his second week of trial, Sirhan assumed an almost jaunty air, growing used to the courtroom now, fascinated that he was so much the center of attention, seemingly oblivious of the fact that he was on trial for his life. At one point David Fitts was asking a potential juror, Lawrence Morgan, his stock question: Would he have the courage to face Sirhan three or four months from now and tell him face-to-face that for the murder of Senator Robert F. Kennedy he must die in the gas chamber?

As Fitts spoke, Sirhan leaned forward around Parsons and smiled broadly at Morgan. Fitts's question was no longer a shock. "You can see him now," said Fitts to Morgan. "He just leaned over and even smiled at you. He may smile at you all through the trial."

"I smile at you, too, Mr. Fitts," Sirhan blurted in a clear, good-natured tone.

"Yes, you do. You smile a lot," said Fitts. Judge Walker told Fitts to restrict himself to the questions. It was perhaps unwise of Fitts to draw attention to the fact that a man on trial for his life was assuming such insouciance in the courtroom, for that was not normal behavior.

Nor was it normal for a defendant to be more worried about my book than the progress of his own defense. Yet, on the afternoon of January 18, when Cooper, Berman and I paid Sirhan a call and brought a Xerox copy of his notebook up to the cell, Sirhan was much more worried over the book that I hadn't even then begun, than he was over his own notebook, which would play such a large part in his own conviction.

"I would like to have a little influence on your book," said Sirhan.

"A little influence!" I said. "The book is mainly about you, and I can only report what you tell me. Of course, if you want to write your own book . . ."

Berman's rejoinder didn't please Sirhan either: "Judging from some of your writings, Sirhan," said Berman, with a wave at the Xeroxed pages in Cooper's lap, "your book would be somewhat incomprehensible."

Cooper laughed, more out of embarrassment over that notebook than over Sirhan's discomfiture, for Cooper had tried and tried that afternoon to get Sirhan to tell him how and when he had written in the notebook and what it all meant. " 'Put blinkers on the son of a bitch.' What's that mean?" Cooper's voice was stern.

"I don't know." Sirhan's voice was soft, almost a whisper.

"Blinkers?" asked Berman. "Don't you put those on a horse?"

"Yeah," said Sirhan.

"Lookit here," said Cooper, continuing to read from the notebook. " 'Long live Communism. Long live Communism. Long live Communism. Long live Nasser. Nasser. Nasser. Nasser. Nasser.' "

"Nasser was no Communist," said Berman.

"Yeah," said Sirhan.

" 'Nasser is the greatest man who ever lived in this world. Nasser is the greatest man who ever lived in this world. Nasser is the greatest man who ever lived in this world. Lived. Lived. Lived.' What about that?"

"All this repetition!" said Sirhan, exclaiming over the notebook as if it were the first time he ever saw it.

" 'Peggy Osterkamp,' " read Cooper. " 'I love you. I love you. Oster-kamp. Miss Peggy. Peggy. P. P. P.' What is—who is this?"

"This must have been a long time ago!" said Sirhan, indicating that he had had Peggy Osterkamp on his mind in 1966, but not in 1967 or 1968 when, apparently, he had written much of the other material in the book.

Cooper ran into some of the little Arabic in the notebook: He asked Sirhan to translate on the spot. Sirhan started to read hesitantly from something that sounded like a letter to his mother asking her to forward his mail. When he got to a part in which he had told his mother not to tell any-one where he was or give anyone his address, he bogged down. Apparently, he did not want his visitors to know that he'd ever given his mother such instructions.

But as Sirhan hummed and ummmed, Cooper became impatient. "Well, we'll leave this here and you can figure it out later." Cooper read on: " 'Tonight. Tonight. Tonight. We. I must buy a new Mustang tonight. Tonight. Tonight. Tonight. Tonight. Meet me tonight.' "

Sirhan looked at me with an embarrassed smile. "I must be psychotic," he said.

"Huh?" asked Cooper.

"I must be psychotic," repeated Sirhan. He laughed.

Cooper ignored this. " 'Hello Tom. Sol. Sol. Perhaps you could use the enclosed $. Sol. Perhaps you could use the enclosed $. Sol Sol Sol Sol. Dollar sign. Dollar sign. Dollar signs.' What are all these dollar signs? Why would you send him money?"

"I don't know, Mr. Cooper."

" 'Illuminati. Illuminati.' What is that?"

Sirhan paused. "Illuminated," he said softly.

Cooper waited for more than that. Sirhan offered no more.

"Aren't they the elite in the Theosophical Society?" I asked.

"Yes."

" 'Hello, Tom,' " Cooper read. " 'How will I contact you after I arrive at the airport. I am comming up sometime Tuesday afternoon. Sirhan. Sirhan. Afternoon. Did you really? Please pay to the order of Sirhan afternoon afternoon afternoon the amount of fifteen thousand dollars. Sometime in the afternoon.' "

Sirhan said he had no explanation for this.

I asked if Sirhan had planned to go up to the Bay Area and visit Tom. Sirhan said he could have planned it, but he denied ever going there.

" 'Let us do it. Let us do it. Let us do it do it it it. Let us do it. Please pay to the order of. 50. 50. 50. 50,000. 5. 500,000. Very good. Very good. One hundred thousand dollars.' "

"Whew!" said Sirhan.

"How much did you say you made a week?" asked Berman acidly.

"Seventy dollars a week," said Sirhan.

" 'Please pay to the order of Sirhan Sirhan the the the the amount of 15 15 15 15 death life 15. $15,000. Must die. Die. Die. Die. Dollar sign. Life and death.' "

"For Christ's sake," said Berman. "Were you smoking hashish?" Sirhan said very seriously that he hardly ever smoked anything.

Cooper found some pages containing translations of the bits of Arabic and Russian scattered through the notebook. He pored over them.

I asked Sirhan if he remembered the time when he had seen Kennedy's face in the mirror. Sirhan remembered. I asked: "Is it possible you wrote in your notebook when you were in a trancelike state?"

"I don't know," said Sirhan.

Cooper interrupted and warned Sirhan sternly: "I don't want him to suggest anything to you." He brought up a line from the Arabic: " 'Let me make love to the boy if I don't find a clean-cut girl to make love to.' What's that mean?"

Sirhan hesitated.

"It says here," said Cooper, " 'possibly verse from Arabic licentious poem.' "

"Yeah, that's exactly what it was. 'If I cannot find a girl, let me make love to a boy.' " He laughed.

Cooper kept reading indiscriminately. " 'And if the world as we know it, if the world as we know it . . .' Just a lot of goddamn nonsense!"

"Not as much as you think," said Berman. "Go on. Go on."

"Here, right here," said Cooper, "you've written in Arabic, right between 'one hundred thousand dollars' and 'one hundred thousand dollars': 'he should be killed.' What about that?"

Sirhan looked at Cooper in silence.

"That could be interpreted," I said, "that you were getting $100,000 to kill Kennedy."

"Where is that money?" asked Cooper. "You holding on to it?" He laughed and indicated that it was not a question he expected Sirhan to answer, for he went right on reading.

" 'Workers of the world, unite. You have nothing to lose but your chains.' "

"He didn't write that," said Berman. "Give Mr. Marx some credit."

Cooper straightened the papers on his knee, handed them over to Sirhan and asked him to study them. Sirhan said Parsons had given him a book he wanted to read. It was a book by Moshe Menuhin, a Jew who was sympathetic to the Palestinian Arab cause, that came to Parsons from Jabara.

"The hell with that!" said Cooper. "This notebook is more important."

Sirhan asked whether the D.A. was going to put the notebooks into evidence. His lawyers indicated they were. "What?" cried Sirhan. "It's unconstitutional!"

"Maybe it is," said Berman. But he and Cooper both confessed they themselves would like to see the notebook in as evidence of diminished responsibility. Both urged him to figure out how and under what circumstances he had written the notebooks.

"A question I have," said Berman, "what kind of writing involves this constant repetition of a word?" It was a good question. And Sirhan had every reason here to tell Berman the truth. He was either unable or unwilling.

"Yeah," said Sirhan bemusedly, "that's what I've been wondering."

Sirhan wasn't helping his own cause, nor would he ever do so in any important way. He was especially resistant to appeals for candor by the doctors who saw him. Why? Because, as he expressed it here to Berman and

Cooper, "they" would say he was "psychotic." The more doctors that said it, the better it would be for Sirhan in the trial. But he didn't want it. "Are they gonna say I'm psychotic? Crazy or something?" Though Dr. Diamond had had his doubts about the prosecution psychiatrist, Dr. Seymour Pollack, who didn't believe that psychiatrists should even address themselves to such legal questions as "premeditation" and "intent," Dr. Diamond had had a conference with Dr. Pollack, secured his promise he would not argue with the law of diminished capacity as currently interpreted by the California Supreme Court and told Cooper that it was okay to let Dr. Pollack see Sirhan alone. Dr. Pollack's first meeting with Sirhan was scheduled for the next day, Sunday, January 19.

"Well," said Cooper in exasperation, "suppose they do? Suppose they do? I can't get this through your head. We don't want you to do anything but tell the absolute truth. I don't care how bad you think it might hurt you. Don't try to cover up anything."

Sirhan nodded, indicating that he surely wouldn't.

Outside Sirhan's high-security area, Cooper stood with Berman and me, waiting for the elevator. He sighed heavily. "I can't figure," he said, "I can't figure this kid out."

Dr. Seymour Pollack was surely one of the world's ambivalent men. He was a husky fellow with a florid complexion and slightly bloodshot eyes and looked more like the fifth member of a bowling team from Hamtramck than one of the leading psychoanalysts in Southern California and the director of the University of Southern California's Institute on Psychiatry and the Law. His professional credentials ran on for pages, and his colleagues in the medical profession had respect for him. But in this case he was forever unsure of himself, always ready to concede that he was entirely wrong. As Emile Zola Berman put it, Pollack had "a rabbinical regard for both sides of every question." His vacillation would ultimately lead to a death sentence for Sirhan.

On Sunday, January 19, Pollack presented himself in Sirhan's cell as an affable, cheery fellow, punctuating his preparatory remarks with frequent chuckles that did not signify happiness but embarrassment. "I genuinely want to help you," said Pollack. He added immediately: "But, at the same time, my involvement may hurt you." He explained that he would be giving his material to the district attorney and he wanted to make sure that Sirhan understood his position. Sirhan said he did.

"Then why did your lawyers let you talk to me?" asked Pollack.

"Because they are going to propose a defense of diminished responsibility," said Sirhan. It was a straight, honest answer. He embellished it with a little speech. "Bob Kaiser always keeps telling me to hide nothing from my doctors. That's what I'm doing. I have nothing to hide."

"All right," said Pollack. "What do you want to talk about?"

This was a funny way to begin and Sirhan was puzzled. "What do you want to *know?*"

"Well," said Pollack, "how do you explain all this?"

Sirhan launched into his long story, one that he had told more than half a dozen times now. When he got to the end, he skipped over Sunday, June 2, and Monday, June 3. Pollack brought him back to Sunday. Sirhan skipped right back to Tuesday. Pollack determined that Sirhan had practiced shooting on Saturday, tried to shoot on Sunday and shot again on Tuesday. To Pollack, this seemed like a change of pattern for Sirhan. "You hadn't been firing that often," he pointed out (correctly).

Sirhan gave no explanation. He skipped again to a narration of the events on Tuesday. Sirhan said he had consulted the morning paper. He didn't like the entries at Hollywood Park that day.

"Were the horses running on Election Day?" asked Pollack.

Sirhan was stumped.

"All right," said Pollack. "Okay."

"On Election Day, the bars are closed," said Sirhan, thinking furiously. "Let's see, where was I?" He was upset because Pollack had caught him in a lie. Others had caught him in lies, but he could usually wiggle out of those. This could be a provable lie. What if those damn horses weren't really running on Election Day?

"What of the Ambassador?" asked Pollack. "Do you remember anything at all?"

"That," said Sirhan, "is where Dr. Diamond is trying to help me."

"You have no recollection at all of wanting to shoot Kennedy?"

"No! No!" said Sirhan.

Pollack tried to pick up the story after the shooting. Sirhan remembered the Miranda warnings about his right to remain silent. He recalled kicking a cup of chocolate out of an officer's hand. But his memory even of those events was not exactly clear.

"When did you realize that you'd shot Senator Kennedy?" asked Pollack.

Sirhan said, "Maybe when Mr. Wirin came up to see me. I don't know."

Pollack sighed and paused. "Well, now that it's over, how do you feel about it now?"

"I don't know what the hell's coming off," said Sirhan.

Pollack studied Sirhan for a moment. "You know, the picture of you your mother gives me is really quite different than the picture you give me." Sirhan didn't know how to respond to that. "Your mother," explained Pollack, "is a very sincere woman."

Sirhan here asked Pollack to turn off his tape recorder, and Pollack did so. When the recorder came back on, Sirhan was asking Pollack whether or not he was a Jew.

Pollack said he was, and he told him there wasn't much difference between an Arab and a Jew. Said Pollack: "I've often felt that the Arabs are much put upon. But that's neither here nor there."

"No," said Sirhan, "it's all here."

Pollack said Sirhan's mother told him Sirhan had Jewish friends.

"Yes," said Sirhan, "but that was before I found they were Jews."

Pollack said he still could not understand how Sirhan's feelings about the Jews—which didn't seem that intense to Pollack—could have caused him to kill Kennedy.

Sirhan tried to explain about his early life in Jerusalem, but his tone was flat and didn't indicate that he was upset in any important way. It was an involved rationalization and post-factum justification, but it didn't have the ring of truth.

Pollack said to Sirhan, "It's obvious you feel very deeply and very strongly about all this." It was not obvious at all, but perhaps Pollack was only trying to draw Sirhan out a bit, for he added, "Do you really believe your revenge was strong enough to kill?"

"That, sir, is what I don't understand!"

Pollack asked, "Why Kennedy? I can see your killing Moshe Dayan. But why Kennedy?"

Sirhan gave no real answer, partially because Pollack didn't pause long enough to give him a chance to answer. Instead, Pollack tried to get at Sirhan's motivation by a simple process of elimination. He explored Sirhan's Communism, found it was a solitary thing, little more than a vague demand for a more equitable distribution of this world's goods. He asked Sirhan about the money he had with him when he was arrested.

"Seventeen oh five. It was a lot of money," said Sirhan, and he paused. So then did Pollack.

"Tell me now," said Pollack, "now that you think about it. What would you rather have done?"

"What do you mean?" asked Sirhan. "If I were free?"

"Yeah," said Pollack.

Sirhan said he certainly would have become more involved in occultism. Pollack wondered if others interested in killing Kennedy had steered Sirhan into the occult.

"Oh," said Sirhan, "hell, no, no!"

Pollack said he could see Sirhan's killing Kennedy if he, Sirhan, were an Arab soldier. But he was not an Arab soldier. Pollack said if he were an American soldier in Vietnam, he could see killing a Vietcong, but he couldn't see himself killing a Vietcong on the streets of New York. That seemed a good parallel. "Why shouldn't I kill that Vietcong here?" asked Pollack searchingly.

"Really, sir, I haven't looked at it from that point."

Pollack asked Sirhan if he would not kill Moshe Dayan if he had the chance.

Sirhan said he didn't know.

Pollack said that during World War II, American soldiers sacrificed many people to save some American lives. "I think that's what your point is. By having one man dead, thousands of Arabs, tens of thousands of Arabs might be worth it."

"Oh, I don't know, doc," said Sirhan, unwilling now for even Pollack to identify him as an Arab hero.

Pollack sighed. Then he spied a Xerox copy of Sirhan's notebook and riffled through the pages. He was surprised that Sirhan hadn't seen them until the previous day. "You recognize them, don't you?" asked Pollack.

"They seem strange to me," said Sirhan. "Everything about them seems strange." When Pollack asked him about specific entries in the notebooks, it was the same old story. Sirhan didn't know. Or, if he did know, he wouldn't say. Who was Peggy Osterkamp? He didn't want to get her involved.

Pollack asked Sirhan about his medical background. "Have you ever had any spells or blackouts?"

"No," said Sirhan. He did remember kicking the television once when George Putnam was on the air. . . .

Pollack said, "You did have some kind of spells occasionally?"

"If I did, sir, I don't remember," said Sirhan. Sirhan may have been holding back with Pollack on certain things, but here, when he had a chance to give Pollack information that might have helped him, he didn't even bother.

Pollack hesitated, wondering what more to talk about. He tried to make some small talk, asking Sirhan when he had last seen his mother or brother. Sirhan didn't want to talk small talk. So Pollack, who had heard about Diamond's success with hypnosis, put Sirhan under himself. His method was different from Diamond's. He had Sirhan look at the back of his watch and he started to count. While Sirhan's lids became heavier, he counted from 1 to 25, then from 26 to 50, then from 51 to 75. He put Sirhan in hypnosis all right, but he got not one word out of him. Pollack seemed particularly anxious for Sirhan to tell him about the first time he ever went to the Ambassador Hotel. No answer. Pollack tested the authenticity of the trance. He suggested that Sirhan's throat become dry. He suggested that Sirhan lift his left arm. "Can you tell me why you won't talk with me? Can you tell me why you won't talk about what took place? Are you afraid? Are you afraid, Sirhan?"

Sirhan only mumbled.

"Why won't you talk with me?" No answer. Pollack brought Sirhan back and told him that he would return on the next day. His parting was abrupt.

Chief Deputy District Attorney Buck Compton had miscalculated. On the last day, he passed his peremptory challenge, assuming that Cooper would exercise a peremptory of his own and keep the seesaw going. Cooper didn't, and, for a moment on January 21, it looked as if the prosecution was stuck with the jurors now sitting in front of them in the box, most especially stuck with Miss Dora Jacobi, a dumpy little woman with gray hair who, in her *voir dire,* had gone out of her way to inform the court that she was a psychiatric social worker and teacher who knew a good deal about such arcana as Rorschach inkblots and their interpretation. There had even been a discussion in chambers about Miss Jacobi: the judge said that someone from the Los Angeles County Department of Public Welfare and Supervisor Kenneth Hahn had phoned him to say Miss Jacobi was "psycho." Cooper said he wasn't impressed with hearsay evidence such as that. As far as he was concerned, Miss Jacobi was a fine juror and the prosecution had, in effect, agreed with him by passing its peremptory.

Cooper was right, said Judge Walker in open court. What did the prosecution propose to do? Compton flushed a deep red and started to bluster: "I'm not going to play games," he said. Walker cut him off and told him what he must do. Make a motion to withdraw his acceptance of the jury; in other words, admit he'd made a mistake and ask for the indulgence of the court.

Compton swallowed his pride and did so. Walker granted his motion and said, "The peremptories are now with the People."

Said Compton: "Excuse Miss Jacobi." A new venireman was called and the jury selection was still wide open once more.

Sirhan was not disappointed by the dismissal of Dora Jacobi. He was worried about Pollack and called McCowan over to whisper a command: "Find out if they were racing on Election Day," said Sirhan. "I told Pollack that I looked at the entries and didn't like 'em. That's why I went to the range." Now he wanted to make sure that his story hung together.

Shortly before noon on January 24, as a heavy rain beat down on the old gray Hall of Justice, both prosecution and defense accepted a jury of eight men and four women, seven Republicans and five Democrats. Cooper, Parsons and Berman had fifteen peremptory challenges left, but they preferred to gamble on this jury because "they're a great cross section of people. Intellectually and economically, they're a conglomerate group." They were:

Ronald G. Evans, an installation man for the Pacific Telephone & Telegraph Company, who already seemed bored with the entire proceeding.

Miss Susan J. Brumm, a telephone operator in her mid-fifties, who once served on a first-degree murder jury that voted to acquit the defendant.

Albert N. Frederico, a plumber for the city of Los Angeles. He was the only one on the jury who had voted for Robert Kennedy; he said he read no newspapers or magazines at all; and he furrowed his swarthy brow whenever the attorneys spoke in words of more than two syllables.

Mrs. Marylou Busby, a mathematics teacher at Downey High School. Mrs. Busby was an attractive woman with a firm set to her jaw, a Nixon voter and a regular reader only of Barron's weekly financial newspaper and the financial section of *The New York Times*.

Laurence K. Morgan, a computer programmer for the I.B.M. Corporation. Morgan wore socks the color of highway signal flags and described himself as "deeply religious." He said he read only religious periodicals.

Mrs. Irma Martinez, a pretty, petite clerk for the Southern California Gas Company and the wife of a truck driver. Mrs. Martinez was a Humphrey Democrat.

Alphonso Galindo, a civilian mechanic for the U.S. Navy in Long Beach. Galindo was a Republican and a Roman Catholic with a strong impassive face.

Bruce D. Elliott, a systems analyst for T.R.W., Inc., an aerospace corporation that would have a large share in putting America's first astronauts on the moon. Elliott was a bachelor in his late twenties with a doctorate in mathematics and would be elected foreman of this jury.

Mrs. Nell Bortells, a business representative for the Pacific Telephone & Telegraph Company. Mrs. Bortells, a Rockefeller Republican, wore her hair swept back so severely that it seemed to pull her eyebrows up and back, giving her a look of perpetual surprise.

Benjamin Glick, the owner of a clothing business in West Los Angeles. Glick was a thoughtful-looking man with an animated face, silver hair and horn-rimmed glasses.

Gilbert F. Grace, an employee of the Los Angeles Department of Water & Power. He was a Mexican-American who had anglicized his name, a Democrat who had voted for Nixon.

George Broomis, also an employee for the Department of Water & Power. He was a Mexican-American, a Republican, a slim, alert man in his late forties.

Sirhan, without a coat or tie for the first time in court, told McCowan he was pleased with the jury. In the crowded corridor outside, Mrs. Sirhan told members of the pencil press who crowded around her: "They're nice people when they stand and say they are sure of themselves. To consider taking a life, you have to be sure of yourself. It is up to their conscience now. I see they are nice people. I am satisfied with them. Now the answer is up to God." Mrs. Sirhan had heard the judge admonishing the jury not to read the papers concerning the trial, but maybe somehow, some way they would hear this. So she added a little sermonette: "Before everything else we get our power and our strength from God. That's how I get my strength every day."

To Cooper, Sirhan was obviously ill, and so the advance planning of the assassination didn't necessarily mean "premeditation" in the legal sense of the word. His behavior fit nicely under California's law of diminished capacity. But Sirhan's failure to remember writing in the notebook or, even killing Kennedy, would not sit well with the jury, for they would surely think Sirhan was lying. Since his whole defense was predicated on an excess of candor, Cooper wished that Sirhan could remember. Either Dr. Diamond had to help Sirhan remember or find out why he couldn't. Maybe, said Cooper, Diamond had better find out first about the notebook.

But when Diamond went up to see Sirhan on Saturday, January 25— taking me along as an investigative aide—Sirhan informed him immediately that the notebook would not be used in evidence. Diamond ignored

that. Sirhan shrugged. He just didn't want to discuss the notebook. He only
wanted to clear up one thing: the line in Arabic about making love to a
boy. That wasn't an original thought of his. He had just jotted down a
verse from an Arab song. He wasn't a homosexual as that might imply.
And anyway, in Arabic the masculine "him" is often used in place of the
feminine "her."

Diamond let that pass. He preferred to go on to another page, page 41
of the notebook. "What about this '$15,000'? Does that amount ring any
bells?"

"No," said Sirhan. "The only amount that rings any bells is $1,705, the
money I got from the Industrial Accident Commission."

" 'Please pay to the order of.' What's that?" Sirhan didn't know. "That's
what you see on a check, isn't it?" Sirhan admitted it was. Diamond read,
" 'Kennedy must fall Kennedy must fall . . .' What do you think of that?"

Sirhan's response was quick, matter-of-fact. "He fell."

"That he did. But what do you think of your writing this a couple of
weeks before? Do you remember writing that?" He didn't. "It's going to be
very hard to convince a jury you could forget something like this, Sirhan.
It's not gonna make much sense to them."

"Well, sir," said Sirhan.

"They're going to think you're lying just to protect yourself."

"Sir. Look, they can throw me into that gas chamber anytime they want,
sir, and I wouldn't give a damn."

"I don't think that's true, Sirhan. You've got a lot of feelings locked up
inside you, Sirhan."

"You wanta take me up on that?" said Sirhan belligerently.

Diamond let that go and flipped through some more of the notebook.
"Can I hypnotize you again, Sirhan?" asked Diamond abruptly. Sirhan
shrugged. Quickly, Diamond put Sirhan under and stuck a safety pin into
the skin on top of Sirhan's hand. Sirhan seemed to feel no pain. Diamond
asked what was troubling him. Did he really want to die in the gas chamber? No answer. Was he afraid? No. Did he trust Diamond? Yes. "Sirhan," said Diamond, "did you tell anybody you were going to shoot the
Senator?"

"No," said Sirhan. His voice was soft and dreamy.

"Did you tell that girl you had coffee with at the Ambassador?"

"No."

"Sirhan, when did you get the gun?"

"When I was working," said Sirhan very indistinctly. Diamond had him
repeat it.

"Why did you buy a gun?"

Sirhan paused some five seconds. "I liked guns."

Diamond was unhappy with Sirhan's mumbles. He had him sit up and open his eyes, and started asking him a series of questions about the notebook. Still in hypnosis, Sirhan denied any knowledge of when or how he had written that Kennedy must die. Diamond showed Sirhan a page of the notebook. Is this your notebook? Is this your writing? Sirhan said it was. Did he remember writing that Kennedy must fall? He didn't. "Were you in a trance when you wrote that, Sirhan?" No answer. Diamond found the page of Sirhan's notebook dated May 18 and read, " 'My determination to eliminate RFK is becoming more the more of an unshakable obsession.' " Sirhan started to moan painfully. "That's your handwriting, Sirhan. Remember, Sirhan, remember what you were thinking about. Who told you to write that?"

Sirhan was unresponsive.

Diamond read more from the page. " 'RFK must die. RFK must fall. RFK must be assassinated.' Did you write that, Sirhan?"

"I don't know."

Diamond tried to get Sirhan to re-create the moment when he wrote in the notebook. "You're back in your room. You're thinking of killing the Senator. You're writing in your notebook. Are you watching TV? Huh? Remember the jets to Israel. Remember the jet planes, Sirhan?"

Sirhan started to moan.

"Remember the bombs and the Jews, Sirhan?"

Sirhan's moans turned into a childlike whimpering. His face became contorted with fear and sadness. His eyebrows furrowed, his jaw tightened, his eyes clenched, his face flushed. Diamond let the reaction take its natural course, and without any further suggestion, Sirhan started weeping more strongly. Then, after a minute or so, his sobbing subsided.

Diamond wondered whether Sirhan's deep feelings about the bombs could come out in a waking state. He gave Sirhan a hypnotic suggestion that he let his feelings come out, and woke him.

Sirhan started to shiver, looked confused, moved his head from side to side. He trembled. Then he spied the safety pin stuck in his hand and thrust it away from him as if his hand were some monstrous appendage. Diamond invited him to pull out the pin. Sirhan made a tentative reach for the pin, then recoiled. After more urging, he pulled it, crying little cries of pain and imagined pain.

"There!" said Diamond, apparently delighted to see that Sirhan had gotten the pin out all by himself.

"A hell of a sensation!" said Sirhan. He shook his head violently back and forth. "It wasn't the pain. Just the idea of . . . Uhhh!"

Diamond treated it all very matter of factly. "Simple mind over matter," he said.

All of a sudden, Sirhan decided it hurt. Just as quickly, he was convinced by Diamond that it didn't. Diamond asked Sirhan to tell him about the bombs.

"What bombs?" Under hypnosis the merest mention of the bombs had triggered a real hysteria in Sirhan. Now he said, "What bombs?"

Diamond's hypnotic suggestion failed to work. He asked Sirhan to remember how he felt about the bombs that he had seen explode back in Jerusalem. Sirhan only intellectualized, delivered a flat rhetorical question about the injustice of it all. "I asked you how you *felt*," said Diamond.

"I told you guys," he said. "Oh, shit, doc. I don't know. It helps not to remember."

Diamond told Sirhan he had to sort out his feelings, learn what he feared, what he hated. Sirhan said he knew: the Jews. "Why did you kill Kennedy?" asked Diamond. "He wasn't a Jew."

"I, I, I don't know," stammered Sirhan. "Those bombers, sir. They fucked me up."

Diamond put him under again, suggesting this time that he keep his eyes open so he could read the Xerox copy of his notebook. He thrust the most incriminating page of his notebook in front of him. "Read what it says, Sirhan." Diamond pointed to a line near the top of the page.

" 'RFK must dee.' "

"No," said Diamond. "It doesn't say 'dee.' "

"Die," said Sirhan. Under Diamond's urging, he continued to read. He read very poorly, like a second or third grader, and his voice was a barely audible whisper. He paused—psychologists would say he blocked—when he got to one particularly long word.

"Spell it out, Sirhan," ordered Diamond.

"A-S-S-" spelled Sirhan.

"What does that word spell, Sirhan?" No response. "Sirhan, read like a grown-up. 'Robert F. Kennedy must be' what's the next word?"

"Killed."

"No, that isn't what it says. Open up your eyes and look. 'A-S-S-' What does that say?"

Finally, Sirhan got the word out. "Assassinated."

"Right. Read on."

Sirhan continued to read, in low, measured tones. " 'RFK must be assassinated. RFK must be assassinated.' "

"When did you write that, Sirhan?"

Sirhan didn't seem to hear. " 'RFK must be assassinated. RFK must be assassinated.' " Like a stuck phonograph record.

"When did you write that, Sirhan? Sirhan, pay attention to me. When did you write that? A long time ago?"

"I don't know."

"Sirhan, what happened to RFK?"

Sirhan didn't know.

"What happened to Kennedy?"

"He can't."

"What?"

"He can't."

" 'I can't'? Yes, you can."

"He can't."

" 'He can't'? He can't what?"

"The bombers."

"What happened to Kennedy?"

No answer.

"Who killed Kennedy, Sirhan?"

"I don't know."

"Yes, you do know, Sirhan. Open your eyes and look at me, Sirhan." Diamond tried to wake up Sirhan "halfway." He remained unresponsive. Diamond decided to awaken him again, but he added a fillip or two this time. Diamond gave Sirhan a suggestion that he would feel warm and that his left hand would be paralyzed. "I want to prove to you the power of mind over matter."

Sirhan woke up and looked around curiously, as if he wasn't quite sure he knew where he was. "What happened?"

"We've been talking about the notebook."

"They can't use that," said Sirhan. Diamond waited. At length, Sirhan reached for a cigarette, but he couldn't light it. "Did, did you sterilize that pin?" he demanded hotly.

"Yes, why? What's the trouble?" said Diamond.

Sirhan shook his left hand. "It feels numb."

Diamond explained that he had paralyzed his hand. He asked him how it felt.

He shook it. "Like a fuckin' loose octopus," he said.

Diamond gave him the safety pin and asked him to prick himself in the hand. He did and felt nothing. "Move it up your hand," said Diamond. Sirhan continued to jab himself, then jumped with pain when he jabbed himself above the wrist where sensations were normal.

With that power of mind over matter, Sirhan joked, maybe Diamond could get him out of here. He was impressed and he wanted to talk to Diamond about some experiences of his own with the occult. But first, he insisted on Diamond's shutting off his tape recorder. He had done the same with Dr. Pollack. Why did he want the recorder off? Because he was afraid that if his own experiments with the occult were "on the record," they could be used to prove he was crazy. And, of course, he wasn't crazy. Diamond nodded understandingly. He understood too well: Sirhan fit into a classic pattern which Diamond had once described in a paper for *The Journal of Social Therapy,* entitled "The Simulation of Sanity."

There, Diamond wrote that the faking of insanity is a very rare occurrence and, when it does happen, it is likely to be a sign of serious psychopathology. On the other hand, he said the simulation of sanity is very frequent, even in persons accused of serious crimes where the mental illness would have been an adequate defense.

> . . . a major criminal action does, in my opinion [wrote Diamond], carry a heavy medical, even though not legal, presumption of mental illness, and the examiner must be exceedingly cautious in assuming that a defendant is telling the whole story of his thoughts, feelings and inner life.
>
> All of us like to believe that our actions are the result of our own free will, and we are reluctant to admit that much of what we do is the result of unconscious compulsions rationalized by *ex post facto* intellectualizations. The paranoid schizophrenic is especially averse to admitting that his actions are due to mental disease and will insist, even in the face of the threat of the death punishment, that his criminal actions were intentional. To conceal his delusions he will confabulate logical reasons for his crime and resist all attempts of the psychiatrist to discover his psychopathology. Such schizophrenics pretend to be mentally healthy because to admit mental illness would destroy their self-esteem and break down the remnants of their contact with reality. Often, too, their delusions and hallucinations involve highly secretive material of a supernatural or sexual nature that must not be communicated to another person. So they would far rather go to prison or even to the gas chamber than to violate the dictates of their delusional systems.

That seemed to be a rather neat description of Sirhan Sirhan, and Diamond had written it thirteen years before.

Diamond put Sirhan in and out of another trance, suggesting again that

Sirhan remember everything about the notebook, that he be able to read it and tell him how he had written it and when. Then he brought him out of the trance. Sirhan read: " 'Kennedy must fall. Kennedy must fall. Please pay to the order of Sirhan Sirhan the amount of Sirhan Sirhan. We believe that Robert F. Kennedy must be sacrificed for the cause of the poor exploited people.' " He couldn't remember the writing or what he was thinking of when he wrote it.

"Was it in your room at home?"

"It had to be at home."

"Think very hard. An image should come to you."

Sirhan said he was reading at his desk at home when he heard a news report about Kennedy's speaking at a temple or a Jewish club somewhere. Maybe he wrote this page after he had heard that broadcast.

They examined various pages of the notebook. Sirhan recognized some of it as schoolwork. He didn't know much about the rest. He wondered if the D.A. had written the dates in. No, Diamond assured him, the writing was his. "When you were practicing the Rosicrucian exercises," said Diamond. "did you ever practice writing?"

"I've read about—I don't know, there's a special name for it—"

"Automatic writing."

"Yeah, where you have a blank sheet of paper and you can transfer it telepathically or somehow."

Diamond riffled through the pages and had Sirhan read another out loud. " 'A declaration of war against American humanity,' " read Sirhan, this time not quite so childishly. " 'When in the course of human events, it has become necessary for me to equalize and seek revenge for all the inhuman treatments committed against me by the American people . . .' " His voice trailed off. He whistled. "This sounds—big. But shit, this is not like my handwriting. There's a difference in style in my handwriting."

"It looks a little sprawly," I said, "like you're a little out of control when you wrote this. Although it's your writing, it's bad writing. Like maybe you were tired."

Diamond asked Sirhan to read right down to the bottom of the page, and continue to the next. Sirhan read haltingly. " 'The author . . . expresses his wishes very . . . bluntly that . . . he wants to be . . . recorded by . . . historians as the man . . .' " Sirhan stopped and whistled, as if he were reading this for the first time.

"Yes," said Diamond. "It says 'man' and it's underlined. Go on."

" 'The man who triggered, triggered'—what's this?"

" 'Triggered off.' "

"Whew! It looked like a *b* and an *o* here. 'The last war.' "

"What do you think of that, Sirhan?" asked Diamond.

Sirhan sighed. "I don't."

"Well, think." Sirhan thought and thought. "Think, Sirhan! When did you write that?"

"I can't, doc. My mind's a blank. I don't remember this."

The declaration Sirhan just read had a date of June 2, 1967. I wondered if Sirhan hadn't made a mistake on the date and written 1967 when he meant 1968. My surmise was wrong. But it led to a discussion of Sirhan's activities on Sunday, June 2, 1968. Diamond wondered why Sirhan had lied to me about his presence at the Ambassador then. Sirhan said he had an inborn distrust of journalists. But, he added righteously, he told Parsons and McCowan the truth.

"It took you a long time," I said.

"That was the next time they came up," said Sirhan.

"But that was in September or October. They'd been coming up to see you since June. June, July, August, September. Four months. You withheld that information from them for four months."

"Yeah, but, they, it never came up. We were more involved with that, with, uh the events of that—that Tuesday."

"In other words," I said in a level tone, "I pushed you farther than they did."

Diamond interjected. His voice was kind. "Sirhan, is there anything important that you haven't told us, that you're still holding back?"

"Goddamn, doc!"

"Yeah, I don't like to push you."

"This bugs the shit out of me! You think I'm holding back, but God I'm not, doc."

"Yes, but you see there's this that has to be explained, Sirhan." Diamond tapped the pages in his hand.

"If this is gonna be admitted in court," said Sirhan, "I'm gonna change my plea, doc. I told you guys this before." He was vehement. "If this is gonna be admitted in court, I'm gonna say 'fuck you one and all.' "

"Why?" asked Diamond.

"This was taken without benefit of the Fourth Amendment!" said Sirhan. "I don't give a fuck what it is!"

"Well," said Diamond, "they may well introduce that in evidence."

Sirhan said if they did and the judge allowed it, he would ask for the gas chamber. He was going to die anyway, because of the prejudice against him. And he didn't want to spend his life in prison.

"Do you think you're a cold-blooded killer?"

"No. I don't have the guts to—to, to step on a—a cockroach."

"What about these notes? That's a cold-blooded kind of thing there. A declaration of war."

"I don't like it," said Sirhan softly.

"Did you see Kennedy kind of like an enemy soldier?"

"I saw that bastard as a mass murderer, sir. He was to the Arabs like Hitler was to the Jews, sir."

"Why Kennedy? Why not Johnson?"

"That's what I don't understand myself. But Kennedy, sir, I liked him. I really liked him. He failed me, sir, that's all."

"Is that what you felt like when you wrote the notebook?"

"But I don't remember the writing of those things in relation to my feelings."

"There's no connection?"

"I don't see it. I don't feel it."

Diamond said Sirhan's "convenient loss of memory" wouldn't look good to the jury. "It's all right for you to spout off here that you want to go to the gas chamber, but that sort of thing doesn't go in court." To get him to remember, maybe he could play on Sirhan's greatest fear. "They'll really think you're a mental case then."

"I'm not mental, sir."

"All right, you don't want people to think that, but they'll really think you're a crazy nut."

"That's the problem. If I do say I'm mental, this whole defense of diminished responsibility, they're gonna say, hell, he's begging for his life. That's the problem. I don't wanta beg for it, sir. If you don't have fucking justice in America, piss on you. And if America's the best country in the world and I cannot have what it gives, I don't wanta live at all."

"Well, that's big talk, Sirhan." Diamond still spoke softly.

Sirhan folded his arms. "Like I say, doc, take me up on it."

Diamond said he didn't want to take him up on it. He didn't want Sirhan's life. "I'm on your side. I'm trying to help you."

I said I couldn't understand Sirhan's wanting to give up just because the notebooks were being introduced. After all, they showed a certain obsessive frame of mind that might indicate some diminished capacity.

"All right," said Sirhan, "but in school I learned, sir, and goddamn it, I learned those Bill of Rights, the whole twenty-two amendments. There was no search warrant."

Diamond said the judge would decide on the notebook.

I asked Sirhan if he had ever gone to any trials.

Sirhan said he hadn't.

"Honest?"

Sirhan mentioned Munir's trial. "Other than that, I didn't."

"Munir says that you and he used to go to trials together."

"Oh, no! We used to go to court. You know, just to look at the legal processes."

"Those were trials, weren't they?"

"Like you know the milkman attacked this guy's daughter? I watched that, you know."

"What did you think of it?" asked Diamond.

"I didn't know the facts," said Sirhan diffidently. He obviously didn't want to talk about it. Then he conceded that he "was always interested in going down to the courtroom."

Diamond regarded Sirhan curiously. Just when he thought Sirhan was telling the truth, he would tell another lie. He decided to put Sirhan into a trance again. "I want to help you, Sirhan. You're my patient and I'm your doctor. I want to help you. I have to go in the courtroom and I have to tell everybody about your thoughts and feelings. I want to tell them an honest story. I want the world to see you truthfully, Sirhan. I want the world to see you as you are. You don't want them to have the wrong idea about you." He told Sirhan that he would wake up and tell the truth, that he would wake up feeling warm and comfortable and that he would be truthful. "Wake up, Sirhan. Wake up. One, two, three."

Sirhan shook his head in some confusion, but he had a smile on his face. Diamond had him poring over the notebook again. "Sirhan," said Diamond, "are you afraid that if they saw this notebook they'd think you're crazy?"

"I never meant for this—"

"It is a crazy notebook, isn't it?"

"It's just none of their business."

"But, uh, it became their business when you shot Kennedy. You can't change, you can't get away from that. But," said Diamond good-naturedly, "it is a crazy kind of notebook."

"Hell, I know it, doc. I laughed at it as if I had listened to it or saw it for the first time."

"But they're gonna think you're crazy when they see it. Is this why you don't want them to see it?" Sirhan did not reply. Diamond assured Sirhan that his lawyers were not going to make an insanity plea, which, if successful, would put Sirhan in a mental institution for the rest of his life. His defense was something different.

Sirhan wondered if anyone else had ever gotten into trouble by reason of their experiments with the occult. Diamond said he thought so. Sirhan made it clear he didn't want Tom Rathke involved. Diamond wondered what Rathke's involvement really was. Sirhan said that Rathke went for the occult too. "He's the one I want to protect," said Sirhan. "But he's not crazy. I'm not crazy." Furthermore, he didn't want to involve the Rosicrucians.

I pointed out that Sirhan's notebook writing was in part suggested by an inspirational article in the *Rosicrucian Digest* called "Write It Down." "So, in a very remote way, at least, the Rosicrucians are involved, aren't they?"

"Yeah, but I don't want—oh, shit—I don't want to put any blame on them in that way, oh, hell, no. No, shit, no. Hell. No."

"We're not trying to put any blame on them," said Diamond. "But we do want to make sense out of it. I mean, one way of looking at it is that you were just a cold-blooded fanatic who decided to assassinate Senator Kennedy to prevent him from sending jet bombers to Israel. And that you made up your mind, bought a gun and practiced to do it and did it."

"That isn't—that isn't—"

"I know—"

"Let me say why. This whole thing happened in late May and I had the gun long before that."

"All right," said Diamond. "I don't think that's all that happened. You don't think that's all that happened. But that's what the district attorney thinks happened."

"And it's simple for him to tell that story," I said.

"Sir, it's his own conscience he has to live with, I mean, if that's what he wants to say, and if that's what he really believes, then I . . . let him do it. I can prove it—"

"No, I'm not willing to let him do it," said Diamond. "It's going to be his word against your word, and I want your word to be truthful. I'm convinced that the truth will win in this case. But you've got to tell the truth. And just to say, 'I can't remember' doesn't sound very good."

"Doc," said Sirhan, "I honestly can't." There were many times when Sirhan sounded as if he were lying. But here he sounded as if he were telling the truth.

Diamond paused a moment and looked searchingly at Sirhan. "How come, Sirhan, you've got such a bad memory? What's your trouble? Are you a mental case? That's a sign of mental illness, isn't it?"

"Those writings, sir, I cannot."

"I mean, I've written notebooks twenty years ago and I can remember them. What's the matter with your mind? You have so much memory trouble. You don't remember the notebooks. You don't remember writing them. You don't remember going to the hotel. You don't remember all kinds of things. Are you a mental case, Sirhan? You don't believe that, do you?"

"No."

"Of course not."

"No . . . I didn't even know I was as smart as I was, doc."

"You've got lots of abilities that you didn't appreciate."

Sirhan's chin sunk to his chest. "I don't understand," he said gloomily.

"You're one mixed-up kid, huh?"

"Maybe you should get rid of me." Sirhan laughed.

"Get rid of you! Where we gonna get rid of you, huh?"

"Maybe the death chamber will take care of it."

"No," said Diamond. "I've fought too long against capital punishment. I've devoted all my life fighting against it. I'm not gonna lose the battle on account of you. Hmmm?"

Sirhan said he couldn't see the state letting him go—ever. He'd rather have the gas chamber. Why? "To save my sanity," he said.

"It's up to you," said Diamond soberly.

"Maybe—let me read your minds—maybe you're saying Sirhan is trying to hide something, trying to protect something. But I'm not."

"That's what people are going to think."

"Maybe *they* are crazy."

"It's a crazy world we live in," conceded Diamond. But he appealed to Sirhan's belief in a purpose and a power in life. "We're not just here as puppets or machines," said Diamond. "We have minds which can master and rise above these things. Isn't that a fair statement of what you believe in?"

"I think so, doc. But again I ask—why?"

"Who knows the why of these things?" said Diamond. But, he said, Sirhan still had to play the game because he wasn't going to get the gas chamber. "Do you know how many people there are on Death Row now? You know how long it's been since there's been an execution?"

Sirhan said he would not appeal. Diamond said he didn't have a choice about that. In California, there is an automatic appeal for anyone getting a death penalty. And there was a possibility that he'd spend the rest of his life on Death Row in San Quentin. Did he want that?

Said Sirhan: "I'd just reconsider another means of eliminating myself." I wondered at Sirhan's phraseology. *Reconsider? Another* means? Was killing Kennedy a nutty way of eliminating himself?

Diamond sighed, feeling that he had come to a kind of impasse with Sirhan. He started to restack the notebook papers, and Sirhan made a last request. Maybe the doctor could get him a sedative to take before he went into the courtroom. He was nervous and jumpy down there.

Diamond said that was against the law. Also, if he were under sedation, Sirhan would look to the jury "like a cold, malignant bastard."

"Oh," said Sirhan, "but, hell, I move around too much, too jumpy."

I shook my head in bewilderment, and gave Sirhan a little lecture. "I think you realize that the defense in your case is gonna be the truth. As much of the truth as you can get across to the jury. But just the idea of having sedation in that courtroom is the wrong idea, you see what I mean? That would be a lie. If you were doped up, you'd be sitting there as a liar before the jury. So you see how your instinct here is the wrong instinct, as far as your defense is concerned? Huh?"

"I thought it would make a better impression," said Sirhan.

"No," said Diamond. "The best impression is the truth. You as you are."

Diamond was depressed at his failure to crack the code that would give him the key to Sirhan. He knew the psychologists, Schorr and Richardson, had detected signs of psychosis in Sirhan, a permanent state of schizophrenia or near-schizophrenia, but, so far, he couldn't see it.

The next day when Dr. Diamond appeared in Sirhan's cell with Dr. Pollack and me, Sirhan insisted that Pollack and I get out. He had something to tell Diamond—in private. He was through. He didn't want any more doctors bugging him. He'd thought it all over. He was going to plead guilty as charged. He'd rather go to the gas chamber than have anyone "fuck around" with his mind. "You guys are goofing up my mind. I don't understand it."

"What do you feel we are doing?" asked Diamond.

Sirhan didn't know what all the doctors were up to. Or rather, he had strong suspicions that they would portray him as "a fanatic or some stupid person or something like that. I'd rather die and say I killed that son of a bitch for my country, period." And *say I killed for my country*

To Diamond, it was more complicated than that. The judge would probably reject Sirhan's plea. It didn't matter to Sirhan. That was going to be his "new role."

Diamond didn't argue with Sirhan. Naturally, he was disappointed, for he believed that if Pollack could see Sirhan in hypnosis, he would find new evidence of Sirhan's mental illness. He called in Pollack and me, and with Sirhan's premission, told us how Sirhan felt about "all the doctors bugging him and making him into a mental case."

Pollack assured Sirhan that he, for one, didn't think Sirhan was crazy. Sirhan was pleased with that: his only friend was the psychiatrist for the prosecution!

"You don't really trust the psychiatrists, do you, Sirhan?" asked Diamond.

"You know more about me than I know about myself," said Sirhan, "and that's what I don't . . ."

"What puzzles you most about yourself, Sirhan?" asked Diamond.

"Nothing," he said quickly.

"Would it help," asked Pollack, "if, after Dr. Diamond hypnotizes you today, you listen to the tape yourself?"

"You don't understand, doc. I don't wish to cooperate any longer."

Diamond pointed out that, through hypnosis, he was trying to illuminate some of the dark places in Sirhan's memory. That, quite possibly, would help the doctors and the lawyers discover how everything fit together. Diamond told Sirhan he wanted Pollack to see him under hypnosis, to see "another Sirhan, a part of you you don't seem to know anything about. I think you, too, ought to know about these feelings, Sirhan. They may be the best feelings that you have. They're deep down inside you, and they may be the real key to what's causing everything."

Sirhan shook his head, puzzled.

I turned to him and told him that what he demonstrated was his own childhood reactions to the war in Jerusalem, something he had been trying rather unsuccessfully to tell everyone all along.

"Really," said Sirhan, "you guys are talking something strange to me. I don't—"

"You don't remember yesterday, Sirhan? You sobbed and sobbed and sobbed?" said Diamond.

"Goddamn. That's not me, doc."

"That *is* you, Sirhan."

Sirhan said he didn't understand. This was a crucial moment for Diamond. He knew from past experience that his own patients frequently made their biggest self-discoveries at moments when they seemed most brittle, most resistant. "Sirhan, let's have one more. Let me show this to Dr. Pollack. Let me show it to you. And I'll play the tape for you."

Sirhan voiced a half-laugh, half-sob. Which way would he go? "It sounds weird, sir."

"I'd like to put you to sleep one more time," said Diamond softly.

Sirhan looked at Diamond intently. He turned to me sitting on his right. He put his head down, almost between his knees. He lifted his head and regarded Pollack sitting across from him with a large microphone in his hand and a Uher tape recorder spinning slowly at his feet. "Okay," he said.

Diamond put him under, warning him this time not to go so deeply to sleep. And asking him to remember, later, what happened under hypnosis.

Then Diamond and Sirhan went through the most exhaustive and exhausting session of them all. Sirhan went into a deep trance. "Remember the bombs, Sirhan? Remember the bombs? Sirhan, remember the bombs?"

Sirhan started to whimper, and his whimpers turned to heavy sobs, as before. His jaws tightened and his lips twisted and tears flowed and Sirhan grabbed protectively at his groin and twisted his knees. Diamond woke him up right in the middle of the trauma, and Sirhan awoke to find himself crying. He was very frightened. He trembled and shivered. "Oooo! Whew! Whew! Whew!"

"What happened, Sirhan? What happened!"

Sirhan's voice was low and breathy. "They . . . they killed him."

"What did you see, Sirhan?"

"That poor man. I saw that poor man. They killed him." Sirhan had apparently replayed in his mind's eye the scene in the street outside his home in Old Jerusalem, where the grocer was blasted to bits by the bomb that struck him outside his shop. Those who have undergone hypnosis and recreated scenes from their past often report that they saw it all "like in a Technicolor movie." It is probable that Sirhan, here, saw that street scene in vivid color.

"Can you see him now, Sirhan? Close your eyes and look at him right now."

Sirhan closed his eyes and gave a sudden start. He started to sob again. "It's too bloody," said Sirhan. "Get me out of this, doc, get me out of this." Diamond reminded him that he was not under hypnosis. But Sirhan nevertheless re-created that scene. He saw the man "in his coffin," and he recoiled, almost banging his head on the steel wall behind him. I caught him and wrapped my left arm around his shoulders.

"Sirhan, these are your feelings. These are the feelings you've been running away from. Don't be afraid to cry, Sirhan. Real tears, Sirhan. Let it all come out, Sirhan." Now Sirhan's whole body shook with sobs and the tears streamed down his face and his nose started running. "The whole world has to know the truth, Sirhan. No lies, no cover-ups. The whole world has to know the truth. Only you can let them know what the truth is, Sirhan. You mustn't be afraid of your feelings. You're awake now. You're not hypnotized, Sirhan. These are your feelings and you can't hide them."

Sirhan kept crying and Diamond encouraged him to keep it up, for Diamond believed it was good therapy.

Dr. Pollack broke the spell. He started in with a line of rapid-fire questions that made Pollack sound more like a D.A. than a doctor: When Sirhan went to the Corona rifle range. Whether he went alone. Where he went when he left. Who was home when he got there. What he did then. What sections of the Sunday newspaper he read. Where he left the gun. Where in the room. Why under the cushion. When he went to the Ambassador. Whether that was the first time he'd been to the hotel. Pollack's tone was high and his manner nagging. "You actually saw Kennedy there on Sunday? How long did you stay there? What did you do? That was about what time? Was it dark? How long did you stay there? What time did you get home?" Pollack found that Sirhan's memory for detail was pretty good until he got to late Tuesday night. Then things became hazy.

Diamond put Sirhan in hypnosis again. He sat on the steel bed, leaning against Sirhan's left shoulder so he wouldn't sag. I did the same on Sirhan's right and Dr. Pollack leaned forward, his large microphone thrust forward. Sirhan was drifting into a deep trance, so deep his responses were only mumbles. Diamond tried to pull him out, not all the way, but enough so he could understand and be understood.

"Sirhan, open your eyes and wake up. One, two and wake up." Sirhan stirred and mumbled and his eyelids fluttered. "Open your eyes. Now, Sirhan, we were talking about on Tuesday night you'd gone back to your car. You're tired. You'd had four Collinses to drink and you're too drunk to drive and you go back to the car and you see your gun on the back seat. Do you remember?"

"Ummmm," said Sirhan. He was still in pretty deep.

"Open your eyes, Sirhan. Open your eyes. Now you see the gun on the back seat. Now what did you do with the gun? Where did you put it?"

Sirhan mumbled, almost unintelligibly. Five or six words, then the phrase "so they can't steal it."

"So they can't steal it. Yeah, you were afraid. They were going to steal your gun. So what did you do with it? Did you put it in the band of your pants?"

Sirhan mumbled, unintelligibly, a sentence of possibly a dozen words ending with "me."

Pollack spoke up. "I think possibly it would be worthwhile waking him up. Having him remember."

"All right," said Diamond. He gave Sirhan a command to "remember where we left off, remember everything." Then he woke him up.

Sirhan came out of it—slowly and shiveringly. The cell was warm but again he was cold. Finally, he saw Pollack. "How the hell did you get here?" he demanded.

"Don't you remember my coming in here?"

"You frighten me," said Sirhan.

Soothingly, Pollack said, "I don't mean to frighten you."

"Wake up, Sirhan," ordered Diamond. "Wake up. And try to remember. It was just a little while ago that Dr. Pollack was talking to you and I was talking to you and Bob Kaiser was talking to you. We're not doing any tricks, Sirhan, really we're not."

Diamond and Pollack both reminded him of what he had just told them minutes before, under hypnosis. "Don't you remember that feeling, that somebody was going to steal the gun?"

"You said the Jews were going to steal the gun?"

"I don't remember."

Pollack said, "But you'd left the gun there a little while ago. You weren't afraid then that they'd steal it, were you?"

"I'm confused."

Diamond sighed, asked Sirhan to recall what happened when he got back to the Ambassador.

"There was a policeman there."

"There was a policeman there. All right. You're awake, Sirhan. And you can remember. So there's a policeman there. And then what? Did you talk to the policeman?"

"It was dark. Oh, hell, it was dark."

"It was dark? I thought there were a lot of lights there," said Pollack. "How can you drink coffee in the dark?"

"I don't know. It was dark."

"It was dark."

"There were a lot of lights, too. A hell of a lot of lights."

Diamond interjected softly and his warm tone was a marked contrast to Pollack's badgering insistence. "This is consistent with what he said before, too. There were a lot of lights there, but he was in the dark."

I asked Sirhan if he was outside on a fire escape while he was drinking his coffee. Or on a terrace. He said he wasn't. He said he was drinking coffee with a girl, out of a big cup, not a paper cup, and there was a lot of silver around.

"And what did you call the girl?" asked Pollack.

"Hell, I don't know. She was tired, too. She wanted coffee, just as much as I did."

"Did she tell you her name? What did you call her? Girl? Did you tell her your name?" Pollack seemed too impatient to ask one question at a time.

"Coffee was all our discussion."

"All right." Pollack laughed nervously. He turned to the subject of the gun. Sirhan didn't remember. Diamond tried to lead him back on the track again. He reminded him of the teletype machines (which were in the Colonial Room, adjacent to a swinging door leading to the Ambassador pantry). Sirhan had told him he went through that door. Suddenly he remembered. "I followed that girl through that door. She led me into a dark place. I was trailing her, that's all."

"Did she know you were following her?"

"I don't know. There was a big silver thing with coffee in it. She was sitting next to it, to the coffee."

"Is she the one who gave you the coffee?"

"She asked for it."

"All right. Then what?"

"And that's what I wanted."

"More coffee?"

"No. That's when I first found it."

"Oh. Then what?"

"Then I gave her a cup."

"You gave her a cup?" asked Pollack incredulously. "She was sitting right there!"

"He drew it for her," I said. Sirhan nodded.

"I'm sorry," said Pollack. "I didn't understand."

"And I made some for me and we sat there. Then she moved and I followed her."

"And then what?"

"There was a policeman."

Diamond explained to Pollack the man Sirhan saw might have been a fireman. "There were a number of firemen around."

"And then what happened?"

"Damn."

"Hmmm?"

"I was tired."

"Did you put the coffee down?"

"I remember lying on the table; I had my elbows on it. I was just resting and all of a sudden I was choked."

"Oh, wait!" said Diamond. "You skipped something. You skipped a lot. Look. You're back in the press room. Do you remember the mirrors, Sirhan? Do you remember the mirrors when you saw Kennedy's face?"

"Oh, yeah. . . ."

"Okay. You remember the mirrors at home. Now, do you remember the mirrors you saw in the Ambassador Hotel?"

"At Rafferty's."

"At Rafferty's party? Right. And what do you remember about that?"

"There was a mirror behind the bar, I think, and there was a pillar that had four sides to it. Four sides had mirrors."

Pollack took him away from the Rafferty party in the Venetian Room back toward the area of the Embassy Room, the location of the Kennedy party. "Were there mirrors there, too?"

"There were a lot of lights, a hell of a lot of lights." The corridor leading to the Embassy Room is lined with mirrors and large crystal chandeliers are in front of the mirrors, reflected and re-reflected to infinity.

"But dark, too, at the same time?" At a time when Sirhan was able to remember, Pollack was quick to interrupt, to challenge.

"The lights bothered me," said Sirhan.

Diamond explained to Pollack where the lights and the mirrors were in relation to the pantry—a few feet away. Sirhan wondered where the coffee location was. I suggested there might have been a coffee setup in the pantry itself. Sirhan remembered there were a lot of cups stacked up near the coffee. But he couldn't remember what kind of table he was resting his elbows on.

"What did you say to yourself when you saw the policeman?" I asked.

"I don't know."

"Did you think he was going to arrest you?" asked Diamond.

"I was drunk," said Sirhan, implying that was sufficient cause for an arrest.

"You were drunk. But what if he knew you had a gun on you?"

Sirhan paused. "I don't remember, doc."

"Where was the gun at that time?" asked Pollack. "You must have had it on you."

"I don't know, doc. I don't know."

"You sure?"

"Could you make a guess?" asked Pollack.

"My pocket?" It was nothing more than a guess.

Diamond tried to forge ahead, trying to get Sirhan to remember the critical moments of the killing. "You told me when you were asleep you saw Kennedy walking toward you. You told me you wanted to shake hands with him."

Sirhan smiled ruefully. "I wish to hell I did. Ohhh, goddamn!"

"Well, try to remember," said Diamond sternly. "Concentrate. You saw Kennedy coming toward you and you wanted to shake hands with him."

Pollack said, "Why would you want to shake hands with that son of a bitch? That I don't get. Why would you shake hands with that son of a bitch?"

"I don't know."

"Hmmm?"

"That's the part of it I really don't . . ."

"Sirhan!" interjected Diamond. "You know that you told me once you really loved the Kennedys?"

"I did. I liked 'em. I liked 'em."

"You liked him. He was gonna be the hope for the Arab people?"

"I thought so."

"Who?" asked Pollack. "Jack Kennedy or Bobby Kennedy?"

"Bobby."

Pollack couldn't believe. "Bobby? Bobby was gonna be the hope of the Arab people? Huh?"

"He was for the underdog," explained Sirhan. Pollack sagged.

Again, Diamond tried to get to the critical moments. "Now, when you saw Kennedy coming, try to picture in your mind . . ."

"Why not hypnotize me again, doc? On that part alone?"

That request startled Diamond and Pollack. At the beginning of this session, Sirhan had said he wanted no more hypnosis, no more examinations. Now, here he was, asking to be put under again.

"All right," said Diamond. "Try to stay almost awake, huh? No deep sleep, so that you can try to remember things." Almost offhandedly, Diamond put Sirhan under again, this time in a light sleep. "You're in the kitchen there, lot of noise. And you see Kennedy coming. Now what do you see? Sirhan, open your eyes. You're back in the kitchen, Sirhan. Kennedy is coming toward you. Look at his face." Sirhan had no reaction. "Sirhan, you asked me to hypnotize you and I did. And you said you would talk. Sirhan, open your eyes and talk. What do you see?"

Sirhan mumbled. Then, faintly: "They're running at me."

"They're running?"

"At me," I said, repeating what I heard Sirhan say so indistinctly.

"They're running at you. Who's running at you?"

"People."

"People. Why are they running at you." Indeed, after Kennedy's speech in the Embassy Room, people did start rushing into the pantry, not *at* Sirhan, but *past* him toward the Colonial Room. "Concentrate, Sirhan. Concentrate. Why are they running at you? Remember, Sirhan. Why are they running at you? Sirhan, think back. You see Kennedy. What did he look like? Look in his face, Sirhan. Look at Kennedy."

Sirhan stirred uneasily and moaned.

"Look! Open your eyes. Open your eyes. Sirhan, look at Kennedy. Look at him. Open your eyes, Sirhan. Sirhan, you must look at him. I order you to look at him. Open your eyes, Sirhan. Sirhan, open your eyes. Open your eyes and look at Kennedy." Sirhan moaned again, this time with more agitation. "Sirhan, don't shake your head. Look at him. You must remember. Open your eyes. I order you to open your eyes and look at Kennedy. Look at him. There he is. He's coming, Sirhan. He's coming toward you, Sirhan. Don't shake your head. He's coming toward you, Sirhan. What do you see?"

Sirhan moaned again, breathed hard. He mumbled something that sounded like "Bobby." Then: "Son of a bitch."

"Were you mad, Sirhan?" Diamond got no reply. "Sirhan, that son of a bitch is coming. What do you see?"

"What's *he* doing here?"

"Huh?"

"What's *he* doing here?"

" 'What's he doing here,' " Diamond repeated. "Go on."

Sirhan was breathing hard. Then, softly, "You son of a bitch."

" 'That son of a bitch,' " repeated Diamond, incorrectly.

" '*You* son of a bitch'?" I said.

" 'You son of a bitch.' You're talking to Kennedy. You call Kennedy a son of a bitch? Sirhan, open your eyes and look at Kennedy."

Diamond turned to Pollack and whispered: " 'You son of a bitch' has been verified by an eyewitness to the shooting. That's the first time he's talked about that." Then to Sirhan: "Sirhan, open your eyes. Open your eyes and look at Kennedy. There he is right there."

At this point, Sirhan reacted with a sudden spasm of his whole body, something that startled Diamond, Pollack and me into similar spasms of surprise. Then all of a sudden, Sirhan was choking in the cell. "Uhhhhh. Uhhhhh. Unnnnn. Uggggg." A deputy sheriff who was watching from out in the corridor stirred in his chair.

"Are they choking you, Sirhan?" asked Diamond.

"Rorig, rorig," he seemed to say. Unintelligible. Possibly a word in Arabic. Sirhan struggled and his face became a bit blue.

"Hmmm?" asked Diamond. Sirhan continued to breathe very hard. He was gasping for air. "All right, Sirhan. It's all right. They're not really choking you. Sirhan, open your eyes. You haven't shot him yet." In the hypnotic re-creation, he already had, but Diamond wanted him to go through it again. "He's still there, Sirhan. There is Kennedy, Sirhan. Open your eyes, Sirhan. Sirhan, open your eyes. 'You son of a bitch,' you said, Sirhan."

"He can't. He can't."

" 'He can't?' Huh? He can't do what?"

"He can't."

"He can't do what?"

"Can't send those bombers."

"He can't send the bombers. You're not gonna let him, are you, Sirhan? Hmmm?"

"He can't. He can't. He can't. He can't."

"Sirhan! Did you know that Kennedy was coming this way?"

"No."

"Did you expect him?"

"No."

"Sirhan, were you waiting for him?"

"Uhhhh."

"Yes or no, Sirhan?"

"No. Uhhhh."

"No. Are you sure you weren't waiting for him?"

"No."

"But you see him now. He's coming now. He's coming down the hall. Look at him, Sirhan. Open your eyes."

"He's running at me." Sirhan was very agitated now.

"Huh?"

"He's running at me."

"C'mon, look at him."

Sirhan was trembling violently now, half hissing, half panting. "You can't. You can't. You can't. You can't." He was panting like someone approaching a sexual climax. He accelerated the cadence. "You can't. You can't. You can't. You can't."

"Are you reaching for your gun, Sirhan?" Sirhan grabbed crudely, moving his right hand over to his left hip bone.

Diamond shot me a knowing look. A witness in the kitchen thought she saw Sirhan grab there for his gun, but this was the first time Sirhan gave any indication he knew where it was. Sirhan continued to pant.

"You can't. You can't. You can't. You can't."

"Are you reaching for your gun?" asked Diamond again.

The gasps were faster and faster now. "You can't. You can't. You can't. You can't. You can't."

"You can't do that. You can't send the bombers."

"Whew! Whew!" Sirhan started a breathy whistling.

"Are you gonna stop him, Sirhan?"

"Whew! Whew!" Now Sirhan was grabbing for his gun again, but instead of grabbing at his left hip, he was grabbing at the front of his pants, at his penis. "Whew! Whew! Whew! Whew! Whew! He can't."

"All right, he can't. How you gonna stop him?"

"He can't."

"All right. He can't."

"He can't," sighed Sirhan. "He can't. He can't. He can't." He was still grabbing for his penis.

"Sirhan, open your eyes and look at Kennedy. Sirhan, open your eyes. He's coming. Reach for your gun, Sirhan. It's your last chance, Sirhan. Reach for your gun. Where is your gun?" For the record, Diamond noted out loud, Sirhan was reaching into the waistband of his pants and also into "his lap."

"All right, what happened, Sirhan? Take the gun out of your pants. You've got the gun in your hand now. Let me see you shoot the gun, Sirhan. Shoot the gun. Shoot the gun. Shoot the gun. Sirhan, take the gun and shoot it." Then Sirhan's right hand pounded climactically on his right thigh—five times. His right forefinger squeezed and twisted three more times in a weakening spasm. Then he was still.

Diamond and Pollack and I sat there in silence. Then Diamond started to bring Sirhan out of the trance, suggesting he feel good and warm and relaxed when he woke up. "You won't be worried," said Diamond reassuringly. "And you won't be frightened. You got a lot of bad feelings out of you and you'll feel clean inside, Sirhan. You'll feel clean and you'll trust us. We're doctors, Sirhan, and we want to help you. We're Jews, Sirhan, but we want to help you because we hate war, too, Sirhan. We hate war, Sirhan, just like you hate war."

Twelve

In interviews on January 27, 28 and 31, Pollack tried to get Sirhan to agree with him that his interest in the occult and his angry feelings toward society were normal, that he saw theosophy and Rosicrucianism as simple "brotherhood philosophies like Catholicism" and that his psyche was really not so different from that of a black psychiatrist he knew.

Sirhan conceded he was a member of a minority, that he had taken his school lessons about equality in America most literally—and didn't see why he shouldn't, even though he was an Arab.

"You look Jewish!" Pollack laughed.

"Maybe if I was a Jew," said Sirhan, "I wouldn't be here right now."

"Why?"

"You guys run the whole country."

"Yeah, you believe that. I know you believe that," said Pollack. "It isn't true." Then Pollack added his usual disclaimer: "In my opinion. You see, Sirhan, the big difference between you and me—I believe I'm right. But you know what bothers me? I may always be wrong."

Sirhan immediately conceded that he, Sirhan, could be wrong about the Jews, to prove to Pollack that there really wasn't much difference between the two of them. Then Sirhan and Pollack both lied to see who could view most objectively the proposition, "Resolved that the Jews run the United States of America." Pollack conceded that the Jews had a considerable political influence, but he pointed out that they numbered only five and a half million people. Sirhan conceded that five and a half million in America was not a very great number, but he pointed out that the Jews seem to have a disproportionate influence on the mass media. He was sure that Otis Chandler, publisher of the Los Angeles *Times,* and Harry Luce were Jews, facts he assumed from *Time*'s and the *Times*'s coverage of the Arab-Israeli conflict.

Pollack sighed deeply. "What I don't understand is how—you know how I think about you, don'tcha—I look at you as a very emotionally-filled, intense kid. I look at you as filled with feeling. But I can't conceive of you doing this."

Pollack explained further. Judging by what he knew so far, Sirhan was "stuck." The notebooks showed that he was terribly disturbed by the Arab-Israeli conflict and that he had wanted to kill Kennedy for a long time. (The notebooks didn't show that: they showed a much more free-floating anger, hardly zeroed in on the Arab-Israeli war, and only a late resolve to kill Kennedy.) To Pollack, that could only mean first-degree murder.

Sirhan insisted that he really didn't know what he was doing when he killed Kennedy.

"I believe you wanted to kill Kennedy," said Pollack. "I believe you even planned to kill him. What I'm not sure of is that you planned to kill him that night."

Sirhan again tried to describe the feeling he had that he was on a sort of slide carrying him inexorably to the assassination.

"What you're doing," said Pollack, "is discounting the real Sirhan, the intense—what shall I say?—freedom fighter?"

Sirhan smiled and gave an honest description of himself. " 'The little punk.' That's what I call myself."

Pollack said he was a punk then with a lot of feeling. "What bothers me," he said, "is your discounting the notes you made. And that you had such strong feelings about them. You—you didn't want the Arabs to be hurt more. You wanted America to take a different stand. You felt it necessary to bring this to the attention of the world." This was a pretty good paraphrase of a line that Abdeen Jabara had been urging on Sirhan.

Maybe Sirhan could take it from Jabara, but he couldn't take it from Pollack. "Oh, shit, sir. I could have slapped him in the face, I could have broken his nose, I could have thrown my cup of coffee at him. Why? Why not? Why the hell didn't I do that?"

"Because that wouldn't stop the jet bombers. That's why. Because the jet bombers were very important, not for just you. Because the jet bombers are and were not just for you, but for the Arab people. And I think that you believe as I do that—if we were told, the Arab people, to think about these things, that there are probably a lot of people are glad that Kennedy died."

Now Sirhan agreed with him and that pleased Pollack. Pollack added: "If you were say, if you were Jewish and had done what you did, then I'd be"—Pollack laughed nervously—"up in the air trying to figure it out. Then I wouldn't have a good explanation." Now that he had a good explanation, Pollack had only to clear up a few minor matters. He asked Sirhan why he kept his diary so secret. Sirhan said it was not a secret and it was not a diary.

"Some of the things you wrote were a year old," said Pollack. "Why would you have been angry with Kennedy in '67?"

Sirhan said he wasn't angry with Kennedy in '67. It wasn't until May, 1968. He started riffling the pages of his notebook, looking for the citation. Finally, he found the note headed 2 June '67, 12:30 P.M., and gave it to Pollack who read it:

A declaration of war against American humanity. When in the course of human events it has become necessary for me to equalize and seek revenge for all the inhuman treatments committed against me by the American people. The manifestation of this declaration will be executed by its supporters as soon as he is able to command a sum of money ($2,000) and to acquire some firearms the specifications of which have not been established yet.

The victims of the party in favor of this declaration will be or are now the President, Vice etc. down the ladder.

"There's nothing about Kennedy there," said Sirhan.

"In other words," said Pollack, "what you were referring to here was not just Kennedy, but the whole shebang. You felt that the whole system was against the Arabs." (There was nothing in this declaration about the Arabs, either.) "Again, there's probably some truth to that. But one of the things that troubles me is that you feel that wasn't you."

"It was me at the time I wrote it," said Sirhan, "but I don't feel it."

"Not now."

"No."

"I don't really think you thought the whole thing out. You certainly didn't work out a good way of killing him, in the sense that it was, ah, a good plan."

"That's what I don't understand," said Sirhan. "If I'd wanted to kill a man, why would I have shot him right there where they could have choked the shit outta me?"

"It might be that you wanted to be caught, if you wanted the world to know it was an Arab who did it." Sirhan made a face. "You don't think so?" asked Pollack.

"I may have done more damage to the Arab cause," said Sirhan ruefully. (As a matter of fact, Sirhan did not shout after he killed Kennedy,

"I'm an Arab, I'm an Arab." He didn't even give his name and it is unlikely that Sirhan ever said that night, "I did it for my country.") "I'm not a killer. I'm not a killer," said Sirhan. "If I'd wanted to kill him, would I, sir, be so stupid as to leave that notebook there, waiting for those cops, sir, to pick up?"

Pollack said that was a very good question and a point that should be argued. "It would seem not. It would seem that if you'd planned to kill him, you wouldn't leave things around."

"That's what puzzles me," said Sirhan.

"Only you're not a killer," said Pollack. "You see, a person who isn't a killer doesn't think about all those things. If I were to kill somebody, I could do something as stupid as that, too, and I'm not stupid either. And, looking at it from your eyes, I don't think killing Kennedy was stupid. You see, I think Kennedy's assassination was a political assassination."

Sirhan was glad to agree with him. Sirhan said he would just as soon they shoot him right then and there. He was just as good as dead anyway. He didn't want to fight it anymore.

"It's almost as if you're being a martyr," said Pollack. "Is that really what you'd like? To have the world see that, through your death, the U.S. is really pro-Israel?"

"We're all going to die someday."

"As long as you make a mark?"

"No, not necessarily, sir."

Pollack paused. "Well," he said, "you've made a mark. As far as the Arab world is concerned, you've made a mark, haven't you?" Pollack, too, was buying the Arab propaganda.

"I wish I'd never have. There are better ways to make marks than shooting people."

"Well, that's the way you feel now," said Pollack, "but that isn't the way you felt then? For a year or two you felt very very strongly." He said he thought Sirhan had changed a lot since then.

"In what way?" asked Sirhan.

Pollack wasn't sure how to describe it, but he said Sirhan would have a hard time killing *him,* for instance.

Sirhan agreed. "I'd have a hard time slapping you in the face, never mind killing you."

That was one of the things that bothered Pollack. He felt that he himself "genuinely represented society," which put him "in the D.A.'s camp." On the other hand, he was "a human being" who hated the thought of Sirhan's dying. He didn't believe in capital punishment. "But," said Pollack, "I can't find you mentally sick in order to save you. I don't believe you're mentally sick. Maybe Diamond finds you mentally sick, but I don't find you mentally sick. But you realize, don't you realize that if I don't find you mentally sick, it's—bad for you? Aren't you aware of that?" What Pollack was trying to say was that even the California Supreme Court would have difficulty reversing a first-degree verdict unless there was unanimity among the doctors on the case.*

Sirhan laughed and said, "Well, then I'm a psycho."

"I don't see it," said Pollack.

"I don't see it either," said Sirhan, switching quickly to a low, depressive tone, agreeing with a point of view that would mean a death verdict for him. On January 29, Dr. Pollack had said as much to Mary Sirhan during one last visit to the Sirhan home in Pasadena, and she knew then that Pollack wasn't going to help. Next day in the narrow hallway outside the courtroom in the middle of a large crowd of newsmen, she told Cooper that Pollack was out to destroy her son, and then broke into great heaving sobs. Cooper tried to comfort her, but her motherly intuitions were probably correct.

Here in the cell now, Pollack went on asking some of the right questions and, in fact, got answers that showed more of Sirhan's contorted reasoning. He focused on Sirhan's conceptions of Robert Kennedy. Sirhan seemed to put Kennedy "in a very colorful position." But even if Kennedy were President of the United States, said Pollack, "he wouldn't have the power you give him."

Sirhan replied that he was convinced of Kennedy's power because he had supported Israel for twenty years. "They had him in their bag."

"Well," said Pollack, "why did you pick Robert Kennedy? Why RFK instead of, say, Hubert Humphrey?"

Sirhan pondered a moment. That was the key question. "I liked him, sir. I think that is the crux of it, sir. He was a hero, an idol. I really went for him, sir, but he failed me, sir. He betrayed me, sir."

"Betrayed you?" said Pollack. "Well, that idea—that is twisted thinking. That is twisted thinking." He paused, possibly to let the representative of society gain the upper hand now over the psychiatrist in him who threatened to take over. Society won. "I think that what failed you, what betrayed you, were your own unrealistic expectations, your own ideals. You wanted more than the world was going to give you. Of that I have no

---

* Pollack could have been mistaken. The Supreme Court could decide to accept Pollack's *medical* judgment (i.e. that Sirhan was psychotic) and cast aside his *legal* judgment (that Sirhan was responsible before the law).

—no question about. That image failed you. That image failed you. It is almost as if you feel the U.S. was the hope of the world and it had let you down. But it didn't. Your hopes, your dreams let you down." True enough but not deep enough: Pollack ignored Sirhan's illogical and unreal equation of Kennedy with the United States. It was normal enough to have dashed hopes. It was not normal to murder a real person who symbolized those hopes. "Many people share your feelings," said Pollack, "so I don't see you as crazy. And that doesn't help you."

"But the defense of diminished responsibility, though . . ."

"It's still crazy," interrupted Pollack.

"No," said Sirhan. To him, "crazy" meant commitment to a crazy house.

Pollack insisted on his unprofessional imprecision. "It's a kind of craziness, in the sense that you didn't know what you were doing." Pollack added that he couldn't see the value even of that defense to Sirhan. Even if he "won" with that defense, he'd be in prison for life. "And you don't want that."

Sirhan admitted he didn't. So the conclusion was inescapable. "You don't even have to take me to court, sir. You could shoot me right here for what I did. My own conscience is against me."

Pollack asked him to explain that.

Sirhan said simply that what he did was against his upbringing. "My childhood, my family, the church, prayers, the Bible, Thou Shalt Not Kill —all that. And here I go and spatter this guy's brains. It's just not me."

Pollack sighed and sank into silence.

Sirhan tried to take a cosmic view of the whole affair. He said he would go before the jury and admit he killed Kennedy. " 'You can kill me, too.' I'm gonna tell the jury that. That they can kill me. I'd wanta die for what I did. But goddamn it, learn the lesson, sir. Let the death of Kennedy and my death as human beings make you aware of what the forces were, what are the forces, that caused me to kill Kennedy."

"What were the forces?" Even to Pollack that was still a mystery.

But Sirhan's reply was the pat answer he had learned that would establish him as an Arab hero. "The injustice of what Kennedy would have done," said Sirhan, "had he lived."

"How did that affect you?" asked Pollack.

"Of what he would have done to the Arab people."

"How did that affect you?"

"They're my people, sir. They're my people."

"How did that affect you," insisted Pollack, "with respect to the way

you wrote what you did and didn't know what you wrote? How did it af-
fect you so that you came down and didn't know that you were there?"
Pollack's tone here was terribly earnest. "Is that what you're telling me?
Now I'll agree, I honestly believe everything you said about the forces that
moved you." He looked up and saw Sirhan grinning at him. "Heh, heh.
What are you grinning about? Heh, heh. That's what I don't understand.
Not the forces."

Pollack wasn't the first one to notice Sirhan's smile at the most inappropriate moments. Dr. Diamond had called it a "schizy grin." But Pollack
passed it over, looked at his watch, realized it was close to 6:30 P.M. He had
to be going. But before he did, he again told Sirhan where he stood. "As a
psychiatrist representing society, I have to put my feelings aside. I have
my responsibility to society and—suffer with it. When I look at the material and—I'm not a judge—but to me, so far, the evidence appears that
you carried your gun down to shoot him. People don't carry loaded guns
unless they intend to use them." Pollack had set up a dichotomy here, as if
his duties were opposed: as if to represent society properly, he had to put
aside his training as a psychiatrist, which had taught him to dig beneath
the surface of his subject and assume instead a common-sense approach,
which judged on impressions alone.

Even Sirhan could see something was wrong with that stance. "Well,"
he said, "a layman could come up with the same conclusion."

"That's right."

"Really, you're not telling me anything new."

"That's right."

"Or surprising."

"That's right."

" 'That's right! That's right!' " mimicked Sirhan. Well, if that was all
there was to it, the denouement was obvious. "They saw me shoot him. So,
kill that son of a bitch."

"No," said Pollack, "that's not the law. That's not the way the law looks
at it. Otherwise, you would have been dead long ago. Maybe you think
you are being persecuted, but—"

Sirhan said at once that he didn't feel persecuted. Minutes later, when
Pollack said he thought that Sirhan's belief about the Jews "is almost like
Hitler's belief about the Jews," Sirhan responded: "Well," said Sirhan, "I
feel toward the Jews as they felt toward Hitler. Hitler persecuted them and
now they're persecuting me in the same style—"

"I don't believe the Jews are persecuting you," said Pollack.

"I believe the Jews have something . . ." Sirhan raved for a moment about the Jews' influence on the mass media. "They don't give the Arabs peanuts!" he shouted. "Just because we're Arabs in this country, we have no power, no prestige, no influence, no money—nothing really. We can be treated like dogs, like ants. Had it not been for me, sir, Munir would be out there in one of those camps. He would have been deported."

"How?" asked Pollack. "What do you mean?"

"With me and Kennedy."

"How? You mean that Munir was going to be deported?"

"Yes, sir, because of that conviction."

"Yes, but how did you stop that?"

"Well, they figured 'Sirhan.' The whole world knows 'Sirhan' now. If they had deported his younger brother from America, that would show an injustice on the part of America." He added bitterly: "But even without me, what's the difference? Munir was just a good-for-nothing Aye-rab."

"Have you talked about all of this with Dr. Diamond, too?" asked Pollack.

"No, sir. I don't think I have. Not as much as I have with you."

Pollack paused and sighed. "Ah, what a crazy, mixed-up case."

Maybe Pollack felt it was mixed up because he, the representative of society, a society that wanted to see Sirhan dead, was gathering material that could forestall a death sentence for Sirhan. Pollack gathered more on the next day when Diamond tried to verify the hunch that Sirhan wrote some of his notebook material in a less-than-conscious state. After more than an hour of resistance from Sirhan, who was adamantly ready to ask for the gas chamber if the notebooks were introduced in court, Diamond put Sirhan under a light hypnosis, asked him if he could hear the voices of both Dr. Pollack and Kaiser, gave him a yellow legal pad and a ball-point pen and asked him to write his name. Without any further instruction, Sirhan wrote "Sirhan B Sirhan Sirhan B Sirhan Sirhan B Sirhan." Over and over again, Sirhan kept writing slowly, thirty seconds to a line, and Diamond, a victorious gleam in his eye, let him write.

It was the final discovery, the key to the mystery of the notebook: like many a practitioner of the occult, Sirhan was adept at automatic writing. At one point, Sirhan found himself at the right side of the page, his name unfinished. He continued, right to left, writing his name in Arabic for a line and a half, then slipped back into English, left to right. "Sirhan Sirhan Sirhan Sirhan Sirhan Sirhan." When he arrived at the bottom of the page, he stopped and waited for further orders. (See Appendix D.)

It was February 1, 1969. Diamond asked Sirhan to write the date at the top of a new page. Sirhan wrote "Friday 31 January 68." Diamond asked, "Is this 1968?" Sirhan wrote a nine next to the eight. Then he wrote again, "Friday 31 January 69 Friday . . ." He would have kept on going, but Diamond stopped him and asked him to write something about Kennedy. He wrote "RFK RFK RFK RFK RFK."

Diamond asked him to write more than Kennedy's name. Sirhan wrote another line: "Robert F. Kennedy. Robert F. Kennedy."

"What about Kennedy, Sirhan?"

Sirhan wrote "RFK RFK RFK RFK RFK must die RFK must die RFK must die" nine times, until Diamond stopped him. This was a pretty good reduplication of the page in Sirhan's notebook where he wrote, over and over again, that Kennedy must die.

"When must Kennedy die, Sirhan?" asked Diamond.

"Robert Kemedey is going to die," he wrote. "Robert is going to die. Robert is going to die. Sirhan Sirhan. Robert is going to die."

"Who killed Kennedy?" asked Diamond.

"Who killed Kennedy?" wrote Sirhan.

"Stop writing," said Diamond. "Write an answer, not the question."

"I don't know," wrote Sirhan. "I don't know."

"Is Kennedy dead yet?" asked Diamond. "Stop writing 'I don't know.' " Sirhan wrote again: "I don't know."

"Is Kennedy dead?"

"No No No," wrote Sirhan. "Now."

"When is the 'now'?" asked Diamond. "What is the date today?"

Sirhan wrote, "Friday 31 January Friday."

"Is Kennedy alive?" asked Diamond.

"Yes yes yes." Diamond concluded that for Sirhan, emotionally, Kennedy was still alive.

"Doesn't Kennedy talk to you?" asked Diamond.

"No no," wrote Sirhan.

"Did anybody tell you to shoot Kennedy?"

"No No N."

"Did anybody give you money to shoot Kennedy?"

"No no no."

"Did anybody help you to shoot Kennedy?"

"No No No."

"Was anybody with you when you shot Kennedy?"

"No No N."

"Who was with you when you shot Kennedy?"

"Girl the girl the girl."

"Do you know the girl's name?" Sirhan groaned. "Write out the name of the girl." No response. Only groans. "Start a new line, Sirhan. Is this the way you wrote at home?"

Sirhan wrote the question. "Is this the way you wrote at home?"

"Don't write the question. Write the answer. Is this the way you wrote the notebook at home?"

"Yes yes yes." Diamond gave Pollack and me a triumphant look and let Sirhan go on writing. "Yes yes yes yes yes."

"Is this crazy writing?" asked Diamond.

"Yes yes yes yes yes yes yes yes yes."

"Are you crazy?"

"No no no. N—"

"If you're not crazy, why are you writing crazy?"

"Practice practice practice practice practice."

"Practice for what ?"

"Mind control mind control mind control mind—"

"Mind control for what?"

"Self improvement self improvement," wrote Sirhan laboriously. His lids became heavier now. His hand began to cramp.

"Who taught you how to write this way?"

"I I I I." Eleven times.

"Did you learn this yourself? Did you read it in a book?"

"Yes yes yes."

"Did someone tell you about it? Did your friends tell you about it?"

"No No No."

'Who wrote your notebook, Sirhan?"

"I I I."

"Are you asleep now?"

"I I I I I."

"Listen carefully. Are you asleep?"

"Sleepyes," wrote Sirhan. "Sleey," wrote Sirhan. Then he tried to cross out the misspelled word.

"Are you asleep now? Are you hypnotized?"

"I am sleepy."

"Are you hypnotized?"

"Yes yes yes."

"Were you hypnotized when you wrote the notebook?"

"Yes yes yes."

"Who hypnotized you when you wrote the notebook? Write his name down."

"Mirror mirror my mirror," wrote Sirhan. "my mirr my mirror."

Now things were becoming clearer for Diamond. He could put Sirhan into a hypnotic state so easily, because of Sirhan's prior hypnotic experience. But he had had great difficulty talking in this state. Now, Diamond saw, Sirhan had far less difficulty answering Diamond's questions when he wrote them down on paper, an indication that his previous experience with hypnosis was a solitary, self-induced affair and that his form of expression under hypnosis was not verbal, but written. Diamond took advantage of the opportunity to ask Sirhan the answers to other puzzling questions. "Who taught you to do this?"

"AMORC," wrote Sirhan.

"What does that mean?" asked Diamond. Sirhan hesitated. Diamond told him not to "run away." "Put your pencil on the paper and write the name of the person who taught you how to do the mirror writing, who taught you how to do this. Write so we can read it."

Sirhan wrote "AMORC AMORC."

Then Diamond understood. AMORC meant Ancient Mystical Order of the Rosae Crucis, the Rosicrucians. "Did they show you how to do it?" asked Diamond.

"No."

"Did you read it in a book?"

"Yes yes yes."

"Who gave you the books?"

"I bought the books I bought."

Diamond took Sirhan back to the Ambassador on a mind trip. "Write how many drinks you had," demanded Diamond. "Don't go to sleep. Write it down. Write the number."

Sirhan wrote "1234 1234 1234 1234."

"What kind of drinks?"

"Give me a Tom Collins. Collins."

"Were you drunk, Sirhan?"

"Were you drunk?" wrote Sirhan.

"That's my question. Write the answer."

"Yes Yes Yes."

Diamond had Sirhan answer further questions about the night of the assassination. Sirhan confirmed his earlier story: that he went back to his car, decided to go home, then went back for coffee. Where? To the party. Whooo party?

"Kathleen Kathleen Kathleen Kathleen," wrote Sirhan.

Kathleen was, apparently, the daughter of the Republican Senatorial candidate, Max Rafferty, whose followers were partying in the Venetian Room. "Did you meet Kathleen?" asked Diamond.

"No no no."

"Did you know the name of the girl?" asked Diamond.

"Kathleen."

"Not Kathleen Rafferty," said Diamond. "The other girl. The girl you drank coffee with."

"She did not tell me her name," wrote Sirhan.

"Did this girl tell you to shoot Kennedy?"

"No No No."

"Did this girl know you had a gun on you? Did she know you had a gun?"

Sirhan sank back, almost totally asleep now. Diamond revived him and Sirhan wrote, "I don't know."

"Could she have seen the gun in your pants belt?"

"She wanted she wanted coffee."

Pollack asked Diamond to ask Sirhan what he was thinking of when he shot Kennedy. Diamond said, "Were you thinking then of shooting Kennedy?"

"No no," wrote Sirhan, sliding off the legal pad entirely and writing in the air.

"Listen carefully," asked Diamond. "Were you shooting Kennedy then?"

"No," wrote Sirhan. "No." He groaned and stopped writing, for he had come to the end of the page. In this hypnotic session, it was clear his mind was out of control when he killed Kennedy. Awake, he rejected that Sirhan, the Sirhan being driven along by mysterious inner and outer forces. "This is political," he had said. "This is a politically motivated. Heh-heh. This is political, heh heh, politically motivated." That was a much neater explanation than the story he told in his trance. He didn't like the implications of the story that came out in hypnosis: that he had programmed himself (or been programmed by another) as an automatic assassin, couldn't believe it, wouldn't believe it. He preferred Dr. Pollack's diagnosis: he was just a normal, garden-variety assassin.

Diamond woke him up. Sirhan came out slowly. He did not recognize the writing as his. And when Diamond asked him to read parts of it, Sirhan read "1234" (his count of the drinks he had consumed) as "Twelve thirty-four."

With Diamond's discovery of Sirhan's skill at automatic writing, Pollack had what he admitted was "a possible key" to the notebook puzzle, for if Sirhan wrote in the notebook in a trance, or semitrance, how *could* he remember? Furthermore, Pollack had studied hypnosis a good deal. He knew that Sirhan's new ability to remember how he had written the notebook was good evidence that his previous amnesia about the notebook was not intentional avoidance at all, neither a lie nor a fake, but something far more complicated, perhaps even sinister.

Dr. Pollack, the prosecutor's man, got strong new data about Sirhan's other abnormalities from Sirhan's psychologists at a meeting the next day, February 2, in the library at Grant Cooper's office. There, Drs. O. Roderick Richardson and Martin M. Schorr presented their conclusions and submitted to a kind of cross-examination by Drs. Diamond, Marcus and Pollack. It was an unusual move by Cooper, part of his overall strategy of total disclosure. If Sirhan was sick, then the more the D.A. knew of it the better. All the doctors were pretty well agreed that Sirhan was sick. Dr. Pollack raised some questions about Sirhan's cultural underlay. He would like to see some psychologists who had tested Arabs evaluate the raw data of both Richardson and Schorr. That would be easy enough, Diamond said, but now what about Pollack? Where did he stand?

Pollack described his own ambivalence. He was the D.A.'s man, but he found himself liking Sirhan. "I'm doing my damnedest to bend over backward to find something that would exonerate him, and so I have to watch myself. . . . How the hell can I be so deceitful? Here I am, a prosecution consultant, and yet at the same time—you get my point?"

It soon became clear where Pollack was having trouble. It wasn't so much whether Sirhan was or was not psychotic. Maybe he was. But what were the legal implications of this diagnosis? "If Sirhan were frankly psychotic," said Pollack, "he still wouldn't necessarily have diminished capacity at the time of this episode."

Diamond flatly disagreed. As one of those who had helped pioneer the legal concept of diminished capacity in California, he knew that the law was on his side and said so.

Pollack admitted that the law, for the time being, was on Diamond's side. "I think the Supreme Court has accepted conclusions from Dr. Diamond and others. . . . It's almost as if the individual today is found suffering from diminished capacity as a result of being psychotic, not as a result of how and in what way his psychotic thinking interrelated with his act, but rather merely because he was psychotic. And it is that kind of conclu—uh, thinking that I'm very critical of, as Dr. Diamond says. We are in very definite opposition on that point." Pollack said he didn't believe that Sirhan killed out of "a psychotic motivation." And so, he didn't see how Sirhan's killing could be compared to Ronald Wolff's,* whose case helped establish the law on diminished capacity.

Diamond said there was no essential difference between the motivation of Sirhan and that of Wolff, "except that this man's [motivation] would have been approved by a segment of society and no segment of society would approve Wolff's."

"Sirhan's motivation," insisted Pollack, "was not psychotic."

"What was his motivation?" asked Marcus.

"To kill Kennedy in order to prevent Kennedy from sending fifty jet bombers which would kill thousands of Arabs."

"You imply this is rational?" asked Marcus.

"As rational," said Pollack, "as any Arab feeling that it was necessary for some action to be taken to prevent the Arab refugees from being destroyed." The other doctors did not agree with Pollack, but allowed him to proceed anyway with what he called "the major question": did Sirhan intend to kill Kennedy?

Diamond asked him what he meant by the word "intend."

Responded Pollack: "Clear purpose."

"No," said Diamond. "Now we're getting hopelessly confused. This is a dead-end street if you cannot accept the Wolff decision. The Wolff decision does not talk of 'clear purpose.' " Diamond thumped on the table for emphasis. "If someone hears voices telling him to kill his next-door neighbor because he is the anti-Christ, and he does so, he has 'clear purpose.' But he does not, in the language of Wolff, have the capacity to meaningfully and maturely deliberate and make a kind of decision as a mentally normal person would. Now, are you prepared to evaluate Sirhan in that type of framework?"

Pollack stared down at the table and Marcus leaped into the silence to point out that Pollack was confusing the three requisite intentions for first-degree murder, which were: (1) specific intent to kill, (2) premeditation and (3) malice. Marcus, at least, was willing to grant that Sirhan had the capacity to form a specific intent to kill. And now, both Marcus and Diamond asked Pollack how he stood regarding Sirhan's capacity to "mean-

* See p. 410 for the background of the Wolff case.

ingfully and maturely reflect on the gravity of his contemplated act," according to the language of Wolff?

Pollack sat there silently. This was the most important legal question of all, for the language of Wolff now defined "premeditation" in California, and Pollack would either answer the question in the negative as Diamond and Marcus did, or he would have a fine battle on his hands there and then, a battle that could have helped Cooper and Berman (who were now sitting in on the conference) define the legal issue in a clearer way than they had so far been able to do for themselves.

Dr. Schorr ruined the moment by asking a question of his own, which was well-intended but off the mark. "Do you see *any* evidence of diminished capacity?" he asked.

Pollack said there was some evidence that Sirhan was psychologically disturbed at the time of the crime and possibly under the influence of alcohol. "I have raised questions about how much weight to give this material with respect to impairing his capacity to have the intent in the *Wolff* sense —I have forgotten the exact phraseology. I have raised questions."

"Seymour," said Diamond, " 'raise questions'?"

"I haven't yet decided," said Pollack defensively. "I raised questions with respect to the alcohol, with respect to his being in a dissociated state—"

"Seymour," said Diamond, "can I interrupt because I have to go very soon. Frankly, it is of no interest to me what questions are raised. A great many are raised. To hear you say 'questions are raised' communicates no information to me that I didn't already have. I'm thoroughly familiar with the questions. You're not saying anything."

"I'm considering these. I didn't come here with a firm—"

"So you really don't have an opinion?"

"At this point, that's correct. Do you have an opinion, Bernie?"

"Yes, I do. Do you feel there is going to be information available, further tests, interviews with the family that would make it possible for you to have an opinion about this? Let's say about diminished responsibility. Can you imagine an additional test, or is it one of those situations where you can never decide because the information is not forthcoming?"

Pollack said he wondered about an amytal interview. He was worried about some of Sirhan's lies and distortions, but he really didn't think sodium amytal would get Sirhan to open up, and, anyway, Judge Walker had decided that he would not make any orders for sodium amytal or lie detector tests.

Diamond said, "Is there anything the defense can make available to you?"

Pollack thought he would not need any more interviews with Sirhan. He conceded that there was some evidence of a dissociated state. He was still weighing the pros and cons.

"Yeah, we understand," said Diamond. "But what I want to know, is it worthwhile to pursue this any further? You give me the impression, Seymour, that nothing would get you off the fence."

Pollack said he doubted he would get any more material from Sirhan. "It's going to depend on my thinking about this and arriving at a more firm opinion, rather than—new material."

"Well," said Diamond, "your problem is you want to think about it?"

"I don't have any firm opinions," insisted Pollack. "Do you think I'm lying to you?"

"No. I don't know. I do not think you are lying. But not having any firm opinions, you have nothing to share with the group."

Marcus edged into Diamond's sputtering rage with a suggestion. "How about tentative opinions?"

"—so that I would be interested in tentative opinions," continued Diamond, "not quibbles or questions raised. Otherwise, you are wasting my time and everybody else's time."

Pollack didn't even have tentative opinions then and there, and the others turned to Schorr who was itching to make a fuller presentation of his own findings.

Schorr's presentation was windy and filled with self-congratulations. He exposed his charts and graphs and poked at them with a chrome-plated telescopic pointer extended to its longest and tried to establish his tests as more complete than Richardson's. Diamond fumed at this performance, but Pollack was impressed with Schorr's exegesis, and, by the end of the meeting, Pollack sounded more convinced of Sirhan's schizophrenia.

Pollack left, phoned the district attorney's office and said that Sirhan was psychotic. When Evelle Younger heard this, his course was clear: he'd better make a deal with Cooper for first-degree murder with a guarantee of a life sentence, something he knew Cooper would be satisfied with.

The attorneys still had to pick six alternate jurors and Cooper had to present the remainder of his legal motions. In arguing that Sirhan was not indicted by a jury of his peers, Cooper put both Sirhan and his mother on the stand, briefly, to testify that they were poor. Sirhan took the oath with an upraised, clenched fist, a gesture identified with student and Third World revolutionaries. It was an identification that certainly wouldn't help Sirhan. His mother tried to counterbalance her son's anarchistic image with an extemporaneous little prayer. Cooper finished with his questions, Mary Sirhan rose to leave, then turned to the jury: "I thank God that gives me the strength and I thank you nice people, as I never get hungry and I have a roof over my head."

Later that day in chambers, Chief Deputy D. A. Lynn Compton told Judge Walker his office was willing to accept Sirhan's plea of guilty to first-degree murder in return for a promise of life in prison. It was an altogether ordinary deal that would mean a trial of one or two days or no trial at all, the kind of deal entered into every day in the overcrowded criminal calendars of the county courts. Without such bargains, criminal justice would be bogged down in a morass of delays. But this was not an altogether ordinary case. Judge Walker felt that a full trial would answer the public's right to know, something the public hadn't enjoyed after Lee Harvey Oswald had killed President John F. Kennedy. He simply would not deprive the public of a full-blown murder trial.

The judge's position was a setback for Cooper. But he returned to his office and searched the law books to see if there were any precedents for forcing a plea on an unwilling judge. Apparently there were none. He would have to rely on the forcefulness of the district attorney, Evelle Younger himself, for he knew that Younger wanted a plea as much as he did.

On February 8, Sirhan hypnotized himself under Dr. Diamond's direction by staring at a twenty-five-cent coin propped against a cigarette pack in his lap. In fifteen minutes, his head sagged. Diamond suggested that he ask about the weather when he woke up. Sirhan was soon out in the anteroom, asking a deputy if it was raining outside.

"Why did you do that, Sirhan?" asked Diamond with mock curiosity.

"What's so unusual about that?" said Sirhan. "Asking about the weather?"

"Whose idea was that, Sirhan?"

"Huh? Wuh, wuh, uh." Sirhan could tell from the smile on Diamond's face that something funny was going on. But he couldn't believe that Diamond had programmed him to ask if it was raining. Diamond punched the rewind button on his Sony tape recorder. He would show Sirhan how he instructed him under hypnosis. But his tape was blank. He had forgotten to put the machine on "record" in the first place. Sirhan was overjoyed, for this only proved what he had suspected all along: Diamond was bluffing. He reaffirmed his contention that Diamond had never really hypnotized him. To prove that right now, he told McCowan (who had been curious to see Sirhan in hypnosis and came along with Diamond on this visit) that he would give him a finger signal when he was supposedly "under." That would mean that he was definitely not hypnotized.

Diamond put Sirhan in hypnosis once more. Sirhan looked at McCowan through his heavy lids. The middle finger of his right hand quivered but he couldn't budge it. Then Diamond suggested that Sirhan would come out of the trance and climb the bars like a monkey.

Sirhan went out and climbed on the bars. He was up there, he explained to Diamond, "for exercise." Diamond replayed the tape, let Sirhan hear how he'd been programmed. "It wasn't your idea at all, Sirhan. You were just following my instructions."

Sirhan was silent for a time. He shivered. "Ohhh, it frightens me, doc."

"It is very scary," admitted Diamond.

"Oh," said Sirhan, as if realizing something for the first time. "No. No."

"But it's very real," said Diamond. "It's not a fake. And it's not a trick."

"But goddamn it, sir, killing people is different than climbing up bars."

"There's this difference, Sirhan. I couldn't force you to do something you were opposed to. But if you wanted to do it, you could do it under hypnosis. Do you know, Sirhan, if five men had wanted to stop you from climbing those bars, they couldn't have done it?"

Sirhan shook his head. It was scary.

But Diamond didn't want to take the responsibility for putting any far-out idea in Sirhan's head. "Now, get this straight, Sirhan. I do not believe that anybody hypnotized you and told you to kill Kennedy. I think you did it to yourself. You get the distinction?"

"Yes, sir. Yes. I understand."

"I don't think any Rosicrucian came down from San Jose. That's non-sense."

"That's one of Kaiser's—"

"Yeah, and I've told Bob Kaiser that's a crazy, crackpot theory. That just isn't true. And as far as I can figure out—"

"That's what it was—"

"There wasn't anymore. And it seems to me this is entirely a matter of your studying on your own. You've been afraid to talk about this business.

You don't want people to think you're crazy. I'm satisfied. You don't have to be crazy to do these things."

"You can do them when you're crazy, too," said Sirhan. Diamond agreed with that, but insisted that Sirhan had programmed himself with thoughts about Kennedy—like a computer. "It frightens me," said Sirhan. "It frightens me."

Diamond agreed that it was frightening—and dangerous stuff for people to play with alone. Suddenly Sirhan saw Diamond as a kindred spirit, a believer in the power of mind over matter. "You know, when they say you can move mountains, sir, I believe that shit. I believe that shit." He asked that Diamond shut off the recorder, then explained how he had forced a horse named Press Agent (owned by his former boss, Bert Altfillisch) to crash the rail during a scheduled race at Hollywood Park. What was so unusual about that? Well, he wasn't on the horse. He was sitting in the grandstand, and he did it all simply by concentrating very hard and *willing* the horse into the rail. The power of mind over matter. Diamond tried to look properly impressed with Sirhan's power. He wondered why Sirhan had asked him to shut off the recorder. Because, said Sirhan, it was a crazy notion and he didn't want it "on the record."

They talked for a time about the occult. Twice more, Sirhan asked Diamond to turn off the recorder. He wanted to tell Diamond about a personal experience with voodoo, and he didn't want that "on the record" either.

On Monday, February 10, when the attorneys were very nearly agreed on a complete panel of twelve jurors and six alternates, Younger strolled into the courtroom at 9:15 and disappeared with his deputies and the defense attorneys into Judge Walker's chambers.

"I understand that the defendant is prepared to plead guilty," said Younger, "and accept the life sentence. Is that right, Mr. Cooper?"

"Yes," said Cooper, adding that his colleagues agreed with him.

Younger turned to Judge Walker: "We favor it, Judge, and the law requires your approval. Now that we have gotten our psychiatrist's report, a man whom we have great confidence in, we are in a position where we can't conscientiously urge the death penalty, number one. Number two, we don't think under any circumstances we would get the death penalty even if we urged it, and, number three, we don't think we can justify the trial under those circumstances. It appears that the result is a foregone conclusion. Our psychiatrist, in effect, said the defendant is psychotic and his report would support the position of the defense because of diminished capacity. And the death penalty wouldn't then be imposed. So the alternative . . . are we justified in going through the motions of a trial, a very traumatic and expensive trial, when we say we can't conscientiously ask for the death penalty anyway? I don't think we are."

Compton added by way of correction that Dr. Pollack didn't support the defense contention of diminished capacity, but he did think Sirhan was psychotic and he had warned the D.A. he would testify for the defendant in any penalty trial.

Judge Walker asked Cooper if he had any observations. Cooper gave the judge a quick run down on the diagnosis of the psychiatrists and psychologists who were advising the defense.

Younger added that he and the defense counsel and the police would work together putting into the record all pertinent material, witness statements, psychiatric reports—in short, everything that would be in the record if there were a three-months' trial—so that the public would not think there was any "hanky-panky."

Judge Walker said he'd given the matter a great deal of thought. "I appreciate the cost. I appreciate the sensation. But I am sure it would just be opening us up to a lot of criticism, and criticism by the people who think the jury should determine this question. We have a jury. Whatever expenses we incur from here on out would only be negligible with what I think would be incurred if we did otherwise." Judge Walker suggested instead a plea of guilty in open court and a trial on the penalty. "I think you have got a very much interested public," said Walker, then added quickly, "I don't let the public influence me. But, at the same time, there are a lot of ramifications. And they [he didn't say who "they" were] continually point to the Oswald matter and they just wonder what is going on because the fellow wasn't tried."

Cooper suggested that instead of the attorneys merely filing reports at the time of the plea, both sides could put on "a very skeleton outline of the case . . . put on certain witnesses to testify—"

To Judge Walker, that sounded like a mock trial and that was too much. "Well, then," he said with even more finality, "they would say it was all fixed, it was greased. So we will just go through the trial. Let's get the trial over. I don't think it would be a three-month trial. If you want to go back to what was originally suggested, a plea to murder, and try the penalty and punishment—"

"We couldn't do that," said Cooper.

"Well, maybe you could," said Compton to Cooper, somewhat later in the morning. He took Cooper, Parsons and Berman to his office and proposed a new deal. If Sirhan would plead guilty to first-degree murder and let the matter go to the jury for penalty, then the D.A. would make a positive recommendation of life in prison instead of death. Cooper said he'd have to think it over and talk it over with Sirhan and his family, but he made sure he got it all on the record by reporting the new offer to Judge Walker in the presence of the court reporter and the deputy district attorneys at 2:00 P.M.

Judge Walker was more amenable to such a move, but he was worried about the newsmen's curiosity over Evelle Younger's visit that morning. "I think we are in a very precarious position with all this discussion and dragging our feet. We've got a lot of smart people out there."

"I know," said Cooper. "They've already asked. Their antennae are up."

Indeed they were. Normally, when reporters on the courthouse beat hear of plea bargains, they know enough to avoid writing stories about them, for that can only jam the wheels of justice, even lead to higher court reversals. Analogously, police reporters who hear of a narcotic stakeout, for example, avoid writing advance stories about it that would tip off the suspected pushers. For all their vaunted "objectivity," newsmen are on the side of the law.

But now, as suspicions began to arise that both sides were talking of a plea, in this, the biggest case of the century, the usual rules didn't seem to apply. Some old pros, like John Douglas of the Los Angeles *Herald-Examiner* and Mary Nieswender of the Long Beach *Press Telegram,* sat on the story. Bob Greene wrote a careful piece for Long Island's *Newsday,* reporting that Judge Walker refused to consider a plea and that the lawyers were considering ways of circumventing the judge. But Dave Smith of the Los Angeles *Times* heard nothing of the judge's reluctance and worked the next few days to get a confirmation (probably from Evelle Younger himself) that a plea was still possible, even probable. Indeed—at midday, February 11—as Smith was putting the finishing touches on his story, Cooper was then proposing to Sirhan in the presence of Berman, Parsons, McCowan and Mary and Munir Sirhan that he consider pleading guilty to first degree in return for the district attorney's promise, a positive recommendation to the jury of life in prison.

Younger undoubtedly believed that Cooper would prevail, but there were other—crazy and not so crazy—factors Younger didn't reckon with. Mary Sirhan didn't like the idea of a plea at all. She was praying for acquittal. Munir, who was in jail once for nine months, thought even ten years in prison too long. He'd rather die. Sirhan asked for time to think it over.

Dave Smith of the Los Angeles *Times* knew nothing of this, of course, when he took his story to Bill Thomas on the metropolitan desk of the *Times*. Sirhan was expected to plead guilty now to first-degree murder and that was news. The *Times* had been stymied by the court order regarding publicity; Thomas turned back now to the court order itself and discovered the order did not bind the press, but the officers of the court and their agents. So, the *Times* laid aside the newspaper profession's long-standing policy of intelligent self-control and leaned instead on the letter of the law.

This is the story that appeared in the *Times* late in the evening of February 11, just twenty-four hours before the Sirhan jury would be sequestered at the Biltmore Hotel.

SIRHAN CHANGE OF
PLEA SEEN LIKELY

ADMISSION OF GUILT MAY SHORTEN
TRIAL AND BRING LIFE SENTENCE

By Dave Smith
Times Staff Writer

Sirhan Bishara Sirhan probably will plead guilty to first-degree murder in the slaying of Sen. Robert F. Kennedy, it was learned Tuesday.

The switch from an earlier plea of innocence could come when the trial reconvenes Thursday morning, and would result from either an understanding or a firm belief that a life term would be the maximum penalty.

Such a change of plea would make it unnecessary to try Sirhan on the question of guilt or innocence and would reduce the trial—once expected to consume two or three months—to a penalty hearing, possibly of only a few days' duration.

The only likely obstacle would be Sirhan's own refusal to change his plea.

Defense attorneys huddled Tuesday afternoon with Sirhan, his mother, Mary, and brother, Munir, to discuss the possible advantages of a guilty plea.

Sirhan has been described as fearful that a change of plea could rob him of the chance to publicly air his reasons for the assassination.

REASON FOR SWITCH TOLD

The willingness of the three defense lawyers to change the plea is said to be based on their conviction that, while psychiatric evidence would not warrant a death penalty, they could not hope for a jury verdict of less than first-degree murder.

They are confident that the psychiatric evidence by both sides would block any effort to secure a death penalty. Instead, they feel, it tends to support the defense contention that Sirhan's diminished mental or emotional capacity mitigated the degree of premeditation that must be proved to warrant a death penalty.

Reporter Smith was wrong. The lawyers were willing to change the plea simply because they would rather rely on the district attorney than take a chance on the jury. And the psychiatric evidence Smith was writing about had legal weight only in the guilt-or-innocence, not the penalty, phase of the trial.

When Cooper picked the *Times* off his porch at 6:00 A.M., he realized that any jurors who saw the story—it was bannered on page 1—would have a hard time finding Sirhan guilty of anything less than first-degree murder. A trial now was doomed before it began. All the more reason, Cooper believed, to go ahead with the plea and try the issue of penalty alone.

But Berman didn't see it that way. He came down to breakfast at the Ambassador Hotel coffee shop with a somber expression on his face. "I haven't slept all night," he said to me. "If we plead this kid guilty, we're destroying his right to a fair trial, and he'll never even have the possibility of an appeal." I showed him the article in the Los Angeles *Times* that turned Berman's gloom into despair.

He hurried to Cooper's office and told him that if Cooper went ahead with the plea, he would pack up quietly and return to New York. He couldn't bargain away the defendant's rights.

Cooper worried the tobacco in his pipe for some moments. He'd come within an inch of saving Sirhan's life without going through the agonies of a three-month trial and now everything seemed to be toppling in on him. The story in the *Times*. Berman's threat to leave. And then the phone rang. It was Dr. Bernard Diamond in Berkeley. How could Cooper plead Sirhan guilty to first-degree murder when he knew what the doctors had found—even the prosecution doctor? When Cooper told Diamond that the doctors' testimony could come out during the penalty phase as evidence of "mitigation," Diamond exploded. "Not *my* testimony!" he cried. "The 'ev-

idence in mitigation' belongs in the primary phase, not the penalty phase.
That's a victory we won ten years ago. Now you're turning back the clock!
If you go directly to the penalty phase after a plea of first degree, don't ex-
pect me to be there!"

"Another factor to consider," Cooper said as he hung up. "If we plead,
we won't have Diamond." He phoned Parsons and discovered he, too, favored going ahead with a full-blown trial and would recommend that to
Sirhan at 10:00 A.M. "Well," said Cooper, "let's go and see Sirhan. He's
the one who has to decide."

A clomping herd of newsmen greeted Cooper and Berman when they
arrived at the Hall of Justice, and Cooper was uncharacteristically curt
with them. "No comment," he growled, as he approached Russell Parsons,
who was posturing before a dozen cameras in the main lobby of the courthouse. Cooper forged ahead into the dozens of lenses and lights ahead of
him, forcing the news crews to backpedal up a short, dangerous flight of
marble stairs.

"I have no comment," chimed in Parsons. "I just told you that and I've
told five newspapers all over the world since six o'clock this morning."

"This is something that somebody made up?" asked Charles Arlington
of KFWB.

"I never said that," said Parsons.

"No comment," said Cooper, plowing toward the jail elevator.

The sheriff's deputies had set up a conference table in Sirhan's outer
cell. Cooper, Berman, Parsons, Abdeen Jabara and I sat down, and then
Sirhan sat. And I pushed the "record" button on my casette recorder.

Cooper told Sirhan about the phone call from Diamond. Berman said he
couldn't give counsel that would leave open the door to the gas chamber.
Parsons agreed.

Cooper stuck to his guns. Now that the L.A. *Times*'s story had appeared, his hopes of anything less than first degree were nil. And then
they'd be going into the penalty phase without the D.A.'s positive recommendation of life in prison.

Jabara thought the *Times*'s story was "beautiful grounds for reversible
error." Cooper agreed, and Berman asked Sirhan what his answer would
have been this morning even if he hadn't seen the article in the *Times*.

Sirhan had his own unrealistic deal all worked out: "I would have pled
the first degree with a guarantee of life and having a chance to tell my
story on the witness stand, plus another guarantee of parole after seven
years. I absolutely want guarantee of that."

The group exploded. "You'll never get that," said Cooper.

"You can't, you can't get parole," said Parsons.

"The Parole Board," said Berman, "has nothing to do with a deal here."

"No power at all," said Cooper. "Nor would the judge ever make such a recommendation." He turned again to Jabara. Jabara said he thought they ought to go to trial. He was impressed with Dr. Diamond, and he thought they could get second degree. He knew, moreover, what his Arab cohorts felt: that a real legal contest would focus world attention on the plight of the Palestinian Arabs. In New York, Dr. M. T. Mehdi, Chairman of the Action Committee on Arab-American Relations, heard news reports saying Sirhan might plead guilty and offered a new team of lawyers. The present lawyers, he said, "failed to understand that the Sirhan case is a historic political event and not an ordinary legal problem."

Cooper couldn't see how any historic or political dimensions could help Sirhan (and his feelings would be borne out): "You can't overlook the fact that the man that was shot and killed was a candidate for the office of President and was a U.S. Senator and a very popular individual. Second degree," he added, "would be an empty victory. We as lawyers would be big heroes, but what's it going to help Sirhan? It's still life imprisonment. The minimum doesn't mean a damn thing." Technically, he said, Sirhan would be eligible for parole at the end of three and a half years, but practically speaking, he'd be in prison until the Parole Board decided to let him go. In other words, an awfully long time. But, Cooper added, he'd go along with the majority if that's the way the majority felt.

Sirhan sighed. There didn't seem to be any exit. If only the judge—

"The judge," said Sirhan, "is overplaying his authority."

Cooper said that the district attorney himself, who used to be a judge, couldn't persuade Judge Walker to change his mind.

"Well, hell," said Sirhan, "I might as well fight it all out."

In the riotous corridors of the Hall of Justice, Cooper still had no comment for the newsmen who were wondering now if the long-awaited trial would begin on the morrow or not. Not even the district attorney's office could help the newsmen now, not until David Fitts got a call from Cooper at 2:15. "Dave," said Cooper, "I'm afraid we're going to have to go to trial and—I'm sorry about this, Dave—but, as a result of that goddamn article in the *Times* this morning, we're gonna have to ask for a mistrial."

The district attorney's office tried to obviate that by renewing its request, again in the chambers, that the judge accept a first-degree plea of guilty. Chief Deputy Buck Compton believed first-degree life would achieve "essential justice to both sides." The question of a "format or public exposure of the evidence" was really not relevant to the court's just decision. The question is, said Compton, are the People arbitrarily waiving the appropriate penalty? Does the court think the penalty should be death?

It didn't matter what Judge Walker thought. The decision was too much for him. He wanted the jury to make it.

Compton persisted. "We are willing to assume the full responsibility for the decision. We are not asking that your Honor has to be the one who says it was your idea or that you have any responsibility for it other than just to prove it in form as being acceptable to both parties and accomplish the essential justice in the case."

Judge Walker was stubborn. "I think the jury should determine the penalty. That's my decision. If you want to enter a plea on that premise, all right. Let's go ahead and try the lawsuit."

In open court in the absence of the jury, Judge Walker wouldn't hear of a mistrial. It didn't make any difference to him if the airways were saturated with news that Sirhan was going to plead guilty. He proposed asking the jurors if the news had influenced them. Cooper said no juror could be expected to say he'd violated the judge's admonition not to read the papers or listen to the radio or watch television on the case. "I think jurors are as fair-minded and as honest as any people who walk around," said Walker, "and I think their answer should be given full credence."

"They are human beings, your Honor," said Cooper.

Walker proposed bringing all the jurors down and putting them in the jury box, then taking each one into chambers to see whether he or she had read or heard about yesterday's news in the Sirhan case, because he didn't want the jurors mingling together and talking about this before he and the attorneys had had a chance to question them. As soon as he said this, he clapped his hand over his mouth and Cooper reddened with embarrassment, for Judge Walker had just refuted his own contention about the high probity of the jurors. Walker admitted it: "I have put myself in the same position as defense counsel."

But it didn't make any difference. Walker brought the jurors into chambers one by one. Juror No. 1, Ronald Evans, admitted he'd heard on the radio Sirhan might change his plea to guilty. Cooper asked if that wouldn't make it difficult for Evans to bring in a verdict of second degree or manslaughter. Evans said it would. Cooper promptly asked again for a mistrial. The judge said he wanted to hear the other jurors. None of them admitted as much. Mrs. Busby said a friend had mentioned something to her about it, but she refused to discuss it. Mr. Morgan had seen the paper and had seen something about a change in plea. Mr. Elliott had seen something about a guilty plea. Mrs. Bortells said she had heard Sirhan was going to plead guilty. Mr. Glick had heard on the radio that Sirhan was going to plead guilty. Mr. Broomis said his wife had told him Sirhan was pleading guilty. Mr. Stitzel's wife had said he might not be locked up as long as he thought. Why? Stitzel said he wasn't curious enough to ask. Mrs. Landgreen had heard about a guilty plea on her car radio while she drove to the hotel where the jury would be sequestered. On a kind of cross-examination by the prosecuting attorneys, however, all eight of these jurors said they could still judge impartially. And on those grounds, Walker denied Cooper's motion for a mistrial and said the prosecution could begin its case. In open court, before the full jury and the defendant, Alice Nishikawa read the indictment that Sirhan Bishara Sirhan did "willfully, unlawfully, feloniously, and with malice aforethought" kill Senator Robert Kennedy at the Ambassador Hotel on the morning of June 5, 1968.

David Fitts stood to present the prosecution's opening statement, squeezed his way past a $6' \times 6'$ scale model of the Ambassador Hotel's lobby floor, took a position directly behind another $3' \times 6'$ mock-up of the Ambassador's seventy-four-foot-long pantry, which was placed directly in front of the jury box, and told the jury that the gun that killed Senator Robert Francis Kennedy was purchased on August 10, 1965, "while smoke from the fires of Watts still hung heavy in the air." It was a rather poetic beginning to a chilling narration of the facts amassed by all the law-enforcement agencies employed in the case. Fitts fiddled nervously with a silver, orange-tipped pointer, but his voice was calm, and he completed his preview of the entire case without a reference to his notes. For the first time, Fitts revealed that Sirhan was seen at the Ambassador Hotel on June 2, two days before election night. On June 4, said Fitts, when most people went to the polls, the defendant went to a gun range to practice rapid fire. One witness, he said, saw Sirhan lurking in a corridor near the Embassy Room later that evening. Another saw him in the pantry asking whether Senator Kennedy was coming this way.

Fitts pulled on the orange tip of his pointer. It expanded like a telescope and gave Fitts a six-foot reach so he could lean over the pantry mock-up and point out the exact location where Kennedy was shot: at Coordinate 13-E, eighteen inches from the corner of the first serving table.

At that point, said Fitts, Sirhan stepped from a tray rack toward Senator Kennedy, reached into his waistband, extended his right arm, brought his right hand near Robert Kennedy's head and fired eight shots. It is probable, he said, that the first shot resulted in the death of Senator Kennedy twenty-five hours later. It was a painful story, even now six months later, and the judge called a recess.

After the recess, at the request of the newsmen straining to hear from their seats in the auxiliary courtroom, Fitts attached a Lavalier microphone around his neck and proceeded to tell of the pandemonium in the pantry, the attempts of a dozen men to grapple with Sirhan, his words ("I can explain."), his arrest and incarceration.

At Sirhan's home in Pasadena, said Fitts, police found some six * notebooks that belonged to the defendant. At this point, Cooper interrupted and asked to approach the bench. The judge hadn't yet ruled on the admissibility of these notebooks, whispered Cooper. He asked that Fitts not mention them. The judge agreed and Fitts wound up with a single sentence. "In conclusion, ladies and gentlemen, the evidence will show the defendent Sirhan Sirhan was alone responsible for the tragic events at the Ambassador Hotel in the early morning hours of the 5th of June, that he acted alone and without the concert of others."

Then Emile Zola Berman faced the jury to present what the public would feel was a fantastic, almost incredible defense to the indefensible crime.

When Sirhan killed Kennedy, said Berman, he was out of contact with reality, possibly in a trance. But Berman was barely into his fifteen-minute opener when Sirhan, at the far end of the counsel table, started to murmur. Berman paid no attention. In raspy, nasal tones, Berman told the jury Sirhan was "immature, emotionally disturbed, mentally ill."

"No, no," said Sirhan, and began to rise from his chair.

Inspector William Conroy leaned over to McCowan. "Talk to him, Mike." McCowan rose, pushed Sirhan back into his chair with both hands and the two of them had a vehement, whispered colloquy while Berman plunged ahead, describing Sirhan as a victim of spells, trances and mystic delusions. "In his fantasies, he was often a hero and savior of his people. In the realities of life, however, he was small, helpless, isolated, confused and bewildered by emotions over which he had no control."

Sirhan was still shaking his head and murmuring. He didn't like this helpless, bewildered Sirhan that Berman was trying to sell. In fact, he had

* Actually three notebooks.

greeted me before this morning's session with a request to dig up documentation on "CIA-planned executions abroad in foreign countries." How could an Arab equivalent of a CIA executioner be "small, helpless, isolated, confused and bewildered"?

"Jesus Christ," whispered Russell Parsons, "calm down, for my sake. We gotta have some defense." Sirhan did calm down a bit and Berman continued, telling the jury that Sirhan's mental deterioration was the end product of a process that started at the age of three when war broke out in Palestine and culminated at one point during the Six-Day War in June, 1967, when his fanatical obsessions, hatred, suspicion and distrust found expression in a notebook entry declaring war "against American humanity" and promising to assassinate the President, the Vice-President and so on down the ladder, wanting to be recorded by history as "the man who triggered off the last war." Berman looked over the top of his rimless spectacles at the jury. "From which, I gather, he meant the last war ever to be.

"The killing," Berman said, "was unplanned and undeliberate [a slight exaggeration of the facts, as Cooper saw them], impulsive and without premeditation or malice, totally a product of a sick obsessed mind and personality."

When Berman finished, Judge Walker called a recess. Reporters ran to the telephones and Sirhan was hustled back to a windowless "holding tank" behind and to the right of the judge. Parsons and McCowan gave him a chance to blow off steam and, after the recess, Sirhan had changed his tune: "Nice going, Zuke!" he cried to Berman.

The New York Times said the same thing, in effect, the next morning when it reprinted the complete text of Berman's statement alongside a glowing, two-column profile on the affluent Jewish lawyer from New York who was defending the Palestinian Arab refugee in Los Angeles. But George Lardner, Jr., of the Washington *Post,* took a slightly cynical view of Berman's opener, which claimed all the ingredients that could be used under California's laws of diminished capacity: obsession, anger, fear, even liquor. "It promises to be a bizarre trial," wrote Lardner. "Only the hashish seems to be missing."

The prosecution's case was hardly bizarre. Just a straightforward, ploddingly thorough presentation of 14 witnesses who saw Sirhan shoot Robert Kennedy, four of the five others who were shot, 6 witnesses who saw Sirhan practice rapid fire at the San Gabriel Valley Gun Club, two who sold him the .22 revolver, two who saw him at the Ambassador on the night of June 2, ballistics experts and doctors and a coroner who testified on the cause of death, policemen who participated in the arrest and interrogation of Sirhan on the night of the killing and, finally, two policemen who found Sirhan's notebooks in the bedroom at 696 E. Howard Street in Pasadena, and a handwriting expert who identified the writing in them as Sirhan's.

Defense attorneys made it easier than they had to: they weren't contending that their facts were any different then the prosecution's, and for the most part avoided any tough cross-examination. They established the fact that no one knew of Kennedy's route through the pantry until the last minute and that Sirhan seemed abnormally strong when he was set upon by the bystanders, which included the two massive black athletes, Roosevelt Grier and Rafer Johnson.

Juan Romero, the little busboy with the jet-black shock of hair, told a poignant tale. He held Kennedy's head in his hands for some minutes in the pantry telling him, "Come on, Senator, you can make it," putting a rosary in his left hand and moving away when Ethel Kennedy finally made it to her husband's side. It was a story that certainly wasn't calculated to foster sympathy for Sirhan, but when Russell Parsons took Romero on cross-examination, he had him tell the whole thing once more. Cooper leaned over to me, sitting directly behind him inside the rail. "This," said Cooper, "is a good example of how not to cross-examine."

Some of the witnesses were obviously well coached. Some referred to Sirhan in terms only a policeman would use: "the suspect." Thomas Vincent DiPierro identified a picture of a blonde coed from the University of California at Santa Barbara named Valerie Schulte as "the girl in the polka-dot dress" he had seen in the pantry moments before the shooting (a statement he would later claim the police had "forced" him to make). The police and the district attorney's office were trying their best to lay all talk of conspiracy to rest, a move that won the concurrence of the defense, whose task was complicated enough already without throwing conspiracy into the hopper. Nor did newsmen challenge the identity of Valerie Schulte as the girl in the polka-dot dress.* They turned their attention now to a parade of personalities from the world of Bobby Kennedy: Jesse Unruh,

---

* Valerie Schulte could hardly have been the girl described earlier by DiPierro: he had originally said the girl was a brunette, wore a black and white polka-dot dress, was already in the pantry when DiPierro entered with Kennedy and that she stood next to Sirhan on the tray rack and had some words with him. Miss Schulte was a blonde, wore a green dress covered with large yellow circles, came into the pantry some fifteen feet behind DiPierro and never approached Sirhan.

with eyes like a basset and a deep-toned articulate delivery; Roosevelt
Grier in moustache and goatee, yellow boots, yellow shirt and yellow tie;
Jack Gallivan, a young man who bore some resemblance to Ted Kennedy,
who had served as an advance man for Bob and was now working for
ABC's "Wide World of Sports"; Frank J. Burns, Jr., a soft-spoken attorney
and Unruh's chief assistant in Southern California; Bill Barry, Bob Kennedy's bodyguard, flicking the tips of his fingers and fidgeting nervously on
the stand; Rafer Johnson, broad nose, broad shoulders, very serious, very
well spoken, very much at ease; Paul Schrade, the U.A.W. official who
was shot in the forehead, now wearing a heavy Van Dyke beard; George
Plimpton, the author, in a neat gray suit, tan and well-groomed.

No network news cameras, of course, were allowed in the courtroom to
capture the celebrities' statement on film. And so the television news crews
set up a gauntlet in the eastern corridor of the eighth floor where they
waited with their lenses and lights for each witness to appear after his testimony and demand that he or she repeat the essentials of what they had
said on the stand. When the witness was a celebrity in his own right, the
newsmen became a news mob, pushing for position and shouting impreca-
tions at one another. Roosevelt Grier, a deeply sensitive man who suffered a personal loss with Kennedy's death, couldn't understand. Later, on
a Broadway curbside, he complained bitterly to Al Stump a veteran reporter covering the trial for the Hearst Syndicate, "The press is only
around when there's something sensational like this," said Grier, "but when
it comes to reporting the day-to-day jobs we all have to do, nobody seems
to be around. People have to stay on the job." Grier didn't like the laughter inside the courtroom either. "People forget too quick," he said.

When Plimpton was on the stand, he admitted under cross-examination
by Berman that Sirhan's eyes seemed "enormously peaceful." Explained
Plimpton: "He struck me . . . as compared to the rest of us, enormously
composed. The rest of us, of course, given this sudden tragedy, were not
composed. We reacted in a number of different ways. His reaction seemed
startling to me because in the middle of a hurricane of sound and feeling,
he seemed almost—the eye of the storm—peaceful and I had the sense—"

"I don't want to ask you for your sense," interrupted Judge Walker. "I
just want a description."

"That is what I mean," said Plimpton. "Peaceful. He seemed—purged."

Plimpton's description gave a bit of corroboration for the defense contention that Sirhan killed while he was in a kind of trance. But the prosecution overrode the effect of Plimpton's observation with Sirhan's garbage
man, Alvin Clark, who reported that Sirhan told him more than a month

before the assassination that he intended to shoot Robert Kennedy. Sirhan thought Clark's testimony was a joke and barely suppressed his laughter at Clark's embarrassment when Berman asked Clark about a statement he had made to the FBI. "Do you recall being asked to testify . . . and you said you wouldn't want to take the oath because you hated Sirhan so much [for killing Kennedy] you'd say anything to see Sirhan convicted?"

"Yes," admitted Clark.

"That's all," snapped Berman.

"Are you telling the truth now?" asked David Fitts, on redirect examination.

"Yes," said Clark, simply.

But Sirhan was sober when Jesus Perez, a helper in the kitchen, and Martin Patrusky, a waiter, both said Sirhan had asked them a half hour before the shooting if Kennedy was coming that way. Cooper didn't challenge that fact or confront the witnesses with pictures of Michael Wayne who was also in the pantry before the shooting and was mistakenly taken for Sirhan by other police witnesses. Sirhan was upset. He leaned over to McCowan and whispered that he hadn't said any such thing to Perez and Patrusky. But when McCowan reminded him that he couldn't remember what he'd done in those moments before the shooting, Sirhan nodded and gulped, realizing that his loss of memory really wasn't helping very much now.

Furthermore, Sirhan had finally alienated his own attorney. On four consecutive noon-hour visits alone with Cooper, Sirhan had been so evasive that Cooper had difficulty believing Sirhan was telling him the entire truth. After the first two of these visits, on the morning of February 19, Cooper climbed in my car, weary and disgusted. He still didn't know why Sirhan had killed Kennedy or whether anyone else was involved or whether Sirhan was given money or the promise of money to do the job.

Cooper also doubted the arresting officers who claimed they had noted no evidence of Sirhan's intoxication. Arthur Placencia, the youngest of the policemen, admitted he had checked Sirhan's eyes, but he wouldn't tell the jury why he'd checked them or what his examination revealed. Finally, he admitted, under cross-examination by Cooper, that Sirhan's pupils were dilated, even when he shone a flashlight into his eyes. Cooper subjected Placencia's partner, Travis White, too, to a grueling cross-examination and drew an admission from White that Sirhan's eyes were "not completely normal."

White attributed the abnormality to fright and said he intended to check Sirhan's pupils again "after he was able to calm down."

Cooper wheeled suddenly and challenged White: "As a matter of fact, you didn't give him any eye examination that morning, did you?"

"Yes, I did," gulped White.

"Nothing further," said Cooper.

But if Cooper scored any points with his cross-examination of Placencia and White, Fitts overwhelmed the jurors with something much more striking: a dark blue jacket with five bullet holes in it and two photographs in color, close-ups of Robert Kennedy's skull, taken while he lay on the operating table of Good Samaritan Hospital.

Over Cooper's objections, Fitts passed the items to the jury. The pictures were not pretty. Kennedy's head was shaved, his nose was pressed into the table and a hand sheathed in a rubber glove was pointing to the hole where Sirhan's bullet had entered the brain. Some jurors studied the photos closely. Others handed them on quickly. None of them could have failed to touch the pictures without a sinking feeling in their hearts.

On the morning of February 20, yet another page 1 story on Sirhan's aborted guilty plea appeared in the Los Angeles *Times,* and Cooper, in chambers, moved again for a mistrial. "Well," said Judge Walker, "let me say that I gave some of that information out myself." He explained that the *Times* had gotten only part of the story in its edition of February 12. He wanted the *Times* to have "the other half," namely, that he, Walker, had turned down the plea with a promise of life, but agreed to a plea if the defendant would submit the matter of penalty directly to the jury. That wasn't exactly all of the "other half." Still unreported anywhere were Evelle Younger's words: "We can't conscientiously urge the death penalty . . . we don't think under any circumstances we would get the death penalty even if we urged it . . . we don't think we can justify the trial."

It was Cooper's position that the judge shouldn't have been talking to the press, and assigned it as judicial misconduct, renewing his demand for a mistrial on the same grounds as before: prejudicial publicity.

Judge Walker noted that the jury was sequestered. "I have checked with my bailiff," he said. "This paper hasn't been anywhere near the jury, isn't that right?"

"That is right," said Bailiff Willard Polhemus. Walker denied the motion.

But Compton took the opportunity to point out that certain members of the Eastern press—notably Bob Greene of *Newsday*—came out with the story before the L.A. *Times* went to press with it. And the D.A.'s office hadn't supplied Greene. "We shouldn't be singled out," said Compton, "as the sources for this information."

"Are you finished, Mr. Compton?" asked Cooper.

"Yes."

Cooper said that from his reading of the *Times*'s article, "it looked like it emanated from the D.A.'s office because Evelle Younger was quoted in the article. . . ."

"I may state this," said Judge Walker, "the story was given to me that your man, your investigator-writer, was the one that did it."

Cooper's voice took on an incredulous tone. "Kaiser?" he said. He laughed. I had been complaining that McCowan, Parsons and Berman had each been relaying Sirhan's private comments to the press in violation of my exclusive contract with Sirhan and the attorneys. I was the unlikeliest leak of all. In fact, my position inside and my reluctance to reveal anything at all to the press had already drawn the enmity of some reporters, most particularly of *The New York Times*'s Lacey Fosburgh, who found she could wheedle information out of everyone except me.

On February 24, the prosecution had Sergeant William E. Brandt on the stand. He was one of the officers who had discovered Sirhan's notebooks, and as David Fitts began leading up to the point where it was clear he would introduce the notebooks as evidence, Sirhan started whispering vehemently to Parsons. "Those notebooks are private," he said. "They're my property. The police had no right to take them. They had no search warrant."

Cooper asked for a recess. Judge Walker looked at the clock. It was 3:55 P.M. He simply called for adjournment and asked to see Cooper in chambers. Cooper went into the holding tank to see Sirhan, then went in and told Walker: "Our client wants to object to the notebooks." Walker only cleared his throat and scowled.

On the next morning, Sirhan came to court without a tie and jacket, stripped down, as it turned out, for action. He demanded to see the judge in chambers. The attorneys trooped in, and Sirhan was escorted in shortly by Deputies Davis and Torcaso. "Put out your cigarette, Sirhan," said Cooper sternly. "The court is in session." Sirhan crushed his Winston in an ashtry on the judge's desk. "Mr. Sirhan," said Cooper, "you wanted to make a statement?"

"Your Honor," said Sirhan, "if these notebooks are allowed in evidence, I will change my plea to guilty as charged. I will do so, sir, not so much that I want to be railroaded into the gas chamber, sir, but to deny you the pleasure, sir, of after having convicted me, turning around and telling the world, 'Well, I put that fellow in the gas chamber, but I first gave him a fair trial,' when you, in fact, sir, will not have done so. The evidence, sir, that was taken from my home was illegally obtained, was stolen by the district attorney's people. They had no search warrant. I did not give them permission, sir, to do what they did to my home. My brother Adel had no permission to give them permission to enter my own room and take what they took from my home, from my own room." It was a long speech for Sirhan, and Judge Walker, sitting there in his shirt sleeves and galluses, only raised a bushy eyebrow at Cooper.

Cooper suggested he and Sirhan have a private talk.

"No, sir," said Sirhan. "I am adamant on this point." Finally, Cooper persuaded him to go into the holding tank for a ten-minute chat. Then Cooper went back to Judge Walker's chambers and told the judge Sirhan would rather go to the gas chamber than see the notebooks introduced in court. Compton wondered if this wasn't some kind of act. Walker said he was convinced it wasn't and had Sirhan escorted in once more.

Now Walker was vested in his black judicial robes and he told Sirhan: "The court has ruled on the admissibility of this evidence. If there is error, the upper court can reverse this case."

"Yes," said Sirhan. "I understand."

Walker said Sirhan had three excellent attorneys. "They've been at this business for many years."

"I understand, sir," said Sirhan.

"—and I know them personally, at least two, for thirty years. I am not saying you are going to go to the gas chamber. You are not going to go to the gas chamber unless that is the determination of the jury, and even then I have an opportunity to set it aside, if it is warranted. Let me say this. Guide yourself by your attorneys. That is what they are here for. They are excellent, conscientious attorneys. They are doing you an excellent job."

"I understand that," said Sirhan.

"So keep that in mind before you come in here and say these things to the court," warned Walker.

"Well," said Sirhan, "I wanted to say it here because I didn't want to say it in court last night and I almost blew up."

"I know you did," said Walker, "and that is why we recessed early. I want you to understand that if you plead guilty, before I take a plea from you, I would examine you for at least twenty minutes. I have to, under the law. You understand that?"

"Yes," said Sirhan.

"I have it all worked out," said Walker. "Four pages of questions that I will ask you before I will even accept a plea and that is what the law requires. Now keep those things in mind." Walker rose. "Now, let's go to work."

Sirhan came out of chambers looking rather proud of himself. He smiled and laughed and waved to his mother and his brother sitting in the second row, and chatted with Parsons and McCowan. "Mike," he said, "you watch me. I am going to embarrass that judge yet. Publicly."

Over at the prosecution table, David Fitts thumbed through the pages of the notebooks he intended to offer in evidence, and when court resumed with Sergeant Brandt once more on the stand, he did offer two of Sirhan's notebooks as People's exhibits 71 and 72 for identification, and a small $3'' \times 5''$ notebook with only a few names therein as People's 73. Also a brown U.S. Treasury envelope with writing on it: "RFK must be disposed of like his brother was."

Fitts put another officer, James Evans, on the stand to affirm further that the notebooks were found in Sirhan's bedroom. On cross-examination, Cooper asked if Evans had a search warrant. He didn't. Did he find People's 72 lying on the floor? He did. Did it appear to be stolen property? It didn't. He didn't know the contents until he looked inside? He didn't. He knew where the defendant was at the time? He did. Did he go and ask the defendant's permission to take the notebook? He didn't.

Officer Thomas R. Young of Pasadena was assigned to guard the Sirhan home after the assassination. At 8:00 A.M. on June 6, he went through the Sirhan trash can out in the backyard and discovered another envelope from the Argonaut Insurance Company. It, too, had writing on it. The back of the envelope was covered with a kind of repetitive doodling: "RFK must be be be disposed of d d d disposed disposed d of disposed disposed of properly Robert Fitzgerald Kennedy must soon die die die die die die die die die die."

Then Fitts put on Laurence W. Sloan, the district attorney's handwriting expert, who had testified in court some 1,500 times since he began his career as a calligrapher in the late 1940's. He identified various documents as written in Sirhan's handwriting, including eight pages from the two large notebooks that Sirhan had objected to being introduced in court, and

Fitts offered them in evidence. At this point, Judge Walker sent the jury out of the courtroom to their waiting rooms on the ninth floor, and Cooper stood to lodge an objection. He admitted that four of the pages seemed relevant, pages 15, 35, 39, and 47 of People's 71. But he objected to pages 123, 124, 125 and 126 of People's 72. Pages 123 and 124 amounted to Sirhan's manifesto advocating "the overthrow of the current president of the fucken United States of America" (see Appendix C), and the second pair was a similar manifesto urging anarchy and the assassination of the President "who is your best friend until he gets in power then he is your most exploi[t]ing fucker suck every drop of blood out of you and then if he doesn't like you, you're dead."

Cooper said these were highly inflammatory, irrelevant and immaterial to the issues. The judge said he was inclined to agree with Cooper. Compton argued that the language was relevant: "The defendant, your Honor, has used a very colorful adjective to describe the United States—"

Sirhan stood up and shouted a warning to the judge: "Wait a minute, your Honor!" he cried. "It hasn't been admitted into evidence yet!" McCowan grabbed Sirhan and shoved him down in his chair. "Let me go! Let me go!" shouted Sirhan.

Judge Walker agreed with Cooper about pages 123 and 124. "The inflammatory nature of these documents far outweighs their probative value." He put the pages "in the record," but did not admit them in evidence. Compton soon clarified that. He wanted the judge's permission to give the disputed pages to the press. "I think in the interest of the nation and the public that they know this defendant's attitude and thinking about this country. Not that the jury is going to hear it, as the jury is not going to know. . . . The public should know what motive he had."

Fitts added an argument of his own. "This purports to be a little political dissertation. If Sirhan's so sick . . ." Fitts's voice trailed off but his implication was clear: how can he write such cogent material?

"Well," said Judge Walker, "I realize that the court cannot suppress anything from the press if they want to get it. It is a matter of record in the case and it will remain that and the press can deal with it accordingly. The record will note that the jury is sequestered in the tightest security. All papers are being censored, all radio and TV programs are being monitored." The manifestos had been effectively suppressed by court order since June 7. Now, Judge Walker was saying that the time had come to tell the world. It was another frank admission from Walker that the trial was being played to world opinion as much as, perhaps even more than, to the jury.

Cooper asked the court to admonish the prosecutor not to make known to the public "matters to which the court has sustained an objection in matters that are inflammatory and matters that are irrelevant." He suggested that the press could have the notebook after the trial. "There's nothing going to be withheld."

"The jury is locked up," said Walker dryly. And that took care of that. At the noon recess, Compton gave the press photostats of the pages in question, and Cooper, ever the politician with the press, handed out copies of his own. He wouldn't be outdone by Compton.

After lunch, moments after the afternoon session reconvened, David Fitts began to describe the notebooks' contents to the jury, which was now back in the courtroom. Sirhan promptly raised his left hand in an imperious gesture: "Your Honor, excuse me for interrupting—"

McCowan and the attorneys swooped down on Sirhan, the judge called a recess and Sirhan stalked off to the holding tank. For a half hour, the attorneys tried to reason with Sirhan, omitting to tell him for the time being that they themselves were determined to offer all the notebook pages in evidence, evidence of his sickness and his obsessions. Then they called Mary Sirhan and Munir.

"What? What? What is it?" asked Mary Sirhan. McCowan explained to her that Sirhan wanted to ask for the gas chamber. Maybe she could talk to him? She burst into sobs and McCowan ushered her and Munir into the holding tank. Mary Sirhan emerged in ten minutes, too choked to talk, even to the sympathetic fat man, Bob Greene. "They are throwing even the trash at him," she cried. Finally, the attorneys emerged and so did Sirhan, wiping the tears from his own eyes, somewhat subdued now. He made an effort to smile at a pleasantry offered by McCowan.

"If your Honor, please," said Berman, when the jury had reconvened, "the defense moves for a continuance until tomorrow morning at 9:30." Walker granted the motion. Cooper went out to tell the press that Sirhan was asking for the gas chamber. "Sirhan blew his top," Cooper told Val Clenard of KMPC, "but we're still running the case." And Berman sent me to a telephone to seek Dr. Diamond's advice.

Dr. Diamond, summoned from a class at Berkeley, was considerably less excited than the attorneys. "It's not so bad," said Diamond. "This only makes the defense theory that much more meaningful." As far as Diamond was concerned, the attorneys should let Sirhan blow his top—preferably in front of the jury. And stop babying him.

For months now, Parsons and McCowan had been soothing Sirhan and telling him the kind of lies one tells a spoiled five-year-old. Cooper wouldn't do that but neither would he stop Parsons and McCowan. Berman told Sirhan on this particular afternoon: "Stop pointing your finger like that! Put your goddamn finger down! It looks like you're aiming at the judge just like you aimed at Kennedy."

But it was Parsons who triggered Sirhan's outburst the next morning by handing Sirhan a list of tentative defense witnesses that I had prepared for him. "No, no, no," murmured Sirhan at the counsel table as proceedings began. He slashed at the list with a ball-point pen and hissed his objections to Parsons and turned to shoot angry glances at me. McCowan gave me a high sign and we met in the deserted corridor while the judge and jury poured over the six notebook pages that were admitted in evidence.

"What's bothering him now?" I asked.

"The witness list," said McCowan, with an idiotic smile.

"You're not serious."

"Yep," said McCowan, straightening his face. "Russ gave it to him."

I couldn't figure it. The witness memo I had written was intended for the attorneys, not for Sirhan. Why then did Parsons, who was trying so hard to keep Sirhan "calmed down," let him see it?

At the lunch hour, Sirhan waved the memo in Cooper's face. "You're not gonna call these witnesses," he said. The witness list was unexciting in itself and the witnesses' potential testimony would be inconclusive at best.

Cooper tried to reason with Sirhan. Sirhan was adamant. He did not want Prestwood called. Nor Peggy Osterkamp. Now Gwen Gumm. Nor the Strathmans. Nor Ivan Garcia. Nor Walter Crowe. Nor Tom Rathke. Nor any of the Rosicrucians. And who the hell was this mystery girl? *

"Lookit," said Cooper, "we need some of these witnesses to show your state of mind."

"This is political," insisted Sirhan. "Politically motivated."

---

* "The mystery girl" was a long-shot possibility. Aziz Shihab, a Palestinian Arab, an assistant city editor of the San Antonio *Express,* had written a little book called *Sirhan.* In it he presented a story that Sirhan had broken off an unhappy love affair in March, then met the girl by chance at the Ambassador on the night of June 4. It was the girl's rejection that night, wrote Shihab, that triggered Sirhan's psychotic break and his shooting of Kennedy. I was then phoning Shihab in Texas to see if he could or would reveal the identity of the girl. If Shihab's story were true, the girl would obviously be a key witness. For his own reasons, Shihab later declined to help Cooper find the girl. It is possible she was only conjured up by Shihab's sources in Los Angeles. Sirhan's brother Adel had broken up with a girl in March, 1968. But an understandable misidentification of Adel's girl as the one who rejected Sirhan, coupled with newspaper stories of a mysterious girl who was with Sirhan at the Ambassador, may have stimulated some overactive imaginations.

Cooper conceded that it was. But how did a childhood trauma suddenly erupt twenty years later in the Ambassador pantry? Sirhan shook his head. He couldn't see it. Cooper told him it didn't matter whether he could see it or not. He had to defer to his lawyers' judgment. "If we're going to proceed in the case," said Cooper, "we've got to call the witnesses we want. Otherwise, we'll have to withdraw from the case."

"If that's the way it is," said Sirhan, "that's the way it is."

Cooper went back down to the judge's chambers at 2:00 P.M. and, while Sirhan sat alone at the counsel table, reported to Judge Walker. "I don't see why this has to be on the record," Fitts complained.

"I can tell you why it's on the record," said Cooper. "As a result of this conflict with my client, I should ask to be relieved of the case, except. Except this. Believing as I do that he has diminished capacity—not that he's insane—I don't think he is in a position to exercise judgment and therefore I owe him a duty. But in view of the fact that he has blown up in the courtroom before, and, if we call these witnesses, he'll blow up again. I didn't hear him say this, but Mike said he said, 'By God, if you call these witnesses, I won't testify.' And we are left with egg all over our faces. Now, I want this defendant to know how I feel. I don't want him blowing up in the courtroom and ruining my case." It was a strange position for Cooper to take: On the one hand he was contending that Sirhan was too sick to have anything more than diminished responsibility for his crime, and at the same time expecting him to maintain control in the courtroom.

"I can appreciate that," said Judge Walker.

"And for that reason, I'm going to ask to be relieved and I want him to know I mean business and we will not have this behavior in the courtroom."

"I know that," said Walker. "I do too."

"I wanted to do it on the record."

"I could give him a lecture," said Walker, "but it hasn't done much good."

"It did some good," said Parsons, "because this morning he changed a little bit. He talked with Munir and then he shook hands with me and said he was sorry and asked me to apologize to Mr. Cooper. But I've been watching him like a hawk all morning."

"Several of us have," said Fitts dryly.

"I guess all of us have," said Parsons.

"Except me," said Berman. "I turn my back to him."

"I do, too," said Cooper.

"But in any event," said Parsons, "he has improved a little bit."

"Until this afternoon," said McCowan.

Berman pointed out that Sirhan was somewhat mollified by the way the six notebook pages were handled in court that morning. They were not read out loud but merely passed among the jurors. Apparently, Sirhan didn't want them read in his presence. "But in any event," said Berman, "let's go ahead. I don't see how we can get out of the case merely because the client is obstreperous."

"Let's go ahead today," agreed Walker.

They did go ahead. Sirhan sat there glumly while the prosecution ended its case with the testimonies of V. Faustin Bazilauskas, the doctor who had treated Senator Kennedy at Central Receiving, who turned out to be a salty and opinionated fellow whom Berman chose not to cross-examine; and Dr. Thomas D. Noguchi, the county coroner, who was ready to give all the goriest details until Cooper objected.

"I think this witness can express his opinion that death was due to a gunshot wound." said Cooper, "but all these details . . ."

Compton said that surely Cooper wasn't suggesting that he was limited to asking one question.

"Maybe you can omit some of these details," said Judge Walker, "without damaging the value of the doctor's testimony?"

Compton turned to Dr. Noguchi in obvious exasperation. "Doctor, did you find a gunshot wound in his head?"

"Yes."

"Where was it located?"

"Right in the mastoid area behind the right ear, sir."

Quickly then, Compton led Dr. Noguchi through the other essential details: the head wound was inflicted from a distance of one to two inches. Two other wounds were inflicted from farther away, both on an upward trajectory. Dr. Noguchi handed 123 additional photographs of the atuopsy to Compton, and the prosecution case was finished in midafternoon, February 26. It had taken exactly nine days.

Cooper asked the judge for Thursday and Friday to get his witnesses ready. He suggested the gentlemen of the press, too, could use a break, for they were tired. Walker said he wasn't worried about the press. He gave Cooper one day off and said the defense should begin its case on Friday, February 28, at 9:15 A.M.

Sirhan knew who had prepared the memo on the potential witnesses: Kaiser. He wanted to see me, and he wanted Abdeen Jabara too. Lieutenant

Carpenter set up a table for Sirhan, Jabara and me outside his cell, between a humming refrigerator and a chrome coffee warmer.

Sirhan insisted I turn off my tape recorder and then demanded immediately: "What the hell you writing about me in that book?"

"I haven't written a line yet," I said. "I've been busy working for you." That made Sirhan smile, somewhat pleased with the image of himself as employer. "What's bothering you?" I asked.

Sirhan accused me of fouling up his defense with extraneous witnesses he didn't want. Jabara took my side. He, too, had feared that the defense would not pay attention to the political ramifications of the case, but now he was persuaded otherwise. He had spent all day Sunday and two hours on Tuesday with Mary Sirhan, Parsons and McCowan, reviewing Sirhan's life in Jerusalem. "The other witnesses on that list are only incidental," said Jabara.

"Yeah, well, I don't want 'em. Fuck it. I want to plead guilty as charged and go to the gas chamber."

"You don't know what you're talking about," I said. "And stop acting like a baby."

My hard words made Sirhan meek for a moment. "I feel hemmed in," he said softly.

"Naturally," I said.

Sirhan was silent again. Finally he said, "I'm adamant. I'm gonna plead guilty. I'm gonna stop the trial." Then he rambled. He didn't want the trial to go on, but it wasn't because of his stated reason to Judge Walker that his "constitutional rights were violated," but rather because he was afraid of what the psychiatrists and psychologists would testify in court. He didn't want the doctors to say he was crazy.

"So you're going to plead guilty instead and go to the gas chamber? That isn't crazy?"

"I don't care," said Sirhan. "I'm adamant. I want to show up this judge. I want to prove to the world that you *can't* get a fair trial in America. This will really fuck up the Arabs and the U.S."

"Is that what you want?" I asked, flipping on my recorder.

"If that's what you want," said Jabara, "I don't want any part of it."

"Really," said Sirhan. "I don't know what to think. I'm—fucked up right now. I don't know what's going on."

I said if he didn't know he'd better take the advice of those he'd learned to trust.

"I'm resolute," said Sirhan. "They're not gonna shove that shit down my throat."

"Well," said Jabara, "the decision's yours. I—I—"

"I don't think it is his," I said. "I don't think he's got any control over the situation."

To tell Sirhan he didn't have control of the situation was the ultimate affront. He sputtered: "I—well—uh—that—wuh—wuh—wuh—with—"

"If you get up and plead guilty," I said, "the judge is gonna say, 'Sit down and listen to your attorneys.' "

"I don't fuckin' think so, Bob."

"You don't?"

"That FBI doesn't know everything. What if I said that? They'd wanta cop—they'd wanta say now—"

"Now you're talking."

"Now I'm talking. You're goddamn right. Now I'm talking."

"All right. If you've got more information—"

"What if I came up with something like that?"

"Then . . ." I paused. Was this the break I'd been waiting for? "Then you could stop the trial right now. That's the only way you could stop the trial."

"I don't have to—I don't have to substantiate it. That'd make it. That'd make 'em stop the whole thing."

I said his new information would have to be checked out. "But if you've got information about, maybe other persons—"

"No—"

"Then that's a horse of another color."

"Well," said Sirhan, "that's just one diversion I could use if I wanted to."

"Fine," I said, deeply disappointed that the moment of truth had not really arrived. "Use it. It would make better reading. Make my book just that much more sensational."

"Well, uh— That's what I don't want you to do in your book, Bob."

I laughed. "No, I want to write the truth."

"You want to write the truth, but I don't want you to write everything about the truth."

"Oh?"

"Seriously."

"Why not?"

"Because I don't know what you've written so far."

"You only want partial truth? Half truth?"

"Look—"

"What are you? Some kind of an abstraction?"

Sirhan chuckled and said to Jabara, "A great moralist here! No, seriously, Bob, I would like to read what you have written so far."

"You will be able to. I assure you of that. And you will be able to lodge all kinds of objections to what I have written."

"I would like to have some power to affect those lodge-ments."

"The power you have," I said, "is the power of your reasoning. If your reasoning is good, I'll follow it. If your information is good, I'll follow it. Whatever facts you have to overturn the impressions or opinions that I have, I'll change my opinions."

"You see," said Sirhan, "if you're going to express opinions, you're not talking about truth. That's what's—"

"In other words," I said, cutting Sirhan off in the middle of a point that was well taken, "we're reasoning beings, aren't we? And we give weight to reason?"

"Yes," admitted Sirhan.

Mike McCowan came into the area and sat down. He, too, tried to reason with Sirhan about the witnesses. "They're necessary," he said, "to establish a bridge between your childhood traumas and your current feelings."

Sirhan didn't buy that.

I said the list wasn't final.

McCowan corrected me. "It is. And if Sirhan insists they not go on, he's going to have to get some new attorneys."

"I'll be my own attorney," said Sirhan.

I laughed. "If you had appendicitis, would you try to take out your own appendix?"

A sly smile broke over Sirhan's face. "Hey, a Russian doctor did."

"But you're not a Russian doctor," I said.

"Nor an Arab lawyer," said McCowan.

Sirhan went back to my book again. He thought that the contract allowed him to censor it. I shook my head. Sirhan looked to McCowan. "I never read the contract," said McCowan.

"It was read to him in the cell here," I said, "in the presence of you and Mr. Parsons, was it not? Didn't you read it, line by line?"

"I wasn't here that day," said McCowan.

"You were not?"

"I was not here that day."

I turned to Sirhan. "He" —pointing at McCowan— "was not in the cell when Mr. Parsons read the agreement line by line?"

"I don't remember," said Sirhan.

"I wasn't here," insisted McCowan.

"You were," I said. "I've got a note on it."

"Well, I don't care whether you've got a note or not. I'm telling you right now, I wasn't here that fuckin' day."

"When the contract was read—to Sirhan?" The sheriff's log would show that Sirhan signed the contract on August 28 in the presence of Parsons and McCowan, who both remained in the interior cell with Sirhan from 12:42 P.M. to 1:24 P.M.

"Jesus Christ, I can't make it any plainer, Bob. I wasn't here." I waited—in vain—for a cock to crow.

"You see," said Sirhan, "that's what I don't understand. I asked Mr. Parsons . . . do I have the right to okay it and approve it and all that shit? And he said, 'It's all in the contract.' "

"I thought he had a copy of it in his cell," said McCowan. "To be honest with you."

"So I didn't have that. So that worries me."

I sighed, wondering now why McCowan was lying. "Well," I said to Sirhan, "everything worries you."

"Yeah, sure. But if you were in my shoes, Bob, wouldn't you be worried, too?"

"Yeah," I said, "but I didn't kill Kennedy."

"No." Sirhan paused and added in a light breathy tone: "Did I kill Kennedy?"

"I don't know," said McCowan acidly. "I'm still searching."

Sirhan wondered where he stood. I said I would make sure Sirhan got a copy of the contract. Then he would see that it was not Sirhan's book but mine, and that he didn't have any right "of approval."

"Then I guess I was misinformed by Mr. Parsons."

"It was read to you by Mr. Parsons, line by line, and you signed it."

"I was not—I was not in a—in a normal state of mind at the time. I was too excited."

I chuckled. "Really."

"What are you trying to tell Bob?" asked McCowan.

He said he wanted to make sure I wasn't writing some of the fanciful stuff written in a book called *Sirhan* by Aziz Shihab, which he called "shit."

"I didn't write that," I shouted. "One of your Palestinian Arabs wrote that."

"I'm too tired," said Sirhan. "Too fuckin' tired."

"Okay," said Jabara, "let's leave him."

I had one last word of advice. I urged Sirhan to keep as flexible as he could. A fixed idea—that was crazy. Being flexible was not crazy.

McCowan had his advice too. Sirhan had to follow his lawyers' plan. If he couldn't, he was finished. Lieutenant Carpenter set a paper cupful of coffee in front of Sirhan. Sirhan offered it to me. "Have some coffee, Bob?"

I regarded it with mock suspicion. "Will you taste it first?"

Thirteen

"Kennedy was doing a lot of things behind my back."

On Friday, February 28, the defense began its case at the beginning—
Jerusalem in 1948. Baron Sarkees Nahas, a U.S. citizen born in Jerusalem
and a former officer for UNRWA in Palestine, set the scene. He identified
certain key places on a large map of the city and described the ravages of
the Arab-Israeli conflict upon it. Then Ziad Hashimeh, a boyhood contemporary of Sirhan, from the same crowded apartment in Old Jerusalem (whom
Jabara had discovered living in Chicago), described the Sirhans as he knew
them. From Hashimeh came a story of Bishara Sirhan's cruelty that had
never come from the Sirhan family itself.

"Did you ever see Sirhan's father strike him?" asked Cooper.

"Oh, yes, quite a few times," said Hashimeh.

"I take it because he was a bad boy or something?"

"Well, no, the husband, the man was too emotional, you know?"

"Mr. Sirhan?"

"Mr. Sirhan. Yes, he used to be too emotional."

"How often did you see him strike Sirhan?"

"Well, I can't give you a specific answer. I tell you, I didn't count them
but quite a lot of times, quite a bit of times he beat him."

"Did he cry?"

"Yes."

"Did he strike him with his hand?"

"He used all sorts of sticks and hands."

"Well, would he strike him on the bottom?"

"Bottom, back, everywhere."

"And you say Sirhan did cry?"

"Yes. Yes."

Mary Sirhan sat in her second row seat, her neat little notebook full of her notes on the trial now forgotten, her face in her hands. This would be a terrible day for Mary Sirhan, a woman who had seen now a good many horrible days.

John T. Harris, an official for the Pasadena School District, took the stand to report on Sirhan's school records and the results of his various intelligence tests. When he took the Pintner Test for General Ability he was thirteen; he achieved a test level of eight years, eight months. He was fourteen years and ten months when he took the Terman-McNemar Test and scored a mental age of twelve years, eight months, with very low scores in verbal reasoning, abstract reasoning and the ability to see objects in three dimensions. At the age of seventeen he had an IQ on the Stanford Binet of 89, just under the normal range of 90–110.

During Harris' testimony, Sirhan shot smoldering looks at me and regarded two pretty girls sitting on my right with worried frowns. Finally, he turned to Parsons and demanded he ask the judge for a recess. He wanted to talk to the judge in chambers. Parsons approached the bench and Cooper followed. "He will not talk to me in chambers," said Judge Walker.

"I told him I didn't think it was possible," said Parsons.

Wearily, Cooper said, "Do you want to excuse the jury now and have this out in open court? We have to face this sometime."

"Yes, why don't we do it now and get it over with?" said Walker. He gave the jury his usual admonishment and retired them to the jury room.

Cooper went back to the counsel table and said that Sirhan had objected to his calling this witness, approximately a dozen witnesses, in fact, whom he felt had relevant testimony to give. He started to speak for Sirhan, then stopped and said he would let him speak for himself.

"There was something you wanted to say?" asked Walker.

"May I address the court in chambers, sir?"

"No."

Struggling to keep control, Sirhan held on to the arms of his chair and said: "I, at this time, sir, withdraw my original pleas of not guilty and submit the plea of guilty as charged on all counts. I also request that my counsel disassociate themselves from this case completely."

"Do I understand—stand up. Do I understand," said Judge Walker, "that you want to plead guilty to murder in the first degree?"

"Yes, sir, I do."

"All right, and what do you want to do about the penalty?"

"I will offer no defense whatsoever."

Three wire-service men in the courtroom sat there in agony, trying to scribble the unbelievable words they were hearing, and watch Sirhan and each other at the same time. Finally, Reuters broke for the door and the AP and the UPI, not to be scooped, followed.

"The question is," said Judge Walker, "what do you want to do about the penalty?"

"I will ask to be executed, sir," said Sirhan.

"Now, I know of nothing in the law that permits a defendant under any circumstances to enter a plea of guilty to murder of the first degree and ask for execution," said Walker.

"Well, I have, sir."

"Well, now, just a minute. Why do you want to do this?"

"I believe, sir, that is my business, isn't it?"

"You just believe it is your business?"

"That is my prerogative."

"No, it isn't. Now, when we come to accepting a plea, you have to give me a reason."

"I killed Robert F. Kennedy willfully, premeditatedly, with twenty years of malice aforethought, that is why."

"Well, the evidence has to be produced here in court."

"I withdraw all evidence, sir."

"There is no such procedure."

"To hell with it."

"Well, the court will not accept the plea. Proceed with the trial. Let me give you to understand here and now that this court will not put up with any more of your interrupting. You are to follow the advice of the court and just sit down there. Any further interruptions by you in this trial will result in you being restrained. You understand that?"

"Sir?"

"I mean by that that you will have a face mask put on you which will prohibit you from talking and, further, your arms will be strapped to your chair and the trial will proceed. You understand that?"

"I understand. However, sir, I intend to defend myself *pro per*. I don't want to be represented by these counsel."

"You have retained counsel. Counsel is staying in the trial."

"What I have said, I don't want anyone to have a trial shoved down my throat, sir, and you are not going to shove it down my throat, sir, in any way you want."

"You say you want to go *pro per*?"

"Yes, I will."

"What are the defenses; let me ask what are the elements of the crime of murder?"

"Sir, I don't know. I don't understand all of this legality. You let me—"

"I am conducting these proceedings, not you. What are the defenses to murder in the first degree?"

"I don't know."

"I find you are incapable of representing yourself. Sit down and keep quiet, and, if not, I intend to keep you quiet." Some two dozen members of the press trooped out to phone their news desks.

Sirhan was still adamant. "No, sir, I still maintain my original point. I plead guilty to murder and ask to be executed."

"I thought I made it clear. The court will not accept the plea."

"I am sorry. I will not accept it."

"The law tells me what I can do and cannot do," said Walker. "Now, you understand from here on out you keep quiet, and if not, I will see to it that you are kept quiet."

"I am sorry, but my original position stands."

"Get the jury down."

"Why not let me go into chambers? I insist."

"You are not going to go in chambers. I let you go in there once and that was the beginning and the end. That procedure is over as far as I am concerned. We will proceed with the trial. Again, I will tell you to keep quiet and consult with your attorneys." Walker took an afternoon recess.

In the holding tank, Sirhan was puffing furiously on an L & M, and Cooper was telling Sirhan he'd be glad to get out of the case but he didn't think the court would let him. Cooper left to talk to the judge as Deputy Joe Torcaso brought a yellow calfskin muzzle and some leather straps into the holding tank. "You see that?" I said. "That's for you. You don't want that, do you? That's demeaning."

"I told you not to bring those two girls in here," screamed Sirhan. It was not so much the revelation of his IQ of 89 that triggered Sirhan's rage. Somehow it was the presence of two girls who had nothing to do with the case.

"Who are you talking about?" I asked.

"Those two girls sitting next to you."

"Who *are* they?"

"As if you didn't know!" cried Sirhan. "One of them is Gwen Gumm and the other is Peggy Osterkamp."

I was dumbfounded. Miss Gumm had visited Cooper's office only the day before. I told him neither of the two ladies was Miss Gumm. Sirhan called me a liar. One was Peggy Osterkamp and the other was Gwen Gumm, said Sirhan, forcing me to judge that Sirhan was in a kind of paranoid, dissociated state there and then. I went back out to the courtroom and asked the two girls for their identification. One was Sharon Karaalajich, a clerk-typist for the Los Angeles Police Department, and the other was Karen Adams, a beautician from Columbus, Ohio, who was visiting her sister in Los Angeles.

I printed the girls' names on a sheet of notebook paper and handed it to McCowan as the attorneys readied themselves for the next round. McCowan put his arm around Sirhan and showed him the note. Sirhan read it, looked back at the girls and shook his head furiously. He wouldn't be fooled.

Judge Walker returned to the bench. The jury was still out. Cooper rose. Cooper told Walker that Sirhan had advised him "definitely, positively and unequivocally that he does not desire us to continue to represent him. None of us," said Cooper, "have any desire to continue representing a client who does not desire our services. I think I should state this into the record historically. We were asked to represent him, and each one of us has volunteered our services without compensation, and we feel that with the work that each one of us has done, including two investigators who have worked long hours month on month on end, we have prepared what we feel, based upon the facts and the law, is a legitimate defense of diminished responsibility. So this record may be perfectly clear further, your Honor, the defendant has sufficient capacity to cooperate with his counsel. We can converse with him, and it isn't that we cannot make ourselves understood to him. It is just that there is a very violent difference of opinion as to how the defense should be conducted. Now, all of us, having had some years at the bar in criminal cases, cannot allow a defendant to run the lawsuit. And so long as I am counsel, I am not going to let a client run the lawsuit. I am perfectly willing, . . . I might say anxious to withdraw from the case and let him either represent himself or be represented by another counsel. I hasten to add this. Neither one of us wants to desert him. We are still willing, if your Honor please, to represent him as conscientiously as we know how. With that, I must leave it up to the court."

Walker said, "I know of no law that permits counsel to withdraw in the middle of proceedings except for good cause. I have examined the law and I don't feel that this situation has good cause. Are you gentlemen willing to proceed in the defense?"

"Yes, your Honor, please, if you desire, we will," said Cooper "I don't

want it misunderstood that we are deserting him, your Honor. I just
wanted to make our position clear to him."

"Well, I appreciate your position," said Walker. "I think you have prepared a good defense, if not the only logical defense that could be presented."

"We are prepared and we will go forward."

"All right. We will proceed," said Walker.

Cooper finished quickly with Harris, the administrator from the Pasadena schools, and Parsons called Mary Sirhan to the stand. Still blinking
back tears after all this, she climbed into the witness box, a tiny figure in a
black suit embroidered with gold.

"You are the mother of Sirhan Bishara Sirhan?" asked Parsons.

"Yes." Her voice was small and quavering, and she looked down stol-
idly.

"When was he born?"

"He was born in 1944. March."

"March, 1944?"

"Yes."

"And where was he born?"

"In the city of Jerusalem."

"Were you living in Jerusalem at the time?"

"Yes."

"And how long had you lived in Jerusalem before he was born?"

Mary Sirhan looked as if she were about to burst into tears. "Well—I'd
say thousands of years. My family—from generation from generation from
generation." Now people in the courtroom started to weep.

Parsons turned to the map behind her. "Does this bring home to you
that this is a pretty fair representation of the city of Jerusalem?"

"Yes," said Mrs. Sirhan. "The City of Peace." Her voice started to
break, but Parsons continued.

"Is that what you call Jerusalem?"

"Yes, all over the whole world, the City of Peace." Now she started to
sob. "Please don't mind me if I look this way."

"Well, do your best," said Parsons. Sirhan sat in his seat thoughtfully,
pushing his right thumb into his upper teeth. Then he started to smile.

Cooper asked to approach the bench. "She didn't want to go on this afternoon, your Honor."

Walker understood and took a recess until Monday. After the jurors
left the courtroom, Walker said that he was sure the newsmen understood
why he'd called the recess. "But in case there's any question in your

minds, I can't conceive of any worse circumstances under which a mother could be called to the stand and I think she showed great courage."

The attorneys filed out quickly, hardly eager to comment on the day's events. The press was loath to ask them. It was a lugubrious afternoon, made gloomier by another drenching thunderstorm, just one of many that would make this the rainiest Southern California winter since 1887.

On the next day, Saturday, March 1, Dr. Diamond flew down from San Francisco for another talk with Berman, for it would be Berman's task to examine the medical witnesses and tie their testimony to the current decisions of the California Supreme Court on diminished capacity.

Berman thought it would be simple enough to examine Diamond. All he needed to do, he said, was prepare the right "wrap-up question." He tried one out on Diamond: "Do you have an opinion because of mental illness and emotional disorder, Sirhan did not have, and lacked the capacity to have, the mental states for deliberation, premeditation and malice?"

"Well," said Diamond, "the answer to that question is 'no.' But it isn't going to do you any good, Zuke, if Pollack gets up and says, 'Yes, Sirhan did have the capacity to do this.' What you're going to have to prove is that Pollack is using the wrong criteria in deciding this question. This isn't going to be an easy thing because Pollack is very shrewd. That's why I want you to go over these decisions."

Diamond then launched into a three-hour seminar on the historical development of diminished capacity in California. He went through all the significant cases of the last twenty years: *Wells, Gorshen, Wolff, Conley, Goedecke, Nicolaus, Bassett* and *Castillo,* showing the court's advanced acceptance of psychiatric factors that lessen (but do not exculpate) criminal responsibility for murder.

Diamond helped in the appeal for Wesley Robert Wells, a prisoner at San Quentin who conked a guard in the head with a heavy cuspidor and was given a mandatory death penalty when he was convicted of assault with malice aforethought. Wells's lawyer, Charles Garry, argued before the California Supreme Court that the trial judge shouldn't have excluded the testimony of the prison psychiatrist who was ready to swear that Wells was suffering from "a state of tension." If the doctor had testified, Garry reasoned, the jury might have acquitted Wells. The California Supreme Court ruled that the trial judge erred by excluding the doctor's testimony and that began a new page in the history of psychiatry and the courtroom. To help Garry back up his claim that psychiatric testimony was relevant to determining the man's mental state, especially on the question of malice, Diamond did some research on the question, and found, to his surprise, that malice aforethought, as defined by modern courts, had nothing to do with forethought and very little to do with malice, but rather with a conscious act of free will. Diamond wrote his conclusions in an article for the *Archives of Criminal Psychodynamics:* if by reason of mental illness an individual is not capable of making a free-will decision, he is not capable of malice.

The California Supreme Court cited the article in 1959 in its second significant decision on diminished capacity, *People* vs. *Gorshen*. By chance, Diamond was the psychiatrist to testify at this trial that Nicholas Gorshen, a San Francisco longshoreman, shot and killed his pier boss, Red O'Leary, with neither premeditation nor malice—even though Gorshen had announced to everyone on the dock that he was going home to get his gun and kill O'Leary, went home, got his gun, came back and killed him— with policemen standing at each elbow. Gorshen wasn't insane, but he was a chronic paranoid schizophrenic (Diamond testified) who committed the crime to prevent himself from going insane. The judge decided Gorshen was guilty of second-degree murder. "It would be a perfect first degree," he said, "if it wasn't for the fact that he was never in trouble and because of the statement of the psychiatrist." The California Supreme Court affirmed that verdict. Gorshen could not, and therefore did not, deliberate.

The law, like most human institutions, evolves. In 1964 the California Supreme Court amplified its Gorshen decision in the case of *People* vs. *Wolff*.

Ronald Dennis Wolff, a fifteen-year-old diagnosed as "schizophrenic," killed his mother with an ax handle so he could be free to bring girls home, rape them and/or take their pictures in the nude. He planned the murder ahead of time, hid the ax handle under his pillow and afterward turned himself in to the police, evidence that he knew what he did was wrong. But in analyzing the case, the California Supreme Court said:

> . . . there is no question that the defendant had the intent to kill; but the mental infirmity of this defendant presents a very serious factual problem as to the quantum of his personal turpitude and depravity as inherently related to the degree of murder . . . In the case now at bench, in the light of defendant's youth and undisputed mental illness . . . the true test must include consideration of the somewhat limited extent to which this defendant could *maturely and meaningfully reflect* upon the gravity of his contemplated act. . . . Certainly, in the case now at bench, the defendant had ample *time* for any normal person to maturely and appreciatively reflect upon his contem-

plated act and to arrive at a cold, deliberated and premeditated conclusion. He did this—in a sense—and apparently to the full extent of which he was capable. But, indisputably on the record, this defendant was not and is not a fully normal or mature, mentally well person. He knew the difference between right and wrong; he knew that the intended act was wrong and nevertheless carried it out. But the extent of his understanding, reflection upon it and its consequences, with realization of the enormity of the evil, appears to have been materially . . . vague and detached.

The court reversed Wolff's conviction for first-degree murder and reduced it to second degree. In effect, the court redefined "premeditation."

Sirhan, too, could premeditate, said Diamond, but only in a sense. Like Wolff, he "was not and is not a fully normal or mature, mentally well person." Without that capacity to premeditate, Sirhan could be convicted of no more than second-degree murder.

Furthermore, he probably didn't have malice either, in the sense now defined by the Supreme Court in the case of Junior Lee Conley. In *Conley,* the court said that a man acts with malice when

. . . with wanton disregard for human life, [he] does an act that involves a high degree of probability that it will result in death . . . If, because of mental defect, disease, or intoxication, however, the defendant is unable to comprehend his duty to govern his actions in accord with the duty imposed by law, he does not act with malice aforethought and cannot be guilty of murder in the first degree.

The court then cited the *Gorshen* case as an example of what it meant, even amplifying the significance of *Gorshen* beyond its original decision in the case.

The situation of an individual who kills with intent, deliberation, and premeditation, but without malice aforethought is illustrated by the evidence in the *Gorshen* case. Had the trial court in that case believed the defendant's testimony, it might have concluded that he acted without malice when, after an altercation with his foreman and after consuming a large quantity of alcohol, he went to his home, got his pistol, fired a shot in his living room, drove back to his place of employment, and then after being searched by two police officers (who did not find his gun) and while still in their company shot the foreman. The psychiatric expert urged that because of personality disintegration and paranoic schizophrenia the defendant believed the act necessary to prevent his own insanity and that the defendant was incapable of having the "mental state which is required for malice aforethought, or premeditation or anything which implies intention, deliberation, or premeditation." [*People vs. Gorshen, supra,* 51 Cal. 2d 716,723.] The defendant had testified that he had forgotten about "God's laws and human's laws and everything else." [Id.] Confronted with this evidence, the court or a jury could conclude that the defendant killed intentionally, with premeditation and deliberation, but did not do so with malice aforethought. Although legally sane according to the M'Naughton test, such a defendant could not be convicted of murder if mental illness prevented his acting with malice aforethought.

A year later, in *People* vs. *Goedecke,* the Supreme Court reduced a first-degree murder conviction, with a death penalty attached, to second degree. According to the court, Raymond Henry Goedecke, who was eighteen when he killed his father, mother, brother and sister, "was not a mentally and emotionally normal individual." The court's reasoning was the same as in *Wolff:* Goedecke knew the difference between right and wrong, but

the extent of his understanding, his reflection upon it, and its consequences, with realization of the enormity of the evil, was materially vague and detached and fell short of the minimum essential elements of first degree murder, especially in respect to the quantum of reflection, comprehension and turpitude of the offender. Here, the defendant was so precariously balanced on the edge of insanity that in the few seconds following his inflicting of mortal wounds upon his father, the jury found him to have plummeted into insanity so that the continuing rain of blows upon the three remaining members of his family was found to have been delivered by him while insane.*

If Sirhan's attorneys wanted to play safe by tailoring the defense to fit even the more stringent guidelines of Justice Mosk, they would have to do more than make a showing of Sirhan's mental illness; they would have to show that Sirhan's particular canted view of reality had everything to do with his shooting Kennedy. In the trial, Dr. Pollack would obviously lean on Mosk's minority opinion.

In *People* vs. *Nicolaus,* the Supreme Court also reversed a first-degree

---

* Justices Stanley Mosk and Marshall McComb dissented, however, from the majority, pointing out that no one had disputed the extent of Wolff's schizophrenia, while there was a serious conflict among the experts regarding the extent of Goedecke's mental illness and, moreover, other strong evidence that his murder was "studiously planned and executed." Goedecke had thrown police off the scent by disarranging the house to simulate a burglary, disposing of the knife he had used and feigning shock when he discovered his victim's bodies "—all in marked contrast to the prompt and meek surrender of the defendant in *Wolff.*" Wrote Mosk: "Reliance upon *Wolff* should not be employed to absolve an emotionally unstable parricide from guilt of first-degree murder where the evidence supports the judgment. As we said in *Wolff* on the sanity issue, 'to accept defendant's thesis would be tantamount to creating by judicial fiat a new defense plea of "not guilty by reason of schizophrenia." To do so . . . would be bad law and apparently still worse medicine.' "

murder conviction, with a penalty of death, to second degree. Reason: Robert Henry Nicolaus, who had killed his three children by shooting them each in the head several times to keep them from growing up in what he called an immoral environment, "was not a normal person either mentally or emotionally." There was some psychiatric conflict over this judgment at the trial. But the court found significant omissions in the testimony of the prosecution psychiatrist. One of those who said Nicolaus was not mentally ill failed to make "any references to defendant's previous bizarre and abnormal conduct given in detail in the histories relied upon by the defense psychiatrist." Furthermore, said the court, "Both prosecution psychiatrists were of the view that defendant could and did deliberate and premeditate the killings, but neither expressed an opinion as to the extent of defendant's ability to maturely and meaningfully reflect upon the gravity of his contemplated act."

Again, in August, 1968, the Supreme Court reduced the first-degree murder conviction of Fred Kipp Bassett on the same grounds. Bassett, who was eighteen when he methodically executed his mother and father and exulted as they lay dying because "all crumbs deserve to die," was diagnosed as a paranoid schizophrenic caught in the grip of a complicated delusional system. "The evidence is overwhelming," said the court, "that while he planned the parricide with precision and knew that it was wrong, his diminished mental capacity was such that he could not maturely and meaningfully reflect upon the gravity of his contemplated acts." Almost wearily, the court said, in a unanimous decision written by Justice Mosk,

> In these circumstances we must once again shoulder the burden of dissecting a lengthy record and weighing the "substantiality" of the prosecution's evidence of mental capacity. [The court referred here to *Goedecke* and *Nicolaus*.] This is a responsibility we are empowered by statute to perform, and we will not hesitate to act, as here, to prevent a grave miscarriage of justice.

The court reviewed the prosecution's case-in-chief and the case for the defense—a showing of the defendant's mental illness, which precluded his capacity for premeditation. If the case had gone to the jury on that evidence alone and had resulted in verdicts of murder in the first degree, the court "would have been compelled to find it insufficient under the authority of *People* vs. *Wolff.* . . . To forestall such a ruling, the prosecution undertook to create a 'conflict' in the psychiatric evidence . . ." and produced "testimony from various non-expert witnesses that defendant appeared normal."

The court dismissed the substantiality of the nonexpert witnesses in a footnote: "a person can suffer from paranoid schizophrenia for a long time without his illness being detectable by untrained, lay observers." It also attacked the substantiality of the evidence offered by the prosecution psychiatrists.

> There is no doubt that their *conclusions* were so phrased as to support the jury's implied finding of mental capacity . . . But . . . a man's life, in our system of justice, cannot be made to depend on whether or not the witnesses against him correctly recite by rote a certain ritual formula . . . In the case at bar, therefore, we cannot call a halt to our inquiry merely because the prosecution's experts uttered the "correct" words; we must press on, and determine the substantiality of the proof which that testimony purported to represent.

The court took a closer look at the facts and reasons given by the psychiatric witnesses who found Bassett did not have diminished capacity and rejected each of them. Two doctors did not examine the defendant at all and gave "no reasons whatever for their conclusions." Such an opinion was "no better than the reasons upon which it is based." A third doctor (Marcus Crahan) testified that Bassett was "legally insane" at the time of the crime but that he did have the capacity to premeditate and deliberate, to reflect maturely and meaningfully on the gravity of his contemplated act and to harbor "malice aforethought." The only inference the court could draw—"however reluctantly"—was that Dr. Crahan was misled concerning the meaning of the crucial term "premeditation."

> Whatever that word may have signified prior to our *Wolff* decision, we there made it clear that the true test in this regard is not simply an adequate time to deliberate, or a manifest intent to kill, or even an abstract appearance of "rationality" in the defendant's planning, but rather the depth of his appreciation of the "enormity of the evil" he proposes to commit. If, as Dr. Crahan testified, defendant was so insane that he could not understand the "nature and quality" of his contemplated act, it follows *a fortiori* that he could not "maturely and meaningfully reflect" upon its gravity. We conclude that testimony which purports to maintain two such self-contradictory propositions cannot be deemed "substantial" proof of either.
>
> When the foundation of an expert's testimony is determined to be inadequate as a matter of law, we are not bound by an apparent conflict in the evidence created by his bare conclusions.

It was on precisely this basis that Diamond knew Pollack to be most vulnerable. Pollack didn't understand the law and a proper cross-examination would make that abundantly clear. He tended to confuse the specific intent to kill with "premeditation" as defined in *Wolff*. He equated malice with "clear purpose," failing to understand that "malice" as defined in *Conley* implied a reasoned act by a person of sound mind.

Did Sirhan have a sound mind? Pollack didn't seem to think so. Diamond referred to Pollack's February 5 report to Evelle Younger, which had been handed over to the defense the day before. Pollack called Sirhan psychotic. That, coupled with Pollack's conception of the law, Diamond said, was good enough to get a favorable verdict from the Supreme Court (though he had his doubts whether it would mean much to the jury or to Judge Walker).

Berman studied Pollack's report. It seemed that Pollack couldn't make up his mind. Though he called Sirhan "psychotic" and a "borderline schizophrenic with paranoid and hysterical features," his paranoia had nothing to do with killing Kennedy. "In other words," said Berman in a comic paraphrase of Pollack, "he can think pretty good about killing, but, generally speaking, he's a nut!"

Over in the District Attorney's office, David Fitts and John Howard studied Pollack's report. "He contradicts himself, " said Fitts. "He's consistently inconsistent." Fitts and Howard wondered bleakly how they might keep Pollack off the stand. The trouble was, if they didn't call him, they knew Cooper would.

On Sunday, March 2, the psychiatrists and the psychologists for the defense met again in Cooper's office. Berman had planned to begin with Dr. Richardson and end up with Dr. Diamond. But Dr. Schorr objected. He wanted to be the lead-off batter and let the others move him around the bases and across the plate with the first score for the defense. Berman was inclined to squelch Schorr's ambition. But Richardson said it didn't matter to him; if Schorr wanted to begin, okay.

Baron Sarkees Nahas arrived at Cooper's office with Ambassador Issa Nahkleh, director of the Palestinian Arab delegation (which maintains a diplomatic presence, but no vote) at the United Nations, a dark, courtly gentleman, who had come from New York to observe the latter stages of the trial. Cooper took Nahkleh up to the Hall of Justice to see Sirhan, urging Nahkleh to help Sirhan cooperate with his lawyers. Nahkleh asked Sirhan what seemed to be troubling him. Sirhan told Nahkleh that he didn't want certain witnesses called. Why not? Sirhan was less than coherent here and Nahkleh tried to reason with him. In the back and forth, Nahkleh, the ambassador, found a diplomatic compromise. Would Sirhan cooperate if the lawyers crossed only the two girls off the witness list? Was that agreeable to Cooper? It was. Was it agreeable to Sirhan? It was.

Then Diamond, with McCowan and me, arrived at the cell at Cooper's request so he could demonstrate to Nahkleh what Sirhan was like under hypnosis. Diamond soon had Sirhan weeping and moaning, traumatized anew with a suggestion he think about the war in Jerusalem—something that was so painful to Nahkleh that he was soon demanding Diamond pull Sirhan out of the trance. Diamond wanted to demonstrate a couple of other phenomena about Sirhan: that under hypnosis he was an adept at automatic writing and that he could be programmed to do certain things after he came out of his hypnotic state. Diamond suggested that Sirhan come out of his trance and sing an Arab song when Diamond took his handkerchief out of his pocket.

Soon Sirhan was humming a tune by Om Kolthoum. The group enjoyed that little display. But the man Diamond wanted to impress the most, Grant Cooper, was positively uninterested in Diamond's hypnotic tricks and spent most of the interview talking to one of the deputies nearby. Cooper had already made up his mind that he didn't need any farfetched trance theory to save Sirhan's life. Sirhan had a mental illness—a political paranoia—that had some influence on his killing Kennedy, and that was enough.

Diamond knew he didn't need a trance theory either. But he was convinced that Sirhan was in a trance when he killed Kennedy. Was he supposed to cast aside an adequate explanation for the crime merely because it was fantastic?

On Monday, March 3, Russell Parsons ran Mrs. Mary Sirhan through her story. It was the seventh time she had told it and by now it was beginning to sound a little rehearsed. After the midmorning recess, Cooper introduced Issa Nahkleh to the court. He was a member of the English bar, said Cooper, admitted to practice at Lincoln's Inn and also a member of the Palestinian bar. Cooper moved his admission into the case for the duration of his stay in Los Angeles, where he had come to observe and advise. Judge Walker granted the motion and McCowan and Berman edged over to make room for Nahkleh at the counsel table. Berman fumed. He hadn't counted on working together with the director of the Palestinian Arab delegation at the United Nations.

Adel Sirhan took the stand. He testified that Sirhan had changed somewhat after his fall from the horse, that he spent a good deal of time alone in his room, that he became increasingly morose and angry over the news reports emanating from the Middle East.

On cross-examination, David Fitts tried to break down the picture of a Jerusalem in constant siege. There were periods of relative tranquillity when life went on normally, were there not? asked Fitts.

"I wouldn't call it normal," said Adel.

"Didn't Sirhan go to school every day, often unaccompanied?" asked Fitts.

"Not too often," said Adel.

"Didn't you go to soccer games," asked Fitts, "to take your mind off the horrors of war?"

"Nothing could take my mind off war, sir, but that particular soccer field was so far in Arab territory you'd feel safe if you went there."

"Was it unsafe to walk around the walls?" asked Fitts. Adel said that it was. Fitts said, "You wouldn't believe it if I told you I walked around the wall in February, 1951, would you?"

"No, sir," said Adel. "Fear was planted in me by the war. It was still there when I left."

Irvin G. Lewis, the administrative dean for student personnel services at Pasadena City College, took the stand to give Sirhan's record at PCC. He entered in September, 1963, got one F in ballroom dancing, a C in Russian, a C in basic communication, and four D's during his first semester. He got five C's and an F in his second semester. In his third semester, he got a C in Russian, and four D's. In the fourth semester at PCC, he had five F's when he was dismissed on May 18, prior to the end of the semester, for poor attendance.

At the recess, Cooper went into the holding tank to remind Sirhan of his promise. He wouldn't call Gwen Gumm and Peggy Osterkamp as witnesses, and Sirhan would cooperate while he was on the stand. It was an important element in the defense strategy for Sirhan to put his own self-image on the record, if not for the jury, at least for the Supreme Court. It wouldn't help much if Sirhan simply told the jury he wanted to go to the gas chamber, as Cooper suspected he might do even now as he was about to take the stand.

The deal suited Sirhan. He enjoyed the illusion that he was running the case now, and keeping those girls off the stand was something he had intended to insist on. He told Cooper he'd be good. At 3:05 P.M., Sirhan took the stand in his own behalf, after another oath with clenched fist. His voice was weak and he smiled nervously. "Did you shoot Robert F. Kennedy?" asked Grant Cooper.

"Yes, sir," said Sirhan. His hands were flat on the counter in front of him and he sat on the edge of his chair. Then he fiddled with a cord in his left hand.

"Did you bear any ill will toward Senator Kennedy?"

"No."

"Do you doubt you shot him?"

"No, sir, I don't."

Cooper picked up People's exhibit 71-15 and read " 'May 18 9:45 A.M. 68 my determination to eliminate R.F.K. is becoming more the more of an unshakeable obsession. . . .' Did you write that?" asked Cooper.

"Yes, I did," said Sirhan. "That is my handwriting."

Cooper read the page all the way through to the end. " 'RFK must die RFK must be killed Robert F. Kennedy must be assassinated before 5 June 68 Robert F. Kennedy must be assassinated I have never heard please pay to the order of of of of of of of of of of of of this or that.' " For some reason, Sirhan smiled. One of the air conditioners started to flutter. Clacketty-clacketty-clacketty-clack.

Cooper took Sirhan back to the age of four to see what he recalled of his boyhood. Sirhan recalled the life of a refugee, the ration cards, the food lines. "It was pretty damn cold," said Sirhan.

"Pardon me," said Cooper sternly. "You watch your language, Sirhan."

Sirhan remembered being sickened when he had drawn some water from a well and brought up a human hand in the bucket. What else did he remember? He remembered a military outpost at the Zion gate where the Arabs were in control of the city wall, and an Arab soldier had let him look at the Jewish part of the city through his large binoculars. " 'That's our land out there, our land,' the soldier told me," said Sirhan. "I didn't understand what he meant, but now I understand."

Judge Walker adjourned court for the day.

The next morning on the stand, Sirhan relaxed his grip on the counter in front of him. He sat back a little in his chair and fiddled less with the cord to the microphone around his neck. Surprisingly, he described to the court and the world what he'd previously insisted telling Diamond and Pollack "off the record": his experiments with the occult. He talked about the books he had bought and the books he browsed in at Broughton's, and he told of his experiments with candles and mirrors and his powers of thought transference, citing the time he had forced his mother, with his concentration alone, to get up and go to the bathroom, and the time he had used his mental powers to run Bert Altfillisch's horse into the rail in a race at Hollywood Park.

This was a new Sirhan, keen now instead of diffident, seizing the forum he had made for himself and making the most of it. Cooper asked him what he knew about the history of the Arab-Israeli conflict. Sirhan launched into an impassioned discourse on the growth of Zionism under Theodor Herzl and Chaim Weizmann. He faltered for a moment, said, "I'm too nervous," took a proffered drink of water, gathered his thoughts and then raced ahead with a coherent, surprisingly articulate lecture on the Arab-Israeli conflict. He told of the deals England had made with the Zionists and with France, and he unreeled a string of statistics about the "Zionist take-over" in the Middle East after the immigration or importation of European Jews into Palestine. It was a recitation that amazed the reporters who had, up to this point, seen Sirhan in terms of an 89 IQ.

"What impact on me, sir? I had no country, no place I could call my own. I was sick and tired of being a foreigner, of being alone. I wanted a place of my own where they speak my own language, eat my own food, share my own politics and my own—something I could identify as Arab, a Palestinian Arab." * Sirhan's face became flushed and his fist pounded lightly on the counter in front of him. "I wanted my own country, my own city, my own land, my own business. I wanted my own everything, sir." Sirhan spoke without interruption for almost twenty minutes. He recalled that he had seen photographs of Israeli soldiers standing on the banks of the Suez Canal at the end of the Six-Day War and became enraged. "If I had seen those guys personally, I would have blasted them . . . I would have killed them." He learned that soon after the war, American Jews sent $370 million to aid Israel. "It burned the hell outta me. I said, 'What gives?' The goddamned Zionists picked up millions of dollars and sent it out the back door to another country. What gives? I was unemployed. I didn't have a job. What gives?"

Benjamin Glick smiled in the jury box and shook his head in disbelief, and the judge adjourned for lunch. Berman avoided Cooper's usual noontime confab in the elegance of the Pavilion of the Music Center and had lunch with McCowan at the Redwood Room. "I'm going to withdraw from the case," said Berman. No one, he said, had told him that an Arab lawyer would be sitting with him at the counsel table. At 1:40 he went back to the Hall of Justice and told Cooper he was going back to New York. Cooper asked him to wait until four o'clock, at least.

* It is interesting to compare these remarks with Sirhan's contradictory statements to me on December 28, 1968. See page 276.

Cooper proceeded to offer Sirhan's entire notebook (People's 71) in evidence. Fitts could hardly believe it. The defense had argued vociferously against its admissibility; now Cooper was putting it in the record. Cooper felt that each and every crazy page would help him prove his point, that Sirhan was mentally ill and he started to read it all out loud. Sirhan made not one objection.

Cooper came around once more to People's 71-15. "Do you remember writing that?" asked Cooper. "There's a date there. May 18. Do you remember your feelings about Robert F. Kennedy?"

Sirhan recalled that that evening he had brewed himself some tea, went into the living room to watch television and saw a documentary about Robert Kennedy. It told of his career as a politician and of his achievements, his being Attorney General of the United States, his close association with President Kennedy, his brother, and his becoming a Senator from New York. The documentary told of Kennedy's wish to help the poorest, weakest members of society and then, all of a sudden, Kennedy's face flashed before him as a reporter in Israel in 1948, "helping to celebrate their independence." Sirhan was overcome suddenly by the awful truth and he was seemingly the last one to know: "Kennedy was doing a lot of things behind my back," he shouted, with a contorted expression on his face, and a little murmur traveled through the newsmen in the courtroom.

"It burned me up," continued Sirhan, without prompting. "If he were in front of me, the way I felt then, so help me God, he would have died right then and there. I must have been burned up, sir. I was burned up."

It was the TV that provoked him to write down in his notebook that Kennedy must die. "I was pissed off," he said. "Those must have been my feelings. Those were my feelings at the time." Then a week or ten days later, he said, he heard more about Kennedy's current support for Israel. He heard the announcer on KFWB say that Robert Kennedy was at some Zionist club in Beverly Hills and that he had promised to send fifty jet bombers to Israel.

The only trouble with this story is it was on May 18 that Sirhan wrote in his notebook that Kennedy must die, while the television documentary was seen in Los Angeles for the first time on May 20. Furthermore, Kennedy didn't advocate sending fifty jet bombers to Israel until a speech on May 26 at the Temple Neveh Shalom in Portland, Oregon. At the Temple Isaiah in West Los Angeles on May 20, Kennedy tried to avoid taking a strong position one way or the other on American foreign policy in the Middle East, saying first that he hoped for peace in that part of the world and a negotiated settlement between Israel and the Arab states. He said he was concerned about the Soviet show of strength in the Mediterranean. "We must assist with arms, if necessary, to meet the threat of massive Soviet military buildups. We can't render Israel defenseless in the face of aggression. But, in the long run, an arms race helps no one, least of all the people of that region who have lived under war for two decades. What we need is an agreement . . . to defuse the Middle East and to stop on all sides further arms shipments . . . a small, but important, step toward peace in the world." Kennedy envisioned a joint Arab-Israeli development in the Middle East, a sharing of the waters of the Jordan to make the deserts bloom and a solution to the homelessness of the refugees. Someone in the audience asked Kennedy how he stood on the city of Jerusalem. "I stand—here in Los Angeles," he said, evading the question entirely.

It is doubtful that Sirhan heard anything about Kennedy's "promise" to send fifty jet bombers to Israel until John Lawrence told him about it *after* the assassination (see p. 126), and Sirhan's occasional claims while he was in hypnosis that he had killed Kennedy because of these fifty jets bear no more credence than similar claims when he was fully awake.

At the 2:45 P.M. recess, Berman fumed in the corridor, puffing furiously on a cigarette. "This is very very embarrassing to me," said Berman the Jew. "I thought we weren't going to make a political thing out of this." He blamed Nahkleh and Nahas for persuading Cooper to let Sirhan use the witness stand as a forum for his views on Israel. "This makes it a political assassination," said Berman the lawyer, "and that's no defense to murder."

Sirhan resumed the stand, and Cooper continued to plow through the pages of the notebook. On one page, Cooper found President Johnson and former UN Ambassador Arthur Goldberg marked for possible death. "Did you ever have it in mind to kill President Johnson?" asked Cooper.

"No," said Sirhan, "but I hated his guts at one point. He said the United States supports the territorial integrity of all nations, and he stressed *all* nations." Sirhan tapped his right forefinger on the counter in front of him for emphasis. He added that Ambassador Goldberg had repeated Mr. Johnson's phrase. "And he said allll nations. He made that a hell of a long 'all.' "

"Should he have died for that?" asked Cooper.

"Why not?" demanded Sirhan. "He didn't stick to his word."

After the day's adjournment, Berman confided to a few favored newsmen that he was thinking of resigning because of the political turn the case had taken. At the hallway gauntlet of lenses and lights, Harvey Sachs of KABC immediately turned to Cooper and challenged him. "Why did you come up with this unexpected testimony?" asked Sachs.

"It wasn't unexpected," said Cooper. Indeed, it was not. Berman had said at least eleven times that the defense couldn't bring in experts to tell the history of the Arab-Israeli war, but Sirhan could tell what he knew.

"What he knows is what's relevant," Berman had said. Now, Berman was surprised that Sirhan knew so much—and stated it so strongly.

In the elevator going down to the first floor, Berman told a radio reporter, "Oh, Sirhan is obviously mad," oblivious of Mrs. Sirhan standing right behind him. "That notebook shows nothing but madness," he continued, "sheer madness." But when the elevator hit the ground floor, Mrs. Sirhan darted after Berman.

"What are you saying?" she demanded. "I don't like that. You cannot say that, that my boy is mad. What he did, he did for his country." Now it seemed Mrs. Sirhan was convinced this was the most honorable posture she could assume. Sirhan wasn't a mad weasel or a hired gun. He was an Arab patriot.

"I'm not saying he's mad," stuttered Berman. "I'm just saying he's not normal." Mary still had "mad" in her ear and fire in her eye when Munir pulled her eastward through the corridor while Cooper drew Berman away to the west.

Cooper drove Berman back to his office for a chat. He urged him not to go back to New York. Withdrawal now would be disaster. With misgivings, Berman agreed to stay. But something had gone out of him, and his contributions to the case, from this day forward, began to dwindle.

But Cooper saw Berman's acquiescence then as a victory for the cause. He sighed a happy sigh. He had had a hard day, but so far he had managed to keep all the pieces in place. And then he received good news from Berkeley. Dr. Diamond phoned to say that his spies at the university discovered that Dr. George DeVos, a psychological anthropologist selected by Dr. Pollack to evaluate the raw data of Drs. Richardson and Schorr, had come to a conclusion: Sirhan was a schizophrenic. "Many Arabs are indeed paranoid," DeVos was reported to have said. "But Sirhan goes way beyond them!"

But not, apparently, much beyond his brother Sharif. That night, Sharif phoned home and told them he was going up to San Francisco to get a machine gun so he could come home and shoot the entire family. Sharif had been planning to testify on Sirhan's behalf. Cooper had said he would put him on right after Adel. But then the family told Cooper that they believed Sharif intended to blurt out something to the jury that would hurt Sirhan, and Cooper informed Sharif that he wouldn't be needed, after all. Now, it seemed, Sharif was going to get even.

The next morning, someone with a foreign accent phoned Cooper's office and said, "Get some guards out to Cooper's house. They're going to blow it up."

Parsons had the Sirhan family move to a hotel, the Royal Host Hotel off Olympic Boulevard. Cooper ignored the threat and spurned police protection.

" 'Ghattas. Sirhan. Ghattas. Sirhan S Sirhan. Ghattas. Please pay to the order please pay to the Sirhan Sirhan Sirhan fifty fifty fifty very good fifty fifty fifty five five fifty thousand.' " Grant Cooper had Sirhan on the stand for the third day and was still reading from Sirhan's notebook. As Cooper read, Sirhan leaned way back in his chair and started to survey the courtroom from his coign of vantage. "Pay attention now," admonished Cooper. "It's your trial, you know." Sirhan straightened up in his chair. "Did you have $50,000 in your mind?"

"I guess so," said Sirhan, pointing at the notebook.

Cooper went on reading hurriedly, as if he didn't expect to get any important clarifications from Sirhan. " 'Kennedy must fall. Kennedy must fall. Kennedy must fall. Please pay to the order of Sirhan Sirhan the amount of Sirhan Sirhan and do not forget to become any more of a—' "

Cooper read on. And on. Sirhan had no clarifications. He conceded he must have written these things. That was all. Cooper came to page 123 of the second notebook, People's 72, which was mostly blank. "You appear to have written the following," said Cooper. " 'I advocate the overthrow of the current president of the blank United States' in which is a very nasty word."

"Very," said Sirhan.

Cooper looked up at Sirhan over the top of his black horn-rimmed spectacles. "You wrote that, did you not?"

"It's my handwriting, yes."

"What caused you to feel that way?"

"I don't know."

"Wasn't the United States good to you?"

"It wasn't good to the rest of my people."

"I am asking you was it good to you?" If Cooper sounded like a prosecuting attorney here it was because he wanted to ask the questions rather than let the D.A. do it, and thereby maintain his forthright stance before the jury. Better admitted now than exposed later on cross-examination.

"Very good to me," admitted Sirhan.

"Why did you write this?"

"I don't know, sir." One of Sirhan's intellectual heroes, C. Wright Mills, had kept notebook jottings that often served as starting points for his books and articles, and Sirhan's friend, Walter Crowe, had kept a notebook of his own. It is conceivable that Sirhan, who was always easily led, started his own notebook in emulation of Mills and Crowe. But he wasn't going to admit this to anyone.

Cooper read on, read two pages he had earlier opposed giving to the press, pages 125 and 126 of People's 72. As he read them, Sirhan looked bored. He tapped the side of the judge's bench, played with a big microphone to his right. "Now, pay attention, Sirhan!" said Cooper.

"Yes, sir," said Sirhan meekly, sitting back in his chair, squinting and tying knots in his microphone cord. Dr. Schorr, observing now from a seat in the courtroom, fancied that Sirhan was "fondling his mike cord aimlessly like some primordial umbilical link to a world mother."

Finally, Cooper finished with the notebook and took up an exhibit the D.A.'s office hadn't seen, but would certainly have used in evidence against Sirhan if they had: Sirhan's copy of the *Rosicrucian Digest* for May, 1968. There was an article in it by Arthur J. Fettig called "Put It in Writing." Cooper asked Judge Walker if he could introduce it in evidence as Defendant's J.

"You can mimeograph it if you want to," said Sirhan, looking at Walker with smiling contempt. He was now enough at ease on the stand to assume his ordinary, snotty manner.

Cooper shushed him. "Did you read this?" he asked.

"Yes," said Sirhan.

Cooper walked around behind the counsel table and read the article into the record. In the context of this trial, and considering the use Sirhan made of the advice, it was pure irony. Excerpts:

Plan to dare something different—something exciting! But here's a word of advice: put it in writing! Put your plan, your goal, your idea in writing, and see how it suddenly catches fire. See how it gains momentum by the simple process of writing it down!

Sometimes writing it down feeds the data into your subconscious mind a little clearer, and when you let your mind know exactly where you want to go, you simply get there a lot quicker. Writing it down brings it into focus—clarifies it—makes you pin down exactly what you wish to achieve.

Try it. Pick a goal. Set a target date. Now, start working to make it come true . . . Read that goal every morning when you get up and every night before you go to sleep. Read it, believe it, and start doing the things you feel you should to make it come true. This simple formula of writing it down and believing works. It works for the young and old. Once you get moving, your momentum will carry you over many of the obstacles that might have previously stopped you . . . I dare you to write it down!

Cooper's luncheon at the Music Center was something of a scene. As soon as the members of the defense team had piled their plates at the buffet table and sat down, Issa Nahkleh voiced his grief. Newsmen had told him that morning that Berman threatened to withdraw from the case because Sirhan was given a chance to air the Arab-Israeli conflict. Now Nahkleh was insisting that Cooper put some more material in the record, particularly on the plight of the Palestinian Arab refugees. "There are only pieces of it in the record now," said Nahkleh. "I want the rest of it in to create a balance in the jurors' minds."

"Now lookit," said Cooper.

Berman said nothing.

Nahkleh had a piece to say and didn't want to be interrupted. "My friend Mr. Berman's objections," said Nahkleh, "were motivated by political reasons, not by a sincere desire to help your client. He threatened to withdraw from the case—"

Now Cooper interrupted. "So did you, Mr. Nahkleh. This morning." He did so when Cooper told him there was already enough Arab-Israeli material in the record.

Nahkleh ignored that sally. He insisted that Cooper put in more on the Arab refugees. "It is not for propaganda," said Nahkleh. To prove his purity, he suggested excluding the press from the courtroom. "Let only the jury and judge hear it."

McCowan pointed out that making this a purely political assassination wasn't helping Sirhan and that that was Berman's only concern.

"Political assassination," chimed in Berman, "isn't exactly diminished capacity."

Nahkleh flared at Berman's intervention here. He turned to Cooper. "Mr. Berman has stopped you from doing what you must. He's acting for political motivations."

"You're sending Sirhan to the gas chamber," said Berman.

"No," said Nahkleh, "this boy is a refugee."

McCowan said, "Look. It's already been covered. Mrs. Sirhan and Adel and Sirhan all talked about it."

"Lookit," said Cooper, trying desperately to make peace. "Even our Supreme Court disagrees occasionally."

"This is our best defense," said Baron Nahas.

"You haven't read the cases on diminished capacity, Mr. Nahas," said McCowan.

"Lookit," said Cooper. "As trial lawyers we have pride. We want to win. We're very much concerned that if we keep adding more material on the Arab-Israeli conflict, we will be making a serious mistake. There is a Jew on the jury, you know, and we don't know where the sympathies of the others lie."

"Only twenty or thirty minutes more," pleaded Nahkleh.

"Well," said Cooper, "we can articulate this in argument later." He was giving a little, but not now.

Nahkleh was stubborn. After lunch, in the crowded elevator, he insisted that he understood the defense of diminished capacity. He had talked to Dr. Diamond for three hours on Sunday afternoon, and he attended part of the Sunday conference. Berman was whispering into Cooper's other ear: "Don't let Nahkleh go back in that holding tank to see Sirhan."

Back in the Hall of Justice, before readjournment, Berman was giving yet another hallway interview to Harvey Sachs of KABC, who was nodding sympathetically. In the courtroom, Nahkleh was talking furiously to the reporter for the Long Beach *Press Telegram*. "You don't *know* how the refugees have suffered," said Nahkleh. She, too, was a good listener. Jew to Jew and Gentile to Gentile.

For the rest of the afternoon, Cooper took Sirhan through further descriptions of his experiments with the occult and his Rosicrucian meeting on May 28 in Pasadena. He got Sirhan's story on the purchase of the gun. "I liked guns. It was cheap," he said. He first shot it in March, 1968. He practiced perhaps six times.

Sirhan recalled his view of Robert Kennedy at the Ambassador on June 2. "Kennedy sang with a movie star, I think. I was really thrilled, sir," he told Cooper. "That was the first time I saw him, sir. And my whole attitude toward him changed because every time I heard him before, I'd associated him with the Phantom jet bombers he was going to send to Israel and I pictured him as a villain every time I heard him in relation to the Zionists and to his support for Isreal. When I saw him, sir, that day, that night, he looked like a saint to me . . . I liked him." Sirhan said he didn't look around the kitchen that night. The two witnesses who said he did "were liars."

Finally, Cooper asked Sirhan to recall everything he did on June 4. The practice at the gun range. Sirhan said he wasn't firing his gun rapidly. A man at the post next to him with a National Rifle Association emblem on his sleeve was doing the rapid fire. The supper at Bob's Big Boy Restaurant. His discovery of the ad about the Jewish parade on Wilshire. He was infuriated. "I was off to go down to see what those goddamned sons of bitches were up to. I was driving like a maniac." Senator Kuchel's party. "It was pretty dull, to tell you the truth." Sirhan looked up and fended off the audience in court with his right hand and smiled. "Forgive me, any of the Kuchel supporters here." Then he walked into the Ambassador by the same route he had taken when he'd been there on Sunday. He noticed quite a few people "of his own complexion. People of Spanish origin. Black people. The whole place was milling with people, sir. There were many TV cameras. A lot of bright lights, sir."

"I have nothing further today, your Honor," said Cooper.

Sirhan didn't recall much about the night of June 4. He had a few Tom Collinses. He didn't remember picking up his gun. "You're sure?" asked Cooper.

"I have sworn to tell the truth, sir, and that's what I'm telling you."

He remembered finding a big shiny coffee urn. He didn't know where it was. Somewhere in the Ambassador. "Were there any bright lights around?" asked Cooper.

"No, sir, there weren't," said Sirhan. Sirhan knew that it was Dr. Diamond's theory that he was confused by the bright lights and the mirrors near the Embassy Room and it was the lights and mirrors that put him into a kind of trance state. Here in court, he added, perversely throwing doubt on the story he knew Diamond would tell, "There weren't any mirrors either." *

The next thing Sirhan remembered, he was being choked. "Did you know that when you were blacked out you walked up to Senator Kennedy, pointed a gun to his head, pulled the trigger . . . and he later died?"

Sirhan smiled, shrugged his palms turned upward. "Yes, I was told this."

"—you now believe it is true?"

"Obviously, sir."

* Sirhan confided to McCowan after the trial that he had waited for Kennedy in a corridor directly behind the stage of the Embassy Room. That corridor was not well lit, and police photos taken directly after the shooting show a large shiny coffee urn and piles of cups on a table in the short hallway.

"After you were arrested, you refused to give your name, didn't you?"

"Yes."

"You wouldn't discuss anything about the case?"

"They never brought it up, sir." Sirhan added that it was "such a friendly discussion . . ."

When did he first realize that he'd shot Kennedy?

He knew Kennedy was involved in this because he had heard his name when he was before the lady judge (Joan Dempsey Klein) on the morning of June 5. He said he didn't really realize that he'd shot Kennedy until A. L. Wirin came to see him in the county jail.

"That is about the whole story, isn't it?" asked Cooper, with some weariness in his voice. This was Sirhan's fourth straight day on the stand.

"Yes, sir."

"Now let me ask you this, Sirhan. You have told this jury that when you came to the Ambassador Hotel that night, you didn't come there with the intention of shooting Kennedy. Is that right?"

"That is correct, sir."

"You don't remember shooting him?"

"I don't remember shooting him."

"Yet let me recount these facts to you. You have heard all of the things that were in your notebook?"

"Yes, sir."

"You wrote them?"

"Yes, sir."

"You don't deny it?"

"No, I don't."

"You bought the gun January, February, March of 1968?"

"Yes, sir, I did."

"Prior to that time in your notebook in June of '67, you said you didn't know what kind of weapon you would use for killing the President and the Vice-President and the like?"

"Yes, sir."

"You saw Kennedy?"

"Yes, sir."

"And you were also angry at him at the same time you felt he was a saint?"

"I was ambivalent toward him, yes."

"You went out target practicing on the afternoon of the fourth of June, right?"

"Yes, sir."

"You took your gun with you over to the Ambassador Hotel; is that right? I mean over to—"

"Yes, sir."

"Obviously, you took the gun in there."

"Yes, sir, obviously."

"You didn't take any ID with you. In other words, you left your wallet in the car. Is that right?"

"I always leave my wallet in the car."

"I understand that. But you did leave it there?"

"Yes, sir, I did."

"And you did kill him?"

"Yes, sir, I did."

"How do you account for all the circumstances?"

"Sir, I don't know."

"Is that the best you can explain it?"

"What I have told you, sir, is the truth, the whole truth, and nothing but the truth, sir."

"You may cross-examine," said Cooper.

Compton stood and brushed his hand through his blond, crew-cut hair. Sirhan looked at him unblinking. "You nervous?" asked Chief Deputy District Attorney Lynn Compton.

"A little bit," admitted Sirhan. His voice was very soft, and he gripped the counter tightly.

Compton asked him immediately whether he had ever blacked out in Jerusalem. Sirhan said he didn't remember. "The only occasion then was at the Ambassador Hotel?" asked Compton.

"No," said Sirhan. "When I wrote in the notebooks and the fall from the horse . . . sir." Sirhan drew a figure eight on the counter with his left forefinger. Compton asked him about his hatred for the Zionists. Sirhan quoted an Arab proverb: " 'A friend of my enemy,' " he said, " 'is my enemy.' " But he denied that he ever had any hatred, as such, for the United States. He was grateful to the United States. However, from June, 1967, on, he was "resentful."

"Yet you don't deny that at some point in your career, you felt very strongly about the overthrow of the United States Government?"

"As I said, at that time, sir."

"At the time you wrote the material down."

"Yes, sir, when I wrote it down and only at that time, sir. I don't remember entertaining it after or before. I don't even remember that itself right then." Sirhan clenched his right fist and unclenched it, then put his right finger in his mouth.

Compton said, "Now, you told us yesterday or the day before that at one point in your life you acquired a fondness for Senator Kennedy?"

"Yes, sir, I did." Sirhan smiled winningly, gestured with his left hand, then started picking at his right forefinger.

"Can you tell us in point of time when that began?"

"Sir, I always associated him with, sir, with President Kennedy, and to me, he was the next President at the next election. I was hoping he would become President. I was hoping he would continue what his brother, what had started, sir, namely, sir, that——"

"Well, you have answered my question. There was a period of time, if you recall, after President Johnson said he wasn't going to run again that Senator Kennedy was not announcing his candidacy. Do you remember that?"

"I honestly don't, sir."

"Well, do you recall there was a time then when Senator Kennedy came out and said he was going to be a candidate for President?"

"Yes."

"Do you recall about when that was?"

"No, I don't, sir."

"Do you recall whether at the time he said he was going to be, that you felt that you were for him and wanted him to?"

"I was for him, very much so."

"So then, there was a time the love turned to hate. Was that at a time when Senator Kennedy was a candidate for President of the United States? Right?"

"Yes, it was during the time he was. But exactly specifically when it turned into hate, not only that, hate really, because I still loved him, but when he came out with his support for the state of Israel, when he said he would give them fifty Phantom jet bombers to Israel."

"At that time, he was a candidate for President of the United States?"

"Yes."

"You say it wasn't until all of that, that hate then?"

"No, but it was enough for me, sir, that anything that has to do with Israel or the Zionists or support of Israel, that is enough cause for me, sir, to hate him."

"But not all of that?"

"Well, enough, sir, to have an impression only."

"Enough to kill him?"

"I don't know about that, sir."

"Well, didn't you just tell us here a few days ago that if you had him right there, you would have blasted him?"

"At the time he came out and said he would send those fifty jet bombers, I would have done that."

"You would have done that?"

"Yes. I am a very impulsive person." Sirhan blinked hard and snapped his fingers. "Whatever my objective would be, it is just good for that time only."

Sirhan said that he'd always believed in nonviolence and Compton challenged him on this. "The other day you told us, if you recall, that you saw a picture of a newsreel soldier standing on the east bank of the Suez Canal and you said that if you had been there, you would have blasted him."

"Yes, sir," said Sirhan. "And again, if you were trying to kill me now and I had a chance, I would kill you, and you would be first, sir. That is the way I feel about it. When it comes to self-preservation, sir," Sirhan pointed his right hand at Compton, "I come first, not you."

"So this peaceful approach to things only goes so far. Is that right?"

"Gandhi said that himself, sir." Sirhan smiled. One point for Sirhan.

Compton pushed Sirhan very hard on the notebook. He took a photocopy of People's 71-15 up to Sirhan. Sirhan said he had no doubt that he wrote that page on May 18. "You wrote that because you read in this book from the Rosicrucians that if you write things down and think about them enough, they will accomplish the goal. Right?"

"That's what the book said, yes," said Sirhan.

"Now, my question is," said Compton, "was your writing this down in your book done with the idea that if you thought about it hard enough, and wrote it down enough times, that it would happen by some force other than through yourself?"

"I don't know, sir. You read that article, sir, in the *Rosicrucian Digest,* sir. That's the best explanation to it."

"Well," said Compton, "I'm asking you, what did you think? That if you wrote things down and thought about them hard enough, that they would occur by some other force, or that it would help you accomplish the goal?"

"That you would be helped by some force," said Sirhan. It was an admission Sirhan had made before to the doctors, but only "off the record."

"Without you having to actually do it yourself?" asked Compton.

Sirhan said, "I don't know, sir. I'm not that well versed on it. I'm only a student of it. I only read what they tell me and I do the exercises as told, sir."

"Well," said Compton, "do you ever remember looking in the notebook at things you had previously written out?"

"Again, sir, I don't remember."

"You don't remember ever going through that and saying, 'Gee whiz! Look here. I wrote Senator Kennedy must be assassinated, and I don't know why I wrote that.' Did you ever go through that experience?"

"No, sir, I never have."

"Or this passage about overthrowing the government or assassinating the thirty-sixth President? You don't ever recall looking back in that notebook and rereading them?"

"No, sir, I don't."

"Do you have any recollection at all of the last time you saw this notebook before you were shown it here during court?"

"No, sir, I don't."

"I show you this envelop from the Argonaut Insurance Company, People's exhibit 73. Have you seen that?"

"Yes, sir."

"That is your handwriting?"

"Yes, sir, that is mine."

"Do you recall when you wrote that?"

"No, sir, I do not."

Compton tried hard to get Sirhan to acknowledge something about the notebooks. Anything about the notebooks. He suggested that Sirhan must have had more than several notebooks when he was going to Pasadena City College. Compton said, "You had several books and you took a lot of them."

"Were you with me at the time?" asked Sirhan. "How in hell do you know I had several books?"

"I am asking you," said Compton.

"Then don't tell me, sir. Ask me. That is better. But don't put words in my mouth."

"I am asking you, did you have several notebooks?"

"I said I don't know."

"You don't remember? You have no remembrance of that at all?"

"No, sir."

Compton asked Sirhan if he remembered writing his name down when he signed in at the range.

"No, I don't remember exactly, sir. Sir, you are asking me—this is just in the process—this is part of the process, sir. I don't exactly remember when I opened my gun and when I put in every bullet. You are asking me when I wrote my name, sir, is the same as asking me every bullet that I put in that chamber. That's stupid."

"I confess," said Compton, "that sometimes I do ask stupid questions."

"Yes, sir, you do," agreed Sirhan, taking a long drink of water from the paper cup given him by the court bailiff.

"Thank you," said Compton. "Now, Mr. Sirhan, let me just ask you a couple of brief questions. You told us earlier this morning that, as far as you were concerned, you were willing to fight for the Arab cause, right?"

"Yes, sir, the Palestinian Arab cause."

"And do you think that the killing of Senator Kennedy helped the Arab cause?"

Sirhan responded, "Sir, I'm not even aware that I killed Mr. Kennedy."

Compton said, "Well, you know he's dead."

"I know he's dead," said Sirhan. "I've been told that."

"In other words," said Compton, "the killing of Senator Kennedy would have only helped the Arab cause if you did it, right?"

"How do you mean that, sir, if I did it?"

"Let me ask you this. Again, I will repeat the question. Do you think that the killing of Senator Robert Kennedy by anybody helped the Arab cause?"

"I'm in no position, sir, to explain that," said Sirhan. "I am no political observer to say."

"There's no question in your mind but what you did it?"

"All the evidence has proved it," said Sirhan. "Your evidence."

"Are you glad he's dead?"

"No, sir, I'm not glad."

"Are you sorry?"

"I'm not sorry, but I'm not proud of it either."

"But you are not sorry."

"No, sir, because I have no way of, no exact knowledge, sir, of having shot him."

"Well, the other day, right here in this courtroom, did you not say, 'I killed Robert Kennedy willully, premeditatively, with twenty years of malice aforethought'? Did you say that?"

"Yes, sir, I did."

Cooper interrupted. "Pardon me, if your Honor please, I think that in fairness that question should be put in context, if your Honor has that in mind."

"Approach the bench," said Walker. At the bench, Judge Walker said to Compton, "If you recollect, that was done outside the presence of the jury."

Compton said, "But it is his statement. All the statements he made at the police station were outside the presence of the jury, too."

"Well, if your Honor please," said Cooper, "I have given some thought to this myself because I naturally expected that the question would be asked by a good prosecutor, and we have good prosecutors, and I didn't object to it because I didn't feel it was an objectionable question. But I do feel that the circumstances—I suppose I can bring it out on redirect."

"That's the place to do it," said Walker.

"I will do it on redirect, your Honor. No, I, I didn't object to it, your Honor."

"Okay, then," said Walker.

Back in hearing of the jury, Compton said, "One last question, Mr. Sirhan. You said you would be willing to do what you could to help the Arab cause and fight for it. Are you willing to die for it?"

"When did I say, sir, that I wanted to attempt to fight for the Arab cause?"

"This morning, I think," said Compton. "May I ask you again. Are you willing to fight for it?"

"I'm willing to fight for it," said Sirhan.

"Are you willing to die for it?"

"I'm willing to die for it," said Sirhan.

Cooper took him on redirect and he said, "Sirhan, the response to one of those questions put to you, and let me get the exact words here. 'I killed Robert Kennedy willfully, premeditatively, with twenty years of malice aforethought, that is why.' Do you remember making that statement in this court last Friday?"

"Yes."

"In the absence of the jury?"

"Yes, right."

"And twenty years ago, how old were you?"

"Four years."

"And at that time, did you entertain any malice against Senator Kennedy?"

"I didn't even know what malice was, sir."

"Now, let me ask you this. Late Friday, you were very angry at your lawyers."

"Yes, I was very angry."

"At your lawyers?"

"Yes."

"You were angry at who?"

"Mr. Berman, Mac, yourself and all defense attorneys."

"Now let me," said Cooper, "would you please tell the jury what you were angry about?"

"I was angry with my defense attorneys. I had a disagreement with them about the strategy of my defense with respect to calling certain girls to the witness stand."

Cooper asked Sirhan how many witnesses he crossed off the witness list. He said about a dozen. Whether he remembered Cooper's coming to visit him in his cell and trying to calm him down and reason with him. He did. Cooper went over the whole scene on February 28. The judge reminded the court that this was not done in the presence of the jury. Cooper said, "No, the jury was not present. The jury's hearing this for the first time right now." Cooper than read the jury a transcript of Sirhan's blowup in court on February 28. Anyone who asked for the gas chamber, Cooper reasoned, must be seen by a jury to be somewhat less than normal.

Compton resumed his cross-examination of Sirhan. He pointed out that when Sirhan was angry with his lawyers, he did take a piece of paper, the witness list, make some marks on it and sign his name. Sirhan said no, he had actually signed his name to another paper, one that Cooper dictated to him and told him what to write. Compton said, "But you remember what you were writing?"

Sirhan said, "I don't remember exactly the writing."

"You don't have a clear recollection of writing it down either?"

Sirhan said, "He dictated these to me, sir, and I was mad. I was mad."

Compton laughed. "That is all," he said and gave the jury a triumphant look. To Compton, Sirhan's lack of memory was incredible. He didn't buy it and he didn't think the jury would buy it.

Moments later in front of the television gauntlet, Compton told newsmen, "He remembers the things he can safely remember. He is lying. There is no question in my mind about it."

But some of the newsmen were impressed with the case for the defense. After adjournment, Harvey Sachs of KABC said, "It does look like a verdict of second degree. The jury has to think he's nuts now." Sachs won general agreement from his colleagues around him. But Bob Greene of *Newsday* disagreed. "Mercurial, yes," said Greene. "Nuts, no."

On Friday, March 7, the defense put on the rest of its "other witness" list. Robert Prestwood, a racehorse owner whom Sirhan used to work for, testified about Sirhan's intense desire to become a jockey; and John Strathman, a burly, bearded fellow, stated that he had noticed changes in Sirhan since his fall from the horse. Said Strathman: "Sirhan seemed a little more lonely and a little less interested in what I had to say. To be frank . . . he was no longer interested in talking about any of the things we used to talk about. He seemed to be in a hurry, not that I knew where he was going, but that is the way he seemed."

On redirect, Cooper said, "You did notice a very definite change in him after his fall from the horse?"

And Strathman said, "Uh-humm. I would say so."

Patricia Strathman, his wife, took the stand. "After Sirhan's fall from the horse," Mrs. Strathman said, "well, Sirhan seemed to be brooding more, not as open. He never was—he would never tell his most intimate secrets, but he seemed even more confined." She also told the court about Sirhan's experiments with extrasensory perception, or the occult.

Millard Sheets testified. Sheets, a horse owner, was the one who had found Sirhan crumpled "like a bird" against a rail at the Granja Vista del Rio racetrack that foggy morning on September 25 and cradled Sirhan's head in his lap until an ambulance arrived.

John Weidner, Sirhan's boss at the health food store, described his last altercation with Sirhan, which ended when Weidner had to call the police to get Sirhan out of the store.

Then came four witnesses who had seen Sirhan drinking on the night of June 4. The police had maintained Sirhan wasn't drunk. The defense had to offer independent witnesses who could corroborate Sirhan. But it paid a high price for the testimony of three. Only Gonzalo Carillo-Cetina—a waiter at the Ambassador—was simply helpful. He said he saw Sirhan drinking, period. The others all added material that, Adel Sirhan noted bleakly at the end of the day, "didn't help."

Hans Peter Bidstrup, an Ambassador electrician, said Sirhan came into his booth near the Venetian Room about 10:00 P.M. When he saw Sirhan, he said, "Here comes another drunk." But John Howard broke him down somewhat on cross-examination.

"You told us he didn't stagger. Is that correct?"

"No."

"You told us he didn't slur his speech. Is that correct?"

"That's right."

"You told us his eyes were not bloodshot. Is that correct?"

"That's right."

"Then, what then do you base your opinion that he was intoxicated upon?"

"Well, mainly the glass in his hand."

"You mean everyone who has a glass in his hand is intoxicated, in your opinion?"

"Well, it was half empty."

"Do you think one half a drink would make that man intoxicated, or any man?"

"I wouldn't know," said Bidstrup.

Howard asked Bidstrup whether Sirhan had asked him about Robert Kennedy. Sirhan had asked him how long Kennedy was staying at the Ambassador. And he had asked him a question about Mr. Kennedy's security, whether or not he had bodyguards. And finally, that Sirhan had seemed startled by the sudden appearance there of a fireman in uniform.

On redirect examination by Cooper, Bidstrup finally admitted that Sirhan seemed "half-drunk and very tired."

Enrique Rabago, an unemployed auto mechanic from Buena Park, had gone to the Ambassador with Humphrey Cordero to join in Kennedy's victory celebration. Rabago, a chunky, gregarious fellow, soon struck up a conversation with Sirhan. Sirhan had a glass in his hand from which he was taking normal sips. He was neither drunk nor belligerent. "I would say he was educated and arrogant," which was a pretty good description. Then Rabago added that he had expressed some worry over the outcome of the election. McCarthy, he observed, was ahead.

"Don't worry if Senator Kennedy doesn't win," Rabago said Sirhan said. "That son of a bitch is a millionaire. Even if he wins, he won't do anything for you or me or the poor people."

Cordero said he noted that Sirhan had a glass in his hand. "It looked to me like a highball." He was cross-examined by John Howard.

"You had a chance to observe Mr. Sirhan?"

"That I did."

"And he appeared intelligent to you?"

"It didn't sound like he was on drugs or dope or drink or anything."

"He looked pretty sound to you that night when you talked to him?"

"I couldn't see anything wrong with him other than he was just a little disgusted with the party."

Cooper's last lay witness was Richard Lubic, a cable television promoter who had been with Kennedy in the pantry when he was shot. Cooper asked Lubic to show him on the scale-model mock-up where he was standing when the shots were fired. Lubic came down off the stand and pointed to the exact spot, somewhat to the right of Senator Kennedy. The shots, said Lubic, sounded like a starter's gun at a track meet. Cooper asked him whether he heard anything before the shots were fired.

"I heard a voice say, 'Kennedy, you son of a bitch!' Then the shot." No further questions, said Cooper.

In a news conference after the day's adjournment, George Lardner, Jr., of the Washington *Post,* observed that Cooper's day-long parade of witnesses sounded "tailor-made for the prosecution."

Cooper said, "I realize there's stuff in there that's very bad for Sirhan, but I don't care. It's all a predicate for the testimony of the psychiatrists."

"How," wondered Lacey Fosburgh of *The New York Times,* "would the testimony of Richard Lubic help the defense?" Cooper gave Miss Fosburgh a fatherly hug and told her she'd see in due time.

In a Sunday story for *The New York Times,* Miss Fosburgh wrote about "the air of tension and violence" that seemed to hover over Sirhan. There were, however, "some baffling incongruities" about him.

> In the courtroom, for example, he can be both gentle and nasty, shy and arrogant. One minute he will seem ingenuous; the next, frightening.
>
> And for this reason, one of the curious things about this historic trial is that there is a mystery.
>
> No one awaits a secret witness or the disclosure of the real murderer. But gradually developing more each week is a mystery about Sirhan.
>
> Who is he? What is he? Why did he kill Robert Kennedy, a man he saw for the first time only two days before the assassination and thought was a saint?

And on Monday morning, Bob Greene had a reflective piece in *Newsday* to prepare his readers for yet another view of Sirhan from the psychologists. Greene said they would contradict the "highly romanticized picture of himself" which Sirhan had presented to the jury.

Fourteen

"People take lives in warfare, don't they?"

There was an abstract issue that might have made the trial worthwhile. The trial could have helped educate the public about a new solution to the most difficult question in the law: the criminal responsibility of the mentally ill. But this was a courtroom, not a college classroom, and the issue was soon tossed into a quagmire of ambiguity by the defense attorneys who either didn't understand the defense of diminished capacity or didn't think they could sell it to the jury, and by a team of prosecutors who couldn't or wouldn't treat the question with anything more than scoffing hee-haws. And so, instead of fostering a new rapprochement between psychiatry and the law, the Sirhan trial would provide cynics all over America with a new example of psychiatry's "inherent self-contradictions."

One of the troubles was that some of the doctors—encouraged by the attorneys on both sides—went beyond their professional expertise. One of these was Dr. Martin M. Schorr. He started off impressively enough. His battery of tests indicated that Sirhan was a paranoid schizophrenic guided by inner beliefs that didn't match the realities of the outside world.

On the Wechsler Adult Intelligence Scale, Sirhan had a verbal IQ of 109, which ranked him higher than 75 percent of the population. But he had a nonverbal IQ of only 82. The wide gap between verbal and non-verbal led Schorr to suspect either brain damage or psychosis.

The Minnesota Multiphasis Personality Inventory showed Sirhan was more paranoid than ninety-five out of one hundred people one might choose at random. It also showed him as highly hypomanic—"apt to be very aggressive, restless, on the go, in a state of flux . . . sort of like a roadrunner, if you want an image." Sirhan scored low on the test's "lie scale." "Most people," said Schorr, "would lie more than Sirhan did on this test." At the end of the counsel table, Sirhan smiled. This didn't sound so bad.

Indeed, when McCowan went to visit Sirhan in his cell during the lunch hour (because he felt Sirhan needed "special support" during this week), Sirhan told him that he'd come to some compromise with himself over the testimony of the doctors. "It's all right if Schorr says I'm psychotic," said Sirhan. "I just don't want him to say I'm crazy." Or, as he said to me at the counsel table: "Better a live dog than a dead lion."

After lunch, Schorr had copies of Sirhan's Rorschach score sheet and summary sheet distributed to the jury, along with copies of the ten standard Rorschach inkblots and a location chart of Sirhan's responses (See Appendix F). It was clear that Schorr valued the Rorschach more than any of his other tests. The test, said Schorr, "is a most diagnostically revealing X ray of the personality. It gets behind the image of a person, into the reality as he perceives himself." The reason the test was so good, said Schorr, was that it was almost purely "projective." There was no way, he said, for the subject to tell the examiner what he wanted to hear, no right or wrong answer. The responses came from the subject's apperceptive mass. And they gave the examiner the best possible insight into that person's subconscious depths.

Schorr proceeded to show on a series of colored slides how Sirhan had responded to the inkblots. The jury, all of whom had been taking copious notes during the trial, started marking their copies of Schorr's exhibits.

Sirhan, said Schorr, had come up with an inordinate number of "unusual responses." He saw a crushed frog, a trachea, a monster charging at him, a fried chicken leg, scarred seals, a staring face, a rotting red apple, spurting blood, a liver.

But Schorr's intricate scoring system for the Rorschach confused everyone in the courtroom, and Berman, sensing that he wasn't getting across to the jury, told Schorr to remember that he had "an average jury" in front of him. In contrast to the two hour and thirty-seven minute "trial" the day before of James Earl Ray,* maybe this jury was learning more

---

* In Memphis, Tennessee, Ray had pleaded guilty to the sniper slaying of Dr. Martin Luther King and was sentenced to a ninety-nine-year term in prison after the state merely read its case to the jury. *The New York Times* hardly thought that was enough in a case of this magnitude. "No one was demanding blood; everyone is demanding facts. Are we going to get the facts from Ray's lawyers, past or present, one of whom is trying to peddle the story to magazines? Are we going to get the facts from William Bradford Huie, the author who has 'bought' the 'rights' to Ray's story? What a mockery of justice for the facts to emerge in marketed justice!"

The Times's editorial writer seemed to assume that "the facts" would necessarily emerge in court: "Unless proceedings are convened in court—federal, if not state—we shall never know the adjudicated truth."

than it really wanted to know about Sirhan. In his second day on the stand, Schorr responded to Berman's suggestions with some colorful comparisons. Sirhan was "like a marionette on a string." This was better. This was something the jury could understand.

But when Dr. Schorr reported on the results of Sirhan's Thematic Apperception Test, he slipped back into his profesional jargon. The TAT, said Schorr, showed Sirhan's "ambivalence and alienation, homicidal and suicidal fantasies, dependence and domination by the mother."

In one TAT card, Sirhan had seen a man who had been slipped a Mickey Finn: "He looks drunk but he doesn't drink. I don't like this card." In another, Sirhan saw someone standing under a streetlight: "He's lonely. No hope, no family, no country. He thinks of killing himself. He reminds me of me." In another, he wasn't sure whether the figure was a boy or a girl reaching for a gun on the floor. "She wants to have it, but she can't reach it. . . . She is thinking of taking her own life. I don't like that card." In still another, Sirhan saw a man leaving a nude girl in bed and going home to his mother. And then there was a card that was completely blank; there Sirhan saw the face of Moshe Dayan looking down at people. "But there's a bullet that's crashing through his brain at the height of his glory." Sirhan was not "part of the scene." He was the scene. "I'm the one killing him."

In the Bender Gestalt test, in which Sirhan was asked to reproduce a set of figures, Sirhan had a high concern for accuracy, but he placed them on a sheet of paper in an irregular sequence and there were "collisions" between the figures, a production normally seen in psychotic individuals.

Summing up, Schorr said Sirhan had two personalities, each quite different from the other, which tended to dissociate under stress, "like Jekyll-Hyde," or Eve White–Eve Black (from the psychiatric classic, *The Three Faces of Eve*). He used his notebooks, said Schorr, as a "sort of escape valve to discharge his hostilities, he has to keep constantly writing, furiously writing. He is unaware of the killer in himself, but is aware of his own ambivalence."

Schorr summed up Sirhan as "a Semite but not a Jew, an Arab but not a Moslem, a man who has family but not a father, a man who immigrated to this country but is not a citizen, a man without identity."

Berman stood, ready with his magic question, faced Schorr, waited for

The Los Angeles *Times*, for its part, demanded a kind of Warren Commission to investigate the entire James Earl Ray affair.

Editorial reactions like these were exactly what Judge Walker had feared if he accepted a plea in the Sirhan case.

the clacketty-clacketty-clack of the air conditioner to subside, and asked Schorr if Sirhan had the mental capacity maturely and meaningfully to premeditate, deliberate and reflect upon the gravity of his contemplated act of murder on June 5, 1968, and whether he had the mental capacity to comprehend his duty to govern his actions in accord with the duty imposed by law and thus have the capacity to act with malice aforethought?

Schorr's answer was, "No." Berman said, "You may cross-examine."

In his cross-examination, John Howard wondered if, through his tests, Schorr could have predicted the assassination of Robert Kennedy.

"On June 3?" asked Schorr.

"Yes," said Howard. "Ahead of time."

"Well," said Schorr, "with a reasonable degree of certainty, murder is predictable." In fact, based on his psychological testing of a young man in a San Diego County Honor Farm named Joseph Bernard Morse, Schorr had done just that: he had predicted that Morse would kill, and asked the authorities if there wasn't some way of detaining him. There wasn't, the state released him and Morse killed his mother and his sister shortly thereafter. Later, moreover, he garroted a fellow prisoner in his cell. With unusual modesty, Schorr failed here to report this prophetic judgment to Howard.

In general, Schorr scored more points under Howard's cross-examination than he had done under Berman's direct examination. But he couldn't resist going beyond his premises. He said he believed Sirhan was in a dissociated state when he killed Kennedy, that he was still in a dissociated state when he cried out that he was being choked, still in a dissociated state during his interrogation by the police. John Howard wondered what triggered Sirhan's dissociation. "Well," said Schorr, "the triggering may have been when he saw the gun in the car. It desn't take much to dissociate when we start with a premise that he is psychotically disturbed. In my opinion, the gun gives him an aggressive personality he does not possess. Sirhan needed to be treated like a man, needed to act like a man. He needed a destiny."

By then, Schorr had said it all, had presented the results of his five diagnostic tests and stood up well under Howard's questions. Howard, it seemed, was ready to leave Schorr alone, under the theory that a lawyer never asks a question unless he knows in advance what the answer is going to be. But, on the morning of March 12, Schorr insisted on reading part of his final report of December 18. The report was a jazzy psychodynamic summary that had little to do with Schorr's test data, an unnecessary, though literate, explanation of what made Sirhan tick. Dr. Marcus had warned Schorr earlier that he would be better off if he didn't try to bring such material into court. But now, Schorr insisted. He said to Howard: "I have to read my final report, and you are free—that gives you latitude to ask questions about that. I gave a copy to the district attorney's office."

Howard said: "Would you want it to refresh your memory? Do you need it now?"

"The December 18 report," said Schorr. "It summarizes everything."

"If you need it, we have it right here," said Howard.

"Yes, I would like to read it, if I may."

Fitts started to object, "I thought the purpose of this was to refresh the witness's recollection."

But Schorr insisted and Berman let him go. "I have to read the report in its entirety," said Schorr, "in order for the jury or for you to see."

"I read it," said Howard.

"Well, the jury hasn't heard it," said Schorr. He read from page 3 of his December 18 report:

> By killing Kennedy, Sirhan kills his father, takes his father's place as the heir to his mother. The process of acting out this problem can only be achieved in a psychotic, insane state of mind.
>
> Essentially, the more he railed and stormed, the more the mother protected Sirhan from his father, and the more he withdrew into her protection. He hated his father and feared him. He would never consciously entertain the idea of doing away with him, but somewhere along the line the protecting mother fails her son. The mother finally lets down the son. She, whom he loved, never kept her pledge and now his pain had to be repaid with pain. Since the unconscious always demands maximum penalties, the pain has to be death. Sirhan's prime problem becomes a conflict between instinctual demand for his father's death and the realization through his conscious that killing his father is not socially acceptable. The only real solution is to look for a compromise. He does. He finds a symbolic replica of his father in the form of Kennedy, kills him, and also removes the relationship that stands between him and his most precious possession—his mother's love.

"Who wrote that?" asked John Howard.

"I did," said Dr. Schorr.

"Uh-huh," said Howard. He smiled. Howard hadn't wanted the jury to hear that. Now that they had, he was curious to know where Schorr had gotten it. He was reasonably certain Schorr didn't write it himself.

It was a striking statement. In the corridor at recess, news reporters crowded around me for another slower reading to make sure they had gotten it all down correctly. As I read, Mrs. Sirhan edged close to the crowd and stood there listening, straining for each word's meaning. When I finished, Mrs. Sirhan said, "I don't want that. I don't want that." I explained that it was already in the court record, that the reporters would get it later anyway. "It's all right if the prosecution gives that to the press," said Mary Sirhan. "I don't want you to do it." She went back into the courtroom and wrote a note and sent it to Sirhan through McCowan. Sirhan read the note and for a moment looked close to tears himself. He turned to his mother and tried to pantomine a reply. Mrs. Sirhan kept shaking her head. She didn't understand. At lunchtime, she cornered Russell Parsons and demanded a private meeting with her son. "I want to see him alone. I must talk to him alone. I must understand all of this." Parsons offered to let her talk to Sirhan in the presence of his three lawyers. She shook her head, completely unhappy now, with Dr. Schorr, with the entire situation.

The New York Times was also unhappy with Dr. Schorr when it discovered that he had cribbed his last statement from a recent work by Dr. James A. Brussel, *A Case Book of a Crime Psychiatrist.* On Thursday, March 13, *The Times* printed the words of Dr. Schorr and Dr. Brussel side by side in a special box. And a sidebar by Israel Shenker quoted Brussel's publisher, Bernard Geis, who said he "would definitely sue." But Dr. Brussel, a prolific author and former assistant commissioner of mental hygiene for New York State, said he was flattered by the quotation.

The trouble was, Schorr didn't give Brussel credit. It was an unpardonable oversight and one that was destined to discredit Schorr's raw data and his two other reports, totaling twelve pages, detailing the results of Sirhan's psychological tests. His four-page cadenza written on December 18, half cribbed from Dr. Brussel, gave Howard the opening he was looking for.

On Friday March 14, Cooper and Berman went to Houston, Texas, for a meeting of the American College of Trial Lawyers. I took the opportunity to see how Sirhan was viewing the proceedings and discovered that he rather liked the notion that he was a "schizophrenic." "I'm more than a double personality," he said. "I'm a triple. But I don't consider that mental illness. That's why I would have made a good diplomat. I learned that from the Jews, by the way."

Sirhan discussed the highlights of the trial. He knew the names of all the jurors. He didn't like juror number 8, Nell Bortells, because she didn't seem to have any reactions. He liked Mrs. Busby, the schoolteacher who sat in the middle of the first row. He was proud of his performance on the stand, prouder of the way he had thwarted Buck Compton on the cross-examination by remembering nothing, offering no opinions. He replayed the night of the assassination, now seen from the point of view of others who testified on the stand. He jeered at Bill Barry, Kennedy's "bodyguard." "Where the hell was Bill Barry?" asked Sirhan. "Where the hell was he? It was his fault."

What about Unruh? "That son of a bitch!" said Sirhan. "I fixed him." How? "He was banking on the wrong horse." He observed other witnesses very closely. He noted that witnesses DiPierro and Gallivan had referred to him in "police language." "They called me 'the suspect,' " snorted Sirhan.

He was proud of himself for humbling Cooper. "Now," he said, "I'm running the trial." How? "I kept those two girls off the stand, didn't I?" And he had managed to deceive his own doctors, his lawyers, the judge, the jury. Did he fake his blowups in court? He smiled. "Later, Bob, later."

This was a different Sirhan from the Sirhan of the summer. That Sirhan had been, on the whole, simple, naïve, confused. This Sirhan was shrewd, devious, knowing, impressed with his new self-image as an Arab hero. Letters like this one from Sussex, England, may have helped a bit:

> Sirhan Sirhan, I think you're fantastic, and I admire you an awful lot. 4 million people in Cairo think the same. I'm an Egyptian girl living in England, which is a country just about as bad as America, so it will serve them right if any of the Al Fatah hi-jack thier aeroplanes, which there bound to do. I think you're the most wonderful and courageous and lovely person in the world . . . I'm 13, by the way, and I love you. I left Egypt when I was 7 and I'm longing to get back to Cairo.

He had feared that a psychiatric defense might send him to the funny farm forever. Now he believed the defense would win him a verdict of second-degree murder, and a short prison term.

The prosecution, moreover, didn't prove very much against him. "The FBI," he said, "haven't done a goddamn thing. They haven't turned up a thing. There's a lot they don't know about this case." His tone was boastful.

I wondered what it was that the FBI had failed to discover, and what would, in Sirhan's mind, have kept him in prison longer if they had discovered it.

Sirhan interpreted my silence correctly: "But there's no conspiracy!" he said. "There's no conspiracy!"

※　※　※　※　※

For the better part of three days, everyone in court listened to the police recordings of Sirhan's conversations with the law on the morning of June 5. It was a move on the part of the prosecution to confute Schorr's judgment that Sirhan was in a dissociated state before, during and after the shooting of Robert Kennedy. The jury heard a Sirhan who was, generally, pretty cool, more adept at questioning the police than they were at questioning him, too breezy really for someone who had just assassinated a Kennedy, yet so lacking in curiosity that he never once inquired why he was under arrest.

Finally, on March 18, after some bitter wrangling between defense and prosecution over the admissibility of Dr. Brussel's entire book as evidence, a battle which the prosecution lost, Howard confronted Schorr with a copy of his December 18 report and a copy of Brussel's book.

Schorr did the only thing he could do: he confessed.* He said Brussel was a recognized authority in the field. He used some fine language in his book. "So I used whatever was pertinent in the material, not involving myself in any of his cases, only with the language which involves the paranoid mechanism, only to try to highlight it for the purpose of illustrating to you what this is all about."

Just before lunch on Tuesday, March 18, Howard drew from Schorr the admission that Sirhan could premeditate. It was a contradiction of Schorr's earlier testimony and it couldn't fail to confuse the jury.

On redirect examination, Berman might have clarified the difference between premeditation in the popular sense and premeditation as it was now defined by the California Supreme Court. The best thing he could think of was to get Schorr off the stand and tell him to get lost—quickly—and avoid giving any more interviews to the press. After six days on the stand, Schorr was glad enough for the advice. But he was damned either way, interviews or no. *Newsday*'s Bob Greene led his next morning's story like this:

> Los Angeles—Dr. Martin M. Schorr had the sick look of a man who has just taken a hard right to the belly yesterday when he stepped off the elevator on the first floor of the Hall of Justice at exactly 12:07 P.M.
>
> He is just getting used to contact lenses and he had to tilt his head backwards to focus correctly before he started walking. A mob of interviewers

---

* It was a fateful turn for Schorr, said Mary Sirhan, but a divine sign. "God agreed with me," she said, pointing skyward. "If anyone had asked me, I would have told him to leave it out." (Meaning, of course, Schorr's analysis of Sirhan's Oedipal problems.)

tried to hold him back. But he kept shaking his head and broke into an awkward trot toward the street door. His petite, gray-haired wife, Dolores, put her arm around his waist and squeezed. He sagged a moment and then squeezed back. And then, holding one to the other, they left the building without looking back. . . .

Unaccountably, Berman let the prosecution continue to talk about "premeditation" and "malice" in imprecise popular terms, despite a memo he had gotten from Dr. Diamond warning him not to let the expert witnesses or the prosecution ever use the term "premeditate" unless the term were coupled with Sirhan's incapacity to "maturely and meaningfully reflect on the gravity of his contemplated act." That was the only way, Dr. Diamond had said, that California law defined "premeditation." If the expert witnesses were allowed to offer the opinion that Sirhan could not "premeditate," the jury would think the defense was playing semantic tricks on them: the jury knew Sirhan *thought* about killing Kennedy *ahead of time*. But was Sirhan able to reflect maturely and meaningfully on the gravity of his contemplated act? That was the question that had to be drummed in.

If anyone could recoup the setback suffered by the defense at the hands of Dr. Schorr, there wasn't a better man to do it than Dr. O. Roderick Richardson. He was tall, husky, direct and open in his responses, a skilled psychologist who knew what his tests could do and couldn't do, ready to admit the reasonableness of David Fitts's quibbles over his interpretation of the Rorschach, but firm in his opinion that Sirhan was just as sick as Schorr had said he was—possibly sicker: "Schizophrenic process, paranoid state, acute and chronic," said Richardson in a summary.

Furthermore, he had given his raw data (see Appendix G) to two other psychologists, Dr. Steven Howard and Dr. William W. Crain, and they had made blind diagnoses that generally agreed with his.

Sirhan was initially angry when he read Richardson's report at the counsel table, but he soon lost interest in the proceedings. It was his birthday, March 19, and he enjoyed the attention it brought: a special birthday profile in the Los Angeles *Times* by Dave Smith, birthday cards from his family and his four attorneys—and a turndown by the sheriff of his mother's request to send up a cake. That, too, made him feel good in a perverse way, for it fed what Richardson was describing on the stand as his delusions of persecution.

On cross-examination, Fitts made some rather unsuccessful attempts to challenge the validity of any projective psychological tests and even suggested to Richardson that Sirhan was only having "a little fun with him."

Richardson said it really didn't matter. "The minute you begin to respond to the Rorschach, even in a silly way, you are giving us a kind of map of your receptual and cognitive approach, something about your unconscious ways of perceiving. And I never—when my friends want me to give them an interpretation of a Rorschach card, I say, 'No, please, because I like you and I want to know you as my friend and I don't want to see your psychological innards, so to speak.' That is why we say we don't give—I wouldn't want to have my friend's Rorschach responses, even the silly ones, any more than I would want to have his X rays around."

Fitts rubbed his nose, went back to the counsel table and consulted his notes. He challenged Richardson's interpretation of a pastoral scene on the TAT card where Sirhan had shown some anxiety over "sex reversal" by reason of the fact that the girl was holding the books instead of the man.

"Wasn't Sirhan influenced by his Arab culture?" asked Fitts.

"Yes," said Richardson, "but—"

Issa Nankleh rose at his end of the counsel table and objected. "Not any more," shouted Nahkleh. "Now, women, too, become educated." Cooper lifted a hand to restrain Nahkleh, and the judge asked Cooper to see him in chambers after the adjournment.

"I understand," said Cooper.

Cooper took the next two expert witnesses himself, wishing to handle them crisply and with dispatch—for he knew the jury was tiring of all these inkblots. Drs. Steven J. Howard and William W. Crain, both clinical psychologists, had evaluated Richardson's raw data without prior benefit of Richardson's diagnosis. Both agreed with Richardson's conclusions. Dr. Howard said that "Mr. Sirhan is a very sick man, a borderline psychotic who goes in and out depending on the minor stresses which occur in daily life. He's been this way most of his life."

In cross-examining Dr. Howard, David Fitts wondered whether—psychotic or not—Sirhan could still plan to shoot Senator Kennedy. Dr. Howard, who spoke with a slight Slavic accent (he was born in Poland), replied that he could. Fitts suggested that war was a "psychologically normal activity" but Dr. Howard wouldn't concede that.

"People take lives in warfare, don't they?" asked Fitts.

"And some of them come apart as a result," said Dr. Howard. "I as-

sume there are other people in the United States who feel as Sirhan does,
but they don't go around killing people."

"That is true," said Fitts. "I have nothing further."

Fitts couldn't best Dr. Howard on the psychopathology of war. He
didn't even try with Dr. Crain. Cooper asked Crain only one question, and
offered him for cross-examination. "No questions," sighed Fitts, who had
just been handed a five-page report written by Dr. Crain which couldn't
help the prosecution's case. Indeed, Crain's report underlined most forcefully the long-standing nature of Sirhan's sickness:

". . . his plans," said Dr. Crain, "to assassinate appear to have had their
base in a very deep and long-standing effort on the part of Sirhan to right
past wrongs regarding his own life experience . . . Mr. Sirhan's 'premeditation' began, in my judgment, when he was a very small child."

It was Crain's inference about Sirhan's longtime and sick premeditation
that moved me away from my stance as a relatively uninvolved observer
into an active participant. I knew of Sirhan's abiding interest in assassinations, a fact which I thought would bolster the guesses of Dr. Crain (and
of Dr. Eric Marcus, who was convinced that Sirhan fit the mold of the
classic assassin, a paranoid with a political fixation). Parsons and Mc-
Cowan knew, too. But Sirhan's high-school history books, with marked
passages on the assassinations of Archduke Ferdinand and President
McKinley, were still sitting in Parsons' office. At lunch I asked Dr. Marcus, who was ready to testify next for the defense, if the introduction of
those books would bolster his theory. "Of course," said Marcus, blinking
hard and wondering why they'd been concealed up to now.

I leaned over to McCowan and said, "We'd better get those history
books in evidence." McCowan agreed with me.

Dr. Eric Marcus took the stand and gave his qualifications. He'd gotten
his B.A. and his M.D. from UCLA, and he'd taken his psychiatric training
at UCLA's Neuropsychiatric Institute. He was a member of all the major
psychiatric associations, a past president of the Southern California Society for Psychiatry and the Law and a member of the National Council on
Crime and Delinquency. He had examined Sirhan in his cell four times,
once when he was under the influence of alcohol, he had interviewed Mrs.
Sirhan and Adel, he had reviewed Sirhan's notebooks, he had done a good
deal of study on assassins and assassinations, he had consulted the results
of Sirhan's psychological tests and he had conferred with all of the doctors
who'd seen Sirhan, including Dr. Pollack.

"You're one of those psychiatrists who don't like to put labels on people, aren't you?" asked Cooper. Marcus said he was. "Then what do you mean," asked Cooper, "by calling him mentally ill?"

Marcus explained that mental illness was a broad general category. In simple terms, if a man was mentally ill, he couldn't think logically or handle his emotions. For the purposes of courtroom psychiatry, he said, he didn't like to get into arguments over nomenclature.

"Did Sirhan have a mental illness on June 5, 1968?"

"He did."

"Why do you say that?"

Marcus predicated his opinion mainly on Sirhan's notebooks and the psychological tests. The writings, he said, looked like the writings of insane murderers now incarcerated at Atascadero (a California hospital for the criminally insane). Sirhan started to frown and fume and stir in his chair.

Marcus said that such a mentally ill person could form an intent to kill, plan a murder and entertain malice aforethought. But Sirhan didn't, said Marcus. His thinking rose from his paranoid view of himself as "a savior of society who was out to destroy America's political leaders and start World War III." This, said Marcus, was sick thinking, so sick that Sirhan wasn't capable of malice in its technical legal sense.

Now Sirhan conferred heatedly with Parsons. Parsons poured a long monologue into Sirhan's ear. By the time he'd finished, Sirhan had seemingly forgotten what it was he was angry about.

Was Sirhan a political assassin? He was not a political assassin, said Marcus, like the Puerto Ricans who attempted to kill President Harry Truman at the Blair House in 1948; he assassinated a politician, to be sure, but he was, as far as Marcus could tell, like all the sick assassins who had been trying to kill American presidents since the attempt in 1831 on the life of Andrew Jackson. He wasn't an Arab patriot. In fact, Sirhan made no mention in his notebook of Kennedy's support for Israel. Furthermore, as Sirhan's schoolbooks indicated, Sirhan had been thinking about assassinations for a long, long time.

On cross-examination, Fitts tried to suggest that some of Sirhan's "sick" activity was basically normal. Sirhan's reading, for instance. Didn't the range of his reading simply suggest that Sirhan was simply going through a process of "self-education?"

"What would be his major?" asked Marcus dryly. "Would it be political assassinations? Or religious pursuits? Or was he going to become a philosopher? It was a mishmash. That is what they do in hospital libraries all day long."

Sirhan was a schizophrenic, said Dr. Marcus. He tried patiently to explain what a schizophrenic was.

Fitts wondered whether there were not certain schizophrenic processes in normal people. He took himself as an example: "An individual who generally tries to set the image in his household of a kind father, for instance. He puts up with the importunities of his children, he is vexed with them at times, he tries to be tolerant of them. And yet, given a sort of a stress situation, such as perhaps having to work on a long trial, he blows up at the kids and does things for which he may be sorry later."

"No," said Marcus. "That's not what schizophrenia means. What you're describing is a sort of middle-class, neurotic phenomenon. That happens to me and others. No, I wouldn't call this schizophrenic. Schizophrenic has a specific meaning. It means there is something wrong with the way your brain operates. It's as if, using an analogy, you are using a telephone switchboard and the plugs are crisscrossed so that things are not adding up."

Marcus called attention to Sirhan's mistaken political beliefs, "assuming, for instance, that he could start World War III. That was one mistake. He made some other mistakes. His mistake was that if he could assassinate President Johnson and the Vice-President, and on down, that somehow he would make a new order of being in the world. I consider those as very gross errors in judgment."

"But there's lots of people in the world who think there's something wrong with our system, aren't there?" asked Fitts.

"Oh, yes."

"As a matter of fact, in other political ideologies," said Fitts, "it's common practice for people to dispose of their enemy in any way possible. Isn't that true?" Fitts said he was thinking of Machiavelli.

"Anybody," said Marcus, "who thinks seriously about those things and who has made attempts—most of those people are either in prisons or mental hospitals."

Fitts wondered about Stalinist Russia and its political pogroms. Were Stalin and his leaders all mentally disturbed?

"Well," said Marcus, "I don't know about all. There's some question about the leaders, such as Stalin and others. Once you achieve a position of power, you are considered as sane by definition, since you run the show and you hire and fire the psychiatrists. Some things are open to question when you get to the very top."

Fitts took Marcus back to the night of the killing. Could a psychotic Sirhan have asked others in the kitchen pantry if Kennedy was coming that way? Marcus said that was possible. Sirhan could have gone to the Ambassador to assassinate Kennedy. It could have been planned that way. But the planning was done within Sirhan's delusional, bizarre system.

"He made a decision that night not to drive because he had too much to drink," said Fitts. "Doesn't that imply some degree of social responsibility?"

"That," said Marcus, "is one of the peculiarities of the schizophrenic. It's like The Boston Strangler saying to one of his victims, 'Pardon me for breaking in.' "

"Sirhan told you he didn't remember the shooting, didn't he?" asked Fitts.

"Yes."

"You don't believe it, do you?"

Marcus paused and gave the matter some hard thought then and there, actually humming in the process. Finally, he said to Fitts: "Yes, I believe it."

Marcus' hesitation here prompted Fitts to probe more deeply, and his instincts were right. No one on the defense team could ever really say he was sure Sirhan was telling the truth. And Marcus was the man to ask, for he was proud of his impartiality. "Was Sirhan suffering from a bona fide amnesia?" asked Fitts. Marcus said he didn't know whether Sirhan had real amnesia, retrograde amnesia or whether he was malingering altogether. "It could be any of those?" asked Fitts.

"I would say," said Marcus, "it would be a toss-up between malingering and retrograde amnesia."

"Well, with the retrograde amnesia, that would still be, so far as Mr. Sirhan is concerned, a period of forgetfulness, wouldn't it?"

"Yes."

"And if it were a retrograde amnesia, Mr. Sirhan would then be making the same inquiries as if it were a real amnesia?"

"Right."

"So that leaves us then with only a working hypothesis of malingering, doesn't it?"

"Apparently so," said Marcus.

"Then to go back to the question that I asked you earlier, when Mr. Sirhan claimed this amnesia in his interview with you, he was lying to you?"

"That's quite possible," said Marcus.*

"I think that's all," said Fitts.

---

* There was another, unexamined, possibility: that Sirhan was programmed to forget.

Cooper got up immediately and said: "Doctor, does that change your opinion as to your diagnosis?"

"No," said Marcus. "We haven't been discussing diagnosis for quite some time."

It may not have had anything to do with Dr. Marcus' medical diagnosis. But it had everything to do with the progress of the trial. And Marcus knew it, for at lunch he apologized to Dr. Diamond, who had just flown in from San Francisco, for making this damaging admission in court. Marcus realized that he had made no real effort to determine whether Sirhan's lack of memory was due to amnesia, retrograde amnesia or malingering. Diamond was the one who had tried to get to the bottom of that mystery, and Diamond should have been the one to give an opinion in court.

Diamond agreed. Furthermore, said Diamond, amnesia wasn't exactly the issue. A man could be in a dissociated state and still not be amnesic.

When court resumed, Cooper tried to repair the damage. "Do you have an opinion," he asked Dr. Marcus, "as to whether he was or was not malingering?"

"I'm really not sure," said Marcus. "My examination of him really didn't get into this area. I was more interested in his overall life pattern, especially during the last several years. This would take specific studies of him dealing specifically with his state of mind at that particular moment."

And, under a second cross-examination by Fitts, Marcus found the opportunity to add, "Sirhan may have been dissociated and still have not lost his memory."

"Well, that's a pretty good one to me," Fitts said. He pointed out that Sirhan had responded to the Miranda warnings by police early in the morning of June 5 with silence; that he had, furthermore, refused a demand somewhat later by Sergeant Melendres to tell the police what had happened "the last several hours at the Ambassador Hotel." Then he said to Marcus, "Do you remember that every time it was asked, the defendant said, in substance, you're pressing me too close?" Marcus said he'd like to see the transcript of that interrogation. He didn't remember that. He didn't remember it because Fitts was giving an inaccurate report. Sirhan got no more questions that morning as direct as the one asked by Melendres.

But Marcus did have an observation to make concerning that police interrogation. Sirhan's entire demeanor during that morning was "inappropriate for someone you know has just committed the crime of the year."

Fifteen

"Too illogical even for the theater of the absurd."

When Dr. Bernard L. Diamond took the stand late Friday afternoon, he felt abandoned. He'd been reading copies of the court record, sent to him almost daily by Cooper's office, and he was rather displeased with the handling of the case. Why had Cooper been so willing to concede that Sirhan was lying in wait? Why had he failed to put on Munir Sirhan, who could testify better than anyone concerning his brother's psychological deterioration? Why had he let Sirhan be indulged by Parsons and McCowan? Didn't he see that they were only helping Sirhan appear on the stand as something other than he really was? Why had he failed to question Sirhan closely on the stand about his feelings when he was arrested, why he hid his identity, why he kicked the hot chocolate out of the policeman's hand, why he would rather plead guilty and go to the gas chamber than have two girls he hardly even knew testify in the trial? Why had Cooper bothered to put Sirhan on the stand if he wasn't going to demonstrate his psychopathology?

And what was wrong with Berman? Berman was supposed to begin by asking Dr. Diamond to tell the jury about his qualifications as an expert witness, qualifications that would have dazzled any jury. Diamond was a Fellow of the American Association of the Advancement of Science; a Fellow of the American Psychiatric Association and the American Orthopsychiatric Association and of the American Sociological Association; past president of the Northern California Psychiatric Society; formerly president of the San Francisco Analytic Institute and Society; a member of the Committee on Psychiatry and Law of the American Psychiatric Association, chairman of that committee in 1962–63; on the Committee on Law and Psychiatry of the Group for Advancement of Psychiatry; chairman of the Committee on Social Issues of the American Orthopsychiatric

Association, and member of its board of directors at the present time; a member of the California Commission on Insanity and Criminal Offenses, 1960 through 1963; recipient of the J. Elliot Royer Award of the Regents of the University of California for the Advancement of Psychiatry in 1964; the recipient in 1968 of the Isaac Ray Award of the American Psychiatric Association for the Advancement of Psychiatry and Law; consultant to the Department of Justice in Washington for the National Institute of Law Enforcement and Criminal Justice; the author or co-author of some thirty-one articles in various medical and legal journals dealing with psychiatry and the law.

But Berman forgot to ask Diamond what made him an expert and then started to stumble through a set of prearranged questions. Diamond decided to wing it alone. He launched into a kind of lecture to the jury in a conversational tone; he told them of all the baffling mysteries he confronted in Sirhan: his lack of recollection about the notebooks, his failure to remember the events of the night of June 4; above all, his failure to demonstrate any of the signs and symptoms of the profound mental disease which Diamond eventually diagnosed: a chronic, paranoid schizophrenia, a major psychosis, which put him in a highly abnormal, dissociated state of restrictive consciousness at the time of the shooting.

Then Judge Walker adjourned for the weekend.

On Monday morning, Diamond continued on the same tack. The psychological tests had given him an X ray of Sirhan's mind. But in his early interviews with Sirhan, he found none of the obvious signs to substantiate the profound psychological disturbance revealed on the tests. Diamond thought he knew why. He knew that people who are paranoid have no trust. They are abnormally suspicious of others, they suspect that others are out to do them in, and they often fake sanity. Diamond quoted his paper on the "Simulation of Sanity." He had a duty, he thought, to sort things out, to sift all the half-truths, evasions and lies and figure out the mystery of Sirhan.

By talking with others, Diamond found some clues: Sirhan's early dissociated states suffered under the shock of the war in Jerusalem, his family breakup, his lonely adolescence, his psychological deterioration after his fall from the horse, his rage at the time of the Six-Day War, his escape into the occult. All these were possible signs and symptoms that all was not well deep within him. But what *was* going on deep within him? Normally, said Diamond, he spends hundreds of hours with a patient until gradually things begin to emerge. "That," said Diamond, "is certainly the most reliable method. That's what I usually do. I don't go around hypnotizing people. But in the medicolegal field and in battlefield medicine, you have to utilize shortcuts."

He had three shortcuts available: a lie detector (which doesn't really provide information), sodium amytal or pentothal (which is risky) and hypnosis. He preferred hypnosis. He used it, he said, not as a method of learning "the truth," but as a means of gaining access to the patient's mind. It was particularly useful in overcoming, not intentional lies, but unconscious evasions. "To a considerable degree," said Diamond, "when a resistance is overcome through the use of hypnosis, and an individual talks about something he was unable to talk about when awake, this is clinical evidence that the resistance against bringing it up in a conscious state was *unconscious in itself* and was not an intentional withholding or an intentional lie. So that the overcoming of a memory loss, an amnesia, through hypnosis techniques is considerable evidence in itself—but not of course final proof—that the amnesia is genuine and was not a fake or pretended loss of memory."

Sirhan, he found, went into hypnosis rather easily, and, as time went on, Diamond began to suspect that Sirhan had been hypnotized frequently before, though he was puzzled by Sirhan's inability to speak under hypnosis. Diamond told the jury about Sirhan's "abreaction" on January 26—his reliving of the night of the assassination. There was no absolute guarantee, he said, that the reliving equated the actual event as it happened. But he was convinced that what Sirhan *did* relive of the assassination happened pretty much the way he lived it. The significant material which Sirhan remembered was not all that startling, but it indicated that Sirhan hadn't been holding back on purpose; it was material he had every reason to recall in a waking state, for it helped establish his disorientation that evening: (1) He picked up his gun in the car "because he didn't want the Jews to steal it." (2) He gave a description of the girl he was with while he was having coffee. (3) He was dazed and confused by the lights, the mirrors and the people. (4) He stared at a teletype machine. (5) People rushed at him. (6) He cried out, "You son of a bitch." (7) He shot Kennedy.

At that precise moment, said Diamond, Sirhan was in a highly abnormal, psychotic state, a dissociated state. It was only by reason of a remarkable concatenation of circumstances that he had a loaded gun with him at the precise moment when Kennedy (and all that name and face symbolized for Sirhan) would come upon him. Diamond wasn't saying this was all a terrible accident. It wasn't. Sirhan programmed himself to do this, like a robot. Sirhan was some kind of automatic assassin. And that is where the notebook came in. Diamond tried to explain the notebook to the jury. It, too, was a product of Sirhan's illness; even more, of a series of self-induced trances wherein Sirhan wrote "like a robot." Diamond told of how he had reduplicated that, too, in Sirhan's cell (see page 364.) Diamond gave the jury a complete account of that four-hour session. He went through all of his questions to Sirhan, and all of Sirhan's written responses, right down to the end of the fourth page, when Diamond asked, "Were you thinking then of shooting Kennedy?" and Sirhan wrote, "No no no."

Diamond folded up his notes and smiled with the obvious satisfaction of a pro who knows he has done a good job. In the back of the courtroom, Bob Greene, who seemed to see humans as mirrors of the animal kingdom, said Diamond looked "like a hawk preening himself after swallowing a big fat mouse." But Greene and everyone else in the crowded courtroom were themselves spellbound.

Diamond wasn't sure the jury could believe his account. He wasn't even sure Sirhan himself believed it and said so. "I still hope to be able to convince Sirhan. I might say that I don't wish to give you the impression here that Sirhan is cooperative in the least. Sirhan never talked to me very much. I don't think he ever really believed that I was working for the defense, despite the reassurances of his attorneys." Diamond said he was engaged in a kind of "power struggle with Sirhan" which "still goes on to this day." He was still evasive with Diamond about "his Rosicrucian magic"; he still "tells lies when it comes to indicators of his mental illness."

Berman asked Diamond to state his ultimate conclusions. "I agree," Diamond said, "that this is an absurd and preposterous story, unlikely and incredible. I doubt that Sirhan himself agrees with me as to how everything happened. Sirhan would rather believe that he is the fanatical martyr who by his noble act of self-sacrifice has saved his people and become a great hero. He claims to be ready to die in the gas chamber for the glory of the Arab people. However, I see Sirhan as small and helpless, pitifully ill, with a demented, psychotic range, out of control of his own consciousness and his own actions, subject to bizarre, dissociated trances in some of which he programmed himself to be the instrument of assassination, and then, in an almost accidentally inducted twilight state, he actually executed the crime, knowing next to nothing as to what was happening."

Diamond's sum-up should have agitated Sirhan. Instead, Sirhan looked bored. None of the doctors, he later explained to me, knew what they were talking about. And nobody who counted believed them anyway. The morning mail had proved that much. There was a time when he was worried over what the public would think about him. But not anymore. People were sending him small contributions. And, more importantly, letters like the one he had gotten only this morning, a letter "of praise and adoration" from a high-school senior in Pennsylvania. These made him feel good.

After a day's recess to prepare for the cross-examination of Dr. Diamond, David Fitts challenged Diamond's notion of free will. Didn't Diamond once write that free will was "illusory?"

"I never said there was no such thing as free will," said Diamond. In fact, he said, he and Professor Louisell of Boalt Hall, the Law School of the University of California at Berkeley, had written an article in which they described their concept of free will and showed that there is less difference between psychiatry and the law than is usually believed. Normal people, he said, have free will as it is usually described. Abnormal people, sick people like Sirhan, do not.

Fitts dropped that line of questions and started to attack Diamond on what was, in effect, the doctor's weakest point: his deduction, really, that Sirhan was in a dissociated state at the time he killed Kennedy. Diamond admitted that the dissociated state was a key part of his hypothesis. Diamond said that he did not think that Sirhan's schizophrenia alone would have caused him to commit this killing. "In other words," said Fitts, "you have to add the ingredient of the dissociated state."

"You have to add every one of the ingredients that I talked about, starting with Jerusalem in 1948," said Diamond.

But didn't Diamond put too much credence in the Sirhan family's accounts of the Arab-Israeli war and its effect on Sirhan? "Don't you suppose," asked Fitts, "that Mrs. Sirhan, having her son in trouble, has some disposition to magnify the horrors of war and the effect on her son in the hope that they will have some impact on this jury and on your psychiatric opinion?"

"Sir," said Diamond, "I don't think it is possible to magnify the effect of the horrors of war on children."

"Well, it depends, of course," said Fitts, "on what they actually were. Isn't that true?"

"I think I am familiar with war," said Diamond, "what the war conditions were. I went through five years of World War II and I have a family —for example, my daughter and granddaughter live in Israel and my son lives there, and I am fully aware of what conditions are. I don't feel that they were exaggerated."

"Well, in any event," said Fitts, "you would probably agree with me that Mrs. Sirhan wouldn't be the sort of person who could describe or recognize such a state and explain it to you in such terms that you, with reasonable medical certainty, could be assured that it had happened. True?"

"I don't understand what you mean by 'reasonable medical certainty.' That's one of Dr. Pollack's phrases that I don't use."

"All right. You don't know whether he was just a frightened little boy back there in Jerusalem or not, do you, Doctor?" asked Fitts.

"It's my opinion," said Diamond, "that he was much more than a frightened little boy. War does much more than frighten little boys. It psychologically damages them."

"You think it psychologically damaged all the other four-year-olds over there in Jerusalem, too?" asked Fitts.

"Yes, to some degree it did."

"He more than others?"

"I don't know the others."

"You are perfectly aware, of course," said Fitts, "that before you got to him a number of people had attempted to elicit information from him?"

"Yes."

"Including his own lawyers?"

"Yes."

"Including investigators?"

"Yes."

"It's quite possible that they discussed a great number of things with him that were known to them, that they brought to his attention and asked about?"

"None of them," said Diamond, "had elicited certain information that I found that I was interested in. None of them could tell me or present a story of this that made any sense to me. That is why I undertook this investigation of him—because I felt that of all the people who had seen him, including psychologists and psychiatrists and his lawyers, nobody else really had the proper, whole story of Sirhan. The first story I got was essentially the story everybody knew. I was not satisfied with that."

Fitts said: "And in his conscious state, all the stories that you got from him were constructed ones, weren't they—in his aware state, his usual state?"

"What do you mean 'constructed'?" asked Diamond.

"There's no question in your mind that any anticipation of the trial, and the things that he knew of this sort—that he had adopted an attitude of what he was going to say, and what he was not going to say?"

"Well," said Diamond, "no. That was the difficulty. He was talking in

many ways which to me seemed very strange. He was admitting information which certainly would not help him and was concealing information
which might help him. Some very important elements of the story were missing and all these various people who talked with him had not gotten the
real story. That's why I felt it was very essential that some other technique
or means be used to gain access to Sirhan."

"Well, isn't it rather usual for, let us say, just a sociopathic personality
—a man who commits a crime and gets himself in jail—to concoct a story
that might not please everybody because he thinks it's the only way to help
himself?"

"Sirhan had one quite the opposite of that," said Diamond. "Sirhan had
concocted a story which couldn't possibly help him."

"In view of what?" asked Fitts. "How couldn't it help him?"

"Because Sirhan was quite prepared to admit to me or anybody who
would ask him that he had killed Senator Kennedy, that he hated Senator
Kennedy and that he had done this to prevent Senator Kennedy from getting elected to the Presidency and sending fifty bombers to Israel. This, he
would tell to anybody who would listen. This did not impress me as [the
statement of] a sociopath who is inclined to help himself by concealing his
crime. These are the things that he *would* talk about. What he *wouldn't*
talk about were all these things which were related to his psychological
state, and what I regarded as a mental illness."

"All right," said Fitts. "Assuming for the moment that Sirhan wanted to
kill somebody, do you think that the fact that he used a .22 revolver is an
indication of some mental impairment on his part?"

"It's an indication," said Diamond, "of a lack of knowledge of how you
go about killing people."

"You can't quarrel with success, though, can you, Doctor?"

"Yes," said Diamond, "I can quarrel with success."

Fitts sneered at Diamond's easy acceptance of Sirhan's own story, that
he had kept his gun loaded "by accident."

"The only information I have," said Diamond, "is that the gun was
loaded on the range before the range was closed, and I have no information which indicates that anything else happened."

"But, of course," Fitts said, "to accept that as the gospel truth, you give
full faith and credence to whatever Sirhan has told you."

"Sir," said Diamond, "I do not believe that I know the gospel truth
about this case. I have tried my very best to examine him and reconstruct
what is necessarily a psychiatric theory of what has happened. I certainly
never proclaimed this to be the gospel truth or to exclude all possibilities.

I present this simply as my opinion of what is the most likely and most probable explanation of this crime. It's not the gospel truth and there are alternative explanations."

"It still does bother you though, doesn't it, that having painfully or otherwise extracted something like 500 rounds from this gun—that he didn't bother to extract eight live rounds from the gun when he left the range?" asked Fitts.

"Yes," said Diamond, "it bothers me, because it indicates his irresponsibility about guns and the irresponsibility of society—allowing guns to be in the hands of people like Sirhan. This is what puzzles me."

Fitts came back to the question of Sirhan's "dissociation."

Diamond was obviously nettled, and he turned sideways on the witness stand so that he wouldn't have to look at Fitts. But he tried to explain what schizophrenics look like when they are "dissociated." "They do not do like in the Hollywood movies—look around with a blank expression on their faces and say, 'Where am I?' I have never seen an authentic case of amnesia or dissociation or hysteria or schizophrenia behave that way. That's Hollywood stuff. The typical kind of behavior is a sort of on-guard, cautious attitude, a looking around, being very reserved, a kind of looking around to see what people's reactions are, to try to kind of figure it out, being evasive— and sometimes very gradually, sometimes over a period of hours and hours and hours, a slow restoration to memory of what is going on." Diamond said that's the way he believed Sirhan was in jail on the night of the assassination. He added: "And I know it is not permissible, but I assert to you with clinical honesty that I would have no difficulty in triggering off such a state right now with Sirhan in front of everybody."

Fitts ignored that. "Doctor," he said, "in your summation you said, 'I agree that this is an absurd and preposterous story, unlikely and incredible.' You said that, didn't you?"

"Yes, I did say it."

"Who were you agreeing with?"

Diamond paused. He couldn't very well say that Grant Cooper thought his story preposterous. "I agree with the world," said Diamond.

Bob Greene of *Newsday* drained the last of his special fizz, a relaxing five-o'clock concoction of gin, fruit juice and vanilla ice cream prepared by Hilton bartender Eddie Diaz, eased his bulk off the stool in the Steak House bar and told Helen Dudar of the New York *Post,* Theo Wilson of the New York *Daily News,* John Hemphill of the Nashville *Tennessean* and Harry Rosenthal of The Associated Press he'd see them for supper about eight o'clock. He knew he'd have no trouble getting the space he needed to tell the story today. There was nothing an editor liked better than a battle, and this had been a good one.

"Who won?" asked *Newsday*'s National Editor Mel Opotowsky. Greene cradled his room phone in his third jowl, lit a Pall Mall and said that both Fitts and Diamond scored their touchdowns. But Diamond did so with arrogance.

"He get mad on the stand?" asked Opotowsky.

"He did," said Greene.

"You still call it a draw?"

"In a debate," said Greene, "Diamond is the winner."

"But?"

"But Diamond let Fitts get to him. I think he lost the jury."

The next morning, Fitts still had Diamond on the stand. He produced a transcript of the February 2 meeting of all the doctors in Cooper's office, and noted that Diamond had said then that he didn't believe Sirhan was psychotic. "All my clinical material," Diamond had said (and Fitts read it now to the court), "points largely to this dissociative hysteria rather than a psychotic picture. I picked up a lot of paranoid stuff . . . but I don't see it as a psychotic type of affair."

"Isn't it true," said Fitts, "that you did not find Sirhan to be a psychotic?"

"No, sir," said Diamond, "it is not true."

Fitts shot a significant look at the jury. "That's all," he said.

On redirect examination, Berman had Diamond explain. After his review of all the psychological tests and his conferences with the psychologists, Diamond saw that Sirhan was "a schizophrenic beyond a doubt, indicating a psychotic state, and thoroughly and completely resolved the doubt I had when I made the statement, which was whether these dissociated states were the product of a highly hysterical reaction or a product of the schizophrenia. I came to the conclusion that the dissociated states were . . . the product of a true psychosis, a chronic, paranoid schizophrenia."

Berman then asked Diamond what he meant when he had said that the entire story was unlikely and incredible. Diamond read a summary he had written late the night before:

> When I first had personal contact with Sirhan, I was prepared for the usual case of the paranoid fanatic who dreams of glory through violence and death. In part, this is what has been found to be so.

I was not prepared for what else I discovered—an astonishing instance of mail order hypnosis, dissociated trances and the mystical occultism of Rosicrucian mind power and black magic. That this primitive, psychotic, voodoo thinking could have resulted in the death of Senator Kennedy and so affected the destiny of the entire world is, in my opinion, the ultimate in preposterous absurdity, too illogical even for a theater of the absurd.

I have investigated Sirhan's mind by every psychiatric means within my power. I have related my findings and upon them I base my opinion that Sirhan Bishara Sirhan lacks the mental capacity required by the legal definitions of the crime of murder. At this time, I have little expectation of belief, but I think it to be important that there exist a full record of how the assassination of Robert Kennedy came about.

Everyone was tired. Berman fumbled through his papers, read haltingly through something in the trial transcript of uncertain relevance, then asked Diamond (again) what he meant when he said the entire story was unlikely and incredible.

With some embarrassment, Diamond tried again to explain what he meant by the preposterous character of his analysis. "It is unlikely," he said, "that this chain of events could have resulted in a tragic crime that affected the destiny of this country and of the entire world. This is a script that would never be acceptable in a class-B motion picture and yet it is the result of my psychiatric findings." Then Diamond left the stand, somewhat shaken—but not surprised—by the spectacle of Berman's own peculiar dissociation.

Briskly then, Grant Cooper proceeded to examine two psychologists whom Dr. Pollack had hired to reevaluate the raw psychological data of Drs. Richardson and Schorr. They were Dr. Georgene Seward from the University of Southern California, and Dr. George DeVos from the University of California at Berkeley. While Dr. Seward testified—she agreed with both Schorr and Richardson, as well as Diamond, that Sirhan was a paranoid schizophrenic—Sirhan pored over the written reports of Drs. Seward and DeVos. He didn't like DeVos. DeVos had written about Sirhan's underlying sexual pathology.

Dr. Seward didn't indulge in speculations of this type, but Sirhan didn't like her report either. She said, "This is not the performance of a healthy Arab, but of a very sick, young American." And she pointed in her testimony on the stand to the possibility of "latent homosexual tendencies." Sirhan glared at her, leaned over to Parsons and snapped, "What kind of a son of a bitch do they think I am?"

Of all the experts at the trial, Dr. DeVos had perhaps the longest string of academic credits, ranging from his undergraduate days at the University of Chicago, his research in psychology and cultural anthropology at Nagoya National University in Japan, the University of Michigan, the University of California at Berkeley, the French Ministry of Justice at Vaucresson, France, and the University of Hawaii. He was the author, notably, of *Oasis and Casbah: Algerian Culture and Personality in Change,* a psychological study of Northwest African Arabs. DeVos said there was no cultural underlay that would have made Sirhan seem sicker than he really was. Nor did he think that it was possible for Sirhan to have fooled the psychologists. He said he'd never seen anyone "fake" on the Rorschach. His diagnosis of Sirhan's tests indicated "paranoid psychosis." And that was just about all that Cooper let him say. At the counsel table, Sirhan brightened, happy because DeVos hadn't brought up any of "that homosexual crap."

Then Cooper read into the record a transcript of the February 25 conference in chambers at which Sirhan challenged Judge Walker and said he wanted to go to the gas chamber. It was the only significant "in chambers conference" the jury had not yet heard. And Cooper wanted them to hear it before he rested his case. As he did so, Berman read along carefully, Parsons sat there glumly with his chin in his hands, Fitts fiddled with a small piece of folded paper, Howard doodled on his yellow legal pad and McCowan rocked back and forth in his chair at the counsel table with a satisfied look on his face, winking at some of the jurors, smiling, raising his eyebrows and sucking on a paper cup. When Cooper finished reading he said: "The defense rests, your Honor." John Howard promptly asked for permission to show the twelve-minute film taken at the Ambassador Hotel on the night of June 4, the last speech of Senator Kennedy and some of the confusion that followed. Howard argued that the film would show that Kennedy's speech contained nothing that could be construed as a "triggering mechanism" for the dissociated emotional state in which the defense claimed Sirhan killed Kennedy.

Cooper made strenuous objections and Judge Walker concurred on two grounds: (1) that no one had ever claimed Kennedy had said anything that night that precipitated Sirhan's dissociated state, or even claimed that Sirhan had actually heard the speech; and (2) the film, which Walker had seen, could have an inflammatory effect on the jury, far outweighing the film's probative value.

Howard didn't protest. The city had spent money on the film; he felt he had a duty at least to ask permission to show it in court. Well, he had asked and the judge said, "No."

Sixteen

On Friday, March 28, the prosecution began its rebuttal. It put on George Murphy, the huge, florid, balding investigator for the district attorney's office, who had spent a good deal of time with Sirhan on the morning of June 5. "Sirhan," he said, "seemed as normal as anyone I ever handled on a homicide charge."

Sergeant Adolph B. Melendres, a graying, paunchy veteran of the Los Angeles Police Department, who had worked eighteen years in homicide investigation, said Sirhan "was completely sober" and "very intelligent. He appeared very calm to me." Cooper tried to get Melendres' response stricken from the record on the grounds he was not an expert on mental psychopathology. But the judge let his answer stand.

Sergeant Frank Patchett, a handsome detective with steel-gray hair, who was also with Sirhan on the morning of the fifth, told the court, "I asked Sirhan if he was ashamed of his name because of what he had pulled that evening." He said Sirhan said, "Hell, no."

Here Judge Walker announced that President Eisenhower had died that morning. He asked for a minute of silent prayer. Everyone closed his eyes except Sirhan's security detail—and Sirhan himself, who looked around at the clock, examined his fingernails and twisted his fingers. At lunchtime in his cell, I asked Sirhan how he felt about the news of President Eisenhower's death. "I was saddened," said Sirhan. "I was really moved."

"Bullshit!" I said. "I saw you fiddling around and looking at the clock. You were the only one in the courtroom with his eyes open."

Sirhan gave me a cunning smile. "Well," he said, "I wasn't the only one. I know a writer-investigator who had his eyes open too!"

I asked Sirhan whether the image of Sirhan, the political assassin, had been tarnished by the testimony of the psychologists and psychiatrists. Sirhan didn't think so. He'd heard now that the Al Fatah had established him as a native hero in the Middle East. That commando organization was, in fact, distributing tens of thousands of posters featuring a picture of Sirhan over the words, "I did it for my country." I asked him how he felt about that.

"Well," said Sirhan, "the shot was expended. I might as well make the best of it."

That led me to ask—once again—why Sirhan had killed Kennedy.

Said Sirhan: "Because he was there." Sirhan pointed up to the roof. He believed in a God who metes out retribution for injustice. "Kennedy got what was coming to him," he said. Did Sirhan see himself as an instrument of divine wrath? He shook his head and smiled. "God didn't tell me to shoot Kennedy," he said calmly.

I told Sirhan that Dr. Pollack, who was going on the stand shortly, insisted in his reports that Sirhan had seemed normal in the last days before the assassination. Sirhan nodded. "Normal" was a good word. He liked that. "You weren't more reclusive toward the end?" I asked. Sirhan said he wasn't. In fact, he said, he had never had a better time in his life. "Well, then," I said, "who were you associating with in May of 1968?"

Sirhan smiled and said nothing, obviously amused with my attempts to lift the veil of secrecy he had dropped over this last month of his life on the outside. Anyway, he didn't want to tell me anything new. He was angry with me. He said I had told the D.A. that he had lied about being at the Ambassador on the night of June 2, and that hurt him. I said I hadn't told the D.A. McCowan had told Cooper in a written report dated November 22; Cooper gave the report to Dr. Pollack, and he gave it to the D.A. Sirhan didn't believe it.

Ahh, I thought, the hell with it. Why should I try to humor him? I left the cell, letting my anger and exhaustion turn me away temporarily from my resolve to accomplish the impossible: gain enough rapport with a paranoid-schizophrenic Palestinian Arab assassin to learn the entire truth.

The prosecution had a fourth rebuttal witness. He was Laurence W. Sloan, the handwriting expert. He had compared Sirhan's automatic writing done in the cell with Drs. Pollack and Diamond on February 1 with samples of Sirhan's notebook writing. He found "significant variations" between the two. He saw a "qualitative breakdown" in the automatic writing. He did not see the same qualitative breakdown on, for example, People's exhibit 72–15, the page in which Sirhan had written "Robert Kennedy

must be assassinated by 5 June 68." It was his opinion that Sirhan's notebooks "were not done under a state of hypnosis."

On cross-examination, Cooper got Sloan to admit that there were definite changes between different pages of the notebook, that there was some
quality deterioration on some of the pages of the notebook, and that, in
fact, even the key page in the notebook, People's 71–15, evidenced some
lessening of quality toward the end. "Did you ever read any books on automatic writing, Mr. Sloan?" asked Cooper.

"No," said Sloan.

"Did you ever examine any writings of paranoid schizophrenics?"

"No." said Sloan.

A jury's common sense could overrule the Rorschach. All the jury
needed was a little guidance. It came, not surprisingly, from the prosecution's man. Dr. Seymour Pollack, a forensic psychiatrist, like Diamond,
whose expertise was legal as well as medical. Pollack agreed that Sirhan
had a substantial mental illness, but insisted on the stand that he wasn't
sick enough to come under the California law of diminished capacity.
Though his testimony was full of contradictions, he clung stubbornly to his
conclusions. Cooper's cross-examination in open court couldn't shake him.
Neither could the contempt of his colleagues in psychiatry who saw the
profession categorized once more as a whore. It wasn't that Dr. Pollack
was not a good psychiatrist. He just couldn't agree with the legal concept
of diminished capacity.

There had been a good deal of discussion on the prosecution team about
Dr. Pollack. Should he be allowed to testify or not? His February 5 report
was a mishmash and his thirty-page report delivered on March 21 was, if
anything, more confusing. Howard pointed out that if the prosecution
didn't put him on, the defense would, and then the prosecution would have
to treat him as a hostile witness. "Okay," said Fitts to Howard. "You handle him."

Pollack's credentials were good enough. He had served his psychiatric
internship at Bellevue Hospital in New York, his psychiatric residency at
the New York Psychiatric Institute, a part of the Columbia College of
Physicians and Surgeons. He had taught at UCLA's School of Psychiatry
and was a professor in psychiatry at the University of Southern California
since 1956. He belonged to all the usual psychiatric associations, including
the Group for the Advancement of Psychiatry, on whose Committee on
Psychiatry and the Law he served. He was, moreover, the director of the

University of Southern California's Institute of Psychiatry and Law. He had spent about 200 hours on the Sirhan case—ten times what he spent on an average criminal case—twenty hours alone with Sirhan and five more with Dr. Diamond and Sirhan. He had listened to the police interrogations of Sirhan, seen the psychological reports of Drs. Schorr and Richardson, conferred with the other psychiatrists, read the jail logs since Sirhan's incarceration.

On February 5 Pollack had decided that Sirhan was psychotic. But even as he conveyed this information to the district attorney, he indicated that he didn't like the apparent implications of his judgment. Sirhan was sick, but he was still responsible to society for his actions. Though Deputy District Attorneys David Fitts and John Howard agreed with Dr. Pollack (for how could America survive, they reasoned, if nutty assassins were not given the ultimate penalty?), they spent several grueling private sessions with Pollack, pointing to his inconsistency with the law as it stood. Pollack was stubborn. He said Sirhan was sick. But he wasn't *that* sick. "What do you mean?" asked Fitts. "You said in your report that Sirhan was psychotic." In several thousand well-chosen words, Dr. Pollack said that Fitts didn't understand.

But now, in the trial, Pollack had come to another more logical formulation. Sirhan was *not* psychotic, and therefore knew what he was doing when he killed Kennedy. It took Pollack more than two days to say that on the stand in a woolly, wordy account which he read—interspersed with elaborate interpretative asides—from the second report he had dictated on March 21.

Much of what he said was obviously intended to counter Dr. Diamond's analysis. To do this, however, Pollack was often reduced to saying simply that he had no evidence of what Dr. Diamond had discovered. Such a stance implied either that Pollack was not as insightful as Diamond or that he didn't want to admit the implications of what he actually saw. There were, for example, Sirhan's "childhood traumas." Sirhan's conscious statements to Pollack about the war in Jerusalem were flat and matter-of-fact. And Pollack might well have concluded that Sirhan was merely "a frightened little boy." But those conscious statements were far, far removed from the cries of anguish that came from Sirhan when Dr. Diamond hypnotized him in Pollack's presence.

Pollack said that Sirhan's bizarre political judgments about President Johnson, Ambassador Goldberg, TV Newsman Clete Roberts and the American political system, and his belief that he could change American policy in the Middle East by killing Kennedy, "were not psychotic delusions." And at this point, Sirhan smiled delightedly and leaned forward to whisper to Parsons.

Pollack said Sirhan focused on Senator Robert Kennedy as an individual who should die, "not only because of the Kennedy promise to give Israel the jet bombers that would cause death to thousands of Arabs, in Sirhan's opinion, but also because Sirhan wanted the world to see—he wanted the world to see how strongly our United States policy was in the pro-Israel, anti-Arab movement in the face of—in spite of our government's professed interest for the underdog and world justice." He repeated the same idea—twice—and then concluded: "In spite of my belief that Sirhan at no time expected to be a martyr, I don't believe he wanted to be caught. I don't believe he expected to be punished for his political views or political acts."

McCowan walked out of the courtroom, signaling with an eyebrow for me to follow. In the corridor, *sotto voce,* McCowan said: "Sirhan just asked me, 'Should I flip now?' I told him if he did, I'd break his neck."

Sirhan had seen that Cooper was using Sirhan's outburst in court as evidence of his "diminished capacity." Though the previous outbursts were genuine, Sirhan didn't like their implication, and was taking the position now—in fact, had told his brother Adel in my presence—that he had planned them all along. It was just an act. By "flipping out" again, Sirhan believed he wouldn't hurt his case any, and yet he would also "prove" to his brother and his family that the outbursts were all merely part of a clever plan. *His* plan. "He's getting wise," I said.

"Your fuckin' A," said McCowan.

"What else is new?" I asked.

"Oh," said McCowan, "now he's talking about extorting $150,000 from Jimmy Hoffa. Either he gets the money or he tells the world Hoffa put him up to shooting Kennedy." I laughed. Sirhan had been using the same story for months now; first it was Lyndon B. Johnson, then Richard Nixon, now James Hoffa. There was no reason to suppose Sirhan knew that in actual fact a fellow prisoner of Hoffa's in the Lewisburg, Pennsylvania, Federal Penitentiary had told the FBI that he overheard Hoffa and his cronies in prison talking in May, 1968, about a "contract to kill Bob Kennedy." Hoffa wouldn't even discuss the matter with the FBI, and his friends in prison denied ever hearing of such a contract. It is almost absolutely certain, however, that even if Sirhan was chosen as a hired gun, he would be the last person to know the identity of the man at the top.

"How did Sirhan come up with the name of Hoffa?" I asked.

"He said, 'Kennedy put him in prison, didn't he?'"

A deputy stuck his head outside the door of the courtroom. "He did it again, Mike!"

Inside the courtroom, Pollack had said that Sirhan was lying when he claimed he couldn't remember writing in his notebooks.

Sirhan stood up in court. "Your Honor, sir—"

Judge Walker said: "You sit down or I will do what I told you I was going to do." Four husky deputies jammed Sirhan back into his chair and Judge Walker called a recess.

Sirhan carried through with his act and said, as he was being ushered back to the holding tank, audibly enough for L.A. *Times'* reporter Dave Smith to hear him, "I told the truth and I don't like him to call me a fuckin' liar." At the doorway, Sirhan wheeled, shot Pollack a smoldering look and said, "That son of a bitch."

Parsons went into the holding tank to calm him down, and Mary Sirhan and Adel sat anxiously in their seats, waiting to see if he would be bound and gagged when he returned to the courtroom. "He doesn't lie," Mrs. Sirhan insisted. "From the time he is a small boy I always teach him not to lie, and he never does. The poor boy."

The trial resumed and Parsons apologized to the judge. Parsons said that Sirhan could not control himself when the witness testified that he had told "a falsehood." At the noon break, the judge called the attorneys back up to the bench and said that any time they felt that Sirhan was getting to the point where he was going to break to let him know. "I will call a recess because I don't want these outbursts."

Parsons said: "I'm holding his hand all the time and I am there and I look at him all the time."

"I purposely don't look at him all the time," said Judge Walker.

After lunch, Pollack said that he had "reasonable medical certainty" that Sirhan wasn't in a trance when he killed Kennedy. Then he admitted, under no urging from anyone, that it was also—remotely—possible that he "actually had a dissociate mind at the time of the act, which was accompanied by a genuine amnesia." But Diamond's theory that Sirhan wrote his "kill Kennedy" material while he was in a trance was even less likely. He claimed that Sirhan's automatic writing was the result of "previous suggestions" * to Sirhan by Diamond.

Pollack was impressed with the psychological tests. "I was impressed more than the prosecution was," said Pollack, "and I am positive of my psychological test results. What impressed me more was that in my inter-

* There is no evidence that Diamond ever made such a suggestion to Sirhan.

views with Sirhan, this kind of thinking wasn't demonstrated." In other words, Pollack never got beneath the mask of normality which Sirhan habitually wore, not even when he put Sirhan under hypnosis on January 19. At that time Sirhan "blocked" so effectively that Pollack did not elicit a single response from him.

There were times, Pollack admitted, when Sirhan presented himself in an irrational fashion. However, he had studied the police reports of the witnesses at the Ambassador Hotel and found that none of them described the "confusion and bewilderment which I assume would have been present in Sirhan if he were awakening then from an altered state of consciousness."

For these reasons, Pollack said, it was his judgment that Sirhan intended to kill Robert Kennedy.

John Howard listed the mental states necessary for first-degree murder: (1) specific intent to kill, (2) premeditation, (3) malice. Did Sirhan have the capacity for all three of these mental states? Pollack said that he did. When he was asked to explain, he made a very good case for No. 1, that Sirhan had the capacity for the specific intent to kill—which was something the defense was ready to concede. He made a somewhat poorer case for Sirhan's capacity to harbor malice aforethought, leaning on the statutory definition of malice, and omitting the Supreme Court's added requirements under the *Conley* decision.* And Pollack gave no explanation whatever to account for his opinion that Sirhan had the capacity "to maturely and meaningfully premeditate, deliberate and reflect upon the gravity of his contemplated act of killing the Senator."

This was the most crucial legal point in the entire case: Sirhan's capacity to premeditate. Pollack glossed it over, and Howard, naturally, let him go.

But so did Grant Cooper. Cooper cross-examined Pollack for two full days, but never adequately underscored this curious oversight. He came close to it when he reminded Pollack that Sirhan had told him he expected to get only two years in prison for killing Kennedy. "Was that mature and meaningful thinking?" asked Cooper.

Pollack hedged. Sirhan, he said, "had the mental capacity for a mature and meaningful formation of the intent to kill Senator Kennedy."

Cooper said that none of the defense experts claimed Sirhan lacked the intent to kill.

* See pp. 111 112.

Dr. Pollack said, "I believe Dr. Diamond—if I recall his testimony that I read—placed Sirhan in a state of unconsciousness, in a trance." Diamond had said Sirhan was in a dissociated state. He hadn't said he was unconscious. But Cooper ignored the distinction and so, apparently, did Pollack.

Cooper didn't want to defend Diamond's admittedly "preposterous" story. "All right," said Cooper. "I don't have to agree with all of the psychiatrists." What he wanted to know was what Pollack thought about Sirhan's capacity not to form a specific intent to kill, but to premeditate.

Said Pollack, "Sirhan . . . wanted to kill Senator Kennedy. He appreciated the changes that would take place if he killed Senator Kennedy. He appreciated the change and that is why he wanted to kill him." Pollack added: "If Sirhan's deliberations had been accompanied by psychotic or substantially disturbed thinking in the sense that I had meant it—from psychotic delusions—Sirhan would not have had the capacity for meaningful deliberation. I believe that." Then Pollack muddled through a monologue that explained nothing.

And he ended not with an assertion but a question: "Where do you draw the line" he asked, "between mature and immature deliberation? Where does society draw the line? They're going to have to decide."

"You're trying to help them, aren't you, Doctor?" asked Cooper.

"I don't decide intent," said Pollack. "I talk about capacity for intent." And Pollack couldn't say that Sirhan's capacity was sufficiently impaired. He had, he admitted, seen some evidence of that in Sirhan's notebooks and in the psychological reports. But if those reports were valid, Pollack insisted, he should have been able to pick up even more material, and he had not been able to do so. He said he might have been able to find more evidence if he had had more time.

Cooper pointed out that Pollack had told the district attorney on February 5 that more intensive examination of Sirhan "would probably reveal more definite signs and symptoms of psychosis." Cooper reminded Pollack that the defendant was on trial for his life. Why didn't Dr. Pollack ask for more time to examine Sirhan?

Pollack said that Dr. Diamond opposed any further interviews.

Cooper had forgotten that Diamond had pleaded with Pollack to tell him what more he needed (see page 372), and that Pollack himself had decided that further interviews would be fruitless. Now Cooper looked over the top of his dark horn-rimmed glasses and frowned. "Why didn't you call me, Doctor?" asked Cooper. "You have done it many times before, have you not, at my home? We have talked, we have been friends for a long time and you have discussed this case with me frankly, haven't you?"

Pollack reddened and looked down at his notes. "Yes," he said.

"Did you ever think of calling me?" asked Cooper.

"I didn't call, Mr. Cooper," said Pollack, in a very low tone. "I should have called."

Cooper pointed out that even without additional interviews, Pollack had reported on February 5 that Sirhan "revealed a degree of paranoid thinking with accompanying emotional responses that led me to suspect that there were psychotic characteristics in his personality. When I stressed him in my interviews with him, I believe that his disturbance in thinking went beyond the paranoid trends which are characteristic of the nonpsychotic, paranoid personality."

Said Cooper, "This morning didn't you tell us that he was not psychotic?"

"Not clinically psychotic," said Pollack.

Dr. Pollack admitted that Sirhan's ideas were "bizarre." "But they are not bizarre to many people who believe in them, just as many people believe in astrology; just as many people believe in many of these cults."

"But now some doctors," said Cooper, "some psychiatrists, would say that these are symptoms of a psychosis, wouldn't they?"

"No," said Dr. Pollack, "only if there were evidences that these ideas were delusional."

And Pollack wasn't ready to concede that, for Sirhan, such ideas were delusional. Pollack said that Sirhan had discussed his experiments in the occult with him quite freely—but said nothing about Sirhan's extreme reluctance to do so, and did not mention that when Sirhan did talk about the occult, he asked Pollack to turn off his tape recorder *because* he didn't want anyone to think he was crazy.

Cooper changed his tack:

COOPER: Let me ask you, Doctor, what kind of thinking was it for someone—here is someone who has had a year and a half in college and is familiar with the court, and who reads newspapers, and who thinks he would get two years in jail for a killing—assassinating a Senator who was a Presidential candidate?

POLLACK: The same kind of thinking that is exhibited by, say, a black nationalist who believes he should not be given too much jail or prison or punishment because he killed someone who has been involved in our racial discrimination in America; the same kind of thinking that is exhibited—

COOPER: Doctor, let me stop you there. Have you ever read or heard or seen or can you quote any authority that anyone who has killed someone in cold blood—and there is no question he killed Kennedy in cold blood—

POLLACK: All right.

COOPER: And put that gun within two inches of him, pulling the trigger, and kept pulling it, is that right, no self-defense, and can you tell me a black nationalist that ever killed somebody in that fashion and who said he only deserved two years in jail?

Pollack couldn't. But comparing Sirhan to the anarchists in America who were establishing their own law at gunpoint wouldn't hurt the prosecution's case at all. In fact, Fitts would play on the jurors' fears of black violence to argue for Sirhan's conviction.

On Good Friday morning, Cooper was anxious to get a few more items on the record and dismiss Dr. Pollack before the judge's contemplated recess at noon for the Easter weekend. "Doctor, yesterday afternoon you mentioned in response to one of my questions that it was your hope or recommendation that the defendant would be sent to the Medical Facility at Vacaville, and you recall that?"

"Yes," said Pollack.

"I take it that you had in mind that the Medical Facility at Vacaville is a maximum security penitentiary?"

"Yes, I did. I know that it is." Cooper moved on to another subject. Pollack interrupted. "My question of Vacaville had nothing to do with the maximum security, Mr. Cooper, but with the medical aspect."

Cooper knew that. Because lawyers are forbidden to discuss penalty in a trial's primary phase, Cooper couldn't tell the jury about the high security arrangements that would be made for Sirhan should they spare his life, but since Pollack had introduced the subject of Vacaville, Cooper tried to make the most of it. "I understood," said Cooper. "But you also know that it is a maximum-security institution?"

"Yes."

"Where he can get psychiatric treatment?" *

"That is correct."

Cooper asked Pollack to comment on Sirhan's outbursts in court. They were normal enough, said Pollack, for a paranoid personality. "Do you think the defendant was faking?" asked Cooper.

---

* And where, according to a release from Vacaville, printed prematurely by the San Francisco *Examiner,* Sirhan would enjoy a three-room suite with living and dining quarters and a television set, even then being prepared for him—a story that was picked up by the wire services and infuriated many who said the state ought to gas Sirhan quickly and be done with it.

"No. His outbursts were genuine. He wasn't putting on a show for you or me."

Cooper asked him about Sirhan's explosion when he, Pollack, was on the stand (and Sirhan was, for the first time, putting on a show).

"I don't think he was putting on a show for me," said Pollack.

Cooper asked about Sirhan's inappropriate conduct in court, "For example, laughing when things are serious."

"I've gotten to like Sirhan," said Pollack. "He may still feel I'm an S.O.B. . . ."

"Was his behavior inappropriate?" persisted Cooper.

Pollack said he had not seen "the degree of inappropriate response we see in a psychotic person."

"Was his conduct normal for a person on trial for his life?"

"No," admitted Pollack. "It was more impulsive, more volatile."

"In other words," said Cooper, "he didn't have as good a control over his brakes as the normal person?"

Said Pollack: "I suspect he wishes he could control himself better."

The prosecution had a second doctor for rebuttal, a clinical psychologist from the University of Southern California named Leonard Olinger. Olinger was a slight, prissy fellow who had not examined Sirhan, but he was able to throw further doubt on the psychological reports by criticizing the methods employed by both Drs. Schorr and Richardson. Olinger said that both "overlooked some positive strengths in Sirhan." Furthermore, they knew they were examining an assassin and therefore couldn't help reading a good deal into the data.

Olinger put up charts on the chalkboard and explained them: a list of ten procedural precautions, of eight neurotic traits, of eight indications of schizophrenia. He discussed the "collisions" on Sirhan's Bender-Gestalt, and his supposedly paranoid answers on the MMPI, some of which indicated a "good contact with reality." He pointed to the generally depressing nature of the TAT cards selected for Sirhan's analysis and said Sirhan had "fairly common responses" to the inkblots. There were "apparent inaccuracies" in Dr. Schorr's scoring. He got "41 percent small detail" "right out of the air." He shouldn't have scored "dove" or "fried leg" or "bears" as Fm but F. Sirhan's nine responses to Richardson's first card was "a highly productive record, hardly impaired." At this Sirhan smiled broadly and leaned over to tell Parsons he liked these guys the prosecution was bringing in now.

But the jurors looked unhappy. Dave Smith would write in the Los Angeles *Times:*

> For more than a month, they have listened to such psychiatric verbal shorthand as C-prime response, small animal movement, inanimate movement, large human response, pure form response, large M and small fm, large F and little c and TH column. It is debatable how efficiently the jurors have been able to translate such arbitrary terms into their meaningful emotional equivalents. But the mere effort has exacted a toll that was apparent Monday as they listened to still more of the same with faces that ranged a gamut of expression from boredom to stupefaction.*

Olinger said he suspected that Sirhan had never said in response to Card 8 of Richardson's Rorschach, "The color shocks me." Why? Because, among psychologists, the phrase "color shock" has a technical meaning (it is a definite sign of psychosis), and in all his thousands of testings, he'd never heard a patient put the two words together. "It is almost as if the person had been instructed or advised or otherwise informed about this particular term," suggested Olinger with a smile.

Despite all these criticisms (and more), Olinger gave Sirhan a diagnosis of "borderline schizophrenia, with primary neurotic features." Sirhan would probably fit best, he believed, in a category that wasn't listed in the American Psychiatric Association Handbook: pseudo-neurotic schizophrenia. And he had the capacity to "maturely and meaningfully premeditate and deliberate to commit the act of murder."

On cross-examination, Cooper drew an immediate admission from Olinger that he had volunteered his services to the district attorney's office. He reminded Olinger that he had testified that a psychologist should be objective, shouldn't have preconceived ideas, shouldn't attempt to fit his subject to a Procrustean bed. "In other words," said Cooper, "he should not consciously or unconsciously be swayed by knowledge of the patient or in this case knowledge of the subject of Sirhan."

"That's correct," said Olinger.

"Now, you have told us, Doctor," that you volunteered your services as consultant to the district attorney's office in this case."

"Yes, sir."

"And I think, am I correct, that you heard some of Dr. Schorr's testimony and you didn't like what you heard, so you called the district attorney and told him that you didn't like it?"

---

* Issa Nahkleh, the Palestinian envoy, was also bored. He found an excuse to leave the trial and go back, for a time, to New York.

"That's not quite exactly correct, sir."

"Well, you tell me," said Cooper.

"Some of the testimony that was reported to be given sounded as if it were unwarranted by the material that was being presented in support of it."

"All right," said Cooper. "First, Doctor, had you ever seen any of the material?"

"No, sir, I had not."

"What had you read about the testimony of Dr. Schorr? Do you remember what? Was it a newspaper you read it in?"

"I don't believe I can recall where I read it."

"Did you hear it on the radio?"

"Probably."

"On television?"

"Probably."

"That was only a small part of his testimony, wasn't it?"

"Yes, sir."

"And from the small part that you read in the newspapers, you felt that his testimony was, would you say, unreliable?" asked Cooper.

"Yes, sir."

"So, feeling that it was unreliable, you called the district attorney's office and volunteered your services?"

"Not quite."

"Well, you volunteered to help them."

"Sort of."

"Well, you volunteered to give them some advice?"

"Information. Information."

"All right. Then—but you don't remember what you read. Do you remember the substance of what you read?"

"Only in a general way."

"Now I take it that after a phone call, you had a consultation with one or more than one of the deputies in this case?"

"Yes, sir, I did."

"And whom did you see?"

"I saw Mr. Fitts and Mr. Howard."

"And discussed your point of view with them, did you, for some period of time?"

"It wasn't so much the point of view."

"Well, you discussed with them what you had read and your opinion of what you had read in the newspapers?"

"My reactions to what I had read."

"How long did you spend with them that time?"

"On the first meeting about three hours."

"Have you been able to fix that date for us, Doctor?"

"I believe it was the—I think we can fix the date—in a sense it was the Saturday when the story broke about the plagiarism, about the portions from Brussel's book that were utilized by Dr. Schorr."

"You term that 'plagiarism'?"

"Yes, sir, I would."

"Now, since you have had an opportunity since that time to study this more carefully and in depth—that is correct, isn't it?"

"Yes."

"—you have learned that there was nothing in the protocol—I mean, in the test material itself, and I will use the words 'that was plagiarized' from Dr. Brussel? You knew that?"

Olinger couldn't recall.

"You also knew, did you not," asked Cooper, "that if you didn't find something wrong with Richardson's and Schorr's conclusions, you couldn't testify for the prosecution. Isn't that true?"

"Couldn't or wouldn't have to," said Olinger.

"How do you account, Doctor, for the fact that Georgene Seward, a full professor at the University of Southern California—that her evaluation of paranoid schizophrenia was the same as Dr. Schorr's and Dr. Richardson's?" Howard objected. The court overruled.

Olinger said: "I account for it on the fact that I believe she was not privileged to be exposed to the full range of information that I had made available to me."

"All right," said Cooper. "You knew that she was sought out and employed by the prosecution, didn't you?"

"I since learned this."

"And that Dr. DeVos, a full professor at the University of California at Berkeley came to the same conclusion without knowledge of the diagnoses of Dr. Schorr, Dr. Richardson and Dr. Seward?" Howard objected. Cooper showed from Volume 91, page 7308, line 23, of this trial's transcript that Howard's objection would have to be overruled because the psychologists *had* testified that they did not know the diagnoses of the others. "I take it, Doctor, that you are of the opinion that Dr. Schorr's conclusions were wrong?"

"Some of them."

"Well, [that] his ultimate conclusion was wrong, that he was a paranoid schizophrenic?"

"Yes."

"Dr. Richardson's diagnosis was wrong?"

"Yes."

"That Dr. Howard's diagnosis and evaluation was wrong?"

"Yes, sir."

"That Dr. Crain's evaluation and diagnosis was wrong?"

"Yes, sir."

"That Dr. Seward's diagnosis and evaluation was wrong?"

"Yes, sir."

"That Dr. DeVos' evaluation and diagnosis was wrong?"

"Yes, sir."

Judge Walker adjourned for the day. In the hallway on the eighth floor, the lenses and the lights were focused on Buck Compton. Somehow the complexion of the case had changed again, and the newsmen suspected the verdict would be first degree. If it's first degree, someone asked Compton, are you going to ask for the death penalty? Compton said he would not. He would let the jury decide.

But J. Miller Leavy, the ripping, slashing prosecutor who had convicted Caryl Chessman and was now a top administrator in the D.A.'s office, complained bitterly after he had heard Compton say this on television. "If we can't ask the death penalty for Sirhan, then how can we demand it ever again?"

Wrote Dave Smith in the Los Angeles *Times:*

The stated aim [of the prosecution] was to find and enlarge weak spots in the ornate psychiatric facade erected by the defense.

But the more likely aim appeared to be to thoroughly sicken the jury on all psychiatric testimony, pushing jurors from confusion through boredom and to such exasperation that they might wave aside all expert testimony and weigh the case solely on these facts:

That Sirhan hated Zionism and its allies, wrote of his intention to kill Kennedy, did so and isn't sorry.

As the prosecution prepared its final arguments, Chief Dep. Dist. Atty. Lynn Compton confirmed what has been common knowledge since early February—that the prosecution will not press for the death penalty for Sirhan. Nor will they ask the jury not to impose it.

At 7:30 A.M. on April 7, Cathy Fulmer, the go-go dancer who had told the sheriff's office she might be "the girl in the polka-dot dress" sought by the police after the assassination, checked into a cheap motel on North Broadway in Los Angeles. She signed the register as "Sunday Rossi," left a wake-up call for 5:30 P.M. and went off to her room. She never woke up and died the next day at County General Hospital. Cause: overdose of drugs. In Miss Fulmer's purse, police found six Seconal tablets, twenty Benzedrines and four marijuana cigarettes. Scrawled in lipstick on the motel mirror were the words: "Lord you gave me a mountain and I'm love to climb." It was signed "Sunday." Below it was another message: "A wooden box will do." The police could not say whether the writing was hers, but the official coroner's verdict was suicide.

As always, the stuffy little courtroom was jammed, but now there was an air of high expectation in the gallery. Now was the time for the lawyers to sum up with all the skills they had, to put it all together for the jury, to construe the facts as they saw them. The prosecution would have the first and the last word and Parsons, Berman and Cooper would each have his turn in between.

David Fitts led off. "The rules of the game are such," Fitts told the jury in a brilliant summation done without a single note, "that we poor prosecutors didn't know much about this psychiatric defense until after the jury had been selected." Fitts knew, of course, that this was the only conceivable defense Sirhan's attorneys could offer for the obviously "premeditated" murder of Senator Kennedy. He also knew that recent decisions of the California Supreme Court have made it difficult for D.A.'s in California to make first-degree murder convictions stick with any but perfect or near-perfect psychological specimens.

But Fitts pretended to be as uninformed as the jurors in front of him. Through most of the trial, Fitts had expressed himself with great erudition —he seemed to have an encyclopedic knowledge of classical music, Moorish architecture, modern linguistics, the history of art and Middle Eastern diplomacy, among other things—until the psychologists and psychiatrists appeared for the defense. Then Fitts was a dunderhead who had never heard of Mesmer, Freud or Rorschach, or, indeed, the defense of diminished responsibility in California. Now, figuratively, he put himself in the jury box alongside the plumber and the aerospace technicians and the civil servants who sat there and he, too, was horribly put upon when the defense started subjecting the court to "lessons in psychology" that began "in a most peculiar way."

Fitts looked like the British actor Trevor Howard, and he could sneer as well as Howard did in the 1968 remake of *The Charge of the Light Brigade*. Now he sneered impressively, making the name, "Dr. Schorr," into an expletive. Fitts shook his head and smiled painfully at the thought that Dr. Schorr might have left a bad taste in the mouths of the jury regarding the whole psychological profession. Dr. Schorr's cribbing from Dr. Brussel, his pleading with Parsons to serve on the case, his destruction of the recordings he had taken in Sirhan's cell in a case of this historic magnitude—all of it was "disgraceful and deplorable."

It wasn't that he objected so much to the psychological tests themselves, though Fitts admitted they had caused him many sleepless hours while he stayed up studying Schorr's big M's and little m's. Jurors Busby and Frederico laughed out loud in obvious sympathy. But the tests, said Fitts, are no better than the person who administers the tests, and the jurors knew by now what kind of man Dr. Schorr was. "As *you* study the Rorschach and the TAT," said Fitts to the jury, "I wonder what sort of results you come up with?" This, too, brought smiles from the jurors, who had in fact been taking little Rorschach tests on their own, and had seen some of the same figures Sirhan saw.

"In the father card," exclaimed Fitts, waving his arms and trying to look like Rorschach Ink Blot 4, "Sirhan saw a Frankenstein monster. Maybe Dr. Schorr's got a good memory. There are no notes whatsoever to indicate that Sirhan said 'Frankenstein monster.' What are we getting here?" Fitts waved a copy of Schorr's protocol in the air. "Dr. Schorr? Or Sirhan?" He slapped it back down on the table in disgust. "I say it's deplorable.

"As for Schorr's plagiarism," said Fitts, "maybe Dr. Schorr selected the language of Dr. Brussel because it was persuasive. Well," said Fitts, "persuasion may or may not be important." Or maybe Dr. Schorr was "concentrating more on entertainment." In any event, Fitts suggested that "entertainment in a report is not appropriate in a capital case. So far as I'm concerned, Dr. Schorr is consigned to oblivion."

Fitts said he rather liked Dr. Richardson, but then damned him with faint praise, as a "pretty good mechanic." Fitts asked the jury to use their common sense in evaluating Dr. Richardson's evidence that Sirhan was suffering from various delusions.

Nor did Fitts see how four other truly competent psychologists could say "me, too, to the whole shebang." He suggested they did so because they were reluctant to come to court and knock their own profession. "It was," he said, "like a typical malpractice suit, wherein it is very difficult to get one doctor to testify against another. But even in the malpractice field," said Fitts, "you *can* find doctors with guts enough to do so."

He turned to the three psychiatrists in the case, said they were not exactly like three blind men examining an elephant, but it was strange that all three reached different conclusions. Dr. Marcus offered no diagnosis at all and Dr. Diamond had a super diagnosis, but both, said Fitts, "simply bought the story Sirhan had concocted." Dr. Pollack saw yet another Sirhan.

Over at his end of the counsel table, Sirhan could hardly suppress his smiles. It was Pollack who had bought his concoction, not Marcus or Diamond, and he was overjoyed that Fitts had as much antipathy to Marcus and Diamond as he did.

Fitts sighed over the difficulties he had had in communicating with Diamond, subtly allying himself ("a poor prosecutor") with the largely unlettered jury against "a professor who wears three hats at the University of California at Berkeley" and then attacking the weakest element in Diamond's diagnosis: the evidence of Sirhan's "dissociation" on the night of the crime: "He said the usual Sirhan was harmless, even with a loaded gun in his belt. So it seemed to me that this dissociation thing was the key. And I was interested in eliciting data on it from Dr. Diamond, who said that Sirhan was in a dissociated state at the Ambassador on June 5. Did Sirhan suffer truly dissociated states? At any time earlier? During his childhood? After his fall from the horse? While he was engaged in Rosicrucian exercises? I thought it fair to ask Dr. Diamond what his information was and how good it was. Well, his source was Mary Sirhan, and Munir, and Sirhan himself. In all instances, it depended on what Sirhan said or his family said. Very flimsy data indeed for someone who calls himself a scientist to therefore conclude that Sirhan was in a drunken state, saw himself in a mirror and killed Kennedy in a trance or an unconscious state." Fitts said Diamond was very proud of the work he had done with Sirhan under hypnosis. But Fitts charged that it was all pretty pointless: who cared whether or not Sirhan "climbed the bars of his cage like a monkey?" But it was on this "insubstantial edifice of fact" that Dr. Diamond concluded Sirhan was in a dissociated state.

And what did Dr. Diamond think of his own conclusion? Fitts read Diamond's own words: the story was "absurd and preposterous . . . unlikely and incredible." "Well," sighed Fitts, slapping the transcript back down on the counsel table, "I can't improve on Dr. Diamond. If that is what he thinks of this story, and that's what he said about it, why need I say anything more? You understand it's impossible to have the last word on Dr. Diamond, so let him have the last word." Fitts shrugged sadly at the transcript.

Was Fitts ready to throw out the doctors completely? Could Fitts know more than they about mental illness? No, said Fitts. Sirhan was sick. But so what? "Frankly," said Fitts, "I'm glad Sirhan is sick. I can't imagine anybody running into the Ambassador Hotel with a gun in his waistband and pumping eight shots into Senator Kennedy and *not* being what I'd consider sick. But our jails are full of people who have committed atrocious acts, rape, child molestation and murder. And they're probably sick, too." Seventeen jurors in the box (twelve jurors and five alternates) were as frightened as any seventeen members of the middle class might be by the wave of violence that had wracked the nation for the past five years, and Fitts played on that fear by implying that society could not condone a separate kind of law for psychotics. "We have this plague of violence in America," he said, "and it's not getting any better."

And Sirhan Sirhan was not a sympathetic psychotic. He was the first assassin in history to receive such a thorough dissection in open court, and knowing Sirhan better didn't make you love him. After only a few hours with Sirhan, the medical director of the county jail described him as "emotionally immature, zealous, inflammatory, dogmatic, irreversible, envisionary, full of hatred, money hungry, power proud, opinionated, arrogant and egocentric." Dr. Richardson had another descriptive litany: "Paranoid, blaming, suspicious, critical, unreasonable, demanding, attacking, opposing, resistant, rebellious, power-oriented, legalistic, very vulnerable and socially inadequate." When Sirhan heard during the trial that his brother, Saidallah, had been struck by a car and was in serious condition in a Pasadena hospital, he expressed no concern at all for Saidallah, or for his brother, Sharif, who became so violent with one of the nurses at the hospital that he was placed under arrest. "What are they trying to do to *me?*" Sirhan demanded.

Earlier, Fitts had summarized Sirhan: at the Ambassador, a cold-blooded killer; in custody, a clever liar. Fitts recalled Sirhan's buying the murder weapon under clandestine circumstances, his threats to kill Kennedy found in the notebooks, his purchase of hollow-nosed ammunition, his stalking of Kennedy two days before the murder, his rapid-fire target practice on the day of the assassination, his inquiries at the Ambassador about Kennedy's security guard just before the killing and, finally, his arrival in the pantry with a loaded gun hidden in the waistband of his trousers. "Kennedy's going through the pantry," said Fitts, "was no fortuitous circumstance. Sooner or later, Senator Kennedy would pass through the pantry and become a target for this assassin's bullet." Fitts reminded the jury of Sirhan's statements after the shooting and the cute way he avoided giving statements to the police, concealing his identity and leaving his wallet in the glove compartment of his car. Fitts scoffed at Sirhan's statement that he always left his wallet in his car and quoted one of Sirhan's employers who said he had seen Sirhan pull his wallet from his pocket on several occasions.

Over at his end of the counsel table, Sirhan murmured, "He's lying. He's a goddamn liar. I don't wanta hear this. I'm not gonna put up with this shit." Wearily, Judge Walker called another recess. Parsons soothed Sirhan in the holding tank. And Cooper retired to the auxiliary courtroom on the fourth floor to watch the rest of Fitts's summation on television. Whatever the reason for Sirhan's outbursts in the past, now Cooper knew Sirhan was faking. And he didn't want to be a part of it.

Fitts, too, guessed that Sirhan was indulging in theatrics. He pointed to him after the recess and said to the jury he was certain Sirhan knew what he was doing. He said that Sirhan had denied or pretended amnesia on every major piece of evidence that would show that he had premeditated the assassination. He listed the testimony of trash collector Alvin Clark, the notebooks, the five witnesses who said Sirhan was engaged in rapid fire at the rifle range on the day of the killing, his denial to his own defense investigators that he had been at the Ambassador viewing Kennedy two days before the killing and his disagreement with the testimony of two witnesses who said they saw him at the Ambassador on June 2.

"How can we reconcile all of these witnesses with the denials of Mr. Sirhan?" Fitts asked rhetorically. "I submit that he was fully aware that these acts were perfectly reasonable for a man about to assassinate a Senator. And that he knew that they were proof of premeditation. That is why he has denied them so forcefully. As for Sirhan's outbursts in court," said Fitts, "when he has indulged in them he has made sense. Both in his denials and his outbursts, he has never been divorced from reality."

Fitts admitted that Sirhan was "less than a full man. How much less, I don't know. But he is the Sirhan you have seen in court. He is the man who testified on this witness stand, eagerly, with a certain dramatic flair, with an intelligence somewhat unusual in the criminal courts—if you will accept my word for it—with an ability to anticipate. Indeed, he could hardly wait for the next question on the part of his lawyer. In certain respects, with a sense of the theatrical, Mr. Sirhan in the course of his testimony deliberately chose to use certain four-letter words and then he would smile at the judge and say, 'Pardon me.' Do you think that man at the counsel table [Fitts pointed at Sirhan] didn't know what he was doing? I am certain that he did. The question," said Fitts, "is whether or not, given that degree of mental impairment, or if you will, diminished capacity, Sirhan yet had the ability to harbor malice, that has been described to you, and to maturely—whatever it means to you—and meaningfully— whatever it means to you, not what it means to a doctor, but what it means to you—premeditate and deliberate upon taking the life of a fellow human being. That's your job. Thank you very much."

As Fitts left the courtroom surrounded by newsmen, he was met in the hall by Cooper, who shook his hand and congratulated him for a brilliant summary. He talked a bit to the television cameras, trying not very successfully to condense his four-hour summary into two minutes, and headed down the hall. Others congratulated him. Then near the elevator, a little old lady came up to Fitts and said consolingly: "Well, you did your best. That's all you can do." Fitts was agape. He knew he'd made a marvelous summary. So what was she talking about? And who was she? An agent planted by the defense? It was a good guess. But the defense was hardly that imaginative outside the courtroom.

Or in it, either, for that matter. Parsons, aching with sciatica as he led off for the defense, made a bathetic, overdramatic declaration that neither a death sentence nor life imprisonment would be a just verdict for Sirhan. Parsons told the jury that its verdict would spell a message "in every hamlet, on every desert in the Arab Republic, and in Europe, that a man can get justice in America. And justice is not the death penalty or life imprisonment in this case, because that isn't warranted—not for this poor, sick wretch who did not know what he did.

"It's going to take a little courage to return a proper verdict in this case," Parsons told the jury. "A little courage to see that justice is done. But justice must be done because this trial is going down in the history books. . . ." Apparently, however, Parsons had already given up, for he next spoke as if the jury had already reached a verdict of first degree: "I don't believe in the death penalty," Parsons said. "I don't believe you can take the life of another man." His voice quavered. "Only God can do that."

Parsons conceded that Sirhan took the life of Kennedy, just as Kennedy's brother, President John F. Kennedy had been assassinated five years before. "That was a horrible act," Parsons said, and added, "There isn't a man in America who shouldn't say a prayer for the remainder of that family—every night."

Sirhan, who had been smiling through most of Parsons' delivery, laughed out loud here, then quickly covered his mouth with his right hand.

Parsons had not confronted Fitts on a single one of the many incriminating points Fitts had made. Berman hardly did any better. He insisted that Sirhan was not faking insanity when he asked for the gas chamber. "If you could see his face, his clenched fist, the tautness of his body," said Berman, "you could see he wasn't putting on an act. There were two girls —due to the tremendous investigation of Mike McCowan here—we wanted to put two girls on the stand, and all kinds of stuff of that nature. We placated him because these two had very little, if anything, to offer. We think we know something about human nature. This is a product of a sick mind. It doesn't matter what definition or distinction you make. You're here to see whether this was a man or a rambunctious child in the body of a man. You're the ones who can see that he gets the psychiatric help and assistance he needs." Sirhan was sawing his thumb with his two front teeth, a malevolent look on his face, and a slight smile.

"In the name of humanity," said Berman, "we do not assign to first-degree murder a mental cripple. As you know, I ask you plain and simply. I am not a beggar. I don't beg from people. But I ask you with all understandable belief in the name of humanity, we do not send for the crime of first-degree murder a mentally sick man. And finally, may I remind you of the basic rule of a free society that once one's rights are tampered with, or trifled with, all men's rights are in jeopardy. I cannot say much more with all of my energy and intellectual honesty than I have said, and I leave it with you. The responsibilities are yours. The judgments are yours. And the intellects are yours. And the options are yours. And you stand for what is right, despite the gruesomeness of this crime. Your Honor, please, I have concluded."

It was a fumbling, stumbling presentation capped with an unnecessary reminder of the horror that the court had lived with for three months. Sirhan turned to his brother Adel sitting behind him in court and shrugged derisively.

At the recess, Cooper went into the holding tank to see Sirhan and told him, "Trust me. You won't like what I say. But I'm trying to get second degree. Trust me."

Without a Lavalier mike around his neck, with his left hand stuck casually in his jacket pocket, Cooper faced the jury. He paid some courtly thank-you's to Judge Walker, recognized the fairness of the prosecution, told a funny story, assured the jury that he knew they were going to do an honest and conscientious job because they had suspended their judgment thus far. "At the outset," he said, "we are not here to free a guilty man. He is guilty of having killed Senator Robert Kennedy. But contrary to what my friend David Fitts said yesterday, it is not the duty of a lawyer to free a guilty man. The duty and obligation of a lawyer is to represent only those causes which are legal or just. A duty to represent them. Not to free a guilty man. We are not asking for an acquittal." Then Cooper startled the jury and everyone in the courtroom by declaring, "Whether Mr. Sirhan likes it or not, he deserves to spend the rest of his life in the penitentiary." There was no reaction from Sirhan at the counsel table. But down in the second row of seats, Mary Sirhan started to murmur.

Cooper said there was only one issue before the jury—whether the defendant had diminished capacity or not. "That's the guts of the case," said Cooper, "the sole issue." He told the jury that first-degree murder was premeditated murder with malice, that second-degree murder was unpremeditated murder with malice and that manslaughter was murder that was both unpremeditated and without malice. He said the expert psychiatric witnesses in the case indicated that Sirhan did not have the capacity to kill with malice aforethought. But he, Cooper, was not going to ask for a verdict of manslaughter. "Because of the conduct that brought him to the bar of justice in this case," Cooper said, "I wouldn't want Sirhan Sirhan turned loose on society. There are two Sirhans. There's a good Sirhan and a bad Sirhan. And the bad Sirhan is a nasty Sirhan."

Cooper conceded that the murder of Kennedy was willful, deliberate and premeditated. But, he added, you can have that in second-degree murder and in manslaughter. How? Because of the law of diminished capacity, something, he said, that had never really been explained. He told the jury about the *Wolff* case, wherein Wolff showed some premeditation and deliberation and some degree of thinking. But, said Cooper, was it mature and meaningful thinking? In the case of young Wolff, a paranoid-schizophrenic, the Supreme Court decided that it definitely was not.

Cooper pointed to some facts on the record illustrating Sirhan's lack of mature and meaningful thinking, he pointed to the significance of Sirhan's outbursts in the courtroom and he spent a good deal of time considering Sirhan's intoxicated condition on the night of the assassination. Cooper apologized for Dr. Schorr, but pointed out that he hadn't plagiarized the basic body of his testimony, that Dr. Richardson had come to the same findings, and that four other psychologists—two of them chosen by the prosecution—had also corroborated them under oath. As for Dr. Pollack, Cooper was constrained to point out that Pollack hadn't been completely honest. On direct examination, he said that Sirhan was a paranoid personality. "Not once did he say Sirhan was a psychotic. Not once did he tell you he had a substantial mental illness. On cross-examination, one of the purposes is to bring out the whole truth. But suppose there was no cross-examination? You wouldn't have known he'd written this letter of February 5 [to the District Attorney], would you? [saying] that he [Sirhan] was anything but a paranoid personality—that he was a psychotic person."

Cooper hastened to excuse conduct on Pollack's part that was nothing if not peculiar: "He found himself in a rather difficult position." Cooper quoted from Pollack's February 5 view of Sirhan: " 'He has been successful in hiding his psychotic symptoms from public view and able to avoid revealing such symptoms to psychiatrists in clinical interviews. . . . When I stressed him in my interviews with him, I believe that his disturbance in thinking went beyond the paranoid trends which are characteristic of the nonpsychotic paranoid personality . . . it is my opinion that more intensive professional exploration of this defendant's thinking and personality characteristics would probably reveal more definite signs and symptoms of psychosis.' " And he quoted Pollack's conclusion: " 'This mental illness should be considered a substantial mitigating factor on the issue of penalty. * Should a conviction of murder of the first degree be obtained, I hope that Sirhan is able to avoid the death penalty and is sent for treatment to the California Medical Facility at Vacaville . . . I have no doubt that substantial mental illness was present and still exists in Sirhan and merits consideration in this case.' "

But, said Cooper, a verdict of second-degree murder would be enough to send Sirhan to Vacaville for life.

Compton rose and shouted that this was very improper argument. Judge Walker agreed and admonished the jury not to consider the matter of penalty. It was already discussed too much, he said. But, since it had already been discussed, it was Fitts who then whispered the suggestion to Judge Walker that the jury be instructed on the legal consequences of each possible verdict. The judge ignored him. Cooper came back to the jury and said

---

* An anomaly that could only be explained by Pollack's refusal to recognize the implications of the *Wells-Gorshen-Wolff* decisions in California. If mental impairment was relevant in the trial's penalty phase, it was also relevant to the question of criminal intent. Unless, of course, Pollack thought Sirhan was sicker now than he was when he killed Kennedy.

that he was only trying to put the whole matter in proper perspective, that he certainly didn't believe that Sirhan should be given a medal for what he had done. "But I feel that the evidence and the law justifies under your oath as jurors a verdict of guilty of murder of the second degree, and it would certainly take care of the situation."

It was not Cooper's best day in court. Quite possibly the very worst. He, too, avoided challenging the prosecution's own interpretation of the facts, nor did he endorse the interpretations of either Drs. Diamond or Marcus. He concentrated, instead, on the only real thing in his favor, the law of diminished capacity. But his explanation of the law was wordy and contorted. What had been a subtle and complicated defense from the beginning was now turning out to be most incomprehensible. And the man who would give the jury its last evaluation of that defense was the former right guard for UCLA, Chief Deputy D.A. Lynn Compton.

With a Lavalier microphone on his chest and his hands in his pockets, Compton sat on the edge of the counsel table and crossed his legs. "I haven't been here every day to hear all this stuff," said Compton. "I've had a few other things to do. Had to get the budget out to run this office. We get thirty to 35,000 felons a year through here and I thought to myself, 'Do any of 'em have mature, meaningful judgment?' The college kid caught with marijuana? The heroin shooters? The guy who shoots up a liquor store for $15, or smashes the window of a jewelry store to steal a diamond? None of these reflect mature, meaningful judgment. The courts are full of 'em. That's what this case is all about. What about this guy who smashes a store window for the diamond? He can do it for one of three reasons. Either he's hungry or he needs money or he wants to replace the missing diamond in the forehead of an idol at home that will satisfy the evil spirits. That's a crazy reason. But what difference does it make? He still stole the diamond. The point is: does any person maturely and meaningfully make a wise decision? Not by my standards or yours." *

Compton pointed to the chalkboard where Cooper had carefully written the names of seven doctors who had said that Sirhan was a schizophrenic and suffered from diminished capacity. "I was going to erase the names of those seven doctors on the board," said Compton. "Well, I hope I can erase them from your consideration and leave you to think about them

* There is no defense of diminished capacity for any crimes other than murder or attempted murder. Compton's argument here was a misstatement of the law and Judge Walker later admonished the jury to disregard it.

over the weekend." He didn't explain how the jury should cope with these contradictory instructions. "All of these magnificent seven said 'no malice.' Malice is one of the necessary ingredients in second-degree murder. And yet, Cooper, Mr. Cooper, says, 'Find him guilty of second-degree murder.' Apparently, he rejects the psychiatrists too. I can be frank to admit that right now as I stand here, I can't answer this, what should be a simple fundamental question: did Robert Francis Kennedy, a young, highly successful man at the peak of his career, former Attorney General of the United States, Senator from New York, and a candidate for the Presidency of the United States—did he breathe his last breath on that dirty floor of the pantry at the Ambassador Hotel with the mops and the dirty dishes—did that man leave a widow and eleven children and expire with a bullet in his brain because he favored the United States support of the Israeli state, or because he somehow inadvertently and unwittingly became a substitute father image in some complicated Oedipus complex that occurred in Sirhan's mind? I admit that I don't know. And if you believe Dr. Diamond with his mirror act and all of the testimony about this defendant being in some kind of a trance and being so completely out of it that he just didn't know whether he was afoot or horseback, it would be inhumane to punish him for any crime, manslaughter, second-degree murder or anything else, because how can you take a poor guy who doesn't know anything about what he's doing and say, 'You're guilty?' It can't be done. So if you buy those so-called experts, you have to turn him loose. But if you don't buy it, like I don't buy it, and Dave Fitts and John Howard don't buy it, there's nothing left but a plain old cold-blooded first-degree murder. I'll leave that with you."

Wrote Bob Greene of *Newsday:* "The jury seemed in a state of shock as Compton stalked away and court adjourned. Cooper had been courtly, charming, friendly, sympathetic. For the jurors, listening to Cooper had been like sitting warm and snuggly in father's lap. Compton was like an ice cold shower. He brought them back from the vagaries of psychiatric abstraction to the reality of blood on a pantry floor, from possible pity for Sirhan to sorrow for the lonely young widow of McLean, Virginia."

On Monday morning, Compton continued his inelegant—and eminently effective—argument. "The whole idea of the jury system is that we want just twelve average people, I mean with good sense. All we ask is that you go at this thing like you were sitting in your own living room and somebody sat down and said, 'Look, here are some facts, here is some evidence. We would like to have you decide it. It's just that simple.'

"Now again, as I say," continued Compton in his easy, almost offhand manner, "I'm not the most articulate guy and I'm a little—oh, I guess, embarrassed—to follow a Stanford man like Mr. Fitts, with his great command of the language and his great literary knowledge and talk about a lot of things I don't know about. But at some time in my life I have heard that Charles Dickens once wrote a book in which one of his characters said something about, 'The law is an ass.' And I think that's true and I'm a lawyer. And I think the law became an ass the day it let the psychiatrists get their hands on law." So much, said Compton, had been made of this defense of diminished capacity. "And it's no big deal. It has been overcomplicated. It has been dealt with as if it is all separate and apart from what we are dealing with, and it really isn't."

Compton asked the jury to consider the facts. He went through the prosecution litany of Sirhan's actions before the crime and asked the jurors to apply "good old common sense." Those actions added up to premeditation. The only possible source of doubt seemed to lie in an assessment of Sirhan's state of mind, and again Compton asked the jury to apply common sense. "You saw him on the stand. He was alert. You saw him fence with me. You remember once, he said he wasn't sure 'whether Senator Kennedy was in Oregon then or not.' Up to then, nobody had even mentioned Oregon. But he knew. That was significant to me: he knew because he was keeping track of Kennedy. He stalked Kennedy because he wanted to kill him." Sirhan smiled an embarrassed smile.

Compton literally snorted over the testimony of the psychologists who said that Sirhan's mental condition was deteriorating. "If he was a vegetable on June 5, he should have been a gibbering idiot by the time you saw him on the witness stand. But he was no such thing. You saw him." *

---

* According to at least one accepted psychiatric theory, propounded by R. D. Laing and Gregory Bateson, schizophrenia is "a special strategy that a person invents in order to live in an unliveable situation." For Bateson and Laing, a psychotic episode is like a journey. "Once begun, a schizophrenic episode would appear to have as definite a course as an initiation ceremony—a death and rebirth—into which the novice may have been precipitated by his family life or by adventitious circumstances, but which in its course is largely steered by endogenous process. In terms of this picture, spontaneous remission is no problem. This is only the final and natural outcome of the total process. What needs to be explained is the failure of many who embark upon this voyage to return from it. Do these encounter circumstances whether in family life or in institutional care so grossly maladaptive that even the richest and best organized hallucinatory experience cannot save them?" Applying this theory to Sirhan, the killing of Kennedy in the Ambassador pantry was the end of a psychotic journey. And the Sirhan seen in the courtroom was a Sirhan in some state of "spontaneous remission."

Not that Compton had much regard for the psychologists and psychiatrists who, he said again, didn't really belong in the courtroom on the issue of guilt or innocence. "I ask you," said Compton, "can inkblots really show *what* Sirhan's state of mind was on June 5 at the Ambassador Hotel? I can't for the life of me believe that anyone can crawl inside his head and say what he was thinking on June 5 by asking him what he's thinking when he sees a boy with a violin." He told the jury to disregard the fact that the defense put on psychologists originally hired by the prosecution, suggesting that all the psychologists are members of the same club. Of course, he said, they have to rely on their tests; it is all they've got. "But I say reject the tests. Put them out. Because I think it would be a frightening thing for the administration of criminal justice in this state if the decision turned on whether or not, when Sirhan is shown some inkblot, he saw clowns playing patty-cake or kicking each other in the shins."

"This man has no delusions," said Compton. "He's not Nasser. He's not Napoleon. He's Sirhan." Compton said that Sirhan thought that what he did was right. All right. Maybe he did. But, said Compton, that was no excuse. He quoted from the *Conley* case:

> An intentional act that is highly dangerous to human life, done in disregard of the actor's awareness that society requires him to conform his conduct to the law, is done with malice regardless of the fact that the actor acts without ill will toward his victim or believes that his conduct is justified . . . Thus, one who commits euthanasia bears no ill will toward his victim and believes his act is morally justified, but he nonetheless acts with malice if he is able to comprehend that society prohibits his act regardless of his personal belief.

Compton failed to read the very next sentence of *Conley,* which was, of course, the whole point of the trial: "If, because of mental defect, disease, or intoxication, however, the defendant is unable to comprehend his duty to govern his actions in accord with the duty imposed by law, he does not act with malice aforethought and cannot be guilty of murder in the first degree."

Compton instanced members of the Ku Klux Klan who lynch Negroes or college students who set bombs on campus. "They all think it's morally right," said Compton "but they can't be excused or diminished."

And he scorned all the doctors, even his own consultant Dr. Pollack. "There aren't any *prosecution* psychiatrists anyplace," he said. But he saved his deepest disdain for Dr. Diamond—"the ubiquitous Dr. Diamond, the walking lie detector, the handwriting expert, the gun expert, the psychiatrist, the psychologist, the lawyer. Nobody knew what happened until Dr. Diamond descended on the scene." Compton smirked at the jury, in a bad imitation of Diamond's smile. "He did it with mirrors. On spotting nuts," said Compton, "I'd take Sergeant Melendres over Diamond." And then, by distorting a fact or two and leaning hard on a common man's sense of plausibility, Compton implied that Dr. Diamond had trumped up his entire analysis.

"Well," he sighed, "why would the psychiatrists come in here and lie? I'll tell you why. Their whole reason even for being is to find something wrong with someone." He was sure psychiatrists could find something wrong with the jurors, too, an unsubtle play on the fears of each juror that a psychiatrist could threaten *his* future. "What better way," said Compton "to foist their theories on the whole world than the case of *People* vs. *Sirhan?*

"Is Sirhan a bad guy?" asked Compton. "Some of his defense attorneys say they like him." Compton turned and glared at Sirhan and Sirhan dropped his gaze to the table. "I don't like him. He's vicious." And then he asked the jury if the nation could survive 200 like him. "Could the nation survive 200 assassins?"

Judge Walker and the attorneys had discussed the relevant law the jury needed in this case. Now Walker was ready to read his legal instructions to the jury.

"Murder [read Walker] is the unlawful killing of a human being with malice aforethought." Fair enough, elemental enough. But he defined murder of the second degree in a style that was sure to confuse the jury:

> Any murder which is perpetrated by one who does not have the mental capacity to maturely and meaningfully premeditate, deliberate and reflect on the gravity of his contemplated act, or his inability to form an intent to kill, perpetrates any kind of willful, deliberate and premeditated killing with malice aforethought.

At 2:55 P.M.—fifteen weeks to the day after the trial began—the twelve jurors * climbed nineteen worn wooden steps to a dingy jury room domi-

---

* It was a jury of seven men and five women. During the trial, two of the jurors were replaced by alternates. A death in the family took away Ronald G. Evans, the

nated by a battered conference table and a fading blackboard. There was an electric clock on the east wall next to an alarm button which the jury foreman could punch to summon the bailiff—for the door of the room couldn't be opened from the inside—and a large coffee urn on a table next to the north wall. Two small windows that hadn't been washed, it seemed, since the Chessman trial overlooked a construction chasm to the south.

Judge Walker remained behind in the courtroom and chatted from the bench with the newsmen who remained, the first time he allowed himself to relax with the press. "They're making nominating speeches now," he said, "for their selection of a foreman." Then he told a story about the twelve lawyers who comprised one famous old jury that was locked up for some four days. When the judge tried to find out how they were doing, he was told they were still making the nominating speeches. But seriously, said Walker, a jury that had been together so long didn't really take much time to elect a foreman. He was right. One of the youngest members of the panel, and its only bachelor, Bruce D. Elliott, twenty-eight, was elected on the first ballot. He had his Ph.D. in electrical engineering from the University of Illinois and some guessed he was chosen because he had more formal education than any of the others.

McCowan had been telling himself and anyone else who would listen that the jury would come in with second degree. But an informal poll of newsmen, taken the next morning by Jim Brodhead of *Time,* resulted in a prediction of first degree by a majority of nineteen to five.

If Brodhead had asked Sirhan, the count would have risen to twenty. I saw Sirhan at 11:30 in his cell on the thirteenth floor—again at Sirhan's request. He was tearing up notes he had written to himself so he could flush the pieces down the toilet. He knew what the verdict was going to be. He wasn't happy. "What's new?" he said to me without looking up from his bunk.

"Concerning?" I was deliberately churlish because I knew what was coming.

"The book."

"What about it?"

"There'll be no book!" he shouted.

---

juror who said he'd have a hard time finding Sirhan guilty of anything but first-degree murder after he'd read the news stories about Sirhan's plea bargain, and Laurence Morgan developed a bleeding ulcer. They were replaced by George A. Stitzel, a press foreman for the Los Angeles *Times* and Mrs. Ruth Stillman, an insurance adjuster.

"That's what I was trying to tell you the other day," I said. "There will be a book. You've just got a lot to lose by not cooperating."

"Bullshit!" He looked up, his face full of hatred. "You're not gonna put any words in my mouth!"

"I'm not putting words in your mouth. I've got 'em on tape. I've got my notes."

"I thought I told you—" Now Sirhan was trying to take control of a situation he had no control over "—to work out a termination of the agreement."

"I did. It was unacceptable to Cooper."

"Well, shit! He can go to hell. You can go to hell too. To hell with both of you. I'll sue."

"Go ahead and sue," I said. "It won't do you any good. We had a contract. Otherwise, I wouldn't have put a year of my life into this. Contracts are honored in our society."

"To hell with your society," said Sirhan whom society had just given a trial that cost $609,792.

"Okay," I said. "You're the only one who has anything to lose."

"I've got nothing to lose."

"Have it your way." I pointed to the torn-up bits of paper.

"What are you doing?"

"Get out!"

"You're the one who asked me in here."

"Get out!"

I stood, flushed now with anger with myself for giving Sirhan the chance to issue even one picayune little order. I left when Sirhan shouted a third time: "Get out!"

"That was quick," said Craig Carpenter, whom Sheriff Pitchess had made a captain a few days before.

"Yeah," I said, still burning with rage. Later, after I cooled down, I reflected on this new Sirhan, now so different from the meek Sirhan who had existed on the outside. Now, he was a dramatic model of Frantz Fanon's recipe for manhood among emerging peoples:

> Violence is a cleansing force. It frees the native from his inferiority complex and from his despair and inaction; it makes him fearless and restores his self-respect.

Killing Kennedy made Sirhan the mouse into Sirhan the rat, and that, I said to myself, was progress of a sort.

* * * * *

Now everyone had to wait. Helmeted sheriff's deputies stood guard in the Hall of Justice, hoping that "the little punk" would get murder one. On the thirteenth floor, Sirhan lay back on the cot in his air-conditioned cell, unable to read, exhausted now by the tensions of fifteen weeks of trial. In Pasadena, Mary Sirhan sat in a chair near the living-room window, where the light was good, and read from an Arabic Bible. Judge Walker waited and worked in his chambers, trying, with Court Coordinator Harold Frediani, to work out the logistics of a speeded-up criminal calendar, now unbelievably backlogged. In their offices nearby, the three prosecutors, Buck Compton, David Fitts and John Howard, fingered the files on other waiting cases, but sat there, for the most part, in a state of general lassitude. Cooper tried to clear the correspondence, at least, from his desk. Berman had packed and departed for New York. Parsons couldn't stay away from the courtroom, anxious, if anything, to talk to the newsmen who had taken to ignoring him in the latter weeks of the trial.

And old pro Bob Greene pumped Parsons for what he was worth. Parsons told Greene that he was trying to arrange some sort of "swap" for Sirhan between the Arab nations and the United States.

Parsons had done nothing more than talk about such a possibility with Sirhan. But Parsons said that Issa Nahkleh was now in New York to discuss such an exchange with King Hussein of Jordan. Hussein was in the country to garner American support in his fight against more militant fellow Arabs and would have found the name of Sirhan—whom the militants were making into a poster hero—as palatable in his inner council chambers as a plate of Texas hawg jowls.

But Parsons told Greene that "Nahkleh went to New York to discuss the possibility of just this type of exchange with King Hussein. We worked all this out. Why do you think he has been out here? He hasn't been here for fun, you know. He's been here to help us with just this sort of thing. At first, I was going to go to Jordan myself, but then we decided that this would be better." Whom would the United States want in such an exchange? asked Greene. "I'm sure they have a lot of people we want," said Parsons.

Greene reported Parsons' revelations straight. But his editors in New York added a kicker: Nahkleh hadn't seen Hussein.

Seventeen

"He has no special claim to further preservation."

At 2:05 P.M. on April 16, Foreman Bruce Elliott punched the buzzer twice, a signal that the jury wanted some clarification.

In fifteen minutes, Judge Walker and the lawyers on both sides were in court; the jury filed in and Elliott said the jury was having trouble with his instructions on second-degree murder. (See page 493.)

Walker didn't see why the jury should have any difficulty with that. Nor did he ask the jury what their trouble was. Grant Cooper said he guessed they might be having trouble with the word "or." Walker reread the same instruction to the jury and paused. Well, maybe it wasn't exactly clear. Walker flipped through his sheaf of instructions and read the jury another instruction they'd heard before that said it better:

> "If you find from the evidence that, at the time the defendant shot and killed Senator Robert F. Kennedy, his mental capacity had been substantially reduced, whether caused by mental illness or intoxication or a combination of mental illness and imbibing of intoxicating beverages, or any other cause, and if you find that to the extent that you have a reasonable doubt whether he did or could maturely and meaningfully premeditate, deliberate and reflect upon the gravity of his contemplated act or form an intent to kill, you cannot convict him of a willful, deliberate or premeditated murder of the first degree, but you may find him guilty of murder in the second degree, if you are convinced beyond a reasonable doubt that he had the mental capacity to harbor or entertain malice aforethought."

Any high-school English student could judge that the court was trying to say too much in one sentence. But it would have to do: "Does that clarify it for you?" asked Walker. The jurors nodded. "All right," he said, "you may retire to the jury room."

At 10:47 A.M. on Thursday, April 17, 1969, Bruce Elliott pushed the buzzer three times. After sixteen hours and forty-two minutes of deliberation, the jury had reached a verdict.

At 11:00 A.M., Sirhan breezed into the courtroom, trailing a cloud of smoke after one last puff on his cigarette. He took his seat at the counsel table. Parsons slapped him encouragingly on the knee, and Sirhan smiled thinly.

At 11:09 A.M. the jury filed into the box. None of them was smiling and no one looked at Sirhan. "Ladies and gentlemen of the jury," said Walker, "you have a verdict?"

Bruce Elliott stood. "We have, your Honor." He handed a sheaf of papers to Bailiff Willard Polhemus who passed them to Judge Walker. Walker glanced at them and, impassive, handed them to Clerk Alice Nishikawa who read aloud:

We, the jury in the above entitled action, find the Defendant Sirhan Bishara Sirhan guilty of Murder, in violation of Section 187, Penal Code, a felony, as charged in Count 1 of the Indictment. We further find it to be Murder in the first degree. This 17th day of April, 1969. Bruce D. Elliott, Foreman.

"Ladies and gentlemen of the jury, is this your verdict, so say you one, so say you all?" The jurors murmured their assent.

Harry Rosenthal of the AP and Jack Fox of UPI dashed for the doors. Judge Walker let them go. The clerk's voice droned through the recitation and repetition of guilty verdicts for Counts Two through Six.

Sirhan stared straight ahead. Cooper asked for a poll of the jury on Count One. Alice Nishikawa called the jurors' names one by one: "George A. Stitzel, Susan J. Brumm, Mr. Frederico, Mrs. Busby, Mrs. Stillman, Mrs. Martinez, Mr. Galindo, Mr. Elliott, Mrs. Bortells, Mr. Glick, Mr. Grace, Mr. Broomis." Each in turn confirmed with a firm, "Yes."

Sirhan's family got the news at home on one of the news bulletins that were interrupting programs on all the TV channels. "We feel terrible," Adel Sirhan told a reporter who called him immediately on the telephone. "There is nothing more I can say. We didn't expect this verdict."

Alice Nishikawa impressed the verdicts with the official seal of the court, and everyone seemed to freeze while the thumps of the sealing machine echoed through the silent courtroom. Then the attorneys huddled in front of Judge Walker. Cooper made a motion for a separate jury on the penalty phase of the trial. He was literally "going through the motions," for he had to make a complete record on an issue that might turn out to be a constitutional question—that is, can a man get a fair hearing if he was tried, over his objections, by "a hanging jury"?

Sirhan called for McCowan and McCowan slipped over in his chair. "What are they doing up there?" he demanded. McCowan told him Cooper and Parsons were asking for a new jury. "Hell, I don't want a new jury," said Sirhan. "I want this jury." He pointed vehemently at the jurors. "And I want 'em to give me the death penalty."

As if to accommodate Sirhan, Judge Walker denied the motion for a new jury.

Cooper and Parsons came down from the bench. Cooper put a hand on Sirhan's shoulder, reminding him of his promise not to carry out his threat, made minutes before, to ask for the death penalty then and there.

The judge dismissed the jury until Monday morning. Sirhan was up and on his feet immediately before the judge could say, "Remand the defendant" and moving toward the holding tank, motioning for Cooper, Parsons and McCowan to follow.

In the holding tank, he reminded Cooper that he hadn't embarrassed him. Now, in return, he wanted a favor from Cooper. He wanted him to put on "further evidence" on the Arab-Israeli conflict during the penalty hearing. It was a strategy that could hardly help Sirhan in face of the final argument the prosecution was preparing. But Cooper said he'd make the motion immediately (hoping fervently to himself that the judge would deny it).

Down in the fourth-floor auxiliary courtroom, some seventy-five newsmen jostled for position around a table that flowered with eleven microphones for a commentary on the trial by the attorneys for both sides. First, Buck Compton, John Howard and David Fitts eased into the chairs in front of the mikes. Out of the Babel of questions that burst forth, Compton fielded one about psychiatry. "Well, I don't think it should be interpreted as a repudiation of psychiatry in general.* I think it has to be inferred from the verdict that they did not accept the diagnosis of most of the psychiatrists. And the facts were quite overwhelming in pointing to premeditated murder."

---

* But that is exactly where Emile Zola Berman put the blame. Interviewed in New York, immediately after the verdict, Berman said, "I just regret that the sciences of psychology and psychiatry are held in such low esteem." Coming from the man who was given prime responsibility for making these disciplines relevant at the trial, that was quite an admission.

Someone wondered (again) if he would ask for the death penalty. Compton had a clarification. "I think this is a unique case without precedent. I think the jury will express the conscience of the nation to this kind of a crime. We have no precedent. What is the appropriate penalty for a political assassination in this country? I don't know. I think the jury will give us that answer. I never said we weren't gonna ask for the death penalty. Or that we were gonna reject the death penalty. We're simply going to point out to the jury what we see as the relevant factors for their consideration."

Someone asked if the prosecution's position was compromised because it once agreed to a life sentence.

Compton chose his words carefully. "It certainly imposes on us an obligation to not assert that the death penalty is an absolute must, because we conceded otherwise in the past. There's no question about that."

John Howard, who would present the argument for the prosecution, tried to amplify. "The jury," said Howard, "will have absolute discretion. In our argument, we will attempt to point out at least facts in the prosecution case that may suggest one punishment."

For example?

"Lack of remorse. What is the effect of assassination on the democratic process? Something like that." This clearly was a new tune and Cooper stood near the doorway with a sour look on his face. He didn't like the melody.

When the newsmen asked to talk to the losers, Cooper was uncharacteristically curt. He said Sirhan was disappointed. How? asked the newsmen, who had grown used to daily reports from McCowan and the lawyers on Sirhan's ups and downs. What did he say? "The conversations we had were privileged," said Cooper. How did he express his disappointment? "By the expression on his face." He didn't say anything? He didn't say a word? "What he said to us at that time is privileged. And he requested that it be privileged."

Someone asked Cooper how he accounted for the verdict. He said he had no way of knowing what went on in the jurors' minds. But he wasn't going to quarrel with their decision. "I don't know of any other way we could have tried it," he said. Sergeant Charlie Collins, one of the LAPD detectives who had worked on the case almost from the beginning and had seen it through every day of trial, stood on the fringe of the crowd. "All I can say," said Cooper, "is we did our best and we lost, that's all." And Collins nodded.

The defense team had a weary, gloomy lunch at the Music Center. It was a long trial, fought against great odds and they had lost. This was Cooper's second loss in two consecutive full-length trials. "I've never had to argue a penalty phase before," he said bleakly, his mind already running to what lay ahead.

"I have," said Parsons. "Three or four times. And I never liked it."

Inevitably, however, thoughts ran backward. Cooper admitted that he himself had never really bought the full psychiatric testimony and so he wasn't surprised that the jury hadn't done so either. "I can't blame the jury," he said, "or Judge Walker. I don't think he even wanted to see the psychiatrists in the courtroom."

McCowan confirmed that impression. He reported that after the verdict, Judge Walker declared, "I would have liked to argue before that jury for just one minute."

"You didn't have to," said McCowan. "Buck Compton gave your argument for you."

"That's right," McCowan said Walker said. "He did."

In court, in the absence of the jury, Cooper argued that when the jury deliberated over their penalty judgment, they should know the full truth about the plea bargain. Some of the jurors admitted they had heard part of the story. He wanted them to know that the district attorney himself didn't think Sirhan should get the gas chamber. Compton argued that the legal precedents were against Cooper. Judge Walker agreed.

Cooper asked if during the penalty trial he could put on witnesses to testify that the death penalty was not a deterrent to crime. Walker denied that, too. "This is a matter for the legislature," he said.

Cooper asked if he could put on two expert Arab witnesses who could testify further about the Arab-Israeli war. "This jury," said Cooper, "may not be aware of the historical events. And it would be evidence in mitigation, for it would show that the defendant was telling the truth."

"Beautiful, sir," said Sirhan.

Walker turned down that motion as well.

Adel Sirhan went into the holding tank for a fifteen-minute chat with his brother as Parsons looked on. He emerged, unwilling to tell me any of the family reactions to the verdict or the details of his chat with Sirhan. I drove him home to Pasadena, and Adel ruminated out loud about "the good Sirhan"—the Sirhan who liked to help people, who bought groceries for a poor old man who couldn't afford them, who fixed flat tires for passing strangers, who, at Hollywood Park Race Track, would give a fellow railbird $2 or $5 to play a hunch. But Sirhan the assassin? Not even his own brother understood that Sirhan.

Penalty phase. Monday, April 21, Cooper called for Mary Sirhan. She rose from her seat in the second row, from which she had watched and wept through most of the trial, and marched bravely up to the stand with dignity, a diminutive homely woman in a light blue skirt and matching jacket, climbed into the jury box, adjusted the microphone on her bosom and moistened her lips. She frowned and blinked at Cooper from a face ravined by tears enough for ten. She had buried eight of her thirteen children, lived through two wars, been abandoned by her husband. Now, she was asked to testify at the death penalty hearing of her son, the assassin. Cooper asked her one question: had Sirhan ever been in trouble with the law?

"He has never been," she said. "And that is not from me or from him. That is because I raised him up to the law of God and His love."

Cooper turned to Howard and told him he had no further witnesses. It was the shortest penalty hearing in California history, but what more could any witness add? Under California law, juries are given no criteria to decide between life and death. The only thing left to a lawyer is rhetoric.

John Howard's rhetoric was persuasive. He was a big man who spoke in his smallest voice, anxious, he told reporters later, not to appear bloodthirsty. Indeed, he made no specific request for Sirhan's life, but it was clear from his pithy argument that he felt the jury had no other choice but death.

"Robert F. Kennedy," said Howard, "was struck down at a moment when he represented the hopes and the ideas of an important segment of this nation. History may well record that, but for this defendant, Senator Kennedy might have succeeded to the highest honor and responsibility which the American democratic process can bestow. Beyond doubt, the tragedy which occurred in the early morning hours of June 5, 1968, at the Ambassador Hotel was politically motivated. The question now to be resolved is the proper penalty for political assassination in the United States of America."

Howard reminded the jurors they had been asked to consider what 200 such assassinations might do to the country. He said: "A half-dozen would suffice to leave this country bereft of democratic leadership. If death is to be the reward for political aspiration, you will know your candidates as two-dimensional images on the television screen or as disembodied voices over the radio.

"In resolving the question of this defendant's guilt," continued Howard, "you have found him lacking in honesty, in integrity and even in the courage of his convictions. At the same time, he obviously enjoyed the star status and the opportunity to engage in dramatic theatrics. To ease your task I should like to be able to concede that at some time in the course of this trial the defendant demonstrated the slightest degree of remorse. You in the jury box have had a better opportunity than the prosecution to observe the demeanor of this defendant. Perhaps you observed his reaction when Mr. Russell Parsons in his address to you urged in all sincerity that America pray for the ill-starred Kennedy family. You could not have failed to see the smirk on this defendant's face when he declared from that witness stand, 'I don't know who killed Senator Kennedy.' "

Howard told the jury that they could "eliminate Sirhan from society altogether, or merely eliminate him from your society. This defendant will regard permission to live as a further triumph, for life imprisonment is an entry into a form of custodial society that can only suffer from the inclusion of this defendant. You may not be obliged to hear this defendant boast that he committed the crime of the century. Others will."

This was not what Cooper expected, not at all. He leaned on his left elbow, his head cocked inquisitively at Howard, who was obviously asking for the death penalty.

Howard said he had noted in the paper that 202 Americans were dead in Vietnam this week. "That took only a small part of the news, while the Sirhan trial dominated the paper and the front page." Enough was enough, Howard implied. "We have lavishly expended our resources for the sake of a cold-blooded political assassin while content to send patriotic Americans to Vietnam with a $70 rifle and our best wishes. Sirhan was entitled to a fair trial, which each of you has now given to him. He has no special claim to further preservation. I would ask on behalf of the prosecution that each of you in your hearts have the courage of your convictions. Have the courage to write an end to this trial and to apply the only proper penalty for political assassination in the United States of America."

It was a gloomy Russell Parsons who stood then to face the jury. "Without asking you to invoke the death penalty," said Parsons, "it's quite plain what they speak." Parsons said he wasn't seeking sympathy for Sirhan, he was seeking justice. "The world is waiting to see if we've got guts enough to see that justice is done. My God," he exclaimed, "could I have been wrong? Do we execute sick people in California? If we do, we are only following Hitler who believed in killing the lame, the halt and the sick.

"This man is sick," thundered Parsons. "He doesn't know right from wrong, and I don't believe we've got down to the bottom rung yet, where we execute sick people in California." Parsons wondered where he had failed. He mentioned Drs. Schorr, Marcus, Richardson and Seward, and asked the jury "what was wrong" with their testimony. He mentioned Drs. DeVos and Diamond, "both from one of the great institutions in our land, the University of California at Berkeley" (though, he conceded, the university had had "some bad luck" lately). He reminded the jury that Diamond was a "professor with three hats—he even hypnotized him." And then he asked the jury to apply the law of diminished capacity to the question of whether or not this man should live or die.

"I don't know," said Parsons, in rebuttal to Howard, "where he bragged to anybody. He hasn't bragged to anybody. I don't think he's got sense enough." In other words, if he had good sense, he would brag about killing Kennedy? "I have lived with the kid since June," said Parsons. "I hope I could have better done my job as a lawyer. That's what I was appointed for. And so, ladies and gentlemen, I want to thank you for your consideration. The evidence points to only one just verdict in this case."

"May it please the court," said Cooper. He rose, walked slowly over to a podium in front of the jury, put his hands in his pockets. "Shortly after midnight on the morning of June 5, 1968, a young, vigorous Senator, fresh from his victory in the California primaries for the office of the Presidency of the United States, met his untimely death at the hands of a mentally ill, young Palestinian Arab."

Over at the counsel table, Sirhan chewed on a stick of gum and looked totally unconcerned. It was as if the horses were going to the post for the last race and he had decided not even to bet.

"On the floor of the drab, dirty, dreary pantry at the Ambassador Hotel," continued Cooper, "lying in a pool of his own blood, clutching a crucifix, he whispered his last words to his brave and loyal wife kneeling beside him. He died the next day, the victim of hate, hate generated in the bowels of war in a far-off land, hate engendered at an early age in the child Sirhan, hate that consumed what was once a healthy mind, hate that reduced that mind to one described by the evidence as 'a substantial mental illness.' "

Cooper told the jury of its alternatives, life in prison for Sirhan or death by cyanide gas "in a gruesome little green room at San Quentin." He said the law gave them no guidelines. "The law makes no distinction between life imprisonment or death. Either punishment—" Cooper shook his head vigorously "—will equally satisfy the demands of the law for murder of the first degree." The jury had absolute discretion. That meant that if a juror's conscience allowed him to exercise sympathy for the defendant or passion against him, the law allowed him to do what he wished. The jury had the power of a king, of a benevolent monarch or of a despotic dictator.

Cooper said he assumed that the jury's verdict of first degree was based partly on Dr. Pollack's opinions and reasoning. He pointed out that Dr. Pollack also believed that Sirhan should not die in the gas chamber because he was mentally ill. He asked the jury to be consistent by following Dr. Pollack now.

"Some one of you," continued Cooper, "may suggest that your verdict should express the conscience of the community. But this is not the law. The only thing in this penalty proceeding that is explicit is that your verdict must express the individual opinion of each juror. It is your individual judgments, not the judgments of the community, that must be expressed. The reason that the law looks to you and not the community is obvious. The community has not sacrificed three months of their lives to hear all the testimony, to see the witnesses face-to-face, to hear the arguments, to hear and understand the law. The community only hears smatterings of the arguments from the news media. Moreover, and of significant importance, theirs is not the responsibility. It's easy to express an opinion on life imprisonment or death in the chitchat of idle conversation. But it is another thing when that decision is yours and yours alone.

"So far as my knowledge goes, probably the first recorded murder of record is when Cain slew Abel. How many thousands of years ago that was I do not know. But I do know that since that date there have been thousands upon thousands of murders committed in other lands and in ours. In response to those murders there has been retaliation in the form of revenge and in the form of lawful death penalties. But the murders have continued and still continue and, unfortunately, will continue, regardless of what you do here. Violence begets violence. Violence breeds violence.

"If the death of Sirhan Sirhan would restore Senator Kennedy to his coun try and to his family, I would be the first to demand his life. Taking the life of a human being, as Sirhan took Senator Kennedy's life, is a degrading act. It not only degraded Sirhan, but it degraded the country as well. But so also when the law, through the intervention of a jury, takes the life of a human being, it too degrades us all. Violence, the taking of a human life by the law, also begets violence. Has it solved the incidence of murder? Do you honestly believe that the execution of Sirhan Sirhan will ever prevent another mentally disturbed individual from committing another political assassination? Is it not more probable that by sending him to the medical facility at Vacaville, a maximum-security penitentiary in every sense of the word, a place where he can be studied scientifically and psychiatrically, something more can be learned about the human mind and what causes people to want to kill and to kill?"

Then Cooper took a bold step. He focused on the division and the hatred and the violence that seemed to be overwhelming the country and told the jury they could do their bit to stop it—right here, by sparing Sirhan's life. He quoted no less an authority than Senator Robert Kennedy himself. "Will you listen to his words?" he asked the jury. "Will you heed his advice? Will you not please weigh carefully . . . what he said just two months before his death?"

"It was the night of April 5, 1968. It was at the City Club in Cleveland, Ohio, the night after the Reverend Martin Luther King was slain at the hands of a sniper.

"In that setting at that time—with human understanding the young Senator said:

> Whenever any American's life is taken by another unnecessarily—whether it is done in the name of the law or in the defiance of law, by one man or a gang, in cold blood or in passion, in an attack of violence or in response to violence—the whole nation is degraded.

"At that speech in Cleveland, Senator Kennedy singled out certain forms of violence most of us take for granted, stating:

> We calmly accept newspaper reports of civilian slaughter in far-off lands. We glorify killing on movie and television screens and call it entertainment. We make it easy for men of all shades of sanity to acquire whatever weapons and ammunition they desire.

"Why? Why? Why? Well, there are a lot of people to blame, but that won't do any good. Senator Kennedy himself said in this same speech:

Some look for scapegoats, others look for conspiracies, but this much is clear: violence breeds violence.

"Now, in a most particular way, and as a kind of posthumous tribute to Senator Kennedy, this jury can do something to break this circle of violence—by simply saying in this case, under these circumstances—do not take the life of this mentally sick individual—even in the name of the law.

"Oh, yes. It would be legal if you did. But it would still be violent and perhaps vengeful. Society doesn't need that. Or, as Senator Kennedy put it in that Cleveland speech:

We must recognize that this short life can neither be ennobled or enriched by hatred and revenge. Our lives on this planet are too short and the work to be done too great to let this spirit flourish any longer in our land.

"The day before that Cleveland speech at Indianapolis, Indiana, moments after he had gotten the news of Dr. King's death, Senator Kennedy spoke in the same tone of reconciliation. His words then were spoken in a different context—in the context of urban violence and the divisions in this country between black and white. He said:

What we need in the United States is not division; What we need in the United States is not hatred; what we need in the United States is not violence or lawlessness, but love and wisdom, and compassion toward one another, and a feeling of justice toward those who still suffer within our country, whether they be white or they be black.

"But the words apply in this case just as well—even better—for Sirhan, as you know, though culpable, is a product of division and of hatred and of violence. And if the United States is divided, so is the world. If the United States is full of hatred, so is the world. If the United States is full of violence, so is the world."

Sparing Sirhan's life, said Cooper, would fit very well within a vision that was Kennedy's own: "To tame the savageness of man and to make gentle the life of the world."

Cooper turned from the jury and faced Sirhan. Sirhan, the actor, watched Cooper's display with a good deal of curiosity. "And now, Sirhan Sirhan, I've done all the best that I could do for you, for the American system of law and justice which I serve and revere." He turned toward Mary in the courtroom. "And to you, Mary Sirhan, his mother, I can do no more. I now entrust the life of your son to the hands of this American jury. Mary Sirhan, may your prayers be answered."

Before Judge Walker let the jury go, he warned them:

If, upon consideration of the evidence, you believe that life imprisonment is the proper sentence, you must assume that those officials charged with the operation of the parole system will perform their duties in a correct and responsible manner and that they will not parole this defendant unless he can be safely released into society. It would be a violation of your duty as jurors if you would fix the penalty of death because of the doubt of the [California] Adult Authority to properly carry out its responsibility.

The jurors retired to their dingy deliberation room. Parsons and McCowan took Mary Sirhan and Adel into the holding tank to see Sirhan for an eight-minute visit. And I chatted with Munir in the near-empty courtroom. Munir was optimistic. He reported that a woman with a Mexican accent who said she was the wife of one of the jurors had phoned the Sirhan home and said that under no circumstances would Sirhan get the death penalty from this jury. "I guess," said Munir, "she ought to know." Who was she? "I don't know," said Munir. "She said . . ."

The door of the holding tank opened. Mary and Adel and Parsons and McCowan emerged and Sirhan, the perfect host, was seeing them to the door. Then he spied me talking to Munir. He pointed at me and shouted at Munir, "Don't talk to him! Don't talk to him!" Adel hurried out into the courtroom, grabbed Munir by the arm and whispered to him in Arabic.

In the jury room, Foreman Elliott took a preliminary poll to see where matters stood. Five voted for death, three for life imprisonment, and four were undecided. They discussed the pros and cons. Howard was right, said one of those who favored death: Sirhan never showed any remorse. Another said he was impressed with Howard's implicit view that there was only one proper punishment for political assassination in America: death. In their deliberations over guilt or innocence, two of the jurors had held out for second-degree murder. Now, in a second vote at the end of the day, only those two voted against a penalty of death.

On Tuesday, Alphonso Galindo, a Roman Catholic, and Susan Brumm, a grandmotherly soul who kept referring to Sirhan as "that kid," were still holding out for a life sentence. "The death penalty is still on the books, isn't it?" one of the others demanded. Galindo admitted it was. "And we all believe in capital punishment, don't we?" Galindo admitted that all of the jurors had sworn that they did. "Well, what crime do you need if not *this* one?" he was asked.

Martin Kasindorf of *Newsweek* reported that "a much perplexed Galindo slept on that—or tried to."

On Wednesday morning, another ballot, and Mrs. Brumm came over.

In his cell, Sirhan had just told Parsons and Nahkleh, "They've been out too long. They're going to come in against us."

Finally, at 10:55 Wednesday morning—after eleven hours and thirty-four minutes of deliberation—Galindo gave up and said quietly, "Let's all go home."

Elliott hit the buzzer three times. The attorneys and the press were summoned, and Sirhan was moved down the elevator and through the guarded corridors. Cooper paced back and forth in front of the counsel table with his hands in his pockets. "I don't like it," he said to Bob Greene. "I don't like it. I can feel a chill in my bones." He walked away, then returned to Greene at the rail. "The weak ones crumbled, just like they did the first time. They couldn't stand the pressure."

Howard and Fitts were professionally pessimistic, like the Notre Dame coaching staff before a big game. They'd be surprised if the verdict was life. So would McCowan. He sat at the counsel table with his hands folded, like a preacher at prayer. In the corridor, Adel Sirhan puffed nervously on a cigarette and reporters who had grown to like this natty little fellow looked the other way when they saw him. Thank God, they thought, Mrs. Sirhan stayed home.

The jurors edged through the jury box to their seats. Their faces were strained and, again, they avoided looking at Sirhan. Mrs. Nishikawa again took the verdict in her hands and read aloud:

We the Jury in the above entitled action, having found the Defendant Sirhan Bishara Sirhan guilty of Murder in the first degree, as charged in Count 1 of the Indictment, now fix the penalty at death. This 23rd day of April, 1969. Bruce D. Elliott, Foreman.

And again the wire services broke for the door.

Cooper demanded a voice poll of the jury. Each juror answered, "Yes," when asked if the verdict represented his opinion. When it was Miss Stillman's turn, she covered her eyes and said, "Yes," so low it could hardly be heard. Miss Nell Bortells, looking as if she would burst into tears, choked out her reply.

Cooper's voice was husky when he gave notice immediately of a motion for a new trial. Parsons shook his head in disgust. McCowan put his face in his hands. Sirhan turned in his seat to look at his brother, Adel, shrugged his shoulders, stood and swept the jury with a contemptuous look, threw back his shoulders and swaggered into the holding tank. "It's all right," he said, comforting Cooper, Parsons and McCowan. "Even Jesus Christ couldn't have saved me."

The attorneys met the press once more in the auxiliary courtroom on the fourth floor. Cooper and Parsons were both depressed. "Things are bad in this country," intoned Parsons, "and it's very difficult to get a fair trial."

"Nobody's saying he didn't get a fair trial," said Cooper. "But the underlying feeling of the entire United States caused a backlash that has seeped into the minds of the jurors." Indeed, on the cover of *Newsweek,* delivered to the jurors after their deliberations on Tuesday, was a picture of three blacks swathed in cartridge belts and carrying rifles as they emerged from their seige of Willard Straight Hall at Cornell University. "The jurors," said Cooper," are governed by the same emotions—love and hate—that you and I have, and they can't help but be affected by unrest."

Cooper also agreed with one newsman that the prominence of the victim made a definite difference. "If the victim," he said, "had not been Robert Kennedy, the court would have accepted the plea of second degree. I mean it. I believe it. It never would have gone this route."

Compton noted that juries deliberating the death penalty are often swayed as much by their overview of the defendant in the courtroom as they are by the evidence itself. "I don't believe," said Compton, "that the defendant's conduct was such as to evoke sympathy or endear him to the jury."

But others, somewhat more removed from Sirhan, had different judgments. In San Diego, a young woman wrote Sirhan a simple little note: "I am praying that society might forgive you and that God might forgive society." *The New York Times* concurred in the sentiment. So did Eric Sevareid, commenting that night on CBS News, and so did certain members of the Kennedy entourage, including Jesse Unruh, the man who had helped save Sirhan in the Ambassador pantry, so society could give him "justice." All were somewhat surprised that justice—in 1969—would mean death.

Sirhan, who had done his homework on American assassins, was hardly amazed. He knew that all of the country's major assassins—no matter how nutty—were done away with in one way or another. Only Richard Lawrence, who tried to murder President Jackson, survived to live out his life in a mental institution. When it came to the assassin of a President, or a near-President like Robert F. Kennedy, society didn't give a damn about a psychosis that diminished criminal responsibility.

Society had "progressed" in a good many areas since the trial of President Garfield's assassin, Charles Guiteau, in 1881. But now in the Sirhan trial, as Charles Rosenberg wrote of the verdict returned for Guiteau:

> Society . . . must protect itself; the merciless prosecution of the vicious must not be impeded—no matter how lamentable the circumstances conspiring to form their vicious character.

Eighteen

"Robert Kennedy was a Fascist pig.
Eldridge Cleaver said so."

At the main entrance to the Biltmore Hotel, a crowd stood and applauded the jurors as they debarked from their yellow bus, and others inside the hotel shouted their congratulations to a jury that had done its duty. Newsmen who followed the jurors up to their corridor found them celebrating boisterously over a buffet lunch, joking with the man they regarded as their host, Judge Walker, laughing with one another and exchanging addresses and telephone numbers.

Martin Kasindorf of *Newsweek* discovered that many of the jurors had come to loathe Sirhan during the fifteen weeks of trial. "Sirhan is a conniving brat," said one juror. Another called him "an animal" and thought that someone ought "to cut a little piece out of him every day." What were the factors that allowed them to rationalize their hatred for Sirhan into a verdict of first degree? "Not even the experts could get together among themselves," Benjamin Glick told Kasindorf. Albert Frederico, the city plumber, agreed with Glick. "All those psychiatrists!" he exclaimed. "They really had us all stirred up. It was confusing. It stunk!" Mrs. Brumm said she was voting for second degree, but her thinking changed when another juror pointed out that Sirhan had never been in trouble before the killing; therefore he must have had the mental capacity to control himself.

Kasindorf reported: "As the prosecution had hoped, the jurors administered to themselves the Rorschach 'ink blot' and other psychological tests that defense experts used . . . The tests backfired on the defense when several of the jurors found some of their responses startlingly similar to Sirhan's 'paranoid' reactions."

David Larsen of the Los Angeles *Times* interviewed Juror George Stitzel. The most damaging evidence against Sirhan? "As far as I was concerned," said Stitzel, "it was the notebooks." That made clear in his mind "the overriding gravity of the crime, the cold-blooded murder of an individual—a planned murder." But he was startled when Larsen told him that the prosecution had agreed before the trial to accept a plea of first degree with life in prison. How would he have voted in the penalty phase if he had known this? "I honestly don't know," said Stitzel.*

On May 21, Judge Walker would go through the formality of hearing Cooper's motions for a new trial before he pronounced judgment. In the meantime, Sirhan was given a chance to mark everyone connected with the trial on his mental report card. No one fared very well. No one could. He refused to shave, he asked for no newspapers or magazines, he became surly with his guards. When his mother visited him for the first time after the death verdict, he announced to the deputies that he wouldn't see her unless he could do so in the privacy of his inner cell, and when Captain Craig Carpenter refused, he let her go away with Parsons, only a muttered phrase in Arabic passing between them. On May 1, he started reading the *Encyclopedia Americana* from the beginning.

On May 2, I went up to see Sirhan. He had told Cooper that he had changed his mind about me. He was anxious to cooperate and curious to see what I had written thus far. I presented some 200 manuscript pages for his inspection, a distillation of thousands of pages of official reports and a good deal of my own investigation. When he read about Roosevelt Grier and Rafer Johnson, he sneered. "The Negroes bought RFK's image, but the blacks didn't. The Uncle Toms bought it, but not the militants." He sneered, too, at President Johnson's establishment of a Commission on Violence, and spoke in the classical language of the juvenile delinquent: "They just want to make more laws, tie you up with more fuckin' chains. Fuck the law! If every man had the right to work, equality and justice, none of this would have happened."

But Sirhan agreed with my suggestion in the text—that violence and the rhetoric of violence had had their influence on him. "That," he said with enthusiasm, "shows some insight."

I asked Sirhan if, now, after all, he saw himself as the man who—wittingly or unwittingly—struck the first blow of the Third World against the West.

---

* But another juror was apparently never in doubt. Mrs. Irma Martinez confessed to Michael McCowan not long after the trial that she could never have voted for a life sentence. She had a cousin, she explained, who was killed in south central Los Angeles when a man threw a fire bomb into a neighborhood bar. The bomber, said Mrs. Martinez, is walking the streets today—a free man.

"I think I did," said Sirhan quietly. He tried to explain, hesitantly, haltingly, how he thought. "In the first place," he said, "Robert Kennedy was a Fascist pig. Eldridge Cleaver said so."

"Did you know that before you shot Kennedy?" I asked.

"No," he said, "I read it—afterward. But I knew it myself."

"Did you identify with the black militants?"

"I did. Very much so." He flexed his right arm. "This arm can give a little," he said, "it's flexible. But if you keep bending it, it's gonna break."

"The militants are impatient."

"They are."

"Are you? Were you?"

"You're goddamn right. We don't have enough to eat or clothes to wear. And then we strike out because there's nothing else to do."

"You strike out in despair?"

"Yes," he wailed. "But it doesn't do any good. We are crushed." He fell silent and reflected on that image a moment. As a kind of an afterthought, he added, defiantly, "But, hell, I gained something. They can gas me. But I am famous. I achieved in a day what it took Kennedy all his life to do." He added his standard disclaimer: "I'm not proud of what I did, but . . ."

He said his emotions were "shallow" and it didn't take much to trigger his anger. And then, he turned immediately to a discussion of the book and the movie by Truman Capote, *In Cold Blood*. He had never talked about *In Cold Blood* before, but now it was obvious that the work had made a deep impression on him. He said he identified with Perry, and it was easy to understand why. Perry was small and dark and he'd been kicked around. Sirhan's voice rose with excitement as he recalled Perry's confrontation with a parole officer who let him leave prison before he was ready. " 'Why did you let me go too soon?' " It was Sirhan's paraphrase of Perry's anguish. " 'You had me and you let me go!' " Then Sirhan said it on his own, his own face contorted now: "You had me and you let *me* go. And look what I did!"

"Who had you?" I asked. "Who had you?"

Sirhan shook his head. He didn't know.

On May 5, I went back to the cell to see what kind of marks Sirhan had given to all the principals at the trial. Sirhan thought the defense attorneys put on a pretty good case, as good as they could under the circumstances. He was even ready to concede—for the first time—that Dr. Diamond's theories might be correct. But he thought the prosecution attorneys were "crooked." They knew he never carried his wallet with him. And yet Fitts told the jury he did and made his leaving it in the car just another proof of premeditation.

Inevitably, the conversation drifted to the situation in the Middle East. I noted that the current issue of *Look* magazine had a feature on the young men of Al Fatah. Did Sirhan see it? No, he wasn't reading much these days. Did he want to see it? Not really. He wasn't even sure that he approved of a magazine article on the militancy of the Arabs, for then, the Zionists could point to it and use it as further excuse for more of an arms buildup, and more U.S. support. And then, the Arabs would be forced to retaliate in turn. "The more the Arabs are gonna be provoked and some other psychotic or some other punk or some other fanatic is gonna blow some politician's brains off and uh, start the whole cycle again."

I asked Sirhan about the escalating circle of violence in the Middle East. What was his solution? He suggested bilateral disarmament and "let 'em fight it out hand to hand."

I asked him what he would do if he had dictatorial power to impose a solution on the Middle East.

"I don't think dictatorial powers can do it," said Sirhan. "It's the masses' problem; it's the people's problem. Not the—not the leaders in the Middle East. It's not Nasser and Hussein who call the shots. It's the average man on the street who calls the shots. That's more democratic, I think, than in America."

"Well, what you're saying is, that the skirmishes, the little wars, and, if there's a big war, even the big war is going to be what the people want?"

"I think it would have to be. Because they aren't satisfied. They haven't had anything. They've had promises, promises. Just talk doesn't satisfy. They want action. They want results. Hey!" Sirhan smiled. "I produced action for them. I'm a big hero over there. I don't feel that here. I'm not proud of what I did. But that's how they regard me. That's how much they want action. And that's what the United States does not understand. This is what bugs me about the American people. They got so many psychologists, so many psychiatrists and—learned people. And they don't know what these masses need. They don't need—guns. They need—recognition. A little appreciation for themselves. That's what I think they need basically."

"So if you were all powerful, how would you go about giving them—recognition?"

"Education. Industry. Agriculture."

"All right. But you can't have that when a country's at war."

Sirhan said that you had to have some education before you could go to war. It seemed to be the complete obverse of the point he was trying to make, and I said I wasn't sure whether Sirhan was for war or against war.

Sirhan said he was for it, if needed. "I'm for violence whenever—as long as it's needed."

"Even though it tends to have a very very bad effect on children and other living things?"

Sirhan had no answer for that. Or if he did, I couldn't understand how his reply was in any sense an answer.

"Well, well, whatever one human being can put in the mind of another, he can take it out. If a man can wound a mind, he can heal it at the same time."

I tried to shift gears with Sirhan. "You think it's just as easy?"

"I think it's just as easy. Because nobody tried to heal the scars that I had. You just aggravated them and moved them from chronic to malignant. And it eventually burst."

"What could have changed your path? What could have deflected you from this way to this way?"

"More acceptance on the part of American society. Showing a little bit of the dream that you have. Don't tell me America's the greatest. Show me, prove to me. Don't let me look at it. Let me feel it." Sirhan told me this was one more thing that helped build up the pressure inside him— "The pressure of not being employed, of not living a decent American life, an average American life."

"In fact," I said, "you *did* have a job in a health food store."

"I did. But that isn't what I want in life. I want identity. I want something to associate with and—I like that."

"You had a car. A lot of people in this country, and most of the people in the rest of the world, don't have their own car."

"Sure, but as much ambition as I had, as much aggressiveness? It was an American ideal, being aggressive, wanting to get ahead. I thought I had that, but I couldn't show what I had. And, uh, what's a '56 De Soto?"

"You really bought the American dream?"

"I really bought the American dream wholeheartedly. And I thought I could achieve it. But it—wasn't a dream. It was a nightmare. That's the best description I have for it. It wasn't a dream. It was complete disillusionment. I couldn't buy it anymore after I saw that. . . . The dream is not there. It's just words. A mirage is what it was. It wasn't reality. To me! For a rich man, maybe, it was reality. To Kennedy, it must have been a reality. Not to me, sir."

I wondered whether the reality could be achieved by violence.

Sirhan said violence in the right place and at the right time had done wonders. "Even Gandhi could tell you that." I asked him if he made any distinction between violence toward property and violence toward persons. He hadn't thought of it.

"I mean," I said, "had you ever thought of burning down Kennedy's house instead of killing Kennedy?"

"What would I have achieved? I've had my own house destroyed. . . ."

"I mean, talk about a gesture that would have been significant—"

"As far as for me to have satisfied myself with Kennedy, I think all I would have needed to do was just to give him a good punch in the nose at that Ambassador. I think that would have satisfied me. It was a symbolic way of defeating him. It would have been enough for me—had I been conscious and awake at the time that I saw him."

"Yeah. Yeah." I wasn't agreeing with Sirhan, only trying to keep him talking.

"The way that I performed," continued Sirhan, "I think that I must have been a coward. That's the way cowards go. They use guns, because they don't have it on their own. I thought—I thought I had it on my own."

"It sounds to me like you'd be in favor of restrictive gun laws."

"Well, I guess, for psychotics, I am. For myself, I am. Well. Obviously. Although I disagree with those who say that I used the gun as a phallic symbol. If I wanted to express myself sexually, I certainly would have used a different gun than the one I used. That's the part of the psychologists I don't buy." Sirhan's voice then took on an earnest tone as he explained: "This was an assassination in the classical sense of assassinations —where the assassin was—dulled—mentally at the time that he commits the crime. The word assassin itself means hashish—*hashshashin,* persons who are drugged, under the influence of some narcotics, liquor. I wasn't under the influence of marijuana, hashish or heroin or whatever. Just a few mirrors and a couple shots of Tom Collins was enough to put me in that same state, the same state, mental state, as the ancient assassins were."

"The *hashshashin* being an ancient sect which had to drug themselves in order to commit the murders they had to commit? Right?"

"Right."

"Implying that no man in his right mind would do—"

"Would do such a thing!" Sirhan eagerly agreed. He added: "You know. I can't see it. You know this Lee Oswald and this fellow that shot King. I don't see it. That's not—" Here Sirhan paused for a moment, catching himself saying something he didn't want to say. Whatever he was going to say, his next words indicated that he felt somehow different from Oswald and Ray. They shot from ambush. They succeeded in eliminating a fellow. "But," wondered Sirhan, "where's the satisfaction?"

I simply waited for Sirhan to amplify on his own. Direct questions at a time like this were useless.

Sirhan used an example, possibly a personal one. "It's just like wanting to have some sex and, instead of going out with the most beautiful broad, you go into nigger territory and pick the ugliest whore they've got. What have you satisfied yourself? Sure, you got a piece of tail. But, you know, where's the satisfaction of it? Nobody knows it, because you're too ashamed, too frightened to tell everybody about it. Whereas, if you go out with Raquel Welch, hey, you want the whole town to know about it."

"In a sense," I said, "your act was less cowardly than that of the guy that killed President Kennedy or Martin Luther King?"

"Hey, when you shoot a man in the back? There you go! At least, Kennedy saw me. I think. I don't know." I waited. Silence was best. Let him talk. He did. "You see. This is what I don't understand. How did the man himself feel? You know, when he saw me pulling the trigger? And he saw me. I—I can't imagine that. I don't remember it. I don't feel it. Hell, just the sight of that man with the—you know, the fright—would have scared me from pulling that trigger."

I pointed out that the first shot hit Kennedy behind the right ear. So Kennedy didn't see him, nor did he see Kennedy's face until the second shot.

"I don't know about that," said Sirhan. "I don't know. Because the face —" Again, Sirhan blocked. "I don't know. I must have faced him. How the hell else would I see him from profile? Uh, uh, I don't know if I could see him or distinguish him."

I paid Sirhan a visit on May 19 and with me was Jack Perkins of NBC-TV, which had offered what amounted to $1,000 a minute for an exclusive TV interview with Sirhan. Sirhan's hair looked like a bird's nest, he hadn't shaved in five days, and he had his pants down when we walked in on him. "Who the hell's this?" demanded Sirhan, jerking a thumb at Perkins. I told him. "Oh," said Sirhan. He remained standing. "I want to see Parsons first. It's urgent." I said I'd tell Parsons. In the meantime, Perkins just wanted to say hello, get acquainted a little bit so he wouldn't start absolutely cold on the interview, now scheduled for May 22, the day after Sirhan's last hearing in Los Angeles.

Sirhan settled down a bit and started pumping Perkins. He was impressed with the potential size of NBC's audience. "Whew! Twenty million? Twenty?" And characteristically vain: "I don't want the camera full face," said Sirhan. "My profile looks better."

Perkins told him a producer was coming out from New York especially for this interview. "What's his name?" asked Sirhan.

"Polikoff."

"Polikoff? Sounds like a goddamn Jew! Shit!" He found out that Perkins had covered the trial for the Huntley-Brinkley News. How, he wanted to know, did Perkins evaluate the psychiatric testimony. Perkins said he didn't buy it. That seemed to please Sirhan.

On May 21, District Attorney Evelle Younger came into the courtroom. "If the court please, may I interrupt? For the record, I am Evelle J. Younger. . . ." He told Judge Walker that during the plea bargain before the trial he had asked Senator Edward Kennedy if the Kennedy family had any thoughts about a proper penalty in the Sirhan case. He was told by a family attorney from New York the family had no recommendation to make. In the past week, this same attorney phoned and asked if it was now proper for the family to express their opinion about Sirhan's sentence. Younger urged him to have Kennedy send him a letter which he could deliver in open court. Now he had a handwritten letter from Senator Kennedy himself.

Judge Walker accepted the letter, but did not read it, and asked Cooper to proceed with his motion. Cooper had thirteen numbered arguments in the brief he submitted in support of his motion for a new trial. He charged Walker with judicial error in admitting the notebooks in evidence, in not accepting Sirhan's plea of guilty, in ruling off the panel venireman who couldn't conscientiously levy the penalty of death, in letting the trial go on despite improper publicity, in accepting an indictment from a grand jury that was improperly constituted.

He argued at length to show that the district attorney's office had misled him on a second plea bargain; they promised that if Sirhan pled guilty the prosecutors would urge the jury to hand down a sentence of life, but, if he went to trial, they would make no recommendation either way. It was partially on that basis, said Cooper, that Sirhan's attorneys advised him *not* to plead guilty, but, apparently, they were simply giving Sirhan bad advice, for the prosecution went right ahead and asked for the death penalty. "We had a chance to get the district attorney's recommendation of life in prison," said Cooper, "and we gave it up, based on a false premise. We gave up a very valuable tool, and misled our client in the process."

John Howard stood and explained that the district attorney's office was "misinformed and uninformed" about the strength of the psychiatric evidence. During the trial, they had taken "a hard new look" at it. And their posture had changed.

Judge Walker looked at the transcript. He didn't think the prosecution *had* asked for the death penalty.

"Well, your Honor, if that wasn't an implicit call for death, then our argument folds." Cooper wasn't going to quibble over words. Howard had told the jury Sirhan had "no special claim to further preservation," and asked them to apply "the only proper penalty for political assassination in America." Cooper flatly asked the judge now to reduce—"if that is the proper word"—Sirhan's penalty to life in prison. He compared Sirhan, a young man who'd never been in trouble, concededly mentally ill, and headed now for the gas chamber, with James Earl Ray, a many-time loser, who got life in prison for killing Martin Luther King—a contrast which, Eric Sevareid noted, would "sit poorly with a great many people." Cooper also quoted an editorial in *The New York Times:* "State-inflicted death as punishment for crime repudiates the findings of modern penal science and rejects the quality of mercy that is the mark of a just society. It represents a retreat to the law of the jungle. . . . In this particular crime of violence with its warped background of frustrations and fanaticism, justice and the American people will surely be best served by a reduction in Sirhan's sentence to life imprisonment, an option still open to the presiding judge."

Then Cooper read into the record the letter from Senator Edward Kennedy. It was written in the Senator's own hand and surely the judge could not ignore it. It read, in part, "My brother was a man of love and sentiment and compassion. He would not have wanted his death to be a cause for the taking of another life. Moreover he was a young man totally committed to life and living. He stood against injustice, poverty and discrimination for those evils lessened life. He grew to despise war for war denies the sacredness of life. And he had a special affection for children for they held the promise of life. If the kind of man my brother was is pertinent, we believe it should be weighed in the balance on the side of compassion, mercy and God's gift of life." (See Appendix H for the full text.)

In response to Cooper's plea, Walker said, "Well, the law of this state says that a defendant convicted of the crime of murder in the first degree in a proper case shall suffer either life in prison or the death penalty. It is the feeling of the court that the jury was right, and I have no reason to change my feeling now, so the motion for a new trial and all points will be denied. Will the defendant please stand up?"

Sirhan stood.

"Is your true name Sirhan Bishara Sirhan?"

"It is."

Walker read a history of the case, from the indictment to the present moment. "This is the time for judgment and sentence," he read from a prepared text. "Is there any legal cause why judgment and sentence should not now be pronounced?"

"None," said Cooper, "other than the points just urged."

"There being no legal cause why judgment and sentence should not be pronounced, it is the judgment and sentence of this court that for the crime of murder in the first degree of which you, Sirhan Bishara Sirhan, have been convicted by verdict of the jury, and the jury having determined in their discretion that you should suffer the penalty of death, that the said penalty be inflicted within the walls of the state penitentiary of San Quentin, California, in the manner prescribed by law at a time to be fixed by this court in the warrant of execution." He said the sheriff of Los Angeles should deliver Sirhan to the warden of San Quentin within ten days.

Sirhan stood there with his hands on his hips. The judge had not given him the usual Hollywood chance to say "one last word," nor did he seize the opportunity. He would have a chance to talk to twenty million on TV tomorrow.

His mother wept quietly in the second row of seats. She, too, had written to Judge Walker, citing Biblical references in her plea for mercy. Now she would go up to the cell to see her son, probably for the last time in Los Angeles.

No one present in the cell—not Cooper, nor Parsons, nor McCowan, nor Mary, nor Munir Sirhan, nor I—felt very good about the judge's refusal to change a jot or tittle, not even when urged to do so by Ted Kennedy. But Sirhan was unconcerned. "I don't care about the death penalty," he said. "What's bothering me is Kaiser's book."

Cooper pointed out that this would probably be the last chance for Munir, Mrs. Sirhan and Sirhan to talk together for some time. For the next half hour, Sirhan, Munir and their mother talked about money: the proceeds from the book, the threat of a civil judgment against Sirhan by others who were shot in the Ambassador pantry, Nahkleh and the Arab money. "Got all you can," said Sirhan to Munir. "Go after it."

Finally, Cooper suggested that maybe Mrs. Sirhan might want to kiss her son good-bye. He got up to ask Captain Carpenter for special permission. "Fuck that!" said Sirhan.

Cooper went ahead and got Carpenter's okay. Mary moved around to the south end of the table that was set up outside Sirhan's cell. Sirhan moved to her side. She threw her arms around him, put her lips to his neck and began to murmur something in Arabic. Then she began to cry and Sirhan started to blubber as well. He pushed away from his mother, moved into his inner cell for perhaps a minute, while everyone else stood there waiting. Sirhan emerged, wiping his eyes, shook hands with his brother, and Cooper clasped him around the neck.

A battery of cameras and lights awaited the party in the jail's first-floor reception room. A black deputy slid open the iron gate, Mary and Munir slipped off to the right, and Cooper and Parsons stayed to talk to the press.

"What reaction did Sirhan have to Kennedy's letter?" cried one of the newsmen.

Cooper paused. "He thought it was very—magnanimous of the Senator. He was very pleased." I choked a bit. Later, Cooper laughed. "I couldn't tell 'em what he really said, could I?"

"I guess not," I said.

Sirhan had greeted the news of Kennedy's plea for mercy with a snarl. "Ahhh," he said, "it's just politics."

NBC had two camera crews, a producer and Correspondent Jack Perkins waiting for Sirhan the next morning when he was ushered out of his cell for his chat with the world. The cameras and the lights made his heart beat faster and almost at once he complained: "I'm too nervous!"

"Are you?" asked Perkins.

"I'm too nervous!" he cried again.

Perkins had intended to plunge right into the events of June 4, the assassination itself, but he slowed down the pace immediately and started to draw Sirhan out more gently. "You worked at a horse ranch here for a while?"

"Yes, sir."

"And enjoyed that, did you?"

"I loved it. That was the most enjoyable experience of my life . . . horses."

"Why do you like horses? Why do you like horses?"

Sirhan stammered. "They're not—they're—they're easy to be with, sir. I love to be with them."

"What about people?"

"They're equally good to be with, but—"

"You're not suggesting that you don't get along with people?"

That is exactly what Sirhan was suggesting but he didn't like the implications of that suggestion, so he rhapsodized for a moment or two about the thrill and the challenge of racing.

They talked about Sirhan's experiments with the occult, they talked about his feelings for—and against—Robert Kennedy, they talked about his obsessions over the Arab-Israeli conflict. Perkins drew an admission from Sirhan that he had never felt discriminated against in America because he was an Arab, nor ever felt impelled to hide the fact that he was an Arab.

"I'm still proud of being an Arab," said Sirhan, "a Palestinian Arab, at that."

And how did Kennedy offend Sirhan's Arab feelings?

It was, said Sirhan, a television documentary that implied that Kennedy favored the Israelis because they were "underdogs in the Middle East." But they weren't underdogs. "They're militarily victorious, and they have the know-how and the technology of the West, sir." The Arabs, he said, were the real underdogs—"backward and uncivilized." Kennedy should have favored them. Then Sirhan backpedaled. "The backward Arab" was a picture painted by the Zionists for the American public. It was "totally erroneous."

"Now, uh," said Perkins, hardly knowing how to deal with such an inconsistent fellow and deciding to change the subject, "you bought a gun?"

"Yes, sir."

"Why did you buy a gun?"

"I like guns," said Sirhan. Then he laughed.

That, too, seemed to unsettle Perkins. He moved on to other subjects, finally got to the matter of the notebooks. "You were planning to kill Senator Kennedy," said Perkins flatly.

"Only in my mind," said Sirhan.

"Well, that's the only place you can plan it," protested Perkins.

"Not to do it physically," said Sirhan. "I never thought of doing it. I never, I never, I don't see myself, sir, as doing it. I don't have the guts to do anything like that."

"You don't have the guts?"

"It's against my nature, sir, to do that."

"Well, you did it!"

"I did it, but I was unaware of it, sir."

Perkins went back to the mystery of the notebooks. Sirhan was, as usual, less than cogent about them. They were still a mystery to him, part of his experimentation with the occult, perhaps. Still: "There's something here, sir, that has something to do with it, and I don't know what it is." Again, he disowned the writings.

"They're the writings of Sirhan Sirhan," said Perkins.

"Yes, sir, but they're not the writings of me now, sir."

"Well," said Perkins, "if you were writing in your notebook now what would you write about Robert F. Kennedy?"

Sirhan paused for at least half a minute. Finally, he said, "To me, sir, he's still alive."

"How?"

Again a long pause. "To me, my whole life stopped on June 5. On June 5, reality to me stopped right then, I guess. This whole—all the time from then, for the past year, from June 5, '68 on, is unreal to me, sir. I still don't believe what has happened."

"To you, Robert F. Kennedy is still alive?" Perkins' tone was incredulous.

"No, I don't believe he's dead, sir. To me, he's not—I mean, if I went out in the streets right now—"

Perkins cut him off. "You're playing words with me, aren't you?"

"No, I'm not."

"But you do believe it?"

"He's dead," admitted Sirhan.

"Do you wish he were alive again?"

"Very much so, sir, every morning—"

"Would you vote for him for President?"

"I'd vote for him for 'God'—if there was such a thing, voting for a supreme being. Every morning when I get up, sir, I say I wish that son of a gun were alive, because I wouldn't have to be here now."

"Oh, well," said Perkins with a broad smile. "That's why you wish he were alive? So you wouldn't be in jail?"

"No," said Sirhan softly. "I wish he were alive, sir, just to be President."

Perkins asked him how he compared himself to Lee Harvey Oswald and James Earl Ray. Sirhan said he felt there was no comparison. They knew what they were doing. They used telescopic lenses, they both planned to get away. "Does that make you any less guilty?" asked Perkins.

Sirhan reiterated his old position. He was legally guilty, but he didn't "feel guilty." No one in his right mind, he added, could have done such a thing.

"Are you mentally ill?" asked Perkins.

"I'm not mentally ill, sir, but I'm not perfect either."

"Do you think you'll ever be executed?"

Sirhan stammered. He would rather die than spend his life in prison, but his lawyers didn't want him to say that on television. He had an automatic appeal pending before the California Supreme Court and there was no sense jeopardizing that.

"Are you prepared for the execution if it comes?" persisted Perkins.

Sirhan said what his lawyers wanted him to say: "Sir, I don't fear death, but in this case, yes, I don't seek it. I intend to fight it, sir, to the last breath."

"Sirhan," said Perkins earnestly now, "what, what good do you think you could do if your life were spared? What good could you do anyone in jail?"

Sirhan was almost incapable of thinking of anyone else. It was his own good he was worrying about. "My heart, sir, has been broken. It has been shattered by the experience that I have gone through. I think, sir, that infamy and the hatred that has come my way as a result of this, sir, is enough of punishment for me. I've learned my lesson already, sir."

But if he were released from jail?

Sirhan knew that some Arabs had made him into a hero. Knowing that, he said, "Somehow I think I could convince them—I shouldn't say convince them—that I could help towards a peaceful settlement in the Middle East somehow."

Perkins looked at his watch. The cameramen had almost two hours of Sirhan on film now and the sheriff's deputies were going to terminate the interview shortly. He had to ask Sirhan if he were in this thing alone. "In your notebook, Sirhan, you said, 'We believe that we can effect such action. We believe that Robert F. Kennedy must be sacrificed.' You used the word, 'we.' Now was there ever anyone else in your mind—"

"I don't—"

"—or was there a plot or a conspiracy?"

Sirhan gave a characteristically indirect answer. "The FBI, the Secret Service, the Los Angeles Police Department and the investigators of the prosecution's, district attorney, they all worked like a son of a bitch to, to uncover any evidence."

"They didn't find any," said Perkins. "But you're the best one to tell us. Was there?"

"Sir, I don't even know that the man is dead—"

"All right."

"—for myself. So if there is any conspiracy, I'm completely unaware of it."

Now Perkins' director was telling him there was time for one or perhaps two more questions. Perkins knew that Sirhan had always had interesting —if varied—answers to a question thrown at him by the psychologists who tested him. Now he tossed it out: "Sirhan, if you had three wishes now, what would they be?"

Sirhan paused. "The first wish—" He choked. "The first wish, I wish that Senator Kennedy were still alive." His voice started to break. He added hastily: "I wish that every day that I've been here. The second one —" He started to sob and he put his right hand to his forehead and covered his eyes. One camera zoomed in for an extreme close-up of the assassin's trembling hand. He looked up again. "The second one, that there should be peace in the Middle East." Again his voice broke, and again he covered his eyes. One camera held the extreme close-up on Sirhan. The other slowly drew back to a long shot of the entire scene: Sirhan hunched over in his chair, Perkins across from him, nodding slowly, the heavy Kleig lights, the other camera, the deputies and the lawyers behind it, watching and wondering how to interpret the last breakdown of Sirhan Bishara Sirhan.

It was the last recorded public view of Sirhan. That night, forty-eight hours ahead of the sheriff's office schedule, he was awakened, moved by Inspector Ralph Welch, Captain Craig Carpenter and Deputy Joseph Torcaso to a launching pad a few blocks from the Hall of Justice, whisked off by helicopter to the Van Nuys Airport and into a twin-engine Beechcraft, where two officers of the State Department of Corrections and a pilot from the Air National Guard were waiting. By 3:00 A.M., the Beech was in the air and at 5:20 it landed at Hamilton Air Force Base. A six-car caravan met the plane and, with the sun coming up over San Francisco Bay, wound its way to the California State Prison at San Quentin. There, prison authorities took official possession of the unlikely assassin and handed Inspector Welch a "body receipt" in return. On the official scrap of paper were scrawled the words, "Misc. items and $24.20" and two signatures: "Lt. C. Loften, San Quentin" and "Sirhan Sirhan."

Nineteen

**"The case is still open. I'm not rejecting the
Manchurian Candidate aspect of it."**

Why did Sirhan kill Kennedy? The simple answers—either that Sirhan
was crazy or that he killed Kennedy to keep the United States from sending fifty jets to Israel—didn't satisfy me. I had to look deeper.

I would be less than honest, however, if I did not admit that my difficulties in understanding were immense. There were, in the first place, too
many Sirhans.

There was a very clever, evasive Sirhan, a Sirhan who, despite all the
probes of police, attorneys, investigators, psychologists and psychiatrists,
kept a head full of secrets.*

There was a mystical Sirhan, who practiced the arts of the occult, tel-
ekinesis and the control of mind over matter. He started on his mother's
kidneys, but he was working up to 707's.

There was an ingratiating, apple-polishing Sirhan who would do anything to make a friend. He stopped on freeways to change tires for total
strangers, he bought drinks for the house and played Chinese checkers
with old ladies.

There was a studious Sirhan who read heavy philosophical tomes and
solemn journalism like the *U.S. News and World Report.* "Ever read any
books on the John Kennedy assassination?" I asked him several times.
No, he said, never. Later, I learned, tricked him into admitting, that he
had read not only William Manchester's book, *The Death of a President,*
but a shelf full of books on assassinations.

---

* After a certain amount of time with Sirhan, it wasn't difficult to tell when he
was lying or holding back. Sometimes it was a lowering look. Sometimes a stammer.
One colleague of mine, hearing Sirhan on tape, has made the intriguing suggestion
that Sirhan peppered his speech with a telltale little word whenever he was acting or
simply lying: "sir." As in: "What I have told you, sir, is the truth, the whole truth, and
nothing but the truth, sir."

And there was a schizophrenic Sirhan. This professional diagnosis was less helpful than I thought it would be, for not even the research teams working under grants from the National Institute of Mental Health knew what schizophrenia was, or how it could have led Sirhan to assassinate Kennedy.

And none of these Sirhans—even added together into the sick, complicated mess that he was—quite explained to me his presence there in the Ambassador pantry at 12:15 A.M. on June 5, 1968, with a smoking Iver-Johnson .22 in his hand.

What did? I believed there were some coconspirators, some witting, some all too unwitting.

The unwitting coconspirators had a disproportionate influence on Sirhan because Sirhan was a *tabula rasa* upon which ideas could be imposed with ease, or, better, a piece of video tape on which certain images could be electronically imprinted and certain sounds electronically etched. He was erasable and replayable. On a Monday I would give him a new word. On Tuesday he would use it on me, sometimes appropriately.

What he ended up playing back at me mostly were the catchwords of the world's young revolutionaries who were frustrated by their inability to achieve affluence, equality, and education overnight, and who elbowed one another for a place in front of network cameras from Berkeley to Berlin. Months after he killed Kennedy, Sirhan said the blow had been struck for "his kind of people"—the revolutionaries of the Third World.

The revolutionaries may protest over this. They may say they didn't want to kill Kennedy. But a black militant group known as the Revolutionary Action Movement (RAM), according to testimony at the New York conspiracy trial of Herman B. Ferguson in May, 1968, had Kennedy marked for execution. Whether Sirhan knew this or not, he did hear other simplistic rhetoric aimed at Kennedy and other Establishment liberals set upon a policy of incremental change, too lawful and too logical. Sirhan heard the angry rhetoric of a Rap Brown and, as Brown suggested, bought himself a gun; he read the rhetoric of the Black Panthers in Oakland who called Bob Kennedy a fascist pig, and the words made him feel justified in having killed the pig.

The full weight of this affinity between Sirhan and the angry blacks didn't come to me until the summer night in San Francisco, 1969, when I watched a trembling black militant named Bobby Seale stand up at a dinner of mostly white liberals and excoriate them until he was hoarse and cry that somebody ought to shoot "the pig Alioto and the shit Reagan and the [I-forget-what-adjective] Nixon." Seale ended by apostrophizing his heroes, Stokely Carmichael and Eldridge Cleaver and Huey Newton, and at that moment I wanted to jump up and shout, "And don't forget Sirhan Sirhan!" For Sirhan belonged. He could not only spew forth his hatred for America verbally and with pen and ink, he could shoot, too, and did.

In a way, then, some black militants were unwitting coconspirators in the assassination of Robert Kennedy. But maybe others were, too. There was a general climate of violence in the United States in 1967 and 1968, contributed to by "good people" and "bad people"—by those television producers who packaged violence, and by those of us who enjoyed it, by the FBI and the Anti-Defamation League in Montgomery, Alabama, who paid informants $36,000 to lure Ku Kluxers into a lethal trap, as well as by the black militants and the Ku Klux Klan and the Missouri Minutemen. It was, furthermore, the policy of the President of the United States and of Congress to export violence by the megaton to Southeast Asia and the policy of the national network news shows to celebrate this violence every evening in living color.

So the climate of violence was, surely, one answer to the question of why Sirhan killed Kennedy. But what brought him to the flash point?

At the beginning, I suspected the more active, knowing involvement of others who wanted Kennedy out of the way. So did the Kennedy family, struck yet another time by another "faceless man." So did the police and the FBI, whose first thoughts raced to "conspiracy." So did the public at large. The police and the FBI ended up with a good many unanswered questions, but could hardly admit to that without stirring up the masses, and so the public was given a trial where it could learn "the adjudicated truth" about the assassination.

That is the way Judge Herbert V. Walker billed the trial; the principals were ready to settle out of court on a life term, but Judge Walker insisted on going ahead (at a cost of $609,792 to the taxpayers) to satisfy the public curiosity—and did not, in fact, satisfy the public curiosity. What he did do was provide a showcase for the American trial system in general. But this was something of a charade, like putting the Bible on the coffee table when the preacher comes to call, for the adversary trial system wasn't working in America. Ninety percent (or more) of all criminal filings in the United States were settled by pleas to a lesser charge and, if they did go to trial under the current procedures, there was no guarantee that "truth" made any solid appearance.

Movie trials produce truth and so always does Perry Mason, but most adversary proceedings have a way of inhibiting the free flow of information to the jury and to the public it supposedly serves. The Sirhan trial was no exception. In general, neither defense nor prosecution probed publicly into whatever questions they had about the involvement of others, for the simple reason that such questions would only complicate their task at hand —which was to prosecute and defend Sirhan on a charge of murder.

The prosecuting attorneys had additional reasons. One of their ancillary purposes in the trial, Chief Deputy District Attorney Lynn Compton told police on July 22, 1968, was to "restore public faith in law enforcement." Compton could hardly do that by advertising how many unanswered questions he and his staff and certain members of the LAPD still entertained (or should have entertained) on the basis of the evidence they had.

The defense attorneys, who had to proceed with the information Sirhan himself chose to give them, could have used more time. With it, they might—in private—have probed more vigorously than they did into some of Sirhan's inconsistencies and discovered the truth. Without that time, and not knowing the truth, they were forced to skim over Sirhan's evasions on the stand. In court, Sirhan said he first made up his mind to kill Kennedy when he saw a television documentary premiered in Los Angeles on May 20, 1968. His attorney, Grant Cooper, naturally enough, did not then ask Sirhan how it happened that he wrote "R.F.K. must die" two days before that—on May 18. Nor did the prosecuting attorneys, who believed their chances of getting a conviction were better as long as Sirhan remained "an Arab hero" working alone.

I did not believe that Sirhan killed Kennedy in order to strike a blow for his side in the Arab-Israeli conflict. A bona fide avenging Arab hero would have shouted something like *"sic semper tyrannis"* or "no more jets to Israel" when he was seized in the Ambassador Hotel pantry. He would have poured forth his story to the police when he submitted to questioning during the early-morning hours after his arrest. Instead, he worked out his role as Arab hero little by little, as the months rolled by after the assassination. I still wondered why Sirhan said nothing in the pantry, why he was a "Silent Sam" with the police, why he hid so many details about himself and his crime from his own attorneys. I wasn't satisfied with the prosecution theory that Sirhan told his Arab hero story on the stand to save his life, for it got him (as he was warned it would) a verdict of first-degree murder and a sentence of death.

I had an easier time accepting Dr. Bernard Diamond's theory that Sirhan had—by his automatic writing—"programmed himself exactly like a computer is programmed by its magnetic tape . . . for the coming assassination." Dr. Diamond's theory implied that Sirhan had no conscious plan of action when he went to the Ambassador. On the stand, Dr. Diamond admitted that this theory was absurd and preposterous, but I admired his courage in propounding it. Dr. Diamond was an expert in the law, in psychiatry and criminology, and he had a great deal of clinical experience. Though I knew that Dr. Diamond might be inclined toward evidence supporting a legal defense he had helped pioneer, the defense of diminished capacity, I also knew he didn't have to make Sirhan into an unconscious assassin to prove diminished capacity. It would have been sufficient to say, as Dr. Eric Marcus did, that Sirhan's premeditation was not the product of a healthy mind and let it go at that. Dr. Diamond would not let go. He had to find a theory into which he could fit *all* the facts. And he was the only one on either side of the case who seemed to bother doing that.

After the trial, I discovered further evidence to corroborate Dr. Diamond's hypothesis.

I found, first of all, new evidence that Sirhan appeared to be in a trance the night he killed. In a police report, I read that at 10:30 P.M. or so on June 4, Mrs. Mary Grohs, a teletype operator for Western Union who was working in the Colonial Room of the Ambassador Hotel, saw Sirhan "staring fixedly" at her teletype machine. The report was a brief one, and so I phoned to ask her what she had seen on the night of June 4.

She was very defensive. "I certainly didn't smell any alcohol," she said.

"Well, okay," I said. "But what did you see?"

After some hesitation, Mrs. Grohs gave this report. "Well, he came over to my machine and started staring at it. Just staring. I'll never forget his eyes. I asked him what he wanted. He didn't answer. He just kept staring. I asked him again. No answer. I said that if he wanted the latest figures on Senator Kennedy he'd have to check the other machine. He still didn't answer. He just kept staring."

"In retrospect," I asked, "do you think that he might have been in some kind of trance?"

"Oh, no!" she said. "He wasn't under hypnosis." I hadn't mentioned the word "hypnosis," but perhaps Mrs. Grohs had read the newspapers during the trial when the possibility was discussed. Or perhaps she had been coached. I didn't ask her if she'd ever seen anyone under hypnosis before. I did ask her why Sirhan didn't respond to her. "I just assumed," she said, "that he couldn't speak English."

"But he could couldn't he?"

"What?"

"Speak English."

"Huh?"

"He spoke pretty good English at the trial, didn't he?"

"Yes."

"Then why do you think he didn't answer you?"

"What was your name again?" asked Mrs. Grohs. "I want to talk to the police about you. They told me not to say anything about this."

I asked Dr. Diamond for his assessment of this exchange. He was angry. He and the prosecution psychiatrist—and the jury—should have heard the testimony of Mrs. Grohs. But he was pleased to know that there was one eyewitness, at least, who, however reluctantly, could support his theory that Sirhan was in some kind of dissociated state on the night of the murder.

Ten thirty P.M. was earlier than Dr. Diamond had suspected Sirhan "went under." Perhaps, Dr. Diamond conjectured, Sirhan was in a trance through much of that evening. This supposition might even better account, he said, for Sirhan's only half-plausible explanations of why he went to Los Angeles that night, why he first went to the Ambassador without his gun and then returned to get it from the back seat of his car, and how he ended up in the Ambassador pantry at midnight. As Dr. Diamond had proved in experiments with Sirhan, Sirhan could easily be programmed to climb his cell bars or sing an Arab tune; afterward, he would present half-plausible (but false) reasons of his own for each action. Sirhan's "reasons" for his action before the shooting were like that: only half-plausible.

After the crime, Sirhan's pupils were dilated—evidence that he was under some alien influence. And he was unbelievably detached when the police led him through an all-night interrogation, a most unusual posture for a young man who had just gunned down one whom he later said was "a god to me." I thought it likely that Sirhan was then in a kind of twilight state and that he didn't start coming out of it until 9:00 A.M. on June 5, when Dr. Marcus Crahan found Sirhan shivering in his cell. Sirhan had similar chills in his cell each and every time he came out of his hypnotic trances with Dr. Diamond.

To explain this behavior, Dr. Diamond had posited his theory: Sirhan, already hypnosis-prone from his experiments with the occult, went into a spontaneous trance at the Ambassador. Triggered by the drinks he had had and the bright lights and the mirrors in the lobby, he went out to his car, got his gun and, programmed by his instructions to himself in the notebook but with no knowledge then that Kennedy would move through the pantry, just happened to be there when Kennedy appeared. It was a million-to-one shot. Dr. Diamond didn't believe Jesus Perez, the busboy witness, who reported that Sirhan asked him whether Kennedy was coming through the pantry. And neither did I. I think he confused Sirhan with another young man in the pantry named Michael Wayne who looked like Sirhan. Wayne did ask several people in the pantry, including Perez, which way Kennedy was coming.

Dr. Diamond's theory, as he admitted on the stand, was only a theory, a hypothetical framework to help explain the facts. After the trial, however, I discovered new information (also withheld from the defense) that clashed with Dr. Diamond's theory.

On May 20, 1968, a bartender named Albert LeBeau, a husky blond fellow, had been set to guard a stairway leading to the second-floor banquet room of Robbie's Restaurant in Pomona during an appearance there by Senator Kennedy. At 12:30 P.M., a young man whom LeBeau believed was Sirhan started to force his way up the stairs. It was an abnormally hot day, and Sirhan had a heavy jacket hooked over his right arm. In retrospect, LeBeau thought, the coat, which was draped over Sirhan's right elbow and completely obscured his right hand, would have concealed a gun very nicely. There was a girl with him, five feet, four inches, twenty-five to thirty years old, light brown hair, fairly attractive, no bangs, satin blouse. She did all the talking, insisting she and her young man were with the Kennedy party, until finally LeBeau let both of them through. A few minutes later, LeBeau found the pair inside, toward the back of the room, the young man standing in a suspicious crouch, the coat still over his arm. LeBeau challenged them: if they were with the Kennedy party, what were they doing in the back of the room? The young man turned on him savagely and demanded: "What the hell is it to you?"

The records show that Detective Sergeants Sandlin and Strong of the LAPD questioned LeBeau about his story. Yes, LeBeau said, he was fairly sure the young man was Sirhan. Would he swear it under oath? No, he couldn't swear under oath. End of investigation. The district attorney didn't need to put Sirhan in Pomona on May 20 to get a conviction. And the detectives certainly didn't need to go back to headquarters with more talk of a mystery girl. Headquarters was sick of having to tell the press they couldn't find the "girl in the polka-dot dress," and the LAPD had knocked itself out persuading witnesses at the Ambassador that they'd never seen such a girl.

I believed LeBeau. His account was corroborated in part by two others at the restaurant and he had no apparent reason for making up such a story. The police, never anxious to confess their own incompetence, had reason to cover it up. For if LeBeau was right, then Sirhan had a female accomplice. *And the police couldn't find her.*

I also believed Dr. Joseph Sheehan, a professor of psychology at the University of California at Los Angeles, and his wife Margaret, who told police they were sure they had seen Sirhan after a Kennedy rally at the L.A. Sports Arena on May 24. He was dark and sinister-looking, and he hung around afterward on the fringes of the obviously more affluent groups who lingered at the arena, as if he were looking for someone. They made a special note of him at the time because he had looked so malevolent, and Dr. Sheehan remarked that it was too bad the Senator "had to run the gauntlet of people like that."

It was becoming clearer to me that Sirhan stalked Kennedy and that he wasn't necessarily alone. I believed he did so on May 20 and May 24, and I believed he tried again at the Ambassador at a Kennedy rally on Sunday, June 2. At the trial, Sirhan maintained that his presence at that Sunday rally was innocent of any ill intent, but the fact was that he tried at first to deny that he was even there. Shortly after his arrest he had told his brother Adel to tell the police he was home all day that Sunday; and he also denied being at the Ambassador on Sunday when I first asked him about it. Only later, having reflected on my report to him that the LAPD might have some movie footage which would prove he was in the crowd, did Sirhan admit to his attorney, Russell Parsons, that he was there.

And if Sirhan was after Kennedy on May 20 and May 24 and June 2, why not also on June 3? Sirhan changed his story three times about his movements on June 3. First, he said he was home all day. Then he admitted to me that he'd gone to Corona. Later still, he told me it wasn't Corona at all, but "someplace in that direction." And still later, he told Investigator Michael McCowan with some satisfaction that he'd put 350 miles on his car June 3 and no one knew where he'd gone. In this context, his sneering judgment of the FBI made more sense: "The FBI doesn't know everything." Maybe, as McCowan speculated, Sirhan drove to San Diego that afternoon. Driving from Pasadena to San Diego and back might explain the 350 miles. Why San Diego? That night at the El Cortez Hotel in San Diego, one of the candidates was scheduled to speak, but he begged off, overcome with exhaustion. The candidate was Senator Robert F. Kennedy.

But if Sirhan had deliberately stalked Kennedy for two weeks, why was he in a trance on June 4 (as some evidence seemed to show)?

I thought the new evidence would indicate that Sirhan's "trance" was no accident but a by-product, rather, of his intense resolve. His moves that night had a far more specific finality than any revealed in his notebook. In the notebook Sirhan said he would kill Kennedy, but in no place did Sirhan indicate how he thought he would do the deed. In fact, Sirhan went out of the Ambassador to get his gun, got it, came back and worked his way through a crowd and past some guards, took up a stand in the pantry, waited for Kennedy, recognized him, walked up and shot, point-blank. When he did so, according to the best eyewitness in the pantry, Freddy Plimpton, Sirhan had a look on his face of "intense concentration." That figured. Sirhan had resolved to kill Kennedy, had already failed on more than one occasion. On this night, he focused, oblivious to all distraction, ready to reach Kennedy no matter what the obstacles.

How did he come to be so focused? As late as May 5, 1969, Sirhan himself was still groping for an answer; he told me then in his cell that he may have been like the original assassins, the *hashshashin,* members of a secret Mohammedan cult who drugged themselves before they committed their appointed murders. "It must have been something like that with me," he said.

I believed him. "Something like that. . . ." I had sat in on most of the hypnotic sessions Sirhan had had with Dr. Diamond. Although those sessions produced far less information than Dr. Diamond had hoped they would, they convinced me that—although Sirhan didn't tell the whole truth while hypnotized—he was not faking when he said he couldn't remember the details of the assassination. But why couldn't he?

If he had programmed himself to kill Kennedy, he should have had some recollection, if not of the killing, at least of the programming. He didn't remember that either.

It had been my guess, during the weeks that Dr. Diamond was making his investigations, that Sirhan programmed himself during his autohypnotic sessions at home. Dr. Diamond tested that theory and concluded on February 1, after he put Sirhan through some experiments in automatic writing, that that was precisely what Sirhan had done.

But there were those (myself and Dr. Diamond included) who asked how it happened that Sirhan had learned such occult arts. Sirhan was evasive about this. Before the trial, he told me his friend, Tom Rathke, the groom, had introduced him to the occult. During Dr. Diamond's probe, he said he'd learned it all from a book called *Cyclomancy.* Where did he get the book? It was recommended to him by Tom Rathke.

Was it possible that one of the friends with whom he had studied the occult had put Sirhan up to killing Kennedy, possibly without his knowledge? Sirhan didn't like that suggestion. Nor did I. It was a farfetched theory, fetched in fact from Richard Condon's novel, *The Manchurian Candidate.* There, Raymond Shaw, the antihero who had been brain washed in North Korea, was moved by the phrase, "Why don't you pass the time by playing a little solitaire?" to riffle through a deck of playing cards until he came to the queen of hearts and then wait for further instructions, then kill without knowing why he had killed or even that he had killed. But a good investigator looks into every possibility, no matter how fantastic. And Sirhan had played around with mind-bending exercises. . . . I thought the line was worth pursuing. And so, marvel of marvels, did Sirhan. He finally asked me, on December 31, to investigate further. Could anyone have had such an influence over his mind?

I did some research on crime and hypnosis and discovered interesting real-life examples of murder-by-proxy, through hypnosis. In 1951, in Copenhagen, Bjorn Nielsen had programmed Palle Hardrup to go into a trance at the sight of the letter X, rob a bank and kill anyone who got in his way, almost completely unaware that he had been used. Unlike the fictional Raymond Shaw, Hardrup had some notion of what had happened. In jail, he recalled enough about his former associations with Nielsen to suspect that he had been used. And he was moved to confide his suspicions to a psychiatrist who, as I have reported earlier, spent almost a year cracking the "locking mechanism" that obscured Hardrup's recollections.

On February, 8, 1969, during the trial, Dr. Diamond programmed Sirhan, under hypnosis, to climb the bars of his cell. Sirhan had no idea what he was doing up on the top of the bars. When he finally discovered that climbing was not his own idea, but Dr. Diamond's, he was struck with the plausibility of the idea that perhaps he had been programmed by someone else, in like manner, to kill Kennedy.

In this, Sirhan seemed sincere enough, but the idea was too much for Dr. Diamond. To him, that was "a crackpot theory." It was, unless I could find a Kennedy-hater with hypnotic skills who used them on Sirhan. And I couldn't find such a man.

I sought out some of those persons who had played occult games with Sirhan. One of them admitted that he had written a menacing letter to Chief Justice Earl Warren which brought investigators from the FBI. And he told a somewhat different version of his recent association with Sirhan than Sirhan had told me. But this didn't argue to his complicity in a plot, and I found no reason to believe that any of those I talked to were involved in the assassination.

But I still had a feeling that somewhere in Sirhan's recent past there was a shadowy someone. So did Roger LaJeunesse, the FBI agent in charge of the Sirhan investigation, who confided to me: "The case is still open. I'm not rejecting the Manchurian Candidate aspect of it." LaJeunesse had attended the trial, he heard Dr. Diamond's testimony and he seemed convinced that Sirhan was indeed in a trance on the night of June 4. And he knew, better than I, that Robert Kennedy had enemies who could have chosen Sirhan, with his antiauthority feelings and his inert paranoia, as a possible tool. Sirhan was a man with nothing to lose, with enough conscious and unconscious hatred within him to draw the attention of anyone looking for a likely gunman.

Who would have wanted to use Sirhan? I didn't know. But the police and the FBI now had evidence that Sirhan associated with extremists from both the Right and the Left and that he had some connections with the so-called underworld. The police and the FBI were the agencies with the legal mandate and the resources to investigate these ties, if they would. I could only hope they would, that, secretly, they were applying wit and imagination even then while PR-minded spokesmen continued to force the facts or reveal only those that enhanced their own image—as Robert Houghton, the LAPD's assistant chief, did in his report on the assassination (*Special Unit Senator,* Random House, 1970).

We looked for a conspiracy, Houghton said, and we didn't find one. He looked the other way when his own detectives browbeat Thomas Vincent DiPierro, until DiPierro reneged on his story of seeing "the girl in the polka-dot dress." His suspicions were not aroused by the story of the Pomona bartender who saw Sirhan stalking Kennedy on May 20 in the company of a pretty girl. He overlooked the insurance executive who saw Sirhan at target practice in May at Rancho California, again with a pretty girl (his detectives told him the eyewitness failed to pick Sirhan's face out of a picture file of Sirhan and some look-alikes, but that would have been pretty difficult, seeing that the detectives interviewed the man by telephone). He brushed aside the puzzle of Edward Van Antwerp, who mysteriously disappeared from Corona twelve hours before RFK was shot and reappeared two weeks later in Eureka, California. Van Antwerp had told the FBI he never knew Sirhan when, as a matter of fact, he had roomed with Sirhan for five months. Houghton did not find it strange that the FBI and his own operatives took ten months to find the man who brought Sirhan to Corona in the first place, Frank Donnarauma, alias Henry Donald Ramistella of New Jersey. He overlooked the direct, naïve approaches which investigators made to Jimmy Hoffa and the likes of Hoffa who were not above suspicion: ("Tell us about your contract to have Senator Kennedy killed, Jimmy. No? No contract? Oh. Well, sorry to have bothered you, Jimmy.") And he approved the facile dumb-cop analysis that anyone who had facts running counter to their lone-assassin theory was "psycho."

It wasn't easy for Houghton to ignore the evidence in Sirhan's notebook that Sirhan associated the killing of Robert Kennedy with some kind of payoff to himself. Whenever the name of Kennedy appeared there, it was always accompanied by "please pay to the order of Sirhan" and that phrase appeared nowhere else in the notebook—only on "kill" or "Kennedy" pages. That should have aroused the suspicions of anyone over eight, much more of a cop who was always ready to expect the worst. But Houghton made the supreme effort. He ignored that, too, in part because he assumed that Sirhan had to have the money in hand before he struck, and Houghton couldn't find any extra money.

It was entirely possible that Sirhan was gunning for Kennedy on a simple promise of money, sweetened by a small down payment. He could have bet that at the track, or stashed it, or, indeed, given it to his family. But if he had, they certainly wouldn't tell the police about it. The Sirhan family did not go out of their way to help the police. But then, the police were naïve to expect help from the Sirhans.

Grant Cooper once asked Sirhan about the money angle, and Sirhan answered Cooper's question with another question: "If I got the money, where is it?"

Here, Sirhan seemed genuinely evasive. But it was clear that in his notebook he was repeating instructions to forget any promises of money: "I have never heard please pay to the order of of of of of of of of of of of this or that 80000."

Sirhan never could explain the references in his notebook to money. But where did the instructions come from? Sirhan or another?

It was possible that they came from another; and that then Sirhan drummed them into himself. But no one could say with certainty. It would take a psychoanalyst as skilled as Dr. Diamond perhaps another year of interviews with Sirhan to test this theory thoroughly—to put Sirhan through more hypnotic sessions in an effort to see if, indeed, his memory had been blocked by some kind of locking mechanism; and, further, to explore with Sirhan the significance of his assertions that he could, for instance, "blow the top off this case" if he chose to say what he knew, to see what was prompting his successive stories that Lyndon Johnson or Richard Nixon or James Hoffa had put him up to killing Kennedy, to find out why he thought that "the FBI did a lousy job of investigation" and "didn't know everything." And it would take me another year to run down all the investigative avenues that still intrigued me.

That would have been another book. And, in the chaotic summer of 1970, two years after the death of the man we now realized we needed more than we had known, I was having enough trouble getting this book published. Sirhan had fired Cooper and Russell Parsons because they couldn't force me to let Sirhan censor my book. And he found new attorneys who promised they would try. They asked courts in California and New York to enjoin publication. New legal battles began. Finally, the California court denied their petition. As Judge Richard Schauer put it when he turned them down in Los Angeles, "Now the cat is out of the bag." Sirhan was very unhappy.

Appendixes

APPENDIX A: Official Los Angeles Police Department List of Victims and Witnesses in Ambassador Hotel Pantry

1. ROTHSTEIN, ALLEN
2. KADAR, GABOR
3. BRUCE, RAE
4. PANDA, RONALD
5. JAYNE, DAVID
6. WILLAMAN, EARL
7. MAMEY, NORMAN
8. CLARK, SONIA
9. LA GUERRE, MICHELLE
10. MANKIEWICZ, FRANK
11. CUMMINGS, JAMES
12. MOONEY, GEONINE
13. LOCKE, SUZANNE
14. MURRAY, BARBARA
15. SULLIVAN, ACQUILINE
16. TOIGO, ROBERT
17. RICH, WALTER
18. WEST, ANDY
19. JACKSON, LARRY
20. UNRUH, BRADLEY
21. MULLIGAN, GLORIA
22. HOLME, BARBARA
23. HEATH, THADIS
24. RICH, TIMOTHY
25. HARDY, CAPT.
26. BEILENSON, DELORES
27. ELMORE, RALPH
28. RUBIN, BARBARA
29. DEAN, LARRY
30. CETINA, GONZALO
31. CASDEN, ROBIN
32. DUTTON, FRED
33. DiPIERRO, VINCENT
34. BEILENSON, ANTHONY
35. UNRUH, JESSE
36. BENNETT, RONALD
37. DREW, RICHARD
38. WITKER, KRISTI
39. BARRY, WILLIAM

40. YARO, BORIS
41. PATRUSKY, MARTIN
42. SCHULTE, VALERIE
43. CESAR, THANE EUGENE
44. LUBIC, RICHARD
45. ROMERO, JUAN
46. BURNS, FRANK
47. PEREZ, JESUS
48. UECKER, KARL
49. FREED, EVAN
50. MINASIAN, EDWARD
51. AUBRY, RICHARD
52. PLIMPTON, FREDDY
53. HAMILL, PETE
54. LAWN, CONSTANCE
55. GUY, VIRGINIA
56. KAWELEC, STANLEY
57. URSO, LISA
58. PLIMPTON, GEORGE
59. ROYER, JUDY
60. WAYNE, MICHAEL
61. GALLIVAN, JACK
62. ROSEN, RICK
63. KLASE, ROBERT
64. TIMANSON, UNO
65. GRIFFIN, BOOKER
66. JONES, JOSEPH
67. LEE, MURIEL
68. WITCOVER, JULES
69. MURRAY, DAVE
70. HEALY, ROBERT

V–1 KENNEDY, ROBERT F.
V–2 SCHRADE, PAUL
V–3 GOLDSTEIN, IRA
V–4 STROLL, IRWIN
V–5 EVANS, ELIZABETH
V–6 WEISEL, WILLIAM

D   SIRHAN, SIRHAN B.

APPENDIX B:
Ballistics Test

In light of certain reports still circulating in the underground press that there was more than one gun fired shortly after midnight in the Ambassador pantry, here, for what it is worth, is the official Los Angeles police summary of their trajectory study of the shots fired from Sirhan's revolver. All the bullets and all the wounds of all the victims seem well accounted for.

Form 15.7 (Rev. April 1962)

Los Angeles Police Department
EMPLOYEE'S REPORT

DR

SUBJECT			
Kennedy - 187 P.C.			

DATE & TIME OCCURRED	LOCATION OF OCCURRENCE	DIVISION OF OCCURRENCE
6-5-68	Ambassador Hotel	Rampart Division

TO: (Rank, Name, Assignment, Division)	DATE & TIME REPORTED
Lt. D.W. Mann, O-I-C, Criminalistics Section, S.I.D.	7-8-68

DETAILS:

The weapon used in this case was an Iver Johnson, Cadet Model, .22 caliber, 8 shot revolver (2½" barrel). This weapon had eight expended shell casings in the cylinder at the time of recovery from the suspect. A trajectory study was made of the physical evidence which indicated that eight shots were fired as follows:

#1 – Bullet entered Senator Kennedy's head behind the right ear and was later recovered from the victim's head and booked as evidence.

#2 – Bullet passed through the right shoulder pad of Senator Kennedy's suit coat (never entered his body) and traveled upward striking victim Schrade in the center of his forehead. The bullet was recovered from his head and booked as evidence.

#3 – Bullet entered Senator Kennedy's right rear shoulder approximately seven inches below the top of the shoulder. This bullet was recovered by the Coroner from the 6th cervical vertebrae and booked as evidence.

#4 – Bullet entered Senator Kennedy's right rear back approximately one inch to the right of bullet #3. This bullet traveled upward and forward and exited the victim's body in the right front chest. The bullet passed through the ceiling tile, striking the second plastered ceiling and was lost somewhere in the ceiling interspace.

#5 – Bullet struck victim Goldstein in the left rear buttock. This bullet was recovered from the victim and booked as evidence.

#6 – Bullet passed through victim Goldstein's left pants leg (never entering his body) and struck the cement floor and entered victim Stroll's left leg. The bullet was later recovered and booked as evidence.

#7 – Bullet struck victim Weisel in the left abdomen and was recovered and booked.

#8 – Bullet struck the plaster ceiling and then struck victim Evans in the head. This bullet was recovered from the victim's head and booked as evidence.

A Walker's H-acid test was conducted on Senator Kennedy's suit coat in the area of the entrance wounds. This test indicated that the muzzle of the weapon was held at a distance of between one to six inches from the coat at the time of all firings.

DATE & TIME TYPED	DIVN. RPTG.	CLERK	EMPLOYEE(S) REPORTING	SER. NO.	DIVN.
7-8-68 10 a.m. S.I.D.					

SUPERVISOR APPROVING	SERIAL NO.			
Lt. D.W. Mann	#2M5	Officer DeWayne A Wolfer #6727 S.I.D.		

Here is Sirhan's notebook, as photostated by the F.B.I., minus a good number of pages which were blank and a few more which appeared to be classroom jottings of no particular significance.

2/474974

0147497/

Gwendolyne Juan   4474974   4474974
                          4474974   4474974

gl Gu   Gwendolyne Gun 4474974
      Gu   ghattas 9,101 N. 9th St. 4473744
                  Arcadia, Calif
                          4474974

ghattass   Sirhan Sirhan

ghattas. Sirhan ghottas, ghottag. 44·
                          447470
                  Seven   4474974
                  Arcadia

ghottas Eighty four Dollars. 44 4 44

gl go G And fifteen   4   4 44
         Eighty four Arcadia 4 4474974
                          7   7   7
  ξ ξ Cξng Ei Eighty   4474974
                              4474 74
G gl Sirhan S Sirhan 974 74
                              Sirhan
         Eighty fine Sirhan S 85:07
Calif
Arcadia Calif. Sirhan Sirhan Eighty   S Sirhan
      Calif Calif Calif
Arcadia Calif. Eighty fine cafi 1/1

age .   دعني ما عبد لنتخا النفي تُنصب ان ط أجد عشأ ظيماً أراه ر

residence   البند

car   دعباد ترحتي أن لا يبنوى تا عمل انذانب هونا داننا نباننهيم الاحقون المنلي

Why not married?   فخالديسمانمر مؤشم ،،

وطي دلبد أنا يبي سا و د عل ار بلكم ومتني مدار انذنج

منا ها سي انا فنا ولد و فا دظنيك وبك فمرتها أبو مبدده ينما فاني ب

مسويدنا ات تالد فرهيي ق ما لنتسنيم بعاد نسور ورت سا ذنل فلد نسمي وفا بند فدا

why not why not car   دلد تير ت..

or any the   SIRHAN   N N I N N

ـhau   - Sirhan   (RathKe)   Tom   walter   walter   Tw Tombittalhle

ـhau   Sirhan   Sirhan   Suhan Sirhan   Sirhan Sirhan

رموني عينيله لباي الى راجوSirhanعدين نزي الالم مءِجابه

اليد شنه هنل ما شوقلم عنيجي   Sirhan   نر تالم نم نلم

Sir   Ş   Ş Ş Ş   Sirhan   Sirhan

Ş   Ş   Sirhan   Sirhan   Sirhan

Sirhan Sirhan Sirhan Sirhan Sirhan

Sirhan Sirhan Sirhan Sirhan

La Canara La

Enter Enter Enter Enter Enter

Enter Enter Enter Enter Enter

Dear Sir

Dear Sir
        I am prompted

Golden   Sirhan   Sirhan

9 Gate fields   Golden Gates Sub fields

Race R   Mr   Mrs.   B   Gale Johnston

Results   c/o. Old English Rancho.

Results   Results   G2

Results   Jalousie #   Sirhan B. Sirhan

Sv   II   II II   Sirhan Sirhan Sirhan

      II   D   S

Results   D Desert Dome.   S   Sirhan Sirhan Sirhan

At At   Sirhan Sirhan

gol   Laguna Doll   Sirhan   Sirhan

ghettos   Jerry Lambert.

ghettos   So L Lag ghettos   L Lambert.

Si   La Laguna Doll   Jockey — Jockey

                    Su Sirhan Sirhan

Tyrone   S   S S S S Sirhan Sirhan Sirhan
Chapmann

Chapmann   Lir C S S S Sirhan Sirhan
Chapmann

Chapmann   John Strathmann Sirhan Sirhan

Chapmann Sirhan Sirhan Sirhan Sirhan

Chapmann Sirhan Sirhan Sirhan Sirhan S Su

Jockey   Alcohol,

Alcohol will love to love long love love
this this this type of feed.

f feed feed feed

(Sirhan Sirhan)   feed feed feed feed.

S feed

feed feed-

Feed Feed Feed feed feed feed.

| ▦   S

J Jee Jeerry J Sirhan 15   15

4474974 44 ghottan к ghottan   15

Sirhan ghettan Sirhan Sirhan f ghottan
S S   Sirhan Sirhan Sirhan Sirhan Sirhan 15

Sirhan Sirhan 15 15   σ 15 15 15

         15   15 15 6 15,
Sirhan 15 15 15 15 Sirhan Sirhan
  15   15-30   5-10   5-10   σ 5-10
5-10   5-10   5-10   3 4 5 6 7 8 9
  Sirhan Sirhan

May 18 9.45 AM - 68

my determination to eliminate ~~eliminate~~ R.F.K. is becoming more the more of an unshakable obsession

please pay to the order

port wine :   port wine   port wine   port wine

R.F.K. must die - RFK must be killed Robert
F. Kennedy must be assassinated R.F.K
must be assassinated R.F.K. must be
assassinated R.F.K must be assassinated
R.F.K, must be assassinated R.F.k. must
be assassinated R.F.K. Must be
assassinated assassinated ~~as the~~ Robert F.
Kennedy Robert F. Kennedy Robert
F. Kennedy must be assassingted
assasinated Robert F. Kennedy
must be assassinated assassinated
assassinated assassinated
Robert F. Kennedy must be assassinated
Robert F, Kennedy must be
assassinated before 5 June 68
Robert F. Kennedy must be
assassinated I have never heard
please pay to the order of of of of of
of of of of of of this or that   HL

8   o o Do o □
please pay to the order of

① (circled)

A List of Grievances against U.S. and
its fecade of "Freedom and Justice for all"

Definitions: per Websters Die.

Freedom: "...a being free, a political
Liberty, a being able to act,
use, etc, without hinderance
Frankness.

Justice: a being righteous, fair,
rightfulness —
the use of authority to uphold
what is right
The administration of law.
do Justreto, to treat fairly
or with due appreciation
(per a citizen of U.S.

My line of thought in this
presentation or is not
steady in flow-due to the
multiplicity of grievances and
charged emotion that
generate within me

personal def. of)

⓪ (circled) Freedom is but an imaginary and
an allusive concept ~~granted to the
American people~~ of political life
granted the American, sheep like
bourgeois masses, by their selfish
(capitalistically permissable) sinister, and
power hungry (wether democratically given to them
or not is immaterial) overlords — (who
are bribed, paid homage to, and toyed with
by ~~one~~ lobbyists.) who are ~~do~~ in turn
treated the same way — by lesser power
hungry (political + Economic), patriotic (understated)
individuals (bastards)

Editorial by Geo. putnam
Fri. June 2 10:30 P.M

An individual freedom of speech is
guaranteed as long as he remains
aligned, and in accord with what
his decadent leaders- want him to be
exp (We.—the leaders— Want to be in power
and legistlate decree as we please and
do what ever is materially expedient
to us. and our families—at your cost.
should you dissent, we will find
some means to kill you—(economically—
socially—politically etc) We will
use some of the loop-holes—that we
have constructed in our legistlation,
(which by the way we established with or
without your concent—even tho we tell you
that you live in a democracy where the
people decide on all important matters
con. that concern them, not their appointees
in congress (the No. 1 clique in degeneration and
stagnation and decadence which incidentally we
are proud of)

American Capitalism will fall
an give way to the worker's dictatorships

2 June 67 12:30 pm

WO

A Declaration of Against the

when in the course of human events
it has become necessary for me to
equalize and seek revenge for all the
inhuman treatment ~~that I~~
~~received by those who~~ committed
against me by the American people.

the manifestation of this Declaration will
be executed by its supporter (s)
as soon as he is able to command
a sum of money ($2,000) and to
acquire some firearms, the specifications
of which have not been established
yet.

The victims of the party in favor
of this declaration will be or are
now — ~~the~~ the President, vice,
etc - down the ladder.

The time will be chosen by the
author at the convenience of the
accused.

the method of assault is immaterial — however the type of
weapon used would influence
it somehow.

the author believes that
many in fact multitudes of people
are in harmony with his
thoughts and feelings

the conflict and violence in the
world subsequent to the
enforcement of this decree,
shall not be considered lightly
by the author of this
memoranda, rather he hopes
that they be the initiatory
military steps to WWIII —
the author expresses his
wishes very bluntly that he
wants to be recorded by historians
as the man who triggered off
the last war —

life is ambivalence
life is a struggle
life is wicked
if life is in any way otherwise, I have
never seen it
I always seem to be on the losing
end, the one exploited to the
fullest

Tom, My warmest salutations.

I do not know what has prompted you to
write to me

The
Random

Blinkers

Long Live Nasser

f   insecticide

Tell them to put blinkers

til till tell them to put

till tell them to put Emphasis on this
on of — b' held

hundred   65   65

he doesn't like authority
authority — he doesn't like

authority he dosen't like authority

Cash Cash Cash Cash Long

Cash Cash Cash Cash

dollars 50   65 live Nixon

2   Niarkos.

Sirhan

1. читав- контианц — Я читаю.
2. понимал порусски — Я читаю русскую книгу.
3. читав книгу — Я писал письмо
4. слушал ... — Я спал —
5. курев сигарена — Я про кофе —
6. слушал на радио забтрокал —
7. побоюсь с другом Я приложивал
   к наш. ... live live live live
NASSER to Long live Nasser   75
       living   "cottage" Long live live
NASS prepare grally "the soup" Long live Long
            696   595
∞ midterm 10 November — Tuesday. — 695
NASSER уХаживаешь Nasser NASSER
NA
WASSER clean living Long live Nasser
Alley fighter Long live
       at night Long live Nerd
Long live communism Long live Communism
   Long live co communism
       NASSER
Long live Nasser NASSER
       NASSER NASSER
NASSER NASSER NASSER
NASSER NASSER NASSER

Racing Luck

No

(Long Live NASSER NASSER)

Racing   Long Live Nasser   racing Luck

Nasser   N   N NN N N   Luck

500,000   500

N N N N N N   500 Luck

500,000

500,000   N   N N Nasser is the

greatest man that ever lived in this

world, Nasser is the greatest man that

ever lived in this world Nasser

is the greatest man that ever

lived lived lived. N N N N

Howard

Hughes.   N How Hughes.

N N Nasser is the greatest man that

Racing   ever ev ever lived

Rich intrist   rict   intrils

R R Pinecraft Restaurant of racing

rules of   according to the rules.

50 50 5 50 to one

16   50 to one   Rich intrist

5   5 to one   (00 to 1)

god   what may
                  ever may be said in   in pro praise

Whatever may be said in praise of poverty,
the fact remains that if is not possible to
live a really complete or successful life
unless one is rich Unless One is is is is rich
No man can rise to his greatest possible
in talentor. I have often wondered what or how
it feels to be rich Rich rich rich rich

meder Black Magic Magic   Black Magic god   good

(Black magic)   B P Black Magic

your   44   I am quite. I am quite convinced
       44
(— 1 2 3 4 5 6 7 8 9 10 11 12 13 14 15 16 17 18, 19 20
busixxx 22 23 24 → ???   ⬛ ⬛ god

that ⬛⬛ ✛ ✛ E god god
          praise of god poverty is not
there of absolutely (acceptable) acceptable to us
that us there is no us us   London
that of in l   us usgods us us London ✝   ✝
London in   London
London l   ✝   god l godll god ✝
       London 4   ✝   god l....   ✝ ✝

everything else NW ✝ ✝ of of proper of of
                  ✝ l of of ✝ ✝ ✝ of of
she should maintain the proper

Peggy P P Peggy y ggy

the incredible power of Kizuma

love   Kizuma is the ancient Eastern technique
your children directing the thoughts and actions of others
Bol & Peggy an more incredible psychic means
   of radiating thought
Bol & Peggy   Bol & Peggy & Peggy

the greenery Peggy Peggy   Peggy
here is we
beautiful   P   P   Peggy

the right kind ggy Osterkamp Peggy
is the

            Osterkamp Osterkamp
is the proper   Peggy   Miss Peggy Osterkamp
type of   13290 Archibald Ave
greenery   G P   Corona, Calif
                              80113

    Pe Peggy Peggy P
  P P   Peggy —
    Baby —   Baby

p· Peggy Osterkamp is
                    I love you I love you
Osterkamp
sterkampMiss Peggy P P P P Iloveyoo
Iloveyou Love   you
P M Miss Peggy Ostertramp
            80327 Ar   I love you
    MISS PEGGY OSTERHAMP   Peggy I love
P P P P   1340 you
        Miss P M   1340 N. II N. ARCI
Mi MISS PEGBY OSC OST TERKAMP

N   Miss   MISS PEGGY OSTERKAMP
    N IN N NA   ~~TI~~ ARCHIBALD AVE.
                    CORONA, CALIF
I love you you yo   18037
    MISS MISS M m MISS PEGGY OSSS
O S OSTER R R RKAMP
            :   69 69 696 E. HOWARD ST.
y y you P
            Miss Peggy Osterkamp
    MISS   696

your yo y you you you I
children
~~Osfgeggy~~ love you I I I love
            y
    love you children Peggy Peggy

وكرم, وكرم سرحان
عثمان   good Morning
SIRHAN SIRHAN
عثمان   696 E HOIN WARD HOWARD ST
عل   SIRHAN SIRHAN   د سرحان د
عثمانس   SIRHAN SIRHAN   سرحان س
Morning   عثمان لي بي   س   سرحان ن
دكرم   سرحان سر سرحان ب
Mr   S SIRHAN SIRHAN g g g good   سرحان ن
SIRHAN SIRHAN   سرحان ن
696 E. Howard = SIRHAN GHATTA A ASS
Pasadina   g g goodbye goodbye
91104   goodbye we   Ellen good   Morning
C a cal we we your children Ellen gruder   العرب
cal Ellengruder Jol & Peggy,   Kalldlen we
Carf 10 91104   Jols Pe Pe Peggy we we
good we   we we we   we
g good Jol and P P Peggy Peggy we we
Morning   الدين   العرب الاسلامية
Morning good morning good Mo

M Morning to you all all all
plea please notify us us
us us us us all ——

Bad Spur
Jet Spec P P Peggy
Pe

الوالده المحترم) حفظها الله وابقاها .
وبجر)

~~ ~~

إن كل شيء من قبلي على ما يرام وإني بأحسن
الصحة والعافية - وآنأمل وآنتمنى أن تكون نفس الحال عندكم
وبجد . إن جهودي على حتى هذا الكتاب عشره دولارات
وهي نسبي محمد شراءً طويح بريد تلصقيها على كل
المراسلات التي بحثت إلي عندكم في بابا دينا وحماصه علاقات
وصحف الروزيكلوشا من شنر وغيرها من مراسيل . وإني أيضا باستطلاع
(شيكي) من دائره المدينه الأمريكيه فارسلوا . إبلاغي Peggy P P
صندا الخلتت يحوي أيضا أداة مكتوب عليها عنواني واستعملوها
فقط بحث الرسائل إيضا . ومن محمد وأرجوكم بطريقه خاصه أن
لا تفاخوا أي شخص عن موضوع من من مه مرضد مرة.

سرحان سرحان سرحان   وكم جزيراتكر سلفا سرحان
            سرحان
سرحان ن   وكم لا   ولكم ولكم سرحان
    سرحان سرحان ولكم   neru
    سرحان   neru
سرحان   Нинищка سرحان Нинищка
            رسالات
    Нина سرحان neru
neru   سرحان   m   Neru
        سرحان   m   m   neru
n   سرحان سر سرحان   m   neru л
        سرحان سرحان   Néru
néru л m   neru

TRANSLATION FROM ARABIC AND RUSSIAN

My reverend mother, God keep her and bless her (Bart Spur) and (Jet Spec P
P Peggy)
[Translator's Note: The following phrase was crossed out in the original—I am
in very good health and all is well] (Pe)
Everything with me is at its best and I am in the best of health. I wish and
hope that the same will be with you. Enclosed find ten dollars for the purpose
of buying stamps to be placed on all letters you may send to me from Pasadena
and especially envelopes and publications from Rosicrushay from Shener and
other mail. I am also waiting for a (check) from the American Treasury Department which you are also to send (P P Peggy). This envelope contains also
papers with my address written on them which you are to use only for sending
the letters to me here. I especially beg of you in a special way to discuss the
matter of my location with no one at all at all. Many thanks in advance Sirhan
Sirhan Sirhan Sirhan Sirhan Sirhan your son your son your son Sirhan Sirhan
Sirhan Sirhan your son *Peggy Peggy Ninischka* [*sic*] [Translator's Note: di-
munutive form of Nina] Sirhan *Ninischka* [*sic*] Sirhan Sirhan Sirhan letters
Sirhan *Nina* Sirhan *Peggy Peggy* S *P* S *P Peggy* Sirhan Sirhan S *Peggy P P* S S
Sirhan *P* Sirhan *Peggy Peggy Peggy*

Translator's Note: Parentheses indicate words appearing in English in the
original. Words appearing in Russian are italicized.

$\frac{25}{100}$
$\frac{00}{00}$

لتعيش ﻫﻢ العربية ابا ابا ابا ابا ابا

Peggy
Corona Breeding 7 Farm $\frac{25}{5}$

Osterkamp   Osterkamp

Peggy Corona Breeding Farm   Osterkamp

Co Corona B B Breeding Farm | Constitution
                                | Constitution

Con   Please pay to the order of

Peggy   united states   the
        Sirhan — Sirhan Sirhan   Of will ever
                                  Sirhan need to

Re   Sirhan Sirhan Must begin to work on uphold
     solving the problems and deffinities
PP   of assassinating the 36th president
     of the glorious United States

PP   United States United States Kenmore
                                   Kenmore
Burt Unfortunately So Janice So S Kelvinator
     Nobody No   No   So No ikefonator
     So Nobody   So No Sirhan   Sirhan
           Syrha S Sirhan Sirhan Sirhan
Norvell My   Sor Sirhan   Sirhan
                         696 E Howard st.

     Sirhan Sirhan Sirhan   Burns
            Cahf   California   Me
         Pasadena, California
California 696E green St.

the socalled president of the
United States of America must be advised
of their punishments for their own
treasonable crimes against the the
the state more over me believe that
the glorious United States of America will
eventually be felled by a blow of an
assasins bullet — by bullets
bullets
by an assasins bullet

Today I must plan to come frome in
a new car today I must plan to
drive he home in a new new new Mustang
in in a new mustang in a
tonight we 10 N I must by a new mustang tonight
Tonight tonight tonight
tonight No meet me tonight
tonight come you
tonight tonight
must Must

mustang

Must

muster

mustang

mustang

Mustang   Dinar

the   Blue Denim

united states

the

Dinar

their   abouts

if abouts

abouts

abouts   D D Dinar   Dinar

he does not
feel like giving
them a a
a a a.
a a
a ride
A ride or there
abouts

دینار

or or their
their

انبوب انبوب انبوب ب انبوب
مجنون استان استان دینار دینار دد دینار
دینار د دینار دینار دینار دینار استان

لیره لیو لیره

Where do you usually the hang
around at hollywood park—

must be aware of her commitment
of to their allies to to their
allies
there abouts, long line socialism

this seems to be the right amount

Hello Tom

perhaps you could use the
enclosed $

Perhaps you could use the
enclosed $

perhaps you could use the

Hello Tom ——
            perhaps
Perhaps you could use the

enclosed $

you

the

cr.ose   سرحان سرحان

أمر حياتي   حياتي   حياتي

1453
400
————
18 53   Do we look like foraigners to you
        who are not able or unable —

1873   there   demonstrate
        Sukroot   [F)   ⊠   Illuminati | Mathmatically

AL   HILAL
        Master Kuthami   Illuminati

        Um   Kolthoum   Illuminati

        abdel wa wahab

        Sout Sawtushark   5   5

        waheed uddeen   50 BASEM

▽ ▽ NorthernValley —   △

✡   WAJIEDDUDDIEN
        WAJIEDUDDIEN   ✡

        trime   ✡

        Saffurie

saffire Stone Stone

Saffire Stone   Tom —

Lodestone   Eleven Dollars—

Dollars—   Would like to come

Would You   up— for several days—

Ambassador Goldberg   Stone—

Must die die on yobe die meet

die die die mile the airport—

Ambassador Goldberg must die

Stone

Ambassador   Fine thank you

Stone goldberg must be illuminatid— Stone

Fine   fine thank You   Stone

Fine   Stone SIRHAN IS AN ARAB

die Sirhan you you you you

Stone   ARAB ARAB you

Sirhan Sirhan Sirhan   ARAB

Sirhan Sirhan   you   you   Sip

AVE 110 Howard St.

Sirhan PASADENA, CALIF.

Sirhan O.S. you   Sirhan   Sirhan

Perhaps you could use the

Sirhan

enclosed $ Sirhan Sirhan Sirhan

Sirhan Sirhan   green   Sirhan   St

Stone Stone Sirhan   green   ort Stone

Stone

ghattas

Sirhan ghattas

Eleven Oclock — Sirhan

Sirhan Eleven Oclock — Sirhan

Sirhan Sirhan

Eleven Oclock   Sirhan

Livermore   Sirhan Sirhan

Lira   pleasanton pleasanton Sirhan

At at at pleasanton

10 Dollars — D D D   pleasante

Dollars —   Do not really

Loyd   walker

account for this whole problem

Loyd 1,600   1,000 Lloyjskoo pleasanton

walker

you should not be so trying to

loyd   come here or there

Hello Tom 1. race track

perhaps you could use

the enclosed $

I have secured a position
as assistant to the manager of (Corona
Bereeding Farm — (Dezi ARNAZ's)
Pes Sirhan Sirhan Sirhan
$600 p.a. Month — / Sirhan
Hello Tom — S Sirhan
How will I contact you after I
arrive at the airport — I am —
comming up sometime Tuesday
afternoon. Sirhan
Sirhanof Afternoon — Did You really 150.
please pay to the order of Sirhan
afternoon — afternoon — afternoon
the amount of 15000 — dollars —
Sometime in the afternoon
Miss Miss Peggy Osterkamp
Osterkamp — did you really —
it abo 750 750
do 150 Sirhan 750 the
750 750 750 Sirhan
Master approached W
Sirhan Let us do it Let us do it —

Let us do it do it it it Sirhan Sirha
88 417 477
Let us do it Sirhan 8-413-477
84134778413 477
ghattass ghattass
about how much? it will cost.

Long Live Nasser   العيد   العيد الجيد

والى

Live   عرب   عيد   عيد   عيد   ما   عيد   كان   واذا   تصحوا   و العيد   تذكر

Nasser is not truely

acceptable   acceptable ___   العيد   العيد القديم   والعيد   العيد الحب

Physical

Long Live N Nasser

Long Line N Nasser

Long Live Nasser   Nasser   جمال عبد الناصر

Nasser   العيد الجديد

Lo Li   Long-Line Nasser   صر

عبدالناصر   فإن الحظ الحظ   نشاد ثا

Long Line Nasser   تصنا   لاتعرصنا

وها هنا اقم د طبح اصبحي الأبج

gamal abdel N N Nasser   ر   اى الجيد الجديد

جمال عبد الناصر وكان الذى   سرحان   سرحان   الأبج

Standpoint   سرحان سرحان   فى الطرزط ارط   ب دنيانا

الكبرى الكبرى   الألبح

order of   سرحان   سرحان

please pay to the   الكبرى   physical stan

Sirhan   باحلم الكبر   شروطا

gamal abdel Nasser is not altogether

واذا الدنيا كما نعرفى   واذا الدنيا كما نعرفى نعرفى

allmun   المزى   واذا الدنيا   واذا الدنيا كما نعرف شروط   عبد عبدالله

الرئيس جمال عبدالناصر المحترم   الابح

الرئيس جمال عبدالناصر عد   عبدالجيد

الرئيس جمال عبدالناصر   عبد عبد

Darling June une   الجديده الاستاذ   ابو عيو المطر   العاطل الابرح

ان الحياه جميله جميله جميله عبدالكريم وطنى كل اى ى عاينه لا

افدى   عمر عبدالرحيم تنقل بيتنا   فان الحظ شا ثا شاء

الحاد سيداه محمد عبدالحكيم عبدالحكيم   غيط الجيد

امه الحاد اياتينه غايشه عبد عبدالحكيم   المالك وار الدا عليم الحكيم

TRANSLATION FROM ARABIC

The era, the new era (Long live Nasser live) remember the era and wake up and if there is no era era era era era (live N N Nasser is not truly tahoman) and the old era old era (physical acceptable acceptable)—era (tell a dream Long Live N Nasser) the era (Long Live Nasser Nasser) the new era (Long Live Nasser) Abdel-Nasser and if luck, luck, luck wishes it will not be less important (Long Live Nasser) and I here affix my thumb print (Gamal Abdel-Nasser) the new and renewed thumb. Gamal Abdel-Nasser was the one who crushed it Sirhan Sirhan crushed it in our world (standpoint) Sirhan Sirhan in the fabric is a small piece of the thumb. The universe the universe (order of) Sirhan Sirhan in the dreams of the universe (please pay to the) universe (physical standpoint) and if the world as we know it (Sirhan) know it (Gamal Abdel-Nasser is not altogether) and if the world as we know it and if the world as we know it. The dear, and if the world and if the world as we know it Abd Abdallah the thumb the thumb the President Gamal Abdel-Nasser the President Gamal Abdel-Nasser esquire the brother Abdel-Nasser Abd Abdel-Mejid the unworthy the thumb the President Gamal Abdel-Nasser Abd Abd that is the esquire Abu-Eid and AL-Motarer, His Royal Highness, the teacher Mister the one responsible for (Darling June) Life is beautiful beautiful beautiful Abdel-Kerim and everyone went about after his own business, no to to to, Mr. Abd Abdel-Kerim can you say we chose. Luck choses choses.

To Mr. Mohamed Abdel-Hakim Abdallah Hassenein the shameful one. Be sure of his intention Abdel-Hakim AL-Malek and if the esquire Abdel-Hakim Abdel-Majid and if the world as we know it Mr. Esquire.

Translator's Note: All portions enclosed in parentheses appear in English in original.

TRANSLATION FROM ARABIC

Between the two lines, "One Hundred thousand Dollars" and "Dollars—One Hundreds" the words in Arabic read "he should be killed." To the right of the second line appears the word "three." Immediately below this word appear the words "papers, papers."

Sirhan Sirhan   8-413-477

Sirhan Sirhan 696 E Howard ST

gwendolyne Gunn —

Sirhan Sirhan Please pay to the
order of Sirhan
                    Pay —
Order the Ro Rosicrucian Order
Please pay to the order of Sirhan

Long Live

Kennedy must fall Kennedy must fall

please pay to the order of Sirhan Sirhan

the amount of Sirhan Sirhan and do not
forget to become any more of a
~~he~~ ~~murder~~ Senator R. Kennedy
second group of American Sailors -
~~must~~ must be disposed of . . . -
we believe that Robert F. Kennedy must
be sacrificed for the cause of the
~~poo~~ poor exploited people

we believe that we ~~so~~ can effect
such action and produce such results -
~~the~~ hand that is ~~writing~~ doing this
writing is going to do the slaying of
the above mentioned victim
One wonders what it feels like to do any
assasination that might do some
illegal work — ~~please pay~~ to

I believe that I can effect the
death of Bert C. Allfillish

Kennedy must die / kennedy must fall

Kennedy must fall kennedy must fall
kennedy must fall kennedy must
fall I kennedy must fall —

(altfillisch)

Altfillisch

life   to whom it may concern — please
life   pay to the order of Sirhan

life   Sirhan the the the the amount
(life) of 15 death 15 15 15   (Altfillisch)
        life 16 $15,000
must die   die die die   life
die die die $ life + death   life

die (life) Hello (life) (life)
die   life Perhaps you could us
dye the enclosed $ die Line
life life die die die die die die

        Sol life life Sol
Sol (life) Sol life Sol
Sol Sol Sol

Col Soirj uanino   696 E HOWARD ST
PASADENA, CALIF

Sirhan Sirhan   Sirhan Sirhan
Sirhan S. Sirhan Sirhan
Sirhan Peggy Sirhan   Sirhan Sirhan
Sirhan P P P
Sirhan P P P P P
Sirhan   Peggy O. Sirhan   Sirhan   Yong Sirhan
Sirhan   P P P Peggy
Sirhan argy
PEGGY Y Y PE PEGGY SIRHAN
argus Argus
SIRHAN SIRHAN   California
696 E HOWARD ST.
P. P PASADENA, CALIF California

39 5/00 NEBRASKA MASS   Pasadena
39 39. FLA FLA
Fl Florida
the Doe Lectures 46.80   46.80
46.80   46   46.80   46.80
46 80

7¢ per hour   seven cents per hour

razor

Clothes
vitamins —
Blanket
toolsear — gallon container extra tire, tubes
Books — — pens —
I'm have to stay   where does one

to keep up with all of these or all of those
You're goddamned right

you will not be requested to do anything that
may require any great or ungreat

stipulation against the arab people —
is told is is paid to say
is is paid to say say

while any one is or is not required to
perform in any way that or this is
possible —

Jelefer 2 2 200 9 9
200   200 Jelefer
2 2²

Jelefer

( ) I shall begin realizing the sum of
one-hundred dollars— as per the
instructions of the Bible and Thomas
Troward— within the next five days
+ + M before the termination
+ of this month

Jelefer   we we we-we |pointedly
N N C — we eu   **pocn**

90 P P P Pointedly We
20 we we we we
We w We P P 30
and indeed very workable for us—

8   happiness happiness   70 70
60 6 6
8 8   Dona Donaruma
50 80
8   8   Donaruma Frank   8 8
80
8   Donaruma pl please
80   ple please pay to   5
please pay to the order of Sirhan
Sirhan the amount of 5

The Law of of *flamboyantly*
(some more dances with whiskey)
he dosent believe it   no
convictions — and socialy 2
2 2 I close the door
Sirha   there are four rules who (Sirhan) a
    ghatter
Sirhan   S safety   RFK Sirhan
Sirhan   Sir   Next   next

m   Jords Rohn   For
  next   Rohn next
Next
    Rohn   Sirhan   Robert Rhan

Sirhan

next   eight next   Jec Robert
next   Sec next   Cile next next Rhan
          Los Angeles—
Nex [ALL of this]
    Clete Roberts   Clete Roberts
Rohn
P. R.   Clete Roberts Roberts
Rohn   all of his Eilat of aquaba

Explanations

Jet Spec

the Cherub indians

Miss Peggy Osterkamp

Spell out the story with their hands:
M M M   Miss Peggy Osterkamp
California.   25741   Archibald Ave.
Ca   Ca   California   Corona, Calif.

الحرب والاسلام والاسلام والاسلام
الاردن   الحديديه العربيه
العربية

gaudy kamps k k kamps.

Lawrence   charmed
Jet Spec Welk   Jet Spec   a one alter.

a three
Further Do not Bother   Jet

Jet Spec

no   Roman Brother ... Zirhan. 5
no   5   5 hundred   Stokley
emanate from   Jet stokley   show
Zirhan Zirhan   N N   N.Y.
Life is beautiful et spec   New sk
Mahogeny industry industrys.

no   Propensity Yes   Zirhan - Zirhan
yes-   Zirhan ghall   Zirhan Zirhan   ghattan

sing   Does he

Miss   M   M   Miss Peggy Osterk

Miss Miss   Peggie Osterk
O Osterk   Osterkamp
2717 N. Ch
Miss Peggie Osterkamp
2717 N. Archibald Ave.
Corona, California
97702

Miss Gwendoline Gum
1009 9th Ave.   OS O
1   Arcadia, Calif
OSTERKA

Miss Peggy Osterkamp
ER   E   O OSTE

M   M   Miss   M

Osterkamp   M   Miss Peggy Osterkamp
Miss Peggy Peggy Osterkamp 27142

Peggy Miss Peggy Oster Kamp   M Miss

Miss PEGGY OST   OSTERKAMP
2772 ARCHIBALD AVE
Sirhan   CORONA, CALIF.
696 E. Howard St
Pasadena Calif.
Peggy Osterkamp
2772
Archibald Ave

My Sir —
     My Sir please do not
until the [illegible] I use but
     abase abuse   25   I d you also
Sirhan Sirhan Sirhan   share in what
Let's finish some of this work — work ever is sent
fait accompli.   fait accompli to any country
     Chekers
        J The Law of Mentalism
dr   Sin   Sin
    drama Sirhan Sirhan   J [Arabic]
sir | Sirhan S. Sirhan Sirhan [Arabic]   Jet
      | 67   67   67   Jet
      | hope   June 67   the
      | June 67   June 67 [Arabic]   city of
                                    Spec
           Jet Spec [Arabic] [Arabic]
      Spec. Spec.   Spec.
                     [Arabic] [Arabic]
      prepared by Sirhan Sirhan

      Documentations
        0 0.00   [illegible]
      loan   Days
      the T T Deutsch John Days
    Gwen gam — Peggie Osterkamp
           Peggy Peggy Osterkamp

employees Job [Scholarship]   Great assistance.
of this   [Sirhan Sirhan] has been determined
        The importance of will power by the many
Job   oril may be sent so that it can be
        Taken up by thousands. A proof of this is to
        be found in the various suicide and murder
        epidemics — d+z zone zone zone.
Sirhan zone zone backing
        at 3 fort knox and crashed together

Documentations

        up p p p p   The station
Sirhan   that means bus
        Please pay to the order of the
        please pay to the order of
Sirhan   For $ 28 killed   killed pay To
        The granite The granite business order the
Sirhan   Sirhan heard order of
        [Jet Spec.]   Sirhan please

Sirhan Sirhan S § . So used in (order)

        [th g] heat is seldom
                Sirhan Sirhan   Jet Spec
please pay to g Garner Ted Armstrong
the order of

        although   Documentations:
                        H(.....+... 1956: ———
deducing from these fact — .—f
            i 9 .

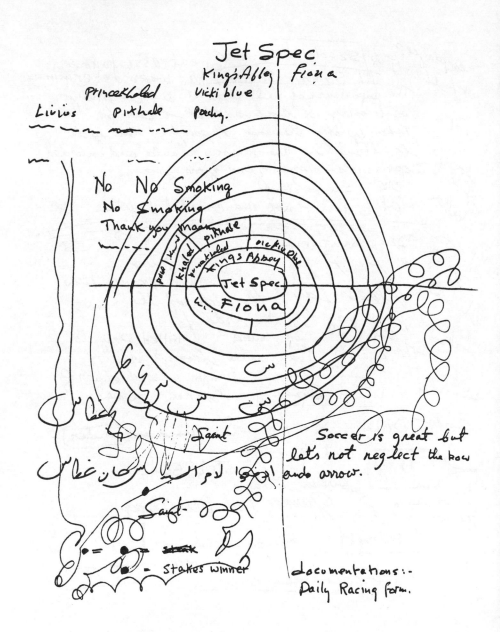

intentional - vs - extentional'.
connotation' vs - denotation.
implicit . Equality before and <u>after the law</u>

I advocate the overthrow of the
current president of the fucken United
States of america, I have no absolute
plans yet - but soon will compose some
I am poor — This country's propoganda
says that she is the best country in
the world - I have not experienced this
yet - the U. S - says that life in
Russia is bad — <u>Why</u> ~~the~~ Supposedly
No average american has ever
lived in a slavic society so how
can he tell if it is good or bad —
isn't his gov't patting words in his
mouth.
Anyway — I believe that the U. S is
ready ~~to start~~ to start decling, not that
it hasn't - it began in Nov 23, 63 —,
but it should decline at a ~~fast~~
faster rate, so that the real utopia
will not ~~the~~ be to far from being
realized during the early 70's in this
country.
I firmly support the communist
cause and its people - wether Russian, chinese

albanian Hungarins or whoever —
Workers of the world Unite, You
have nothing to loose but your
chains and a world to win

Workers of the world unite you
have nothing to loose but your chains
and a world to win —

Workers of the world unite, you have
nothing to loose but your chains

alu Ol Sol

Sol cord

يا عمّال العالم اتحدوا سوف لا تخسرو إلا حنازيركم و على
لا تتحدون

For a person to put his thoughts into words is a difficult task if you were to remember that that person is a troglodyte who is therefore more psychically inclined than his urban contemporary.

America will soon face a downfall so abysmal, that she will never recover from it. This statement is based on several Observations and incidents that the writer experienced

1.

The american politician leads his people through any course that he wants them to - this is possible because the people lack the initiative, or are indifferent to the actions of their leaders — Their leaders say: You have the right to speak against your gov't, and support its changeover — but remember, — though Democratic means Only — If otherwise we will blast the hell out of you — and besides, you wouldn't want to do anything like that, it is stupid costly and Wasteful Just let us run the country hire our relatives to work for us — and earn fat checks —

we know what we are doing in
viet Nam — we're keeping the
economy going through our war spending—
We will keep busy here working
on preagunish matters — to impress you—
all what we really want to do is
fuck you as up — get fat and then
quit—

Well, my solution to this type of
government that is to do away
with its leaders — and declare
anarchy, the best form of govt — or no
govt.

~~I contend that what is the elminate
them to shoot for president~~

the President is your best ~~elect~~
friend until he gets in power they to ~~it your~~
~~most exploing fucker~~ & suck every
~~as~~ drop of blood out of you — ~~fat~~ and
if he dosent like you — you're dead—

APPENDIX D: Sirhan's Automatic Writing

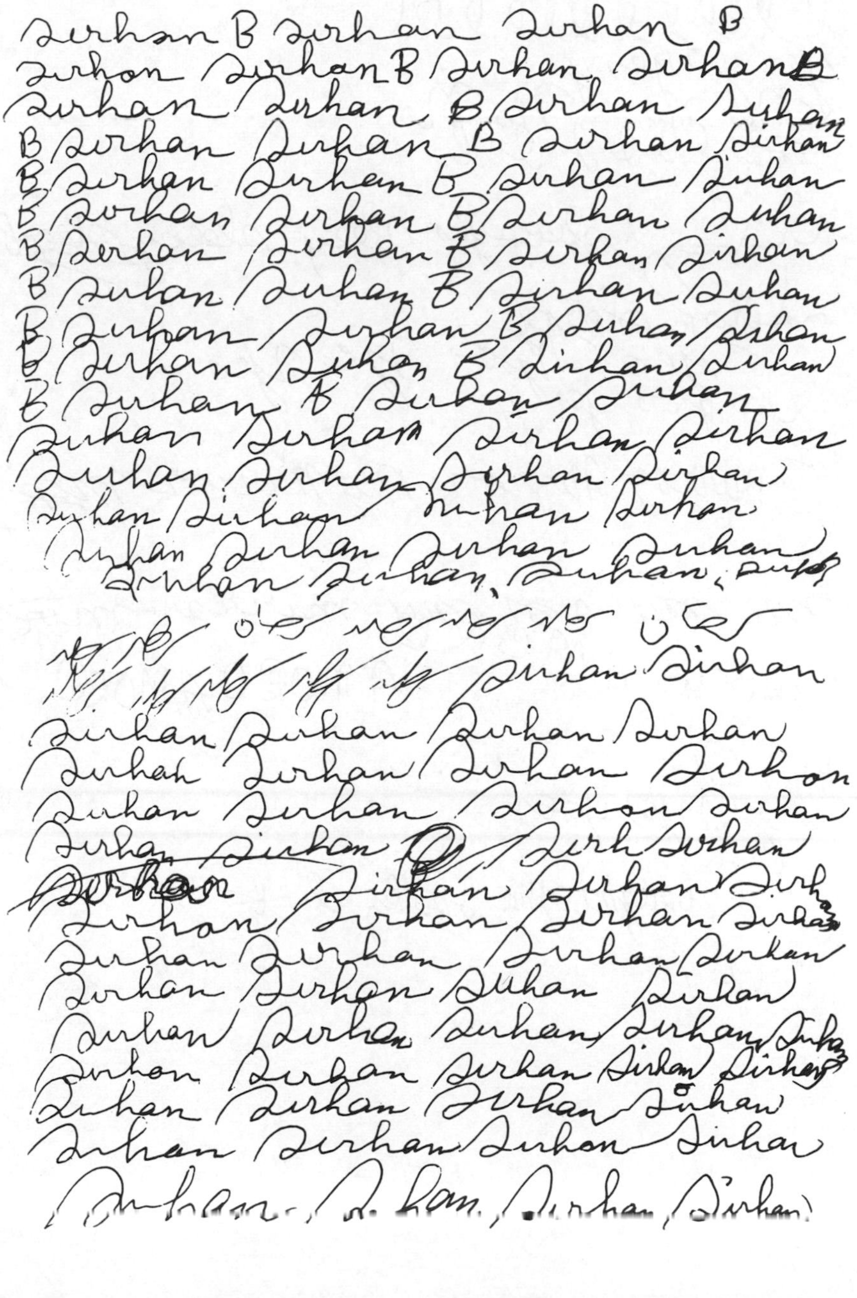

self improvement self improvemt
l l ll l ll l l l .
yes ys yes y
No No l No No
l ll l l l l
_____ I sleepyes sleey sleepy sleeps
lam sleep
yes yes   yes yes
yes yes yes y
mirror mirror My mirror my

my mirror my mirror m
amore AMORE   AMORC AMORC
+ NO
yes yes yes
I bought the books I b
M

Friday 31 January 689   Friday 31 January 69
Friday RFK RFK RFK RFK RFK
Robert F Kennedy Robert F Kennedy
RFK RFK RFK R FK RFK must
die RFK must die RFk must die RFk
must die R.F.K. Must die RF K must die
RFK must die RFK must die RFk
must die Robert Kemedey is going to die
Robert is going to die P Robert is
going to die P Sirhan Sirhan
Robert is going to P
    o Who killed Kennedy? I dont know
I dont know I dont know

No No No N Now Friday 31 January
Friday yes yes yes
No No K
No No d]
No No No
        No No No
- No No N
girl the girl the girl is No No No No
Is this the way you wrote at home
is this so
yes yes yes yes yes yes yes yes
yes yes yes yes yes yes yes yes
No No No
practice practice practice practice
practice Mind Control mind
control mind control

1 2 3 4 1 2 3 4 1 2 3 4
give me a Tom Collins Collins
were you drunk
x 2 yes yes yes
whre is the gon
i dont know
go home go hom aomg
Car Car Car car Car
I want coffe coffe coffe
att the Party ett the party
at ama rad can tomeq

Kathlellen Kathlen Katleen Kathleey
No
N N N N No oo No N N N N
Kathleeen
the did not tell me her name
Mo No
i dont knglo
he wanted she wanted coffeee
No No /
No No

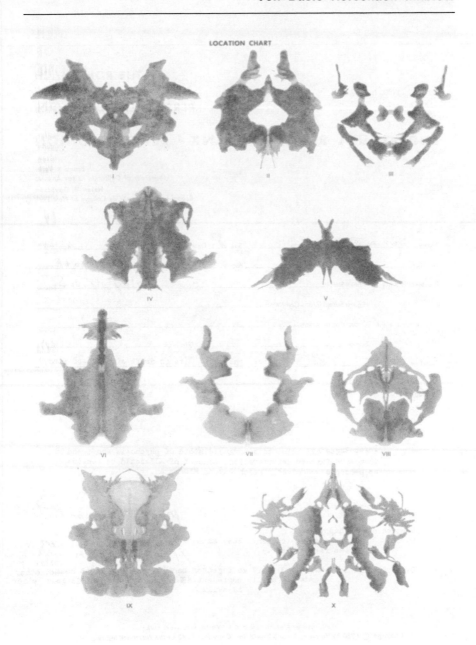

LOCATION CHART

APPENDIX F:
Rorschach Given by Dr. Schorr

THE RORSCHACH
METHOD OF
PERSONALITY DIAGNOSIS

INDIVIDUAL RECORD BLANK · REVISED EDITION

Bruno Klopfer
University of California at Los Angeles
Helen H. Davidson
School of Education, City College of New York

Name _Sirhan B Sirhan_ Sex _M_ Date of Birth _____ Age _24_

Address _____ Phone _____ Date of Administration _11-26-68_

If subject is adult: Marital Status _____ Occupation _college student_

Highest School Grade Completed _____

If subject is a child: Occupation of Parent _____

School _____ Grade _____

Examiner _Martin M. Schorr Ph.D._ (rough draft of 11-26-68 study).

REMARKS

Percentages all point to a paranoid state of psychosis and trend
is toward further deterioration. Concept of NGI could be considered
as percepts conceivably reach beyond M'Naghten.

12-4-68.

Martin M. Schorr Ph.D.

Rorschach Examiner.

Best card = 7 (happy mood)
Worst 9 (colors are too many. They make
me feel violent.)

Conceptualization: Cards 1,3,5,6,7 go together because they represent humanity.
cards 2,4,8,9,10 represent HELL. too chaotic. one is good. other
is evil.

Published by Harcourt, Brace & World, Inc., New York

The Rorschach Miniature Ink Blots in Color:
A Location and Record Form

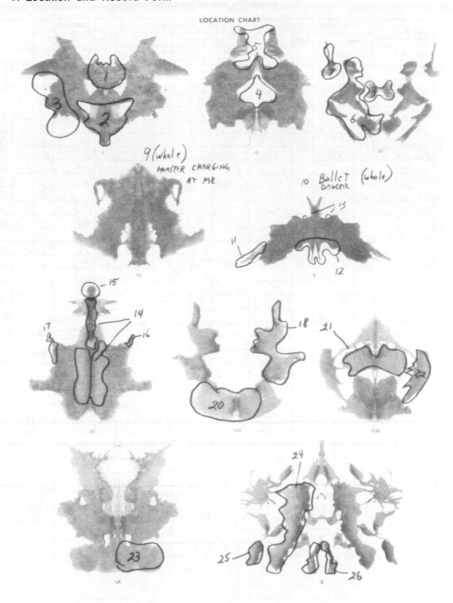

LOCATION CHART

9 (whole)
HAMSTER CHARGING
AT ME

10 Ballet Dancer (whole)

TABULATION AND SCORING SHEET

Card No., Response No. and Position	Reac. Time	LOCATION Main Response W	D,d	Dd,S	Add.	DETERMINANT Main Response Movement	Vista Depth	Form	Texture Ach. Color	Color	Add.	CONTENT Main	Add.	P–O Main	Add.	FLR
I Dove			d			FM						A		O		1
crested Frog				Ddrs		Fm						A		O-		2
cliffs				Ddr				F				N				3
II crown				S				F			C'	obj				4
profile exploding				S		M					m	Hd		O-		5
III watusi		WX				M					C'	H		P		6
8's mouth			D			FM						A		O-.		7
trachea			D					fK				At	(viscera1)			8
IV chasing at sug		W				(M) (monster)					m	(A)				9
V Ballet dancer		W				M					m	H		O+		10
Frid leg			d			FM						Food				11
EARS				dr				F-				Ad				12
second seals				dd		FM						Ad		O-		13
VI coitus				dr		(m)						Sx		O-		14
staring face			d			(M) (BcdsT!)					m	(Ad)		O-.		15
venus				de				Fc				(Hd)				16
launch				dr		Fm						obj				17
VII monkeys, evil			D			(M)		F				(A)				18
Bowl				S								obj				19
Suez				ddr				F				geo				20
VIII Blue Flags			D							CF	m	obj				21
Bears			D			FM						A		P		22
IX red apple crushed			D							CF	m	Food				23
X Blood spurting			D							CF	m	Blood				24
Liver			D							CF	fK	At				25
Green (Land?)			D							CF		geo				26
Total Time T =		**W + D + d + Dd + S = R**				**M + FM + m + k + K + FK + F + Fc + c + C' + FC + CF + C = R**						H 2		P 2		
No. of Responses Main		3 + 9 + 3 + 8 + 3 = 26				6 + 4 + 4 + 1 + + +5 + 1 + + + +5 + = 26						Hd 2		O 2		
Add.												A 6		O- 6		
Sum FLR												Ad 3				
Average FLR																

Blood 1 geo 2.   Sx 1.   Food 2   At 2   N 1   obj 3

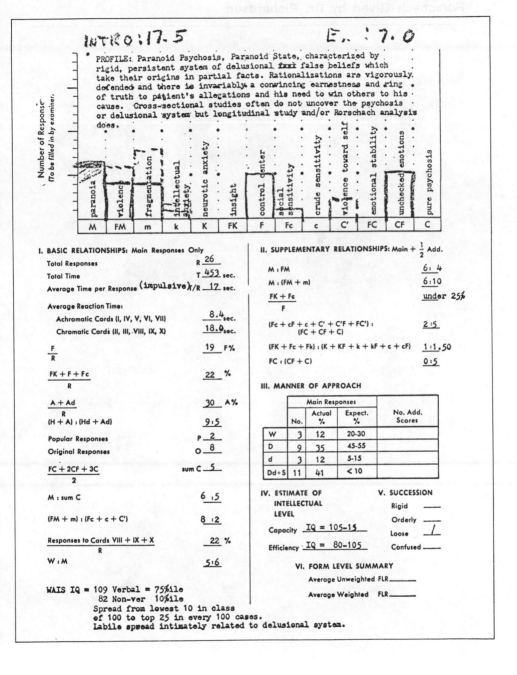

INTRO: 17.5   E. : 7.0

PROFILE: Paranoid Psychosis, Paranoid State, characterized by rigid, persistent system of delusional false beliefs which take their origins in partial facts. Rationalizations are vigorously defended and there is invariably a convincing earnestness and ring of truth to patient's allegations and his need to win others to his cause. Cross-sectional studies often do not uncover the psychosis or delusional system but longitudinal study and/or Rorschach analysis does.

Number of Response (To be filled in by examiner)

paranoia | violence | fragmentation | intellectual anxiety | neurotic anxiety | insight | control center | social sensitivity | crude sensitivity | violence toward self | emotional stability | unchecked emotions | pure psychosis

| M | FM | m | k | K | FK | F | Fc | c | C' | FC | CF | C |

I. BASIC RELATIONSHIPS: Main Responses Only

Total Responses .... R $\underline{26}$

Total Time .... T $\underline{453}$ sec.

Average Time per Response (impulsive) T/R $\underline{17}$ sec.

Average Reaction Time:

  Achromatic Cards (I, IV, V, VI, VII) $\underline{8.4}$ sec.

  Chromatic Cards (II, III, VIII, IX, X) $\underline{18.0}$ sec.

$\dfrac{F}{R}$ $\underline{19}$ F%

$\dfrac{FK + F + Fc}{R}$ $\underline{22}$ %

$\dfrac{A + Ad}{R}$ $\underline{30}$ A%

(H + A) : (Hd + Ad) $\underline{9:5}$

Popular Responses   P $\underline{2}$

Original Responses   O $\underline{8}$

$\dfrac{FC + 2CF + 3C}{2}$ sum C $\underline{5}$

M : sum C $\underline{6 : 5}$

(FM + m) : (Fc + c + C') $\underline{8 : 2}$

$\dfrac{\text{Responses to Cards VIII + IX + X}}{R}$ $\underline{22}$ %

W : M $\underline{5:6}$

WAIS IQ = 109 Verbal = 75%ile
        82 Non-Ver 10%ile
Spread from lowest 10 in class
of 100 to top 25 in every 100 cases.
Labile spread intimately related to delusional system.

II. SUPPLEMENTARY RELATIONSHIPS: Main + $\frac{1}{2}$ Add.

M : FM $\underline{6 : 4}$

M : (FM + m) $\underline{6 : 10}$

$\dfrac{FK + Fa}{F}$ under 25%

(Fc + cF + c + C' + C'F + FC') : (FC + CF + C) $\underline{2 : 5}$

(FK + Fc + Fk) : (K + KF + k + kF + c + cF) $\underline{1 : 1.50}$

FC : (CF + C) $\underline{0 : 5}$

III. MANNER OF APPROACH

	Main Responses			
	No.	Actual %	Expect. %	No. Add. Scores
W	3	12	20-30	
D	9	35	45-55	
d	3	12	5-15	
Dd+S	11	41	< 10	

IV. ESTIMATE OF INTELLECTUAL LEVEL

Capacity $\underline{\text{IQ} = 105-15}$

Efficiency $\underline{\text{IQ} = 80-105}$

V. SUCCESSION

Rigid _____

Orderly _____

Loose $\underline{\quad/\quad}$

Confused _____

VI. FORM LEVEL SUMMARY

Average Unweighted FLR _____

Average Weighted FLR _____

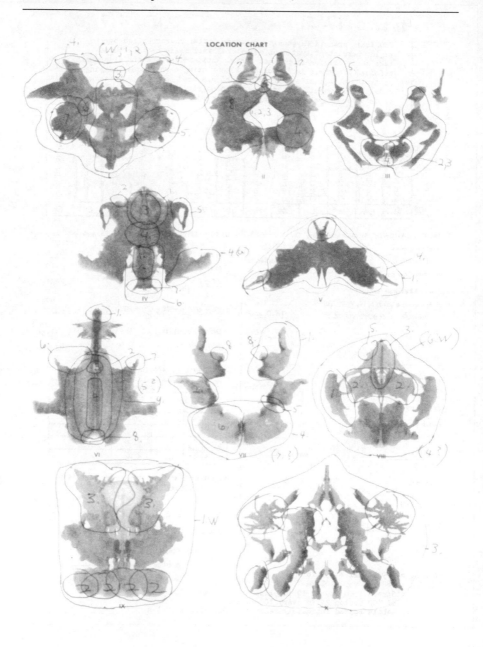

LOCATION CHART

Richardson

RORSCHACH

CARD 1

1. I've seen it before. I still don't know. Looks like the back part of a chicken. You fry a chicken. That's the only thing I can - - -

2. A butterfly in flight. P

3. A frog.

4. Two birds - doves.

5. Coastline.

6. Mountains.

7. Clouds.

8. Cliffs.

9. A ~~bull~~. Bowl

---

1. It's the whole thing, this being the center. I've eaten some chicken. I never used to like that part, if I could avoid it. It's very bony.   Ac'

2. The body is here and here are the wings.   A

3. Looks like the internal dissection of it. From the little of what I remember, this looks like the cloaca.   Ac'

4. (Top dd.) (How does it appear?) as though they have just landed.   A

5. From a top view like from an airplane. Looks like both a photo and an aerial view could be either. I can see islands.

6. Looking down from a plane, the darker areas.

7. Is very dark. Just about ready to start to rain. Dark clouds.

8. This reminds me of cliffs looking far away. The space is the water.

9. It looks like the top of a ~~bull~~, like it's curved here. Bowl

2+1∼+3   5∴J

F+ !)   1∴
            2 . 5.5

CARD 2

1. A crown.	1. It's in the space here, a crown for a queen or a king.
2. A diamond.	2. It looks like a diamond or the top of a mosque. A minaret up here. It's the same space, the cut of it.
3. A satellite, you know, space.	3. It's the same area, you know, just the shape of it.
4. A blood smear on a microscope thing.	4. In here looks like blood smeared around. (Red shading in the dark area, lower right.)
5. A cross.	5. It's at the top, a Rosicrucian cross is the way I think of it.
6. Blood! (Looks intently at the blot.)	6. All of the red especially here (lower D) looks like mixed with other liquids (w).
7. A face of a person. Glass.	7. Profile (red, at top). It projects no feeling to me. (?) Madness (?), anger - - the teeth are showing, they look more like women than men.
8. An elephant or a bear.	8. The GOP elephant (popular area). Maybe it could be just a bear.

CARD 3

1. A couple of dancers.	1. A jovial bunch of Negro drum players - Watusi - although up here - - this much looks like foxes - - more animal than human - - looks like a werewolf (sex?). Oh, men.
2. Lungs.	2. (Center D lower.) Looks like a cauliflower really. I see all the fine edges - - the edge of it looks like a cauliflower. Also looks like the trachea, leading to bronchial tubes.
3. Cauliflower.	
4. Sternum. This is the sternum, isn't it. Long pause.	
5. A rooster.	5. (Side d.) Maybe a turkey - - Red made me think of it.

1+++

CARD 4

Hell!

1. Underwater plantations - - Plant life - - kelp (grimace).

   1. Looks like seeing through kelp, this depth thing here. I see it? Looking through it all. (Additional comment.) Now I feel like saying it looks like a casket to me. It represents death.

2. A medieval castle, abandoned.

   2. (Top dd.)

3. An X-ray of the chest (grimace).

   3. Well, going down the center here (top 1/3) in the shading it looks like the muscles around the neck.

4. (Points at own stomach.) I see these muscles, the abdominal muscles.

   4. (Center line just above CENTER D.) The shading in here looks like the abdominal muscles. (Additional comment.) This much here is way out beyond. It goes beyond. I can't describe it.

5. Very dark - - serpents (grimacing). (Blinks.) (?) Looks ready to strike.

A
A

6. An animal on hind legs.

   7. (Center D.) Say a penquin.

8. The hoof of an animal.

   8. (dd at the bottom of D.)

CARD 5

1. A bird. A big eagle like. Flying head-on.

   1. (W, FM, A, P.)

2. A chicken leg. Fried chicken.

   2. You know these advertisements for fried chicken. Some old man has all these franchises for fried chicken.

3. Horns, look like the ears of a kangaroo.

   3. Looks like horns and ears of a kangaroo, looking straight at me. Right in here.

4. A ballet dancer.

   4. The legs are here, the skirt and all that floating around. (Gestures.) Just the legs and standing on the toes. Just the center bottom legs.

5. A seal.

2

F₋ H²⁺
1

CARD 6

1. A cat.

2. This chicken comes in here again.

3. A lamp.

4. A rocket.

5. An owl.

6. I have a feeling of high altitude.

7. The bust of a female from the chest up.

8. The claws of an eagle or predatory bird.

9. Walking in a very dense forest, a lot of foliage.

10. Vertebrae.

1. (Just the tip of the top d.) Eyes, whiskers.   A ċ

2. No inquiry.

3. It's the brightest spot in the blot. (dd on center line.)

4. (The center line, lower 2/3, F+)

5. No inquiry.

6. From the cliffs. Very high. Looks like looking very high and from a high altitude.

7. (Tip of outer top extension dd.) H ċ

8. Just these claws here.   A ċ

9. Looks like an aerial view what you might see around the equator. (Center, both sides in shading.)

10. No inquiry. (Limits.) Can you find anything of a sexual nature in this particular blot? "Yeah, you mean this being the vagina?" What about an animal skin or a hide that's ofen seen on this card? "Oh, yeah, the whole thing. That's beautiful.' Looks like the fur side - -" Again this foliage.

CARD 7   '4 "

1. ~~monkey with~~ tail.

2. Bears. Stuffed bears.

3. A jigsaw puzzle.

4. A dam.

5. A canal.

6. A map of Egypt, you know the boundaries.

7. The Delta River, no, a delta, a river.

1. Heads, playful. The heads and the tails (tail is the usual ear).   A

2. A bear's head. The expression is wicked, mean, mad.   A ċ

3. A jigsaw puzzle (W no inquiry).

4. A dam. Inquiry - a canal, more like in Egypt.

6. (One side of lower D.)

F+ ⊔⊔⊦

CARD 7 - Continued

8. Towers (very ruminative, here).

8. The towers very distant. (At top of the center.) Very mountainous - - might be a church on a cliff.

CARD 8

1. The California bear.

1. D, F, A, P.   A

2. Flags.

2. (Blue area.) Is that blue or green - - like the United Nations flags at the top of the buildings.

3. The spine. The vertical column. Is it vertical?

3. The spine, the center line - - the spinal column.

4. I don't know, it's a desert plant. Grows very tall - not a cactus. I don't know the name.

4. Patient suddenly verbalizes - "The colors shock me - - no - - I don't know - - I feel very jittery - - I can't hold still, - - it stirs me. I read this magazine article on the 20th anniversary of the State of Israel. It was in color - - that color - - I hate the Jews. There was jubilation - - I felt that they were saying in the article, we beat the Arabs - - it burns the shit out of me, there was happiness and jubilation."

5. Guns - mortars.

6. Boats.

CARD 9   (Head in hands.)

1. In school class - - in biology - - plant life under a microscope - - I don't remember the name of this plant.

1. The smear of a botanical slide (W). The color clashes - I am not used to it - - too many of them at the same time - - it confuses me. It just increases in degrees.

2. Apples.

3. Fire. it's weird, (shakes head). Whew! It has depth - it's too deep. Whew!

A

<u>CARD 10</u>

1. This whole color - - it throws
me off! Monsters! (60 second
interval.) It's really about
all on this one? (You seem upset.) It's frightening - it
frightens me - they all seem the
same - wickedness! Too many entanglements!

1. It's a cacophony of colors, a
hodgepodge. All those legs!
This here looks like some kind
of rat (brown area). No, not
a rat - - it flies - - a bat.
The whole thing looks like
monstrosities. It's more vulgar - I'd avoid it.
Everybody wants to catch on to
you - with all those legs! The
minute you're within reach
you're in their clutches.
(What about the blood?) I seem
to associate the whole thing
negatively with blood.
(What about the red area?) It
looks like liver to me - some
kind of meat. (Grimace.) I'd
rather not even discuss it - -
I'd rather not even discuss it.
All those legs.

2. Blood! (Grimace, puts card away
quickly.)

$F+ = 24$

$F+\% =$

$$56 \overline{)24.30}$$

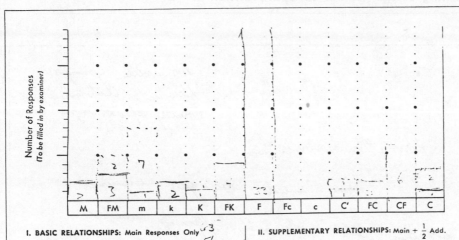

I. BASIC RELATIONSHIPS: Main Responses Only

Total Responses	R _56_
	scorable
Total Time	T ____ sec.
Average Time per Response	T/R ____ sec.

Average Reaction Time:

Achromatic Cards (I, IV, V, VI, VII)	____ sec.
Chromatic Cards (II, III, VIII, IX, X)	____ sec.

$\frac{F}{R}$ _59_ F%

$\frac{FK + F + Fc}{R}$ _66_ %

$\frac{A + Ad}{R}$ _.30_ A%

(H + A) : (Hd + Ad)   _11 : 10_

Popular Responses   P _5_

Original Responses   O ____

$\frac{FC + 2CF + 3C}{2}$ sum C _8.5_

M : sum C   _2 : 8.5_

(FM + m) : (Fc + c + C')   _4 : 1_

$\frac{\text{Responses to Cards VIII + IX + X}}{R}$ _19_ %

W : M   _8 : 2_

II. SUPPLEMENTARY RELATIONSHIPS: Main + $\frac{1}{2}$ Add.

M : FM   _2 : 4_

M : (FM + m)   _2 : 8.5_

$\frac{FK + Fc}{F}$ _.11 ( )_

(Fc + cF + c + C' + C'F + FC') :
   (FC + CF + C)   _1.5 : 0_

(FK + Fc + Fk) : (K + KF + k + kF + c + cF)   _0 : 1_

FC : (CF + C)   _2 : 0_

III. MANNER OF APPROACH

		Main Responses		No. Add. Scores
	No.	Actual %	Expect. %	
W	8	.14	20-30	
D	15	.27	45-55	
d	11	.20	5-15	
Dd+S	20	.56	< 10	

IV. ESTIMATE OF INTELLECTUAL LEVEL

Capacity ____

Efficiency _F+ = .13 %_

V. SUCCESSION

Rigid ____

Orderly ____

Loose ____

Confused ✓

VI. FORM LEVEL SUMMARY

Average Unweighted FLR ____

Average Weighted   FLR ____

Mr. Evelle Younger
District Attorney
County of Los Angeles

Dear Mr. Younger

Some weeks ago you inquired whether the Kennedy family wished to express any views on the possible penalties available to the court under law in the trial involving the death of my brother.

The issue then was the position to be taken by the prosecution on the offer of a plea of guilty and that involved the question whether there would be any trial at all. We felt that any answer to your inquiry at that time would accordingly be inappropriate.

At the time of the hearing on the sentence a similar inquiry was made by defense counsel. The matter was then before the jury and again any response seemed inappropriate.

I now understand that the trial judge will be called upon to exercise his discretion concerning the penalty. Since this is now a question of clemency and the trial proceedings have been concluded. I feel I can appropriately convey to you, for whatever considerate you believe to be proper how we feel.

My brother was a man of love and sentiment and compassion. He would not have wanted his death to be a cause for the taking of another life. You may recall his pleas when he learned of the death of Martin Luther King He said that what we need in the United States is not division what we need in the United States is not hatred.. what we need in the United States is not violence or lawlessness, but love and wisdom and compassion towards one another. Moreover he was a young man totally committed to life and living. He stood against injustice poverty and discrimination for those evils lessened life. He grew to

despise war for was denied the
sacredness of life. And he had
a special affection for children
for they held the promise of life.

We all realize that many
other considerations fall within
your responsibility and that of the
court. But if the kind of man
my brother was is pertinent we
believe it should be weighed in
the balance on the side of.
compassion, mercy and gods gift
of life itself.

Sincerely

Edward M Kennedy

Index